IN SEARCH OF HANNAH CRAFTS

IN SEARCH OF *Hannah Crafts*

CRITICAL ESSAYS ON
The Bondwoman's Narrative

Henry Louis Gates, Jr.

Hollis Robbins

EDITORS

BASIC
CIVITAS
BOOKS

A Member of the Perseus Books Group
New York

Published by BasicCivitas Books,
A Member of the Perseus Books Group

Designed by Brent Wilcox
Set in 12-point Centaur MT

A catalog record for this book is available from the Library of Congress.
ISBN 0-465-02714-8

04 05 06 / 10 9 8 7 6 5 4 3 2 1

CONTENTS

I. THE LITERARY MARKETPLACE
Between the Sentimental Novel and the Slave Narrative

II. REWRITING THE CANON

VI. REVIEWS

Hannah Crafts, *The Bondwoman's Narrative*
Introduction to the Critical Essay Collection

HENRY LOUIS GATES, JR.
HOLLIS ROBBINS

The Bondwoman's Narrative, By Hannah Crafts, A Fugitive Slave Recently Escaped From North Carolina is an autobiographical novel written between 1853 and 1860. Dorothy Porter Wesley, the well-known historian and librarian at Howard University, purchased it in 1948 from antiquarian Emily Driscoll, who had purchased it from a book scout in New Jersey. Henry Louis Gates, Jr., bought the manuscript at the annual Swann Galleries auction in February 2001; it was published for the first time by Warner Books in April 2002.

Hannah Crafts's narrative is a tale designed both to captivate and to provoke its readers. In the preface to her narrative, Hannah Crafts claims to present "a record of plain unvarnished facts" while acknowledging that her text is "a literary venture." She claims that her tale "makes no pretension to romance," even as she writes poetically of "the peculiar institution whose curse rests over the fairest land the sun shines upon." She claims that her narrative has no moral, while noting that those "of pious and discerning minds can scarcely fail to recognise the hand of Providence" in its portrayal of rewards to the righteous and punishments to the wicked. In other words, Hannah Crafts tips her hand to the attentive reader and admits that what will follow is as much art as chronicle.

Yet there are clearly points at which Hannah's story appears to coincide with historical fact, and there is a strong case to be made that she is who she says she is—that she is female, that she is of African descent, that she is a slave who grew up in Virginia, lived for a time in Washington, D.C., and then escaped to New Jersey. Her description of the Virginia landscape—particularly around the tiny hamlet of Milton—coupled with her acquaintance with local lore and unmistakable evidence that she knew John Hill Wheeler and his wife, Ellen, intimately (as well as her knowledge of the famous escape of their servant, Jane Johnson, in 1855) make a persuasive case for the author's authenticity.

Milton is so very tiny—it consisted of two or three buildings—that only a person with firsthand knowledge of this section of Virginia could possibly have situated her story there. It is located near Tyler's Mill and the James River, and several steamboat landings are within walking distance—within a mile or so—as Crafts describes in her novel. The names of several of the neighboring slaveholders she mentions correspond with historical Virginia figures, such as Reverend John Henry and Carter George Cropp. The two masters of Lindendale, the large home around which much of the novel's domestic drama revolves (including a spectacular episode of a prominent slaveholder bringing home his young bride), accord with historic accounts of Richard "Squire" Lee, a well-known Virginia slaveholder. As Paul C. Nagel describes him in his book *The Lees of Virginia: Seven Generations of an American Family* (1990), "Squire" Lee was a famous eighteenth-century bachelor and party-giver, whose wild ways were noted by George Washington in a 1775 letter to his brother. ("Famous bachelor" was a common euphemism for men who openly enjoyed sexual relations with slaves.) At sixty, Lee married his young cousin, Sally, whose son by her second husband built a large home called Linden in Westmoreland County, Virginia, about one hundred miles north of Milton. The Lee family is also distantly related to Reverend John Henry.

Crafts transparently fictionalized her experiences as a slave on a North Carolina plantation in a sly attempt to signal the identity of John Hill Wheeler. Her knowledge of Wheeler's library, her persistent reference to the Wheelers' runaway slave, Jane (mentioned ten times in Chapter 12), and her intimate knowledge of contemporary Washington politics and prominent Virginians (Wheeler purchased Jane Johnson from a Richmond businessman), however, argue in favor of some link between them.

As Gates has pointed out ("Borrowing Privileges," *New York Times*, June 2, 2002), Crafts alludes to a remarkably impressive range of British and American works found in Wheeler's extensive library. The literary echoes in *The Bondwoman's Narrative* of texts owned by Wheeler reverberate throughout Crafts's narrative. For example, her portrayal of the hanging of the old servant Rose ("with something of the martyr spirit burning in her eye") in Chapter 2 may have been influenced by Foxe's *Book of Martyrs* on Wheeler's bookshelf, which includes graphic description of religious persecutions. The many points of similarity between Crafts's text and Nathaniel Hawthorne's *The House of the Seven Gables* (1851)—the storied old house, the glowering portrait, the curse and the old tree, the name Clifford, the preoccupation with documents and inheritance, the sudden, gurgling deaths—may also gesture toward the Wheeler family, whose land was, like the Pyncheons in Hawthorne's tale, first granted to a family named Maule.

Questions of Hannah Crafts's actual identity are put aside in most of the essays that follow. These scholars take it as a more or less settled matter that the author was a woman of African descent who wrote this text after attaining freedom in the North. Just as importantly, all of these scholars accept Hannah Crafts's narrative as a serious and important piece of writing that has dramatically changed how we view the antebellum literary landscape. These essays ask a new set of questions: What kind of text is *The Bondwoman's Narrative?* Is it biographical or entirely fictional? Is it internally consistent? Did the author accomplish what she set out to do? Was she seeking to produce a work of a particular literary genre or to challenge that genre? As a writer, is Hannah Crafts as sophisticated as she appears to be? What is the extent of her class or race consciousness?

The essays that follow are grouped into five categories: 1) essays that explore the idea of Hannah Crafts as a writer self-consciously locating herself within the literary marketplace and within two distinct genres—the slave narrative and the sentimental novel; 2) essays that focus on *The Bondwoman's Narrative's* relationship with individual canonical texts, specifically, Charles Dickens's *Bleak House* (1853), Walter Scott's *Rob Roy* (1817), Charlotte Brontë's *Jane Eyre* (1847), Harriet Beecher Stowe's *Uncle Tom's Cabin* (1852), and William Wells Brown's *The Escape, or, A Leap for Freedom* (1858); 3) essays that explore the theological, legal, and cultural contexts of antebellum American life; 4) essays that situate Crafts's novel in an emerging subgenre that can be called African American gothic; and 5) essays that analyze the identity of the author.

Five essays explore the ways that Crafts's novel both inhabits and resists two popular nineteenth-century literary genres: the slave narrative and the sentimental novel. These scholars read *Bondwoman's Narrative* as a hybrid work—part autobiographical fiction, part sexual psychodrama, part domestic novel, part ghost story, part Christian morality tale, part fable, part picaresque. But it strains against its formal influences, particularly the *Narrative of the Life of Frederick Douglass* (1845) and any of a number of sentimental tales for and about women, in which the heroine survives physical and moral challenges to marry and live happily ever after.

Augusta Rohrbach argues that Crafts is a *craft*sperson familiar with the literary marketplace, utilizing popular literary conventions, and adept at formal elements such as serial plotting. Rohrbach suggests that Crafts's reading ethic—her intimate knowledge of her literary influences—is a function of the fact that books were expensive and usually re-read several times. But although she was familiar with the literary marketplace, Rohrbach argues, her resistance to generic conventions provides an answer as to why Crafts didn't publish *The Bondwoman's Narrative.* Her novel doesn't fit the sentimental genre. For example, the family is a site not of nurturing and love but of power and control. Moreover, the Lizzy chapters offer a "scathing critique of female vulnerability." And her novel is too free and familiar with white literary allusions—Greek tragedies, Shakespeare, Byron—to fit comfortably into the slave narrative convention. Crafts, Rohrbach argues, seems to have presumed that readers would have read the same volumes.

Lawrence Buell explores Crafts's invocations of crucial antebellum texts to demonstrate a creative hermeneutics. Buell teases out biblical-allegorical echoes as evidence of "the amazing fertility of imagination within vernacular African American Christianity." Crafts is an eager if not encyclopedic reader. *The Bondwoman's Narrative*'s combination of subversive biblical revisionism, emphasis on slavery's psychological effects, and embrace of refinement and sensibility situates it partly in the context of women's fiction and partly in the context of the slave narrative. But its "esoteric flamboyance," as Buell puts it, its satire of race stereotypes, and its interest in the inner lives of even minor figures suggest that this is the work of a highly unconventional, confident, and imperturbable novelist.

William Andrews considers the question of why Crafts ended her narrative as she did—cheerfully wed, in her own home, with friends and relatives close by—and argues that *The Bondwoman's Narrative* is best read in the context of slave narratives and sentimental women's novels; it is both and neither. It is both fact and fiction. In either case, he argues, its hybrid status is most evident in its striking departure from other slave narratives: the unreservedly happy ending. "There is simply nothing like it in the entire pre–Civil War African American slave narrative," Andrews argues. In novels, the ending sustains the prevailing ideology. Crafts may have ended her tale optimistically to challenge the notion that a former slave had no business expecting such fulfillment, even in fiction.

Ann Fabian argues that Crafts is a literary iconoclast, breaking the rules that governed texts written by former slaves. Crafts, Fabian argues, "is both humble and confident, a crafty character who uses the disguise of the humble narrator to become the confident novelist." The power of *The Bondwoman's Narrative,* she asserts, lies in its distinctive mix of convention, truth, and crafty imaginings. What is most important and powerful about the novel is that it is an invented world conjured up, woven together, and under the control of a surprisingly confident author who clearly had her readers' expectations in the front of her mind. Imagined fiction is a better option than stories shaped solely by gender or fugitive condition.

John Stauffer argues that *The Bondwoman's Narrative* draws on three literary conventions—the gothic novel, sentimental literature, and the slave narrative—to treat the concept and condition of freedom as problematic, ambiguous, and contradictory. She embraces the evangelical Christianity of sentimental fiction but resists its privileging of the next life over this. She acknowledges the gothic genre's convention of fundamental social inequalities but attacks the institution of slavery and its attendant evils. She escapes to the North, but her flight is reluctant. Stauffer also speculates that one reason her novel remained unpublished is this problematic attitude toward freedom.

The four essays that examine Crafts's engagements with the canon also make a convincing case for Hannah Crafts's blackness. Two of the essays—Hollis Robbins's on the author's borrowings from *Bleak House*, by Charles Dickens, and *Rob Roy*, by Walter Scott, and Catherine Keyser's on the borrowings from *Jane Eyre*, by Charlotte Brontë—make what one might call a textual-critical case, drawing on the ways this author transformed three contemporary British texts to craft her own tale of finding freedom. Crafts's transformations involved appropriating the circumstances represented in a white text and tailoring particular elements to fit the circumstances of a slave. Each of these transformations is a case of moving from white to black, from the British north to the American south, from figural slavery to real slavery. These essays detail the breadth of these borrowings and make the case that Hannah Crafts not only read these texts but knew them well. Each essay makes the case for the author as critic; Crafts, each concludes independently, knew what she was doing in differentiating her heroine from the genteel but impoverished orphan double of British fiction. She is the subaltern who speaks and reminds her literary mentors that slavery is not merely a metaphor.

Robbins argues that Crafts's borrowings from Dickens and Scott constitute a critical response to the British tradition of writing about poor and oppressed communities. Her borrowing proposes a kinship of suffering, squalor, subjugation, and servitude, but she darkens and distills the passages to emphasize the particular problems of slavery. By softening Dickens's Mr. Tulkinghorn to create Mr. Trappe, for example, Crafts suggests that institutional rigidity is far more frightening than the power and predilections of a single individual. But in darkening Lady Dedlock and Mrs. Snagsby to create Mrs. Cosgrove, Crafts suggests that the domestic tragedies caused by slavery are much harsher than those of the British working class. In her delicate and meaningful transformations of Dickens's text, Crafts reveals not only her critical acumen but her sense of how contemporary literature had yet to apprehend the human condition under slavery.

Keyser examines the ideological similarities (and differences) between Crafts's and Brontë's novels, revealing Crafts's considerable literary skill as demonstrated in her reworking of Brontë's novel. Crafts simultaneously admires and chastens Brontë: Hannah and Jane are mirrors of one another, "sisters in their quest for liberty, rationality, and even romantic fulfillment," but as Jane's slave sister, Hannah critiques Brontë's use of race and bondage as tropes. Crafts translates *Jane Eyre*'s engagements with class into engagements with slavery, Keyser suggests, literalizing what Brontë saw as merely metaphorical. In this literary engagement, Crafts shows off her literary skills as well as her sense of individualism and self-confidence. She shows herself free to rewrite this canonical fictional autobiography; she shows herself knowledgeable enough to know the difference between real and metaphoric bondage, underscoring her probable status as a fugitive slave.

Two essays read *The Bondwoman's Narrative* alongside popular American texts about slavery. Jean Fagan Yellin's essay on the influence of Harriet Beecher Stowe's *Uncle Tom's Cabin* and Shelley Fisher Fishkin's essay on the influence of William Wells Brown's well-known play *The Escape, or, A Leap for Freedom* cast light on Crafts's class and race consciousness and make a convincing case that Crafts was critically aware of her own perspective and condition as highly literate and privileged in relation to these fictional depictions of slavery. That is, she represents herself as a slave in a privileged position: she knows the details of her owner's marriage, understands the rules of polite society, knows how to speak in polite company, and knows what remains hidden in the midst of polite entertainment. She is a critic of Southern gentility and the ill-mannered, who speaks from the privileged but insecure position of house servant. She is comfortable in the big house, with putting a master's or mistress's wishes before her own, with watching and listening but remaining silent until asked to speak. But she is also comfortable with giving orders, making decisions, with expressing herself, and with exerting her will; she holds herself to standards and disdains those who do not.

Yellin suggests that Hannah Crafts drew upon the structure and generic expectations of Stowe's best-selling work. If Crafts saw that novels written by whites about slavery could be wildly successful, there was no reason that novels about slavery written by slaves couldn't be equally successful. Perhaps this is one of the reasons that Crafts transforms the "tragic mulatto" stereotype in her own book and rejects the idea of "passing" as white. Within *The Bondwoman's Narrative*, the broad range of African American characters—queer-looking old men, portly women, comic drunken old Jo, the lovers Charlotte and William, the malicious field hands in North Carolina—speaks to Crafts's insistence on the sufficiency of the slave community to people a novel. It is not a novel concerned with differences between "races"; it is not a novel pre-occupied with sentiment and domesticity; rather, it is a novel that condemns systems of exploitation, not just chattel slavery, both within and without the peculiar institution.

Fishkin considers the similarities between *The Bondwoman's Narrative* and William Wells Brown's *The Escape*, first published in Boston in 1858 but read aloud in a range of eastern cities the previous year. She highlights several striking parallels, including the name Hannah, the characterization of a hyp-ocritical, petulant mistress, and the story-within-the-story of the Cosgrove marriage. The centrality of dialogue and the emphasis on humor suggest that Brown's play was a source of inspiration for Crafts. If so, it would suggest both that Crafts had access to abolitionist events and literature and that she took her literary role models from the African American community, as well as from British and American literature. William Wells Brown's imaginative ability to turn the experiences of slavery into literature may well have pro-vided a model for her productive efforts, especially her willingness to turn lived experiences into moments of high seriousness as well as moments of high comedy.

Three essays examine the historical and cultural context of antebellum America and suggest that Hannah Crafts had some fluency in the legal, archi-tectural, and theological debates of the period. Dickson D. Bruce, Jr., reads *The Bondwoman's Narrative* in the context of abolitionist debates about institutions and principles of justice, about the letter of the law and its spirit. Bruce ar-gues that Crafts not only understood but exploited for dramatic purposes contemporary debates about law in a "free" society; she clearly understood the legal subtleties that governed these arguments enough to use them to structure her novel. Bruce focuses on the Henry family period (Chapters 9–12) and Hannah Crafts's creation of an opposition between a rigidly legalistic ap-proach to human affairs and one based on "a deeper, more complex under-standing of moral situations." Underneath Mrs. Henry's outward show of kindness, we are meant to see that she is brutal, blind, legalistic, evasive, and morally bankrupt. Hannah's encounter with the Henrys, Bruce argues, is meant to emphasize "that cruelty was inherent in the system and not simply a problem involving a few bad slaveholders, as the system's defenders tended to claim." In these passages Crafts injects her own voice into the debate in a strik-ingly deep and complex way.

William Gleason argues that Crafts's familiarity with the politics of archi-tectural style is evident in the ways that she interweaves descriptions of home decor with anti-slavery themes. *The Bondwoman's Narrative*, he reveals, is deeply invested in the politics of architectural form and freedom, demonstrates a sophisticated understanding of the relationship between race and architecture, and expresses a powerful desire for independent black home-ownership. Crafts's architectural consciousness, Gleason argues, is most likely a function of her wide reading habits, her interest in such British texts as *Bleak House* and *Jane Eyre*, and her embrace of democratic architectural styles. Crafts's novel shows the clear influence of Andrew Jackson Downing's contemporary notion of the simple moral beauty of neat, modest dwellings. (John Hill Wheeler owned a copy of Downing's 1842 volume *Cottage Residences.*) Gleason argues that although concerns about slavery seem removed from episodes such as the early Henry family chapters (9–10), Hannah's descriptions of the Henry house, "Forget-me-not" (borrowed from *Bleak House*), speak to its backward-looking, anti-democratic aesthetics. The name of the house recapitulates Mrs. Henry's privileging of her promise to her dead father not to own slaves over a request to keep Hannah from being sold. This skillful linking of slavery and architectural ideology is striking and unexpected.

Bryan Sinche examines Crafts's engagement with the outdoors, particularly with the wilderness, as a structural way to demonstrate that Hannah is in God's favor. Crafts cared less about verisimilitude than making a political point, Sinche argues. Her narrative control is evident in these wilderness passages. Rather than showing Hannah to be self-reliant or resilient in the wild—demonstrating survival skills and physical strength—Crafts presents her as the recipient of God's beneficence. Sufficient food is provided to her like manna from heaven. Hannah's second wilderness journey, Sinche argues, "is an affirmation of her belief in Christian morality and a surrender to God's judgment of her life." She is extraordinarily confident of God's protection as she throws herself on the mercy of the woods. For Sinche, Crafts's novel is a tale of moral and physical courage that proposes that Christian virtue is the most important guarantor of complete freedom.

The essays focusing on the genre of African American gothic literature explore a wide range of topics, from the erotic relations between women to a critique of Emersonian aesthetics. But as remarkable as their differences are their moments of convergence. Nearly every essay in this group considers one particular scene in Crafts's novel, in which Hannah stands among the painted portraits of her master's ancestors, to be new, profound, and provocative.

> Though filled with superstitious awe I was in no haste to leave the room; for there surrounded by mysterious associations I seemed suddenly to have grown old, to have entered a new world of thoughts, and feelings and sentiments. I was not a slave with these pictured memorials of the past. They could not enforce drudgery, or condemn me on account of my color to a life of servitude.

As their companion I could think and speculate. In their presence my mind seemed to run riotous and exult in its freedom as a rational being, and one destined for something higher and better than this world can afford. (17)

In this passage, these scholars hear enchantment, subversion, echoes of Nathaniel Hawthorne and Immanuel Kant. Their unanimous judgment of its *power* constitutes a critical consensus about the novel's significance as an aesthetic achievement.

Russ Castronovo suggests that the ghostly themes in *The Bondwoman's Narrative* are an aesthetic response to slavery's horrors. "Ghost-writing" appears in the space between artistic production and the historic context, he argues; Crafts's ghost-writing "recuperates the faded, unacknowledged, and repressed memories of slave community." Ghosts both recall past victims of slavery and make manifest forgotten sufferings. If the privilege of abstract existence was reserved for whites, Castronovo argues, Crafts's ghosts serve to critique the politics and aesthetics of disembodiment-as-freedom. White art never transcends the black labor that helped create it. *The Bondwoman's Narrative*, for Castronovo, is an extended and sophisticated critique of Emersonian aesthetics, the whites-only privilege of inhabiting the abstract rather than the material realm. Hannah Crafts's novel offers a negative materialist critique of this aesthetic ideology, foregrounding the fleshly origins of the spirit.

Patricia Wald considers the ways that Hannah Crafts both uses and resists the ghost story form to articulate ideas about the political and fictional representation of African American women in the antebellum era. In only half-following the ghost story convention, Wald suggests, Crafts jars her readers into reading differently, confounding their readerly expectations. Rather than giving us "the titillating terror of a ghost story," readers are faced with "a far more horrendous story of a barbaric institution." Wald sees Crafts as Rose, the slave woman strung up to die, whose voice gives meaning to slavery's particular cruelties. Slave narratives *haunt*. Hannah Crafts, for Wald, is an author liberated by her ability to express her artistry, whose art is located precisely in the disjunction between gothic convention and her own story.

Christopher Castiglia explores the dynamics of identification and vision in *The Bondwoman's Narrative*, suggesting that the novel challenges the ideology that what is shown on the outside reveals what is on the inside. Crafts reverses the positions of seer and seen in her novel. The novel's preoccupation with vision, Castiglia provocatively claims, is a function of Hannah's psychic blindness toward her own desire for a mother. Her narrative rages against the absent mother in the form of repeated disavowals of other black women. The novel is suffused with desire for an imagined intimacy between women—especially women of indeterminate race. Hannah's relationship with nearly every woman is marked by eroticism (an exception is Mrs. Wheeler). She identifies herself as an orphan to create maternal sympathy from every other older white woman in the novel (Aunt Hetty, Mrs. Henry, Mrs. Wright). Castiglia suggests that her ambivalence toward and distance from other black women in the novel is really a space of imaginative freedom. Her desire for her missing mother is translated into a haunting anxiety toward black womanhood.

Karen Sánchez-Eppler argues that *The Bondwoman's Narrative* is a hybrid work and that its existence disrupts essentialist assumptions about race and literary form. A tug-of-war, Sánchez-Eppler writes, "between the political value of fact and the ontological validations of narration" is the double-bind of slave authorship. The novelistic strategies of slave authors are an effort "to use the tools of fiction to expand the representational possibilities of the slave narrative." Crafts's dismissal of literacy as commonplace is read as a conscious critique of the slave narrative genre's notion that reading and writing were heroic accomplishments. For Sánchez-Eppler, the novel's processes of recomposition and reinterpretation are its great strength; but ultimately, the tale's lack of concern with narrative coherence suggests that it should best serve as a "provocative fruitful ground" for understanding African American fiction during the 1850s.

Robert S. Levine suggests that in its engagement with unstable racial genealogies, Crafts's novel is an early example of "interracial literature." His Hannah Crafts is well versed in the contemporary debates on race and slavery and writes the novel as a critical intervention. Levine reads the scene of Mrs. Wheeler's racial transformation, for example, as evidence that the novel is challenging biological notions of "white" and "black." And Trappe, Levine argues, is a figure of terror recollecting Chillingworth in *The Scarlet Letter*, a threat to whites who live in houses of blackness. But ironically, Trappe is also Hannah's alter ego: both characters observe closely, spy through windows, and catalogue secrets. The secrets always have to do with race and sex. The brilliance of the novel, for Levine, is in the use the author makes of the racial identity dilemma.

Zoe Trodd explores Crafts's interest in the slipperiness of language and suggests that she is suspicious of the Western literary tradition that she simultaneously seeks to join. For Trodd, Crafts is trapped both by the inadequacy of language and the limits of the slave narrative genre. Hannah is uninterested in history, books, and language but comfortable with observation, faces, and the visual image. This novel, for Trodd, is most important for the ways it prefigures twentieth-century texts through its series of strategies designed to reverse the problematic signifier/signified relationship.

Four essays take up the search for the author, Hannah Crafts. Read in conversation with each other, these essays offer some suggestive possibilities for continuing the search for Hannah Crafts. Nina Baym assesses the qualities that would have been needed to write a novel as complex as *The Bondwoman's Narrative* and suggests that it "would have been composed by a person with a long immersion in imaginative literature," as well as access to textbooks on geography and science. The author was clearly part of a "manuscript culture." Baym proposes that Hannah Crafts was probably a "highly literate, omnivorously reading schoolteacher," with time, means, books, accoutrements of writing, pedagogical purpose, and literary sensibility enough to have composed this tale. Absent hard evidence to the contrary, the most likely candidate for authorship, she claims, is Hannah Vincent, a New Jersey schoolteacher, a possibility raised by Henry Louis Gates, Jr., in the introduction to the novel.

By contrast, Rudolph Byrd suggests that Hannah Crafts embodies the concept of the "outsider within," a privileged individual with access to specialized forms of knowledge that flow from distinctive species of marginality. Her experiences, as represented in her narrative, are paradigmatic of many African American women of her era: she claims private knowledge, a special perspective, and a particular angle of vision that attends her position. Her narrative provides the best evidence that Crafts is a mulatto and former slave. Her gleefully detailed portrayals of her white mistresses in particularly unattractive positions (Mrs. Cosgrove up a ladder, petticoats tumbling behind her; Mrs. Wheeler with matted hair and in blackface) are clearly a function of Hannah's subordinate position. No white woman, Byrd argues perceptively, would portray other white women thus.

Tom Parramore suggests that although there is good circumstantial evidence for the author of *The Bondwoman's Narrative* to have once been owned by John Hill Wheeler, not all of the evidence is consistent with the historical Wheeler. While Parramore argues that it is possible Crafts was a servant in Wheeler's household, he thinks it was unlikely; too many things have been fictionalized, such as plantation particulars and travel routes, for him to consider her narrative "true." Parramore acknowledges, however, that if Crafts had known Wheeler, her low opinion of him was probably merited. Wheeler was a religious bigot as well as a racist, and his wife was famously ill-tempered.

Katherine E. Flynn suggests that Jane Johnson, who, with two of her children, famously fled from Wheeler, ought not to be crossed off the list of those who could be Hannah Crafts. Flynn tells the story of Jane Johnson's life before and after her dramatic 1855 escape and increases our store of knowledge about this historically important figure. Though Flynn finds no evidence that Johnson wrote the novel (or even had literary leanings), Flynn's research supports the notion that the author of *The Bondwoman's Narrative* was part of the Wheeler household. Following up on facts established by Gates in his introduction to Crafts's narrative, Flynn strengthens the case that the author of *The Bondwoman's Narrative* belonged to Wheeler before 1855, particularly with the evidence that the author knew of Wheeler's bid for a position in the navy in 1853–1854. Flynn also suggests parallels between the loss of Hannah's status after leaving Washington (being relegated to the slave huts) and the probable reduction in Jane's status in 1854 from "a coveted post as a lady's maid in the nation's capital" to wherever she was left (possibly at the home of a Wheeler family relative) when the Wheelers left for a government post in Nicaragua.

Flynn's research also strengthens the strong ties between the Wheelers and Virginia, crucial to explaining Crafts's familiarity with Virginia geography. Not only did John Hill Wheeler purchase Jane Johnson from a Richmond businessman, Cornelius Crew, in January 1854, but also Wheeler's wife, Ellen Sully, had family ties to Richmond, and the Wheelers visited there often. Richmond, in Henrico County, is adjacent to Charles City County, where a small plantation named Milton is located.

Both Flynn's and Parramore's assessments of Wheeler's character certainly accord with the historical record. In an account that ran in *Frederick Douglass's Paper* on August 10, 1855, Wheeler's bigotry and profanity are shown in full color:

The Wheeler Slave Case

The following is a sketch of a conversation which took place on Sunday last in a drug store in Philadelphia. A young man, J.G.T., was reading aloud an article on the Wheeler Slave Case in *The Sunday Dispatch* of that city. A number of young men were standing by, and near them was Mr. Wheeler, drinking a glass of soda water:

WHEELER: My young friend, I am Col. John H. Wheeler. I am the man whose slaves were stolen.

J.G.T.: I know you are, Sir, though I was not aware that you were present.

WHEELER: Is it possible that you sympathize with that d——d Abolitionist Passmore Williamson?

J.G.T.: Certainly, Sir. All my sympathies are with him.

WHEELER: You think he did right, then, in assaulting me and threatening to cut my throat and stealing my people?

J.G.T.: I do not think your throat should be cut, but he did no more than his duty in taking the people. He acted from the best of motives.

WHEELER: What motives could he have for taking my slaves? I wa'n't disturbing anybody. I was simply passing through on my mission. I am Minister at
Nicaragua. I was taking them to wait on my wife. I won the woman's children, and all the relations are in Washington.

J.G.T.: But they were not your slaves. Judge Kelly decided that last night.

WHEELER: Judge Kelly be d——d! He is an Abolitionist. The Constitution
of the United States recognizes my right to them.

J.G.T.: I do not think it does.

WHEELER: Why, don't it say that fugitive niggers shall be sent back?

J.G.T.: Yes, and it is an infamous thing that it does say so. I for one would obey
no such enactment.

WHEELER: Then you are a traitor, sir a G——d d——d traitor, and you
ought to be taken out of here and hung upon the first lamp-post.

J.G.T.: I am glad you are not my Judge, Sir.

WHEELER: By God! You will be yet. You ought to be down in prison with that
damn'd Williamson. May be it will teach him not to meddle in what don't
belong to him.

J.G.T.: May be it will make a thousand Abolitionists, ready and willing to do
as he did. As for me it would be the proudest period of my life if I were in
his place.

WHEELER: Well, you'll be there one day. You Abolitionists have got to be put
down. If I had had a revolver Passmore Williamson would not be where he
is now; I would have put a bullet through his head. Unless Philadelphia ac-
quits herself, Southerners will not come here, and Southern trade is worth a
million dollars a year to Philadelphia.

J.G.T.: I hope we hold our principles higher than dollars and cents. I don't
think the whole South would buy a true freeman.

WHEELER: My! If I was to act as you Abolitionists, when a man came to me
in my official capacity, I would ask him if he came from the Free States, and
if he did, tell him to go to h——l!

Here Wheeler left abruptly, saying to J.T.G. he would hand him over to
the gentlemen who were listening, evidently supposing that they would be on
his side. So some of these were, in principle, though all agreed, irrespective
of the merits of the case, in pronouncing Mr. Wheeler to be, personally a
black-guard. —*N.Y. Tribune*

Remarkably, the same series of violent acts related in this short account is
portrayed in *The Bondwoman's Narrative* in roughly the same order: a disobedient
servant is hung (23), Hannah's first master has his throat cut and dies (74), a

woman who tried to smuggle a slave to freedom is put in prison (83), a lawyer has a bullet put through his head (235). Moreover, Hannah hears of Trappe's death while standing near a group of gentlemen drinking and talking, one of whom remarks that the person who killed him deserved the thanks of the community "for ridding the world of a villain" (234).

Two letters discovered by Flynn from William C. Nell, a charter member of the Boston Vigilance Society, to Passmore Williamson prove not only that Jane Johnson was alive and well in Boston in 1856 but also that Johnson was literate and corresponding with Williamson. (Flynn also offers convincing evidence that two other women named Hannah Crafts living in Boston after 1855 did not pen the novel—their handwriting is markedly different.) Although there are many questions to be answered regarding the connection between Jane Johnson and *The Bondwoman's Narrative*, it is increasingly certain that some sort of relationship existed between Jane Johnson and Hannah Crafts.

Joe Nickell's essay offers technical evidence about the manuscript, reviews some of the new findings and the new guesses as to Hannah Crafts's identity, and suggests that the search for Hannah Crafts should be continued. As we go to press, Gregg Hecimovich is pursuing the possibility that the author may have been a slave in the household of one of Wheeler's relatives, Henry Bond. The papers of Kate Wheeler Cooper, the highly educated niece of John Hill Wheeler, could offer crucial information on the domestic affairs of the extended Wheeler-Bond family.

Whether Hannah Crafts was Hannah Vincent, the New Jersey schoolteacher, or a servant in John Hill Wheeler's household, the Bond household, or some related household in North Carolina or Virginia we do not yet know, but for reasons of her own, Hannah Crafts took pains to signal her relationship to Wheeler textually. The mounting evidence of this relationship, combined with proof of her firsthand knowledge of regional geography, contemporary local politics, and Wheeler family history, make the case for Hannah Crafts, fugitive slave.

Finally, four reviews of *The Bondwoman's Narrative* close this volume: Mia Bay, "The Bondwoman's Narrative: An 1850s Account of Slave Life" (*New York Times*, May 12, 2002); Hilary Mantel, "The Shape of Absence" (*London Review of Books*, August 8, 2002); John Bloom, "Literary Blackface" (*National Review*, July 26, 2002); and Ira Berlin, "Desperate Measures" (*Washington Post*, June 23, 2002). Each of these reviews offers a sense of the public response to Hannah Crafts's novel in the first six months after publication.

I

THE LITERARY MARKETPLACE
Between the Sentimental Novel and the Slave Narrative

"A Silent Unobtrusive Way"
Hannah Crafts and the Literary Marketplace

AUGUSTA ROHRBACH

Remarkable for its historical value, Hannah Crafts's *The Bondwoman's Narrative* tells a semi-autobiographical tale about a woman's experience as a plantation slave and her subsequent escape. The author uses the form of first-person narrative—a standard feature employed by her fellow African American writers and greatly popularized in their published narratives. Yet, Crafts resisted one of the most prominent norms of black authorship: Her story, though based on fact, is fiction.

Written around 1857, it precedes the other early novel written by an African American female—Harriet Wilson's *Our Nig*—by about two years.[1] Yet, Crafts's novel was never published, leaving us to speculate why. Another important African American woman writer, Harriet Jacobs, author of *Incidents in the Life of a Slave Girl*, famously told Harriet Beecher Stowe that her book "needed no romance" to succeed; Harriet Jacobs found a publisher without Stowe's help. Thanks in part to the support of Lydia Maria Child, *Our Nig* was published, but it was not financially successful, despite its connections to the prominent abolitionist and author. Jacobs fared somewhat better, but authorship never was the boon she had hoped for. From the little we know about Hannah Crafts, she lacked any entrée into the world of publishing. Holding no known ties to the abolitionist movement, Hannah Crafts's work remained a fugitive text—until now.

What might have been some of Hannah Crafts's considerations concerning publication? Unlike Jacobs—and many other African American writers of the era—she does not make a plea in her preface for financial support. Yet, she does wonder about her reception: "How will such a literary venture, coming from a sphere so humble be received?" (3). Her concern, and the terms in which she couches it, suggests a familiarity with the literary marketplace. Calling the novel a "venture," Crafts implies a business interest but does not connect financial need with writing, as others—such as Jacobs—did.[2] Omitting the need for remuneration as an explicit and necessary reason for the text's production keeps the focus on the story as a story, that is, on its aesthetic value. Breaking away from the mendicant narrative tradition, Crafts emphasizes her "craft."[3]

At the same time, however, Crafts utilizes many of the most popular literary conventions of the time, starting with the claim that the novel is a "record of plain unvarnished facts" (3).[4] From the avowal that the novel will appeal to "those who regard truth as stranger than fiction" to the evocation of Providence as the muse of her imagination, Hannah Crafts demonstrates a canny understanding of the literary marketplace and its trends and conventions. And yet, Crafts could not have anticipated the full impact of race when considering genre. Judging from Harriet Jacobs's Pyrrhic victory in the literary marketplace—she died destitute and unknown—no market existed for African American fiction.

She did, however, have a basis for choosing the novel—a popular genre that performed well in the abolitionist market. Writings about slavery—even those tied into the topic ever so loosely—sold well in the antebellum literary marketplace.[5] So why didn't Hannah Crafts's *Bondwoman's Narrative* make it to the marketplace? There is really only one central difference between Crafts and the other novelists discussed here: she is black.

Largely self-taught, Crafts demonstrates her acquaintance with canonical white literature throughout the course of the novel, and there are clues to what she may have read beyond those texts explicitly referred to. The novel's protagonist tells us: "My mistress was very kind, and unknown to Master she indulged me in reading [the books in the parlor] whenever I desired" (36). As it turns out, we know more about the contents of that library than we do about Hannah Crafts herself. Thanks to the literary detective work of Henry Louis Gates, Jr., and Bryan Sinche, we know something about the books to which Hannah Crafts may have had access. John Hill Wheeler, a politician from North Carolina who owned Hannah Crafts, made a catalogue of his 1850 library.[6] In addition to this resource, a catalogue for the library's sale, made in 1883 after Wheeler's death, provides a glimpse into other possible sources for Crafts, as well as an interesting look into the literary life of an upper-class Southern politician of the period.

The titles listed in Wheeler's library catalogue provide a sketch of the literary marketplace of the time. For instance, among his books are copies of speeches by the British abolitionist William Wilberforce as well as the American opponent to slavery Henry Ward Beecher, brother of Harriet Beecher Stowe.[7] These works would have offered Crafts a way to sound out her own thoughts concerning the peculiar institution. However, though potentially inspirational, they say nothing about why Crafts chose to tell her story, nor do such abolitionist writings illuminate the reason for her selection of fiction as her mode.

There are several first-person narratives that stand out in Wheeler's collection. Fictionalized first-person narratives include tawdry sentimental tales such as *The Banker's Wife; or, Court and City, A Novel* and *The Gambler's Wife, A Novel*.[8] These books were most likely part of the parlor library, according to Bryan Sinche, and our narrator tells us directly that she had her pick of those volumes. Indeed, the novel's central story evolves from one of Hannah's forays into the library. Once she got to the parlor library, Hannah tells us, she sat "with a book behind the heavy damask curtains that shaded the window" (36). To protect herself from view and provide light by which to read, Hannah soon reaps another, unexpected gain from this choice—one that makes the remainder of the novel possible. While there concealed, Hannah discovers the secret identity of her mistress as she learns of Mr. Trappe's extortion designs. Observing that "he is the shadow darkening her life," without intended irony, the narrator discovers her mistress's "true" identity (34, 45). Her earlier suspicions that "there was mystery, something indefinable about her" due as much to physical as to behavioral features ("her lips . . . were too large, full and red" for a white woman [27]), prove to be well founded. The mulatto daughter of her father by a slave woman, the new Lady of Lindendale is a slave under the law, as she must "follow the condition of the mother." We learn, with the narrator, that she will be remanded to slavery if Trappe is not appeased. Her secret—uncovered by the lawyer Trappe—sets the plot in motion.

As sensational as Hannah's discovery is, however, we must not overlook the fact that this knowledge comes to the narrator as an indirect result of her desire to read. However, reading produces writing, and black writing posed a special threat to the budding profession of authorship, one populated almost exclusively by whites.[9] Nonetheless, while her mistress is caught in the trap laid by the rapscallion character of the same name (Trappe), Hannah ends up with more freedom than other fugitive slaves in her choice of the novel as her prose style.

To what extent does Crafts's choice of genre affect her larger story? Examining a few of her more explicit creative decisions can help us gain a sense of her intentions. Among the literary features of the novel are the clear signs of serial writing à la Dickens. Crafts laces the novel with clues that the story was of the "to-be-continued" variety; statements such as "Years passed, however, before I learned their fate," concerning the northern white couple who taught her how to read, signal the eventual return of these characters (13). Holding her tale together through the use of cliff-hangers, Crafts's story breaks up nicely into installments. Though she may have intended to serialize the piece, it seems more likely that she was simply influenced by the Dickens works she encountered in bound volumes.[10] Deemed clumsy by some, Crafts's use of the implied serial format has philosophical implications, ones that coincide with her concept of history.[11]

Anticipating the narrative strategies of a later African American novelist, Pauline Elizabeth Hopkins, Crafts uses reappearing characters to outline the contours of her historical imagination.[12] Treating history as a continuous series of events linked ever so slightly by coincidence, Crafts finds ways to uncover cause and effect relationships. For instance, in an early scene in the novel about ancestry and tradition, the tale of the family portraits takes readers into a gothic world of pain and suffering where tradition mutates into a horrible legacy revisited on the family, much in the tradition of Edgar Allan Poe. Privileging an aristocratic model of power, Sir Clifford's edict—that all heirs furnish a portrait of themselves and their spouses for the gallery—emphasizes family as performance. The site of neither nurturing nor love, the family scene portrays the handing down of power in the form of property in general and slaves in particular. Thus, like Poe, Crafts uses family history to limn a larger story about how the sins of the fathers are visited on the sons.[13]

More significant than the gothic details of the portraits themselves is Hannah's reaction to them. Changing as she looks upon them, Hannah's view of the portraits prefigures the ideological divide between black and white. Under her gaze, these former masters become hideous and terrifying. The gallery, a Poe-like tomb of the undead rather than a majestic tribute to ancestors, is a chamber of horrors for Hannah—and ultimately everyone else in the story. A slave's perspective, one seen from the "other side" of history, reveals a wholly different view. Thus, it is in the gallery that we first experience Hannah's point of view on traditional history. Further illustration of this perspective's transformative powers comes into play in the two chapters that follow.

More specifically, those chapters reveal her special power to identify Trappe as a trap. "The bridegroom was probably too happy, and the company too gay," Hannah tells us (28). She, a waiter at the table and an outsider unaffected by the seductive airs of the marriage table, can see things others miss.[14] Despite the fact that he is "an old-fashioned gentleman" and the least likely to attract attention, Hannah "had eyes and ears for only" him (27). Her refusal of romance—and marriage—makes her impervious to the seduction experienced by the wedding guests, and thus she sees through him. Through her ability to read between the lines, we are introduced to the story's central villain and recurring plot line: an unseen enemy wearing the costume of respectability, a costume Hannah immediately recognizes as shabby and without dignity.

Perhaps the best example of Crafts's use of the serial format as a literary strategy comes later in Chapters 14 and 15. Titled "Lizzy's Story" and "Lizzy's Story Continued," these chapters are a tribute to Crafts's skill as a writer and her knowledge of the characteristic conventions of serialization. Lizzy's story is a lurid one about the return of the repressed, told by a character who was left behind when Hannah and her mistress escaped. Ushering Lizzy back into the novel suggests that there is something about Lizzy that makes her ideal to fill this narrative function.

Earlier in the novel, Lizzy is treated as a rather laughable character who takes pride in her white ancestry:

> Lizzy was much better educated than I was, and had been to many places that I had never even heard tell of. She had also a great memory for dates and names which I invariably forgot. She was a Quadroon, almost white, with delicate hands and feet, and a person that any lady in the land might have been proud of. She came, she said of good family and frequently mentioned great names in connection with her own, and when I smiled and said it mattered little she would assume an air of consequential dignity, and assert that on the contrary it was a very great thing and very important even to a slave to be well connected—that good blood was an inheritance to them—and that they heard the name of some honorable gentleman mentioned with applause. . . . And then I said "Of course" which mollified her rumpled vanity. (33–34)

As the story Hannah relates shows, however, white blood is no claim to nobility, morality, or pride. Thus, Lizzy—of all the African American characters we encounter in the story—serves as a perfect demonstration of the hypocrisy of racial pride. But this report also tells us something further about Lizzy: she "had also a great memory for dates and names," an important feature for a tale of "unvarnished facts." Hannah, as she admits here, lacks this ability, telling us that she "invariably forgot" such details. She also tells us that she is adept at smoothing over Lizzy's "rumpled vanity" with a lie—though one that is rather harmless. Thus, through a complex series of rhetorical shifts, Hannah puts forward her substitute narrator as one with better capabilities for remembering facts, while placing herself in the position of fiction writer—one who knows how to speak for effect rather than actual truth.

Crafts cleverly makes way for this narrative intrusion by creating a visual image for the impending scene. At the close of Chapter 13 we leave Hannah and Lizzy hidden "behind some piles of lumber where" they "could be effectively screened from observation" (171). As the gothic tale of sexual license among the planter class unfolds, Hannah is sanitized against the tale by not telling it herself. What is it about this tale of sexual misconduct and marital infidelity that might invite an act of narrative ventriloquism?

For one thing, the story Lizzy tells lays bare any pretensions about the physical and mental and moral superiority of white people. Master and Mistress are shown to be savage, petty, and immoral. But perhaps most significantly, the "story-within-a-story" devise allows Crafts extra leeway for a scathing critique of female vulnerability. The story condemns Mr. Cosgrove for his licentious behavior with female slaves and for betraying his wife by keeping several black mistresses. However, the extramarital sex is not as egregious as the disloyalty. Readers find out, along with Mrs. Cosgrove, that her husband has started an alternate family with a slave woman. To hide his concubine and offspring from his wife, he stashes the slave woman in a secret recess of the house. With this story, Crafts—via Lizzy—adds her take on an arrangement already made famous by William Wells Brown's *Clotel* (1853). Locating the mistress and her children in the house metaphorically suggests the degree to which slavery's corruption has been internalized in the home. Hidden, like a cancer, this arrangement leads to the moral downfall of all concerned—and even death.

Providing still one more remove from an overt critique of American culture, Crafts casts Mrs. Cosgrove as an aristocratic British woman. Assuaging herself with the false notion that she has "freed" a slave, she turns the young mother and her twin babies out of the house to fend for themselves. As they face certain death through exposure, this "lady" lies upon her satin sheets eating toasted biscuits and honey. This scene stands out, as it is one of only two narrative digressions in the novel. Important in part for what is left unsaid, it is an emblem of narrative resistance. Told by someone other than Hannah, the narrative distance is remarkable, but its message is striking. Depicting Mrs. Cosgrove as a frustrated—and infertile—woman, her childlessness is understood primarily in relation to the slave woman whom she sees as her de facto rival. Not only has her husband's mistress borne him two sons, but they're twins—an unmistakable sign of the couple's fecundity.

Hannah's reluctance to narrate this story seems in keeping with her eschewal of marriage while in slavery and her refrain from romance.[15] She recounts only events to which she was an eyewitness, and Hannah was not present at Lindendale, where this scene takes place.

Her history is progressive and forward-looking. The whites in this novel are tethered to a past that "haunts" them.[16] Lizzy's tale is important, in part, because it emphasizes the legacy of slavery *for whites*. Far from being a symbol of white superiority and a boon to white economic power, slavery is responsible for the downward spiral of the heirs of Lindendale. And, as if to underscore the importance of this tale, Crafts hands it over to the one black character who both fits the type of narrator readers would have expected (the slave who tells a story in verifiable detail) and buys into the ideology of whiteness that even many of the most liberal abolitionists held.[17]

Clearly, Crafts learned many of the conventions of contemporary literature from her contact with Wheeler's library. What was the influence of African American authors on Crafts's writing? Among the titles I found in the 1882 catalogue, I was surprised to see an 1833 edition of Phillis Wheatley's poems; its presence in his collection is suggestive of Crafts's relationship to white literary tradition. Though not included in Sinche's list, Wheatley's work foreshadows Crafts's radical appropriation of white forms. Just as Wheatley appropriated the sonnet form for her own purposes, Crafts took on the lineaments of the novel when nonfiction was the norm for African American writers. But unlike Wheatley's work, which was tested and ultimately sanctioned by white community leaders, resulting in publication, Crafts's work never got into print.[18] Perhaps Crafts knew, as Frances Smith Foster argues, that "Wheatley's literary achievements may have facilitated her eventual freedom but . . . it had not protected her finally from the ravages of racial discrimination and poverty." As Foster concludes, "it took more than words to change society and . . . words would be subjected to interpretations engendered by non-literary expectations and assumptions." Among the expectations that Crafts challenges is the racial divide among literary genres. Crafts's novel may have proved too much of an assault on the color lines and conventions of the publishing world. Clearly, her choice of genre would have played a negative role in attracting a publisher.

White authors such as Stowe might have made fact into fiction when it came to racial subject matter, but the reverse was not a possibility, as the example of James Williams shows: In 1838, when James Williams sought publication of what ultimately turned out to be his fictional autobiography, he was branded a liar for his use of the fictional form rather than sticking with the factual narrative open to black writers at the time. As it turns out, *The Authentic Narrative of James Williams, An American Slave* isn't "authentic" at all. Though "dictated" to the abolitionist and poet John Greenleaf Whittier, it is a novel, because Williams was not a slave but a writer savvy enough to realize that this genre was the one with the most currency, especially for a black person.[19]

"Passing" as an autobiography, this novel makes use of a variety of genre styles ranging from the slave narrative to the sentimental and gothic novel.

A testament to self-schooling, *A Bondwoman's Narrative* contains references to the great works of Western literature—from the Greek tragedies to Shakespeare and Byron. Proving Crafts's claim to literacy, these textual references also provide clues to her intended readership. Her literary "samplings" suggest the interpretive communities she wishes to connect with through her acts of intertextuality.[20] Crafts inserts passages from Dickens and references to Byron, along with popular clichés referencing classical authors such as Homer and Virgil, without giving any clear attribution. Her treatment of these literary sources suggests that she expected readers to be familiar with these volumes. But perhaps even more significant for Crafts was the effect that the presence of Dickens, Shakespeare, and Byron had on Crafts's sense of authorship. By incorporating the words of other writers into her text, she put her work on an even plane with theirs.

Whereas Stowe was compelled to "verify" the sources of her fiction with the 1854 publication of *A Key to Uncle Tom's Cabin*, Crafts submits herself to the reverse. "Authenticating" her literacy—and thus her validity as an author—requires a clear demonstration of literary knowledge. Choosing the novel as her form and the works of other famous, respected, and *white* writers as her resources, she asserts the terms of her authorship. Refusing to remain within the sanctioned boundaries offered by the factual narrative, she leaves that literary ghetto behind as she strikes out toward the novel. By claiming the writing and the forms of free whites as her own, she expresses her own sense of freedom.

Importantly, the ease with which Crafts incorporates sources suggests the value she places on them. Crafts's use of literary sources demonstrates a reading ethic associated with an earlier period in publishing history, when books were hard to come by and thus were read and re-read many times. Especially suited for the reading of a sacred text such as the Bible, intrinsic reading assumes a degree of textual inscrutability and thus a philosophy of language consistent with what literary critics call deconstruction. Privileging presence over absence, "intensive" reading practices encourage a reader to consider the idea that the text cannot be fully apprehended in one reading; it is full of hidden relationships and meanings that remain obscure in each individual reading. Lacking the ability to impart total meaning, language as a system of representation—and the texts it produces—remains partial and incomplete. This philosophy of language also suggests that language has an almost inanimate power, regardless of whether it is read. A text unwritten is nothing; a text unpublished will always be something.

Though we do not know which, if any, slave narratives Crafts may have come in contact with, it seems likely that she would have seen, at some point, Frederick Douglass's 1844 *Narrative*. And, indeed, a first edition of Frederick Douglass's *Narrative* appears in the catalogue of Wheeler's library made for the 1882 auction. Assuming for the moment that Crafts knew and recognized Douglass's work as a literary precursor to her own, what links exist between the two? She certainly is aware that textual claims must be substantiated. To that end, Crafts expends much effort in making her position a special vantage point for the observation of slavery and its practices. Repeatedly, Crafts emphasizes her position within the household as a lady's maid as the basis for her knowledge of events told in the course of the story. Yet, because she chose fiction, Crafts also takes for herself an extra measure of freedom. Indeed, the narrator resists verifiable facts such as place names almost entirely. This radical departure from the conventions of slave narratives compels the reader to accept a level of intelligence and artistry that would not be permitted to a black author. Thus her concern is with verisimilitude rather than, as was Douglass's, with verifiability.

In place of verifiable facts, Crafts treats her readers to an unusual degree of social and psychological realism. For instance, though the narrator declares, "I cannot describe my journey; the details would be dry, tedious, uninteresting," she is unsparing in the details of suffering she and her traveling companion experience (266). Thus, though "factual" details are absent, details that heighten a reader's sense of Hannah's emotional and physical discomfort abound. The hut that the two fugitives use as a dwelling offers shelter but reeks of a moldy heap of straw (66). The food they are able to gather is paltry (66). Their bodies, worn from the strenuous journey, appear weak, their clothing, torn (67). When they approach others on their trip, the threat of danger is palpable (56). As the whole narrative testifies, Crafts is much more interested in the psychological and social experiences of slavery and thus forges her brand of humanitarian realism.[21] Heeding—or rather anticipating—Zora Neale Hurston's argument in "What White Publishers Won't Print" that African American writers should spend more time delving into the psychological realm of their characters in order to gain a degree of realism and dimensionality, Crafts makes the mood and physical status of her characters central to the story. Oddly, however, Crafts never mentions her encounters with texts by Douglass, Wheatley, or any other African American writer. Among her literary references, their names and work are notably absent. Instead, we find her referencing and emulating white mainstream fiction of the sort she—like her narrator—might have encountered in the parlor library.

Although Crafts may not have taken lessons in style from her fellow African American writers, she surely noted the impact of publication on the lives of those who were published. In addition to the examples of Wheatley and Douglass, Crafts may have learned about the dangers that celebrity status and public recognition can create—from the experience of a fellow slave in the Wheeler household. I am referring here, of course, to the escape of Jane—an event that made possible Hannah's position as lady's maid and hence the single most important source for this novel.

A local sensation at the time, Jane's escape from slavery, with the help of the Pennsylvania Antislavery Society's president, Passmore Williamson, among others, became a national event. Picked up by several major newspapers, including the *New York Tribune,* the *Philadelphia Ledger,* and the *New Orleans Times Picayune,* the story also appeared in pamphlet form.

This incident—and Hannah's direct link to it—provides us with evidence that Hannah Crafts knew the dangers of publicity. Crafts's choice to eschew notoriety and to remain unpublished reflects her sense of responsibility to family as well as her sense of personal ownership. Adjuring her readers to *imagine* her freedom at the novel's close leaves the condition for freedom's possibility untrammeled by capital, market, and thus slavery.[22] Safe freedom, for the fugitive slave, means remaining unread. Publication would bring publicity, and she did not want her portrait to circulate—as Jane's and Passmore Williamson's did—among the newspapers and drawing rooms of the day.[23] Authorship was a public enterprise requiring full and unmolested citizenship, as the following advertisement from the *Liberator* demonstrates.

Thus, as a witness to Jane's escape and to Passmore Williamson's incarceration, as well as the literary experiences of fellow African Americans, Crafts might have questioned the virtues of publication. If literacy was a crime, authorship was a lifelong sentence. Wheatley died in poverty; Douglass made abolition and civil rights his life's work, as did the many other African Americans who sought publication as a means toward social justice. Instead, Crafts's commitment to "a silent unobtrusive way" guided her away from the hubbub of the literary marketplace, where economics met reform, and toward a new sense of privacy. Miraculously reunited with her long lost—and hitherto unknown—mother, Crafts does not deign to represent the joyous occasion. The event—along with her eventual choice to marry—are kept outside the pages of the novel, protected from readers' prying eyes.

Although Crafts attempted, through literary sampling, to align her story with a variety of reading niches—classical, evangelical, abolitionist, among others—she did not link herself with any organization or with a larger public. Nor did she choose self-publication as an option, as was the case with So-

PASSMORE WILLIAMSON
IN MOYAMENSING JAIL.

JUST PUBLISHED,

A FINE Portrait representing this *Martyr to the cause of Freedom, Truth and Justice,* (versus Law,) taken from life, in the cell in which he has been incarcerated by Judge Kane for alleged Contempt of Court. Size of the Picture, 16 by 20 in. Price, Fifty Cents.

Those desiring early impressions of this interesting Picture can receive them by leaving their names with the Publisher, THOMAS CURTIS, 134 Arch street, Philadelphia, where all orders for the trade must be addressed.

Philadelphia, Sept. 20, 1855.

Advertisement from *The Liberator*, 12 October 1855. Photographed by John Seigfried; image used by permission of Mudd Library, Oberlin College.

journer Truth. Rather, to preserve her privacy and her freedom, she maintained her "silent unobtrusive way" while also exercising her powers of expression. A text that speaks to all sorts of oppression—sexual, racial, and class-based—Crafts's novel retains its intrinsic power despite the fact that it remained unpublished.

This manuscript gives new meaning to the tag line that accompanied many of the works produced by her contemporary black writers: written by herself (or himself). Unaligned with the abolitionist movement, Hannah Crafts eschewed the conventions that promised success to others. Describing herself as having "a silent unobtrusive way of observing things and events" (5), she casts herself with the features of a writer, but just what *kind* of a writer her readers would not know. Writing made this person an author; not publishing kept her free.

Taking stock of Wheeler's library has revealed a great deal about what Crafts might have known about the world of publishing. Crafts's story has been mediated through the lens of fiction, and in making that narrative choice, she chose to give herself that extra measure of freedom from racially imposed standards of genre, perhaps even knowing that this choice would result in not being able to find an immediate market for the manuscript. Hannah Crafts, a mixed-race fugitive slave, author and narrator of *A Bondwoman's*

Narrative, produced a mixed-genre fugitive text. But perhaps most significantly, Crafts preserved that freedom by remaining unpublished. As the inclusion of first editions of Wheatley and Douglass in the 1833 catalogue of Wheeler's library attests, Crafts would not be bought—or sold—again.

Notes

1. Harriet Wilson, *Our Nig* (Rand and Avery, 1859).

2. Asking her readers to "excuse deficiencies in consideration of circumstances" Jacobs makes it clear that she is the sole support of herself and her family: "since I have been at the North, it has been necessary for me to work diligently for my own support, and the education of my children." *Harriet Jacobs, Incidents in the Life of a Slave Girl*, ed. Jean Fagan Yellin (Cambridge: Harvard University Press, 1987), p. 1.

3. For this insight I am indebted to Patricia Wald's "Hannah crafts," published in this volume.

4. For a discussion of "the unvarnished truth" as a distinctive trope in mid-nineteenth-century literature, see Ann Fabian, *The Unvarnished Truth: Personal Narratives in Nineteenth-Century America* (Berkeley: University of California Press, 2000).

5. For a detailed analysis of the antebellum literary marketplace, see Chapter One in Karen Sánchez-Eppler, *Truth Stranger than Fiction* (New York: Palgrave, 2002) as well as her *Touching Liberty* (Berkeley: University of California Press, 1993).

6. See Appendix C, *The Bondwoman's Narrative.*

7. Listed in the catalogue for the 1882 sale of Wheeler's books are *Speeches of William Wilberforce and Others, in 1789, on the Abolition of the Slave Trade* (London), (p. 55), and H. W. Beecher, *Star Papers, or Experiences of Art and Nature* (New York: 1855), (p. 8).

8. Catherine Grace Frances Gore, *The Banker's Wife; or, Court and City, A Novel* (New York: Harper, 1848); and Elizabeth Caroline Grey, *The Gambler's Wife, A Novel* (Philadelphia: T. B. Peterson, 1850). Both of these works appear in Appendix C to *The Bondwoman's Narrative* (327).

9. For a detailed discussion of the threat black writers (and black writing) posed to fledgling white writers in the mid-nineteenth century, see my "Making It Real: Slave Narratives in the Literary Marketplace," *Prospects* 26 (2001): 137–163.

10. See Hollis Robbins's essay in this volume.

11. Ann Fabian, quoted in the "Introduction" to *The Bondwoman's Narrative*, by Henry Louis Gates, Jr., finds "all the clumsy plot structures, changing tenses, impossible coincidences, and heterogeneous elements of the best" of domestic fiction (xxvi).

12. For a detailed discussion of serialization as a narrative strategy consistent with a radical racial agenda and a bold concept of history, see my "'To Be Continued': Identity, Multiplicity, and Antigenealogy as Narrative Strategies in the Magazine Fiction of Pauline Hopkins," *Callaloo* 22:2 (1999): 483–498. See also, Genevieve Fabre and Robert O'Meally, eds., *History and Memory in African American Culture* (New York: Oxford, 1994).

13. It seems very likely that Wheeler, being a man with literary predilections, would have subscribed to the journal in which Poe was published (*The Southern Literary Messenger*) and that Crafts may have read his fiction there.

14. Repeatedly she tells us that she will not marry because of her slave status. For a fascinating analysis of Hannah's refusal to marry, see Christopher Castiglia's essay in this volume.

15. For declarations about marriage and romance as privileges of the free, see pp. lxiii, 120, 131, and 206–207.

16. See Patricia Wald's "Hannah crafts," included in this volume for a discussion of Crafts's use of the ghost story and its reflection on the history of American slavery.

17. For a detailed and fascinating look at the few figures who were relatively free of the racism that crippled the movement, see John Stauffer, *The Black Hearts of Men* (Cambridge: Harvard University Press, 2002).

18. As to whether Crafts knew of Wheatley, literary scholar and historian Frances Smith Foster believes "African American women knew what had happened to Phillis Wheatley and to her work." Frances Smith Foster, *Written by Herself: Literary Production by African American Women, 1746–1892* (Bloomington: Indiana University Press, 1993), p. 18.

19. *Narrative of James Williams, an American slave; who was for several years a driver on a cotton plantation in Alabama* (New York: American Anti-slavery Society, 1838). Henry Louis Gates, Jr., in a lecture delivered at Harvard on December 10, 1999, made a case for rechristening this work as a novel.

20. Literary "sampling" is common among African American writers and should be distinguished from Henry Louis Gates, Jr.'s concept of "pastiche," which he discusses in *The Signifying Monkey* (New York: Oxford, 1988). See my "'To Be Continued': Identity, Multiplicity, and Antigenealogy as Narrative Strategies in the Magazine Fiction of Pauline Hopkins," *Callaloo* 22:2 (1999): 483–498, for further discussion of literary sampling.

21. Humanitarian realism emphasizes suffering—physical, mental, and spiritual—so as to encourage social change in readers. For a detailed discussion of this term and its bearing on the relationship between African American and Anglo-American literature, see my *Truth Stranger than Fiction: Race, Realism and the U.S. Literary Marketplace* (New York: Palgrave, 2002).

22. In "Eaten Alive: Slavery and Celebrity in Antebellum America," Michael Newbury argues that slavery and celebrity share the same model of labor. His analysis turns on the realization that both the slave and the celebrity are embodied forms of property. *ELH* 61(1994 Spring): 159–187.

23. Aside from Crafts's probable knowledge of the historical examples discussed here, she provides evidence within her novel concerning her knowledge of the impact of publication. See her discussion of Byron's sudden fame with the publication of *Don Juan* (213).

2

Bondwoman Unbound

Hannah Crafts's Art and Nineteenth-Century U.S. Literary Practice

LAWRENCE BUELL

*T*he *Bondwoman's Narrative* starts with an esoteric flamboyance rare if not unique in African American writing before the Civil War. In the King James translation of the Bible, from which the author takes most of her Victorian-style chapter mottoes, "bondwoman" in the first instance can only mean Hagar, Abraham's cast-off Egyptian concubine, the mother of wandering Ishmael and not his legitimate younger half-brother Isaac, from whom the children of Israel descended. Hagar was a common name for female slaves as well as a popular, complexly symbolic figure in nineteenth-century literature and art, of which more anon. Hagar is the only named biblical character referred to by the epithet "bondwoman." Her banishment becomes a symbol in the Christian New Testament for bondage to the old theology: "Stop then, brethren, we are not children of the bondwoman, but of the free" (Gal. 4: 31).

However, the author of our novel stipulates that "Hannah," *not* Hagar, "crafts" *The Bondwoman's Narrative.* Given that no black writer before 1865 "quoted more texts in her own work" than did "Hannah Crafts,"[1] one cannot help wondering whether the writer has chosen a pseudonym in order to make author/title into a declarative sentence that will both assert her pilgrimage from bondage to free authorial agent and deepen it by aligning herself, symbolically, not only with *the* "obvious" biblical H-figure for her particular type of case but with a double-helix constellation of H's.

The biblical Hannah lives out a success story more like that of Hagar's rival Sarah, Abraham's long-barren wife. Sarah initially enlisted Hagar as a surrogate, but through God's grace eventually she too gave birth (to Isaac), and she saw to it that Hagar and Ishmael were banished. The biblical Hannah, first wife of Elkanah the Ephraimite, is also shamed by long infertility but at last is granted the favor of mothering the prophet Samuel. Indeed, her prayer to this end is the most extended prayer given to any woman in the Hebrew Bible (I Samuel I: II–18), although ironically it seems initially to fall on deaf ears: the temple priest, overhearing her, thinks at first that she's drunk. Literally Hannah petitions for a son, but her broader plea is that the Lord "look on the affliction of thine handmaid, and remember me." In time this becomes one of the sources of the Magnificat of the Virgin Mary, who upon hearing that her humble self is to give birth to a savior praises God for having "regarded the low estate of his handmaiden" and rejoices that "henceforth all generations shall call me blessed" (Luke I: 48).

What does all this have to do with the antebellum author who calls herself Hannah Crafts? Most fundamentally, it begins to suggest that this was an author who, despite facing obvious impediments to the mastery of the dominant high culture, was capable of invoking the antebellum period's most important literary master text with a subtlety—at best—equal to the classics of high canonical Anglo-American literary scripturism by Emerson, Dickinson, Hawthorne, Melville, Stowe, and others. The Bible was by far the best-selling, most accessible, most cited book in the United States between the Revolution and the Civil War; and Hannah Crafts, an eager if not encyclopedic reader, showed herself as adept in creative hermeneutics as any of the authors aforesaid. Let us now look a little more closely at the results before going on to focus on some of her more specifically "literary" models.

To begin with, the biblical-allegorical echoes I have so far teased out expand the biblical warrant for handmaidens to prophesy (Acts I: 17–18) to bondwomen as well. Hannah Crafts does not so much argue as take for granted what Olaudah Equiano had claimed a half-century before in the first great author-written Anglophone slave narrative—that the children of Africa, "descendants of Abraham," are as honorable as white Europeans are.[2] Bondwoman and handmaiden cannot be pried apart. Indeed Crafts would likely have noticed that the Bible itself montages the two figures. Hagar herself is called "handmaid" before Sarah turns on her, and after Sarah's death she is called by that title once more, almost as if the ostracism had never happened (Gen. 16: 1; 25: 12).

At all events, the author of *The Bondwoman's Narrative* blurs the two categories not just in her role as bondwoman-become-author, not just in the novel's final vignette of the ex-bondwoman enjoying middle-class domestic contentment in an idyllic Northern cottage, but also within the main narrative, by sending her first and last mistresses across the color line, for example. Mrs. Vincent turns out to be part black and therefore marked as potential bondwoman, unbeknownst at first to herself but immediately so perceived by Hannah. This leads to a failed escape scheme during which mistress and bondwoman change roles, Hannah taking the lead as the stronger and bolder person. Mrs. Wheeler powders herself with a white substance that turns her skin temporarily black, so that to her chagrin she is mistaken for a slave—a farcical episode that has the feel of African American jokelore or blackface minstrelsy fakelore, though as Hollis Robbins notes the author might also have come across the story in an 1851 issue of *The Scientific American* in the library of the historical Mr. Wheeler. The serious point behind the joke is of course that the difference between bondwoman and master class is no more than skin deep.

These examples begin to suggest how *The Bondwoman's Narrative,* draft rather than finished work though it is, is one of the most artfully structured of antebellum narratives by African Americans. The two episodes together constitute one of several pairings that create a bilateral symmetry within the text. In other cases as well, an event from the early part of the novel is echoed or reprised toward the end. Before the story can conclude, Hannah must first meet once again the kindly Northern Quaker who taught her to read and must hear about the death of the evil Dickensian lawyer-slavetrader Mr. Trappe, discoverer and exploiter of the secret of her first mistress's parentage, whose machinations produce the first serious destabilization in Hannah's life and drive her mistress to her death.

Hannah must also negotiate another biblical twinship. Mrs. Wheeler, whose mind has been poisoned against her by a rival servant Maria orders Hannah to remove to the slave quarters and "marry" a repulsive field hand. (The fact that Hannah's rival predecessor-successor is a "Maria" may be a slyly disruptive allusion to the biblical link between Old Testament Hannah and New Testament Mary.) Distraught and disgusted, Hannah resorts to the folk superstition—common among whites as well as blacks—of opening her Bible at random, to the "place where Jacob fled from his brother Esau." She resolves to follow the patriarch's example. Presumably the author must have known that it was Esau, like Ishmael, who conventionally signified the unwashed, the racial other. In the eyes of whites at least, blacks were stereotypically Esaus, not Jacobs. A century later, W. E. B. DuBois would reverse the stigma in one of his most eloquent commemorative orations. He portrays Esau, the older twin robbed of his birthright by Jacob's clever impersonation of him, as the honest but improvident laborer, and Jacob as the wily unscrupulous determined power-hunger of Eurocentrism.[3] But just as she has laid claim to Hannah's rather than Hagar's identity, the bondwoman-author aligns herself here, in orthodox Christian fashion, with Jacob's example, escaping to the North in male disguise. Along the way, she quietly self-confirms her claim by staging an encounter with a fellow fugitive by the name of Jacob, who becomes her protector, fellow traveler, and thereby a kind of double, without penetrating her disguise—any more than biblical Jacob's disguise was penetrated by father Isaac when the trickster sought the blind and dying patriarch's blessing clad in sheepskins that gave him an Esau-like hairiness. The fact that Hannah Crafts's literal Jacob is killed by a pursuer as pretended Jacob escapes seems a further invitation to read this part of the plot symbolically.

But I do not want to make the case for this novel's latter-day interest rest solely or even mainly on its feats of heterodox scriptural imagination. The biblical thematics I have been describing are, after all, not so much unique achievements as striking variants on the amazing fertility of imagination within vernacular African American Christianity. The combination that we see here, in *The Bondwoman's Narrative*, was also broadly characteristic: a subversive biblical revisionism (e.g., slaves identifying themselves in spiritual songs of longing and protest with the chosen people Moses was to lead out of Egypt) arising from a conviction of faith much more profound than mere opportunistic strategy, though it was that too of course. Crafts as Hagar/Hannah is in that sense no more remarkable a feat of self-invention than fugitive Moses Roper recalling a longed-for but unexpected reunion with his family as the reunion of Joseph and his brothers (Gen. 42: 7–8), or Jarena Lee proclaiming herself Jonah in an *ex tempore* sermon to an African Methodist congregation in Philadelphia, much less Nat Turner comparing himself to Christ. More striking to a *literary* scholar than Crafts's biblical allegorizing is the more pervasive "literariness" of this text. I want now, therefore, to turn to some ways in which the novel markedly deviates from, even while partially following, the two contemporary literary models on which it most conspicuously draws.

Up to a point, *The Bondwoman's Narrative* reads like a fictionalized slave narrative. This too is an autobiography, ending with escape, focused on slavery's abuses as experienced and witnessed by the narrator. Its most obvious mark of difference from typical autobiographies of ex-slaves is the unabashed nature of the fictionalization. As William Andrews remarks, slave narratives depended for their credibility on a paradox of disguised artfulness. On the one hand, "even the most artless of slave narrators were schooled by slavery in the survival art of self-invention." In contrast, "the reception of [a] narrative as truth depended on the degree to which [one's] artfulness could hide his art."[4] Unlike most slave narrators, Hannah Crafts neither takes pains to claim that she is actually telling the truth nor disguises her penchant for literary stylization. "The ancient mansion of Lindendale was to receive a mistress"; "What an array of costly furniture adorned the rich saloons and gorgeous halls";

"Thus I felt while threading the long galleries which led to the southern turret"—this is the stuff of Radcliffean gothic novels and gothic tales à la Edgar
Allan Poe (13–15). Even more striking about such touches other than their
frequency is that they often seem created as much for the sheer relish of it—
the artist indulging her medium—as for fulfilling a particular instrumental
purpose, like Frederick Douglass's impassioned set piece on the shameful
abandonment of his helpless old grandmother to certain lonely death.

It comes as no surprise, then, to find the bondwoman-narrator drawing a
stark contrast between the power of unleashed imagination and the constraints of slavery, as when Hannah muses with a sense of creeping ominousness on the pictures of her master and his forbears that hang in the drawing
room that is to be part of the quarters occupied by his new (and unbeknownst to him) mulatta bride.

> Though filled with superstitious awe I was in no haste to leave the room; for
> there surrounded by mysterious associations I seemed suddenly to have grown
> old, to have entered a new world of thoughts, and feelings and sentiments. I
> was not a slave with these pictured memorials of the past. They could not en-
> force drudgery, or condemn me on account of my color to a life of servitude.
> In their presence my mind seemed to run riotous and exult in its freedom as a
> rational being, and one destined for something higher and better than this
> world can afford (17).

That an experience of solitary meditation on "pictured memorials of the
past" should be what provokes the most violent feelings of resistance to slavery Hannah expresses in Chapter I, and that the sense of "freedom" thereby
engendered is an apocalypse of mind and *not* a literal emancipation, points to
a contrast between *Bondwoman* and slave narrative more subtle and profound
than the matter of literariness as such.

Hannah's view of her predicament is curiously polarized. Often a slave narrator, "like the archetypal hero of the *Bildungsroman*, moves from the idyllic life
of childhood ignorance in the country into a metaphoric wilderness," produced by the traumatic "recognition of his status as slave."[5] Not Hannah.
Unlike the narratives of Douglass, Jacobs, and various others, she does not
start with a scene of awakening to "the hell of slavery," as Douglass calls it.[6]
From the very start, she knows that slavery is hell. From the very start, she
feels the injustice of her position. But she displays no overriding need to make
a literal break for freedom. She is too practical, too risk-averse for that. For
most of the narrative, such desires get displaced onto other figures. In the
early part of the narrative, it is Mrs. Vincent, not Hannah, who experiences

the shock of awakening (to the fact that she is part black). Hannah is the one who suggests that her mistress flee, but she herself goes along only after Mrs. Vincent requests that she do so. Indeed, Hannah portrays herself as reluctant to leave the old homestead. Only loyalty to her mistress drives her to do it. ("I had been the general favorite of the young people on the estate, but though I loved them much, I loved my mistress more.") To be sure, when the mistress begins to waver ("What will the old people, and the children—the weak help-less ones do without you?"), Hannah then insists. Mrs. Vincent reads her in-sistence as meaning that "you desire freedom for its own sake," as indeed she does. But nothing in the text at this point suggests that Hannah's stated rea-son is not her primary reason: refusal to "leave you to go forth alone. My dear indulgent mistress—never, never" (50–51).

The novel's title is well chosen, in short. To a striking degree the narrator embraces the bondwoman's role almost throughout, be it loyalty or strategy—almost surely a combination of both. Her second mistress, Mrs. Henry, who nurses her back to life after a near-fatal accident, vexes Hannah no end by re-fusing on principle to buy her and thus secure her safety. (Mrs. Henry feels bound, obstinately to Hannah's mind, to the vow made to her repentant slave-holder-father on his deathbed never to traffic in slaves.) But again the impulse to escape at this juncture gets displaced onto her fellow servant Charlotte, who flees north with her husband William when they find that he is about to be sold. When they beg Hannah to accompany them, she declines to risk it: "I have tried elopement once. I know what it is." Hannah's equation of runaway slave with runaway marriage is infinitely suggestive. Into that one word "elopement" gets packed feelings of longing, solidarity, and cautious aversion to running afoul of the law. It's a highly unstable synthesis, but for now it holds. Hannah is tempted neither by William's Patrick Henry–like resolve ("With me it is liberty or death") nor his scoffing at her other excuse—"that I could not lightly sacrifice the good opinion of Mrs. Henry and her family" (141). Hannah consents instead to be handed over to Mrs. Henry's vain im-perious sister, Mrs. Wheeler, whom she nonetheless tries dutifully to serve. Only when Mrs. Wheeler remands her to the slave quarters and into forced marriage does Hannah flee.

It is not that Hannah ever lacks a sense of self-worth. "Though neglected and a slave, I felt the immortal longings in me," she says of herself as a girl in Chapter I, echoing the language of Shakespeare's Cleopatra as she presses the asp to her bosom to commit suicide (7). In other words: I recognize my predicament, and I assert my independence of mind and being in spite of it, though I see no practical way to escape Caesar short of death.[7] No matter whether she is scolded, imprisoned, sold, or threatened, Hannah never comes remotely close to feeling the erosion of self-worth that Douglass feels under Covey or Jacobs feels as a result of being scolded by her grandmother for yielding to sexual advances. One way of reading *The Bondwoman's Narrative* is as a reminder or a thought experiment of how extreme the provocation must be to drive a tolerably well-treated slave to seek to escape from a condition that she knows most of her readers will think (like Mrs. Vincent and William) she *must* inwardly feel is intolerable, a condition that she herself recognizes is unjust. As Hannah sums up just before she takes flight, "Dear as freedom is to every human being, and bitter as servitude must be to all who experience it, I knew too much of the dangers and difficulties to be apprehended from running away ever to have attempted such a thing through ordinary motives" (207). Only Hagar-like expulsion from the bosom of the household could have driven her to take such a step. It makes good novelistic sense that the escape ideal entails a temporary erasure of identity, symbolic death, and a literal near-death experience.

The Bondwoman's Narrative clearly emphasizes slavery's psychological effects over its physical effects. Whippings and still more gruesome forms of torture are indeed described, but the narrator asserts that emotional suffering is worse. "Those that view slavery only as it relates to physical suffering, or the wants of nature, can have no conception of its greatest evils," she asserts (130). Here she is specifically thinking about her fellow servant Charlotte's grief at the prospect of being separated from her new husband, William, but the claim is categorical, not limited to slavery per se. "She had cleared the house of his favourites" but "she could not clear them from her imagination," Hannah remarks of one planter's wife's reaction to her husband's clandestine amours—a reaction so strong it puts them on a collision course that drives her to her death (186). The two most drawn-out tales of emotional suffering precipitated by slavery are the stories of the ordeals and deaths of the last two mistresses of Lindendale, Hannah's mistress-sister Mrs. Vincent and the equally ill-fated Mrs. Cosgrove, of whom more anon.

As these and other episodes show, Hannah takes an interest in the inner lives of the figures around her that goes well beyond the traditional slave narrative. That may be one reason why *The Bondwoman's Narrative* takes the highly arresting but most improbable step of having the arch-villain Trappe taunt his victims with the revelation that he considers himself as well to be "the victim of circumstances," the walking embodiment of the flawed legal and social system that permits him to snatch and sell ostensibly genteel women discovered to have faint traces of African ancestry (97, 98). This is obviously not documentary truth but gothic melodrama—or an uncanny anticipation of the postmodern "neoslave" narrative, like Charles Johnson's *Middle Passage,* where the leading slave catcher inflicts similarly bizarre intimate self-disclosures on the protagonist. But what is most distressing about this particular scene in *The Bondwoman's Narrative* is Trappe's insistence that he has *no* "inner nature" as such. Whatever tenderness of feeling he may once have felt as Mrs. Vincent's suitor or on any other account has been thoroughly suppressed by the zealous embracement of the custom of the country. This is the equivalent for slave-holders of the condition Hannah ascribes, with equal revulsion, to the field hands on the Wheeler plantation, "coil[ing] themselves to sleep on nauseous heaps of straw fetid with human perspiration" (199). In Trappe she has shown how institutionalized slavery can reduce human beings from the master class to things; here she sees a similar effect on Wheeler's slaves. These figures are "scarcely human," reduced to mere automatons, robbed of inner life. "Their mental condition is summed up in the phrase that they know nothing" (201, 200).

Here it is easy to find fault with Hannah. Gates rightly calls her a "snob." She assumes too readily that her reader will share her outrage at her banishment from great house to smelly hut and loutish Bill (the paretic antipode of Charlotte's dashing William). After a lifetime of acquiescence to the bond-woman's role, she hits the road more from chagrin at demotion than from actual hardships suffered. Hannah is all too visibly proud of being not a typical slave but one who has enjoyed positions of respect and trust. Her sense of solidarity with fellow captives is quite selective.

But to boggle overmuch on this detail is to ignore the fact that the authors of the most widely read and cited slave narratives tended to be the George and Eliza Harpists rather than the Aunt Chloe and Uncle Toms, much less the beaten-down Pres at the very bottom of servitude's status ladder. In this respect Hannah has a good deal in common with Olaudah Equiano, Henry Bibb, Frederick Douglass, Harriet Jacobs, James W. C. Pennington, and Moses Roper. One among many telltale signs is her strong emphasis on the milestone event of learning to read—in common with other narratives by literate ex-slaves. Hannah is simply more upfront than most about cherishing refinement of sensibility as an intrinsic value.

That *The Bondwoman's Narrative* stands out even from most "literary" slave narratives in this way is one measure of its affinity with middle-class domestic or "woman's" fiction. Might the author conceivably have known the antebellum fictions of such kind by the popular southern writers E.D.E.N. South-worth and Harriot Marion Stephens that used the Hagar-figure in order to symbolize the stigma of feminine assertiveness—a trait Hannah often shows—in their white, ironically racist, heroines? (In Euro-American art and poetics of the same period representing biblical scenes, Hagar is also made to

look white, despite the name being coded "black" in social history and in famous fictions like *Uncle Tom's Cabin*.)[8] If so, then one of this novel's notable
"firsts" was its resistance to racialist hijacking in the appropriation of the biblical bondwoman-figure. In any case, *The Bondwoman's Narrative* offers a clearly
recognizable variation on the "woman's fiction" plot as defined by Nina Baym:
a modified Cinderella story of an orphaned girl whose feistiness is disciplined
though also in the long run validated by trials imposed by "stepmother"-figures
(in this case Mrs. Wheeler especially and institutionalized slavery more generally), mentored by surrogate parent-figures like her reading instructor and her
first two mistresses, melodramatically threatened with social if not also actual
death but rewarded in the end for steering between the extremes of passivity
and aggressiveness with a companionate marriage in which her individuality
can express itself in the context of the domestic ideal.[9] Especially provocative
is the extreme to which *The Bondwoman's Narrative* takes woman's fiction's
premise that "although children may be necessary for a woman's happiness,
they are not necessary for her identity—nor is a husband."[10]

By contrast to the slave narrative that most resembles woman's fiction, Harriet Jacobs's *Incidents in the Life of a Slave Girl*, *The Bondwoman's Narrative* portrays its
narrator as virtually impervious to the attractions of sex, marriage, and children until the very last chapter. We see sexual predators aplenty among the
planter class and shocking tales of sexual victimization. But never is Hannah's
own virtue threatened, refined female house servant though she is. Possibly the
reason is simply that she is "excessively homely"—or so Saddler the slave
trader exclaims after being set up by Trappe to expect a beautiful woman
(103). But this may be deliberate exaggeration on Saddler's part in order to
bargain down the price he must pay for Hannah. In any case, the novel never
satisfactorily explains her seeming immunity from rape or flirtation. This itself
may be one mark of its fictitiousness. Harriet Jacobs might introduce fictional
devices into her autobiography but presumably felt she had to stick more or
less to the documentary record, embarrassing though it was to discuss her sexual torments and liaisons. Hannah Crafts was freer to edit and invent experience (assuming the novel *was* based on personal experience). But it is also
striking that never during her captivity does Hannah express a strong hanker-
ing of her own for love, marriage, or family. She makes a point of emphasizing that she was always the favorite of the children but never confesses to
yearning for her own. Even at the end she seems quite happy as a childless
schoolmistress.

Hannah also vehemently denounces marriage for slaves as a sham and a
trap, because it has no binding status. It is "something that all the victims of
slavery should avoid as tending essentially to perpetuate that system" (206).

To be sure, this in itself was an abolitionist commonplace, as was reticence in slave narratives on the subject of the protagonist's sexual activity. Hannah's critique of "marriage" among slaves is indeed less outspoken than, say, Henry Bibb's or William Wells Brown's, and her ethic of austerity in itself is no more curious than Frederick Douglass's *Narrative*'s silence about his sex life, if any, in slavery, even as he acknowledges in a footnote the fiancée who helped him escape. But Hannah's sexual imperturbability seems more notable given the sexual entanglement, jealousy, intrigue, tale-telling in which many of the women around her, on both sides of the color line, become embroiled either literally or vicariously. She lives in an environment where the women to whom she feels emotionally close cannot resist sexual involvement or at least sexual gossip. Yet she herself seems immune to such venality, except of course in her capacity as retailer of the stories. What is to explain it?

I, for one, am inclined to take her at face value when she tersely, tardily, and without further explanation mentions sundry marriage proposals that had come her way before Mrs. Wheeler's loathsome command. "I had spurned domestic ties not because my heart was hard, but because it was my unalterable resolution never to entail slavery on any human being" (206–207). This is as much as to say "If I seem strangely nunlike, it is because slavery has forced me to play that part." It's conceivable that the actual writer—assuming the book *is* autobiographical—might have been less chaste than the narrator lets on. But that the text sincerely maintains what the narrator says about the importance of slave women resisting sexual/marital entanglement seems certain. (Fugitive Margaret Garner's desperate infanticide when she saw that recapture of her family was inevitable, the basis of Toni Morrison's *Beloved*, is dramatic corroboration of such thinking both as a fact of history and as a fact of imagination.) So too, I think, with the novel's strategy of producing a deliberately strange effect by planting a sexually unmoved protagonist-narrator in the middle of a plot rife with women on both sides of the color line who experience sexual anxiety, fantasy, temptation, victimization. Because the novel resembles domestic fiction at least as closely as it resembles slave narrative, Hannah is thereby made not only to express but also to model the necessary (for slaves) sublimation, postponement, denial of the ordinary pleasures of domesticity to which free women feel rightfully entitled.

The insistence, the belatedness with which the issue of the narrator's personal domestic desires is broached and the hastiness of the storybook ending (the novel knocks off the subject of Hannah's connubial bliss in two short concluding paragraphs) make one wonder, on second thought, if *The Bondwoman's Narrative* finally means to mimic woman's fiction only to put it in its place. Might the novel be insinuating satirically that woman's fiction tells a white middle-class woman's story and that the only way a bondwoman's narrative can qualify is by miraculous fortuity, a deliverance that amounts to outright forcing of the plot? A husband, a home with an "exquisite flower-garden" and a "dainty orchard of choice fruits" (239), a job she loves, "my own dear mother" miraculously restored after a lifetime of separation, the ideal village and church, reunion with Charlotte and William thrown in, life in the North "all my fancy had pictured it to be" (237)—surely this denouement pours the syrup on suspiciously thick. Or might the novel, more subtly, be trying to "queer" the genre by devices like the protagonist's inherent coolness to men and the conclusion's pie-in-the-sky factitiousness? Maybe. More likely, though, the author invokes the power of the genre more in order to dramatize the irony of the denial to slaves of the social and emotional possibilities the genre expresses, even to women who otherwise perfectly fit the template for a heroine of woman's fiction, so long as they remain in bondage. To the extent that *The Bondwoman's Narrative* does constitute an ironic reflection on the genre itself, it may be in respect to woman's fiction's tendency to assume that a Cinderella-type confinement is the worst kind of "slavery" that can befall an upstanding young woman.

At this point the possibility that *The Bondwoman's Narrative* might be signifying white literature's appropriation of the Hagar-figure suggests itself once again. Certainly, the way this novel plays the marriage card has the effect of beating domesticity at its own game in at least two respects. First, wrapping herself in the flag of marriage as sacred institution enables the narrator to maintain a staunch emotional detachment and unbesmirched moral authority (from a white middle-class standpoint) in defiance of the crushing sexual humiliations to which female slaves are notoriously subject, thus dramatizing how Hagar can be Hannah. And second, in the emphasis she gives to postponing all thoughts of married bliss until precisely the opportune time, she creates a novelistic plot with a denouement that feels (even) more the result of the heroine's own independent devising than in the plots of woman's fiction.

This way of reading *The Bondwoman's Narrative* comports with what may be its single most distinctive and ingenious plot motif: the reiterated portrayal of characters, both black and white, dragged in various ways across the freedom line into slave territory, to their horror and dismay. The introduction of the "tragic mulatta" figure in the case of Mrs. Vincent, plunged into the abyss by the revelation that she is not one hundred percent white, is only one such case. It isn't even the first case. The first is Northern Quaker-bred Aunt Hester, who, together with her husband, is thrown into jail for teaching Hannah to read. After this come Mrs. Cosgrove, the "aristocratic" English immigrant destroyed by her aversion to her planter husband's double sexual standard, and the funny-sinister contretemps of Mrs. Wheeler, who "becomes" a slave temporarily by powdering her face the wrong way. Then there are the cases of white anti-slavery Southerners like Mrs. Henry and especially Mrs. Wright—jailmate of Hannah and Mrs. Vincent after they are recaptured by lawyer Trappe—who are scarred and confined by the social system they seem to have no choice but to live within. (Mrs. Wright has gone insane serving a prison sentence; Mrs. Henry, rather like Hannah before the climax of the novel, never seems to consider the possibility of leaving the South.)

Through these case histories, the author dramatizes many times over and in a more complex and variegated way an anti-patriarchal feminism reminiscent of Harriet Jacobs's *Incidents,* which also represents "white women such as Mrs. Flint" and African Americans as "victimized by white men and by a sexual double standard."[11] However, Hannah Crafts populates her narrative with a veritable host of female figures who see slavery through alienated, "Northern" eyes, a number of whom (especially herself) are not sexual victims as such, even though sexual exploitation across the color line certainly looms very large. This in turn gives an unusual comprehensiveness to Crafts's diagnosis of the wrongs of bondage. Implicitly, and often explicitly too, her denunciation of slavery takes her far beyond "women's sphere" into analysis of the perversities of the legal system and the importance of being able to think, feel, and act as an independent being. It is broadly in keeping with the tendency of what William Andrews calls "novelized slave narratives," like Jacobs's *Incidents,* to stress a dialogue between whites and blacks that demonstrates "that the terms of the master-slave relationship were not dictated from the one to the other [simply] in an 'I talk—you listen' fashion."[12] However, *The Bondwoman's Narrative's* repeated dramatization of free Southerners who for various reasons lose caste, lose privilege, even lose their minds as a result of institutionalized slavery is distinctive. It is Hannah Crafts's equivalent to *Uncle Tom's Cabin's* device of duplicating names across the color line and issuing direct appeals to well-meaning unenlightened white readers: if this were *your* little Harry, and not just some lowly slave mother's, how would *you* feel? Much of the artfulness of *The Bondwoman's Narrative* consists in scripting episodes for white Northern readers that will make them feel vicariously entrapped by slavery, making it impossible for them to rest in the delusion that slave territory exists in a hermetic elsewhere from which free people are immune.

Here too we see another link between *The Bondwoman's Narrative* and the Anglo-American classics of the U.S. literary emergence period—the so-called "American Renaissance." Many of those texts also portray contexts of oppressive constraint and—through detached narrators, personae, or fictive surrogates—a satiric anatomy of these conditions, a sense of intolerable entrapment, a will to escape. Hawthorne invents a "Puritan" woman with a markedly "modern" consciousness, Hester Prynne, and places her within paleolithic New England village culture. Melville sticks his mentally hyperinquisitive, intellectual-relativistic narrator aboard a tightly stratified ship captained by an authoritarian fantast who sees the world in old-fashioned Manichean-allegorical terms. Thoreau imagines trying to create a breathing space for himself at the edges of a society of quiet desperate conformists. The appalling pathology of the social status quo is of great concern in all of these antebellum classics, *The Scarlet Letter, Moby-Dick,* and *Walden.*

Not that their protagonists' sense of marginalization can be equated with that of Hannah Crafts. Between the 1930s and the 1950s, American critics were at great pains to demonstrate how "major" U.S. writers have defined themselves as embattled prophets speaking from society's margins. We now realize how much special pleading was involved in making such a case for, say, the best friend of a U.S. president (Hawthorne and Franklin Pierce—also a close friend of Jefferson Davis—for whom Hawthorne even went so far as to write a campaign biography) or for any other member of the Northern white male intelligentsia with more or less equally good social connections. It's all very well for Thoreau to claim in *Walden* that being a slave driver to yourself is worse than being a slave, but try to tell that to Crafts or Douglass.

On the other hand, it's also the case that a goodly amount of armchair imagination exercised from a niche of far greater comfort than the scene of bondage portrayed went into Douglass's autobiographies and *The Bondwoman's Narrative.* It's also certain that one of the main patterns that place these texts, the Anglo-American texts discussed above, the slave narratives, and woman's fiction generally at the same point in the literary history of the United States is a shared commitment—nuanced of course very differently from case to case—to narratives of entrapment and liberation and to dramatizing through them the effort to reach and sustain independent-mindedness notwithstanding the horror and perverseness of unfreedom. In this sense, *The Bondwoman's Narrative* rightly belongs not only to the literary subspecies of African American novel, fictionalized slave narrative, and woman's fiction but to all of nineteenth-century U.S. literature.

And why end there? With the possible exceptions of Poe and Stowe, the now-canonical white writers who seem to have caught Hannah Crafts's eye were all British: Horace Walpole, Ann Radcliffe, Walter Scott, Charles Dickens, among others. *The Bondwoman's Narrative* belongs not just to the United States but to the Atlantic world, and not just to the "black Atlantic" world either. It is quixotic to stipulate how much of it is written in an "African American" voice as opposed to a "mainstream American" voice, or even a "woman's" voice as opposed to a "man's." Discovered at a point in critical history when nineteenth-century Americanists are proclaiming the need to move "beyond separate spheres," *The Bondwoman's Narrative* is an especially timely find.[13]

Notes

My sincere thanks to Janet Gabler-Hover, Henry Louis Gates, Jr., and Karen Dalton for their valuable and timely help with this essay.

1. Henry Louis Gates, Jr., "Borrowing Privileges," *New York Times Book Review*, 2 June 2002, p. 18.

2. *The Interesting Narrative of the Life of Olaudah Equiano, or Gustavus Vassa, The African, Written by Himself*, ed. Werner Sollors (New York: Norton, 2001), p. 30.

3. W. E. B. DuBois, "Jacob and Esau" (1944), *DuBois on Religion*, ed. Phil Zuckerman (Lanham, MD: Altamira Press, 2000), pp. 187–196.

4. William Andrews, *To Tell a Free Story: The First Century of Afro-American Autobiography, 1760–1865* (Urbana: University of Illinois Press, 1988), pp. 93, 3.

5. Valerie Smith, *Self-Discovery and Authority in Afro-American Narrative* (Cambridge: Harvard University Press, 1987), p. 33.

6. *Narrative of the Life of Frederick Douglass, An American Slave, Written By Himself* (1845), ed. Benjamin Quarles (Cambridge: Harvard University Press, 1960), p. 28.

7. The question of whether Cleopatra should be imaged as nonwhite was a matter of debate in nineteenth-century Anglo-American literature and art; see, for example, Werner Sollors, *Neither Black Nor White Yet Both* (New York: Oxford University Press, 1997), pp. 13–15; and William H. Gerdts, "William Wetmore Story," *American Art Journal* 4.ii (November 1972): 20–22. Shakespeare's Cleopatra, however, whom Crafts quotes here (*Antony and Cleopatra* V. ii. 275–276) is unambiguously depicted as an exotic cultural if not also racial other in the eyes of the play's Roman figures.

8. Janet Gabler-Hover, *Dreaming Black / Writing White: The Hagar Myth in American Cultural History* (Lexington, KY: University Press of Kentucky, 2000), pp. 1–94. According to Gabler-Hover, not until 1882 does an American writer (white) create a clearly nonwhite Hagar; not until Pauline Hopkins's *Hagar's Daughter* (1901–1902) do we find an African American creative writer inventing an African American Hagar.

9. Nina Baym, *Woman's Fiction: A Guide to Novels by and About Women in America, 1820–1870* (Ithaca: Cornell University Press, 1978), pp. 22–48. In the last chapter of *The Bondwoman's Narrative*, Hannah is reunited with her mother, from whom she was evidently separated in infancy.

10. Baym, *Woman's Fiction*, p. 38.

11. Lori Merish, *Sentimental Materialism: Gender, Commodity Culture, and Nineteenth-Century American Literature* (Durham: Duke University Press, 2000), p. 207.

12. Andrews, *To Tell a Free Story*, p. 275.

13. See, for example, Monika M. Elbert, ed., *Separate Spheres No More* (Tuscaloosa: University of Alabama Press, 2000); and Cathy N. Davidson and Jessamyn Hatcher, eds., *No More Separate Spheres* (Durham: Duke University Press, 2002).

3

Hannah Crafts's Sense of an Ending

WILLIAM ANDREWS

The subtitle of *The Bondwoman's Narrative* identifies its author, Hannah Crafts, as a fugitive slave from North Carolina. If she was, then *The Bondwoman's Narrative* is a truly unique text, the first slave narrative to have been authored by an African American woman, and the first slave narrative to have survived in manuscript form.

With a text of uncertain origin, such as *The Bondwoman's Narrative*, there are two general ways to attempt to ferret out its authorship. One can try to track down the author through historical research, or one can attempt to extrapolate the identity of the author by comparing what she or he has written to the work of others. Henry Louis Gates, Jr., the editor of the first published edition of *The Bondwoman's Narrative*, has done a great deal of research in an effort to confirm the existence of a historical Hannah Crafts who can be linked with certainty to the narrative that bears her name. Although several candidates have emerged, each of whom Gates identifies in his Introduction to *The Bondwoman's Narrative*, Gates does not claim to have found *the* Hannah Crafts who authored this narrative. Hannah Crafts may be only a pseudonym adopted by a fugitive slave author as insurance against recapture. Still, Gates advances several good reasons for concluding that the author was a black woman. Given her familiarity with John Hill Wheeler (1806–1882), a North Carolina lawyer, politician, and author who plays a significant role in the narrative itself, it is tempting to conclude that Hannah Crafts was once a slave in the Wheeler household. Although none of the evidence we now have proves conclusively the racial or even sexual identity of the author of *The Bondwoman's Narrative*, my own view is that, in light of what we do know about the narrative and given the richness of the story as a text, we have ample justification for comparing the text to its relevant contemporaries in order to see what leads might emerge as to the identity of the author.

In this brief inquiry into *The Bondwoman's Narrative* I'm especially interested in what the ending of this text might signify with regard to its author. If Hannah Crafts was a black woman writing sometime in the late 1850s, as the evidence Gates has marshaled suggests, why did she choose to end her narrative as she does? Does the story end as it does simply because that's what actually happened to Hannah Crafts? If so, then *The Bondwoman's Narrative* is just what it appears to be—an autobiography. But what if *The Bondwoman's Narrative* ends as it does because that's how its author wanted the story to end? In that case *The Bondwoman's Narrative* is not what it appears to be—it's not an autobiography but a novel.[1]

If *The Bondwoman's Narrative* is an autobiography, then its closest literary kin is the fugitive slave narrative, which was the dominant and most popular form of African American storytelling, factual or fictional, in print in the United States in the middle of the nineteenth century.[2] If, on the other hand, *The Bondwoman's Narrative* is a novel, not an autobiography, then it should be read in the context of the dominant and most popular form of European American fiction in the United States in the mid-nineteenth century, namely, the "trials and triumph" novels by white American women, which the literary critic and historian Nina Baym has termed simply "woman's fiction."[3] What becomes clear after reading *The Bondwoman's Narrative*, however, is that each of these two literary traditions can justifiably claim *The Bondwoman's Narrative*.

Because no one has yet determined who Hannah Crafts was or whether the narrative attributed to her is an autobiography or a novel, it makes sense to discuss *The Bondwoman's Narrative* in relation to both black-authored slave narratives and white-authored "woman's fiction." Because, in my view, *The Bondwoman's Narrative* reads like a hybrid of the fugitive slave narrative and woman's fiction, I will look at the possible influence of both traditions on this narrative with an eye toward suggesting why, given the ways that slave narratives and woman's fiction tended to conclude, the author of this text chose to end her narrative as it does. Hannah Crafts's sense of an ending may shed some light on the motives and goals of the shadowy author of this intriguing text.

Let me pause here to make one note about naming in my ensuing discussion of *The Bondwoman's Narrative*. There is no reason to assume that the author of *The Bondwoman's Narrative* and the character who goes by the name of Hannah Crafts in the story were the same person. We should not assume a book is an autobiography just because its title claims it is. When *The Autobiography of an Ex-Colored Man* appeared anonymously in 1912, many readers mistakenly took that text, which we now know was a novel written by James Weldon Johnson, to be the true confession of an African American who had passed for white. Before Johnson acknowledged his authorship of the novel, he had the ironic pleasure of meeting people who claimed to know who the author of the "autobiography" actually was! To avoid confusing the author of the text with the main character in the story, I will refer to the character in *The Bondwoman's Narrative* as simply Hannah, as she is addressed throughout the text. When I refer to the author of *The Bondwoman's Narrative*, I will refer to her as Crafts or "the author."

The full title of *The Bondwoman's Narrative*, as it appeared on the title page of the original manuscript, is *The Bondwoman's Narrative By Hannah Crafts A Fugitive Slave Recently Escaped From North Carolina* (1). If Crafts was an escaped slave, as the title of her narrative claims, she may well have been inspired to write her story by the international success of slave narratives such as Frederick Douglass's *Narrative of the Life of Frederick Douglass, An American Slave. Written by Himself* (1845), William Wells Brown's *Narrative of William W. Brown, A Fugitive Slave. Written by Himself* (1847), and *The Fugitive Blacksmith; or, Events in the History of James W. C. Pennington, Pastor of a Presbyterian Church, New York, Formerly a Slave in the State of Maryland, United States* (1849). These immensely popular autobiographies deprecated American slavery and celebrated the heroism of black men who forsook their chains and not only seized their freedom but became famous professional men—writers, speakers, and ministers—in America and abroad. Capitalizing on their achievements in autobiography, Douglass in 1853 published the first novella, *The Heroic Slave*, in African American literature. A few months later Brown's British publisher brought out the first full-length African American novel, *Clotel, or The President's Daughter.* Both *The Heroic Slave* and *Clotel* are hybrid texts, part slave narrative and part fiction. As such either or both could have impressed a black woman, especially if she too had been a fugitive slave.

We should remember, however, that in the mid-to-late 1850s, when Crafts evidently wrote *The Bondwoman's Narrative*, the most likely African American literary precedent for a formerly enslaved author came from men such as Douglass, Brown, and Pennington, whose works dealt almost exclusively with male experience. Only two book-length female slave narratives had appeared before the author of *The Bondwoman's Narrative* undertook her task. *The History of Mary Prince, a West Indian Slave. Related by Herself* was published in London in 1831. But Prince's story is not likely to have been widely distributed or well known in the United States twenty-five years later. It is more likely that the author of *The Bondwoman's Narrative* would have heard of Sojourner Truth and/or encountered the *Narrative of Sojourner Truth, A Northern Slave, Emancipated from Bodily Servitude by the State of New York, in 1828*, which was published in Boston in 1850. By the late 1850s Truth was a well-traveled figure among reformers and a popular orator on the abolitionist and women's rights circuits. Nevertheless, whether Prince's or Truth's narratives were known to Crafts, they bear relatively little similarity in terms of style or subject matter to *The Bondwoman's Narrative*. Enslavement for Prince and Truth was exceedingly more physically cruel than what the comparatively privileged Hannah had undergone according to *The Bondwoman's Narrative*. Moreover, unlike Prince and Truth, neither of whom actually wrote their narratives, the author of *The Bondwoman's Narrative* was not only literate but literary, as allusions in her story to classic Greek drama and Dickens's *Bleak House* and a quotation from *Macbeth* testify. As a consequence, while Prince and Truth both required amanuenses and editors to help them get their stories into print, Crafts seems to have had the skills and the opportunity to write her story herself. The result, assuming Crafts was a black woman as the narrative claims, is the first self-authored narrative of slavery by a black American woman.[4]

The question is, what kind of "narrative" is *The Bondwoman's Narrative*? In the mid-nineteenth century, titling a book as a "narrative," such as Douglass's or Brown's, was a way of signaling that it was a true story. In addition to the many autobiographies of escaped slaves that were published under the title of *Narrative of* (Frederick Douglass or William Wells Brown or Sojourner Truth), many white people published their life stories under the same title, for example, *A Narrative of the Life of David Crockett, of the State of Tennessee. Written by Himself* (Philadelphia, 1834), and *Narrative of the Expedition of an American Squadron to the China Seas and Japan, Performed in the years 1852, 1853, and 1854, under the Command of Commodore M. C. Perry* (New York, 1857). At the same time, however, that "narrative" was used to denote a true story, usually an autobiography, the term was also appropriated by writers who wished to mask a fictional account as factual so as to enhance sales of their books. Thus Edgar Allan Poe's only novel is titled *The Narrative of Arthur Gordon Pym, of Nantucket* (New York, 1838), and Herman Melville's first novel, *Typee* (1846), is subtitled *A Narrative of a Four Months' Residence among the Natives of a Valley of the Marquesas Islands, or, A Peep at Polynesian Life*. In Melville's case, because *Typee* was the outgrowth of a month its author had spent living among a tribe of Polynesians in the Marquesas during the summer of 1842, critics then and now have debated whether Melville's first-person narrative is a novel or a novelized autobiography. The more we learn about the grounding of *The Bondwoman's Narrative* in history, if not in a traceable individual's history, the more we are likely to read this narrative as straddling the categories of fact and fiction in ways similar to Melville's. Indeed, the preface to *The Bondwoman's Narrative* seems designed to raise such questions in the reader's mind.

The preface starts out by promising a "record of plain unvarnished facts" (3), in other words, an autobiography. Yet in the next sentence Crafts refers to her narrative as "a literary venture," hinting that in recording "facts" she has also presented them in a consciously "literary" way. In the next sentence, however, she sounds less like a "literary" author than an antislavery journalist intent on accurately portraying the "peculiar features of that institution whose curse rests over the fairest land the sun shines upon." Continuing in this vein, Crafts assures her reader that "being the truth it [the narrative] makes no pretensions to romance." By rejecting "romance," Crafts aims not to rule out the possibility of a love interest in her narrative but to distinguish her story from outright fiction. (In 1850, for instance, Nathaniel Hawthorne entitled his new novel *The Scarlet Letter: A Romance.*) Crafts underlines the historicity of her narrative further by denying that it bears "a moral" imposed by the author: "relating events as they occurred it has no especial reference to a moral." Yet a little farther in the preface Crafts confides almost teasingly that "pious and discerning minds can scarcely fail to recognize the hand of Providence in giving to the righteous the reward of their works, and to the wicked the fruit of their doings." Thus it appears that the narrative does offer its reader, if not a clear-cut "moral," at least a kind of poetic justice that confirms a fundamentally moral view of the world, in which God ("Providence") rewards the righteous and punishes the wicked in the world of human affairs.

A "pious" mind in mid-nineteenth-century America might have held as an article of faith that Providence presided over humankind by actively reinforcing good and punishing evil. But an equally "discerning" mind could have pointed to daily evidence showing that the righteous were not always rewarded for their goodness or the wicked punished for the evil they did in this world. An African American living in the United States in the late 1850s, whether formerly enslaved or free-born, could certainly have cited the federal government's enforcement of the Fugitive Slave Law in the North and the continuing legality of human bondage in the South to argue that "the hand of Providence" was not as active in support of racial justice in the United States as either "pious" or "discerning" minds might have liked. To insist, therefore, in a narrative about the African American experience of slavery written *before* the Civil War, that the righteous and the wicked receive their just deserts required, if not the outright imposition of a "moral" on a true story, at least the representation of the events of Hannah's life so that their ultimate outcome would confirm a belief in a just God presiding over a moral universe. We have good reason, then, to pay particular attention to the way Crafts ends her narrative, because what happens to the characters will either confirm or undermine the idea of the ultimate justice and morality of Providence that Crafts posits in the beginning of her story.

In common with the slave narratives of Douglass and Truth, as well as the early novels of Douglass and Brown, *The Bondwoman's Narrative* relates a story of black women and men suffering in bondage, resisting their exploitation, and seeking liberty and fulfillment in a free land. Many aspects of style and story-telling, coupled with Crafts's exploration of the complex allegiances and aspirations of a female house slave, differentiate *The Bondwoman's Narrative* from other fugitive slave narratives. But the most striking departure of Crafts's text from the slave narrative tradition arises from the unreservedly happy ending that Hannah reports at the end of her story. There is simply nothing like it in the entire pre–Civil War African American slave narrative.

The final chapters of *The Bondwoman's Narrative* confer on Hannah an astonishing shower of good fortune, although she would likely call them "rewards," given her wording in the preface. First, Hannah achieves personal freedom after an arduous, and for the most part solitary, journey through North Carolina and western Virginia. Just when the fugitive needs help the most, a long-lost friend from Hannah's childhood, a white woman she calls Aunt Hetty, miraculously appears to steer the fugitive toward her destination in the novel, "refuge among the colored inhabitants of New Jersey" (230). On the way to New Jersey, a second surprising coincidence occurs: Hannah overhears a conversation between two men about the violent death of her chief nemesis, Mr. Trappe. The last chapter of the novel finds Hannah in an unnamed locality in New Jersey where, in addition to freedom, she delights in "a deep repose a blest and holy quietude" (237). Considering the amazing blessings that have been lavished on her since her arrival in New Jersey, we can hardly wonder at Hannah's calm and complacency. More miraculous than her rescue by Aunt Hetty during her flight for freedom is her reunion with her mother, whom she had never seen previously in her life but whom she meets—"accidentally, where or how it matters not" (238)—sometime after her arrival in New Jersey. In addition to her mother, Hannah's community in freedom consists of one of her closest friends from her past, a fugitive slave named Charlotte, who, together with her husband, William, somehow has ended up in precisely the same place in New Jersey as Hannah. They are all supremely happy, especially when in church, which is pastored by the "fond and affectionate husband" Hannah has married in freedom. Hannah introduces her husband as "a regularly ordained preacher of the Methodist persuasion" who "is, and has always been a free man" (238). Yet she neglects to mention his name. Although no children have been born to this union, Hannah joyfully serves as a school-teacher for black children in her community, whose "tenderness and love" for her she finds impossible to relate. "I could not, if I tried, sufficiently set forth the goodness of those about me" (239), Hannah confesses, summing up her blissful life of "undeviating happiness . . . in the society of my mother, my husband, and my friends" (239).

No slave narrative in the history of African American literature comes to such a marvelously happy, yet curiously hazy, ending. Unlike the typical mid-nineteenth-century fugitive slave narrative, the account of Hannah's escape to freedom in *The Bondwoman's Narrative* is peculiarly vague about dates and places. It is true, as Gates points out, that Frederick Douglass urged his fellow slave narrators not to tell how they escaped from slavery, lest other fugitives find the same routes barred, but the fact remains that slave narratives, with the remarkable exception of Douglass's, provide a great deal of detail about when and where escapes began, what towns and rivers the fugitives traveled through, and where and when the escaped slaves got to freedom. To fail to provide such detail was to invite insinuations from pro-slavery critics of these narratives that their authors had never been slaves at all. Even Douglass, though he does not tell the route of his flight, informs his reader of when he left and where and when he arrived in freedom. *The Bondwoman's Narrative* is singularly indefinite about all of this.

Hannah's life in freedom is represented as idyllic, although again the author gives her reader few specifics. Former slaves prized their marriages in freedom and often documented them in their narratives, but the author of *The Bondwoman's Narrative* never even mentions her husband's name. Nor her mother's. Nor the last names of her friends. Perhaps Crafts veiled all these people from her reader because she did not want them, or herself, to be traceable through their identities, especially because she and her friends Charlotte and William were, apparently, still fugitives at the time of the writing of *The Bondwoman's Narrative.* Yet when compared to other fugitive slave narrators, who regularly tell their readers where they live, whom they married, and what they are doing in freedom—regardless of whether they were still fugitives or had purchased their freedom—Crafts's vagueness about her escape and her life in freedom raises questions about why she shares so little with her reader about aspects of her life that, typically, slave narrators were proud to proclaim.

Most authors of slave narratives were, like Hannah, overjoyed on finally reaching freedom in the North. Many, however, especially those who had lived an appreciable amount of time in the North before publishing their autobiographies, acknowledged that the freedom they had found was far from ideal and that an absence of slavery in the free states did not mean an absence of racism. At the end of *Incidents in the Life of a Slave Girl* (1861), its author, Harriet Jacobs, reflects on the freedom she had finally gained after years in the North as a fugitive. Even as she celebrates her liberty, however, she qualifies it. She is "as free from the power of slaveholders as are the white people of the north," but "that, according to my ideas, is not saying a great deal." Given such testimony in the slave narrative against the many corruptions of freedom in the pre–Civil War North, it is all the more puzzling to find Crafts observing in her last chapter: "I found a life of freedom all my fancy had pictured it to be. I found the friends of the slave in the free state just as good as kind and hospitable as I had always heard they were" (237). Perhaps, but if so, Crafts was alone among fugitive slave narrators in writing so fulsomely about the joys of life in the free states. She evidences no worry over the possibility of recapture, a common source of distress expressed by fugitive slave narrators on arriving in the North. Unlike many slave narrators, who cautioned that it was not always easy to tell who "the friends of the slave" were, even in the antislavery movement itself, Hannah seems to have met no "friends of the slave" who didn't fully live up to her expectations. Wherever she is in New Jersey, therefore, it seems to be a place wonderfully insulated from the threat of recapture and from the racism and discrimination that most antebellum slave narrators describe as pervasive in the North.

All of these divergences from the kinds of endings one finds in the autobiographies of fugitive slaves contemporary with Crafts's suggest that the final chapters of *The Bondwoman's Narrative* are highly fictionalized, if not almost entirely imagined. To make this suggestion is not to dismiss *The Bondwoman's Narrative* from consideration as an autobiography. Important evidence researched by Gates shows that features of Crafts's text may well be autobiographical, or at least founded in historically traceable people and places. It would be hard to make such a claim, however, about the ending of the book. What, then, might have been Crafts's purpose in bringing this ostensible fugitive slave narrative to such an unlikely ending, in which its female protagonist, after undergoing many trials of her faith and after repeatedly sacrificing her own interests for the welfare of others, finally is rewarded so bountifully?

As I have already mentioned, just as the fugitive slave narrative would have been the most applicable literary model for Crafts to follow in writing an autobiography, so white American "woman's fiction" would have been the most prominent and the most popular form of novelistic storytelling for Crafts had she decided not to limit her narrative strictly to autobiography. It's not surprising, therefore, to find throughout *The Bondwoman's Narrative* that there are affinities between the ups and downs of Hannah's life and the experiences of the heroines of white American "woman's fiction." Like most woman's fiction in the United States at mid-century, *The Bondwoman's Narrative* tells the story of an orphan's rise from destitution to self-reliant independence and eventually a fulfilling marriage. Other similarities between the popular heroines of woman's fiction and Hannah include the following: the trials and testing of self that these heroines must undergo in order to discover their inner strengths; the reliance of these heroines on women, rather than men, for guidance and support during their trials; a foundation in Christian faith that these heroines seek not in institutions but in their own spiritual intuitions and perceptions; a concomitant abhorrence of poverty and social degradation; and a sustaining conviction that by maintaining honor, principles, and religious faith a woman can strengthen her character and prepare herself for eventual deliverance and triumph.[5] Most significantly for my purposes in this discussion, like the typical heroine of popular woman's fiction such as Susan Warner's *The Wide, Wide World* (1851), E.D.E.N. Southworth's *The Curse of Clifton* (1852) and *The Hidden Hand* (1859), and Maria Cummins's *The Lamplighter* (1854), Hannah is blessed at the end of the story with marriage, a home, and a community of loving, mutually supportive adults.[6] Indeed, the marriage Hannah enjoys at the end is with an unnamed minister, a profession, as Baym points out, that provides more husbands to the heroines of mid-nineteenth-century American women's fiction than any other.

Marrying "a fond and affectionate husband," establishing a secure home, finding fulfilling, socially respectable work, and recovering her long-lost mother represent almost a fantasy of social and spiritual gratification for Hannah, the likes of which cannot be found anywhere else in early African American autobiography or fiction. The authors of *The Heroic Slave* and *Clotel*, though liberated by fiction to imagine the best of all possible worlds for their fugitive heroes and heroines, do not offer such unalloyed fulfillment to their main characters. Rather than submitting to re-enslavement, Brown's central character, Clotel, dies. In Harriet Wilson's novel, *Our Nig* (1859), which until the discovery of *The Bondwoman's Narrative* was thought to be the first novel written by an African American woman, the mixed-race protagonist, Frado, after years of toil and abuse, seems to receive her reward for long-suffering virtue in the person of a bread-winning husband, but he soon proves feckless and abandons her. At the end of *Our Nig*, Frado contemplates a solitary struggle to care for her infant son. Harriet Jacobs ends her narrative not with marriage but with freedom and then goes on to discount the quality of even her freedom by noting its limitations because of the Fugitive Slave Law. Although several post–Civil War women's slave narratives pay tribute to the slave mother who tirelessly labors to reclaim her children scattered by slavery and war, *The Bondwoman's Narrative* is the only text in African American literature of the nineteenth century that brings mother and daughter together at the end of her story almost magically without even explaining how the once-enslaved mother and daughter found each other.[7]

That *The Bondwoman's Narrative* differs so markedly in its ending even from the African American fiction of its time adds credence to the notion that

Crafts's aim in winding up her story as she does was to reward her fugitive slave heroine not just with escape and freedom but also with the kind of emotional, social, and economic security that the heroines of white "woman's fiction" regularly qualified for. What if, therefore, Hannah's story was specifically intended to articulate what *ought* to happen to a woman of color who virtuously endures spiritual trials and moral tests, often in a very altruistic fashion, who repeatedly places the freedom of others (Mrs. De Vincent, Charlotte and William) before her own, and who decides on "rebellion" against slavery only after concluding "that duty to myself and God actually required it" (206)? Given the sentiments of the author's preface, in which the reader is assured that good and evil will reap their just deserts in the working-out of this narrative, it is hard *not* to think that *The Bondwoman's Narrative* ends as it does in order to confirm that *this* heroine deserves all the wonderful, near miraculous, blessings that she receives at the end of the story.

The rewards Hannah receives in the end for her many good works would not be especially remarkable if hers were the story of a white female servant who had to make her own way in the world. But, of course, Hannah is not white. She is a slave, albeit a privileged one. Thus *The Bondwoman's Narrative* raises the implicit question, "Could a slave woman, practicing virtues typically celebrated in white American 'woman's fiction,' aspire to similar rewards and similar fulfillments as an outcome of her struggles, as was promised to the white girls and women who read *The Wide, Wide World, The Lamplighter, The Hidden Hand*, and other novels of this sort?"

Harriet Jacobs's implicit answer to this question in *Incidents in the Life of a Slave Girl* was an emphatic "No." Jacobs insists that enslaved women could not exercise the same virtues as free white women, nor could black women, in the North or South, expect to enjoy the rewards, the happy endings, that white women could imagine for themselves in their fiction. A slave woman such as Jacobs could dedicate herself to freedom and qualify for it, in part, by refusing to seize it for herself until she had ensured it for her children. Such self-sacrifice might prove Jacobs a model mother in her autobiography, but in the end, Jacobs's reward is an alloyed freedom and a profoundly unfulfilled desire for a home of her own. The same message emerges from the *Narrative of Sojourner Truth*. Truth's dedication to freedom is not rewarded by marriage.

As of the writing of her 1850 *Narrative* she could not claim a home of her own either. The ending of *Our Nig* seems also to suggest that for a black woman, freedom and independence are achievable only by relinquishing the ideal of reliable husband, stable home, children, and loving adult community.

In contrast, in *The Bondwoman's Narrative*, Hannah, the escaped slave, is allowed to fulfill the fantasies of virtue rewarded that undergird the happy endings of much mid-nineteenth-century American "woman's fiction." And though it may be hard to picture a fugitive slave woman in the wish-fulfillment role that Hannah occupies at the end of her story, the author of *The Bondwoman's Narrative* may well have brought her novel to this conclusion precisely to challenge the notion that an African American woman had no business expecting or even hoping for such fulfillment, even in fiction. Perhaps the author of *The Bondwoman's Narrative* believed that a black woman of the mid-nineteenth century, whether a slave or free, as long as she remembered that "even freedom without God and religion would be a barren possession" (109), deserved the same prospect for emotional, spiritual, social, and economic fulfillment in life as white women imagined for themselves. If such a motive led Crafts to end her novel with Hannah's every wish fulfilled, then at least one moral of *The Bondwoman's Narrative* seems to be that even a woman of the lowest American caste, a slave woman, if she held fast to "God, truth, honor" (108), could aspire, *through her own efforts,* to freedom and the social and economic accouterments (husband, home, work, community) that women of the highest caste believed they deserved. For the author of *The Bondwoman's Narrative*, insisting on Hannah's thorough fulfillment in freedom may have seemed the best way to announce to her readers, white as well as black, that an African American woman had every right to aspire to such fulfillment as Hannah achieves and to expect that "Providence" would reward an African American woman in this fashion if she lived up to the moral and religious standards that Hannah consistently summarizes as her "duty."

What sort of an author would write a text like *The Bondwoman's Narrative* to make such a case for African American women's rightful claim to marriage, home, work, and community in freedom? This is the profile of this author that I would propose for consideration in light of the way *The Bondwoman's Narrative* ends. First, the author of *The Bondwoman's Narrative* is most likely an African American woman. Her sympathies with Hannah, particularly in rewarding her so greatly for all that Hannah must endure in the novel, imply a sisterhood between author and protagonist. It is very hard to think that even the most enlightened of white women writers at that time could imagine a female slave who actually felt it her "duty" *not* to lie about her enslavement, even though telling the truth would return her to bondage. It is almost as hard to think of a white woman writer at that time who would picture an escaped slave woman finding total fulfillment in a Northern black community in which neither she nor her husband nor any of her friends and neighbors seems to be active in any way in efforts to end slavery and bring about social reform. Therefore, Hannah is the product of an African American woman's experience and imagination.

But was the woman who wrote *The Bondwoman's Narrative* a fugitive slave? It seems to me that the ending of this novel gives us good reason for thinking that this author may not have been a fugitive slave. The vagueness about Hannah's escape, her idyllic fulfillment in freedom, and her lack of evident interest in the antislavery movement in the North (other than to make clear in her story the many injustices of slavery that she has personally witnessed and experienced) lead me to envisage Crafts as a free African American woman who, if she experienced slavery directly, may have gained her freedom via some means other than flight. While unquestionably opposed to slavery, the author of *The Bondwoman's Narrative* seems to have been a very traditional woman in many other respects, a woman more likely to pen a story privately in her home than to deliver a lecture in a public hall. The Crafts I envisage may well have been more active in a local African American literary society than a national antislavery organization. She would be more likely found in a meeting of black churchwomen than in a gathering of abolitionists. Pious, studious, reflective, and sober-minded, the author of *The Bondwoman's Narrative* may have lived relatively quietly, reading and writing, perhaps for African American periodicals, until she met a former slave on the run in search of refuge in the author's own New Jersey community. Perhaps such an encounter inspired the author to learn this woman's story, to imagine the kind of life in freedom that such a woman deserved, and then to undertake the bold and unprecedented venture of writing that story as an African American woman's novel in the guise of a slave narrative, the better to gain the attention and credence of the American reader. Perhaps Hannah Crafts's story is a tribute to both a real person, the escaped slave woman who recounts her life in this narrative, and an ideal community, the free black women of the North who recorded and rewarded that life, at least in literature, with the ultimate fulfillments of freedom reserved for those sisters who kept the faith.

Notes

1. There is a curious discrepancy in the title of the Warner Books edition of *The Bondwoman's Narrative*. On the dust jacket of the Warner Books edition, the full title is *The Bondwoman's Narrative, A Novel*. But on the title page of the book itself, the title is simply *The Bondwoman's Narrative*. The full title given the manuscript by its author is *The Bondwoman's Narrative By Hannah Crafts A Fugitive Slave Recently Escaped From North Carolina*. See p. 1 of *The Bondwoman's Narrative*.

2. For more information on the slave narrative, see William L. Andrews, *To Tell a Free Story: The First Century of Afro-American Autobiography, 1760–1865* (Urbana: University of Illinois Press, 1986); and Frances Smith Foster, *Witnessing Slavery*, 2nd ed. (Madison: University of Wisconsin Press, 1994). A complete digital library of slave narratives can be accessed on the

internet. See "North American Slave Narratives," William L. Andrews, series editor, http://docsouth.unc.edu/neh/neh.html. All slave narratives referred to in this essay may be accessed and read on this site.

3. Nina Baym, *Woman's Fiction: A Guide to Novels by and About Women in America, 1820–1870* (Ithaca: Cornell University Press, 1978). See also Susan K. Harris, *19th-Century American Women's Novels* (Cambridge: Cambridge University Press, 1990); and Shirley Samuels, ed., *The Culture of Sentiment: Race, Gender, and Sentimentality in Nineteenth-Century America* (New York: Oxford University Press, 1992). Another popular descriptive term for this type of fiction is "domestic fiction."

4. Heretofore the first known autobiography written by a formerly enslaved American woman was Harriet Jacobs's *Incidents in the Life of a Slave Girl* (Boston: the Author, 1861). If *The Bondwoman's Narrative* was written by a former slave, it likely predates *Incidents*, although Jacobs's autobiography remains the first published slave narrative written by a formerly enslaved American woman.

5. See Baym, *Woman's Fiction*, 41–48.

6. Although the end of *The Wide, Wide World* does not have its adolescent heroine, Ellen Montgomery, married to the man she loves, the reader has every reason to expect their marriage. More relevant to *The Bondwoman's Narrative* is the claim to ownership of Ellen by various members of her domineering family that pervades *The Wide, Wide World* and Ellen's struggle to reconcile her Christian faith with her desire to be free of such control.

7. See William L. Andrews, ed., *Six Women's Slave Narratives* (New York: Oxford University Press, 1988).

4

Hannah Crafts, Novelist; or, How a Silent
Observer Became a "Dabster at Invention"

ANN FABIAN

If Hannah Crafts was indeed a woman who had been a slave, then *The Bond-woman's Narrative* is an important book. It is important not because it is a great or even a good or powerful book but simply because it is a novel. Like every novel, *The Bondwoman's Narrative* describes a world its author has invented. "Hannah Crafts," our author, borrows from gothic tales, sentimental novels, Charles Dickens, slaves' narratives, and political gossip, but she weaves all these bits and pieces into something distinctly her own. It is a remarkable thing to make up a world and set it down in the form of a novel, anytime, anywhere. In the United States in the first half of the nineteenth century, it was all the more remarkable for a bondwoman, even for a woman who had once been a slave, to invent a fictional world, to people it with characters she conjured up, to fill those characters with thoughts she imagined, to mete out rewards and punishments as she saw fit, to conceal and reveal as she chose, and, finally, to ask a reader, for a time at least, to consider her fiction a credible invention.

To see why a novel by a "bondwoman" might be so important, we need to visit the world of literary production that slaves and former slaves encountered as they made their way north and into print. Although *The Bondwoman's Narrative* was never published, it is clear that "Hannah Crafts," whoever she was, wrote it with readers in mind and that she knew the peculiar conventions that allowed poor, uneducated, and even illiterate people to become authors of books. She opens, promising a "record of plain unvarnished facts," and then apologizes for writing, asking, "How will such a literary venture, coming from a sphere so humble be received?" (p. 4).

43

In her preface, she suggests that her social position will influence the way readers respond to her work. But such doubts seem to vanish once she starts to tell her story. Happy at last in New Jersey, Hannah Crafts acknowledges her readers once more, concluding with a confident valedictory salute, "I will let the reader picture it all to his imagination and say farewell" (p. 239). Which Hannah should we believe—the Hannah who apologizes or the Hannah who dismisses her readers with an easy wave? Our Hannah, I will argue, is both humble and confident, a crafty character who uses the disguise of the humble narrator to become the confident novelist. She says she is a silent, unobtrusive observer, but with her novel she makes herself loud and conspicuous.

Like so much else in cultural life of the United States before the Civil War, the art of storytelling and the rules that governed the truth and fiction of stories were shaped by slavery and by race. When fugitive narrators told their stories, they often found themselves labeled as either virtuous truth tellers or dangerous liars. Imagined fiction was not really an option. When Hannah Crafts produced her novel and imagined readers for it, she broke many of the rules that governed literary works by people who had been slaves. How she did so makes for an interesting story.

"A dabster at invention"

White abolitionists worked out many of the rules for literary productions by people like Hannah Crafts when they began to publish slaves' narratives in the late 1830s. The first of the slave narratives published by organized abolition, *The Narrative of James Williams,* proved something of a public relations disaster for the American Anti-Slavery Society. The controversy turned on just the kinds of questions about truth and invention that run through Hannah Crafts story. Fugitive narrators called on readers to take action. But how should readers respond if they weren't sure the stories they heard were true? Abolitionists and fugitives from slavery worked hard to establish former slaves as reliable narrators. They knew that audiences and readers in the North sometimes questioned the veracity of people who had often survived by their ability to dissemble and deceive.

On January 4, 1838, the Executive Committee of the American Anti-Slavery Society authorized the Quaker poet and anti-slavery activist John Greenleaf Whittier to "write a narrative of the life and escape of a fugitive slave now in this neighborhood, & that the same be published under the direction of the Publishing Committee, with a portrait and other embellishments."[1] Whittier and James Williams sat down together and produced a book. They recruited Patrick Reason, a talented African American artist working in

New York City, to produce a portrait of Williams, and Whittier wrote down Williams's account of his life as a house servant in Virginia and a driver on a cotton plantation in Alabama.

In his preface, Whittier boasted the visceral appeal of Williams's story. Through Williams, Whittier said, "we see," "we feel," and "we look" on "the secrets of the prison house" of slavery. He used Williams's story to condemn the hypocrisy of slaveholders who were able to live with the "hideous anomaly of a code of laws, beginning with emphatic declaration of the inalienable rights of all men to life, liberty and the pursuit of happiness, and closing with a deliberate and systematic denial of those rights to a large portion of their countrymen."[2]

Williams, Whittier told his readers, was one of their countrymen who now had come forward to bear witness to the brutality of slaveholders. Whittier said he gathered the pieces of Williams's "simple and unvarnished story" just as they fell "from the lips of the narrator." He assured readers that on several occasions Williams had successfully repeated the account of his life to groups of "gentlemen," who now vouched for his veracity.

In the spring and summer of 1838 advertisements for the book, which ran in the anti-slavery press, touted "the perfect accordance of his statements (made at different times and to different individuals) one with another, as well as those statements themselves, all afford strong confirmation of the truth and accuracy of his story."[3]

Williams told Whittier he was "born in Pawhatan County, Virginia on the plantation of George Larrimore, sen., at a place called Mount Pleasant, on the 16th of May 1805." Williams remembered his life in Virginia as relatively easy, but everything changed when his master married an ill-tempered French woman from New Orleans and moved his household to Alabama. On the Alabama plantation, the slaves fell under a sadistic overseer named Huckstep. When Huckstep tried to force Williams to prepare "a burning solution" to rub into the lacerations on the back of a flogged slave, Williams ran away. He made his way back to Virginia; old friends in Richmond helped him on to Philadelphia; and Quakers in Pennsylvania sent him on to New York.[4]

Interestingly, the *Narrative of James Williams* ended with a "Note by the Editor," informing readers that Williams, certain he "would not be safe in any part of the United States," and wary of the "unsettled state of the Canadas," had sailed for Liverpool. It appeared that Williams exchanged his story for money to pay his passage to England. Whittier tried to cover for Williams, invoking again the "gentlemen" who could corroborate the "facts stated by James Williams."[5] But with Williams out of the picture, the story ran into trouble.

Several parties had an interest in whether James Williams told a "true story." Remember, he called slaveholders cruel hypocrites, a stinging accusation to slaveholders who considered themselves men of grace and honor. To make things worse, in opening descriptions of his Virginia neighborhood, Williams named some seventeen slaveholders by name, including them all in his blanket indictment. Naming names was a bold move, and it riled up J. B. Rittenhouse, an Alabama editor who challenged the abolitionist publishers to produce the former slave who dared to libel respectable men.[6]

What was the American Anti-Slavery Society to do? The abolitionists, who were hard-pressed for cash in the depression years of the late 1830s, hesitated to withdraw a narrative they had financed. The Society's Fifth Annual Report praised the narrative as a "publication of much interest." The executive committee determined that the story was well "within the bounds of probability," pointing out that "there could be no imposition in the story without attributing to its author such powers of mind, as few men, either white or black, could justly lay claim to." An editor of the abolitionist *Herald of Freedom* expressed a similar sentiment, suggesting that if Williams invented his story, he was "a dabster at invention, for an 'inferior race,' and in time will be sharp enough for freedom, if he keeps on."[7]

Editor Rittenhouse figured there were problems with Williams's book either way. If Williams had told the truth, then he had made liars out of slaveholders who defended their practices as good for slaves and good for the country. If Williams had invented a story abolitionists now took as true, he had tricked a community into believing not a carefully crafted fiction but a set of lies. It was hard to tell whether Williams was an inventive storyteller, a crafty liar, a libelous accuser, an artless witness of a hard life, or somehow all these things at once.

Rittenhouse set out to take the story apart. He searched for the people and plantations that Williams mentioned and found none of them. He published a letter from his own "gentleman" friend who deemed the story a "foul fester of falsehood," just what the editor expected from a clever, lying slave. He found a slaveholder in Virginia who said he recognized the man in Reason's portrait as a slave named Shadrach Wilkins, who had tried to poison "Dr. Roy and his family."[8] According to the editor, Williams's appearance in print did not mark him as a new and free man; rather he took advantage of print to continue slavish behavior in a new venue. Just as lying had helped enslaved men and women survive, so Williams now used his tricky ways to gull unsuspecting abolitionists.

Rittenhouse perhaps played on racist assumptions of some among Williams's northern readers, and the American Anti-Slavery Society felt the sting of his pen. The society set up a committee to look into his allegations. Committee members confessed themselves predisposed to accept Williams's story as true. "After all the fraud and trickery of the slaveholders and their abettors, to cover up their shameful deeds, the friends of the slave know full well the injustice of setting down as undeniably true all the oppressor says in his favor, and as undeniably false or doubtful, all that the victim relates concerning his own sufferings."9

To all who had met him, Williams seemed an honest man. "He was intelligent, far beyond what slaves usually are. His account of himself, and of what he had seen, whether true or false, proves this. His wardrobe was but indifferently supplied—yet he seemed careless about replenishing it with more than was necessary for his actual comfort. He had no money—and he asked for none." The committee took it as a mark of his honesty that "[f]rom first to last he seemed to have no idea of deriving any pecuniary benefit from the publication, in any form, of his sufferings in slavery, or from the sympathy he had excited in those to whom they were rehearsed."10

Or so they thought. Williams certainly bartered his story for at least enough money to pay his passage to England. By early fall in 1838 committee members had learned enough to conclude that "many of the statements made in the said Narrative were false." They hesitated "to decide of *course*, or hastily, against a *black*, where the testimony was contradicted by a *white*," but they felt they could not "ask for the confidence of the community in any of the statements contained in the Narrative." And so, with regret, the committee directed the publishing agent "to discontinue the sale of the work."11

A few in the abolitionist community dissented. "Where *is* James Williams?" Lydia Maria Child asked, writing to her friend Angelina Grimké in December 1838. "Can he not be found and cross examined?" Child believed Williams. He had lied only about names, she thought, and then only to protect himself from capture. The problem was not with the story but with the controversy about it. The controversy distracted people from "the principles of things." When Child wrote to Grimké's husband, Theodore Weld, a few days later, she was still worried about Williams's story. "[T]o you and I, who look on the *foundations* upon which slavery rests, it is not the slightest consequence whether James Williams told the truth or not; yet the doubt thrown on his narrative is doing incalculable mischief."12

In the future, northern abolitionists would be more careful about the stories they backed. As the historian John Blassingame noted, after the Williams debacle there "were no comparable exposés during the antebellum period."13 But the compromise, which confined fugitive narrators to the facts of their lives, would come to grate on writers, most famously on Frederick Douglass.

When Douglass revised his autobiography as *My Bondage and My Freedom* in 1855, he recalled his first years on the lecture platform. The abolitionist John Collins told him to "give us the facts and we will take care of the philosophy."

"Just here arose some embarrassment," Douglass continued. "It was impossible for me to repeat the same old story month after month, and to keep up my interest in it. It was new to the people, it is true, but it was an old story to me; and to go through with it night after night, was a task altogether too mechanical for my nature."[14] Douglass eluded his abolitionist handlers, of course, by extracting ever deeper philosophical truths from the "facts" of his life. Hannah Crafts escaped constraints too by writing her novel.

"A silent unobtrusive way of observing things"

I have dwelled at some length on the story of James Williams because it suggests some of the cultural complexities a fugitive narrator and aspiring novelist like Hannah Crafts would have faced. What did it mean for a woman like Hannah Crafts to write a novel? Would she have been granted a license to create, or would she have been branded a liar because she bent the details of her characters' lives to suit her arguments?

Apparently our narrator did not turn to the abolitionists who perhaps would have bristled at the impossible fiction she created, yet it is likely that she hoped to use her fiction, as Child thought that Williams had, to get at "the *foundations* upon which slavery rests." She introduces her project this way. "Being the truth it makes no pretensions to romance, and relating events as they occurred it has no especial reference to a moral, but to those who regard truth as stranger than fiction it can be no less interesting on the former account, while others of pious and discerning minds can scarcely fail to recognize the hand of Providence in giving to the righteous the reward of their works, and to the wicked the fruit of their doings" (p. 4).

This is a funny introduction to the world of this novel. Our narrator is playing with conventions, not telling us her story is true, exactly, but rather letting us know that she knows what is expected of her as a humble narrator. No one could read this story as a collection of empirical or literal truths, and yet she is asking us to grant it some kind of truth. A truth that is stranger than fiction. She also hides her own hand, crediting Providence with the rewards and punishments present in the novel. In the novel, the hand of Providence is, of course, the author's own hand.

Still, like a good and careful creator, Hannah Crafts, our author, takes time at the beginning of the story to tell her readers why she is a good narrator, how she learns what she knows, and why we should trust her. We learn first that she is "neither clever, nor learned, nor talented" (p. 5)—not a particularly auspicious start for a book. And things get worse before they get better. "When a child they used to scold and find fault with me because they said I was dull and stupid" (p. 5). However, by the end of the paragraph, we learn that this dull child did have a "silent unobtrusive way of observing things and events, and wishing to understand them better" (p. 5). "In the absence of books and teachers and schools," she continues, "I determined to learn if not in a regular approved and scientific way" (p. 6). "Slaves," she tells us later, "are proverbially curious" (p. 26).

Observation, curiosity, and determination likely assured the survival of many a human caught in slavery. They are also the skills Hannah will depend on as a narrator. In a sense, she translates what she learned as a slave onto the pages of her book. However, she shuns one weapon in the slaves' arsenal; she refuses to lie. As the case of James Williams illustrates so well, skill at dissembling could spell trouble for a slave turned abolitionist activist and writer of books.[15]

To make sure we understand how good an observer Hannah Crafts is, she makes the point over and over again. "I have said that I always had a quiet way of observing things, and this habit grew upon me, sharpened perhaps by the absence of all elemental knowledge. Instead of books I studied faces and characters, and arrived at conclusions by a sort of sagacity that closely approximated to the unerring certainty of animal instinct" (p. 27). We are in the hands of a cunning narrator.

And she is careful not to let us down. She figures an attentive reader would expect a description of the landscape she passes through with the slave trader Saddler. Unfortunately, "[m]y mind was too busily occupied, and my thoughts too confused and agitated for any close observation of what we passed and whither we went" (p. 111).

Of course, she also knows how to read, and she reveals herself a favored confidante of young and old. A kind old woman teaches her to read, and from time to time, we catch a glimpse of our narrator reading in the pages of the novel. "My mistress was very kind, and unknown to Master she indulged me in reading whenever I desired. The next morning I descended to the parlor, and seated myself with a book behind the heavy damask curtains that shaped the window. In this situation I was entirely concealed" (p. 36). Hidden behind the curtains, she learns her mistress's dark secret, the first of the many passing narratives she weaves into her plot.

Textual evidence (and the contents of John Hill Wheeler's library) suggests that Hannah Crafts read or knew the novels of Charles Dickens, slave narratives, classical mythology, and perhaps even the novels of Charlotte and Emily

Brontë. Apparently, she had also read enough business letters to identify a correct one. In one scene, she describes herself reading to Mrs. Wheeler, but she does not say what she read. The Bible is the only book we actually see her hold, and the narrative is full of biblical references. But when she turns to the Bible to bolster her resolve to escape from North Carolina, she doesn't exactly read the book. Instead, she practices a kind of popular scriptural divination, seeking advice by selecting a passage at random (p. 206).

Likely, the writer Hannah Crafts learned phrasing and plot from what she read. Within the novel, most of what the character Hannah Crafts does not learn by observation, she picks up in conversation. "I was quite astonished to see how much I was trusted and confided in, how much I was made the repository of secrets, and how the weak, the sick, and the suffering came to me for advice and assistance" (p. 11). And not just the weak and the sick. Her mistress confides in her too. "Those who suppose that southern ladies keep their attendants at distance, scarcely speaking to them, or only to give commands have a very erroneous impression. Between the mistress and her slave a freedom exists probably not to be found elsewhere. A northern woman would have recoiled at the idea of communicating a private history to one of my race, and in my condition, whereas such a thought never occurred to Mrs. Wheeler. I was near her. She was not fond of silence where there was a listener, and I was pleased with her apparent sociality" (p. 150).

She does not detail for us Mrs. Wheeler's private history. More important to the structure of the novel are the stories she incorporates almost as old-fashioned yarns; we learn Aunt Hetty's story, the story of the old woman in jail, Lizzie's story, and even the story of the demise of lawyer Trappe. Hannah Crafts depends on this old-fashioned and somewhat crude device to expand the reach of her novel. She needs more than one passing story to capture for readers the "*foundations* upon which slavery rests." She needs to able to generalize beyond the knowledge of her narrator, and, more important, if the novel indeed details her own experience, beyond what she could have known on her own. Despite the modest disclaimer of the preface, this novel is an immodest project.

She is careful to use her secrets well. ("'But you will not betray us. We have placed our secret in your hands'" [p. 143].) She knows that information can be deployed to destroy. The villainous Mr. Trappe has made his career as a blackmailer out of racial secrets. "Many and many are the family secrets that I have unraveled as women unravel a web. You may think of it as you please, you may call it dishonorable if you like, but it brings gold—bright gold" (p. 98).

She will not blackmail, she will not betray, and she will not lie. Or so she contends. Hannah Crafts is fastidious with the truth. Her enemies are "adept in the art of dissembling" (p. 203). When she is "sorely tempted to lie," her "better nature prevail[s]," and she confesses to Mrs. Henry that she is a slave. Within the novel, Hannah does not "expose the inconsistencies in Mrs. Wheeler's character" (p. 155), does not regale the North Carolina slaves with Mrs. Wheeler's Washington disgrace. But doesn't the novel turn this all inside out? Hannah Crafts has the last word, exposing all and turning all she has learned into her novel.

Try to imagine Hannah Crafts, or the creator of "Hannah Crafts," composing this novel. Does she have a room of her own? Does she write in the schoolroom after the students have gone home? It is easy to picture Whittier and Williams sitting down to make their book. Whittier is a published poet, an active abolitionist, a man with extensive connections in the world of letters. He writes down the stories Williams tells him. He cleans them up and smoothes them out, shaping them for dramatic effect. Perhaps it is Whittier who misspells the names of Williams's former owners, opening Williams to charges of fraud and libel. Still, their collaborative project makes its way into print.

Evidence suggests that Hannah Crafts wrote her own book. Whittier wrote down a story from Williams's "lips," and if the book retains a trace of the man, it is his voice. *The Bondwoman's Narrative* leaves us a trace of Hannah Crafts's hand. In her corrections and alterations, we can watch her work. We may never know the whole story of this book that never made it into print. Hannah imagined her readers, but she did not publish a book for them. Perhaps the world of abolitionist publishing seemed to her too narrow to accept a story she partly devised, partly witnessed. Hannah Crafts, whoever she was, waited a century and a half for her readers. We can acknowledge the ways Hannah Crafts reworked the pieces of her culture into a world of her own devising. We can accept the possibility that the power of *The Bondwoman's Narrative* lies in its distinctive mix of facts and fictions. We can try to picture Hannah Crafts at home and let ourselves become the readers she tried to imagine so long ago.

Notes

1. Minutes of the Executive Committee of the American Anti-Slavery Society, 4 January 1838, p. 21, Papers of the American Anti-Slavery Society, Boston Public Library, Boston, Mass.

2. *Narrative of James Williams, an American Slave; who was for several years a driver on a cotton plantation in Alabama* (New York: American Anti-Slavery Society, 1838), p. iv.

3. *Narrative of James Williams*, pp. xvii–xx. Advertisements ran throughout the spring and summer of 1838. See, for example, *The Liberator*, 27 July 1838, p. 120.

4. *Narrative of James Williams*, pp. 89, 95–98.

5. *Narrative of James Williams*, pp. 101, 103.

6. Greensborough, Alabama *Beacon*, 10 May 1838. Rittenhouse's charges were reprinted in the Ohio abolitionist paper, *The Philanthropist*, 30 October 1838.

7. *The Liberator*, 13 May 1838, p. 78. See also William Andrews, *To Tell a Free Story: The First Century of Afro-American Autobiography, 1760–1865* (Urbana: University of Illinois Press, 1988), p. 87. The quotation from the *Herald of Freedom* appears in Marion Wilson Starling, *The Slave Narrative: Its Place in American History* (Washington, D.C.: Howard University Press, 1988), p. 115.

8. *The Philanthropist*, 30 October 1838.

9. "Narrative of James Williams," *The Liberator*, 28 September 1838, p. 153.

10. James G. Birney, "James Williams," *The Philanthropist*, 6 November 1838.

11. Minutes of the Executive Committee of the American Anti-Slavery Society, 16 August 1838, p. 92; 18 October 1838, pp. 99–101. The full report of the committee, signed by James Birney and Lewis Tappan, appeared in *The Liberator*, 2 November 1838.

12. "Lydia Maria Child and D. L. Child to Angelina and Theodore Weld, December 26, 1838," in *Letters of Theodore Dwight Weld, Angelina Grimké Weld and Sarah Grimké, 1822–1844*, ed. Gilbert H. Barnes and Dwight L. Dumond (New York: D. Appleton-Century, 1934), vol. 2, p. 732; "Lydia Maria Child to Weld, December 19, 1838," vol. 2, p. 736.

13. John W. Blassingame, "Critical Essay on Sources," in *The Slave Community: Plantation Life in the Antebellum South* (1972; reprint, New York: Oxford University Press, 1979), p. 372.

14. Frederick Douglass, *My Bondage and My Freedom* (1855; reprint, Urbana: University of Illinois Press, 1987), p. 220.

15. For a longer discussion of this issue, see my *Unvarnished Truth: Personal Narratives in Nineteenth-Century America* (Berkeley: University of California Press, 2000).

5

The Problem of Freedom in
The Bondwoman's Narrative

JOHN STAUFFER

I

Hannah Crafts was, until the publication of *The Bondwoman's Narrative*, an invisible woman. With no formal education, she became one of the most literate and literary African Americans of her day. She refuted southern laws and the beliefs of most whites that kept blacks from learning to read and write, devoured almost every book she could get her hands on, including many classics of her time, and wrote the first extant novel by an African American woman. It is a brilliant novel, intricately nuanced and extraordinarily sophisticated in its storytelling technique. It draws on three of the most prominent literary conventions of her day: the slave narrative; the Gothic novel; and sentimental fiction. She uses these conventions to explore a diverse range of social ills, and in one sense she anticipates Ralph Ellison, who exploits the literary conventions of his day to articulate different forms of protest in *Invisible Man.*

Of course the major reason for Crafts's invisibility is that she was a black woman, for whom the act of book publishing was a "virtually miraculous event," as Henry Louis Gates, Jr., notes (lxiii). Crafts wanted to publish her story—the first words of her novel (in her preface) state that she is "presenting this record of plain unvarnished facts to a generous public"—and she carefully preserved her manuscript in the hopes that one day it would be published (3). But for authors of slave narratives, the publishing market was controlled by white abolitionists. And there is no record of Crafts corresponding or interacting with black or white abolitionists, who could have helped her gain the necessary contacts to publish her novel. Nor is there any record of her going on the abolitionist lecture circuit, which gave African Americans public visibility and served as an important test market for publishing a slave narrative. In fact, no abolitionist appears in her novel. She seems completely oblivious to the movement. Why is this?[1]

Perhaps, as Augusta Rohrbach suggests, Crafts eschewed notoriety. That Crafts remained unpublished could have reflected her "sense of responsibility to family as well as her sense of personal ownership" over her writing (Rohrbach, in this volume). Crafts supports this claim in her conclusion. She describes her new life of freedom in idyllic terms; she is happily married to a Methodist minister, lives in a neat little cottage in New Jersey with her mother and old friends from slavery nearby, and keeps school for the neighborhood "colored children" (237). Publishing her narrative would have increased the likelihood of her recapture and disrupted the "deep repose," the "blest and holy quietude," and the "hush on my spirit" that accompanied her new life (237). As a black woman, publishing would also mean having her manuscript edited by whites and a loss of ownership over her craft. Perhaps Crafts forsook fame for her adherence to the craft of writing and preferred the "holy quietude" of her idyllic private life to the risk of exposure, notoriety, and the increased chances of recapture.

Perhaps, too, Crafts missed the market, as Ann Fabian and Nina Baym imply. Assuming that Crafts completed her narrative in the late 1850s, as she probably did, the market for slave narratives, which was at its peak in the 1840s and early 1850s, had already begun to wane as the sectional crisis and efforts to preserve the union overshadowed the demand for stories of fugitives. Crafts's decision to write a first-person autobiographical novel would have made publication all the more difficult in the political climate of the 1850s. The antislavery and abolition movements demanded veracity above all else from ex-slaves; they had to tell the truth for their stories to be politically effective and commercially successful. As Baym notes, "Given the public insistence on veracity in the handling of slave experiences," Crafts may have hesitated "to launch into the marketplace an experimental novel in the first person under her own name" (lxiv–lxv).

The abolition movement also sought to control the discourse of protest. Abolitionists viewed freedom as an unambiguous concept and were unequivocal in championing it as a sacred right and virtue. They saw freedom as the opposite of slavery—which they identified with sin. For abolitionists, "the essence of both sin and slavery was a denial of self-sovereignty" and freedom, as David Brion Davis has noted (Davis, 292). "By affirming man's freedom to overcome all restraints and dominion, and by shifting the locus of fundamental value from external authority to internal impulse," abolitionists embraced universal freedom and pointed the way to reform and social revolution (Davis,

299). The most passionate desire of radical abolitionists in the 1840s and 1850s was the immediate end of all sin. They viewed slavery as the equivalent of America's original sin and believed that the abolition of slavery would bring about an end to all sin and the emergence of universal freedom.

Crafts, however, articulates ambivalent and problematic attitudes toward freedom, which are part and parcel of her experimental style. At times, she resigns herself to slavery and even blurs the distinctions between freedom and bondage. An abolitionist editor would have required Crafts to affirm absolute distinctions between slavery and freedom, abandon her different modes of social critique, and write a factual narrative that was unequivocal in its embrace of freedom and condemnation against slavery.

Unlike the slave narratives of the 1840s and 1850s, Crafts does not universally condemn the institution of slavery.[2] In combining the Gothic novel, sentimental fiction, and the slave narrative, she hates slavery but is often less than resolute in her quest for and belief in freedom. She affirms the evangelical Christianity of sentimental literature (and of southern slaveholders), establishes clear distinctions between heaven and earth, and subsumes her belief in worldly freedom for the absolute freedom that comes only after death. For much of her novel, she acknowledges permanent inequalities in social relations and believes that patterns of dominance and submission define life on earth. Instead of embracing self-sovereignty, her locus of value resides with a distant God or another master or mistress—some place outside of herself. But she also follows the conventions of the slave narrative; at key moments in her novel, she vigorously attacks slavery, and she ends her narrative as a born-again free woman.

Crafts's relationship with other characters reflects her ambivalence about freedom. She is a comparatively passive narrator and prefers ambiguity to the declarative speech acts that pepper slave narratives in the 1840s and 1850s.[3] In the first paragraph of her novel, she describes herself as "a shy and reserved" child who "scarce dared open [her] lips to anyone": "I had none of that quickness and animation which are so much admired in children, but rather a silent unobtrusive way of observing things and events, and wishing to understand them better than I could" (5). Her persona does not much change as an adult narrator; she remains comparatively "silent and unobtrusive" and rarely challenges authority directly. At various points in the novel, she prefers slavery with a kind mistress to striking for freedom with friends, and once she is free, she seems comfortable with the "silence" of a private and anonymous life.

Crafts prefers in effect to be an observer of events rather than a participant in them; in this sense she seeks understanding over action. By contrast, her contemporaries, from Frederick Douglass (whose 1845 *Narrative* she probably read) to Harriet Jacobs and William Wells Brown, are rebels who continually declare their right to freedom. The tension between narrator as participant and observer stems from Crafts's success at combining different literary modes: as rebels, slave narrators are active participants in the events they narrate. But narrators of Gothic and sentimental fiction are more comfortable in the posture of observer; either they are omniscient narrators who convey a deep understanding of the world, or they seek to unmask Gothic ambiguities. And while slave narrators of the 1840s and 1850s universally condemn slavery, narrators of Gothic fiction lack faith in the possibility of a free and equal society.

II

From the beginning of her novel, Crafts relies on and departs from the tradition of slave narratives. She follows the formula of slave narratives by saying that she doesn't know her age, birth date, or parents. Her natal alienation stems from her bondage and race: "I soon learned . . . that the African blood in my veins would forever exclude me from the higher walks of life. That toil unremitted unpaid toil must be my lot and portion, without even the hope or expectation of any thing better" (5–6). But instead of identifying herself with other slaves and characterizing herself as a representative slave, Crafts identifies with both whites and blacks. Her oppression, she notes, was especially difficult, "because my complexion was almost white, and the obnoxious descent could not be readily traced, though it gave a rotundity to my person, a wave and curl to my hair, and perhaps led me to fancy pictorial illustrations and flaming colors" (6). As a woman who could pass for white (and eventually does during her escape), she considers her condition "the harder to be borne" than that of someone with a darker hue (6). At the same time, her "African blood" makes her predisposed toward fancy pictures and flaming colors, which connote an affiliation with African traditions.

Crafts's proclivity for "fancy pictures" foreshadows her use of the Gothic. In the eighteenth and nineteenth centuries, pictures were a frequent and ideal trope in Gothic fiction; writers from Horace Walpole and Nathaniel Hawthorne (both of whom Crafts probably read) to Edgar Allan Poe and Herman Melville referred to pictures in their narratives as a way to represent the surface of things while exposing hidden and haunted depths. For writers of Gothic fiction, a picture revealed the "unvarnished truth" of surface and depth, image and referent, much as Crafts seeks in her narrative to record the "plain unvarnished facts" of her life, as she states in her preface.

A few pages after acknowledging her fancy for pictures, Crafts's narrative turns Gothic as she describes the family portraits of her master's ancestors.

"Memories of the dead give at any time a haunting air to a silent room," she says, echoing Hawthorne's language in *The House of Seven Gables*: "How much more this becomes the case when standing face to face with their pictured resemblances and looking into the stony eyes motionless and void of expression as those of an exhumed corpse" (16).[4] The portraits, like those in Hawthorne's fiction, become prophetic.[5] Her master's portrait appears as "the first scene in some fearful tragedy; the foreboding of some great calamity; a curse of destiny that no circumstances could avert or soften. And why was it that as I mused the portrait of my master seemed to change from its usually kind and placid expression to one of wrath and gloom, that the calm brow should become wrinkled with passion, the lips turgid with malevolence—yet thus it was" (17). Crafts probes beneath the surface of the portrait to uncover hidden and haunted depths. She initially wonders whether her reaction to the portrait is "prophecy or presentiment"; her narrative proves the former (17).

The haunted and prophetic portraits are a source of empowerment for Crafts. "I was not a slave with these pictured memorials of the past," she says. "They could not enforce drudgery, or condemn me on account of my color to a life of servitude. As their companion I could think and speculate. In their presence my mind seemed to run riotous and exult in its freedom as a rational being, and one destined for something higher and better than this world can afford" (17). As Gates notes, Crafts "argues for the transformative powers" of pictures (245). Here she anticipates Frederick Douglass, who relied on pictures as a way to affirm the common humanity of slaves and masters. In two separate speeches, in 1861 and around 1864, Douglass argued that all humans sought accurate representations of both material reality and of an unseen spiritual world.[6] For Douglass, humans' affinity for pictures is what distinguished them from animals: "Man is the only picture-making animal in the world. He alone of all the inhabitants of earth has the capacity and passion for pictures." By pointing to the proclivity for pictures among all humans, Douglass stressed humanity's common origins, and the superiority of imagination over reason. The "full identity of man with nature," he said, "is our chief distinction from all other beings on earth and the source of our greatest achievements." While "dogs and elephants are said to possess" the capacity for reason, only humans sought to recreate nature and portray both the "inside soul" and the "outside world" through such "artificial means" as pictures (Douglass, "Pictures").

In her embrace of pictures, Crafts, too, suggests the priority of imagination over reason. Pictures inspire her to "think and speculate"; they allow her mind to "run riotous and exult in its freedom as a rational being." Like Douglass, she sees the visual arts as having greater transformative power on viewers than books and writing. As she says of herself a few pages later, "I always had a quiet way of *observing* things, and this habit grew upon me, sharpened perhaps by the absense of elemental knowledge. *Instead of books I studied faces and characters,* and arrived at conclusions by a sort of sagacity that closely approximated to the unerring certainty of animal instinct" (27, my emphases). Given their proclivity for pictures, it is no wonder that in their writings both Douglass and Crafts sought to construct pictures with words; their prose style is nothing if not visual, as though conceptualizing stories from pictures in their heads.[7]

The relationship between the "inside soul" and the "outside world" (Douglass's terms) is what distinguishes Crafts's attitude toward pictures from Douglass's. Crafts articulates clear lines of demarcation between the "inside soul" and the "outside world." The separation between these two realms is one of the defining aspects of Gothic fiction, where haunted spirits lurk beneath the surface of material reality. Douglass rarely employs haunting or the Gothic conventions in his writing. For haunting to occur, there needs to be a clear separation between the spirit and material world, between surface and depth, image and referent, and this separation is consistent with Crafts's religious worldview. She is an evangelical and has been born again through Christ. But her evangelicalism is in one sense conservative: like Harriet Beecher Stowe's Uncle Tom, Crafts distinguishes heaven from earth and places her faith in the next life instead of trying to end sin in this world. Throughout the novel, she points to heaven as the place of eternal and universal freedom and bears witness to heaven. Jacob, a fellow fugitive whom she meets during her successful escape, fears that his dying sister will never "see a free land." Crafts responds with an evangelical rebuke: "Have you, then . . . no faith in God, no hope in heaven? Are you not a believer in that free land where the spirits of just men made perfect eternally abide?" (216–217). These are Uncle Tom's sentiments as well—sentiments which do nothing to inspire revolutionary deeds to achieve a new world on earth. As Robert Abzug has noted, evangelicals affirmed rigid barriers between heaven and earth. They stood apart from Frederick Douglass, William Lloyd Garrison, and other radical abolitionists, who sought to prepare for the millennium.[8] By keeping heaven and God's government distinct from life on earth, Crafts cannot imagine an immediate end to slavery. Unlike radical abolitionists, she lacks the eschatology of a millennialist— she cannot break free from the burdens of the past in order to pave the way to a new age.

The burdens of the past are reflected in Crafts's Gothic narrative and her reading of pictures. The past haunts her first master; he kills himself in his drawing room, "that ancient one where hung the family pictures" (72) It was in the drawing room where the haunted Linden tree could still be heard, swaying in the wind and keeping ever-present the sins of the past. The Linden tree had been the site where slave punishments and tortures were inflicted. Sir Clifford de Vincent, the family patriarch and founder of the plantation, had tortured and hung his slave Rose from the Linden tree, and Rose cursed the house with her last words: "In sunshine and shadow, by day and by night I will brood over this tree, and weigh down its branches, and when death, or sickness, or misfortune is to befall the family ye may listen for ye will assuredly hear the creaking of its limbs" (25). When Crafts's master brings home his new wife, who, unbeknown to him, was born a slave, he takes her to the drawing room, hears the creaking Linden tree, and vows to cut it down in the morning. As if in response his vow, the portrait of Sir Clifford falls to the floor. "The invisible hand of Time," Crafts summarizes, "had been there and silently and stealthily spread corrupting canker over the polished surface of the metal that supported it, and crumbled the wall against which it hung" (29). The portraits connected past to present, preventing a sharp break from the past and the attainment of a new age. A picture also revealed the "dark" truth about Crafts's mistress as the daughter of a slave. A photograph exposes the mistress's attempt to ignore her past, rise from her slave birth into a mistress, and create a new world for herself.

Crafts's inability to envision a perfect world leaves her resigned about slavery and the possibility of freedom during much of the novel. "The life of a slave at best is not a pleasant one, but I had formed a resolution to always look on the bright side of things, to be industrious, cheerful, and true-hearted, to do some good though in an humble way, and to win some love if I could," she declares early in her narrative (11). She does not change her view until her successful escape. Hoping for an eternal reward in heaven sustains Crafts in her sinful world; it also prevents her from adopting the radicalism of slave narrators like Frederick Douglass, William Wells Brown, and Harriet Jacobs. In one sense her narrative resembles eighteenth-century narratives such as Olaudah Equiano's more than it does those of her contemporaries. As Francis Smith Foster notes, in the eighteenth century "discussions of the religious and moral contradictions within slavery were contained in the narratives, but the institution of slavery was not totally condemned" (Foster, 47). Like Equiano, Crafts attacks slavery when it wrongs her but does not seem to mind it when its cruelties abate.

Crafts's ambivalence about slavery, freedom, and hierarchy prevent her from defining herself as an equal to her mistress or exploiting her opportunities to become free. When she discovers that her new mistress is the daughter of a slave and legally still a slave, she continues to treat her as her mistress rather than as an equal.[9] Her mistress seeks to collapse the hierarchy more than

Crafts, who seems content as her servant. She tells her mistress to run away before Mr. Trappe, her solicitor, "traps" her by revealing her slave status and selling her. She seeks freedom for her mistress more than she does for herself, as if her mistress deserves freedom by virtue of having experienced it. She agrees to flee with her mistress but ignores her mistress's exhortations to "[c]all me mistress no longer" (48).

During their flight Crafts is more interested in the care of her mistress than in freedom. In fact she suggests that the experience of freedom weakens one's constitution during times of trial and tribulation: "I could not fully appreciate all she had suffered; for tho' a slave myself I had never possessed freedom, wealth, and position as she had, *but I saw its effects* in the utter prostration of her nervous system, her trembling limbs, and tottering steps" (57, my emphasis).

Mr. Trappe summarizes the problem of freedom, hierarchy, and the burdens of the past that Crafts struggles to overcome. After Crafts and her mistress are recaptured and returned to Trappe, he tries to console them:

> There is no need of your taking on so, no use at all in it. You have long known the condition of life to which your birth subjected you, and you ought by this time to have become reconciled to it. Lord bless me, it is nothing so bad after all. We are all slaves to something or somebody. A man perfectly free would be an anomaly, and a free woman yet more so. Freedom and slavery are only names attached surreptitiously and often improperly to certain conditions. They are mere shadows the very reverse of realities, and being so, if rightly considered, they have only a trifling effect on individual happiness.

For Trappe, one cannot transcend one's origins or escape the condition of one's birth. Freedom is a façade, and we are all enslaved to the past. Crafts, too, acknowledges the "anomaly" of freedom on earth; when her mistress dies, she notes that "a gleam of satisfaction shone over her face. There was a gasp, a struggle, a slight shiver of the limbs *and she was free*" (100, my emphasis). Absolute freedom, Crafts suggests, occurs only in the next life, not on earth.

Trappe's summary of life's condition—that we are all slaves to something or someone—wonderfully summarizes the Gothic imagination. It echoes Ishmael's statement at the beginning of his doomed voyage in *Moby-Dick*: "Who ain't a slave? Tell me that" (Melville, 4). As Mark Edmundson states, "Gothic shows the dark side, the world of cruelty, lust, perversion, and crime that . . . is hidden beneath established conventions"; it exposes the world as the "corrupted, reeking place it is" and shows that "life is possessed, that the present is in thrall to the past. All are guilty. All must, in time, pay up." The Gothic mind is "skeptical about progress [or reform] in any form and is "antithetical to all smiling American faiths," including the American faith in freedom and equality (Edmundson, 4–5).[10]

Trappe is the personification of the Gothic imagination: always dressed in black, he is "the shadow of an evil presence," an "evil eye" who was "noting our doings" and concocting "evil plans . . . against us" (62). But Trappe is more than an evil presence and an evil eye. He is the mistress's dark shadow, the physical embodiment of an evil (black) self, and the source of her guilt. "Even when a child the shadow of his presence occasioned within me a thrill of dread and fear," Crafts's mistress says of him (45). He is a devil-like creature, who obscures Crafts's benevolent God. While Trappe resides on earth and has power over Craft and her mistress, her God resides in heaven and is comparatively ineffective.

Trappe can also be seen as the personification of the dark-souled self that is in all of us. He is like the shadows that give contrast and vibrancy to a painting or the photographic negative that is the source of a beautiful print. His presence (and his shadow) cut against Crafts's belief in freedom: if someone like Trappe lurks inside every wall (or body), threatening to expose someone's dark origins—whether of sin or of slavery—then how can we have faith in freedom and the power of self-transformation? The idea of a double self is a major mode of the "terror Gothic" that Trappe evokes. As Edmundson notes, "The idea of a second self—of a horrible other living unrecognized within us, or loosed somehow into the world beyond—is central to the vision of terror Gothic" (Edmundson, 8). Significantly, Crafts does not consider herself free until she learns that Trappe is dead.

Crafts's ambivalence about freedom is underscored when she meets Mrs. Henry. Their meeting occurs after a series of strange events. After her mistress dies, Crafts is sold to Mr. Saddler, a slave trader, who falls out of his saddle (as it were) and dies, leaving Crafts severely injured.[11] When she awakes, she finds herself in a warm bed, attended by Mrs. Henry, a benevolent slave-owner. She has a golden opportunity to redefine herself as a free woman, for her master is dead, and Mrs. Henry does not know that she is a slave. Owing to Crafts's light skin, Mrs. Henry assumes that Crafts is white and free and asks if Saddler had been "a near relative" or "a dear friend." Crafts is "sorely tempted" to declare herself a free woman; but she betrays her "humble condition" and justifies her honesty by saying, "My better nature prevailed" (116).

If Crafts's "better nature" is as an honest woman, it is also as a slave. Being an honest slave meant a perpetual life of slavery. Slaves lied in order to achieve some semblance of power over their masters and assert a will of their own. They stole, evaded work, feigned illness, and ran away—all measures that most radical abolitionists advocated in the 1850s. By choosing honesty over freedom, Crafts ignores the powerlessness that comes with slavery. Had she remained honest throughout the novel about her "better nature," she could not have passed as a white man, run away, settled in New Jersey as a free woman, or married, for these were all dishonest representations of her legal condition.

Crafts does not mind being a slave to the Henrys. Mrs. Henry resembles Stowe's Augusta St. Clair: both are kind, benevolent masters who refuse to sell their slaves or break up slave families, and they genuinely like the company of their slaves. Mrs. Henry "seemed sent into the world to dispense good-feeling and happiness" and "loved to indulge her servants in all innocent pleasures not inconsistent with their duties" (119). Unlike the mistresses that Frederick Douglass and Harriet Jacobs describe in their narratives, Mrs. Henry seems not to have been corrupted by slavery. Crafts's language of slavery further downplays its evils on the Henry plantation: she refers to bondspeople as "servants" rather than "slaves." She appropriates the language of the master and implies, as masters themselves did, a benign paternalism governing master/slave relationships.[12] Her characterization of labor relations on the estate evokes a mythic ideal of benign paternalism: "The overseer was gentle and kind, and the slaves were industrious and obedient, not through fear of punishment, but because they loved and respected a master and mistress so amiable and good" (123). What Crafts ignores in her description of the Henry estate, which every rebellious slave and abolitionist knew, is that violence or the threat of violence is the very fulcrum on which slavery hangs. Without the threat of violence, slavery becomes an absurd concept, which is one reason why slave narratives and abolition writings emphasized, often in graphic and prurient detail, the uses of violence attending the institution.

While living on the Henry estate, Crafts has a second opportunity to escape, but she prefers bondage under a benevolent master to an alliance with slaves in quest of freedom. Her friends Charlotte and William plan an escape and ask for Crafts's help. "Hannah, wouldn't you like to be free?" Charlotte asks. Instead of answering in the declarative, Crafts uses the subjunctive ("Oh I should, I should, but then—") and then makes excuses for why she prefers bondage to striking for freedom (141). She refers to the dangers and difficulties of escape, says that their scheme for running away looked "wild and unpromising" (it proves successful), and ultimately declares her loyalty to her mistress over that of the slaves and the chance for freedom (142). She even betrays Charlotte and William's confidence by telling Mrs. Henry that it was William and not a ghost who was on the plantation, thus revealing William's whereabouts and endangering his plan to escape. And she tells William and Charlotte that her loyalty rests with her mistress:

I answered plainly that however just, or right, or expedient it might be in them to escape, my accompanying their flight would be directly the reverse, that I could not lightly sacrifise the good opinion of Mrs Henry and her family, who had been so very kind to me, nor seem to participate in a scheme, of which the consummation must be an injury to them no less than a source of disquiet and anxiety. Duty, gratitude and honor forbid it. (142)

It is an astonishing statement: a slave narrator who ostensibly writes her book to condemn slavery affirms her duty, gratitude, and honor to her mistress.

Crafts prefers the stability of slavery to the possibility of freedom in the Henry home. She loves the Henry home, twice refers to it in the endearing term of a "forget me not" (121, 122) Her wish at this point in the novel is simply to remain a slave: "I do not ask you to buy me and then set me free." Crafts tells Mrs. Henry:

Let me perform the menial service of your household—Let me go to the fields and labor there—let me be a drudge, a scallion I care not—nay I would accept the situation with the greatest thankfulness—all I ask is to feel, and know of a certainty that I have a home, that some one cares for me, and that I am beyond the grip of these merciless slave-traders and speculators. (124–125)

Here Crafts attacks the slave trade rather than slavery; she resembles eighteenth-century slave narrators like Equiano more than immediatists like Frederick Douglass. She is a gradualist rather than an immediatist, seeking a gradual rather than immediate end to slavery. She does not seize every opportunity, as Douglass does, to become free or achieve independence from her master; and like other gradualists, she views the abolition of the slave trade, rather than slavery itself, as the practical first step toward ending the institution and ameliorating its evils.[13]

Mrs. Henry similarly opposes the slave trade but not slavery, which Crafts conveys in sentimental language. Mrs. Henry is good, pious, and sympathetic to the plight of slaves and treats Crafts with "as much kindness and consideration" as a "guest" (124). Yet the Henrys' sympathy and religious beliefs do not inspire them to free Crafts. Like Crafts, they attack the slave trade, rather than slavery itself, as the corrupting influence on society. Mrs. Henry has vowed never to buy or sell another slave, which gets in the way of Crafts's desire for freedom and a better life. Instead of following the practice of abolitionists and purchasing Crafts's liberty, Mrs. Henry arranges the sale of Crafts to her friend Mrs. Wheeler, who proves to be a cruel mistress.[14] In Crafts's rendering, the sentimental spirit pervading the Henry home manifests itself in benevolent relations between masters and "servants" and in a gradualist rather than immediatist opposition to slavery. The Henry home more closely resembles the Shelby or St. Clair plantations in *Uncle Tom's Cabin* than the eastern shore of Maryland in Douglass's narrative, where southern plantations are always cast as evil and violent.

For Crafts, it is not so much slavery itself but involuntary marriage and sex that constitute the "crime against nature" (207). Marriage, she argues in three different places in her novel, should be reserved for the free; it is "something that all the victims of slavery should avoid as tending essentially to perpetuate that system" (206; see also 205, 131). Slave marriages perpetuated slavery because they produced new generations of slaves and violated Crafts's "unalterable resolution never to entail slavery on any human being" (207). Crafts essentially treats slave marriages, which were technically illegal, as sexual relationships, and she prefers celibacy to an illegal and blasphemous marriage: "The slave, if he or she desires to be content, should always remain in celibacy" (131).

For Crafts, marriage is a sacrament whose vows can only be fulfilled in a state of freedom: "I ever regarded marriage as a holy ordinance, and felt that its responsibilities could only be suitably discharged [its vows fulfilled] when voluntarily assumed" (205). Like other evangelicals, she cannot base her belief in freedom on scripture; instead she focuses on the way slavery corrupts the sacrament of marriage. As many scholars have pointed out, abolitionists consistently lost their debates with proslavery advocates on the biblical defense of slavery; there were too many instances in the Bible that sanctioned slavery. As a result, radical abolitionists—both black and white—collapsed the evangelical Christian cosmos and abandoned evangelical churches and doctrines in advocating an immediate end to slavery.[15]

It is the threat of involuntary marriage, rather than slavery, that compels Crafts to run for freedom. When Mrs. Wheeler demands that she become the wife of the field hand Bill, she defies her mistress for the first time in the novel: "'Never,' I exclaimed rashly and hastily, and without thought of the consequences. 'Never'" (205). Crafts makes clear that she is rebelling against sex and slave marriages, not slavery itself:

Had Mrs Wheeler condemned me to the severest corporeal punishment, or exposed me to be sold in the public slave market in Wilmington I should probably have resigned myself with apparent composure to her cruel behests. But when she sought to force me into a compulsory union with a man whom I could only hate and despise it seemed that rebellion would be a virtue, that duty to myself and my God actually required it, and that whatever accidents or misfortunes might attend my flight nothing could be worse than what threatened my stay. (206)

Duty to herself and her God requires her to uphold celibacy—to keep her body pure and untainted by the sin of sex, except within the sanctity of marriage. The "compulsory union" with Bill, not the forced labor of slavery, threatens the "holy ordinance" of her religious worldview and incites her to rebel.

Crafts frames her rebellion, escape, and newfound freedom in the language of sentimental literature. Gone is the Gothic fear of the dark-souled self and its rejection of progress, freedom, and equality. When she opens Aunt Hetty's Bible and chances upon "the place where Jacob fled from his brother Esau," she interprets it as a sign from God, who tells her to "abandon this house, and the Mistress who would force me into a crime against nature" (207). It is the first instance in the novel in which she defines herself as a prophet and receives instructions directly from God. With the Gothic conventions and Trappe now absent from her narrative, God aids her quest for freedom and a better world. Elsewhere He is a rather distant entity who does little to help her find freedom.

Jacob's story is more than a prophetic sign for Crafts; her narrative itself corresponds loosely to his story in Genesis. Like Crafts, Jacob is at once virtuous and obedient, as well as a trickster: he passes as his older brother Esau in order to receive his father's blessing, much as Crafts passes as a white man to receive the blessings of liberty. In doing so, both characters repudiate their birthrights—the one a subordinate brother, and the other a slave—and subvert social hierarchies. Both characters also flee to avoid violence: Esau threatens to kill Jacob, and Mrs. Wheeler threatens Crafts with sexual violation. Through flight they avoid the threat of "impure" spouses (Hittite women for Jacob, Bill for Crafts) and find desirable spouses and worldly success. They vow to trust in God, and both suffer a period of servitude before marrying their beloved spouses and establishing a prosperous home—fourteen years for Jacob, a few more for Crafts. While Jacob is eventually reconciled with his uncle and Esau, Crafts is reunited with Aunt Hetty and her mother. Both stories, in other words, revolve around escaping one's birthright, overcoming servitude, marrying the right person, regenerating the self, reuniting with one's family, and remaining faithful to God.

As if to underscore the links between Crafts's story and Jacob's story in Genesis, Crafts creates her own Jacob, with whom she keeps "strange company" during her escape. Her Jacob and the biblical Jacob are similar as well: Jacob's beloved sister dies in flight, while still in the land of slavery, much as the biblical Jacob loses his beloved Rachel, who dies in the land of Canaan while traveling with him. Jacob becomes a symbol of freedom in Crafts's story; his presence—in the pages of her Bible and as a character in her novel—facilitates her safe journey to the promised land. Jacob "greatly relieve[s] the difficulties" of Crafts's "toilsome journey" to freedom (224). His death in the novel, as in Genesis, paves the way to the land of freedom—the North for Crafts, Israel for Jacob, which is also the name God gives Jacob. In both stories, Jacob dies before reaching the promised land. And significantly, Jacob's story is told by Hannah, who, in the Bible, is the mother of Samuel and one of the prophets of Israel. Hannah Crafts hopes that her fictive self and her narrative will become, like her biblical namesake and Jacob, a symbol of freedom.

The introduction of Jacob as biblical figure and character marks the climax of the novel. He leads Crafts out of her Canaan to the promised land of freedom and marriage and leads her narrative out of the Gothic and into the sentimental. This shift paves the way to Crafts's conversion to freedom—both as a condition for herself and as a universal belief. In one sense, Crafts evolves over the course of her narrative: from a Gothic to sentimental self; from being born again through Christ in a world of darkness and sin to being reborn as free and married in a virtuous community; and from a craftswoman to a Hannah. Jacob thus represents a crucial symbol and character: he facilitates the shift toward Crafts's total abandonment of the Gothic and her embrace of universal freedom—and the worldview of abolitionists.

But Crafts stands apart from abolitionists on many fronts: she has no contact with them in her narrative nor, apparently, in her life—at least they did not influence her story. She probably knew that to court abolitionists was to sacrifice her craft and to expose herself to notoriety and the construction of a disingenuous public self. Abolitionists would not have looked kindly upon her literary experiments with freedom; and so she remained, like Ellison's narrator, an invisible woman.

Notes

1. I have looked through the papers of the following abolitionists: Gerrit Smith, the wealthy white abolitionist who corresponded with more African Americans than any other white and was enormously generous in giving money and aid to blacks; Frederick Douglass; James McCune Smith, the prominent New York black physician, critic, and abolitionist who was the New York correspondent for *Frederick Douglass' Paper*; and William Lloyd Garrison, who wrote for the *Black Abolitionist Papers*, the *Liberator*, and *Frederick Douglass' Paper*.

2. As Frances Smith Foster notes, the goal of slave narratives in the nineteenth century, and especially in the 1840s and 1850s, was "the total elimination of slavery. Philosophy gave way to specific examples of physical violence and psychological abuse" (52).

3. William L. Andrews discusses the tendency among slave narrators to invoke declarative speech acts beginning in the 1840s: "In declarative acts, 'saying makes it so.'. . . In making declaratives, a slave narrator becomes a godlike authority over the world of his text and seeks to extend his authority to the world outside his text by abrogating his responsibility to the rules that govern and validate normal discourse" (104–105).

4. Crafts's description of the family portraits bears a strong resemblance to Hawthorne's *The House of Seven Gables*, in which the narrator describes the portrait of Colonel Pyncheon, the patriarchal counterpart of Sir Clifford De Vincent: "Those stern, immitigable features seemed to symbolize an evil influence, and so darkly to mingle the shadow of their presence with the sunshine of the passing hour that no good thoughts or purposes could ever spring up and blossom there" (Hawthorne, 25). The scene is also reminiscent of the role of portraiture in Horace Walpole's *The Castle of Otranto*, as Henry Louis Gates, Jr., points out; in both books, the portrait of a dead patriarch falls to the ground.

5. I am thinking specifically of *The House of Seven Gables* and "The Prophetic Pictures."

6. Douglass's second speech on pictures, called "Pictures," focuses on photography and is an elaboration of his 1861 speech, "Pictures and Progress." His second speech is undated, but I have inferred the date of late 1864 from internal evidence in the speech. My discussion of Douglass's understanding of pictures is drawn from my *Black Hearts of Men*, pp. 45–56.

7. W.J.T. Mitchell discusses the dominance of visual language in slave narratives. See Mitchell, *Picture Theory*, pp. 183–198.

8. See Robert Abzug, *Cosmos Crumbling*.

9. There are only two instances when Crafts refers to her mistress by a name other than "mistress." After discovering the truth of her mistress's birth, she says: "I cannot tell why . . . I approached and spoke to her as though she had been my sister or a very dear friend, but sorrow and affliction and death make us all equal" (44). And after her mistress instructs her to "call me mistress no longer," Crafts insists on calling her "mistress," at which point her mistress rebukes her: "'There: there, mistress again when I have forbidden it.' 'Well then, my dear friend,'" Crafts replies (48).

10. In my discussion of the Gothic I have also drawn from Sedgwick, *Coherence of Gothic Conventions*.

11. Saddler's name connotes his role in the novel; much as Crafts is devoted to her craft of writing, and Trappe traps women, Saddler crashes the wagon, falls out of his saddle, and enables the transition of Crafts's life with the Henrys.

12. Crafts's description of the master/slave relations on the Henry plantation bears resemblance to the "hegemonic paternalism" that Eugene Genovese develops in *Roll, Jordan, Roll* and *The World the Slaveholders Made*.

13. On the relationship between gradualism and immediatism, see Stewart, *Holy Warriors*, pp. 35–50; and Davis, "The Emergence of Immediatism in British and American Antislavery Thought," pp. 238–257.

14. The practice of purchasing slaves in order to set them free was common among abolitionists, except for a few Garrisonians, who argued that paying for slaves' freedom was a form of compensated emancipation and legitimated the legality of slavery. See my *Black Hearts of Men*, pp. 142–143.

15. For this argument I have drawn from Abzug, *Cosmos Crumbling*; McKivigan and Snay, eds., *Religion and the Antebellum Debate Over Slavery*; and Miller, Stout, and Wilson, eds., *Religion and the American Civil War*.

Works Cited

Abzug, Robert H. *Cosmos Crumbling: American Reform and the Religious Imagination.* New York: Oxford University Press, 1994.

Andrews, William L. *To Tell a Free Story: The First Century of Afro-American Autobiography, 1760–1865.* Urbana: University of Illinois Press, 1986.

Crafts, Hannah. *The Bondwoman's Narrative.* Edited by Henry Louis Gates, Jr. New York: Warner Books, 2002.

Davis, David Brion. *The Problem of Slavery in Western Culture.* New York: Oxford University Press, 1966.

———. "The Emergence of Immediatism in British and American Antislavery Thought," *From Homicide to Slavery: Studies in American Culture.* New York: Oxford University Press, 1986.

Douglass, Frederick. "Pictures." Holograph, n.d. [ca. Late 1864]. Frederick Douglass Papers, Library of Congress.

———. "Pictures and Progress." *The Frederick Douglass Papers,* Series One, Vol. 3. Edited by John Blassingame. New Haven: Yale University Press, 1992.

Edmundson, Mark. *Nightmare on Main Street: Angels, Sadomasochism, and the Culture of Gothic.* Cambridge: Harvard University Press, 1997.

Equiano, Olaudah. *The Interesting Narrative and Other Writings.* New York: Penguin, 1995.

Foster, Frances Smith. *Witnessing Slavery: The Development of Ante-Bellum Slave Narratives.* Madison: University of Wisconsin Press, 1979.

Genovese, Eugene D. *Roll, Jordan, Roll: The World the Slaves Made.* New York: Vintage Books, 1976.

———. *The World the Slaveholders Made: Two Essays in Interpretation.* Middletown, Conn.: Wesleyan University Press, 1988.

Hawthorne, Nathaniel. *The House of Seven Gables* [1851]. New York: Signet, 1961.

McKivigan, John R., and Mitchell Snay, eds. *Religion and the Antebellum Debate Over Slavery.* Athens: University of Georgia Press, 1998.

Melville, Herman. *Moby-Dick or, The Whale.* New York: Penguin Books, 1992.

Miller, Randall M., Harry S. Stout, and Charles Reagan Wilson, eds. *Religion and the American Civil War.* New York: Oxford University Press, 1998.

Mitchell, W.J.T. *Picture Theory: Essays on Verbal and Visual Representation.* Chicago: University of Chicago Press, 1994.

Rohrbach, Augusta. "'A Silent Unobtrusive Way': Hannah Crafts and the Literary Marketplace." (In this volume).

Sedgwick, Eve Kosofsky. *The Coherence of Gothic Conventions.* New York: Arno Press, 1980.

Stauffer, John. *The Black Hearts of Men: Radical Abolitionists and the Transformation of Race.* Cambridge: Harvard University Press, 2002.

Stewart, James Brewer. *Holy Warriors: The Abolitionists and American Slavery.* New York: Hill and Wang, 1996.

Walpole, Horace. *The Castle of Otranto.* New York: Penguin Books, 2001.

II

Rewriting the Canon

6

Blackening *Bleak House*
Hannah Crafts's *The Bondwoman's Narrative*

HOLLIS ROBBINS

Two-thirds of the way through *The Bondwoman's Narrative*, Hannah, a house slave in Washington, D.C., is sent out on a rainy day to buy her mistress a box of face powder that has suddenly become popular. A "great Italian chemist, a Signor with an unpronounceable name," we are told, "had discovered or rather invented an impalpable powder, fine, highly scented, and luxurious, that applied to the hands and face was said to produce the most marvellous effect" (*TBN* 158). Hannah trudges through the mud, gloom, and driving sleet to the chemist's shop in time to purchase the very last box. Returning through the busy streets to the Wheeler household she glimpses "a coat of seedy black" that she recognizes. It is her former owner and the novel's villain up to this point, Mr. Trappe. She slips on the paving stones and he helps her up. His presence is "ominous of evil," she thinks, and she hurries home. Delivering the powder to her mistress's room, Hannah hears Mr. Wheeler telling his wife that a new post has opened up; the only problem is that he has had trouble with the official in charge of hiring. Would Mrs. Wheeler use her feminine wiles to ask for the office? "I'll go now, this very evening," Mrs. Wheeler decides, buoyed by the chance to try the beautifying powder so soon. At the last minute, she asks for her new smelling bottle.

Two hours later Mrs. Wheeler returns, her face completely black. "It must have been the powder," an unidentified voice (presumably Hannah's) says. "The powder was white I thought," another voice answers. The knowledgeable voice continues:

> The powder certainly is white, and yet it may posses such chemical properties as occasion blackness. Indeed I recently saw in the newspapers some accounts

of a chemist who having been jilted by a lady very liberal in the application of powder to her face had invented as a method of revenge a certain kind of smelling bottle of which the fumes would suddenly blacken the whitest skin provided the said cosmetic had been previously applied. (*TBN* 167)

"You wretch!" Mrs. Wheeler cries. "Why didn't you tell me of this before?" Mrs. Wheeler, in the guise of a colored woman, has been on her knees asking for the post for her husband. The Wheelers, mortified, return to North Carolina to avoid the scandal. Hannah, relegated to the huts and facing a forced marriage to a field slave, finally decides to escape.

The farcical powder scene comes out of nowhere and serves as the pivot of the novel's plot; it is the reason for Hannah's fall from favor and flight to freedom. Initially, the episode seems designed to showcase the vanity of Washington, D.C., and to give Hannah the opportunity to cross paths with Mr. Trappe. Her return with the box to Mrs. Wheeler's room allows her to overhear (and satirize) the couple's job-hunting machinations. The chance to try the new powder so soon is simply good timing; while the weather and Mr. Trappe provide dramatic tension, we fear little from the cosmetic quarter. Mrs. Wheeler's black face is a stunning surprise. Hannah's scientific explanation is even more unexpected. What did she know and when did she know it? How are we to read her comment, "I had never seen her look better" (*TBN* 165)?

The incident seems perfectly believable on its face. The chemical properties of household substances are mysterious enough for most of us to believe the transformation. Upon reflection, the powder appears to be silver nitrate, a colorless translucent powdered crystal which, when put in contact with organic substances such as skin, will turn blackish purple. As a house servant, the character Hannah would certainly have experienced the properties of silver in blackening fingers and clothes during polishing. Moreover, silver nitrate was commonly used in small quantities as an eye medication and in larger quantities as a hair dye. An 1851 article in *Scientific American* (an issue owned by her master, John Hill Wheeler) asserts that pomades made from silver nitrate powder will turn hair black.[1] But Crafts's emphasis on Mrs. Wheeler's smelling bottle as the blackening agent is provocative. The presence of ammonia (the contents of smelling bottles) is completely unnecessary for the process; silver nitrate powder alone will do the trick. In fact, allowing ammonia to come in contact with silver nitrate powder on a rainy day would have had far more serious consequences. The mixture of silver nitrate, ammonia, and water is explosive, and there is evidence that Crafts knew this. An 1853 article on "Fulminating Substances" in *Scientific American* (also in John Hill

Wheeler's collection) discusses the work of French chemist Claude-Louis Berthollet and Italian chemist Luigi Brugnatelli, who, in 1798, made a fine white powder from silver nitrate with tremendous detonating powder:

> Fulminating silver may be made by precipitating a solution of nitrate of silver by lime water, drying the precipitate by exposure to the air for two or three days, and pouring on it liquid ammonia. When it is thus converted into a black powder, the liquid must be poured off, and the powder left to dry in the air. It detonates with the gentlest heat, or even with the slightest friction, so that it must not be removed from the vessel in which it is made. If a drop of water fall upon it, the percussion will cause it to explode.[2]

Is Crafts exacting a clever literary revenge on her former mistress in this scene? Perhaps. But whether or not the mixture is meant to explode, Hannah protests her innocence a bit too much. Mrs. Wheeler asks for the smelling bottle and refers to it as "new," establishing that Hannah did not purchase it or press it on her. Further, Hannah is not shown giving the smelling bottle to Mrs. Wheeler directly. She gives it to Mr. Wheeler, who in turn hands it to his wife. Afterward, Mr. Wheeler not once but twice puts the blame on the "dam—d little smelling bottle." Can this meticulous exoneration of Hannah's role be taken at face value? This is less likely. Hannah was taught to read by a magical godmother of an old woman, a vendor of salves, ointments, unguents, and other healing potions, who instructed the young slave in the "mysteries and marvels" of many things besides reading. However much Hannah seeks to put the blame on others (including Providence), Mrs. Wheeler's abracadabra metamorphosis is clearly the work of a knowledgeable authorial hand.

But even Hannah Crafts is not really to blame: the rain that plays such a crucial role in the scene is the work of Charles Dickens, from the famous opening paragraphs of *Bleak House*,[3] which was extraordinarily popular in American after 1852 among both white and black readers. *Frederick Douglass's Paper* (originally known as the *North Star*) serialized the novel in its entirety from April 1852 through December 1853. "We wish we could induce everyone to read *Bleak House*," Douglass wrote in the June 3, 1853 edition. "Charles Dickens has ever been the faithful friend of the poor—God bless him for that!—and in the portraitures that he, ever and anon, weaves into his books of fiction, we see the touch of a master hand. His delineations are true to the life; and his being able to give them evinces his being intimately acquainted with the dense ignorance, squallid misery, and pressing wants of 'the London poor' . . . 'Tis true that 'the story is long,' but time spent upon its perusal is not ill bestowed." In Douglass's paper, as well as in the pages of other abolitionist periodicals such as *The National Era,* characters and themes from *Bleak House* functioned as a rich source of comic and ironic allusions for the community of antislavery readers, columnists, and letter-writers. Douglass's decision to serialize the novel was controversial (many readers thought the space and ink could be used more productively), but readers responded to the story's humor and satire. It was, perhaps, the "Seinfeld" of its day.

Crafts borrows disparate elements (characters, texts, themes, tropes) from *Bleak House* and a variety of other widely recognized sources and combines them with her own voice such that they are irrevocably transformed and potentially explosive. This modus operandi is perhaps best characterized as literary alchemy, or textual transfiguration, extraction, and transmutation. The balance of this essay will examine this idea more fully and argue that Crafts uses the words of others (primarily Dickens but to a lesser degree Walter Scott and Charlotte Brontë[4]) when she wants to limit the verisimilitude of her own words—that is, when she has not quite seen something firsthand, when she is embellishing, when she is admonishing, or when she would rather not be blamed for what happens in her narrative. She tends to hide behind the diction of others when she is introducing a character, for example, or when her narrative voice is conceiving (or renegotiating) a personal relationship with the reader. Typically this occurs at the beginnings and ends of chapters, at moments of transition between exposition and apostrophe, or when the genre shifts from fact to fiction, from candor to craft.[5]

What are the political implications of this mode of storytelling? Is *The Bondwoman's Narrative* a British text, a Black text, a Bleak text, or an amalgamation thereof? Perhaps such distinctions are not the point in reading a novel that may revise and reconfigure our sense of the African American literary canon. As Henry Louis Gates, Jr., writes in *The Signifying Monkey: A Theory of African-American Literary Criticism*:

> Our task [in theorizing the black tradition] is not to reinvent our traditions as
> if they bore no relation to that tradition created and borne, in the main, by
> white men. Our writers used that impressive tradition to define themselves,
> both with and against their concept of received order. We must do the same,
> with or against the Western critical canon. To name our tradition is to rename
> each of its antecedents, no matter how pale they might seem. (xxiii)

Hannah Crafts, in this view, might best be seen as a writer grappling with a tradition of writing movingly about the poor and powerless. Crafts recognizes something in this tradition, but, she insists, she writes from misery, not merely about misery. The effect of the black powder scene is to change the complexion of the text from a traditional sentimental novel to something darker. Hannah is transformed from a virtuous heroine into a sharp-eyed critic determined to learn and use her storytelling expertise.[6]

I. The (Fictional) Narrator

The face powder scene is the most dramatic example, but the process of textual transformation has been at work from the first chapter. The first-person narrator begins by introducing herself modestly and within the tradition of prefatory self-deprecation. "It may be that I assume too much responsibility in attempting to write these pages. The world will probably say so, and I am aware of my deficiencies. I am neither clever, nor learned, nor talented," she writes. Yet she is brightly optimistic: "[t]he life of a slave at best is not a pleasant one, but I had formed a resolution to always look on the bright side of things, to be industrious, cheerful, and true-hearted, to do some good though in an humble way, and win some love if I could" (*TBN* 11). But she is also largely fictional. Her words are the words of Esther Summerson, who introduces herself at the beginning of Chapter 3 of *Bleak House* thus: "I have a great deal of difficulty in beginning to write my portion of these pages, for I know I am not clever. I always knew that." Esther too is brightly optimistic: "I often thought of the resolution I had made on my birthday to try to be industrious, contented, and true-hearted and to do some good to some one and win some love if I could."[7]

Crafts changes Esther's words in important ways: Esther worries that the task is too difficult; Hannah worries that she assumes too much responsibility. Esther seeks to be content, Hannah to be cheerful. These two changes alone speak volumes about the author's understanding of Hannah's differences from Esther: Hannah will never be content as long as slavery continues, and she has a responsibility to the cause of ending it. The young slave learns obligation early: "the weak, the sick, and the suffering came to me for advice and assistance. The little slave children were almost entirely confided to my care. I hope that I was good and gentle to them; for I pitied their hard and cruel fate very much" (*TBN* 11). Esther also gently tends to the little ones in her care, but they are "downcast and unhappy" pupils, not sick and suffering slaves.[8]

Yet Hannah's fictional being is born of Dickens (via Esther) and carries many of his literary sensibilities, however transformed. Hannah and Esther are neat, modest, good orphans to whom much happens and around whom events revolve. Their role is to be the catalyst for events and to allow others to demonstrate goodness by being good to them. Neither young woman speaks the language of desire particularly well; each novel skips over the particulars of betrothal and marriage to present the final scene of domestic bliss as a fait accompli. Both women are industrious and domestic. (When Hannah is finally forced to perform hard, outdoor, physical labor—and marry a field hand—she decides to flee.) But Hannah's character and narrative trajectory diverge from Esther's after Hannah is forced to lie. It is as if the experience of "penning a libel" about herself has allowed Hannah to exert control over her own narrative voice.

Until the end of Chapter 12, Hannah, like Esther, has presented herself as utterly sincere. Her almost pathological honesty has landed her in jail, extended her servitude, and kept her from aiding Charlotte and William's escape. (Worse, she has been a tattletale, revealing the plans to Mrs. Henry.⁹) But after the duplicitous Mrs. Wheeler forces Hannah to write that she (Hannah) is homely, bigoted in religion, of doubtful ability, and a potential runaway (*TBN* 153), Hannah puts truthfulness aside and avenges herself on paper. She maligns Mrs. Wheeler in the language of necromancy (from Middle English *nigromancie*). Her future mistress, Hannah complains, had "vanities, and whims, and caprices" in the "dead hours of night," requesting items with well-known magical/herbal powers: pomegranate for fertility, nutmeg for luck, and citron for wealth (*TBN* 154). Other times, Mrs. Wheeler would ask for candy, water, salt, and vinegar—commonly used as remedies for bad digestion. In short, Hannah paints Mrs. Wheeler as a constipated witch.

Hannah exerts even more control over her narrative in the chapters following the black powder scene. She spends a day illicitly sharing stories with her former fellow-servant, Lizzie. For two chapters, the novel ventriloquizes the voice of the new master of Lindendale, Mr. Cosgrove, his wife, and his various slave mistresses. Crafts signals the fictional aspect of these tales by borrowing, yet again, from *Bleak House.* Here is how Lizzy describes Mrs. Cosgrove's appreciation of another slave, Lilly, over her present (white?) servant:

> Well our mistress took a great fancy to her at the first sight, I believe, she actually called the girl to her side and caressed and praised her, to the infinite astonishment of the maid who had always been kept at distance. . . . At length Mrs. Cosgrove dismissed her maid. It was a cruel act; for the girl had accompanied her from beyond the seas and had neither friends nor relatives in this country, but who might question her imperious will. (*TBN* 173)

Compare this with Dickens's description of Lady Dedlock's choosing Rosa over the French maid Hortense:

> "Come here, Rosa!" Lady Dedlock beckons her, with even an appearance of interest. "Why, do you know how pretty you are, child?" she says, touching her

shoulder with her two forefingers. . . . My Lady's maid is a Frenchwoman of two and thirty, from somewhere in the southern country about Avignon and Marseilles . . . Ha, ha, ha! She, Hortense, has been in my Lady's service since five years and always kept at the distance, and this doll, this puppet, caressed— absolutely caressed—by my Lady on the moment of her arriving at the house! (*BH* Chapter 12)

There are differences, of course, but the key point is that Crafts protects herself against the charge of lying about Mrs. Cosgrove by this conspicuous borrowing from Dickens. Or, put another way, it is a controlled yielding of the pen to another writer. This is fiction, Hannah seems to be shouting. I am not maligning Mrs. Cosgrove. Crafts repeats this sort of borrowing several times in the Cosgrove section of her tale, most notably when Mrs. Cosgrove becomes obsessed with the idea that her husband is keeping a slave mistress:

She knows of a certainty that he has a secret now. She sees it in his counte- nance, in his eyes, in every crease of his garments. Even his bearing is less frank than formerly. His tread seems stealthy as if fearing to reveal something. She even thinks that he fears to meet her eye, and these various signs and tokens prompt her to dishonorable acts. She takes a strange fancy to nocturnal exam- inations of his letters to private researches in all manner of places, to listening behind doors, and watching at windows. (*TBN* 186)

The content and diction are straight from Dickens:

[H]e is always keeping a secret from her . . . [she] will look anywhere rather than meet his eye. These various signs and tokens, marked by the little woman, are not lost upon her . . . prompting her to nocturnal examinations of Mr. Snagsby's pockets; to secret perusals of Mr. Snagsby's letters; to private re- searches in the Day Book and Ledger, till, cash-box and iron safe; to watchings at windows, listenings behind doors, and a general putting of this and that to- gether by the wrong end. (*BH* Chapter 25)

The difference is, of course, that Mr. Snagsby is innocent and Mr. Cos- grove is not. His sexual relations with his slaves lead to murder, suicide, bat- tery, and death. What is comic marital suspicion in Dickens is brutal reality in the slave narrative.

The breadth and extent of such borrowings suggest that Crafts had the text of *Bleak House* (either in volume form or in back issues of *Frederick Douglass's Paper*) in front of her while she was writing her narrative. Her borrowings come from throughout the novel. But the copied passages are not plagiarism. In the first place, her alleged status as "property" (or fugitive property) complicates and perhaps mitigates her act of violating intellectual property rights, and in the second, her craft in transforming and transmuting these borrowed passages suggests that the more appropriate term for her act is what Henry Louis Gates, Jr., calls "double-voiced discourse," and particularly the mode he calls "the Speakerly Text." Gates describes a narrative voice characterized by "a hybrid character, a character who is neither the novel's protagonist nor the text's disembodied narrator, but a blend of both, an emergent and merging moment of consciousness" (*TBN* xxvi). The value of a hybrid or polyvocal character to Crafts is that it complicates the idea of a speaking subject. It is not necessarily Hannah's voice who is telling her story.[10] Perhaps she takes advantage of the original artist's creative effort, but her borrowings are productive and interpretive. This is no more apparent than in the case of Mr. Trappe, whose differences from his literary forebear reveal an acute sense of the distinction between a personal and an impersonal antagonist.

II. Mr. Trappe and Slavery

Crafts's Mr. Trappe is almost wholly based on Dickens's Mr. Tulkinghorn.[11] Both are successful, underhanded, black-clad lawyers who stalk their prey with documents. Both are revenged and are found shot to death in their rooms, face down on the floor. Crafts establishes the similarity between the two characters immediately.

> "The old man of the name of Trappe" is "a rusty seedy old-fashioned gentleman . . . great black eyes so keen and piercing that you shrank involuntarily from their gaze." (*TBN* 27)

> The "old man of the name of Tulkinghorn" is "an old-fashioned old gentleman . . . rusty to look at." (*BH* Chapters 33, 2)

Trappe stalks Hannah's mistress with the knowledge of her parentage just as Tulkinghorn stalks Lady Dedlock (Esther's mother) with suspicion of her parenthood:

> [E]ach one watched and suspected the other, that each one was conscious of some great and important secret on the part of the other, and that my mistress in particular would give worlds to know just what the old man knew. (*TBN* 28)

But whether each evermore watches and suspects the other, evermore mistrust-
ful of some great reservation; whether each is evermore prepared at all points
for the other, and never to be taken unawares; what each would give to know
how much the other knows—all this is hidden, for the time, in their own
hearts. (*BH* Chapter 12)

Trappe has a room in Lindendale, "a plainly furnished chamber on the second story, old-fashioned like himself and having a quiet impassive air" (*TBN*
32). Tulkinghorn has a room in Chesney Wold, "a turret chamber of the third
order of merit, plainly but comfortably furnished and having an old-fashioned
business air" (*BH* Chapter 12). The echoes are legion.[12]

But whereas Mr. Tulkinghorn is impersonally powerful, an allegorical
presence with a duty to protect the good name of his aristocratic client, Mr.
Trappe's concerns are wholly personal: he wants money and/or love. And
whereas Mr. Tulkinghorn has a professional and perhaps principled commitment to duty (though these principles pay well in the long run), Mr.
Trappe is indifferent to such social concerns. He cares nothing about race
or slavery per se. As a result, he is a much less frightening character. Further,
Tulkinghorn is consistent in his misogyny and snobbery. All women (especially the wife of his client) are alike and to be avoided. By contrast, Trappe
is obsessed with Hannah's mistress, and his manner softens after she is dead.
In fact, Trappe almost entirely disappears from the novel soon after. He returns, as I noted above, only to pick up Hannah off the slippery Washington streets.

Crafts's transformation of Tulkinghorn into Trappe is deeply meaningful.
She seems to be suggesting that the lawyer who actually believes in the laws
protecting his client, who believes too strongly in precedent, formal procedure,
and the status quo is far more formidable than one who is out for himself.
Trappe is certainly not a good character—he is an extortionist and a slave
speculator—but he is not a monster to Hannah. He feeds and clothes her, he
recognizes that she is "the best tempered in the world, kind, trusty, and religious" (*TBN* 105), and he sells her to a man who is rather kind to her, under
the circumstances. Saddler does not put irons on her, speaks frankly with her,
and offers her food in yet another scene borrowed from *Bleak House*:

Saying this he thrust his hand deep into the capacious pocket of his outer
pocket and drew thence a paper parcel, which he threw in my lap. Opening it I
found some nice cake, iced over with sugar, and highly delicious. "It's very
good, eat," he said again. (*TBN* 113–114).

It draws upon Esther Summerson's first meeting with the avuncular Mr. Jarndyce:

> After a little while he opened his outer wrapper, which appeared to me large enough to wrap up the whole coach, and put his arm down into a deep pocket in the side. "Now, look here!" he said. "In this paper," which was nicely folded, "is a piece of the best plum-cake that can be got for money—sugar on the outside an inch thick, like fat on mutton chops. Here's a little pie (a gem this is, both for size and quality), made in France. And what do you suppose it's made of? Livers of fat geese. There's a pie! Now let's see you eat 'em." (*BH* Chapter 3)

Saddler's pleasantries are surprising, under the circumstances. Since there is little reason for a slave to paint a portrait of a slave trader as nicer than he is, this Dickens allusion most likely serves the structural purpose of contrasting the kindly Saddler/Jarndyce character with the real villain of the novel, her final owner, Mrs. Wheeler.[13]

Remarkably, Crafts rarely employs Dickensian rhetoric (with the exception of the gloom at the beginning of Chapter 13) when she arrives in the Wheeler household after her stay with the Henrys. Her prose is straightforward and biting. And, as noted at the beginning of this essay, Hannah's character changes markedly after the first significant clash with this owner and radically after the second. She begins taking control of her narrative voice just at the point when her story seems destined not to end as Jane Eyre's and Esther Summerson's do. Domestic contentment is not the lot of a slave. The only solution is to transform the sentimental tale into an escape narrative.

III. North Carolina and Freedom

In the final chapters of the novel, Crafts's borrowings from *Bleak House* become more pronounced. There is some evidence that the North Carolina chapters are less fact-based than other parts of the story, in which case her use of Dickens is not surprising.[14] That is, she may not have actually seen a great deal of what she describes on the plantation, or she may be masking what "really" happened with his descriptions. Here, for example, is Crafts's description of the slave huts on the North Carolina plantation:

> There was not that division of families I had been accustomed to see, but they all lived promiscuously anyhow and every how; at least they did not die, which was a wonder. Is it a stretch of imagination to say that by night they contained

a swarm of misery, that crowds of foul existence crawled in out of gaps in walls and boards, or coiled themselves to sleep on nauseous heaps of straw fetid with human perspiration and where the rain drips in, and the damp airs of midnight fatch and carry malignant fevers. (*TBN* 199)

Crafts's prose draws on Dickens's description of "Tom-All-Alone's," a squalid London alley where the poor orphan Jo lives:

Now, these tumbling tenements contain, by night, a swarm of misery. As, on the ruined human wretch, vermin parasites appear, so, these ruined shelters have bred a crowd of foul existence that crawls in and out of gaps in walls and boards; and coils itself to sleep, in maggot numbers, where the rain drips in; and comes and goes, fetching and carrying fever . . . . (*BH* Chapter 16)

The transformation of Dickens's slum to slave huts is, once again, meaningful. "Is it a stretch of imagination?" Crafts asks. No, but she admits it is not what she was accustomed to seeing. Perhaps, after one night, it was beyond her ability to describe it in her own words. For whatever reason, she found the words in Dickens's description of an illiterate free British white male. Her borrowing proposes a kinship of suffering, of squalor, of subjugation, of servitude. This kinship is reaffirmed in the distillation of a subsequent passage:

If the huts were bad, the inhabitants it seemed were still worse Degradation, neglect, and ill treatment had wrought on them its legitimate effects. All day they toil beneath the burning sun, scarcely conscious that any link exists between themselves and other portions of the human race. Their mental condition is briefly summed up in the phrase that they know nothing. (*TBN* 200)

from this one:

What connexion can there be, between the place in Lincolnshire, the house in town, the Mercury in powder, and the whereabout of Jo the outlaw with his broom, who had the distant ray of light upon him when he swept the churchyard-step? What connexion can there have been between many people in the innumerable histories of this world, who, from opposite sides of great gulfs, have, nevertheless, been very curiously brought together!

Jo sweeps his crossing all day long, unconscious of the link, if any link there be. He sums up his mental condition, when asked a question, by replying that he "don't know nothink." (*BH* Chapter 16)

What connection can there be between the very poor and the very rich (and their servants), even if there is a link? Dickens asks. The link exists, Crafts suggests, but the slaves are not conscious of it. Jo speaks his ignorance directly, while in free, indirect discourse, Crafts puts the phrase in the minds—not the mouths—of her slaves. Her use of Dickens is not a case of outright copying but, once again, of literary alchemy. Hannah Crafts clearly saw something she recognized in Dickens's description of Jo. But it is darkened, distilled, and transformed.

The question of who Hannah Crafts was has tended to consume many of her novel's early readers. But the question of how we read her novel is, I argue, even more important. Is it, as I asked earlier in this essay, a British text or a Black one? Is the title character to be regarded primarily as a runaway female slave or as a proto-Marxist who has performed the rhetorical act of uniting workers of the world who had little to lose but their chains? Should we, following the appeal of Frederick Douglass, spend more time reading and teaching Charles Dickens? Or should we, following the appeal of Hannah Crafts, spend more time simply reading? "In a right education," Douglass wrote in 1848, "there is a divine alchemy which turns all the baser parts of man's nature into gold . . . . Dr. Johnson was once asked, 'Who is the most miserable man?' and the reply of the sage was, 'That man who cannot read on a rainy day.'"[15] For the literate Hannah Crafts, *Bleak House* must have seemed a magical place where distasteful *illiterate* characters spontaneously combust, leaving nothing but a horrible mass of sticky black powder.

If a roomful of witty and well-read literary scholars wanted to concoct a readable text composed of the highlights of nineteenth-century literature, they might come up with something like *The Bondwoman's Narrative*. It is an amalgamation of the era's greatest hits: the mysterious old house; the portrait gallery; the questionable parentage subplot; the escape; the imprisonment; the carriage accident; the story of the jealous wife and the philandering husband; the cruel, lascivious slave trader; the heartbreaking sale of family members; the kindly old couple whose cottage provides refuge; the reunion of old friends after long years; the ghosts; the documents; the disguises; the injustices; the pranks; the satirical-political asides; the revenge; the achievement of freedom and some financial security; the final scene of domestic tranquility. Each chapter has an ironic epigraph, usually biblical, and is sprinkled with faux-erudite allusions to literary greats. In short, the novel has everything.

Should it be called a slave narrative? Why not? Hannah Crafts's extraordinary literacy did not make her less a slave. Is it a new genre? The rhetorical elements that the author borrows are subjected to processes of amalgamation and pressure that transform them into something completely new. But as with alchemy (called, in ancient practice, a "black" art because of its origins in Egypt, the place of black earth), the final product is an artistic creation far removed from anything found in "real" life.[16] The events of the novel cannot be considered "plain unvarnished facts," as the preface proposes. *The Bondwoman's Narrative* is a diligently constructed work of fiction.

Notes

1. *Scientific American* 6, no. 23 (February 22, 1851):184. URL: http://cdl.library.cornell.edu/cgi-bin/moa/moa-cgi?notisid=ABF2204–0006–25.

2. "Fulminating Substances," *Scientific American* 8, no. 39 (June 11, 1853):310. She may have even known of the importance of silver nitrate in photographic development. One hundred fifty years later, it is commonly used in forensic analysis and in preventing theft.

3. The weather is important for both tone and plot. It adds to the gloom of the scene and provides a rationale for Mrs. Wheeler to leave the house that very evening. But Crafts's borrowing is so obvious as to be parodic. Compare her description of Washington weather at the beginning of Chapter 13:

> Gloom everywhere Gloom up the Potomac; where it rolls among meadows no longer green, and by splendid country seats Gloom down the Potomac where it washes the sides of huge war-ships Gloom on the marshes, the fields, and heights Gloom settling steadily down over the sumptuous habitations of the rich, and creeping through the cellars of the poor Gloom arresting the steps of chance office-seekers, and bewildering the heads of grave and reverend Senators; for with fog, and drizzle, and a sleety driving mist the night has come at least two hours before its time. (*TBN* 157)

to the second paragraph of *Bleak House*:

> Fog everywhere. Fog up the river, where it flows among green aits and meadows; fog down the river, where it rolls defiled among the tiers of shipping, and the waterside pollutions of a great (and dirty) city. Fog on the Essex marshes, fog on the Kentish heights. Fog creeping into the cabooses of collier-brigs; fog lying out on the yards, and hovering in the rigging of great ships; fog drooping on the gunwales of barges and small boats. Fog in the eyes and throats of ancient Greenwich pensioners.

It is as if she wanted it to be recognized as Dickens's idiom.

4. Specifically, Scott's *Rob Roy* (1819) and Brontë's *Jane Eyre* (1847). See Catherine Keyser's essay in this volume for a thorough exploration of the ways Crafts's text draws on Brontë's.

5. See, for example, the outburst following the story of the infanticide and suicide of a young slave mother sold by Mr. Cosgrove, told by Lilly to Lizzy and then to Hannah:

> Dead, your Excellency, the President of this Republic. Dead, grave senators who grow eloquent over pensions and army wrongs. Dead ministers of religion, who prate because poor men without a moment's leisure on other days presume to read the newspapers on Sunday, yet who wink at, or approve of laws that occasion such scenes as this. (*TBN* 178)

Compare Crafts's language to the following from Dickens:

Dead! Dead, your Majesty. Dead, my lords and gentlemen. Dead, right reverends and wrong reverends of every order. Dead, men and women, born with heavenly compassion in your hearts. And dying thus around us every day. (*BH* Chapter 46)

Compare the following passage from Hannah Crafts:

A few words were exchanged in a low tone with some one within, and the bolts revolved, an iron door swung heavily open and we stood within the vestibule of a prison. It was a small, but strong guard room, from which a narrow stair case led upwards, and two low entrances conducted to cells or apartments on the ground floor, all secured with the tyrant strength of bolts and bars. The bleak walls otherwise bare were not unsuitably furnished with iron fetters, and other uncouth implements, designed for still more inhuman purposes, interspersed with broad bowie knives, guns, pistols, and other weapons of offence and defense. (*TBN* 76)

to the following from Walter Scott:

A few words were exchanged between my conductor and the turnkey in a language to which I was an absolute stranger. The bolts revolved, but with a caution which marked the apprehension that the noise might be overheard, and we stood within the vestibule of the prison of Glasgow,—a small, but strong guard-room, from which a narrow stair-case led upwards, and one or two low entrances conducted to apartments on the same level with the outward gate, all secured with the jealous strength of wickets, bolts, and bars. The walls, otherwise naked, were not unsuitably garnished with iron fetters, and other uncouth implements, which might be designed for purposes still more inhuman, interspersed with partisans, guns, pistols of antique manufacture, and other weapons of defence and offence. (*Rob Roy*, Chapter 21)

6. Evoking the shops in downtown Washington that display "paints and cosmetics in every variety, perfumes from China and India, hair of every color in curls or braids, teeth, washes, powders magnetic or otherwise, filters love-tokens, and similar articles . . . to be exchanged for pure gold," Crafts takes a British author's description of an overcast city, adds several artificial women, some elementary chemistry, several conventional moments (a startling recognition of a face in a crowd, a last-minute call for a smelling bottle), a satire on office-mongering, and more vanity, and transforms the elements into a farcical moment of fitting redress. Mrs. Wheeler's transfiguration and subsequent embarrassment cleverly occurs offstage; we are required to imagine Mrs. Wheeler as a pleading black woman on her knees, Hannah's position several chapters earlier (*TBN* 125), and perceive the ridicule and dismay it occasions.

7. Crafts's epigraph to Chapter 1, "Look not upon me because I am black; because the sun hath looked upon me," from Song of Solomon, perhaps comments upon Esther Summerson's name.

8. "At last, whenever a new pupil came who was a little downcast and happy, she was so sure—indeed I don't know why—to make a friend of me that all new-comers were confided to my care. They said I was so gentle, but I am sure THEY were!" (*BH* Chapter 3)

9. Hannah claims that "duty, gratitude, and honor," prevent her from leaving too. "And so to a strained sense of honor you willingly sacrifice a prospect of freedom," William answers. "Well, you can hug the chain if you please. With me it is liberty or death" (*TBN* 142). The

phrase "hug the chain" has as its source a short, sardonic poem by Byron called "Stanzas": "Could Love for ever / Run like a river, / And Time's endeavour / Be tried in vain— / No other pleasure / With this could measure; / And like a treasure / We'd hug the chain."

10. This is the case in free indirect discourse, in which the narrative voice ventriloquizes the thoughts and words of her characters without marks of ownership. As Henry Louis Gates, Jr., puts it, "the principal indices of free indirect discourse direct the reader to the subjective source of the statement, rendered through a fusion of narrator and silent but speaking character." *The Signifying Monkey: A Theory of African-American Literary Criticism* (New York: Oxford University Press, 1988), p. 210.

11. Though as Catherine Keyser points out, he also resembles *Jane Eyre*'s Mr. Brocklehurst.

12. Hannah Crafts: "I am very much surprised that you should . . ." through to "You well know and I know that our agreement being broken, the engagement terminated. That we are placed in a new position" (*TBN* 37). "It was a violation of our agreement" (*TBN* 38), "Why bless my heart, madam" and "It is not your secret, but mine" (*TBN* 38).

In *Bleak House*, Dickens writes: "I am rather surprised by the course you have taken." "Indeed." "Yes, decidedly. I was not prepared for it. I consider it a departure from our agreement and your promise. It puts us in a new position." "It is a violation of our agreement." "Why, bless my soul, Lady Dedlock." "It is no longer your secret. . . . It is my secret." (*BH* Chapter 48, "Closing In").

Again, in *The Bondwoman's Narrative*, Crafts writes: "'You say,' observed my mistress 'that you do not approve of the course I have taken, and it is a clear case that I do not comprehend the motive of yours. Why have you kept my secret so long only to reveal it now . . . ?'" (*TBN* 38).

Dickens's passage reads: "Lady Dedlock, I have not yet been able to come to a decision satisfactory to myself, on the course before me. I am not clear what to do or how to act next. I must request you, in the mean time, to keep your secret as you have kept it so long, and not to wonder that I keep it too" (*BH* Chapter 41, "In Mr. Tulkinghorn's Room").

Again, Crafts: "Finding that she remains silent, and is likely to remain so Mr. Trappe proceeds, and again with reference to the past. . . . She said nothing, she seemed even incapable of speech and both remained silent for a time. At length she spoke. 'I think this interview were better ended. I have no more to say.' 'But a little more to hear' he replied" (*TBN* 39, 40).

In Dickens we find: "She is not the first to speak; appearing indeed so unlikely to be so, though he stood there until midnight, that even he is driven upon breaking silence" (*BH* Chapter 48). "Sir, she returns . . . 'had better be gone. It would have been far better not to have detained me. I have no more to say.' 'Excuse me, Lady Dedlock, if I add a little more to hear'" (*BH* Chapter 41).

13. I have chosen not to spend much time on the Henry chapters in the novel. In these episodes, Hannah's textual kinship with Esther Summerson persists. The structural reason for this, I argue, is to provide a contrast to her self-determination later in the novel. Some examples of the echoes:

> By and by my strength began to be restored, and my bruised and shattered limbs became capable of motion. At first of very little, then gradually and by degrees of more and much more, until I could set upright, and instead of lying all day watching with a strange calmness the motions of the nurse, and quietly submitting to what she thought proper to do for me, I began to be useful to myself, and interested in attending to my own wants. (*TBN* 118–119)

By and by, my strength began to be restored. Instead of lying with so strange a calmness, watching what was done for me, as if it were done for some one else whom I was quietly sorry for, I helped it a little, and so on to a little more and much more, until I became useful to myself, and interested, and attached to life again." (*BH* Chapter 35)

"How well I remember the pleasant evening when I left my room for the first time to enjoy the social conviviality of a wedding party" (*TBN* 119).

"How well I remember the pleasant afternoon when I was raised in bed with pillows for the first time, to enjoy a great tea-drinking with Charley!" (*BH* Chapter 35).

14. Several historians have suggested that Crafts could not have traveled with the Wheelers at this time, that Wheeler had sold his plantation long before, and that in any case, it did not look anything like Hannah describes.

15. "Educate the People," *The North Star*, April 21, 1848. The evidence is undisputable that Hannah Crafts found useful words and ideas from this novel of poverty and squalor which, as D. A. Miller remarks, never really lets its readers feel at home. What is this *Bleak House*, he asks, "neither wholly blackened by the institutions that make use of its cover, nor wholly bleached of their stain, but (in the full etymological ambiguity of the word) irresolvably Bleak?" D. A. Miller, *The Novel and the Police* (Berkeley: University of California Press, 1988), p. 106. *Bleak House* is famous (in academic circles) for being, in J. Hillis Miller's words, "a document about the interpretation of documents," and in D. A. Miller's, a novel that produces the desire for a mystery/detective story. The topic of imprisonment in Dickens, the latter Miller argues, works to ensure that readers sense the lines of demarcation between institutional captivity and the space of "liberal society." If Hannah Crafts was indeed a runaway slave living under the specter of the Fugitive Slave Act of 1850, her connection with *Bleak House* may be based on her keen sense of the permeability of borders between slave and "free" states.

16. Crafts's literary imagination is manifested, for example, in the turrets and drawing rooms, cloaks and embroidery that color her text. These are poetic and imaginative places and things; Crafts uses them to create set pieces of betrayal, concealment, forgiveness, and revenge.

7

Jane Eyre, Bondwoman
Hannah Crafts's Rethinking of Charlotte Brontë

CATHERINE KEYSER

"And what will you do, Janet, while I am bargaining for so many tons of flesh and such an assortment of black eyes?"
"I'll be preparing myself to go out as a missionary to preach liberty to them that are enslaved—your harem inmates amongst the rest."

—Charlotte Brontë, *Jane Eyre* (1847)

A little girl, "shy and reserved," steals away from the play of other children to hide and read her book. As a young woman, she lives on a wealthy estate where mysterious laughter can be heard in the halls and the creaking of a tree lends an ominous feeling of dread. Because of a dark secret that destroys the romantic hopes of the estate's master, the young woman is forced to flee her erstwhile home. She finds herself a temporary sanctuary among loving companions, but because of an untenable marriage proposal, she must once again run away. Ultimately, she marries and lives happily ever after. The above outline of Charlotte Brontë's famous fictional autobiography, *Jane Eyre* (1847),[1] also provides a synopsis of *The Bondwoman's Narrative*, a fictionalized autobiography written in the 1850s by an African American woman who called herself "Hannah Crafts." The family resemblance may seem at first a coincidence, spawned by the Gothic and sentimental traditions drawn upon by both novelists. However, structural similarities, as well as echoes in diction and incident, suggest the profound possibility that in writing *The Bondwoman's Narrative*, Hannah Crafts was thinking back through her literary mother, to borrow Virginia Woolf's phrase.

In acknowledging such a connection between *Jane Eyre* and *The Bondwoman's Narrative*, one can recognize in Crafts's work a canny critical reading of *Jane Eyre* that anticipates the postcolonial and racial focus central to contemporary critical understanding of that novel.[2] The recent recovery of *The Bondwoman's Narrative* provides further historical and literary fodder for the spate of critics in the past two decades who stress in their treatments of *Jane Eyre* the silent voices repressed by the white imperialist narrator and author. Many of these critics' arguments are based on the idea that the autobiography of self-formation is centrally a Western imperialist construction and that the "female individualism" constituted by such a narrative requires the erasure of the racial "other." As Gayatri Spivak argues, "the 'native female' as such (*within* discourse, *as* a signifier) is excluded from any share in this emerging norm."[3] This account is problematized by a text like *The Bondwoman's Narrative* in which the subject-constitution is that of the "native female."[4] Hannah Crafts embraces what Spivak calls "voice-agency," voluntarily "speaking" her story and providing an autobiography with narrative trajectory (childhood to self-formation in crisis to marriage).

Of the author of the recently unearthed novel *The Bondwoman's Narrative*, we know few details, but editor Henry Louis Gates, Jr., posits "that she was female, mulatto, a slave of John Hill Wheeler's, an autodidact" (*TBN* lxxii). Gates further notes that Bryan Sinche's compilation of titles in John Hill Wheeler's library "provides a rare opportunity for scholars to trace with great specificity the echoes, allusions, and borrowings that this ex-slave drew upon to construct her novel" (*TBN* 331). This library included two copies of Brontë's *Jane Eyre*, an 1847 single volume and an 1850 three-volume collection titled *The Brontë Novels* (*TBN* 326). The cross-fertilization of Brontë's interests in marriage, social class, and the legacy of colonial exploitation with Crafts's concern with and depiction of slavery produces in *The Bondwoman's Narrative* a fascinating novel that tells a story "within the extremely popular tradition of the sentimental novel, replete with Gothic element," according to Gates (*TBN* xxxiv). A similar blend of genres exists in *Jane Eyre*, a novel that contains elements of the sentimental, Gothic, and realist traditions. An even more striking generic similarity to *Jane Eyre* is Crafts's use of the fictionalized autobiography, a choice fraught with potential liability, given the emphasis on veracity in nineteenth-century slave narratives.[5]

In both *Jane Eyre* and *The Bondwoman's Narrative*, the construction of autobiography negates the dehumanizing rhetoric used to deny the heroines' rationality. Hannah's master considers the slaves not to be "men and women" but rather to be like "horses or other domestic animals. He supplied their necessities . . . but [dis]counted the ideas of equality and fraternity as preposterous and absurd" (*TBN* 6). This description echoes Frederick Douglass's use of the same comparison between slaves and domestic animals, as Gates suggests (*TBN* 243), and it also recalls Jane Eyre's violent and tyrannical cousin, John Reed, who deems his cousin a "bad animal" and whom Jane accuses of being a "slave-driver" (*JE* 17). Crafts also invokes, as Brontë does later in her novel, the catchwords of the French Revolution, "equality and fraternity," to ironically underline their absence in a slaveholding world. Jane sarcastically deems the missionary role her suitor St. John proposes for her to be "*slaving among strangers . . . Famous equality and fraternisation!*" (*JE* Ch. 33, emphasis added).

This tendency of Brontë's to use slavery as a figurative trope is an aspect of Brontë's novel noted by many critics.[6] Susan Meyer explores this rhetoric in subtle detail in the chapter "'Indian Ink': Colonialism and the Figurative Strategy of *Jane Eyre*" in her book *Imperialism at Home: Race and Victorian Women's Fiction* (1996). Meyer argues:

> The most frequent recurrence of the racial metaphor in [*Jane Eyre*] is the sometimes covert, sometimes overt comparison of Jane to an African slave. The novel uses the idea of the enslaved Africans (eventually made spectacularly present through Bertha) as its most dramatic rendering of the concept of racial domination, and thus most frequently uses the slave to represent class and gender inequality in England. (75)

She further suggests that Brontë literalizes this trope with the introduction of the racialized character Bertha, Rochester's mad wife from Jamaica:

> The metaphor of slavery takes on such a central status that, although the novel remains situated in the domestic space, Brontë imports a character from the territory of the colonies . . . to give the metaphor a vivid presence. This realization of the metaphor through the creation of a character brings Brontë into a more direct confrontation with the history of British race relations. (64)

By shifting the tale to the American colonies and allowing a black female narrator to take on a role remarkably similar to Jane's in her adventures and self-representation, Crafts transforms *Jane Eyre* into a "direct confrontation" with the history of American race relations and literalizes these tropes.

The situations of the two heroines are not, after all, as different as one might imagine. Jane and Hannah share a gendered point of view and similar occupations: service roles in the households of the wealthy. Jane's communications with fellow servants (she often receives information about Thornfield's mysterious master from the widowed housekeeper, Mrs. Fairfax, who finds her counterpart in Crafts's Mrs. Bry), her silent observations of the machinations of the elite, and her feelings of oppression because of her dependent state provide Crafts with a model for the experience of her bondwoman. Both women play a difficult and often contradictory role within the household, living in the domestic space and often addressed intimately by their superiors, yet separated from the family through the very role that provides them with that intimacy. Jenny Sharpe comments on the contradictions of the governess's role, one which places her in an "ambiguous position" that makes her both intimate to the house and excluded from it, "one who both embodies the domestic ideal and threatens it."[7] Equally, if not more contradictory was the role of the house-slave, labeled inherently inferior, even animal, yet kept in intimate quarters with the family.

Another vocational similarity between Jane Eyre and Hannah Crafts is their shared work as teachers. Crafts, in fact, echoes Brontë in Hannah's description of her teaching successes. Just as Jane notes, "My pupil [Adele] was a lively child . . . and therefore was sometimes wayward; but as she was *committed entirely to my care* . . . she soon forgot her little freaks and became *obedient and teachable*" (*JE* 124, emphasis added), similarly, Hannah explains that "the little slave children were *almost entirely confided to my care* . . . How the rude and boisterous became *gentle and obliging*" (*TBN* 11, emphasis added). Both women find a vocation in teaching the disadvantaged, Jane in teaching the students of the rural poor (*JE* 409) and Hannah in teaching "colored children" in the North (*TBN* 237). The implication in both texts is that such education is inherently both civilizing and liberating, as Deirdre David notes in her discussion of *Jane Eyre*.[8] The link between literacy and liberation underlies both of these texts. Through education, Jane provides a method of self-transformation for her impoverished students, literally into a higher *class* of being (and the pun here is not accidental):

> Their amazement in me, my language, my rules, and ways, once subsided, I found some of *these heavy-looking, gaping rustics* wake up into *sharp-witted girls* enough . . . I discovered amongst them not a few examples of *natural* politeness, and *innate* self-respect, as well as of excellent *capacity*, that won both my good-will and admiration. (*JE* 409)

For Jane, what at first appears to be a constitutional ("gaping rustics") and congenital ("heavy-looking") inferiority reveals itself as a deceptive Sleeping-Beauty style of enchantment. Responding to a wave of Jane's magic wand as teacher, these lower-class asexual clods "wake up" into sophisticated and gendered subjects ("sharp-witted girls"), whose very attainment of wit and femininity marks the cultivation of distinctly upper-class cultural capital.[9] Similarly,

Crafts emphasizes that the superficial markers of racial inferiority in her students result from harsh treatment and deprivation rather than innate inferiority and that they too can thrive if given the proper treatment and tutelage:

> What a blessing it is that faith, and hope, and love are *universal* in their nature and operation—that *poor as well as rich, bond as well as free* are susceptible to their pleasing influences, and contain within themselves a *treasure* of consolation for all the ills of life. These little children, *slaves though they were*, and doomed to a life of *toil and drudgery, ignorant*, and *untutored* . . . thus evinced their *equal origin*, and *immortal destiny*. (*TBN* 11, emphases added)

As Crafts's invocation of social class ("poor as well as rich") and cultural capital ("treasure of consolation") suggests, the relationship between these two texts' thematic concerns cannot be reduced to a substitution—Crafts inserting race where Brontë would discuss class—for both texts reflect a complex engagement with the issues of gender, race, and class. For example, Hannah's perception of class is a notable feature of Crafts's treatment of slave society, as Gates points out: "[Crafts] is keenly aware of class differences within the slave community . . . Crafts clings to her class orientation as an educated mulatto, as a literate house slave" (*TBN* lxvi). Similarly, Jane Eyre, when asked whether she wishes to be given to other—potentially kinder—impoverished members of her family, instead clings to her meager status as an educated dependent within a wealthy home in order to escape what she views as the dire fate of poverty:

> Poverty looks grim to grown people; still more so to children: they have not much idea of *industrious, working, respectable poverty;* they think of the word only as connected with ragged clothes, scanty food, fireless grates, rude manners, and debasing vices: poverty for me was synonymous with *degradation*. "No; I should not like to belong to poor people," was my reply . . . to learn to speak like them, to adopt their manners, to be *uneducated* . . . no, I was not heroic enough to purchase liberty at the price of caste. (*JE* 32, emphasis added)

Crafts includes a similar passage *The Bondwoman's Narrative* to explain her heroine's reluctance to join the field slaves:

> This is all the result of that false system which bestows on position, wealth, or power the consideration only due to a man. And this system . . . bans *poor but honest* people with the contemptuous appellation of 'vulgar.' . . . If the huts were bad, its inhabitants it seemed were still worse. *Degradation*, neglect, and ill treat-

ment had wrought on them its legitimate effects . . . Their mental condition is briefly summed up in the phrase that they *know nothing*. (*TBN* 200)

Crafts adapts Brontë's passage from the speculative and subjective ("poverty for me was synonymous with degradation) to the literal: "Degradation . . . had wrought on them its legitimate effects" (*JE* 200). In translating Brontë's passage about social class into a description of the effects of slavery, Crafts indicates the interconnection of slavery, racism, and class: "It must be strange to live in a world of civilisation and, elegance, and refinement, and yet know nothing about either, yet that is the way *with multitudes* and *with none more than the slaves*" (*JE* 201, emphasis added).

The thematic resonance between the two texts is reflected in their consonant styles. For example, the narrator's shifting use of the past and present tenses, an odd element of Crafts's style that Gates notes, also occurs in *Jane Eyre* and to a similar end.[10] The notable scenes in each novel where these tense shifts occur are both set pieces in a specific locale with an isolated figure whose person and surroundings can only be seen by the reader. Brontë asks the reader to "fancy you see a room in George Inn at Millcote . . . [where] I *sit* in my cloak and bonnet; my muff and umbrella *lie* on the table, and I *am* warming away the numbness and the chill" (*JE* 109, emphases added). Crafts takes the isolation of her scene even further, effecting a double removal of the master to his "silent and solitary . . . apartment," which in turn exists only in Hannah's imagination as she mentally recreates this scene. She describes the details in the present tense: "His dinner *is* waiting, a sumptuous dinner served on massy plate. The delicate viands *breathe* a delicious flavor; the wine *leaps* and *sparkles*" (*TBN* 73, emphases added). In these isolated scenes, objects become active ("my muff and umbrella lie," "the delicate viands breathe," "the wine leaps and sparkles"), while the subject is inactive (Jane is waiting; Hannah is musing on the last experience of her dead master). Through these shifts to present tense, Brontë and Crafts directly engage readers with the narrative of the past by placing them in a present-tense scene of suspended action, where the readers become, like the heroines (for Hannah is picturing the master's suicide), waiting witnesses.[11] These scenes accentuate the heroines' restricted freedom of action. Further, these breaks into present tense allow Brontë and Crafts to conflate the role of heroine, who in isolation reads the room, and the solitary reader of the novel. Thus, Crafts creates the effect of identification that Spivak describes in Brontë's novel: "Here in Jane's self-marginalized uniqueness, the reader becomes her accomplice: the reader and Jane are united—both are reading."[12]

Jane and Hannah both must transgress in order to read, since the library is a province ruled and restricted by the master of the house. Hannah informs the reader that she must "steal away" in order to "ponder over the pages of some old book or newspaper that chance had thrown in [my] way" (*TBN* 7). So, too, must Jane dodge the watchful eye of the wealthy Reeds, if she wishes to avail herself of their library and "possess" herself "of a volume" (*JE* 14). The transgressive readings enacted by Jane and Hannah are not confined, however, to their appropriation of forbidden books. Their social invisibility, enforced by conventions of class, race, and service, provides them a screen behind which they can safely observe the social machinations of the elite. Crafts rewrites this scene in which Jane hides from her cousin John in the scene where Hannah, reading, overhears a confrontation between the evil Mr. Trappe and her beautiful yet tragic mistress.[13] Brontë describes Jane's hide-out and her observation of her cruel cousin from behind the curtain:

> I mounted into the window-seat gathering up my feet, I sat cross-legged, like a Turk; and, having drawn the red moreen curtain nearly close, I was shrined in double retirement ... With my Bewick on my knee, I was then happy ... I feared nothing but interruption, and that came too soon. The breakfast-room door opened. "Boh! Madam Mope!" cried the voice of John Reed; then he paused: he found the room apparently empty ... "It is well I drew the curtain," thought I; and I wished fervently he might not discover my hiding-place. (*JE* 14–15)

The comparison with the following scene from *The Bondwoman's Narrative* is striking:

> I descended to the parlor, and seated myself with a book behind the heavy damask curtains that shaded the window. In this situation I was entirely concealed. In a few moments the echo of a light footsteps [*sic*] was heard on the stair; then the door opened, and mistress entered ... Gliding in after her ... came Mr. Trappe. .... Unintentionally I had been made the witness of a private interview ... but I could not recede without exposure and I was not prepared for that. (*TBN* 36–39)

These descriptions share—along with a window seat, heavy curtains, an opened door, and the fear of discovery—their suggestion of the link between invisibility and readership. Jane and Hannah are screened from view by their lack of status within the households and by their solitary habits as readers, as they each withdraw from the venue of action to a marginalized vantage point that allows them to read the scene.[14] Here, both Brontë and Crafts emphasize the literacy of their heroines as an avenue for agency as well as tacitly praising their capacity for observation and their ability to outwit: Hannah has trapped Trappe, so to speak, just as Jane has outshone John.

Hannah and Jane both prefer to read books with pictures, a kind of reading, as Spivak observes, that allows the individualist heroine to rewrite the world according to the demands of her "unique creative imagination."[15] This preference for passion as coded in color and immediacy of visual understanding without verbal translation both narrators judge to be the result of their particular cultural background. Hannah suggest that her "African blood . . . perhaps led me to fancy pictorial illustrations and flaming colors" (*TBN* 6), while Jane associates the power of the illustrations she cherishes with "the tales Bessie sometimes narrated . . . old fairy tales and older ballads," representing the folk culture of rural England. Like Jane, who "cared little for" what she calls "the letter-press" (the literal meaning and word-content) of Bewick's *History of British Birds* yet finds that "Each picture told a story" (*JE* 15), Hannah sees the very words as pictures: "Though I knew not the meaning of a single letter, and had not the means of finding out I loved to *look* at them" (*TBN* 7, emphasis added). As Spivak notes of *Jane Eyre*, the heroine immediately associates reading with looking.

The two heroines are given the chance to test their ability to read people when they enter the social world of feminine adulthood. Jane leaves Lowood School to take a position as a governess at Thornfield, and Hannah, forced out of the seclusion of her frequent visits to the old couple's cottage, enters the world of social intrigues within her master's plantation, Lindendale. Crafts's initial description of events at Lindendale combines two key episodes in Brontë's novel: first, the arrival of guests at Thornfield brought at the master Rochester's request for the rumored purpose of his choosing a bride, and second, Jane's exploration of Thornfield Hall with the widowed housekeeper, Mrs. Fairfax. Jane comments upon the guests' arrival: "Merry days were these at Thornfield; and busy days too: how different from the first three months of stillness, *monotony*, and solitude I had passed beneath its roof! . . . there was *life* everywhere, movement all day long" (*JE* 206, emphasis added). So too Hannah recognizes that with the planned celebration comes "something . . . to break the *monotony* of our existence; something that would give *life*, and zest, and interest, to one day at least" (*TBN* 13, emphasis added).

Brontë and Crafts both also go into great detail in their descriptions of the preparations. The slaves and servants become stagehands preparing the domestic theater for a romantic drama. Jane tries to imagine Blanche Ingram, the rumored love of Rochester, while Hannah anticipates the beauty of her master's bride. Brontë lists the servants' activities: "*carpets were laid down, bed*-hangings festooned, radiant white counterpanes spread, toilet tables arranged, *furniture rubbed* . . . both chambers and *saloons* looked as fresh and bright as hands could make them" (*JE* 188). Crafts does, too, in remarkably similar terms: "floors were undergoing the process of being *rubbed*, carpets *were being spread*, curtains shaken out, *beds* puffed and covered and *furniture* dusted and polished . . . What an array of costly furniture adorned the rich *saloons* and gorgeous halls" (*TBN* 14). When the guests arrive, both Brontë and Crafts stress the necessity of a look-out,[16] and the arriving party is dramatically described by both authors as a "cavalcade": "The *cavalcade*, following the sweep of the drive, quickly turned the angle of the house" (*JE* 189); "Time and again and perhaps a dozen times had some of the younger ones climbed the trees and fences and a neighboring hill in order to descry the *cavalcade* at a distance and telegraph its approach" (*TBN* 25). Both Brontë and Crafts underscore the sense of imminent performance in these preparations and this fanfare. Thus, these heroines begin their experiments with authorship by applying imagination to their experiences of servitude.

This is not to suggest, however, that this luxury is simply an opportunity for the heroine's creative expression. The wealth of the master, represented by the manor itself, is built on the sacrifices of those who serve him, as Hannah reminds the reader through underscoring her own innocence. She admits that "it never occurred to us to inquire whose sweat and blood and unpaid labor had contributed to produce it." Thus, in Crafts's introduction of Lindendale, she includes not only the pomp and circumstance of the guests' arrival but also the heroine's recognition of the plantation's tragic past and haunted present in the form of the same Gothic tropes used by Brontë to describe Thornfield: mysterious maniacal laughter and a possible ghost. Both Jane and Hannah are guided by the hall's housekeeper, *Jane Eyre*'s Mrs. Fairfax and *The Bondwoman's* Mrs. Bry. "I followed her up stairs and down stairs," Jane reports (*JE* 121), just as Hannah describes Mrs. Bry "dragging her unwieldy weight of flesh up and down the staircases" (*TBN* 14). Both heroines ascend in these scenes to the upper level of the house; Jane contemplates the view from "the leads" or "the roof of the hall" and, "leaning over the battlements and looking far down," surveys Rochester's holdings (*JE* 122), while Hannah "thread[s] the long galleries which led to the southern turret" (*TBN* 15).

These upper floors represent what Brontë calls the "shrine of memory." Jane encounters on the third floor the discarded furniture and "half-effaced embroideries . . . wrought by fingers that for *two generations* had been coffin-dust" (*JE* 121). Hannah is similarly confronted with the historical memory of her master's family, as the upper story of Lindendale is literally "adorned with a long succession of family portraits" (*TBN* 15), while the third floor of Thornfield prompts Jane to inquire about the history of the Rochesters. Jane comments:

All these relics gave to the third story of Thornfield Hall the aspect of a home
of the past: a shrine of memory. I liked the hush, the gloom, the quaintness of
these retreats in the day; but I by no means coveted a night's repose on one of
those wide and heavy beds. (*JE* 121)

Hannah also views the upper rooms with "superstitious awe" (*TBN* 17), but
while access to the proprietor's past unearths the plantation's violent secrets, it
also unlocks his hold on the European cultural legacy. Hannah gazes appre-
ciatively at the portraits:

For there surrounded by mysterious associations I seemed suddenly to have
grown old, to have entered a new world of thoughts, and feelings, and sentiments. I was not a slave with these pictured memorials of the past. They could
not enforce drudgery, or condemn me on account of my color to a life of servitude. As their companion I could think and speculate. (*TBN* 17)

This passage comes closest to revealing the tensions for this African American
author, a former slave, in realizing that the master's whip and his Western
ideas, the plantation property and the liberating library, cannot be so easily
separated from one another. While Hannah reviles the white slaveholder's
treatment of her "on account of my color," she finds that in the company of
their intellectual tradition, she can "think and speculate." The oppressive
white slaveholders become impotent as they pass into history, and Hannah becomes "their companion" as she embraces the Western literary legacy,
"exult[ing]" in her "freedom as a rational being" (*TBN* 17).

History, however, is not altogether impotent in either Crafts's or Brontë's account, and its power is communicated through the Gothic trope of haunting.
Mrs. Fairfax confides in Jane that "'one would almost say that, if there were a
ghost at Thornfield Hall, this would be its haunt'" (*JE* 121), just as Hannah
speculates: "There is something inexpressibly dreary and solemn in passing
through the silent rooms of a large house, especially one whence many generations have passed to the grave . . . you feel the presence of mysterious beings"
(*TBN* 15). Both heroines also hear mysterious laughter while pacing these
upper halls (*JE* 123; *TBN* 20). The Gothic sense of awe and dread in both texts
is associated with the sense of a historical crime that still has not been expi-
ated.[17] Through Rochester's financial successes and marital entanglements in Jamaica, Brontë emphasizes the exploitative nature of this colonial arrangement,
and Crafts is even more direct in her treatment of the history of American slavery as the historical crime at the center of Lindendale's haunting. Because of
these unresolved crises, the attempt to perpetuate the family name through

marriage, when that name is written in the blood of the racial other, is thwarted in both novels. Moaning trees create a Gothic sense of gloom and horror, as marriage arrangements escalate for Hannah's master and Jane's Rochester.[18] The present prospect of happiness (the master's new bride and Rochester's love for Jane), this ominous creaking suggests, will not materialize while the past remains to haunt the descendants and heirs of this sanguineous history. Crafts's description of the tree and its moaning parallels Brontë's passage:

> The *moon* was not yet set, and we were all in shadow: I could scarcely see *my master*'s face, near as I was. And what ailed the chestnut tree? it writhed and groaned; while *wind roared in the laurel walk* and came sweeping over us . . . there was a crack, a *crash*, and a close rattling peal . . . The *rain* rushed down. (*JE* 287, emphasis added)

> The *moon* shined only through a murky cloud, and the rising *wind moaned fitfully amid the linden branches.* Then the *rain* began to patter on the roof, with the dull horrible creaking that forboded misfortune to the house. The cheek of *my master* paled . . . The words were followed by a *crash.* (*TBN* 29)

As the echo in these passages of the phrase "my master" suggests, Crafts takes the idea, figuratively suggested throughout *Jane Eyre*, of Rochester as a slaveholder and literalizes it in descriptions of both the first and the current master of Lindendale Hall. These passages recall Brontë's language in describing her Byronic hero. For example, Jane observes that when Rochester is in a mood, "a morose, almost a malignant scowl, blackened his features" (*JE* 167) and that he looks:

> [With a] glare such as I [Jane] have never seen before or since. [It was a look of] Pain, shame, ire—impatience, disgust, detestation . . . Wild was the wrestle . . . but another feeling rose . . . settled his passion and petrified his countenance" (*JE* 162).

Crafts similarly describes a countenance transformed by emotion in her observation of her master's portrait, transformed not by *his* passions but by hers upon perceiving it:

> [A]s I mused the portrait of my master ~~changed~~ seemed to change from its usually kind and placid expression to one of wrath and gloom, that the calm brow should become wrinkled with passion, the lips turgid with malevolence. (*TBN* 17)

Crafts's emphasis on "wrath," "gloom," and "passion" here reveals the proximity between the Byronic ideal of the hero and the Gothic depiction of the
villain.[19] Crafts's description of Mr. Cosgrove, the owner of Lindendale after
her original master, echoes Jane Eyre's famous comparison of Mr. Rochester
to a slaveholding sultan: His claim that he would not exchange Jane for "the
Grand Turk's whole seraglio," and her resulting fear that Rochester will treat
her as a "harem inmate" (*JE* 301–302). Crafts writes: "[N]o Turk in his
haram [*sic*] ever luxuriated in deeper sensual enjoyments than did the master of
Lindendale" (*TBN* 172). Just as Rochester locks his wife in a hidden room to
keep her secret from his mistress, so Cosgrove locks his slave mistresses away
to keep them secret from his wife. Literalizing Brontë's comparisons of
Rochester to a slaveholder in these two masters of Lindendale,[20] Crafts rejects
the love plot between Jane and Rochester (Hannah does not become romanti-
cally involved with her master), thus obviating the problem contemporary critics perceive in Brontë's ending, which "essentially permits the racial hierarchies
of European imperialism to fall back into place" through its romanticization
of this symbolic imperialist couple.[21]

The haunting secrets that plague the masters of these Gothic Halls are, in
both of these novels, associated with the figures of mysterious women. Both
figures, Bertha Rochester and Hannah's first mistress, are described in racialized terms. Jane describes Bertha with horror to Rochester:

> "Fearful and ghastly to me—oh, sir, I never saw a face like it! It was a *discoloured*
> face—it was a *savage* face. I wish I could forget the roll of the red eyes and the
> fearful *blackened* inflation of the lineaments!"
>
> "Ghosts are usually pale, Jane."
>
> "This, sir, was purple: the *lips were swelled and dark*; the brow furrowed; the
> *black* eye-brows widely raised over the blood-shot eyes.[22] (*JE* 317)

Far lovelier is Crafts's mistress, but Hannah too emphasizes her mistress's lips
as a betraying sign of her race: "She was a small brown woman, with a profusion of wavy curly hair, large bright eyes, and delicate features, with the exception of her lips which were too large, full, and red" (*TBN* 27). Recalling
Bertha's "quantity of dark, grizzled hair, wild as a mane" (*JE* 328), the mistress's "profusion of wavy hair" is described by Hannah as in the "wildest disorder" when her secret is revealed, a revelation which in fact drives her mad
(*TBN* 43). However, the madness that Hannah notes in her mistress comes
not from her racial background, as Bertha's madness is said to descend
through her mother's line,[23] but rather from her weakening experience as a rich
white woman. In a canny reversal, Crafts associates strength and resourceful-

ness with the survival skills required to overcome slavery and degrading nervous effects with wealth and position:

> [H]er apparent weakness really surprised and alarmed me. I could not fully appreciate all she had suffered; for tho' a slave myself I had never possessed freedom, wealth, and position as she had, but I saw its effects in the utter prostration of her nervous system, her trembling limbs, and tottering steps. (*TBN* 57)

This "prostration of her nervous system" leads for the mistress, as it does for Bertha, to madness: "After a time my mistress became decidedly insane" (*TBN* 67). In Crafts's description of her mistress's madness, she uses the image of "the foul German spectre—the Vampyre" repeatedly used in *Jane Eyre* to describe Bertha: "'[Bertha] sucked my blood: she said she'd drain my heart,' said Mason" (*JE* 317, 239). Crafts reverses the denigrating message of this imagery, applying the blood-sucking ferocity to the slave-hunter, not to her mistress: "She fancied herself pursued by an invisible being, who sought to devour her flesh and crush her bones . . . 'Oh, horrible. He tears my flesh, he drinks my blood'" (*TBN* 67).

Not only does Crafts portray Hannah's mulatto mistress—the Bertha figure in her text—sympathetically in a way Brontë does not, but she actually places Hannah in the same dire situations as her mistress, so that Crafts's very heroine experiences Bertha's imprisonment. Hannah and her mistress are locked into a prison arranged for them by Mr. Trappe by a coarse jailer with "uncouth features," "hair [as] . . . red as fire," and an "equally red face" (*TBN* 77), in essence a male version of Bertha's jailer, Grace Poole, whom Jane describes as "a set, square-made figure, red-haired, and with a hard, plain face" (*JE* 123). Crafts's description of the second prison Hannah shares with her mistress, a room in a fine white house, recalls another scene in *Jane Eyre*: Jane's unjust and terrifying imprisonment by Mrs. Reed in the ghostly bedroom at Gateshead. Jane's "silent cell" with its "two large windows, with their blinds always drawn down," its wardrobe with "panels" and door locked from the outside leads her to exclaim, "Alas! yes: no jail was ever more secure," just as Hannah laments, "It was evident that we had only been transferred from one prison to another" (*TBN* 93). By juxtaposing these two scenes of imprisonment, one closely crafted on Bertha's confinement and the other reminiscent of Jane's, Crafts reveals her awareness of the close connection between these two characters in *Jane Eyre*, an oft-cited critical crux of the novel, whether Bertha is considered to be Jane's dark psychological double, as in Sandra Gilbert and Susan Gubar's *The Madwoman in the Attic*, or her colonial native counterpart, as in Gayatri Spivak's "Three Women's Texts and a Critique of Imperialism."

Both Jane and Hannah find temporary sanctuary in homes that offer comfort and love after escaping the horrors of imprisonment (Hannah flees literal imprisonment, while Jane flees the spectacle of Bertha's imprisonment). Crafts's fascination with houses throughout her novel betrays the influence of *Jane Eyre,* a novel also consumed with architectural accounts.[24] Crafts uses houses and their décor to indicate the past of slavery as it attaches to a particular locale, the plantation, and also to suggest the utopian peace and contentment, represented by artistry and taste, possible in a new home. The "latticed window, within a foot of the ground, made still smaller by the growth of ivy or some other creeping plant" of the Rivers' Moor House in *Jane Eyre* resurfaces in Crafts's even more ecstatic description of the Henrys' home, Forget-Me-Not, and its "little windows, surrounded by lattice work with the luxuriant growth of honey-suckle and jasmine pressing through it" (*TBN* 122). In Jane's childhood, the decorative object that most enchanted her imagination was "a certain brightly painted china plate, whose bird of paradise, nestling in a wreath of convolvuli and rosebuds, had been wont to stir in me a most enthusiastic sense of admiration" (*JE* 28). Crafts places this "bird of paradise" in the décor of Forget-Me-Not in a possible allusion to Brontë: "I never wearied in looking at [pictures of birds]. Here were *birds of Paradise* just dropping into the balmy recesses of some cinnamon grove" (*TBN* 122).

By crafting this "bird room," Crafts also picks up on the metaphor St. John uses to describe Jane upon her arrival in Moor House: "'My sisters, you see, have a pleasure in keeping you ... as they would have a pleasure in keeping and cherishing a half-frozen bird" (*JE* 390). Even as she celebrates the craftsmanship of this glorious room, Crafts tacitly recognizes the problematic aspect of this comparison, the similarity of a bird in a cage to a woman enslaved. For while both Brontë and Crafts associate the beauty of these homes with the beautiful minds and hearts of the inhabitants within, this enslaving mentality—the Rivers sisters' desire to make of Jane a pet; St. John's demand that she work for him as his missionary bride; Mrs. Henry's refusal to buy Hannah Crafts, even when this is the only way to set her free—determines that ultimately the satisfactions of these would-be homes are temporary.[25]

In order to find a permanent home, these two heroines will have to create their own through marriage. Despite Crafts's implicit rejection of Rochester, *Jane Eyre's* love plot, such a major feature of that novel, does not disappear entirely from the pages of *The Bondwoman's Narrative.* This subplot is actually placed onto another, a character named "Charlotte," whom Hannah describes as "young, well-educated, and possessed of many advantages" (*TBN* 129). While this name choice may be a coincidence, it may also represent Crafts's nod to Brontë, who had admitted her gender and attached her true name to her novel by the time Wheeler's edition of the text was printed. Crafts's description of Charlotte's wedding recalls the scene between Rochester and Jane in the garden of Thornfield when the open pronouncement of their love coincides with a sudden downpour of rain and an ominous thunder clap, signaling their imminent trials (*JE* 287):

> I gazed at them and wondered if they were really so happy—wondered if no shadows of *coming evils* never haunted their minds . . . Did the future spread before them bright and cloudless? Did they anticipate domestic felicity, and long years of wedded love . . . The night had been beautiful and balmy, and the fine moonlight lay . . . over the scene, but a cloud had suddenly risen, and just as the bride, conspicuous in her snowy robes joined the group of dancers, it swept over the moon extinguishing her light, and a burst of thunder announced the approaching tempest. Suddenly and without further warning the winds arose, clouds obscured the firmament, and *there was darkness, lightning, and rain, where only a few minutes before had been youth, and beauty, and love, and light, and joyousness. Did this change prefigure the destiny of the wedded pair.* (*TBN* 120)

In fact, this climactic change does prefigure the immediate destiny of the wedded pair, just as it does the lovers Jane and Rochester. Charlotte's husband is sold by his master to a slave-trader, and the couple are forced to run away in order to stay together.

Hannah openly comments on the reasons for this union's tribulations, explaining that she has "always thought that in a state of servitude marriage must be at best of doubtful advantage. It necessarily complicates and involves the relation of master and slave" (*TBN* 131). Crafts's point here reflects the lesson one might glean from reading *Jane Eyre*. After all, dependable Mrs. Fairfax warns Jane that "Equality of position and fortune is often advisable in such cases" (*JE* 297), and Rochester assures her that "'I will myself put the diamond chain round your neck'" in a phrasing that takes on sinister overtones of enslavement (*JE* 291). Until Jane rights this inequality, coming into her inheritance and claiming her independence, marriage to Rochester is indeed "at best of doubtful advantage." The only successful marriage, Brontë suggests and Crafts confirms, is a union between two equals and two companions. Thus, Hannah's first and lasting experience of romance occurs after she has escaped slavery, and Hannah emphasizes the importance of their free status, commenting that her husband "is, and has always been, a free man" (*TBN* 238). In the conclusion of Brontë's novel, Jane celebrates the companionate pleasure of her marriage: "No woman was ever nearer to her mate than I am . . . All my confidence is bestowed on him, all his confidence is devoted to me;

we are precisely suited in character—perfect concord is the result" (*JE* 500). Similarly, Hannah deems her spouse a dear "companion," a "fond and affectionate husband" who "sits by my side even as I write" (*TBN* 238). The sentimental endings of both novels bring together other happy couples as well as neighbors and friends to surround the successful unions of the heroines and their husbands. Jane gains the society of her cousins, which she so treasured at Moor House (*JE* 501), and Crafts resolves the romantic subplot of her novel with a happy ending for Charlotte and her husband, as well as a fulfilling marriage for Hannah herself (*TBN* 239).

Thus Hannah and Jane mirror one another in contentment as well as tribulation, sisters in their quest for liberty, rationality, and even romantic fulfillment. The sororal similarities between these two characters are borne out in structural similarities between the two texts, as Crafts renders her own version of nodal episodes and locations in Brontë's novel.[26] In her essay that launched the critical recognition of *Jane Eyre*'s racial themes, Spivak seems driven to recover such a sister-text to *Jane Eyre*, a "dark double," to borrow Gilbert and Gubar's appellation for Bertha Rochester. Spivak emphasizes the importance of finding such alternative texts in her initial description of her goals:

> In this essay, I will attempt to examine the operation of the "worlding" of what is today "the Third World" by what has become a cult text of feminism: *Jane Eyre*. I plot the novel's reach and grasp, and locate its structural motors. I read *Wide Sargasso Sea* as *Jane Eyre*'s reinscription and *Frankenstein* as an analysis— even a deconstruction—of a "worlding" such as *Jane Eyre*'s.[27]

Spivak finds Jean Rhys's *Wide Sargasso Sea* wanting because "No perspective *critical of imperialism* can turn the Other into a self, because the project of imperialism has always already historically refracted what might have been the absolutely Other into a domesticated Other that consolidates the Imperialist self."[28] Even Rhys's rewriting, Spivak argues, cannot grant black characters a voice:

> Christophine [the black female character in *Wide Sargasso Sea*] is tangential to this narrative. She cannot be contained by a novel which rewrites a canonical English text within the European novelistic tradition in the interest of the white Creole rather than the native.[29]

In *The Bondwoman's Narrative*, we have a novel that views a canonical English text (*Jane Eyre*) within the African American literary tradition (the slave narratives) in the interest of the black subject. This text is critically compelling both as an addition to the African American canon and as a supplement to our reading of *Jane Eyre*. *The Bondwoman's Narrative* enacts an effective rethinking of *Jane Eyre*, responding to that novel's racial themes, which have been elucidated in the works of modern critics like Spivak. Reading *The Bondwoman's Narrative*, one recognizes with fascination, even awe, Crafts's astute and artful anticipation of these modern readings one hundred and fifty years earlier.

Notes

1. Charlotte Brontë, *Jane Eyre*, ed. Michael Mason (1847; reprint, New York: Penguin Classics, 1996).

2. Gayatri Spivak's "Three Women's Texts and a Critique of Imperialism" (first published in 1985) has been followed by a number of compelling studies on this topic, including Jenny Sharpe's "The Rise of Women in an Age of Progress: *Jane Eyre*" in *Allegories of Empire* (Minneapolis: University of Minnesota Press, 1993); Deirdre David's *Rule Britannia: Women, Empire, and Victorian Writing* (Ithaca: Cornell University Press, 1995); and most sensitively and notably to my mind, Susan Meyer's "'Indian Ink': Colonialism and the Figurative Strategy of *Jane Eyre*" in *Imperialism at Home: Race and Victorian Women's Fiction* (Ithaca: Cornell University Press, 1996), which is a reprint of an essay first published in 1990 in *Victorian Studies*. References to Spivak's "Three Women's Texts and a Critique of Imperialism" are from her chapter in *Feminisms: An Anthology of Literary Theory and Criticism*, ed. Diane Price Herndl and Robyn Warhol (New Brunswick, N.J.: Rutgers University Press, 1991).

3. Spivak, "Three Women's Texts," 799 (author's emphasis).

4. Spivak ultimately concludes that the sub-altern ceases to be sub-altern when voiced. See Gayatri Spivak, "Can the Sub-Altern Speak?" in *The Post-Colonial Studies Reader*, ed. Bill Ashcroft, Gareth Griffiths, and Helen Tiffin (London: Routledge, 1995), 24–28.

5. In fact, this "public insistence on veracity in the handling of slave experiences" could account for the fact that this manuscript is unpublished, as Nina Baym suggests: "[Crafts] might well have hesitated after all to launch into the marketplace an experimental novel in the first person under her own name" (quoted by Gates in the Introduction to *The Bondwoman's Narrative*, lxv).

6. Sharpe notes that "Brontë deploys the feminist metaphor of domestic slavery for staging one woman's rebellion against sexual and economic bondage . . . . Although Jane identifies the master/slave relation as Roman, the idea of a *revolted* slave had to have come from a more recent past. There were the slave uprisings of Jamaica in 1808 and 1831, Barbados in 1816, and Demerara in 1823. Brontë's novel clearly draws on the moral language of the abolitionists." Sharpe, "The Rise of Women," 39.

7. Ibid., 48.

8. David, *Rule Britannia*, 48.

9. In many ways, their change in status mirrors the transformation that Jane herself undergoes in the course of the novel, from impoverished dependent to independent heiress, from plain governess to coveted bride.

10. In the notes to Chapter 5, Gates remarks: "pp. 73–74, Crafts here shifts the tense of her verbs from past to present when describing a scene from the past" (251).

11. The authors underscore the importance of temporality in these scenes through their return to the past tense: "*half an hour elapsed* and still I was alone. I bethought myself to ring

the bell" (*JE* 109, emphasis added); "Four o'clock in the afternoon, and *that hour passed*" (*TBN* 73, emphasis added).

12. Spivak, "Three Women's Texts," 800.

13. Mr. Trappe bears fruitful comparison to Brontë's villainous Mr. Brocklehurst, Jane's tyrannical schoolmaster whom she describes as "a black pillar," "sable-clad" (*JE* 40). Crafts calls Mr. Trappe "the gentleman in black" and explains that "you would see him . . . leaning speechless against a pillar," literalizing Brontë's metaphor (*JE* 31–32, emphasis added). Both novels feature scenes in which their heroines, horrified, recognize the appearance of these villains through a window (*JE* 73; *TBN* 63).

14. See Spivak's suggestive discussion of Brontë's "marginalization and privatization of the protagonist" and its relationship to "the creative imagination of the marginal individualist" in "Three Women's Texts," 800–801.

15. Spivak notes that Jane "cares little for reading what is *meant* to be read: the 'letter-press.' *She* reads the pictures. The power of this singular hermeneutics is precisely that it can make the outside inside . . . 'the drear November day' is rather a one-dimensional 'aspect' to be 'studied,' not decoded like the 'letter-press' but, like pictures, deciphered by the unique creative imagination of the marginal individualist (*JE*, 10)." Spivak, "Three Women's Texts," 801.

16. Mrs. Fairfax assures her fellow servants that she has "'sent John down to the gates to see if there is anything on the road'" (*JE* 189), while Hannah notes "All day long we had been looking for the wedding party" (*TBN* 25).

17. As Meyer suggests, "The story of Bertha Rochester, however unsympathetic to her as a human being, nonetheless does make an indictment of British imperialism in the West Indies and the stained wealth that came from its oppressive rule. When Jane wonders 'what crime . . . live[s] incarnate' in Rochester's luxurious mansion that can 'neither be expelled nor subdued by the owner' (264), the novel suggests that the black-visaged Bertha, imprisoned out of sight in a luxurious British mansion, does indeed incarnate a historical crime." Meyer, "'Indian Ink,'" 71.

18. Here it is also interesting to note that both halls are named after trees: Lindendale obviously for this haunted linden. Brontë explains that "an array of mighty old thorn trees, strong, knotty, and broad as oaks, at once explained the etymology of the mansion's designation" (*JE* 114).

19. In fact, Crafts's villain, Mr. Trappe, also resembles Rochester. Mr. Trappe's "keen black eye" recalls Brontë's description of Mr. Rochester's "dangerous . . . black eyes" (*TBN* 63; *JE* 233). When Rochester enters his party, Jane's "eyes were drawn involuntarily to his face" (*JE* 197–198), and describing a similar scene, Crafts writes: "In all that brilliant company I [Hannah] had eyes and ears for only one man, and that man the least attractive of any in the throng" (*TBN* 27). Brontë also notes that among the guests Rochester is the least conventionally attractive (*JE* 198).

20. Jane in her anger tells the imperious Rochester to go "to the bazaars of Stamboul without delay; and lay out in extensive slave-purchases some of that spare cash you seem at a loss to spend satisfactorily here" (*JE* 302). She also describes Rochester's appearance, tellingly, as one that "quite *mastered* me," further underscoring the implications of her word choice with her explanation: "[Its influence] took my feelings from my own power and *fettered* them in his" (*JE* 198, emphasis added).

21. Meyer, "'Indian Ink,'" 66. Deirdre David argues that "Jane and Rochester become a symbolic couple, produced by and also producing Britain's culture of empire, and defined by

their complete difference from native tropic sexuality . . . Blanche's sterile snobbery, and a languid gentry indifferent to the colonial sources of its wealth." David, *Rule Britannia,* 116.

22. Meyer notes that "Bertha represents the 'dark races' in the empire, particularly African slaves, and gives them a human presence that lends a vividness to Brontë's metaphorical use of race." Meyer, "'Indian Ink,'" p. 72.

23. Rochester laments, "My bride's mother I had never seen: I understood she was dead. The honey-moon over, I learned my mistake; she was only mad, and shut up in a lunatic asylum" (*JE* 344).

24. See Brontë's elaborate descriptions of the design and furnishings of Gateshead (*JE* 21), Thornfield (*JE* 114), and Moor House (*JE* 123).

25. Neither Jane nor Hannah recognize that these households are unsatisfactory, and both beg to be allowed to stay with the family, even if that means slaving for them:

"'Show me how to work, or how to seek work: that is all I now ask; then let me go, if it be but to the meanest cottage—but *till then,* allow me to stay here: I dread another essay of the horrors of homeless destitution" (*JE* 390, author's emphasis).

"[I] threw myself at her feet. 'Mrs. Henry' I said 'you can save me from this. I have an inexpressible desire to stay with you. You are so good, accomplished, and Christian-like, could I only have the happiness to be your slave, your servant . . . '"(*TBN* 125).

26. It is possible to make loose identifications between many episodes and locations of *The Bondwoman's Narrative* and *Jane Eyre,* as I have suggested elsewhere: between the Reed home and the Wheeler household, for example; Thornfield and Lindendale; Moor House and Forget-Me-Not; New Jersey and Ferndean. Both heroines also experience similar episodes of flight and subsequent illness.

27. Spivak, "Three Women's Texts," 798.

28. Ibid., 807 (author's emphasis).

29. Ibid., 806–807.

8

The Bondwoman's Narrative and Uncle Tom's Cabin

JEAN FAGAN YELLIN

It is not surprising that *The Bondwoman's Narrative* echoes *Uncle Tom's Cabin*. After its appearance in 1852, Harriet Beecher Stowe's best-selling novel enjoyed an unheard-of popularity, and publishers who had shunned the slavery issue for fear of losing "the southern market" eagerly published and marketed at least nineteen fictional responses. Who knows how many other writers, both black and white, penned reactions to *Uncle Tom's Cabin*? Among those published were the proslavery *Uncle Robin in His Cabin in Virginia, and Tom Without One in Boston*, and *Life at the South, or Uncle Tom's Cabin As It Is*. Both of these titles were in the library of John H. Wheeler, the man who may have owned a writer who called herself Hannah Crafts—the author of *The Bondwoman's Narrative*.[1]

Even before 1852 there was, of course, a lively antislavery literature. This included pamphlets like David Walker's inflammatory 1829 *Appeal . . . to the Coloured Citizens of the World*, said to have moved Nat Turner to the bloodiest slave insurrection in American history; newspapers like William Lloyd Garrison's *Liberator*, appearing in Boston weekly since 1831; Maria W. Stewart's 1832–1833 speeches; as well as the first-person testimony shaped into narratives by former slaves including Frederick Douglass, Lewis and Milton Clarke, Josiah Henson, and Henry Bibb. The abolitionists' antislavery reading rooms also stocked a few fictional works: Richard Hildreth's *The Slave, or Memoirs of Archy Moore*, patterned on the tradition of French antislavery fiction and Gustave de Beaumont's *Marie, ou l'Esclavage aux Etats-Unis*, and "The Quadroons," a short story by Lydia Maria Child, author of the historic *Appeal in Favor of that Class of Americans Called Africans*.[2] But *Uncle Tom's Cabin* opened the floodgates.

Although the literary gothic was already well established in our national letters (think Edgar Allen Poe), one of Stowe's contributions to our popular culture was linking American gothic literature to chattel slavery—which, with the genocide of the Indians, is its inevitable American subject. In her book, Hannah Crafts pictures the horror rooted in the ownership of human beings. She writes that when only a girl, she learned "a curse was attached to my race" (*TBN*, 5–6). In her early chapters, she pictures haunted Lindendale, built by the "sweat and blood and unpaid labor" of generations of slaves, and its cursed linden tree, where "slaves had been tied to its trunk to be whipped or sometimes gibbeted on its branches," and where old Rose and her faithful dog were tortured and murdered (*TBN*, 14, 20–22). In these haunted passages, Crafts recalls Stowe's treatment of Legree's plantation up the Red River, with its "black, blasted tree, and the ground all covered with black ashes," which, Cassy warned, tell a history no one dares voice (*UTC*, 384). These references also suggest Stowe's story of the killing of George Harris's little dog Carlo, and they evoke the most famous cage in antislavery letters, scene of the torture and murder Crevcoeur had famously described. Similarly, in her later chapters, Crafts's description of the madness of her dear mistress who, driven insane when reduced to slavery, echoes the anguish of Stowe's Cassy, with her "wild, long laugh" and "convulsive sobbings and struggles" (*TBN*, 82; *UTC*, 376).[3]

The Bondwoman's Narrative further recalls the use of the gothic in *Uncle Tom's Cabin* in the section centering on Charlotte and her husband, William. Like Stowe's Eliza, who was "married in her mistress' great parlor . . . [with] no lack of white gloves, and cake and wine," Charlotte had a kind mistress who arranged for a splendid wedding for her favorite slave where "Cakes, confectionary and wine" were "abundantly provided, and all the servants old and young big and little were invited to be present" (*UTC*, 19; *TBN*, 119). Nonetheless, within the sheltering walls of the Henrys' charming Forget-Me-Not home, Hannah senses that Charlotte is unhappy and hears rumors of nocturnal ghosts. She soon discovers that the mysterious sounds are made by Charlotte's bridegroom, William, who explains that he has gone into hiding after learning that he has been sold by his master to a southern trader "because he said I was proud of my marriage" (*TBN*, 142). His situation echoes that of Stowe's George Harris (Cassy's husband), who—ordered to "take Mina for a wife, and settle down in a cabin with her" or be sold down the river—had run off (*UTC*, 23). In both instances, a slave's marriage is at stake.

The Bondwoman's Narrative also echoes *Uncle Tom's Cabin* in presenting the cruelty routinely used to control slave women. When Hannah's jailer advises that "If a woman is stubborn or obstinate ask her as a favor, coax her, flatter her and my word for it she'll be pliable as wax in your hands," the brutal Hayes responds, "They must mind me either way" (*TBN*, 89). Similarly, Stowe's Loker explained his savage methods to Marks: "'Why, I buys a gal, and if she's got a young 'un to be sold, I jest walks up and puts my fist to her face, and says, 'Look here, now, if you give me one word out of your head, I'll smash yer face in.'. . . I tell ye, they sees it ain't no play, when I gets hold" (*UTC*, 70–71). Crafts's slaveholder, discussing his financial losses trading women into sexual slavery in the New Orleans market, comments, "[G]ood-looking wenches . . . are a deal sight worse to manage than men—every way more skittish and skeery. Then it don't do to cross them much; or if you do they'll cut up the devil, and like as anyhow break their necks or pine themselves to skeletons" (*TBN*, 104). Making his point, he tells Trappe about Louise, "the freshest and fairest in the gang, [who] actually jumped into the river when she found that her child was irretrievably gone"(*TBN*, 104–105). This is reminiscent of the death of Stowe's Lucy who, learning that her baby had been sold, drowned herself (*UTC*, 135–137). Both fictional characters testify to unnumbered slave suicides and prefigure the historic 1856 case in which Margaret Garner killed her daughter to save her from a life in slavery. (A century later, Toni Morrison's *Beloved* immortalized the tragic mother.)[4]

Crafts is also like Stowe in presenting variants of the stock character of the Tragic Mulatto, a pathetic white-skinned figure earlier portrayed in Lydia Maria Child's influential fiction, "The Quadroons," as a mixed-race woman who adores her white male betrayer. An instant stereotype, the Tragic Mulatto spawned many variants, including Stowe's Cassy, who at the death of her master-father had been bought and abandoned by the white man she loved (*UTC*, 371 ff). Cassy always knew she was not white, but in Crafts's novel, Hannah's young mistress is one of the numerous Tragic Mulattos in American fiction who reach adulthood before learning—to their horror—that they are not white and they are not free. Telling her story, Crafts makes use of the device of the baby-switch (which Mark Twain will later include in *The Tragedy of Pudd'nhead Wilson*). Hannah's mistress, who in infancy was substituted for her owner's dead babe, remains ignorant of her origins until they are revealed by the evil Trappe.[5]

Unlike most Tragic Mulattos, however, Hannah's mistress does not leave the country or die before she actually marries into a prestigious aristocratic family. When we first meet her, she is already the wife of the master of Lindendale. At her first appearance, Hannah—like the devoted slaves of plantation fiction—adores her. Later, learning of Trappe's threats, she advises her mistress to escape and agrees to run with her—not as her servant, but as "a very dear sister" (*TBN*, 48). Still later, when they are discovered, Hannah's central concern is not for herself, but for her mistress. At first glance, her comment that "even my strong desire for freedom, now become the object of my life, could not have induced me to abandon her," reads like the exclamation of a devoted slave in plantation fiction (*TBN*, 72). But here the mistress is not a free "white" woman, but a "black" slave. What we are seeing is not the affinity of gender bridging the gulf of "race" and of condition, but the sisterhood of two women, both nominally "black" and both enslaved.

Hannah's mistress is not the only Tragic Mulatto in Crafts's book, and the plotline concerning Trappe is not its only plot line involving this stereotyped figure. Lizzy's story of Cosgrove's harem—which in dramatizing a jealous wife discarded for her husband's slave favorites presents a recurrent theme in black writing—includes a series of Tragic Mulatto figures. When Cosgrove's imperious English wife, outraged at discovering her husband's harem, demands that his light-skinned concubines and their children be sold, one of the women kills her baby and herself. Still later, Mrs. Cosgrove searches out another Tragic Mulatto, "a beautiful woman . . . with two children, twins, and a near alike a two cherries at her breast," whom her husband sends away and shelters (*TBN*, 180–181). (Although we are told the end of the story about the jealous Mrs. Cosgrove, we never learn what happened to Evelyn and her twins.)[6]

But Hannah, Crafts's narrator, is the most important potential Tragic Mulatto in the book. She, however, does not follow the stereotypical pattern—although when bought by Saddler, she is threatened with sale as a sexual slave, like other Tragic Mulattos. Nor does *The Bondwoman's Narrative* present her as a pathetic "mixed-race" protagonist whose "black blood" prevents her from the "white" life to which she aspires. On the contrary, Crafts's book offers an early instance of the portrayal in fiction of "passing" in which the "black" protagonist rejects the possibility of becoming "white." Here a light-skinned "black" woman uses her color to escape, first with her adored light-skinned mistress, then—after cross-dressing—with the dark Jacob and his sister, and finally, with Hetty's help, traveling north as a "white" lady. Once safely in the North, however, Hannah rejects whiteness, asserts her African heritage, and makes her home in a vibrant black community.[7]

Like *Uncle Tom's Cabin*'s Cassy and Emmeline, who transformed an attic into a weapon to frighten the superstitious Legree and later into a hiding place, Hannah, too, hides in a garret. There she finds a suit of clothes that enables her to masquerade as a man (*UTC*, 408, 415 ff). By including cross-dressing as a means of escape, both Stowe and Crafts suggest the example of Ellen Craft. (Indeed, it is possible that the author of *The Bondwoman's Narrative* chose the name "Crafts" as an homage to her.) Echoing Stowe, whose little Harry escaped dressed in girls' clothing, Crafts shows Hannah fleeing while masquerading as a man. In addition, she tells of Mrs. Wright's effort to save her friend (another Ellen) by dressing her as a boy. As literary historian Werner Sollors points out, in such instances, "one cultural boundary [gender] often gets crossed in conjunction with another one [race].[8]

Also like *Uncle Tom's Cabin*, *The Bondwoman's Narrative* includes a number of stereotypical African American characters. Describing the people crowding Charlotte and William's wedding, Crafts writes: "Queer looking old men, whose black faces withered and puckered contrasted strangely with their white beards and hair, fat portly dames whose ebony complexions were set off by turbans of flaming red, boys, girls, and an abundance of babies . . . all flaunting in finery and gay clothes of rainbow colors" (*TBN*, 119). Hannah derides the superstitions of the slaves and—echoing plantation fiction—sketches the comic drunken "old Jo, a negro, who loved above all things to indulge in strong portions of brandy." When we first meet him, Jo thinks he has seen a ghost and is in "the most ludicrous state of terror conceivable His eyes, large and glaring, seemed actually starting from their sockets, his teeth chattered and his whole frame trembled as with the ague," and she finds humor in his account to the other slaves of "his night's ghostly visitant" (*TBN*, 133). In a comic scene recalling Stowe's Sam, who regaled his fellow slaves with his confounding of Eliza's slavecatchers, Hannah notes the "ludicrous countenances of the auditors as they were variously excited by fear, wonder and apprehension" (*TBN*, 138; *UTC*, 80–82).

And like Stowe, Craft shows slaves who are not comical, but corrupt. The people at the Wheelers' North Carolina plantation claim that privileged light-skinned Hannah betrayed the mistress's secret, and they delight in witnessing her degradation. Hannah writes that when she was sent to the slave quarter, the slaves "regarded me with curiosity as I entered, grinned with malicious satisfaction that I had been brought down to their level, and made some remarks at my expense. . . . [O]ne of the woman arose, seized me by the hair, and without ceremony dragged me to the ground, gave me a furious kick and made use of highly improper and indecent language" (*TBN*, 209). Similarly, Stowe had commented that when Cassy was sent to do fieldwork, "there was much looking and turning of heads, and a smothered yet apparent exultation among the miserable, ragged, half-starved creatures by whom she was surrounded"(*UTC*, 360).

Not all of the slaves in *The Bondwoman's Narrative*, however, are comic or malicious. Charlotte is an exemplary woman—so exemplary that Hannah, considering whether she should reveal her friend's escape plan, "began to question the use, or necessity, or even the expediency of my instituting an espionage on the actions of one every way my equal, perhaps my superior"(*TBN*, 136).

Later Crafts portrays Jacob—described as "a black man" she encounters in the woods—as compassionate and courageous as he cares for his sick sister, mourns her death, then braves the wilderness to escape (*TBN*, 215).

Despite its many echoes of Stowe's novel, *The Bondwoman's Narrative* is importantly unlike *Uncle Tom's Cabin* in that it does not present an extended discussion of the differences between the "races." Although Crafts praises Mrs. Henry's "hands white and soft and beautiful" and little Anna's "white beautiful arms," she does not echo Stowe's overtly racist description of Topsy and Little Eva (*TBN*, 125, 129).

"There stood the two children, representatives of the two extremes of society. The fair, high-bred child, with her golden head, her deep eyes, her spiritual, noble brow, and prince-like movements; and her black, keen, subtle, cringing, yet acute neighbor. They stood the representatives of their races. The Saxon, born of ages of cultivation, command, education, physical and moral eminence; the Afric, born of ages of oppression, submission, ignorance, toil, and vice!" (*UTC*, 254).

The omission of such racist comments is significant. *The Bondwoman's Narrative* does not, like *Uncle Tom's Cabin*, present a rigid color scheme in which the black people display simplicity, docility, and an aptitude to repose on a superior mind and rest on a higher power, while the "mixed race" characters display the strength of their white fathers and the sensitivity of their black mothers.

The episode presenting Mrs. Wheeler in blackface dramatizes the distinction between the treatment of color in *The Bondwoman's Narrative* and in *Uncle Tom's Cabin*. After Hannah's vain, capricious mistress, Mrs. Wheeler, sends Hannah shopping for an Italian Medicated Powder for her complexion and carefully applies the makeup, she leaves to solicit a prospective patron for a position for her husband. When she returns two hours later, she is apparently a black woman. Unaware of her transformed color, but distressed by abuse she has just received, she reports on her interview. When she identified herself as Wheeler's wife, she says, the prospective patron and his friends snickered, "by courtesy, perhaps." They then announced "That it was not customary to bestow offices on colored people . . . that would be very unconstitutionally indeed" (*TBN*, 168). Seeing her, Hannah recalls reading that the medicated face powder, when combined with the fumes of a smelling bottle, could temporarily "blacken the skin" (*TBN*, 166). Soon all of Washington is abuzz with Mrs. Wheeler's humiliation, which becomes a topic of gossip from the White House to the tea tables. Crafts writes that "it was even broached among milliners that black for the time being should be fashionable style." "Even kitchens and cellars," she continues, "grew merry and chatty over it Faces black by nature were puckered with excessive exultation that one had become so by artificial means" (*TBN*, 169–170).

Nothing in *Uncle Tom's Cabin* is comparable to this episode. Stowe had dramatized the foolery of Sam and Andy as they frustrated Haley's attempt to catch Eliza, but even her active imagination never portrayed black people finding humor in the spectacle of a vain white woman in blackface. African American authors of the period, however, do play with the notion. In *Our Nig*, Fredo imagines the wicked Miss Mary in hell, where "she'll be as black as I am," and then chuckles, "Wouldn't mistress be mad to see her a nigger!" In *The Gairies and Their Friends*, the wicked Mr. Stevens—who has been mistaken for black, has been attacked, had his face smeared with tar and his lips "swelled to the size . . . [of] a Congo negro"—is set upon by a second group of racist toughs who streak his features with lime, laughing that they are "making a white man of him."[9] In *The Bondwoman's Narrative*, Crafts underscores the importance of this blackface incident by using it to move her plot forward. Because Hannah laughs remembering the event, she is accused of gossiping about it and is condemned to the slave quarter and to the brutal Bill—creating the crisis that triggers her final run for freedom.

At times, *The Bondwoman's Narrative* reads like nineteenth-century sentimental novels—fictional works that critic Nina Baym explains "are written by women, are addressed to women, and tell one particular story about women"; and *Uncle Tom's Cabin*, critic Jane Thompson writes, "is the *summa theologica* of nineteenth-century America's religion of domesticity, a brilliant redaction of the culture's favorite story about itself—salvation through motherly love."[10] It is true that, like Stowe, Crafts privileges motherhood. But in its treatment of religion, *The Bondwoman's Narrative* differs significantly from *Uncle Tom's Cabin*—although black Jacob, like Stowe's George Harris, has no faith in God or hope of heaven, and although Saddler, like Stowe's narrator, estimates the financial value of a slave's religion: " Give me a handsome wench, pleasant and good-tempered, willing to conform herself to circumstances, and anxious to please, without any notions of virtue, religion, or anything of that sort. Such are by far the most marketable" (*TBN*, 105–106). *Uncle Tom's Cabin* is a profoundly religious novel, fueled by the conviction that what matters most is the Hereafter. Again and again, it dramatizes the moral choices white Americans must make in response to the 1850 Fugitive Slave Law. But in *The Bondwoman's Narrative*, religion, while present, is not fundamental. Its central concern is not with the immortal souls of the characters, but with the here and now, and it focuses on the dilemmas slavery presents to its slave protagonist.

Crafts does, however, characteristically open her chapters with quotations from the Old Testament, and in her preface, she cites "the hand of Providence," which gives "to the righteous the reward of their works, and to the wicked the fruit of their doings" (*TBN*, 3).[11] Early on, she writes that good Aunt Hetty and Uncle Siah, who school Hannah both in literacy and in Christianity, "led me to the foot of the Cross" (TBN, 10). Later she is able to comfort her despairing new mistress by "reading portions of the Holy Scripture," and jailed in a dungeon, Hannah finds "comfort" thinking of God's love (*TBN*, 54, 79–80). Still later, when the evil Trappe advises her that, as a slave, "submission and obedience must be the Alpha and Omega of all your actions," Hannah ironically comments that his "advice was probably well adapted to one in my condition, that is if I could have forgotten God, truth, honor and my own soul" (*TBN*, 108).

Although Hannah refuses to run away with Charlotte and William—he accuses her of "hugging the chain"—and twice acknowledges herself as a runaway slave, ultimately she testifies that her religion teaches her what the slave narrators testify that it taught them: to take her liberty (*TBN*, 142, 69, 116–117). When she is faced with Mrs. Wheeler's demand that she live with the brutalized Bill, it is Hannah's sense of her God-given selfhood that prompts her decision to run away: "It seemed that rebellion would be a virtue, that duty to myself and my God actually required it" (*TBN*, 206). Opening her Bible to the story of Jacob's escape from Esau, she concludes that living with Bill would be "a crime against nature" and plans her escape (*TBN*, 207). Like the slave narrators, she echoes America's founders in linking religion with freedom and in asserting that resistance to tyranny is obedience to God. This was indeed the stance of Stowe's mulatto George Harris. But it was not that of her black Uncle Tom, who in the face of tyranny practiced Christian resignation and died a martyr—a portrayal that prompted black activists and their white allies to criticize Stowe's novel from the beginning.[12]

The slave narrators routinely pointed to the contradiction between America as the land of the free and America as a slavocracy, and Crafts, too, comments on the profound irony that "without having committed any crime," she is jailed in "one of the legal fortresses of a country celebrated throughout the world for the freedom, equality, and magnanimity of its laws" (*TBN*, 76). Stowe's aristocratic St. Clare argues, "the American planter is 'only doing, in another form, what the English aristocracy and capitalists are doing by the lower classes'; that is, I take it, *appropriating* them, body and bone, soul and spirit, to their use and convenience" (*UTC*, 237). In *The Bondwoman's Narrative*, Crafts's black female slave narrator, too, moves beyond a condemnation of chattel slavery to a denunciation of all systems of exploitation. She attacks

"that false system which bestows on position wealth or power the consideration only due to a man. And this system is not confined to any one place or
country, or condition. It extends through all grades and classes of society
from the highest to the lowest. It bans poor but honest people with the contemptuous appellation of 'vulgar.' It subjects others under certain circumstances
to a lower link in the chain of being than that occupied by a horse" (*TBN,* 200).

At its conclusion, *The Bondwoman's Narrative,* like *Uncle Tom's Cabin,* ties up all
loose ends. Crafts recounts the killing of the evil Trappe by the sons of yet another of his Tragic Mulatto victims, and then—like Stowe—pictures a generational family once fragmented by slavery now united in freedom. Where
Stowe had rounded out her story with the restoration of Mme de Thoux to
her brother George Harris, and of Cassy to her daughter Eliza, Crafts writes
the reunion of Hannah with both her long-lost mother and with her old
friends Charlotte and William. Stowe had not, however, ended her book with
this sketch of a restored family. True to the religious roots of her novel, Stowe,
in a penultimate chapter, advised her white readers, whether in the North or
the South, to act on the slavery question in such a way that they "feel right."
"See," she exhorted, "to your sympathies in this matter! Are they in harmony
with the sympathies of Christ?" (*UTC,* 452). Then, after urging the expatria-
tion of African Americans to Africa (in opposition to the abolitionists, who
protested colonization), she closed with an appeal to the "Church of Christ"
to lead the nation and to avoid God's righteous wrath through "repentance,
justice and mercy" (*UTC,* 456). *The Bondwoman's Narrative* echoes neither Stowe's
colonizationist political program nor her plea for religious renewal but instead
ends with its fugitive slave protagonist teaching black children in New Jersey.
Although the sensation created by *Uncle Tom's Cabin* certainly helped inspire
Hannah Crafts's novel, and Stowe's best-seller certainly helped shape it, *The
Bondwoman's Narrative* makes a very different statement about slavery and racism
in nineteenth-century America.

Notes

1. Harriet Beecher Stowe's *Uncle Tom's Cabin* was serialized in the *National Era,* June 3,
1851–April 2, 1852, and published between covers in 1852. Parenthetical references in my
text labeled UTC refer to the edition edited by Jean Fagan Yellin and published by Oxford
University Press in 1998. Parenthetical references in my text labeled TBN refer to Hannah
Crafts, *The Bondwoman's Narrative,* ed. Henry Louis Gates, Jr. (New York: Warner Books, 2002).
For responses to Stowe, see Jean Ashton, *Harriet Beecher Stowe: A Reference Guide* (Boston: G. K.
Hall, 1977), 137–138. J. W. Page's *Uncle Robin in His Cabin in Virginia, and Tom Without One in
Boston* (Richmond, 1853), and W. L. G. Smith's *Life at the South, or Uncle Tom's Cabin As It Is* (Buf-
falo, 1852) are both included in *Catalogue of the Library of John H. Wheeler, the Historian of North*

Carolina, Comprising American History and Biography, Slavery, Civil War and Confederate Publications, Indians, Mormons, Quakers, Masonry, Scarce and Valuable Pamphlets and Miscellaneous Books to be sold at Auction . . . April 24, 1882 . . . by Bangs & Co . . . New York. It is not clear that Wheeler acquired these spin-offs shortly after they were published in the early 1850s, when the woman who wrote as Hannah Crafts was apparently in his household. When catalogued long after the Civil War, his collection also included Stowe's *Key to Uncle Tom's Cabin* (Boston, 1853) and three discussions of her book: A. Woodword's "A Review of *Uncle Tom's Cabin*" (Cincinnati, 1853); Rev. E. J. Steaves, *Notes on Uncle Tom's Cabin: A Logical Answer to Its Allegations, etc.* (Philadelphia, 1853); and the later Nassau W. Sanor, *American Slavery: A Reprint of an Article on "Uncle Tom's Cabin" and of Mr. Sumner's Speech of May, 1856* (London).

2. *David Walker's Appeal, in Four Articles: Together with a Preamble, to the Coloured Citizens of the World, but in particular, and very expressly, to those of The United States of America* (Boston, 1829); Herbert Aptheker, *Nat Turner's Slave Rebellion* (New York: Humanities Press, 1966); *The Liberator*, Boston, 1831–1865; *Maria W. Stewart: America's First Black Woman Political Writer: Essays and Speeches*, ed. Marilyn Richardson (Bloomington: Indiana University Press, 1987); Frederick Douglass, *Narrative* (Boston, 1845); *Narrative of the Sufferings of Lewis and Milton Clarke* (Boston, 1846); Josiah Henson, *The Life of Josiah Henson* (Boston, 1849); Henry Bibb, *Narrative of the Life and Adventures of Henry Bibb* (New York, 1849); [Richard Hildreth], *The Slave, or Memoirs of Archy Moore*, 2 vols. (Boston, 1836); Gustave de Beaumont's *Marie, ou l'Esclavage aux Etats-Unis*, first published in France, appeared in an American edition in 1838; L. Maria Child, *An Appeal in Favor of That Class of Americans Called Africans* (New York, 1836), and "The Quadroons," *The Liberty Bell* (Boston, 1842), republished in Child, *Fact and Fiction* (New York, 1846). Both Douglass's and the Clarkes' narratives are included in the 1882 catalogue of Wheeler's library; see note 1, above.

3. J. Hector St. John de Crevcoeur, "Letter IX," *Letters From an American Farmer* (1782). For the gothic, see Teresa Goddu, *Gothic America: Narrative, History and Nation* (New York: Columbia University Press, 1997).

4. After her capture Margaret Garner, a Kentucky slave who had escaped to Ohio with her husband and their four children, tried to kill her children to prevent them from being re-enslaved; she succeeded in killing one. Garner was sent back to Kentucky, then sold further south. See "The Garner Fugitive Slave Case," *Mississippi Valley Historical Review* 40 (June 1953): 47–66; Toni Morrison, *Beloved* (1987).

5. Lydia Maria Child, "The Quadroons," note 1, above. For the Tragic Mulatto figure, see Werner Sollors, *Neither Black nor White yet Both* (New York: Oxford University Press, 1997), especially 2221–2245; for the device of the baby-switch, see Sollors, *Neither Black nor White yet Both*, 436, note 85.

6. For the figure of the jealous mistress, see Minrose C. Gwin, "Green-eyed Monsters of the Slavocracy: Jealous Mistresses in Two Slave Narratives," *Conjuring: Black Women, Fiction, and Literary Tradition*, ed. Marjorie Pryse and Hortense J. Spillers (Bloomington: Indiana University Press, 1985), 39–52; and Nell Painter, "The Journal of Ella Gertrude Clanton Thomas: A Testament of Wealth, Loss, and Adultery," *Southern History Across the Color Line* (Chapel Hill: University of North Carolina Press, 2002), 40–92. For the thoughts of a slaveholder's wife in 1861, see *Mary Chesnut's Civil War*, ed. C. Vann Woodward (New Haven: Yale University Press, 1981), 29–31.

7. For the theme of passing, see Sollors, *Neither Black nor White yet Both*, 247–284; and M. Guilia Fabi, *Passing and the Rise of the African American Novel* (Urbana: University of Illinois Press, 2001).

8. William Craft, *Running a Thousand Miles for Freedom* (1861); for cross-dressing, see Marjorie Garber, *Vested Interests* (New York: Routledge, 1992), and Sollors, *Neither Black nor White yet Both*, note 80, 502–503.

9. Harriet E. Wilson, *Our Nig*, (New York: Random House, 1983), 107. Frank J. Webb, *The Garies and Their Friends* (1857; New York: Arno and the New York Times, 1969), 188, 191; thanks to Carla Peterson for this reference.

10. For sentimental fiction, see, for example, Nina Baym, *Woman's Fiction: A Guide to Novels by and about Women in America, 1820–1870* (Ithaca: Cornell University Press, 1978), 22; Jane Tompkins, *Sensational Designs* (New York: Oxford University Press, 1985) 125, 126, 130; Shirley Samuels, "Introduction," *The Culture of Sentiment* (New York: Oxford University Press, 1992), 3–8.

11. The epigraphs, which are not consistent, include both biblical quotations and lines from contemporary writers. Opening Chapter 16, Crafts, like many antislavery women, cites the biblical heroine Esther, who saved her people—although quoting from Esther 7:4 she strangely omits the reference to "bondwoman."

12. Writing of *Uncle Tom's Cabin* in *Frederick Douglass' Paper* of May 20, 1852, the African American professor William G. Allen commented: "[I]f any man had too much piety, Uncle Tom was that man. . . . I do not advocate revenge, but simply resistance to tyrants, if it need be, to the death." On March 26, 1852, William Lloyd Garrison had queried in *The Liberator*, "Is there one law of submission and non-resistance for the black man, and another law of rebellion and conflict for the white man?"

9

The Bondwoman's *Escape*

Hannah Crafts Rewrites the First Play
Published by an African American

SHELLEY FISHER FISHKIN

The author of *The Bondwoman's Narrative* was an engaged and appreciative reader whose reading left an indelible mark on the manuscript she wrote. Indeed, one of the most intriguing aspects of the book is its author's "sampling" or "extraction of sizeable quantities of text from several well-known contemporary texts," as Hollis Robbins puts it in her essay in this volume, "most notably Charles Dickens's *Bleak House* (1852) and Walter Scott's *Rob Roy* (1818)." Jean Fagan Yellin argues in her essay in this book that Stowe's hugely successful *Uncle Tom's Cabin* (1852) served as a viable model for Crafts, as well, while William Andrews explores resonances between Crafts's book and other sentimental novels, on the one hand, and slave narratives, on the other. Yet this list of texts on which Crafts probably drew neglects a literary work that was neither fiction nor autobiography, but which nonetheless seems to have had a big influence on this work of autobiographical fiction. I suggest that Crafts's manuscript—possibly the "first novel written by a female fugitive slave, and perhaps the first novel written by any black woman at all"[1]—was influenced profoundly by the first play published by an African American.

William Wells Brown's *The Escape, or, A Leap for Freedom*, was published in Boston in 1858. *The Escape* was not Brown's first play, but it was the first of his plays to be published.[2] A prominent anti-slavery lecturer, Brown was also well known by this time as the author of the slave narrative *Narrative of William W. Brown, an American Slave, Written by Himself* (London, 1849), the novel *Clotel; or, The President's Daughter* (London, 1853), and the memoir *The American Fugitive in Europe: Sketches of Places and People Abroad* (Boston, Cleveland and New York,

1855). Brown had written his first drama early in 1856 (a satire on a pro-slavery tract), which Brown eventually called *Experience, or, How to Give a Northern Man a Backbone.* Although Brown frequently read the play to audiences over the next year, he never published it, and no copies are extant.[3] He probably first read *The Escape* in public in Salem, Ohio, in February 1857. He also read the play "before a large audience" in the Elyria, Ohio, courthouse on April 4 of that year. The newspaper reported that "No description which we could give would convey an adequate idea of the beauties of this Drama. It must be heard to be appreciated."[4] Brown read *The Escape* in Auburn, New York, later that month, and the local paper called it "an able production" that "was rendered with excellent effect."[5] After he read the play the next day in Seneca Falls, New York, the *Seneca Falls Courier* charged him with demonstrating "a dramatic talent possessed by few who have, under the best instruction, made themselves famous on the stage," and went on to say,

> If you want a good laugh, go and hear him. If you want instruction or information upon the most interesting question of the day, go and hear him. You cannot fail to be pleased. So highly pleased were those who heard it in Auburn, that twenty-eight of the leading men of the city, over their own signatures, extended an invitation to him, through the Daily Advertiser, to return and repeat the Drama ... Such a compliment entitles MR. BROWN to crowded houses wherever he goes.[6]

During 1857 and 1858, Brown read the play in Philadelphia, Boston, Lynn, and Utica, as well as a range of other cities throughout eastern Massachusetts, eastern Pennsylvania, and New Jersey. Brown wrote Marius R. Robinson, the editor of the *Anti-Slavery Bugle* and head of the American Anti-Slavery Society in Ohio that people who "would not give a cent in an anti-slavery meeting" "will pay to hear" *The Escape.*[7] Brown firmly believed that drama had its role to play in the struggle.

It is possible that Hannah Crafts, who evidently settled in New Jersey, heard Brown read the play on one of these occasions. Perhaps she was present in the "large audience" who heard him read one of his plays aloud in Temperance Hall in Trenton, New Jersey, on November 8, 1858.[8] Given the public discussion Brown's readings prompted, she is likely to have heard of it. Whether or not she heard Brown present *The Escape,* however, Crafts might easily have read the play after its publication in 1858. There are striking parallels between Brown's play and two of the most distinctive features of Crafts's book: (1) the characterization of the selfish, hypocritical, and petulant slaveholder's wife, "Mrs. Wheeler," and (2) the specifics of the interpolated narrative of chapters 14 and 15, which Crafts calls "Lizzy's Story." But if Crafts's borrowings, or bricolage, are noteworthy, her departures from Brown's play are interesting, as well, and demonstrate the imaginative strategies by which she made a character and a plot penned by another fugitive slave her own.

Before focusing on the larger, more substantive parallels, it is worth noting that a slave named Hannah is a central character in Brown's play. Since Henry Louis Gates, Jr., has suggested that "Hannah" may be a pen name for the author of *The Bondwoman's Narrative*, it is possible that on a subliminal level, at least, the author of *The Bondwoman's Narrative* may have had Brown's Hannah in mind. In Brown's play, as in Crafts's novel, in addition to being ordered about by an imperious mistress, Hannah finds herself pushed to marry a slave she doesn't love.

Generally charged with having utilized a number of stock characters in the play (most of whom have no counterparts in Crafts's book), William Wells Brown is credited with having created one truly original character when he penned the vain, hypocritical termagant "Mrs. Gaines."[9] The parallels between *The Escape* and the *Bondwoman's Narrative* suggest that Brown's "Mrs. Gaines" may well be a progenitor of Crafts's unforgettable "Mrs. Wheeler."

Mrs. Gaines's preposterous selfishness is apparent from her first exchange with her husband, Dr. Gaines, an equally selfish character who hopes that "the fever and ague, which is now taking hold of the people, will give me more patients."[10] Mrs. Gaines opines,

> Yes, I would be glad to see it more sickly here, so that your business might prosper. But we are always unfortunate. Every body here seems to be in good health, and I am afraid that they'll keep so. However, we must hope for the best. We must trust in the Lord. Providence may possibly send some disease among us for our benefit.[11]

Proud of her ancestry, Mrs. Gaines is irritated with her husband for having invited a neighbor who just enlisted his services at $500 per annum to come call on them with his wife, the daughter of a tanner ("You must remember, my dear, that I was born with a silver spoon in my mouth. The blood of the Wyleys runs in my veins"). She is also vain and self-pitying as she gives orders to her slaves:

Enter HANNAH, L.

Mrs. G. Go, Hannah, and tell Dolly to kill a couple of fat pullets, and to put the biscuit to rise. I expect brother Pinchen here this afternoon, and I want everything in order. Hannah, Hannah, tell Melinda to come here.

[Exit HANNAH, L.]

We mistresses do have a hard time in this world; I don't see why the Lord
should have imposed such heavy duties upon us poor mortals. Well, it can't
last always. I long to leave this wicked world, and go home to glory.

Enter MELINDA

I am to have company this afternoon, Melinda. I expect brother Pinchen here,
and I want every thing in order. Go and get one of my new caps, with the
lace border, and get out my scalloped-bottomed dimity petticoat, and when
you go out, tell Hannah to clean the white-handled knives and see that not a
speck is on them; for I want every thing as it should be while brother Pinchen
is here . . . [12]

Mrs. Gaines's hypocrisy reaches a peak during her lunch with Mr. Pinchen,
as Hannah clears away the breakfast table. The Rev. Pinchen is sharing his experiences as a minister with Mrs. Gaines, who tells him that "It always does my
soul good to hear religious experience. It draws me nearer and nearer to the
Lord's side."[13] After one of Mr. Pinchen's long stories, Mrs. Gaines comments,

Oh, how interesting . . . . And what power there is in the gospel! God's children
are very lucky. Oh, it is so sweet to sit here and listen to such good news from
God's people! You Hannah, what are you standing there listening for, and ne-
glecting your work? Never mind, my lady, I'll whip you when I am done here.
Go at your work this moment, you lazy huzzy! Never mind, I'll whip you well.
[*Aside.*] Come, do go on, brother Pinchen, with your godly conversation. It is so
sweet! It draws me nearer and nearer to the Lord's side.[14]

After Mr. Pinchen describes a dream in which he "entered the celestial empire" and "saw many old and familiar faces," Hannah asks whether he saw her
"ole man Ben up dar in hebben." Mrs. Gaines responds,

No, of course brother Pinchen didn't go among the blacks. What are you asking questions for? Never mind, my lady, I'll whip you when I'm done here. I'll
skin you from head to foot. [*Aside.*] Do go on with your heavenly conversation,
brother Pinchen; it does my very soul good. This is indeed a precious moment
for me.[15]

After Mr. Pinchen leaves, Mrs. Gaines tells Hannah to

Get the cowhide and follow me to the cellar, and I'll whip you well for aggra-
vating me as you have to-day. It seems as if I can never sit down to take a little

comfort with the Lord, without you crossing me. The devil always puts it into your head to disturb me, just when I am trying to serve the Lord. I've no doubt but that I'll miss going to heaven on your account. But I'll whip you well before I leave this world, that I will. Get the cowhide and follow me to the cellar.[16]

Despite her irritation with Hannah, Mrs. Gaines is resistant when she learns that her husband wants to sell her:

Mrs. G. Now, Dr. Gaines, I am astonished and surprised that you should think of such a thing. You know what trouble I've had in training up Hannah for a house servant, and now that I've got her so that she knows my ways, you want to sell her . . .

Dr. G. . . . I can spare Sam, and don't like to separate him from his wife; and I thought if you could let Hannah go, I'd sell them both. I don't like to separate husbands from their wives.

Mrs. G. Now, gentlemen, that's just the way with my husband. He thinks more about the welfare and comfort of his slaves, than he does of himself or his family. I am sure you need not feel so bad at the thought of separating Sam from Hannah. They've only been married eight months, and their attachment can't be very strong in that time. Indeed, I shall be glad if you do sell Sam, for then I'll make Hannah *jump the broomstick* with Cato, and I'll have them both here under my eye. I never will again let one of my house servants marry a field hand—never! For when night comes on, the servants are off to the quarters, and I have to holler and holler enough to split my throat before I can make them hear . . . .

The "Hannah" who narrates Crafts's *Bondwoman's Narrative* introduces us to Mrs. Wheeler in Chapter 12, "A New Mistress." She finds herself in Mrs. Wheeler's employ after she arranges the woman's hair to her satisfaction. Mrs. Wheeler shares Mrs. Gaines's vanity, petulance, and demanding nature. "There seemed no end to her vanities, and whims, and caprices,"[17] Hannah writes. Mrs. Wheeler proves to be as insensitive to her slaves' need for sleep as Mrs. Gaines was:

It never seemed to occur to [Mrs. Wheeler] that a person could be ill or weary, though all the time complaining of feebleness herself. Sometimes in the dead hours of night she would call me out of bed to get her some kind of candy or confectionary. Then she would call for water to take away the saccharine taste; and then again for more candy. Sometimes it would be for salt, and at others vinegar; there was no telling . . .

When Mrs. Gaines had to "holler and holler" at night to rouse a sleeping slave in the quarters, it was probably for a similarly frivolous request. And like Mrs. Gaines, Mrs. Wheeler is given to accusing her husband of caring more about his slaves than about her. (At one point she lashes out at Mr. Wheeler with the comment, "Slaves generally are far preferable to wives in husbands' eyes.")

Mrs. Gaines and Mrs. Wheeler have more in common than their querulous and imperious natures; they undergo analogous comic physical humiliations, as well. Mrs. Gaines in Brown's play and Mrs. Wheeler in Crafts's novel each receive their comeuppance in a scene that involves a physical transformation meant to strike readers as both hilarious and just. At the climax of Act III of Brown's play (following Mrs. Gaines's demand that Melinda, her husband's favorite slave, drink poison or be stabbed) is a physical struggle between Melinda and Mrs. Gaines, described in the following action:

[They fight; MELINDA sweeps off MRS GAINES' cap, combs and curls.]
Curtain falls.

The image of this haughty mistress, who had been so particular about ordering her slave to get one of her "new caps, with the lace border" left not only capless but wigless in this scene—must have evoked much laughter in Brown's audiences, contributing to the play's great appeal. (Henry C. Wright, who had been present when Brown read *The Escape* in Utica, New York, in September 1858, reported that "The audience listened to his reading—or rather, *reciting*— with deepest interest, and the only regret seemed to be, that it was too short, though the delivery of it occupied an hour and a quarter."[18]) In *The Bondwoman's Narrative*, Mrs. Wheeler's mortification stems, like that of Mrs. Gaines's, from her own vanity and self-importance. To oblige Mr. Wheeler's request that she visit a prominent politician to beg a political appointment for him, Mrs. Wheeler calls for "my rich antique moiré, and purple velvent [velvet] mantilla," and orders Hannah to dust her with a generous application of her "beautifying powder"—a rare, imported cosmetic which she had secured by dispatching Hannah to trek through the rainy mud-soaked streets of Washington to purchase it. But two hours after departing for the politician's house in her carriage, Mrs. Wheeler returns, oblivious to the fact now, as when she saw the politician, that she is in blackface. The special powder, when combined with the fumes of her smelling salts, had turned her skin black. In these scenes of supreme physical embarrassment, both insufferable slave mistresses get their just deserts.

We meet another slave mistress, a Mrs. Cosgrove, in "Lizzy's Story," Chapters 14 and 15 in *The Bondwoman's Narrative* (Lizzy is a slave who worked with Hannah at Lindendale, and who brings her up to date on events that transpired since she left). Mrs. Cosgrove, Lindendale's new mistress, has much in common with Mrs. Gaines in *The Escape*, as well. Like Mrs. Gaines, Mrs. Cosgrove is outraged by the fact that her husband has slave "favorites." Like Mrs. Gaines, she demands that her husband sell these beautiful rivals, and her husband seems to oblige. However, like Mr. Gaines, Mr. Cosgrove sequesters one of his favorites in a small, isolated cottage some miles from his home instead of selling her. Mrs. Cosgrove, like Mrs. Gaines, grows suspicious and vows to ferret out the truth. Both women determine the location of the rival, and both women (accomplished horsewomen) set off on horseback to expose and punish her in a fit of jealous rage. Both women are injured by the horseback ride. There are, to be sure, differences between the two stories. Whereas in *The Escape*, the master claims to have sold his favorite slave, in Lizzy's Story, it is the slave mistress who sends the favorite out of her house. In Brown's play, the mistress's injuries from the horseback ride turn out not to be serious (since someone had borrowed her side-saddle, she "had to ride ten miles bare-back" and "can scarcely walk" when she arrives at the remote cottage),[19] while in Lizzy's Story, the mistress's injuries from the ride lead to her eventual death. But the basic structural elements—a lying husband who sequesters a supposedly banished favorite slave in a remote cottage, and a viciously jealous outraged wife injured by the horseback ride she takes to confront her rival—are the same.[20]

Given Crafts's tendency to borrow characters, images, tropes, and plot devices from Dickens, Scott, Stowe, and others, it is not surprising that she found elements of use to her in Brown's *Escape*, one of the most discussed literary achievements of an African American in the late 1850s. However, in Crafts's hands, elements she may have borrowed from Brown get shaped in new ways.

Although Brown's Mrs. Gaines and Crafts's Mrs. Wheeler seem to be, in many respects, avatars of the same egocentric slave mistress, there are important differences in how they are presented. First of all, in *The Bondwoman's Narrative* we get not only the autocrat's edicts but also the interiority of Hannah's response to them. Whereas in Brown's play, the slave mistress's hypocrisy is exposed, the impact of that hypocrisy on her slave Hannah, forced to work for her day in and day out, is left unexplored. Hannah Crafts's attention to her own responses to Mrs. Wheeler's insults to her probity and her personhood underlines the self-serving myopia of the slave mistress and undermines the legitimacy of a system that registers the needs of the master as always superceding those of the slave. She also occasionally comments sardonically on her mistress's double standard—her tendency to condemn practices in others that she condones for herself, noting that it was funny "that Mrs. Wheeler should inveigh so loudly against office-seekers when [she]herself and [her] husband had both tried their hands at the same game."[21] In addition, Hannah

Crafts conveys the intimacy between mistress and slave in ways that were probably invisible to Brown, being a man and therefore not present when such intimacies were exchanged.

Brown, who on alternate evenings would give an anti-slavery lecture or read *The Escape*, reserved his direct social analysis for his lectures and conveyed his critiques in the play through story and song. Crafts, on the other hand, melded critical commentary on society with her fictional narrative, condemning, for example,

> that false system which bestows on position, wealth, or power the consideration only due to a man. And this system is not confined to any one place, or country, or condition. It extends through all grades and classes of society from the highest to the lowest. It bans poor but honest people with the contemptuous appellation of "vulgar." It subjects others under certain circumstances to a lower link in the chain of being than that occupied by a horse.[22]

Crafts extended the power of the stories she told about the degradations of slavery by injecting passages of general social commentary:

> The greatest curse of slavery is it's [sic] hereditary character. The father leaves to his son an inheritance of toil and misery, and his place on the fetid straw in the miserable corner, with no hope or possibility of anything better. And the son in his turn transmits the same to his offspring and thus forever.
>
> If the huts were bad, the inhabitants it seems were still worse. Degradation, neglect, and ill treatment had wrought on them its legitimate effects. All day they toil beneath the burning sun, scarcely conscious that any link exists between themselves and other portions of the human race.[23]

Crafts's willingness to inject moments of high seriousness into her novel—such as the passage quoted above—was equaled by her willingness to insert moments of high comedy.

The humiliation suffered by Mrs. Wheeler in *The Bondwoman's Narrative* is not just wittier and more distinctive than that suffered by Mrs. Gaines in *The Escape*—it is a brilliant send-up of the culture's racial prejudices. Although both Brown and Crafts elicit the reader's laughter with their comic lampoons of insensitive and obnoxious slave mistresses, Crafts gets more than fun out the venture: she gets a sharp and delicious social critique to boot. Those memorable moments in the book when a proud white slave owner finds herself being taken for black without her knowledge reveal much about the society's assumptions about race. This episode prefigures some of the ironies that will inform Twain's

1894 novel *The Tragedy of Pudd'nhead Wilson*, in which a white child (and the man he becomes) is taken for black, and a black child (and the man he becomes) is taken for white, and the society's prejudices are sardonically unmasked in the process.[24] It foreshadows the hilarious anarchy of George Schuyler's 1931 satire, *Black No More*, in which a special treatment process turns black people white and throws all of American society into chaos as a result.[25] It also looks ahead to some of the ironies of Charles Chesnutt's last novel, *The Quarry* (not published until 1999), in which a child who is first taken for white, is found to be black, but later found to be white after all, by which time he has become a "race man" totally disgusted with the white race.[26] Finally, this list of great moments of witting and unwitting racial imposture in American literature would be incomplete without mention of that wonderful episode in David Bradley's 1981 novel *The Chaneysville Incident*, in which a black man (in stolen Klan robes) is taken for white and manages to foil the Klan's efforts to lynch his friend.[27] Hannah Crafts, in short, places herself at the head of a short but distinguished line of authors who use carnivalesque inversion (of "black" and "white") and farce to disrupt the complacency of a racist status quo and to share with the reader a complicit chuckle at the comeuppance imposed on the powers-that-be. The strategy serves to undermine the legitimacy of racist ideologies and social institutions and encourages readers to distance themselves from those who spout those ideologies and uphold those institutions.

The Bondwoman's Narrative, then, is clearly richer and more complex than Brown's *Escape*. But Crafts may have drawn from *The Escape* more than a character here and a plot sequence there. The centrality of dialogue in *The Bondwoman's Narrative*, as well as some of the more theatrical elements of the novel, including, perhaps, the part played by the theatrical device of blackface makeup, may stem in part from the role that a play may have played in its inception.

Notes

1. Henry Louis Gates, Jr., Introduction to *The Bondwoman's Narrative*, by Hannah Crafts (New York: Warner Books, 2002), p. xxi.

2. "Although Brown was the first African American known to publish a play, he was not the first African American playwright. As Bernard L. Peterson, Jr. has noted, 'Although he was technically the third black American playwright of record, Brown was the first to be born in slavery, the first to write a full-length drama on the problems of American slavery, and the first to have a play published in the Untied States.'" Bernard L. Peterson, Jr., *Early Black American Playwrights and Dramatic Writers: A Biographical Directory and Catalog of Plays, Films and Broadcasting Scripts*, cited in John Ernest, Introduction to *The Escape; or, A Leap for Freedom. A Drama in Five Acts*, by William Wells Brown, Edited [1858], with an introduction by John Ernest (Knoxville: University of Tennessee Press, 2001).

3. William Edward Farrison, *William Wells Brown, Author and Reformer* (Chicago: University of Chicago Press, 1969), pp. 278–283.

4. Elyria (Ohio) *Independent Democrat*, April 7, 1857; *National Anti-Slavery Standard*, April 11, 1857, p. 3. Quoted in Farrison, *William Wells Brown*, p. 284.

5. *Auburn Daily Advertiser*, April 28, 1857, quoted in *National Anti-Slavery Standard*, May 9, 1857, p. 2, quoted in Farrison, *William Wells Brown*, p. 285.

6. *Seneca Falls Courier*, April 30, 1857, quoted in *National Anti-Slavery Standard*, May 9, 1857, p. 2, quoted in Farrison, *William Wells Brown*, p. 285. Full quote reprinted in "Opinions of the Press," in William Wells Brown, *The Escape; or, A Leap for Freedom. A Drama in Five Acts*. Edited [1858], with an introduction by John Ernest (Knoxville: University of Tennessee Press, 2001), p. 48.

7. Brown to Robinson, November 29, 1857, Schomburg Collection, quoted in Farrison, *William Wells Brown*, p. 294.

8. Brown's biographer, William Edward Farrison, writes that in November 1858, "Brown went to New Jersey and thence to eastern Pennsylvania, where he remained at least until the middle of December. He lectured in Temperance Hall in Trenton on Sunday evening, November 7, and read one of his plays in the same hall the next evening. *The Trenton Daily State Gazette and Republican* for November 9 took cognizance on its third page of the 'large audience' he had on both occasions and also remarked that 'Mr. Brown possesses a high order of intellect and is a fine orator.'" Quoted in Farrison, *William Wells Brown*.

9. Farrison, *William Wells Brown*, p. 303.

10. Brown, *The Escape*, p. 5.

11. Ibid., p. 5.

12. Ibid., p. 7.

13. Ibid., p. 12.

14. Ibid., p. 13.

15. Ibid., p. 14.

16. Ibid., p. 15.

17. Hannah Crafts, *The Bondwoman's Narrative*, ed. Henry Louis Gates, Jr. (New York: Warner Books, 2002), p. 154.

18. Henry C. Wright wrote a positive account of Brown's reading in *The Liberator* that ran in its October 8, 1858, issue, p. 163. Cited in Farrison, *William Wells Brown*, p. 305.

19. Brown, *The Escape*, pp. 28–31.

20. It is probably a mere coincidence that the portion of Lizzy's Story set in a place called "Rock Glen" parallels the series of events in *The Escape* that is introduced with the words "*Enter GLEN, L.*" Glen is Melinda's slave husband.

21. Crafts, *The Bondwoman's Narrative*, p. 157.

22. Ibid., pp. 199–200.

23. Ibid., p. 200.

24. Mark Twain, *The Tragedy of Pudd'nhead Wilson and the Comedy of Those Extraordinary Twins* (1894; reprint, with an introduction by Shelley Fisher Fishkin, foreword by Sherley Anne Williams, afterword by David L. Smith, New York: Oxford University Press, 1996).

25. George Schuyler, *Black No More* (1931; reprint, New York: Modern Library, 1999).

26. Charles W. Chesnutt. *The Quarry*, edited, with an introduction by Dean McWilliams (Princeton: Princeton University Press, 1999).

27. David Bradley, *The Chaneysville Incident* (New York: Harper & Row, 1981).

III

ANTEBELLUM CONTEXTS

10

Mrs. Henry's "Solemn Promise"
in Historical Perspective

DICKSON D. BRUCE, JR.

One of the most striking episodes in Hannah Crafts's rediscovered novel *The Bondwoman's Narrative* is that comprising chapters nine through twelve, in which Crafts tells the story of the encounter of her main character, "Hannah," with the kindly but slaveholding Henry family. Drawing on an array of sources, Crafts tells a number of stories intended to reveal the brutality of slavery. These notably include an exciting account of the marriage, sufferings, and flight of one of the Henrys' young slave women, Charlotte, and her husband, William, after their marriage is threatened by William's owner. Moreover, the episode is particularly significant as an indication of Crafts's efforts to place herself and her novel within the context of the abolitionist cause and the contemporary debates over slavery. And, though she relates a number of stories detailing the experiences of others, it is in regard to Hannah's own situation that Crafts inserts her voice into those debates in the deepest and most complex way.

The episode begins as Hannah is being conveyed south by a slave trader, Saddler, to be sold into concubinage on the New Orleans market. Saddler's horse, suddenly surprised by another wagon, bolts. Hannah and the trader are thrown from his wagon, Saddler to his death. Rescued from the remains of Saddler's wagon and awaking in the Henrys' home, Hannah, despite some trepidation, identifies herself to Mrs. Henry as a slave, "one of that miserable class." To her amazement, Mrs. Henry responds not by drawing back but, "the Spirit of Christ within her," with perhaps even greater tenderness and compassion, her voice taking on "a softer, perchance more pitying tone." Despite being a slaveholder, Mrs. Henry appears to be the soul of kindness. Mr.

Henry, a clergyman, appears to bring the same mildness and geniality to the household, and under their care, Hannah regains her health. As Crafts characterizes the situation, Hannah becomes not exactly a guest in the Henrys' home, although treated "with quite as much kindness and consideration," but she is not treated as a servant, either. Ambiguously, and calling attention to slavery's pervasive influence, Hannah recognizes that, while "there was a pleasant familiarity of manner" displayed by the Henrys, it was "mingled with a sort of reserve that continually reminded me that I was not one of them."[1]

The precariousness of her situation is ultimately brought home to Hannah when Mrs. Henry calls her aside to tell her that word of Saddler's death, and Hannah's whereabouts, has reached the trader's next of kin, soon to arrive to establish his claim on her. Hannah, mortified, pleads with Mrs. Henry to buy her and retain her as a servant in the household. Mrs. Henry says she cannot and tells Hannah why. Her late father had been a worldly man, a slaveholder and slave trader who, in the throes of death, was filled with remorse for having been "a trafficker in human flesh and blood, in the lives and souls of men" (126). Accordingly, he had exacted from his daughter a "solemn promise" that she was "never on any occasion to sell or buy a servant" (127), leaving an estate to be apportioned among the remaining slaves, who were to be emancipated upon Mrs. Henry's death. To buy Hannah, however merciful the intent, would be to break her vow. All she can propose is to persuade Hannah's owner to sell Hannah to Mrs. Henry's friends, the Wheelers of North Carolina. Mrs. Henry assures Hannah—mistakenly, as it turns out—that the Wheelers will show her the same consideration she has received from the Henrys themselves. Arranging the sale, she unwittingly sentences Hannah to the most brutal slavery the young woman has ever known.

The episode may have meant many things to Crafts. In some ways, the situation she creates here, like the story of Charlotte, calls to mind the difficulties facing the kindly Shelbys, original owners of Uncle Tom in Harriet Beecher Stowe's *Uncle Tom's Cabin*. The Henrys, like the Shelbys, try to be good to their slaves. Nevertheless, they are inescapably bound to the system of slavery in ways that force them to participate in its brutality. Mrs. Henry, however admirable she appears, is no less the vehicle for Hannah's subsequent sufferings at the hands of the vain and capricious Mrs. Wheeler than were the Shelbys for the tragic fate of Uncle Tom. Hoping to show, as she says in her short preface, how slavery "blights the happiness of the white as well as the black race" (3), Crafts portrays Mrs. Henry and her husband as slaveholding characters themselves made miserable by the institution in which they take part.

But such an explanation only hints at the richness of Crafts's story of Mrs. Henry's solemn promise. Based on the available information about Hannah

Crafts, it remains difficult at this point to delve too deeply into her intentions and motives. Still, given what happens to Hannah, it does seem likely that Ann Fabian is true to Crafts's purposes in characterizing Mrs. Henry's vow as an "absurd deathbed oath" (xxvi). Mrs. Henry may be a woman whose motives are innocent and pure, but her fidelity to her vow turns out to be fidelity to a proslavery pledge. In some sense confirming Hannah's sense of that "sort of reserve" which prevents her from really being a guest in the Henry household, Mrs. Henry betrays in the episode a real moral blind spot so far as her understanding of slavery is concerned.

The story of Mrs. Henry's promise fits into a set of dichotomies that structure much of *The Bondwoman's Narrative*. Throughout the novel, as in the story of Mrs. Henry's oath, Crafts creates an opposition between what might be described as a formalistic, even legalistic approach to human affairs and an approach based on a deeper, more complex understanding of moral situations. The world, Crafts stresses, is not the sort of place for which rules should serve as the only guide to right action. Indeed, a rule-governed approach to morality can lead to the kind of moral blindness Mrs. Henry displays and may even serve as a way of evading the morality of one's acts.

Certainly, this kind of critique of legalism is apparent in Crafts's development of the lawyer Trappe, who plays the role of Hannah's nemesis for much of the novel. Greedy, cruel, and indifferent to others' suffering, Trappe is the personification of all that is evil in slavery. In one of the novel's pivotal early scenes, the bride of Hannah's first master has a confrontation with Trappe, a confrontation that ultimately leads to her death, in which he threatens to expose the secret of her African ancestry. The words that Crafts gives to Trappe dramatize his own moral legalism in an especially brutal way. Trappe's threat results from the bride's inability to live up to an agreement to provide him a monthly stipend, including a house and servants, in return for his silence. A would-be sexual blackmailer, as well, he tells her, "My conscience never troubles me," adding that "the circumstances in which I find people are not of my making." "Neither," he says, "are the laws that give me an advantage over them. If a beautiful women [sic] is to be sold, it is rather the fault of the law that permits it than of me who profits by it." He concludes, "Whatever the law permits, and public opinion encourages I do, when that says stop I go no further" (98). Though his character may be infinitely different from Mrs. Henry's, his legalism is not. If anything, his words help to highlight the moral bankruptcy of Mrs. Henry's subsequent failure to protect Hannah, her moral evasiveness in allowing an oath to prevent her from doing what was right.

Both characters stand in sharp contrast, moreover, to one of Hannah's first real friends, Aunt Hetty, who, with her husband, Uncle Siah, embodies a humane Christian spirit. Simple people, they give Hannah the twin gifts of literacy and religion while, as Hannah says, helping her to cultivate her "moral nature" (10). Rather than hiding behind any moral legalism, they defy the law itself by teaching Hannah to read and suffer for it, losing what little they have when they are driven from their home. They further prove their moral courage when, at the end of the novel, they defy the law to assist Hannah in her escape.

Crafts creates a similar contrast through the character of Mrs. Wright, whom Hannah and her tragic mistress meet in jail after their unsuccessful attempt to escape the lawyer Trappe. Mrs. Wright, too, has willingly violated the laws of slavery by sheltering a virtuous young slave woman attempting to escape being sold into concubinage on the New Orleans market. Caught, removed from her family, and sentenced to a long imprisonment, Mrs. Wright has lost her mind by the time Hannah meets her. Her family now dead, she has come to think of prison as her home. And she has learned, as Mrs. Henry has not, that moral action in a slave society cannot be undertaken within the system's constraints, legal or otherwise.

But the opposition Crafts creates between legalism and morality is especially apparent in the character of Hannah herself. Crafts is doing more in her novel than creating a simple contrast between law and virtue in a kind of abolitionist anticipation of Huckleberry Finn's famous pledge to "go to hell" rather than betray his friend Jim. Through the character of Hannah, Crafts goes a long way toward explaining the distinction between law and morality and why it can be so difficult to address. This is because Hannah, more than any character in the novel, is shown to be aware of the difficulty of making moral decisions.

The Henry episode is built around such an awareness. While in the Henry household, Hannah is constantly confronting moral dilemmas for which she knows there are no easy solutions. In her first encounter with Mrs. Henry, realizing Mrs. Henry assumes her to be white, she must decide whether to admit her identity. It is a decision fraught with danger. Later, she must decide whether to protect Charlotte and William once they have been forced to flee; she is also forced to decide whether to join them in their escape. But what Hannah understands is that decisions have to be based, as they were for Aunt Hetty, Uncle Siah, and the appropriately named Mrs. Wright, not on hard and fast rules but rather on an assessment of what, in a particular situation, seems right or wrong. Crafts emphasizes this point, perhaps, by having Hannah refuse to run away from the Henrys because of her appreciation for their kindness. When she ultimately does decide to escape from the Wheelers, it is because, under their cruel regime, any qualms she may have had about leaving the Henrys no longer hold.

In creating a world of moral ambiguity, Crafts appears to have drawn on several sources. At one level, it is tempting to root at least some part of Crafts's situationalism in significant tendencies in slave cultural traditions. To the extent that such sources as folklore and the reminiscences of ex-slaves provide any insight into antebellum popular morality, situationalist views seem to have been important bases for the ways many slaves thought about moral questions. They, too, showed a tendency to reject formalism or legalism in confronting moral dilemmas. The apparent biases Crafts expresses toward the slaves in the quarters—notably in her account of her time with the Wheelers—may seem to make such connections problematic. The situationalism her book portrays, however, may indicate the power of such traditions across the class lines she otherwise represents.[2]

At the same time, Crafts's situationalism did not entirely depart from abolitionist traditions. She built on modes of confronting questions of honesty and dishonesty that Ann Fabian has discussed as an element in the larger fugitive autobiographical tradition. As in those works, the dilemmas Hannah confronts emphasize the difficulty of absolute honesty in the environment slavery creates. Slavery, as fugitive James Pennington said, puts one "not only in peril of liberty, limb, and life itself, but may even send him in haste to the bar of God with a lie upon his lips." Crafts also echoed the situationalism found in abolitionist discussions, at least tangentially related to the Henry episode, of whether purchasing freedom for a slave was tantamount to cooperating with the system. Significant figures from Frederick Douglass and William Lloyd Garrison to Harriet Jacobs argued, albeit with some ambivalence, that, as Garrison said, "Every thing depends upon the manner in which, the object for which, and the persons by whom, this payment is made."[3]

The deeper resonances of Crafts's situationalism—and especially the situationalism suggested by the story of Mrs. Henry's promise—are most clearly appreciated, however, when the novel is placed within the framework of the larger debate over slavery. First, it should be noted, Crafts was not the only antislavery writer to use the story of a vow in the way she did. For example, the Pennsylvania writer, reformer, and minister Baynard Hall, in his 1852 novel *Frank Freeman's Barber Shop*, related the title character's fear of being sold away from his dying mother. Appealing to a local clergyman of antislavery sentiment, he begs the man, Leamington, to buy him so that he may remain in the neighborhood. Leamington, too, puts fidelity to an oath above mercy, exclaiming, "I cannot!—I dare not!—I have solemnly vowed to God never to buy or sell a human being!" It is a vow that puts Frank Freeman in a spot as tragic, in its way, as Hannah's.[4]

At the same time, neither Hall nor Crafts meant for us to see human beings as morally at sea. Although Crafts rejected formalism, she nonetheless celebrated virtue, and such characters as Aunt Hetty, Uncle Siah, Mrs. Wright, and Hannah herself serve to illustrate what she admired. Virtue, as Crafts defines it, means being guided by conscience, empathy, and an appreciation for human needs in a way that transcends human contrivances, rules, and creeds. Hall made this especially clear when, unlike Crafts, he had Leamington go back on his oath. Confronted by his wife, Leamington is made to realize that he "would not offend God by an act of humanity. Surely," she asks, "no vow can bind you if it prevents help to a sufferer—can it?"[5]

The understanding of virtue represented by Hall, and implied by Crafts, was rooted in those themes of sentimentalism and evangelical Protestantism that did much to shape ideals and values in antebellum America and did much, as Ann Fabian says in Henry Louis Gates's introduction to the novel, to shape Crafts's work, as well (xxvi). Literary historians have long noted that the celebration of sentiment was connected to a view that the core of virtue lay in a hope for the happiness of others, encouraging a morality more like Aunt Hetty's, Uncle Siah's, Hannah's, or Mrs. Leamington's than that of Mrs. Henry. What R. F. Brissenden suggested of Laurence Sterne—that he founded morality on the necessity of love and toleration, recognizing that life cannot be reduced to system—applies to Hannah Crafts, as well.[6]

Such ideas were also at the heart of the evangelical Protestantism that, as Fabian suggests, informs Crafts's novel. Evangelicalism was a movement characterized by the minimizing of theology as the basis for the religious life and, in a process traced so thoroughly by historian Ann Douglas, a consequent celebration of experience and feeling. Incorporating the ethic of sentiment, and reinforcing it, the evangelicalism of Crafts's day was quintessentially a religion of the heart, one in which love of God and love of others served as the only true bases for a Christian community. Here, too, the contrast Crafts created between Mrs. Henry and other, more empathetic characters is apposite.[7]

Within this framework, the kind of antiformalism found in Crafts's novel played a significant role in abolitionist perceptions of themselves, their movement, and their society. The formative, mutually reinforcing role of sentimentalism and evangelicalism for antislavery ideas and organization has long been noted. Abolitionists were well aware of the antiformalist thrusts underlying the movement, and work intended to reinforce such tendencies was a staple in the abolitionist press, as well as in abolitionist fiction. One may note, again, Stowe's portrayal of the slaveholding Shelbys in *Uncle Tom's Cabin*. Along these lines, John Carlos Rowe has called attention to Stowe's critique of a rule-bound morality in her 1856 novel, *Dred*.[8]

The underlying bases for such a perspective were outlined especially clearly in a piece appearing in 1848 in that most critical of antislavery sources, the *Liberator*. This was a brief extract from an essay on theology and religion by Massachusetts Unitarian clergyman James Richardson, Jr. The essay proposes the same structure of oppositions on which Crafts and Stowe were later to build their novels. Theology, Richardson wrote, "has little or nothing to do with Practical Religion." He condemned "those who make their vain speculations about the nature of God, of Man, and of Christ, as laid down in creeds and catechisms—speculations purely philosophical in their character, and which have nothing to do with life and practice." He added, "Religion is the Divine and Spiritual manifested in life and action. Theology, or Religious Science, is the mere Theory." Richardson left no doubt which one he found more valuable. Religion, not theology, "infuses pure and righteous influences and a spiritual power into the hearts of men, and thus elevates, refines, and spiritualizes their whole lives."[9]

What Richardson says about religion reflects a bias against formalism that informed abolitionism in many ways. Much of the divisive debate over whether the United States Constitution supported slavery revolved around not only what that document said but also whether that document, or any document, was relevant to such an issue as slavery. Arguments citing higher law dismissed the Constitution as "a covenant with death" and "an agreement with hell," to cite William Lloyd Garrison's famous appropriation of Isaiah 28:18, and demanded a more transcendent authority than human law for dealing with the issue of slavery. Wendell Phillips put the case clearly in 1842 when, as historian William Wiecek notes, he declared, "When I look on these crowded thousands and see them trample on their consciences and the rights of their fellow men at the bidding of a piece of parchment, I say, my curse be on the Constitution of these United States!" His words form a tacit condemnation, one may add, of a man like Trappe, hiding behind legalisms to justify his treatment of Hannah and her young mistress.[10]

But the rejection of formalism extended widely to include abolitionist perceptions of the antislavery cause, as such. Many abolitionists would have agreed with what Frederick Douglass said in his famous 1852 address on the Fourth of July, when he asked rhetorically, "Must I argue for the wrongfulness of slavery?" He wondered, "Is it to be settled by the rules of logic and argumentation, as a matter beset with great difficulty, involving a doubtful application of the principle of justice, hard to be understood?" Then he added, "How should I look today, speaking in the presence of Americans, dividing, and subdividing a discourse, to show that men have a natural right to freedom? speaking of it relatively and positively, negatively and affirmatively." He would look, he told his audience, "ridiculous," because arousing the "feeling" and "conscience" of the nation was the way to make the only real case against slavery. As Crafts's novel indicates, she too agreed with Douglass's point of view.[11]

At the same time, the remarks of Phillips and Douglass help to place Crafts's novel in the context of its time. As their words indicate, their conscientious rejection of formalism stemmed from, at least in part, what they saw as formalistic arguments in support of slavery. Moreover, their argument against formalism takes on its greatest significance when put in the specific context of antebellum debates over slavery. At various points in the novel, Crafts sets up dialogues between characters that, in many ways, encapsulate those debates. In this, she joins many abolitionist writers, including those fugitive autobiographers who, as William Andrews has shown, used reconstructed dialogues between themselves and their owners to insert themselves into the national dialogue on the antislavery side.[12]

As with the fugitives' narratives, the terms of the debate within Crafts's novel are implicit in the shape and content of her story. In general, the evidence of proslavery and antislavery writing indicates that its authors were quite familiar with each other. As Henry Louis Gates has found from examining the library of John Wheeler, Hannah Crafts's likely last owner, abolitionist literature made its way to the South. The same may be said about the movement of proslavery writings to the North. Slavery's defenders often demonstrated their familiarity with antislavery works, and abolitionist writers usually bent their own efforts to respond to proslavery arguments.[13]

There was much in *The Bondwoman's Narrative* that responded to proslavery arguments. Slavery's defenders often presented, for example, portraits of plantation life intended to illustrate slaves' contentment with their lot. As was always the case in abolitionist fiction, Crafts's descriptions of despair and discontent among slaves may be read as an effort to refute proslavery assertions of slave contentment. Her account of the Cosgrove harem complemented an array of portrayals of slaveholder licentiousness written in response to proslavery claims of slave-owner virtue. Crafts's story of Charlotte and William joined similar episodes, widely diffused, intended to counter proslavery assertions that black people were incapable of true affection. Hannah's refinement, piety, and chastity constituted an exemplary reproach to proslavery stereotypes of African American women. Her encounter with the Henrys, even more than her experience with the Wheelers, emphasized that cruelty was inherent in the system and not simply a problem involving a few bad slaveholders, as the system's defenders tended to claim.[14]

But the Henry episode and its rejection of formalism adds another dimension to the way in which Crafts's novel fits into the debate over slavery. As many historians have stressed, ideals of system and order dominated proslavery thought. Building on a view of the world as a fragile, uncertain place—and evoking anxieties created by both abolitionist challenges and racial fears—slavery's defenders asserted the need for a social and political organization governed by clear rules of hierarchy, order, and stability. In so doing, they developed a rhetoric of structure that gave the proslavery argument a formalistic, legalistic bent.[15]

That Crafts was aware of that proslavery formalism is shown particularly well when, late in the novel, she briefly departs from her narrative to describe the degradation of the Wheeler plantation's slaves. She writes, "It must be strange to live in a world of civilization, and, elegance, and refinement, and yet know nothing about either, yet that is the way with multitudes and with none more than the slaves." Significantly, however, she also identifies a target for her comments, asking rhetorically, "What do you think of it? Doctors of Divinity Isn't it a strange state to be like them" (201).

The barb Crafts aimed at the "Doctors of Divinity" points toward a very specific background to her condemnation of formalist tendencies in the proslavery argument. Among slavery's defenders, few had done more to develop the proslavery argument than the South's white Southern ministry. By the time of Crafts's novel they had done much to create a full-blown Christian defense of the institution, one that consisted, above all, in an effort to prove that the Bible provided slavery's ultimate support.

The scriptural defense of slavery they created had many parts. Proslavery theologians continued to cite, for example, the old story of Noah's curse of Ham as a justification for the enslavement of Africans—although, as Eugene Genovese has shown, some questioned its credibility. Far more significant were those scriptural arguments that stressed ownership of slaves by the ancient Israelites, Jesus's failure specifically to condemn slavery, and the apostle Paul's apparent approval of the institution. Proslavery writers even interpreted Paul's ordering the escaped slave Onesimus to return to his owner, in the book of Philemon (verses 8–20), as Biblical support for the Fugitive Slave Law. These efforts on the part of the Southern "Doctors of Divinity" (which many of them were) should not be discounted. As historians have shown, the scriptural defense of slavery was probably more important than any other, even, as Genovese has argued, that based solely on race.[16]

At the heart of the dispute was, however, a more fundamental question of what religion should be and of how scripture should be read and understood. The proslavery argument was built on a strict, literal interpretation of the Bible, one excluding anything like "opinion" or "speculation" where Biblical interpretation was concerned. As Donald Mathews has shown, proslavery clerics tended to reject emerging critical tendencies—the "higher criticism"—in approaching the Bible. What the Bible said, they argued, had to be taken at face value, as a literal account of God's relationship to humanity and history, including His obvious acceptance of slavery in the Old Testament and the New. The prominent Episcopal proslavery writer Thornton Stringfellow made the point for many when he said that, in regard to slavery, "Christians should produce a 'thus saith the Lord,' both for what they condemn as sinful and for what they approve as lawful, in the sight of heaven." It was an effort, he believed, that would put the weight of argument on slavery's side. Others, echoing Stringfellow's position, suggested that, given biblical authority, opposition to slavery could only be, as one said, "dishonorable to God, and subversive of his government."[17]

As proslavery theologians knew, a very different approach to the scripture was evolving outside the South. One may note, for example, the influential ideas of Horace Bushnell, one of antebellum America's most noted preachers. In an 1849 essay on religious language, Bushnell discussed the impossibility of giving the Bible a literal reading, asserting, "There is no book in the world that contains so many repugnances, or antagonistic forms of assertion, as the Bible." The Bible, he said, had to be thought of as poetry. Language "acts suggestively, through symbols held up in words, which symbols and words are never exact measures of any truth." Expressing views that would have been anathema to proslavery clerics, Bushnell wrote that the worst way to read the Bible was to be insensible to the "poetic life" and linguistic complexities of the scriptures, to treat them as "wooden statues of truths."[18]

Such a point of view was apparent in abolitionist readings of the Bible. Consistent with Bushnell's position, abolitionists, though denying neither the truth nor the authority of the Bible, argued that it was the spirit rather than the "mere letter," as one put it, that mattered in applying the Bible to slavery. Certainly, one should be careful not to exaggerate these differences to the point of caricature. There were many antislavery writers who could be as literalistic as any of slavery's defenders in their approach to scripture. As in the case of minister Joseph Thompson, they even went back to the Greek to question whether biblical forms of servitude could be equated with slavery as practiced in the antebellum South. At the same time, such prominent defenders of slavery as South Carolinian James Henley Thornwell sought to prove that slavery was consistent with the Bible's "spirit." It was not, he argued, "unfriendly to the development of piety and to communion with God" for either slave or slaveholder, and this, he said, was the true spirit of the Bible's message. Nevertheless, in emphasizing the importance of focusing on the Bible's spirit, in decrying its reduction to "mere letter," abolitionists were saying, consistent with James Richardson's *Liberator* essay, that Southern theologians were reading the Bible in a way that ignored its essential, deeper messages of love, humanity, and justice.[19]

If anything, as Crafts's scornful reference to the "Doctors of Divinity" implies, Southern theologians were reading the Bible in a way that involved something more like hair-splitting than real understanding. Such a charge was not unknown. Douglass often referred sarcastically to the "Doctors" and "Bishops" to make a similar point in his frequent attacks on proslavery Christians. In his 1860 narrative, William Craft similarly excoriated the "lukewarm Doctors of Divinity" who put law above virtue. And abolitionists could be particularly hard on such an authority as Thornwell, slavery's most sophisticated theological proponent.

Thornwell was genuinely sensitive to the spiritual and moral claims of slaves. The word of God, he acknowledged, made plain the common humanity of blacks and whites—although he was also prepared to say that the "distinction of ranks in society" was no less providential, including those "distinctions" embodied in what he termed "African bondage." Nevertheless, in 1850 Thornwell defended slavery's Christian character by asserting that "what makes a man a slave" is the slave-owner's claim "not to the *man*, but to his *labour*." The slave continued to own his body and, especially, his soul, which no one could make into "an article of barter or exchange." A correspondent for the antislavery New York *Independent*, writing as "Rev. Dr. Thornwell," poetically imagined the cleric putting a slave on the block. Body and soul, he says, belong to the slave. What, then, does this mean?

> 'Tis a puzzling subject beyond my wit;
> I must have the Doctors to settle it.
> However, it makes no change in the trade;
> 'Twill be a good bargain as ever was made;
> And you'll feel all the better—I do—since I'm told
> It is not the man, but—what is it! we hold.

Impatience with the "Doctors" went beyond the substance of their proslavery arguments to condemn the very formalism to which slavery's defenders laid claim with pride. One can see Crafts inserting herself into this debate not only through her sarcasm about the "Doctors of Divinity" but also through her portrayal of the rule-bound Mrs. Henry.[20]

Such a possibility may be indicated by Crafts's own approach to the Bible. As Gates has noted, almost all the chapters of *The Bondwoman's Narrative* begin with a scriptural quotation, presented in a manner that indicates Crafts's strong familiarity with the Bible and her belief in its relevance to her life (242). This is not the place for closely analyzing relations between individual biblical passages and Crafts's text—although her selection of passages creates an interesting pattern evoking suffering and possibilities for deliverance. It does nevertheless seem clear that Crafts sought to use her epigraphs in ways that directly commented on her text. Thus, for example, she begins her story of Trappe's demise with a piecing together of phrases from Isaiah 3:10–11, promising retribution to the wicked (231, 279). She begins her story of Hannah's escape by quoting Psalm 141, declaring a trust in the Lord (206, 275).

But her most telling use of the Bible may be in the very chapter where she tells the story of Mrs. Henry's tragic vow. Crafts introduces the chapter by quoting Proverbs 31:30, "Favor is deceitful, and beauty is vain: but a woman that feareth the Lord, she shall be praised" (121). In many ways, Mrs. Henry is the embodiment of the woman celebrated in the scripture. The chapter in Proverbs describes, in verses 10 through 31, the virtuous woman and perfect wife whose "price is far above rubies" (verse 10). She is the wife who "looketh well to the ways of her household" (verse 27) and who also "stretcheth out her hand to the poor" and "reacheth forth her hands to the needy" (verse 20). Mrs. Henry, who has given so much to the injured Hannah, has proven her desire to care for the needy. As for the household, Hannah is made to say that one "could never sufficiently admire the order and harmony of the arrangements, which blent [blended] so many parts into a perfect whole" (123).

The analogy makes Mrs. Henry's failure to rescue Hannah, her obtuse fidelity to her oath, all the more striking. As the chapter unfolds, however, the point to be taken from Crafts's use of the scriptural epigraph from Proverbs becomes increasingly clear, especially as Crafts joins Hannah's sufferings to those of Charlotte, the newly married young woman, who, to save her marriage, will ultimately have to run away. Weeping for her own situation, Hannah encounters Mrs. Henry's little daughter Anna, who wonders "what makes everyone so unhappy." She observes to Hannah, "you weep, and so does Lotty, and I can't tell how many more" (129). In keeping with the scriptural image of Mrs. Henry as wife and mistress, Crafts writes of Charlotte that "multitudes of people, white and black, might have envied the situation in which she was miserable" (129–130). But Crafts concludes, "those that view slavery only as it relates to physical sufferings or the wants of nature, can have no conception of its greatest evils" (130). The conclusion, providing an endpoint to the chapter whose epigraph offers such a promising beginning, suggests an ironic reading of the praise for Mrs. Henry that the epigraph appears to offer. Irony was not, after all, unknown in abolitionist and African American traditions. Rather than describing Mrs. Henry, the biblical epigraph serves to highlight her failure. This possibility is reinforced when Mrs. Henry's oath-bound response to Hannah is read in concert with verse 26 of the same chapter of Proverbs. The virtuous woman, it says, "openeth her mouth with wisdom; and in her tongue is the law of kindness," neither of which applies to Mrs. Henry's adherence to her pledge.

Put in historical perspective, the story of Mrs. Henry's solemn promise is an important episode in *The Bondwoman's Narrative.* For one thing, it emphasizes that Crafts herself was familiar with and had a subtle understanding of the debate over slavery—not only in terms of its key provisions but also in terms of more fundamental divisions between pro- and antislavery positions. Whether this familiarity was the product of what she might have gleaned from the Wheeler library prior to her escape, or of her exposure to abolitionism is, at this point, impossible to say. It may also have grown out of what Gates has described, in his introduction to the novel, as Crafts's Southern origins and, especially, her apparent familiarity with slaveholders (lxx). Antebellum white Southerners, and particularly the slaveholding elite, did observe a powerfully formalistic, rule-ridden social ethic, one based on a sense of danger and uncertainty when rules ceased to hold. It was an ethic, and an ethos, embodied in such distinctive Southern practices as the duel. This ethic disposed people toward formalism in approaching an array of issues, including those of politics and theology as well as manners and morals. Mrs. Henry, with her seemingly obsessive commitment to rules, fits well within such a framework.[21]

For another, her presentation of Mrs. Henry's promise helps cast light on Crafts's understanding of the abolition movement itself. As her preface indicates, Crafts did hope to publish her narrative, acknowledging through her modest disclaimer her awareness of the unique role of the African American voice in the antislavery cause. But the work itself suggests, as well, not only a familiarity with pro- and antislavery sources but also her estimate of what should appeal to her potential, largely antislavery audience.

Historians have long debated the role of ideology in the abolition movement, as did many people in the antebellum period. Proslavery writers often sought to tar the movement with charges of "abstraction" and ideological fanaticism, much as abolitionists condemned the callous formalism of slavery's defenders. Ideological concerns were important in abolition. They informed, for example, the debate over whether ransoming a fugitive—however justifiable by circumstances, as Garrison had argued—entailed a compromise with slavery's evil. To engage in such an act, abolitionist Henry C. Wright wrote shortly after Douglass's ransom from Thomas Auld, was to compromise "the principle that God made you free and gave you an inalienable right to liberty" by acknowledging the slaveholder's claim to "a right of property in your body and soul." Crafts's own position, conveyed through her quotidian critique of formalism, essentially declared ideology irrelevant, as she grounded moral action in an ethic and a vision of society based on ties of mutual affection, conscience, and feeling.[22]

One can only speculate as to why her novel failed to receive publication, because there is much to suggest that, in setting forth such a vision, she gauged her audience correctly. Her work complemented that of many major abolitionist writers—poets, novelists, essayists—who placed a similar vision of society at the center of the abolitionist cause. Moreover, it was a vision that appears to have been attractive to significant numbers of antebellum Americans concerned with what they saw as the emergence of an increasingly competitive, aggressive, and unsatisfactory social order. In the way she chooses to focus her appeal to a potential antislavery audience, Crafts thus helps to focus historical attention on the contribution of those concerns, as much as any ideological constructs, to defining the abolitionist cause.[23]

Drawing on an array of cultural and literary sources, *The Bondwoman's Narrative* thus uses the story of Mrs. Henry's promise to create a knowing intervention into antebellum American society and thought, particularly in its proslavery forms. To be sure, similar responses to formalism and legalism go back to the nation's founding and, even before the emergence of abolitionism, had played a role in American thinking about an array of social, cultural, and economic issues. However, through her portrayal of Mrs. Henry's obtuse if unwitting betrayal of Hannah, Crafts provides great insight into how deep fundamental ideological, even cultural divisions could be in the antebellum period. Mrs. Henry's solemn promise reinforces the view that Hannah Crafts created a document from which we can learn much about the world in which she lived.

Notes

1. Hannah Crafts, *The Bondwoman's Narrative*, ed. Henry Louis Gates, Jr. (New York: Warner, 2002), 117–118, 124. Subsequent page references to the novel will appear in parentheses in the text.

2. Lawrence W. Levine, *Black Culture and Black Consciousness: Afro-American Folk Thought from Slavery to Freedom* (New York: Oxford Univ. Press, 1977), 116. See also Dickson D. Bruce, Jr., "On Dunbar's 'Jingles in a Broken Tongue': Dunbar's Dialect Poetry and the Afro-American Folk Tradition," in *A Singer in the Dawn: Reinterpretations of Paul Laurence Dunbar*, ed. Jay Martin (New York: Dodd, Mead, 1975), 107.

3. Ann Fabian, *The Unvarnished Truth: Personal Narratives in Nineteenth-Century America* (Berkeley: Univ. of California Press, 2000), 98; James W. C. Pennington, *The Fugitive Blacksmith; or, Events*

in the History of James W. C. Pennington (London: Charles Gilpin, 1850), 30; William Lloyd Garrison in *Liberator*, January 15, 1847. For Jacobs, see William L. Andrews, *To Tell a Free Story: The First Century of Afro-American Autobiography, 1760–1865* (Urbana: Univ. of Illinois Press, 1986), 251–252.

4. Baynard R. Hall, *Frank Freeman's Barber Shop; A Tale* (New York: Charles Scribner, 1852), 41.

5. Hall, *Frank Freeman's Barber Shop*, 44.

6. R. F. Brissenden, *Virtue in Distress: Studies in the Novel of Sentiment from Richardson to Sade* (New York: Barnes and Noble, 1974), 122–123; see Andrew Burstein, *Sentimental Democracy: The Evolution of America's Romantic Self-Image* (New York: Hill & Wang, 1999), 301; Jane Tompkins, *Sensational Designs: The Cultural Work of American Fiction, 1790–1860* (New York: Oxford Univ. Press, 1985), 132–133.

7. Ann Douglas, *The Feminization of American Culture* (New York: Knopf, 1977), 141–151.

8. David Brion Davis, *The Problem of Slavery in Western Culture* (Ithaca: Cornell Univ. Press, 1966), 480–482; John Stauffer, *The Black Hearts of Men: Radical Abolitionists and the Transformation of Race* (Cambridge: Harvard Univ. Press, 2002), 16; James Brewer Stewart, *Holy Warriors: The Abolitionists and American Slavery*, rev. ed. (New York: Hill & Wang, 1996) 39, 47; John Carlos Rowe, "Stowe's Rainbow Sign: Violence and Community in *Dred: A Tale of the Great Dismal Swamp* (1856)," *Arizona Quarterly* 58 (2002), 43.

9. *Liberator*, January 7, 1848.

10. William Wiecek, *The Sources of Antislavery Constitutionalism in America, 1760–1848* (Ithaca: Cornell Univ. Press, 1977), 228, 237.

11. [Frederick Douglass], *The Frederick Douglass Papers*, ed. John Blassingame et al., 5 vols. (New Haven: Yale Univ. Press, 1979–1992), II: 371.

12. William L. Andrews, "Dialogue in Afro-American Autobiography," in *Studies in Autobiography*, ed. James Olney (New York: Oxford Univ. Press, 1988).

13. *New York Times*, June 2, 2002; see Dickson D. Bruce, Jr., *The Origins of African American Literature, 1680–1865* (Charlottesville: Univ. Press of Virginia, 2001), 273–282.

14. Bruce, *Origins*, 281–282.

15. Robert M. Calhoon, *Evangelicals and Conservatives in the Early South, 1740–1861* (Columbia: Univ. of South Carolina Press, 1988), 176–177, 196–197. See also Dickson D. Bruce, Jr., *Violence and Culture in the Antebellum South* (Austin: Univ. of Texas Press, 1979), 187; and Dickson D. Bruce, Jr., "Racial Fear and the Proslavery Argument: A Rhetorical Approach," *Mississippi Quarterly* 33 (1980), 476–478.

16. Eugene D. Genovese, *A Consuming Fire: The Fall of the Confederacy in the Mind of the White Christian South* (Athens: Univ. of Georgia Press, 1998), 81; Richard J. Carwardine, *Evangelicals and Politics in Antebellum America* (New Haven: Yale Univ. Press, 1993), 54–56; Donald G. Mathews, *Religion in the Old South* (Chicago: Univ. of Chicago Press, 1977), 157–158; John R. McKivigan, *The War Against Proslavery Religion: Abolitionism and the Northern Churches, 1830–1865* (Ithaca: Cornell Univ. Press, 1984), 30; Mitchell Snay, *Gospel of Disunion: Religion and Separatism in the Antebellum South* (New York: Cambridge Univ. Press, 1993), 54.

17. Mathews, *Religion in the Old South*, 175–176; E. Brooks Holifield, *The Gentlemen Theologians: American Theology in Southern Culture, 1795–1860* (Durham: Duke Univ. Press, 1978), 97–98; William W. Freehling, "James Henley Thornwell's Mysterious Antislavery Moment," *Journal of Southern History* 57 (1991), 388; Thornton Stringfellow, *A Brief Examination of Scripture Testimony on the Institution of Slavery* (Richmond: Religious Herald, 1841), 5; McKivigan, *War Against Proslavery Religion*, 30.

18. Horace Bushnell, *God in Christ: Three Discourses, Delivered at New Haven, Cambridge, and Andover, with a Preliminary Dissertation on Language* (1849; reprint, New York: AMS Press, 1972), 69, 88, 72; for the white Southern view, see Holifield, *Gentlemen Theologians*, 54.

19. Snay, *Gospel of Disunion*, 64; Joseph P. Thompson, *The Fugitive Slave Law; Tried by the Old and New Testaments* (New York: William Harned, 1850), 22; James Henley Thornwell, *The Rights and Duties of Masters: A Sermon Preached at the Dedication of a Church Erected in Charleston, S.C. for the Benefit and Instruction of the Coloured Population* (Charleston: Walker & James, 1850), 17.

20. See, e.g., *Frederick Douglass Papers*, II, 98–99; William Craft, *Running a Thousand Miles for Freedom: The Escape of William and Ellen Craft from Slavery*, ed. R. J. M. Blackett (Baton Rouge: Louisiana State Univ. Press, 1990), 18, 49; Genovese, *Consuming Fire*, 82–83; Thornwell, *Rights and Duties*, 24, 32–33; Freehling, "Thornwell's Antislavery Moment," 390–391; Amy Dru Stanley, *From Bondage to Contract: Wage Labor, Marriage, and the Market in the Age of Slave Emancipation* (New York: Cambridge Univ. Press, 1998), 19; New York *Independent*, January 18, 1855.

21. Bruce, *Violence and Culture*, 68–70.

22. Patricia Hickin, "'Situation Ethics' and Antislavery Attitudes in the Virginia Churches," in *America: The Middle Period: Essays in Honor of Bernard Mayo*, ed. John B. Boles (Charlottesville: Univ. Press of Virginia, 1973), 209; Dickson D. Bruce, Jr., *The Rhetoric of Conservatism: The Virginia Convention of 1829–30 and the Conservative Tradition in the South* (San Marino: Huntington Library, 1982), 182; *Liberator*, January 29, 1847.

23. See Ronald G. Walters, *The Antislavery Appeal: American Abolition After 1830* (Baltimore: Johns Hopkins Univ. Press, 1976), xiv, 45; Robert Abzug, *Cosmos Crumbling: American Reform and the Religious Imagination* (New York: Oxford Univ. Press, 1994), 144, 204; see also Burstein, *Sentimental Democracy*, 266, 293; Mary Louise Kete, *Sentimental Collaborations: Mourning and Middle-Class Identity in Nineteenth-Century America* (Durham: Duke Univ. Press, 2000), 116.

"I Dwell Now in a Neat Little Cottage"

Architecture, Race, and Desire in The Bondwoman's Narrative

WILLIAM GLEASON

I learned to see freedom as always and intimately linked to the issue of transforming space.
—bell hooks, "House, 20 June 1994"

Near the end of Hannah Crafts's *The Bondwoman's Narrative*, on the run from the North Carolina plantation of her final owners, the escaped slave narrator Hannah seeks a night's rest in the deep woods. Miles from any human habitations—which through most of her narrative have proven traps rather than havens—Hannah "compose[s]" herself to sleep "in the friendly shelter of a small thicket," feeling "almost happy in the consciousness of perfect security." In the middle of the night, however, Hannah is awakened by the sound of voices. Peering through a gap in the thicket, she sees two figures preparing their own leafy beds near her enclosure. Hannah keeps careful watch until dawn, when she finally begins to drowse. "Presently my thoughts became confused, with that pleasing bewilderment which precedes slumber," Hannah relates. But bewilderment quickly turns to hallucination: "I began to lose consciousness of my identity, and the recollection of where I was. Now it seemed that Lindendale rose before me, then it was the jail, and anon the white towers of Washington, and—but the scene all faded; for I slept."[1]

On one level Hannah's hallucinatory tableau signals the tremendous anxiety that the presence of two strangers near her hideaway might produce. Even though the couple does not appear to pose an immediate threat to Hannah— one of the pair is deliriously ill, the other preoccupied with making his companion comfortable—Hannah's watchfulness suggests that her sense of "perfect security" has indeed been breached, until in her drowsy state she imagines she is no longer in the woods at all but in a succession of built spaces controlled by whites. These spaces—plantation, prison, metropolis—rise before her like specters, ghostly architectural hauntings from her enslaved past. To be returned to one of them at this point in the narrative would likely mean reenslavement, which is why Hannah experiences her momentary dissolution of identity (who am I?) in spatial terms (where am I?). On another level, this tableau also signals the text's deep interest in the shaping power of architectural form and highlights what one might call the broader architectural consciousness of the novel. After all, the succession of spaces that rises in Hannah's confused imagination recapitulates, in the order in which they appear, the locations anchoring three of the main stages of the text: the plantation from which she first escapes; the jail in which she is imprisoned after her recapture; and the cityscape to which she is removed by her subsequent owner. Hannah's hallucinatory tableau, that is, can be read not merely as a sign of one character's anxiety but also as a partial map of the novel's larger fascination with the uses and meanings of physical space.[2] For *The Bondwoman's Narrative*, as this episode makes clear, is a text not only concerned with, but in many ways structured by, the architectural forms of slavery and freedom.

An examination of the role of these forms in the novel will shed light on specific authorial tactics as well as more general mid-nineteenth-century cultural practices. It will be instructive to consider the text's use of built forms not only in the context of mid-century architectural and landscape theory but also in relation to the ideological uses that representations of architecture were frequently put in contemporary debates over slavery. For as we shall see, *The Bondwoman's Narrative* is attentive not only to architecture as fact (to actual examples of and physical developments within American building practice) but to architecture as a powerful literary trope. Of particular interest to me is this novel's sophisticated awareness of the intricate relays between race and the built environment in antebellum America, relays often unarticulated by other prominent shapers of ideas about mid-nineteenth-century domestic space. I will propose a reading of *The Bondwoman's Narrative* as an implicit engagement with—and transformation of—the architectural imaginations of such disparate writers as Andrew Jackson Downing and Charles Dickens, from whose works *The Bondwoman's Narrative* borrows liberally. Following bell hooks, who has observed that "many [black] narratives of struggle and resistance, from the time of slavery to the present, share an obsession with the politics of space, particularly the need to construct and build houses,"[3] I will also trace the persistence in Crafts's text of what one might call cottage desire, a powerful yearning for independent black home-ownership that is activated in the novel's earliest scenes but only finally realized in its closing pages.

Whoever penned this text—"Hannah Crafts" herself, a different escaped slave, or yet another figure[4]—*The Bondwoman's Narrative* emerges today as a fresh and frank examination of the highly charged politics of space at once shaped and navigated by both black and white Americans in the decade preceding the Civil War.

Splendid Cottage, Lowly Mansion

The Bondwoman's Narrative signals its interest in architectural space long before Hannah's hallucination in the woods—indeed, as early as the novel's first chapter. After explaining that her labors are "of the house" (6) rather than in the field, Hannah frames the story of her childhood between two starkly contrasting structures whose interiors dominate the opening chapter. The first of these structures is "the little cottage just around the foot of the hill" (7), to which Hannah is invited for clandestine reading lessons by Aunt Hetty, an elderly northern woman. Hannah has never been in a cottage home before. "I was surprised at the smallness yet perfect neatness of her dwelling, at the quiet and orderly repose that reigned ~~in~~ through all its appointments; it was in such pleasing contrast to our great house with its bustle, confusion, and troops of servants of all ages and colors" (8). In time Hannah discovers that Aunt Hetty and her husband had once lived in a great house of their own before being reduced to narrower means. "Wealth had been theirs, with all the appliances of luxury, and they became poor through a series of misfortunes," Hannah explains. "Yet as they had borne riches with virtuous moderation they conformed to poverty with subdued content, and readily exchanged the splendid mansion for the lowly cottage" (9).

The careful counterweighting in this last sentence, in which the sound pattern of "they had borne" is echoed in the partnered clause, "they conformed," and the phrase "virtuous moderation" is balanced by the chiastically meritorious "subdued content," heightens the ironic nobility of the house exchange described in the final line. For as the narrator suggests, the aged couple's "lowly" cottage, enriched by simplicity, moral goodness, and the invitation to literacy, is a more truly "splendid" space than that of any mansion in the text—certainly more so than Lindendale, the second principal structure framing Hannah's story of her childhood. Built in the colonial period by Sir Clifford de Vincent, the paternal ancestor of Hannah's current master, the "ancient mansion" of Lindendale has been expanded by subsequent generations until there are multiple wings in this grand estate. Despite the mansion's size, Hannah and the other slaves "whispered though no one seemed to know" that Lindendale had become "impoverished" (13). This is not true, it turns out, at least not in the material sense. As the slaves discover when preparing the house for the master's new bride, those portions of the mansion previously off-limits to servants conceal considerable luxuries ("what a variety of beautiful rooms, all splendid yet so different," marvels Hannah [14]). And yet in another sense Lindendale of course *is* impoverished, bankrupted morally by its masters' ongoing abuses of power, epitomized, as Hannah will later make clear, by the original Sir Clifford's brutal torture of the slave Rose and her dog.

Hannah considers this legacy of abuse—and has a presentiment of its present incarnation—in a lengthy interior scene that closes the first chapter. Asked by the housekeeper to shut some windows in a distant apartment of the mansion the night before the new bride's arrival, Hannah "thread[s] the long galleries" of the house on her way to the "southern turret," formerly the De Vincents' drawing room.[5] In a tradition begun by Sir Clifford, this room is "adorned with a long succession of family portraits ranged against the walls in due order of age and ancestral dignity" (15). Every Lindendale master since Sir Clifford has hung paired paintings of himself and his wife in this gallery, with the sole exception of Hannah's bachelor owner, who in defiance of his ancestor's wishes has displayed, prematurely, only his own portrait. Hannah interrupts her housekeeping duties to examine this pictorial mausoleum:

> Memories of the dead give at any time a haunting air to a silent room. How much more this becomes the case when standing face to face with their pictured resemblances and looking into the stony eyes motionless and void of expression as those of an exhumed corpse. But even as I gazed the golden light of sunset penetrating through the open windows in an oblique direction set each rigid feature in a glow. Movements like those of life came over the line of stolid faces as the shadows of a linden played there. (16)

To Hannah's surprise, in their lifelike movements the faces in the portraits assume expressions they "never wore in life" (16), appearing kind, gracious, relaxed. All, that is, except Hannah's master, who undergoes a contradictory transformation. In place of his "usually kind and placid expression," Mr. Vincent's face becomes wrathful and gloomy, "the calm brow ... wrinkled with passion, the lips turgid with malevolence" (17). This puzzling change reinforces the splendid/lowly architectural inversion at the heart of the chapter: just at the moment Hannah is most impressed by her owner's material prestige ("we thought our master must be a very great man to have so much wealth at his command" [14]), he is flashed forth as a gilded criminal. "It never oc-

curred to us to inquire whose sweat and blood and unpaid labor had contributed to produce [this splendor]," Hannah had pointedly observed at the
beginning of the scene (14). The disturbing intimation of her master's hidden
malevolence at scene's end betokens Hannah's rising awareness of the base
corruptions that underwrite mansion glory.

If this reinforcement of the splendid/lowly inversion were all that the portrait scene accomplished in the novel, one might be tempted to write it off as
a kind of Gothic trick, something akin to the painting-beneath-the-painting
transformations in the "Haunted Mansion" ride at Disneyland.[6] But Crafts
immediately complicates the cottage/mansion dichotomy. Despite the looming
presence of the ancient masters and the room's presentiment of "tragedy" (17),
the enslavers' gallery makes Hannah feel oddly free, linking it unexpectedly to
the cottage home in which she had learned to read. Rather than flee the portrait hall, she lingers. "I was not a slave with these pictured memorials of the
past," she explains. "They could not enforce drudgery, or condemn me on account of my color to a life of servitude. As their companion I could think and
speculate. In their presence my mind seemed to run riotous and exult in its
freedom as a rational being, and one destined for something higher and better
than this world can afford" (17). Such feelings recall Hannah's awakening in
the cottage: "I felt like a being to whom a new world with all its mysteries and
marvels was opening" (8). Other unexpected similarities connect the plantation
gallery to the cottage home. Both, for example, are figured as quiet retreats.
Much as Hannah finds pleasure in escaping the "bustle" and "confusion" (8)
of the big house when she steals away to the cottage, Mr. Vincent, she notes,
withdraws to the southern turret when he is tired of the "noise and bustle and
turmoil" (15) of the plantation estate. It is as though the drawing room, in its
"retired situation" (15), is itself a kind of "cottage" space.

I will have more to say in the next section about the specific interest of *The
Bondwoman's Narrative* in mid-nineteenth-century cottage or "country house"
architecture. But let me close here by describing one more example of Crafts's
pervasive use of architecture in the opening chapter, in this case a subtle coun-
terpointing that centers on the misactivation of an architectural metaphor.
Having discovered that other slaves, particularly children, trust and confide in
her, Hannah wishes to instruct them as the aged couple has instructed her.
Hannah expresses this desire in an apt, even routine, architectural metaphor:
"How I longed to become their teacher and *open the door of knowledge* to their
minds by instructing them to read" (12, my emphasis). Two paragraphs (if
some few months) later, however, it is the literal yet *undesired* opening of a door
that shatters this dream:

> The door [to the cottage] suddenly opened without warning, and the overseer
> of my master's estate walked into the house. My horror, and grief, and aston-
> ishment were indescribable. I felt Oh how much more than I tell. He addressed
> me rudely, and bade me begone home on the instant. I durst not disobey, but
> retreating through the doorway I glanced back at the calm sedate countenances
> of the aged couple, who were all unmoved by the torrent of threats and invec-
> tives he poured out against them. (12)

Her surreptitious studies exposed, Hannah must retreat through the very
doorway whose sudden opening, ironically, brings to a close her halcyon days
in the cottage. It is with much additional irony that the overseer bids Hannah
"begone *home*," when it is the cottage, not the mansion, that has become her
true home.[7] Indeed, after this expulsion from the cottage Hannah will spend
much of the novel searching in vain for other authentic "cottage" spaces. Not
until she has escaped slavery altogether will she rediscover the structure she
yearns for, and with it—by starting "a school for colored children" (237)—
reopen the door that the overseer had metaphorically slammed shut.

To Elevate and Purify

Before the middle of the nineteenth century, for any American, slave or free,
to yearn for a cottage would have been decidedly perverse. The term itself
scarcely registers in the American architectural vocabulary before 1800, particularly in the South, and when "cottage" was used it tended to designate
substandard housing.[8] By the 1850s, however, cottage structures were one of
the most popular topics in American architectural treatises and pattern books.
No longer chiefly suggestive of inadequate means, cottages had become respectable, even desirable, rural housing.

A motive force behind this radical reimagining of cottage space in the
United States—for it was not so much the literal buildings that changed as
the ideas behind them—was American landscape architect Andrew Jackson
Downing. Strongly influenced by British models (in England, a similar transformation had occurred a generation earlier), Downing popularized for American audiences the new cottage ideal. After devoting his first book, 1841's *A
Treatise on the Theory and Practice of Landscape Gardening*, primarily to landscape design, Downing turned more fully in his 1842 volume, *Cottage Residences*, to domestic architecture. In the preface to *Cottage Residences* Downing objected that
contemporary American dwellings were too often "carelessly and ill-contrived,"
resulting in "clumsy" and "unpleasing" structures.[9] His remedy for these ills
was to nurture a more thorough appreciation for beauty in even the most

humble of houses, particularly the rural cottage. "So closely are the Beautiful and the True allied," he wrote, "that we shall find, if we become sincere lovers of the grace, the harmony, and the loveliness with which rural homes and rural life are capable of being invested, that we are silently opening our hearts to an influence which is higher and deeper than the mere *symbol*" (ix, original emphasis). In practical terms, Downing called for "compact, convenient, and comfortable" (vii) homes based on "simple modifications of architectural styles" (23) appropriate to domestic life. The first edition of *Cottage Residences* provided ten specific house plans and site designs, ranging from a simple "suburban" cottage to more elaborate villas; later editions would add even more models. Though not all the plans were within the means of working-class laborers, each cottage conformed to what Downing termed the three leading principles of architecture: fitness, or the beauty of utility; purpose, or the beauty of propriety; and style, or the beauty of form and sentiment. Every home, so arranged and appointed, he argued, would "breathe forth to us, in true, earnest tones, a domestic feeling that at once purifies the heart, and binds us more closely to our fellow beings!" (ix).

Both the *Treatise* and *Cottage Residences* were so well received that they quickly solidified Downing's position as the chief American authority on domestic architecture and landscape design. His influence was truly national. Though based in New York's Hudson Valley, Downing found appreciative audiences in both the North and the South, and openly spoke of influencing the "national taste." (*Cottage Residences* is even listed among the books of Crafts's final owner, John Hill Wheeler, in an 1850 catalogue of his library.)[10] In 1850, at the height of his fame, Downing received a presidential commission to plan the Public Grounds in Washington, D.C. That same year he published *The Architecture of Country Houses*, a return to the terrain of *Cottage Residences* but in far more extensive detail. Describing model cottages, farmhouses, and villas from their orderly architectural blueprints to their tasteful decorative furnishings, *The Architecture of Country Houses* further clarified the moral, social, and aesthetic stakes of refined home-building. The opening paragraph of the first section cuts right to the chase:

> Certainly the national taste is not a matter of little moment. Whether another planet shall be discovered beyond Le Verrier's [Neptune, identified in 1846] may or may not affect the happiness of a whole country; but whether a young and progressive people shall develope [*sic*] ideas of beauty, harmony, and moral significance in their daily lives; whether the arts shall be so understood and cultivated as to elevate and dignify the character; whether the country homes of a whole people shall embody such ideas of beauty and truth as shall elevate and purify its feelings; these are questions of no mean or trifling importance.[11]

Downing's shocking death in a spectacular steamboat fire on the Hudson River in July 1852 only enhanced his reputation as the mid-century's leading "apostle" of elevated and purified taste.[12] New printings and sometimes revised and enlarged editions of all his books continued to be issued after his death, including a much-praised "cheap" edition of *Cottage Residences* in 1853. That same year, George P. Putnam also brought out *Rural Essays,* a 557-page posthumous compilation of Downing's monthly editorial contributions to *The Horticulturalist,* his widely circulating journal. Downing's theories saturated America in the 1850s, even in his physical absence.[13]

Composed during this decade, *The Bondwoman's Narrative* bears deeply the impress of Downing's ideas, beginning with Hannah's attraction to the simple moral beauty of Aunt Hetty's plain yet dignified cottage. Like Downing, Hannah is drawn to the modest rather than the ornate, to neatness over disorder. Even under the duress of captivity she is awake to the beauty of rural forms. "Had we been less confused and troubled our ride probably would have been pleasant," she comments while being transported with her mistress by wagon from jail to the rural estate of their tormentor, Mr. Trappe. "The sharp frosty air was clear and bracing, and the sunshine had a warm summer time look, really delightful. Then, too, the country through which we passed has such a cheerful appearance with rickyards, milestones, farm houses, wagons, swinging signs, horse troughs, trees, fields, fences, and the thousand other things that make a country landscape" (90).

And yet throughout the novel the Downingesque buildings and landscapes that emerge almost inevitably betray rather than uphold his rural ideal, a pattern broken only in *The Bondwoman's Narrative's* final chapter, when Hannah at last inhabits a "neat little Cottage" (237) of her own. The most obvious example of architectural betrayal is perhaps Trappe's country house, which Hannah admiringly describes as a "fine cottage residence" (91) when the wagon finally pulls into his drive. But appearances deceive. As Hannah soon realizes, Trappe's house is no home but instead another prison, and a poorly furnished one at that—a gloomy, silent, anti-domestic space. "Was the house uninhabited except by us?" Hannah later asks (93–94). An even earlier and, for Hannah, more deeply disturbing betrayal, takes place in the modest farmhouse at which she and her mistress seek shelter during their flight from Lindendale. Having already sidestepped one house that looks inhospitable, the fugitives are on alert for architectural signs of welcome. To Hannah, the farmhouse's externals look good: "It was a happy-looking rural, contented spot," she declares,

> wanting, indeed, in the appearance of wealth and luxury, but evidently the abode of competence and peace. I felt that the possessors of such a place must

be hospitable people, that they would have a care for two weak weary wandering women, and so exhorting my mistress to be of good cheer and strong in hope, we entered the gate, and advanced by a neatly graveled walk towards the dwelling. Everything seemed imbued with a quiet air of domestic happiness. Even the little dog came to meet us wagging his tail and frisking as if we were old acquaintances. (59)

Once inside the house, Hannah finds her initial judgment ecstatically confirmed. Soon she is ventriloquizing Downing: "It was the sanctuary of sweet home influences, a holy and blessed spot, so light and warm and with such an abiding air of comfort that one felt ~~so~~ how pure and elevated must be the character of its inmates" (60). It is Aunt Hetty's cottage all over again, complete with a kindly old woman and her husband. "Slavery dwelt not there," Hannah concludes firmly. "A thing so utterly dark and gloomy could not have remained in such a place for a day" (60). And yet of course Hannah is spectacularly wrong. The hostess's brother is none other than Trappe himself, who not only "has a room" (61) in the house but is present that night. Slavery, in other words, is in the very next room.

While the surprise reappearance of Trappe may seem a sloppy narrative contrivance, his threat unfolds with a precise spatial terror that meticulously dismantles the Downing ideal. After informing Hannah and her mistress of her brother's presence, the hostess leads the two anxious fugitives into a room "more secluded and retired than the former ones" (61). Hannah provides a detailed inventory of the room: "It contained a bed very white and sweet, some chairs nicely cushioned, a small bureau, a very little stand, and a table. There was one window, only one, and that was low, little, and curtained by whispering leaves" (62). This is a room whose simple furnishings Downing would admire, right down to the leafy curtains. (Downing regarded vines as the sine qua non of cottage decoration because they "always express domesticity and the presence of heart" [79].) But rather than offer sanctuary, the room exposes its inmates to Trappe's surveillant eye, which penetrates the lone window in a harrowing violation of Downingesque space: "The leafy curtaining of our window was slightly rustled, yet there was no breeze," Hannah recounts. "Again there was a slight rustle, and I distinctly saw a human hand cautiously parting and pushing aside the leaves. The large white fingers were certainly those of a man" (63). Terrorized but giving no sign, Hannah and her mistress pretend to retire in the hope that Trappe will leave them until morning. Hours later, when all is still, they "[push] aside the leaves" (64) and creep through the window to escape once more.

This, too, is Aunt Hetty's cottage all over again: the site of apparent refuge violated by the hand of slavery. Just as Hannah had earlier been forced to leave

Aunt Hetty's cottage through the door flung open by the overseer, so must she and her mistress now squeeze through the space parted by Trappe. In the latter scene, Crafts has Hannah reflect on the vexed relation between bondmen and built space in the South. "Were we ever again to sleep in peace?" she asks. "It seemed not. We must fly again. That very night we must set forth. We must leave the hospitable cottage and its inmates without thanks or ceremony" (63). Fleeing the cottage brings a measure of relief but leaves Hannah and her mistress radically unhoused and thus ultimately, Crafts suggests, unfree. "Under the broad heaven, with the free air, the free leaves, the free beauties of nature about us, we could breathe freer than there," Hannah admits, "but could we hope to escape?" (63). Crafts suggests that a true escape from slavery requires more than freedom from incarceration; it demands a habitation, a free home, or at least a safe one. Complete self-ownership, in other words, requires home-ownership. This necessity makes the paradox of the novel's next episode more clear. After fleeing the farmhouse, Hannah and her mistress find shelter in a frightful structure, an uninhabited cabin that has been the scene of murder. The cabin's contents render it almost the precise opposite of the bedroom Hannah and her mistress have just fled: "There was neither floor, door nor window, an old bench, of which one leg was broken, a broken iron pot, and some pieces of broken crockery were scattered about. In one corner was a heap of damp mouldy straw that had probably served as a bed" (65). And yet this horrific space (the straw is later found to be matted with blood) protects the women for months, nearly the entire summer. It is their longest interval of safety since leaving Lindendale; moreover, it is the only space they can be said to "own" in the course of their flight.[14] "True, a more lonely and desolate place could not be imagined," Hannah notes, "but loneliness was what we sought; in that was our security" (66). The stay in the cabin is by no means a summer's idyll. Hannah's mistress becomes increasingly deranged, and the women cannot possibly survive the winter. And yet despite representing in both design and decoration the antithesis of Downing's rural ideal, the cabin, if not a terminus, is nonetheless an unexpected and important model for Hannah, and for Crafts.

The Slave in the Archway

Practical as they may have been, antebellum pattern books typically shied away from discussions of race and slavery, even when specifically addressing southern forms.[15] This is not to say that pattern books ignored the topic of race entirely. Many mid-century commentators hewed to a hierarchical theory of architectural design consonant with contemporary views about the relative abilities of different races in other arenas. In his 1853 volume *A Home For All*, for example, Orson Squire Fowler instructed his readers that people, like animals, build according to a strict scale of racial intelligence. "This law applies equally to man," he explained. "The Bosjowan builds a rude hut, yet of the lowest type of human architecture, because at the bottom of the ladder. The ruins of Pompeii contain only two houses, and these of rulers, above one story high—humanity then being little developed—while the Hottentot, Carib, Malay, Indian, and Caucasian, build structures better, and better still, corresponding with the order of their mentality."[16] Downing, too, believed in a racial theory of architecture. In Section VI of *The Architecture of Country Houses*, for example, he pauses to clarify his use of the term "English" in describing a certain building type:

> In saying that this is a farm-house in the English rural style, we do not mean that it is a copy of any building in England; but that in designing it we have seized upon that manifestation of rural and domestic beauty in architecture which the Anglo-Saxon race feels more powerfully and more instinctively than any other; and of which the English, who have had so much longer time than we have to work out these finer rural instincts, have given such admirable examples. (159–160)

This is only one passage of many in Downing's writings that emphasizes the significance of America's Anglo-Saxon heritage and the importance of racial instinct in establishing a national architecture in the United States.[17]

In discussing southern building practice, however, Downing proves an exception to the rule of silence on slavery. Two of the house patterns in his most extensive treatise, *The Architecture of Country Houses*, are explicitly southern: Design XXVI, "A Small Country-House for the Southern States," and Design XXXII, "A Villa in the Romanesque Style, for the Middle or Southern States."[18] As the first of the two southern examples, Design XXVI receives more detailed attention for its regional idiosyncrasies. Downing singles out two features that distinguish this dwelling as southern: an extended veranda, "so indispensable to all dwellings in a southern climate," and a detached kitchen, "a peculiar feature in all Southern country-houses" (313). Slavery enters the text during Downing's discussion of the kitchen. "This kitchen contains servants' bed-rooms on its second floor,—only such servants sleeping in the dwelling as are personal attendants on the family. For this reason there is not so much room required for servants in the southern country-house itself—but, as many more servants are kept there than at the north, a good deal more accommodation is provided in the detached kitchen or other negro

Fig. I.   Andrew Jackson Downing, Design XXVI, "Small Southern Country House"
(*The Architecture of Country Houses*, 1850).

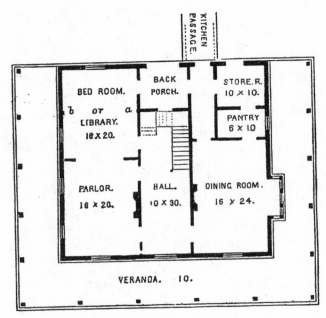

Fig. 2.   Andrew Jackson Downing, Design XXVI, "Principal
Floor" (*The Architecture of Country Houses*, 1850).

houses" (313–314). Although Downing always calls slaves servants, rendering them semantically indistinguishable from northern domestic employees and thereby partially camouflaging the nature of slave labor, he does show here an understanding of the South's complex architecture of segregation.[19] Since Downing's interest lies primarily in the master's house, he leaves any further account of slave accommodations vague. But this is not the last mention of slavery. Two paragraphs later Downing must explain yet another peculiar configuration required by the peculiar institution:

> In the rear of the hall is a back porch—which is a part of the veranda—that may be left open. Adjoining it is an entry or passage-way, five feet wide, for the servants to pass from the dining-room to the detached kitchen, without the necessity of entering the back porch or hall. Alongside of this entry is a large store-room (which is also part of the enclosed veranda), 10 by 10 feet. This is the larder and pastry-room, under the care of the mistress of the house; and adjoining it and the dining-room is a pantry or china-closet. (314)

Here the spatial divisions are unmistakable: the externalized kitchen and passageway belong to the slaves, whereas the mistress controls the interior larder. Although Downing favored spatial segregation in his plans for northern dwellings as well, nowhere in pattern-book literature is the effect of slavery on building design and the circulation of bodies more clear.[20]

It seems all the more noteworthy, then, that the engraving (Figure 1) and the floor plan (Figure 2) for this house—each of which shows the passageway in a different position—introduce a measure of confusion rather than clarity regarding the final home design, a confusion Downing must hasten to dispel. Returning to the detached kitchen yet a third time, he explains:

> We have shown the covered passage to the kitchen, and part of the kitchen itself, in our sketch of the *front* elevation, merely to convey an idea of their effect; though the position of those on the plan is in the rear, and not on the side of the house. This, however, is a matter of mere locality, as the kitchen and other outbuildings will, of course, be placed on the side offering the greatest facilities for their uses, and, at the same time, keeping them most in the background. (315, original emphasis)

Downing's obsessive return, every few paragraphs, to the "detached" and thus ostensibly unseen labors of the southern slave is fantastically amplified by the presence of a most unusual figure in the engraving of the house itself. Framed in the archway of the passage connecting kitchen to villa is a female slave, in all likelihood carrying food to the main house (Figure 3). A startling rarity in pattern-book engravings, the slave is presumably there to illustrate, as though it weren't clear enough from the text, the purpose of the passageway. Ironically, this places her not "in the back-ground," as Downing's text would have her, but very much in the foreground, a position accentuated by her perfect centering in the arch's frame and the absence of any white figures in the drawing. The only other person depicted is yet another slave, framed neatly in the window to the right of the arch, who appears to be returning from the main house to the kitchen. The one figure kept in the background in this illustration, one might say, is the master, who is presumably inside the house receiving the food being ferried from the kitchen. The master remains hidden from view, however, only until the next engraving, a "variation" on the main design in which a planter can clearly be seen standing on the veranda, looking out over his plantation (Figure 4). In this drawing, it is finally the kitchen and its laborers that are put out of view.[21] Downing's compulsion simultaneously to depict and to screen the workings of slavery affects nearly every aspect of his discussion of this southern country house, including his closing estimate of its costs. Whereas for other plans Downing provides exact estimates for materials and labor, in this design slavery's blurry economics make such precision impossible. Without quite fingering the reason explicitly, Downing euphemistically explains that the cost of the house will differ depending on "the locality where it is built" and on "the price of lumber, labor, etc., *which varies largely in the South*" (317, my emphasis).

One reason for Downing's evasiveness about slavery, besides the general tendency of pattern books to avoid the topic altogether, might be an unacknowledged or unarticulated recognition of the threat that human bondage posed to his conception of an independent citizenry, which depends so deeply on individual home-ownership. For despite his insistence on a racial hierarchy of architectural feeling, Downing believed even more passionately in a "free and manly" republicanism that leveled old world distinctions of class, hearth by humble hearth. "But the true home still remains to us," Downing insisted. "Not, indeed, the feudal castle, not the baronial hall, but the home of the individual man—the home of that family of equal rights, which continually separates and continually reforms itself in the new world—the republican home, built by no robbery of the property of another class, maintained by no infringement of a brother's right" (269). If Downing's language veers toward abolitionist rhetoric, it is of course little different in that regard from countless other anti-aristocratic pronouncements never intended to apply to slaves. Nor was Downing in any conventional sense a social leveler.[22] And yet so invested was Downing in an equal opportunity and anti-hereditary politics of

Fig. 3.   Close-up of Downing, Design XXVI, "Small Southern Country House" (*The Architecture of Country Houses*, 1850).

Fig. 4.   Andrew Jackson Downing, Design XXVI, "Exterior of Southern Country House" (*The Architecture of Country Houses*, 1850).

home-ownership, one suspects that talking too much about slavery—especially in a text completed in 1850, amidst intensified sectional animosity—would risk exposing the limits of Downing's rhetoric. Better perhaps to underplay slavery's contradictions than to undermine his most ambitiously democratic claims:

> The just pride of a true American is not in a great hereditary home, but in greater hereditary institutions. It is more to him that all his children will be born under wise, and just, and equal laws, than that one of them should come into the world with a great family estate. It is better, in his eyes, that is should be possible for the humblest laborer to look forward to the possession of a future country-house and home like his own, than to feel that a wide and impassable gulf of misery separates him, the lord of the soil, from a large class of his fellow beings born beneath him. (270)

To the extent that they were heard by African Americans, Downing's words must have resonated deeply with long-standing black yearnings for permanence of place through the possession of a home. In this light, Crafts's interest in putting pressure on Downing's ideology by imagining a succession of pattern-book cottages violated by the hand of slavery seems designed not so much to expose that ideology's hypocrisy as to capture its promise for blacks, to activate its tropes and ideals for its excluded audience. Effectively racializing antebellum architectural discourse, we might say, *The Bondwoman's Narrative* implicitly encourages readers to reconsider Downing's theories from the point of view of the slave in the archway.

I would argue that this is the case even where such concerns about space and slavery seem least pressing, as, for example, in the "Forget me not" chapters. At first glance, Hannah's detailed description of the architectural and decorative features of the Henry family's house might seem charmingly incidental to the novel's larger plot and thus unconnected to racial politics. After all, the description of "Forget me not" interrupts the forward movement of the story for nearly three pages and consists largely of a room-by-room aesthetic evaluation of the house. When one realizes that much of the description in these pages is in fact borrowed from Charles Dickens's *Bleak House* (1852–1853), a text with no explicit connection to American slavery, the quaint irrelevance of this interlude seems confirmed. Yet I would suggest not only that the detailed description of "Forget me not" is germane to the novel's larger escape plot but that through subtle allusions to Downing, Crafts explores the meaning—or rather the unmeaning—of the house to a slave like Hannah.

The allusions to Downing appear in the introductory frame of the extra-ordinary description that opens Chapter 10 of *The Bondwoman's Narrative.* When the narrator asserts that "Every house with its surroundings possesses an air of individuality" (121), for example, her words echo Downing's pro-nouncement in *The Architecture of Country Houses* that "the country house should, above all things, manifest individuality" (262). In the section in which Down-ing makes this assertion, "What a Country House or Villa Should Be," he compares homes built by different types of men: men of "common sense" (262), men of "sentiment" (263), men of "imagination" (263), and men of "the past" (265). "Forget me not"—which Hannah describes as "one of those dear old houses . . . whose construction from first to last bespeaks an as-sociation with the past" (121)—belongs emphatically in this final group. The material details that instantiate the association of "Forget me not" with the past make the house seem merely "old-fashioned," a description Hannah uses repeatedly. In Downing's assessment, however, houses that look back instead of forward risk being out of touch with the currents of the day. "In every age and country are born some persons who belong rather to the past than the present—men to whom memory is dearer than hope," Downing explains. "It is not for these men . . . to understand and appreciate the value of an archi-tecture significant of the present time" (265). However fitting for such men, Downing contends, an architecture of the past is "unmeaning for the many, and especially for all those who more truly belong to our own time and cen-tury" (266).

Crafts encourages us to recognize the dangers of the house's backward glance. If Hannah's room-by-room inventory gives a strong sense of "Forget me not" as domestic space, even as a potential home in which she might live—later in the novel she will remember "Forget me not" chiefly for its "home-bred air of genial quiet and ropose [*sic*]" (198)—once Hannah learns of Mrs. Henry's promise to her dead father "never on any occasion to buy or sell a ser-vant" (127), the architecture of "Forget me not" becomes unmeaning to the escaped slave. Or to use another of Downing's formulations, this is the mo-ment for Hannah when "memory" trumps "hope." It is thus also the moment when Crafts turns the name of the Henry plantation into an element of plot instead of merely an incidental description. For why does the narrator say that "Forget me not" is "not inappropriately named"? Because "forget me not" is the mandate from Mrs. Henry's dead father that prevents her from bestowing on Hannah "the greatest favor that a mild kind hearted man or woman can bestow on members of the outcast servile race" (127). "Forget me not" is the perfect name for this house, and in the end it is with deep irony, rather than quaint appreciation, that the narrator registers this fact. Once Mrs. Henry's house can no longer be Hannah's home, Hannah feels "harassing anxiety" (133) within its walls instead of domestic pleasure. When Hannah finally leaves "Forget me not"—delivered by Mrs. Henry into the duplicitous grip of Mrs. Wheeler—we are treated to no last encomiums on the house, no tearful (or even stoic) farewell. The house of the past has lost its spell.

Black House

If the pattern books dodged the question of slavery, where might an interested reader (or author) turn for a discussion of race and architecture in the 1850s? To the very front lines of the ideological battle over bondage. By mid-decade, representations of built space had become indispensable features of the literature of slavery in both the North and the South, as each side deployed architectural imagery to buttress sectional claims. Journalistic accounts by northerners of their tours through the South, for example, often included detailed descriptions (and sometimes illustrations) of plantation housing, slave and free.[23] Slave narratives, for example, had long dissected the physical contours of segregation and in the 1850s were paying special attention to intrusions on African American domestic space. (Harriet Jacobs's *Incidents in the Life of a Slave Girl* [1861], in its depiction of Jacobs's paradoxically liberating self-confinement in her garret, provides one of the most incisive spatial commentaries of the decade.[24]) The catalytic text in this development was Harriet Beecher Stowe's *Uncle Tom's Cabin* (1852). Stowe not only gave dramatic fictional form to the slave cabin but chose to let that "lowly" space carry the titular weight of her critique. Stowe also animated, usually with trenchant irony, the grander structures of slavery, from the "well-furnished dining parlor" in which Mr. Shelby arranges Tom's sale, to the Moorish excess of the St. Clare mansion, to the decaying estates of the vicious Legree.[25] The surest sign that Stowe's architectural representations had hit their mark is the vehemence and consistency with which her southern debunkers sought to reverse her tropes. Nearly every response to *Uncle Tom's Cabin* stages, early in the text, a socio-architectural rebuttal of Stowe's depictions. In these books, planters' mansions are always tasteful and refined, slave quarters stunningly clean and comfortable. No crumbling Legree plantations or fetid slave huts here, no ma'am—only the honest and open forms of a benevolent institution. Architectural challenges to Stowe and the slave narratives were so central to this genre that they sometimes took visual form, as in the frontispiece to J. W. Page's 1853 novel, *Uncle Robin in His Cabin in Virginia, and Tom Without One in Boston*, "A View of Selma" (Figure 5). This illustration draws on the visual idiom of the pattern books not simply to prove the inherent comfort of the enslaved but, one

Fig. 5. "A View of Selma," frontispiece to J. W. Page, *Uncle Robin in His Cabin in Virginia, and Tom Without One in Boston* (1853).

might say, to model it. Save for the presence of the slave cabins themselves, this drawing would not be out of place in one of Downing's texts, right down to the pair of tiny figures conversing in the left margin.

In its own architectural depictions, *The Bondwoman's Narrative* borrows much not only from Stowe but also, surprisingly, from her southern rebutters. The traces of Stowe's spatial imagination are evident throughout Crafts's text, from its invocation of Rachel Halliday's peaceful Quaker settlement to its use of a tripartite plantation structure very similar to Stowe's.[26] And yet there are also passages in *The Bondwoman's Narrative* that draw uncannily on southern tropes. Compare, for example, these two descriptions of visits to slave quarters, the first from Mary H. Eastman's *Aunt Phillis's Cabin; or, Southern Life As It Is* (1852), the second from *The Bondwoman's Narrative*:

It was just sundown, but the servants were all at home after their day's work, and they too were enjoying the pleasant evening time. Some were seated at the door of their cabins, others lounging on the grass, all at ease, and without care. Many of their comfortable cabins had been recently whitewashed, and were adorned with little gardens in front; over the one nearest the house a multiflora rose was creeping in full bloom. Singularly musical voices were heard at intervals, singing snatches of songs, of a style in which the servants of the South especially delight. (*Aunt Phillis's Cabin*, 29)

After the evening repast I attended Mrs Henry in a very pleasant walk among the negro lodges, and in looking over their little truck patches and gardens, all of which gave evidence of being neatly attended in the absence of weeds and the appearance of thrifty growth in the various plants, vegetables, and flowers, designed for use and ornament. Various groups of persons, young and old, all of whom seemed impressed with a ~~feeling of reverence of the day~~ reverential feeling of the sanctity of the day, and of regard for their mistress, were seated on little low benches at their doors, quiet[l]y enjoying the beauty of the evening. (*The Bondwoman's Narrative*, 138)

The slave cabin tour is a stock device of pro-slavery texts. Sometimes it is rendered by the narrator, as in the example from *Aunt Phillis's Cabin* above. In other texts, the tour is dramatized in the plot, as when a northern visitor takes his or her first peek into the cabins, usually to declare with great surprise (as does the planter's Pennsylvania bride in *Uncle Robin in His Cabin in Virginia*) something like "My dear husband, how very comfortable and neat they all seem to be!"[27] Hannah's peculiar status at the Henry plantation, where she is acknowledged as a slave but not as the Henry's slave, coupled with her experiential divide from field hands, help place her in the outsider's position in this scene. Ultimately, however, Hannah's tour registers less surprise than appreciation, not only for Mrs. Henry's benevolence but also for the slaves' self-sufficiency. Whereas *Aunt Phillis's Cabin* works to obscure slave agency—when Eastman's narrator says that "Many of [the slaves'] comfortable cabins had been recently whitewashed, and were adorned with little gardens in front," the credit for these conditions falls to the magnanimous planter—Crafts's description foregrounds more active slave caretaking: "[all] the little truck patches and gardens . . . gave evidence of being neatly attended." Indeed, like the decrepit old cabin in the woods, these lodges provide a partial model for the neat, independent cottage Hannah herself will eventually own.[28]

If, as I have been suggesting, *The Bondwoman's Narrative* is deeply attuned to literary representations of built space, then the "architectural" text with which Crafts's novel indicates its closest familiarity, intriguingly, is Dickens's *Bleak House*. As Hollis Robbins argues elsewhere in this volume, Crafts's borrowings from Dickens are alchemic rather than plagiaristic; her copies transform their British models instead of simply replicating them. The three-page description of "Forget me not," the most extensive and explicit architectural allusion in Crafts's text, is adapted from Chapter 6 of Dickens's novel, "Quite at Home," in which Esther Summerson describes Bleak House itself for the first time. Here is the opening sentence of Dickens's description, followed by a corresponding excerpt from Crafts's text:

> It was one of those delightfully irregular houses where you go up and down steps out of one room into another, and where you come upon more rooms when you think you have seen all there are, and where there is a bountiful provision of little halls and passages, and where you find still older cottage-rooms in unexpected places, with lattice windows and green growth pressing through them. (*Bleak House,* 61)[29]

> Who does not find a charm about these ancient houses, with their delightfully irregular apartments. . . . [Y]ou pass from one room into another, and go up and down steps, and note a bountiful supply of little halls, entries, and passages leading you cannot tell where. Then every room seems a wonder in itself, with its old-fashioned fire place, and little windows, surrounded by lattice work with the luxuriant growth of honey-suckle and jasmine pressing through it. (*The Bondwoman's Narrative,* 121–122)

Both the directness of Crafts's borrowing and her alterations of the source text are evident here. Key descriptions and actions jump unchanged from Dickens to Crafts, such as "delightfully irregular" and "go up and down steps." Other phrases are slightly revised: "bountiful provision" becomes "bountiful supply"; "little halls and passages" becomes "little halls, entries, and passages"; "lattice windows" become "little windows, surrounded by lattice work." The ellipsis in the Crafts passage above, which marks the omission of seven additional lines of text, indicates the extent to which Crafts reworked her Dickens borrowings to propel, rather than merely puff out, her narrative. A continued side-by-side comparison of the descriptions of Bleak House and "Forget me not" would also make clear Crafts's use of compression and dilation in adapting the Dickens passage to its new narrative context. In the detailed cataloguing of individual rooms that follows the introductory lines above, for example, Crafts excises a number of material details that stamp the Bleak House description as particularly British.[30] She also carries the description of "Forget me not" outside the house to include the rest of the plantation estate, making the American setting clear. "In the lodges of the servants, and every thing pertaining to the establishment the same variety was observable," Hannah notes. "Method and regularity likewise prevailed over the estate. The overseer was gentle and kind, and the slaves were industrious and obedient . . . " (123).

Why so much, so carefully transplanted, from *Bleak House*? I would argue that the identification of "Forget me not" with Bleak House helps Crafts activate a trope of self-ownership through home-ownership that is unavailable through her other sources; that this activation, and the role of the *Bleak House* borrowing in it, become fully clear only at the end of Crafts's novel through the introduction of yet another, more subtle, allusion to Dickens; and finally that the very extensiveness of her allusions—to one of the most widely known imaginary houses in British or American culture in the 1850s—suggests that Crafts wanted the parallels to Dickens understood rather than overlooked.

To test these claims, we will need to move to the end of *The Bondwoman's Narrative*. It is here that Hannah's journey completes the arc of desire initiated in Aunt Hetty's tidy house: "I dwell now in a neat little Cottage," Hannah announces in the final chapter of the novel, "and keep a school for colored children" (237). The unusual capitalization of Cottage elevates this structure to the Downingesque ideal while simultaneously alluding to the end of *Bleak House*, which converges on a nearly identical, but easily overlooked, space: Esther Summerson's cottage. This is the "rustic," "lovely place" (797) given to Esther by her guardian, Mr. Jarndyce, as a physical gesture of his freeing Esther—his former housekeeper—to marry her true love, Allan Woodcourt, instead of Jarndyce himself. Fitted out by Jarndyce exactly according to Esther's taste, the cottage's particular loveliness both anticipates Esther's future bliss and affirms her proprietorship, even though Esther does not yet realize the cottage is to be hers:

> . . . as we went through the pretty rooms, out at the little rustic verandah doors, and underneath the tiny wooden colonnades, garlanded with woodbine, jasmine, and honey-suckle, I saw, in the papering of the walls, in the colours of the furniture, in the arrangement of all the pretty objects, *my* little tastes and fancies, *my* little methods and inventions which they used to laugh at while they praised them, my odd ways everywhere. (797)

Of all the ways that *Bleak House* matters to *The Bondwoman's Narrative* this is perhaps the most important. Like Esther, Hannah Crafts ends her tale not as housekeeper but as homeowner, happily ensconced in an independent cottage, loving husband by her side. Lest the point be missed, Crafts gives Hannah's cottage a twin in the novel's final paragraph. "I must not omit telling who are my neighbors," Hannah interjects. "Charlotte, Mrs. Henry's favorite, and her husband. From the window where I sit, a tiny white cottage half-shaded in summer by rose-vines and honeysuckle appears at the foot of a sloping green.

~~Before it is now~~ In front there is such an exquisite flower-garden, and behind such a dainty orchard of choice fruits"—Esther's cottage is surrounded by a similar garden and similar orchard—"that it does one good to think of it. It is theirs" (239). *It does one good to think of it.* At the end of this novel the idea of African American proprietorship, of the free black home, compels: *It is theirs.* No other literary text whose influence on Crafts's narrative we have been tracing provides a similar image. For Harriet Jacobs the lack of such a structure casts a shadow over her very freedom. "The dream of my life is not yet realized," she admits. "I do not sit with my children in a home of my own. I still long for a hearthstone of my own, however humble" (302). The depth of Jacobs's lament accentuates the importance of Hannah's success.[31]

In trying to image forth black home-ownership, the author of *The Bondwoman's Narrative* pursues in fiction a sociopolitical strategy that black activists like Frederick Douglass pressed outside the text. As Sarah Luria has shown, Douglass "urged African Americans to acquire homes of their own." The reasons, Luria explains, were multiple:

> A home provided a second skin by which African Americans could define themselves by class, taste, and morality rather than by their skin color. A respectable home did more than any speech or law to establish one's social equality. If blacks could acquire middle-class homes, then the chances for social contact with one's white neighbors would be improved greatly and so too the chances for lasting social change. . . . Further, private property offered African Americans the one spot in American life where they might exert significant control.[32]

Like Crafts, Douglass, too, admired Dickens's *Bleak House*, which appears to have been a touchstone for African Americans in the 1850s and after. In the 1880s Douglass even went so far as to dub the one-room, cabin-like structure that he erected as a study behind his Cedar Hill home in Washington, D.C., his "Growlery," after Mr. Jarndyce's home office of the same name. According to Luria, Douglass's unusual study—a cross between a slave cabin and a rustic cottage—was one of several ways Douglass deliberately sought to challenge "conventional definitions of race" in his postbellum Washington home.[33] In the end, Crafts's antebellum transformation of Esther's modest cottage into a powerful image of black home-ownership—of Bleak House into a *black* house, we might say—functions analogously. Much as Douglass would choose a hilltop with a prominent view of the federal capital to deliver his architectural message, Crafts selects one of the most prominent literary texts of the decade to provide the ground for her own.

Conclusion: New Patterns

There is yet a final, fitting way we might think about Crafts's architectural borrowings from Dickens. By selecting from *Bleak House* those passages most applicable to her own story and then reworking them in a fresh context, Crafts treats Dickens's text much the way mid-century builders treated pattern books. As architectural historian Dell Upton has shown, although the architects who wrote pattern books typically prescribed every measurement and relation—offering integrated designs that stood as "cohesive artistic productions"—the builders who were hired to translate those designs into actual physical structures used the pattern books far more selectively. Builders tended to add to existing structures, borrowing and adapting what elements they needed to complete a job, rather than building exactly according to an architect's plan. Crafts, in other words, isn't trying to copy *Bleak House*, either sneakily or sloppily. She is borrowing selectively from Dickens (and other writers), adapting familiar passages to new ends while demonstrating her literary knowledge and transformative skill. In the case of Esther Summerson, Crafts borrows Dickens's original narrative design—the housekeeper turned homeowner—in order to fit out her own depiction of the independent black home.

If Esther's cottage, moreover, is made visible at the end of *The Bondwoman's Narrative* only by the sheer copiousness of the borrowings in the earlier "Forget me not" description—which puts Bleak House as a structure in the mind of an alert mid-century reader—then it seems appropriate that the very last scenes of Crafts's novel point back to the "Forget me not" episode a final time. They do so literally, of course, by having Charlotte and William, the original fugitives of "Forget me not," resurface unharmed. But these scenes also return to "Forget me not" metaphorically, in the surprising advent of Hannah's mother. In narrating this unanticipated plot twist—all Hannah has ever said about her parents is that "no one ever spoke of my father or mother" (5)—Hannah explains that despite being sold from Lindendale while she was still an infant, her mother "*never forgot me* nor certain marks on my body, by which I might be identified in after years" (237, my emphasis). Here Crafts confers an even richer significance on the name "Forget me not": where Mrs. Henry's refusal to forget punishes Hannah, Hannah's mother's refusal to forget ultimately rewards her long-lost daughter. As though to drive this reversal home, Crafts reprises, then revises, the emotional heart of Hannah's pleading interview with Mrs. Henry. In that earlier scene, after Hannah begs Mrs. Henry to purchase her—"You have no idea how good I will be, or how exactly I will conform myself to all your wishes" (126), she insists—Mrs. Henry lifts Hannah from the floor, embraces her, and "compassionate[s]" over her. "She wept," Hannah relates, "and our tears were mingled together" (126). In the novel's final chapter, however, Hannah and her mother share tears of wild joy when their true relation is discovered. "I was then resting for the first time on my mother's bosom—my mother for whom my heart had yearned, and my spirit gone out in intense longing many many times," marvels Hannah.

> And we had been brought together by such strange and devious ways. With our arms clasped around each other, our heads bowed together, and our tears mingling we went down on our knees, and returned thanks to Him, who had watched over us for good, and whose merciful power we recognized in this the greatest blessing of our lives. (238)

In terms of narrative design, the "strange and devious ways" by which Hannah and her mother are brought together seem as much Crafts's as any higher power's. Having thwarted Hannah's desire to live at "Forget me not," Crafts in the end gives her all she wishes and more: her own freedom, her own husband, her own mother, all neatly packaged in her own home. Not even the orphaned Esther Summerson can claim quite as much.

Indeed, the intensity of desire expressed in this final chapter, "In Freedom," surpasses any emotive language the text has earlier offered and encompasses both people and place. "Can you guess who lives with me?" Hannah asks in the first paragraph. "You never could—my own dear mother, aged and venerable, yet so smart and lively and active, and Oh: so fond of me" (237). The conjunctive rush of "ands" that propels this sentence comes to a sudden and powerful pause at Hannah's "Oh," and in the space between the colon and the final phrase ("so fond of me") one senses the depth of pleasure made possible by the mother-daughter reunion.[34] If this pleasure remains nearly inarticulable—"And then I—but I cannot tell what I did, I was so crazy with delight" (238), avers Hannah—it nonetheless permeates the final image of "undeviating happiness" that Hannah feels in "the society of my mother, my husband, and my friends" (239), cottaged side by side in self-owned freedom. "I will let the reader picture it all to his imagination," Hannah concludes, "and say farewell" (239).

Of course Crafts's imagined reader never had that opportunity. Nor have we yet uncovered enough information about Crafts to gauge the degrees of fact and fantasy involved in Hannah's final transformation. Whatever discoveries await, one wonders what kind of effect the completed circuit of cottage desire in *The Bondwoman's Narrative* might have had on African American readers had the manuscript found a publisher. Perhaps Crafts's careful reworkings of Downing and Dickens would have offered black writers new patterns to use in shaping their own spatial imaginings, whether in the crucible of the Civil War, or of Reconstruction, or of Jim Crow. In a more recent imagining of what "housing without boundaries" might look like, bell hooks has declared, "It is my conviction that African-Americans can respond to the contemporary crises we face by learning from and building on strategies of opposition and resistance that were effective in the past and empowering in the present."[35] If Crafts's contemporaries were denied the chance to build on her text, then perhaps it is to us that the opportunity finally falls.

Notes

Portions of the research for this essay were undertaken with the support of a National Endowment for the Humanities fellowship at the Winterthur Museum, Garden, and Library, and I am grateful for the generous assistance of both institutions. I would also like to thank Hollis Robbins and the audience at the Delaware Seminar in Art, History, and Material Culture for their comments and suggestions on an earlier version of this essay.

1. Hannah Crafts, *The Bondwoman's Narrative*, ed. Henry Louis Gates, Jr. (New York: Warner Books, 2002), 214, 215. Subsequent references will appear parenthetically in the text.

2. On yet another level, this scene touches insightfully on the psychology of place attachment among African American slaves, whose legal status as property rather than persons made the question of belonging to a physical place or landscape particularly acute.

3. bell hooks, Julie Eizenberg, and Hank Koning, "House, 20 June 1994," *assemblage* 24 (August 1994): 23.

4. Throughout this essay I will refer to the author as Crafts and will assume, following Henry Louis Gates, Jr., "that she was female, mulatto, a slave of John Hill Wheeler's, an autodidact, and a keen observer of the dynamics of slave life." See Henry Louis Gates, Jr., "Introduction," *The Bondwoman's Narrative*, by Hannah Crafts, ed. Henry Louis Gates, Jr. (New York: Warner Books, 2002), lxxii.

5. The seemingly unusual floor plan of the fictional De Vincent mansion, in which the original drawing room later becomes part of Lindendale's "southern turret," reflects a typical construction pattern for "ancient mansions" in colonial Virginia: a gradual expansion of a modest structure over time. In Virginia (and also elsewhere in the South), the original so-called "mansion"—which despite the appellation may have had as few as four rooms, since larger structures were exceedingly uncommon—may or may not have been incorporated into the final house design. Thomas Jefferson's first house at Monticello, for example, an 18' X 18' box erected in 1770, eventually became his "South Pavillion" once the estate was complete. See Mechal Sobel, *The World They Made Together: Black and White Values in Eighteenth-Century Virginia* (Princeton: Princeton University Press, 1987), 100. Readers who may object that the "turret" design of Lindendale makes it inappropriately European for Crafts's American setting may be surprised to know that it was precisely during the 1850s that literal towers were becoming fashionable (on paper, if not always in practice) in the American South. Consider, for example, Hawkwood, a Louisa County, Virginia, plantation designed for Richard Overton Morris by Alexander Jackson Davis in 1851 (completed in 1852–1854) as an Italianate villa. See Charles E. Brownell, *The Making of Virginia Architecture* (Richmond: Virginia Museum of Fine Arts, 1992), 278–279.

6. In Disney's ride, the flashes from a make-believe lightning storm reveal hideous faces or other unexpected subtexts beneath the benign surfaces of the mansion's paintings.

7. Of course the cottage's proximity to Lindendale and the overseer's apparent jurisdiction within it suggests that it is owned by Hannah's master, already compromising its ability to offer Hannah a home outside of slavery.

8. See John E. Crowley, "'In Happier Mansions, Warm, and Dry': The Invention of the Cottage as the Comfortable Anglo-American House," *Winterthur Portfolio* 32 (Summer/Autumn, 1997): 170; and Carl R. Lounsbury, ed., *An Illustrated Glossary of Early Southern Architecture and Landscape* (New York: Oxford University Press, 1997), 97.

9. Andrew Jackson Downing, *Cottage Residences* (New York: Wiley and Putnam, 1842), vii, ix, vii. Subsequent references will appear parenthetically in the text. Downing did include a brief section on rural architecture at the end of *A Treatise on the Practice and Theory of Landscape Gardening*.

10. See John Hill Wheeler, *Library Catalogue*, John Hill Wheeler Papers #765, Southern Historical Collection, Wilson Library, University of North Carolina at Chapel Hill. For more on Downing's cultural standing, see George B. Tatum, "The Downing Decade," George B. Tatum and Elisabeth B. MacDougall, eds., *Prophet With Honor: The Career of Andrew Jackson Downing, 1815–1852* (Washington, D.C.: Dumbarton Oaks, 1989); and Adam W. Sweeting, *Reading Houses and Building Books: Andrew Jackson Downing and the Architecture of Popular Antebellum Literature, 1835–1855* (Hanover, N.H.: University Press of New England, 1996). In *Avery's Choice: One Hundred Years of an Architectural Library, 1890–1990* (New York: G. K. Hall, 1997), Adolf Placzek and Angela Giral describe Downing's next book, 1850's *The Architecture of Country Houses*, as "arguably the most important work on domestic architecture of the antebellum decades" (159). On Downing's popularity in the South, see Catherine W. Bishir, "A Spirit of Improvement: Changes in Building Practice, 1830–1860," in *Architects and Builders in North Carolina: A History of the Practice of Building*, ed. Catherine W. Bishir, Charlotte V. Brown, Carl R. Lounsbury, and Ernest H. Wood III (Chapel Hill: University of North Carolina Press, 1990), 138–12 and 149–150.

11. Andrew Jackson Downing, *The Architecture of Country Houses* (New York: D. Appleton, 1850), 1. Subsequent references will appear parenthetically in the text.

12. On the steamboat fire and Downing as an "apostle" of middle-class taste, see David Schuyler, *Apostle of Taste: Andrew Jackson Downing, 1815–1852* (Baltimore: Johns Hopkins University Press, 1996). Nathaniel Hawthorne's sister Louisa was also killed in the *Henry Clay* fire.

13. Despite the imposing length of *Rural Essays*, one reviewer declared "there is not a chapter or page which we would spare. . . . It must take its place as a domestic classic." See the *New Englander and Yale Review* 11 (August 1853): 474–475. During the 1850s alone, Downing's four main books were reprinted at least twenty different times. His *Treatise* (already in its fourth edition) was reprinted in 1850, 1852, 1853 (new edition), 1854, 1855, 1856, 1857, and 1859 (new edition); *Cottage Residences* was reprinted in 1852 (new edition), 1853, and 1856; *The Architecture of Country Houses* (first edition 1850) was reprinted in 1851, 1852, 1853, 1854, 1855, and 1856; and *Rural Essays* (first edition 1853) was reprinted in 1854, 1856, and 1857. See Henry-Russell Hitchcock, *American Architectural Books*, new expanded edition (New York: Da Capo Press, 1976), 31–34.

14. Even the party of hunters that discovers Hannah and her mistress avow the cabin is too frightening a place to sleep in. "Faith, I wouldn't stay here a night for all ~~your master's~~ that was once your master's fortune" (69), declares one.

15. As David Schuyler observes in his introductory essay to a modern reprint edition of another pattern book, Henry W. Cleaveland et al.'s *Village and Farm Cottages*, "True, the sectional traumas that threatened the nation are absent, but so they were from most books devoted to the principles of design published during that decade." See Schuyler, "Villages and Farm Cottages: The Ideology of Domesticity," in *Villages and Farm Cottages: A Victorian Stylebook of 1856* (Watkins Glen, N.Y.: American Life Foundation, 1982), n.p.

16. Orson Squire Fowler, *A Home For All, or the Gravel Wall and Octagon Mode of Building* (1853); reprinted as *The Octagon House: A Home For All* (New York: Dover, 1973), 11.

17. See, for example, Andrew Jackson Downing, *Rural Essays* (New York: Putnam, 1853), 121. In a related vein, Downing also believed strongly in regional fitness in architecture, arguing that certain national forms were better suited aesthetically for particular American topographies, such as Rural Gothic for the "broken country" of the North and Modern Italian for the "plain and valley surfaces of the Middle and Southern States." See Downing, *The Architecture of Country Houses*, 274.

18. Alterations to subsequent editions of Downing's texts sometimes changed the numbering of his illustrations. Design XXVI was renumbered XXVII in the 1851 edition of *The Architecture of Country Houses*, while Design XXXII (itself adapted from Design VIII in *Cottage Residences*) was renumbered XXX in 1851. See Jane B. Davies, "Davis and Downing: Collaborators in the Picturesque," in *Prophet With Honor: The Career of Andrew Jackson Downing, 1815–1852*, ed. George B. Tatum and Elisabeth B. MacDougall (Washington, D.C.: Dumbarton Oaks, 1989), 119–120. For clarity, like Davies I will use Downing's original 1850 numbering.

19. For more on the dispersal of slave accommodations, see John Michael Vlach, *Back of the Big House: The Architecture of Plantation Slavery* (Chapel Hill: University of North Carolina Press, 1993).

20. This is not to say, of course, that slaves didn't routinely circumvent such segregatory and circulatory regulations in the South. See, for example, Vlach, *Back of the Big House*, 235–236. On Downing and spatial segregation more broadly, see Sweeting, *Reading Houses and Building Books*, 43.

21. Identifying the figure on the veranda as a southern planter might seem unremarkable given the southern context provided in this section of *The Architecture of Country Houses*. And yet this specific "variation" sketch originally appeared in the first issue of Downing's *The Horticulturalist* in 1846, where it was captioned "Design for a Simple Country House" and given no southern inflection. According to Jane B. Davies, this sketch—recaptioned "Exterior of Southern Country House" in *The Architecture of Country Houses*—was drawn by Alexander Jackson Davis, who contributed many of the designs in Downing's text. Davies confirms, however, that Downing himself designed and delineated the engraving for Design XXVI. See Davies, "Davis and Downing," 121.

22. On Downing and social leveling, see Dell Upton, "Pattern Books and Professionalism: Aspects of the Transformation of Domestic Architecture in the United States, 1800–1860," *Winterthur Portfolio* 19.2/3 (Summer/Autumn 1984): 124–125.

23. See, for example, C. G. Parsons, *Inside View of Slavery: or a Tour Among the Planters* (Boston: John P. Jewett; Cleveland: Jewett, Proctor and Worthington, 1855). Frederick Law Olmsted's travel narratives frequently included illustrations of precisely the type of slave housing and work arrangements that the pattern books tended to ignore. See, for example, the illustrations in his *A Journey in the Seaboard Slave States* (New York: Dix and Edwards, 1856), especially pp. 16,

71, 344, 385, 423, 629. Given Olmsted's interest in both design and slavery, his travel texts might be said to mediate between the architect's (Downing's) efforts to evade discussions of race and the novelist's (Crafts's) efforts to reexamine pattern book ideology from a slave's perspective. My thanks to Bernard Herman for suggesting this possibility.

24. Jacobs depicts the perversion of cottage space by slavery not only through the confining garret but in the "lonely cottage" that Mr. Flint begins building for her "four miles away from the town." In many ways, Jacobs's narrative pivots on this structure: Jacobs evades Flint's cottage trap only by making her "plunge into the abyss" by initiating her sexual relationship with the white Mr. Sands. See Harriet Jacobs, *Incidents in the Life of a Slave Girl* (1861; rpt. New York: Oxford University Press, 1988), 82–87. Frederick Douglass, too, paid increasing attention to domestic space in the revisions he made in expanding his 1845 *Narrative* into *My Bondage and My Freedom* in 1855. One of the most striking additions to Douglass's second autobiography is the lengthy reminiscence of his grandparents' "little hut" at the beginning of *My Bondage and My Freedom*, the log cabin in which Douglass lived so "snugly" during his early childhood and from which "good old home" he dreaded being removed to work on his master's distant plantation. Crafts's account of Hannah's days in Aunt Hetty's cabin bears some similarity to Douglass's tribute to this sheltering yet deeply vulnerable space. See Frederick Douglass, *Autobiographies*, ed. Henry Louis Gates, Jr. (New York: Library of America, 1994), 141–144.

25. Harriet Beecher Stowe, *Uncle Tom's Cabin* (1851–52; rpt. New York: Bantam, 1981), 1.

26. Much as Stowe locates the main action of *Uncle Tom's Cabin* on three plantations—Shelby, St. Clare, and Legree—Crafts places Hannah at Lindendale, then "Forget me not," and finally the Wheelers' plantation. There is also a certain correspondence within the trajectories: like Stowe, Crafts makes the second plantation (at least at first) the most desirable, and it is at the third that her main character is for the first time brought in contact with "vile, foul, filthy" slave huts (205).

27. J. W. Page, *Uncle Robin in His Cabin in Virginia, and Tom Without One in Boston*, 2nd ed. (Richmond: J. W. Randolph, 1853), 23.

28. For more on representations of architectural space by Stowe and her rebutters, including Eastman, see David P. Handlin, *The American Home: Architecture and Society, 1815–1915* (Boston: Little, Brown, 1979), 76–78. As Handlin notes, sectional commentators "often cited the houses of North and South to compare the two societies. The ideas about houses mentioned in this debate had been formulated in the discussion of other issues. But when used to measure the progress of North and South, they assumed some of their most powerful meanings" (76). Crafts's final owner, John Hill Wheeler, had several anti-*Uncle Tom's Cabin* texts in his library in the 1850s, including J. W. Page's *Uncle Robin in His Cabin in Virginia; and Tom Without One in Boston*, according to an auction catalogue prepared after his death.

29. Charles Dickens, *Bleak House* (1852–53; rpt. New York: Bantam, 1983). Subsequent references will appear parenthetically in the text.

30. Some of the "British" details Crafts excises from the borrowed passages actually have a racial aspect, as they link Bleak House to British imperial ventures. For example, Crafts elides Dickens's mention of a "Native-Hindoo chair" and also a series of paintings showing "the whole process of preparing tea in China, as depicted by Chinese artists." See Dickens, *Bleak House*, 61, 62.

31. By having Hannah note in the final paragraph that, in becoming free, Charlotte's husband, William, "has learned the carpenter's trade" (239), Crafts further underscores the im-

portance of black command over built space in her text. As bell hooks has argued, "black folks equated freedom with the passage into a life where they would have the right to exercise control over space on their own behalf. They would imagine, design, and create spaces that would respond to the needs of their lives, their communities, their families" ("House, 20 June 1994," 23). In Jacobs's novel, Linda Brent's father and first love are both carpenters. See *Incidents in the Life of a Slave Girl*, 11, 58.

32. Sarah Luria, "Racial Equality Begins at Home: Frederick Douglass's Challenge to American Domesticity," in *The American Home: Material Culture, Domestic Space, and Family Life*, ed. Eleanor McD. Thompson (Winterthur, Del.: Henry Francis du Pont Winterthur Museum, 1998), 27. Hannah, moreover, uses her respectable cottage home as "a school for colored children," further radicalizing the Downing and Dickens models.

33. See Luria, "Racial Equality Begins at Home," 34–35, 32.

34. Hannah's "Oh" also fittingly recalls the intensity of feeling Hannah experiences during expulsion from Aunt Hetty's cottage ("My horror, and grief, and astonishment were indescribable. I felt Oh how much more than I tell" [12]). In fact, if Hannah's mother replaces Mrs. Henry, she also fully maternalizes Aunt Hetty, Hannah's original aged and "venerable" (229) mother-figure. Pointedly, Crafts has Hannah reunite briefly with Aunt Hetty—who once again resides in "a neat little cottage, tidy and comfortable" (229)—just before she rediscovers her biological mother.

35. hooks, "House, 20 June 1994," 23. The subtitle of hooks's essay is "Housing Without Boundaries: Race, Class, and Gender."

12

Godly Rebellion in *The Bondwoman's Narrative*

BRYAN SINCHE

When Hannah Crafts began writing *The Bondwoman's Narrative*, she clearly had a desire to relate more than simply the "unvarnished facts." Her tale of moral and physical courage in the dehumanizing world of enslavement communicates the main character's strict morality and unwavering faith along with her protest against "the peculiar features of that institution whose curse rests over the fairest land that the sun shines upon."[1] Much more than a tale of slavery, Crafts's novel is a story about one woman and the decisions she makes in an effort to overcome oppression.[2] Yet, Crafts's work is not uniformly satisfying to modern readers, because Hannah simply refuses to overtly resist the indignities of enslavement. Treating her masters and mistresses with deference, courtesy, and even obsequiousness, Hannah appears to gain the reward of freedom by being a model slave. Indeed, this odd facet of the novel is the result of Crafts's desire to see that "[those] of pious and discerning minds can scarcely fail to recognize the hand of Providence in giving to the righteous the reward of their works, and to the wicked the fruit of their doings" (3).

In her effort to portray slavery as the monstrosity it was and still reveal the abiding presence and judgment of a virtuous God—a God that permits slavery—Crafts must make difficult narrative choices.[3] Since the furtherance of a particular political agenda is paramount in her novel, it is no wonder that some incidents within strain the credulity of the reader—verisimilitude was not Crafts's primary goal. Therefore, this essay will not make any determination as to what is truth and what is fiction in Crafts's story; instead, it will assess the narrative logic behind the choices the author has made and examine the ways in which those choices lead the reader to accept the unlikely events within the novel. The author's remarkable ability to utilize her personal experience within slavery to construct a story that validates the God who presides over the peculiar institution, while still condemning the institution itself, speaks to Crafts's unique, if unpolished talent.[4]

An interesting example of this talent is her use of a narrative fulcrum that allows readers to reconceptualize subjugation as rebellion: Hannah's journeys into the wilderness. Though authors such as William Wells Brown and Henry Bibb detail their sojourns into the wilderness as a component of their narratives, their escapes into the wild are an important step in a premeditated escape from slavery.[5] Hannah's removes into the wilderness are undertaken not solely so she can attain freedom, but so she can maintain her meticulously crafted self-image as a virtuous woman. Though she does obtain freedom through her second journey in the wilderness, it is not so much by her own exertions as through God's benignity. Unlike Brown, Bibb, and Frederick Douglass, Crafts does not utilize the wilderness to demonstrate Hannah's determination to escape slavery, nor does she present the protagonist's self-reliance.[6] Instead, she places Hannah in the wilderness so the reader can see that God's favor is the key to her success. Were Hannah to actively pursue that freedom and practice the duplicity concomitant with such a pursuit, she would be rejecting the virtues that define her self-image. However, because she enters the wilderness when she does, and because she relies almost exclusively on God's benevolence within the wilderness, Hannah demonstrates her appreciation for virtue. By adhering to a strict conception of Christian virtue that many slave authors would deem incompatible with resistance to slavery, Hannah follows a different path toward rebellion. This path leads her into the wilderness wherein God's judgment prevails and from which Hannah emerges a free woman.[7]

The escape from the plantation represented a difficult experience for any slave; not only was the escaping servant pursued and hunted, but he or she was forced to travel through confusing, unfamiliar territory in an effort to avoid recapture. In his examination of the wilderness in African American literature, *Ride Out the Wilderness*, Melvin Dixon writes that for the slave, the wilderness "was both obstacle and aid."[8] Within a challenging geographic space,

> It was the fugitive's skillful behavior, action and courage to confront the wilderness that turned potentially hazardous situations into conquests. The wilderness thus became an important test of man's faith in himself and in God's power to bring deliverance or free territory within reach. This was how man *joined* himself with God, with nature and how he *earned* his freedom.[9]

Dixon's use of the masculine pronoun suggests how rare an escape like Hannah's was and helps to emphasize how intense her faith must have been for her to leave her home twice. However, Hannah does not desire to "earn her freedom," nor does she wish to reveal faith in herself. When Hannah departs from each plantation, she does so because she has *already* joined herself with God and is confident in her protection.[10] Not only does her devotion to an inner morality demand that she leave first the De Vincent plantation and then the Wheeler home, but that devotion assures Hannah that she could and would succeed once she entered the inhospitable wilderness.

Thus, Hannah's experiences deviate from the form outlined by Dixon. The wilderness space that is "obstacle and aid" in the slaves' search for freedom is, for Hannah, a site for personal validation. Of course, Hannah is assured of God's protection because she has consistently lived according to the tenets of her personal faith. For the reader to be convinced of the rightness (and righteousness) of Hannah's behavior within slavery, each decision she makes must be tested in a severe environment in which providential favor is absolutely required for survival. In other words, those who purport to be religious must prove it, as Hannah's onetime companions Aunt Hetty and Uncle Siah do. When they are punished for aiding Hannah, she rationalizes: "in conformity to the inscrutable ways of Providence the faith and strength of these aged servants of the Cross were to be tried by a more severe ordeal" (12). Hannah's early experience led her to expect that faith would bring adversity and that adversity would serve to test one's personal faith.

Hannah first enters the wilderness with Mrs. De Vincent as the latter tries to make her escape from Mr. Trappe. When the two women prepare to leave, Mrs. De Vincent is inconsolable, and Hannah tries to "imbue her with the idea that it was a time for thinking and acting rather than giving way to over-strained sensations of any kind" (49). Perhaps this pragmatism is a major reason Mrs. De Vincent chose her to go along instead of the well-bred but delicate Lizzy. When the women leave the house, Hannah speaks: "Say no more, my mind is fixed. We will go and trust in heaven" (51). Thus they enter the wilderness with a firm declaration of fortitude and faith; Hannah's virtuous, enabling confidence allows her to bear the weight of leadership for the pair.

The author demonstrates the strength of the faithful in the contrast between the hopeless and weak Mrs. De Vincent and Hannah, whose mental and physical stamina consistently comes to the fore. When her mistress falls in a heap and declares that they can do nothing but die, Hannah "felt all the more absolute necessity for strong resolution and courage on [her] part" (55). When her mistress cannot think of what to do next, Hannah confidently assumes, "we could not be utterly forsaken, and hopeless and helpless when God was near" (56). Again and again, Hannah declares her faith in God and demonstrates the benefits of this faith through her assuredness and actions. By taking a leadership role in her first wilderness journey, she reveals a font of inner strength that allows her to withstand incredible trials. Though she and Mrs. De Vincent are ultimately captured, Hannah remains purposeful and focused, unvexed by the terrors of the forest. Her mistress's weakness limits Hannah's ability to operate effectively during her first wilderness journey, but she leaves the forest steadfast in her faith, assured of God's protection and confident in her own ability to surmount the struggles associated with her future trials. In other words, Hannah does not view the fact that she and her mistress are captured as a personal failure or as a rebuke from God, even as Mrs. De Vincent suggests, "Heaven . . . has turned against [them]" (70).

After Hannah's departure from the Wheeler plantation, she commences her second journey into the wilderness, during which God's presence and favor are manifest on numerous occasions. On her first morning in the forest, God's dominion over the beasts of the earth serves to bring food to Hannah as she drinks from a cow that needs milking—even in receiving the bounty of God she relieves the suffering of the lowing cow! Within the foreign space outside the confines of the plantation, a place that would seem to deny the concerns and dictates of middle-class society, Hannah attempts to practice the same virtues that guided her life within slavery. Upon "appropriating" a pair of boots since her own shoes are worn through, Hannah begs forgiveness (presumably from the reader and God) and acknowledges, "it was doubtless wrong, and great necessity must be my excuse" (214). Though Hannah's behavior is in keeping with the virtuous standards she has constructed for herself, when viewed in comparison to the behavior of Frederick Douglass or William Wells Brown, her concern with virtue and honesty seems ridiculous. This is not to contend that Douglass or Brown were less than virtuous; rather, it is to suggest that these men could regard any resistance to slavery and any effort to overcome it as a virtuous act. Rather than redefine virtue to suit her own circumstances, however, Hannah is determined to resist slavery *through* virtue and thereby ensure God's assistance during her greatest trials.

Crafts evidences the importance of religious faith within the wilderness by first describing the weakness of Mrs. De Vincent and, during Hannah's second journey in the wilderness, revealing the fate of Jacob and his ailing sister in the forest. Upon meeting the young man in the woods, Hannah immediately "[admired] his fraternal piety and [hoped] that it would meet with its proper reward" (216). However, Jacob's lack of faith in God forces Hannah to "regard him with compassion that in his trials, and difficulties he was unaware of the greatest source of abiding comfort" (217). After Jacob's sister dies and he departs with Hannah, the price for remaining unaware of God is made clear: while in a boat with Hannah, Jacob is shot and killed while his companion remains unharmed. Clearly, the author wants to emphasize the selective power of God and the benefits of faith. Though Jacob and his sister may have escaped from slavery in an effort to ease their earthly burdens, and though their dedication to one another may be admirable, Hannah's flight is rooted in her concern for eternal salvation. Her second wilderness journey, which may be read as an escape to freedom, is also an affirmation of her belief in Christian morality and a surrender to God's judgment of her life. Thus, after Jacob is shot and the boat he and Hannah are traveling in drifts down the river, Hannah need only "[recommend herself] to God" (226) before she awakens on the shore where she is greeted by Aunt Hetty.

This remarkable deliverance, followed soon after by Mr. Trappe's comeuppance, demonstrates God's approval of Hannah's flight and the motives that inspired it. Perhaps Hannah Crafts understood how problematic some of these motives are, and this realization prompted her to include the remarkable wilderness episodes in her novel. Certainly, it seems odd that God would select only Hannah for freedom, leaving Jacob, his sister, and Mrs. De Vincent to die. Such a selection seems to suggest that God is not wholly opposed to slavery—after all, if he was, why wouldn't he allow all the escaping slaves to reach freedom? Within the space of Crafts's novel, God is shown to reward those who are committed to him as opposed to those who are victims of earthly injustice. Therefore, unlike many narratives written by former slaves, *The Bondwoman's Narrative* focuses not on a protagonist deeply committed to overtly resisting slavery but on one primarily committed to becoming a thoroughly middle-class woman. However, as I will argue, this commitment itself represents a profound act of resistance to a system that always denied individuality and, in many cases, asserted the powerlessness of the female slave through physical or sexual violence.

In her recent book, *Sentimental Materialism*, Lori Merish examines the connection among the middle-class home, middle-class virtues, and sympathetic identification with the plight of slaves in the work of Harriet Beecher Stowe. Merish points out that "One of the chief representational strategies through which Stowe represents the full 'humanity' of members of Other races . . . is showing that these characters do indeed 'keep house,' and either reside in, or aspire to, something like middle-class domesticity."[11] In Crafts's work, Hannah's aspirations not only reveal her "humanity" but also guide her life within slavery and motivate her escape from slavery. Of course, middle-class aspirations are not unique to female characters in nineteenth-century novels; as Nina Baym suggests in *Woman's Fiction*, sentimental novels written by or about women often feature the "happy home [as] the acme of human bliss."[12] Thus, Crafts suggests that "middle-class domesticity" is more than simply a marker of "humanity"; it is assertion of Hannah's right to aspire to "bliss," her right to pursue the same life as any other (white) woman.

Hannah's ability to "keep house" as a matriarch of a middle-class household is revealed both through her positive and negative reactions to various female characters and through her willingness to consistently behave as if she were a peer of the middle-class whites she encounters. For example, Hannah attempts to practice the earnest religion embodied by Aunt Hetty and Mrs. Henry and admires the neat and thrifty style with which these women furnish their homes. In order to realize the home life she desires for herself—a life that would signal a peer relationship with other white women—Hannah must prepare herself (and, by extension, the reader) for the ending she is granted, that is, the attainment of her own domestic bliss.[13] Within *The Bondwoman's Narrative*, this preparation takes the shape of anecdotes and incidents that demonstrate Hannah's fitness for middle-class life and reveal her character prior to her escape. Hannah imagines her wilderness journeys and her ultimate success as providential validation not of universal freedom for slaves but of her religion and middle-class aspirations.

Hannah's ability and willingness to endure the extraordinary ordeals within the space of the narrative stem from the worldview Hannah reveals after her first encounter with Aunt Hetty:

> . . . to always look on the bright side of things, to be industrious, cheerful, and true-hearted, to do some good though in a humble way, and to win some love if I could. "I am a slave," thus my thoughts would run. "I can never be great, nor rich; I cannot hold an elevated position in society, but I can do my duty, and be kind in the sure hope of an eternal reward." (11)

The personal program of life that Hannah delineates does not suggest any of Frederick Douglass's rebelliousness, nor does it reveal the steely determination of Harriet Jacobs, a woman who refused to bind herself to traditional values within slavery since she was forced to survive without the niceties of a middle-class home.[14] Despite her enslavement, Hannah is determined to be a dutiful, honest servant who lives by values that can only be fully practiced in freedom without endangering personal harm.[15]

As Hazel Carby has argued in *Reconstructing Womanhood*, most antebellum literature positions black femininity "outside the definition of true womanhood," which was typically reserved for white women.[16] Carby regards the "cult of true womanhood," which valorized tenets such as "piety, purity, submissiveness and domesticity," as incompatible with the slave system that attempted to undermine these very traits in slaves, thereby constructing distance between black and white women.[17] Ironically, however, it is Hannah's willingness to conform her values to the "cult of true womanhood"—despite opportunities to disregard her values and thereby escape bondage—that ultimately allows for her freedom and success in the North. The "school of slavery" that Booker T. Washington describes as preparation for life in freedom does more than simply give Hannah the skills to thrive in a free society; Hannah's adherence to the lessons learned in a very different "school" leads her to escape.[18] The fact that Hannah abides by the same tenets throughout the novel and thereby gains freedom suggests that adherence to a Christian moral code is an effective and providentially sanctioned mode of resistance to slavery.[19]

Obedience to God within *The Bondwoman's Narrative* is an important signifier of the middle-class status Hannah craves. Not only do the women she admires have neat and tastefully decorated homes that evince the simplicity of Hannah's home in the North, but the woman are also strong partners in marriages based upon the religious tenets to which Hannah subscribes. Like many heroines of woman's fiction, Mrs. Henry and Aunt Hetty practice their religion "severed from its institutional setting"; while they are most certainly Christians, "their true religious life is interior."[20]

These role models are concerned not with the church as an institution but with religion as it affects their own lives and salvation. The author reveals that Aunt Hetty and Uncle Siah did not yearn for wealth because they knew "that the peace of God and their own consciences united to honor and intelligence were in themselves a fortune which the world neither gave nor could take away" (9). Similarly, Mrs. Henry's conscience guides her to eschew the purchase or sale of slaves. These women demonstrate to Hannah that, though one may never set foot inside a church, religion can have a profound effect on a life—perhaps even more of an effect—when it serves to focus one's personal morality. Since each free woman demonstrates that personal morality in her kindnesses to Hannah, Hannah logically accepts the religion practiced by such models and incorporates it into her value system. By the time Hannah escapes from the Wheeler plantation, she is wholly guided by her internal faith and her conscience.

The fact that Hannah's internal faith abides through the many hardships she suffers seems remarkable, but several experiences within slavery serve to shape and strengthen her religious commitment. For example, after describing her formative encounters with Aunt Hetty and explaining her outlook on life as a slave, Hannah reveals that by adopting a positive attitude, she was able to enjoy certain advantages. She recalls:

> as I grew older, and was enabled to manifest my good intention, not so much
> by words, as a manner of sympathy and consideration for every one, I was quite

astonished to see how much I was trusted and confided in, how I was made the repository of secrets, and how the weak, the sick, and the suffering came to me for advice and assistance. (11)

Clearly, Hannah played a matronly role on the plantation, and though she does not indicate whether she was the "repository of secrets" for her black peers or her white masters, her later interactions with Charlotte and Mrs. Wheeler suggest that Hannah's mild demeanor helped ingratiate her with both groups. Thus, early in her life, Hannah learned that acting according to her particular worldview was advantageous; it is no surprise that she would have continued such behavior as she grew older. More important than the fact that Hannah takes on a specific role within the confines of the plantation, however, is the fact that she chooses and defines the role herself. She is not assigned the job of de facto mother for the slave community—she willingly accepts the responsibilities concomitant with her outlook. Though her mission, as she defines it, seems to offer little space for resistance to slavery, the fact that she learns to read, becomes religious, and thereby constructs a very personal and specific worldview is itself an enormous act of resistance. From the first, Hannah decides on the terms of her self-definition, and this definition extends well beyond the boundaries denoted by the term "slave."

Because Hannah—to the extent possible—defines the terms of her enslavement and is so often privy to knowledge withheld from other slaves, it is no surprise that she enjoys an intellectual life unique among her peers. Along with her interest in reading, she manifests an appreciation for painting, as she demonstrates when captivated by the De Vincent family paintings. Hannah remembers, "I was not a slave with these pictured memorials of the past . . . In their presence my mind seemed to run riotous and exult in its freedom as a rational being, and one destined for something higher and better than this world can afford" (17). God sees Hannah and knows of her mental liberation; there is nothing providentially approved about *her* continued enslavement. Why then could he not lend his hand to her attainment of freedom? After Mrs. Bry scolds Hannah for viewing the pictures, Hannah muses on her innate ability to transcend the man-made construct of slavery and thus gain intellectual freedom:

Can ignorance quench the immortal mind or prevent its feeling at times that indications of its heavenly origin. Can it destroy that deep abiding appreciation of the beautiful that seems inherent to the human soul? Can it seal up the fountains of truth and all intuitive perception of live, death, and eternity? I think not. (18)

Clearly, slavery cannot stop Hannah from either appreciating beauty or improving her mind. Within the confines of the peculiar institution, she develops a unique freedom of mind and, in doing so, prepares herself for the physical freedom she eventually obtains.

When Hannah aids Mrs. De Vincent in her attempt to escape from Mr. Trappe, Hannah again has the opportunity to practice her developing values. After the two women become lost in their search for the town of Milton, they finally happen upon "a happy-looking, rural, contented spot, wanting, indeed, in the appearances of wealth and luxury, but evidently the abode of competence and peace. [Hannah] felt the possessors of such a humble comfortable place must be hospitable people" (59). Once again, Hannah demonstrates her propensity for linking the appearance of the neat and humble home with the personalities of its residents.[21] As usual, her instincts prove correct; when she enters the house, she finds a "benevolent-looking . . . lady" and an old man reading the Bible. This family, like Aunt Hetty's, focuses on eternal concerns and is indifferent to the trappings of wealth; the family's willingness to aid strangers evidences a desire to "do some good in a humble way," a motif that Hannah has incorporated into her own plan of life. Hannah's uncanny ability to decode the signs of benevolence serves her in both this instance and many others; perhaps the unlikely fortune that seems to attend Hannah's every move is due to nothing more than her own understanding of the markers of virtue and its material rewards.

The author first examines the contrast between external traits and the deeper, more abiding qualities that Hannah is able to sense so keenly in a conversation between Lizzy and Hannah. Lizzy, whose delicate appearance and refined manners are superior to Hannah's, claims, "she came . . . of a good family and frequently mentioned great names in connection with her own" (33). Though Hannah is dismissive of such pretensions, Lizzy asserts:

> it was a very great thing and very important even to a slave to be well connected—that good blood was an inheritance to them—and that when they heard the name of some honorable gentleman mentioned with applause, or saw some great lady flaunt by in jewels and satins the priveledge of thinking he or she is a near relative of [hers] was a very great privilage indeed. (33–34)

Being able to claim important relations and basking in the lighter skin that such relations may provide, while certainly of some value on the plantation, seem to matter little to Hannah. These signs simply speak to a person's external or inherited qualities. For a slave, inheritance was a problematic issue,[22] and therefore Hannah bases her judgment of both herself, and those she meets, on the eternal qualities that she has the peculiar ability to discern.

Hannah demonstrates these abiding traits when a wandering search party discovers her and Mrs. De Vincent. When the men ask Hannah if she is a slave, she affirms her status with scarcely a second thought. For the first time, but not the last, Hannah demonstrates that she would rather be honest than gain her freedom through duplicity. Though she attempts to conceal the fact that Mrs. De Vincent is also a slave, Hannah's responses and demeanor make it clear that she never conceived of their flight as a personal escape attempt; she was merely aiding her mistress while the latter was in need. Though Hannah's willing submission to Mrs. De Vincent and, by extension, the institution of slavery may be frustrating to readers, if we accept Hannah's self-definition, her honesty and resultant recapture can be read as an act of resistance. Because she continues to fulfill the self-image she has created, no matter what the cost, Hannah proclaims her individuality and her freedom from the objectification of those who view her as property. Rather than defy God in order to escape from the men who threaten her, Hannah chooses to remain faithful to her religion and her sense of self. As she answers the men who marvel at her bravery in remaining in a haunted cabin, she also answers the troubled reader who wonders at her willing return to the dangers of slavery: "a good conscience [is] a sure protector" (69).

Hannah's desire to enact and enjoy her personal virtues is further manifested when she reaches the Henry plantation. Upon awaking in the Henry home for the first time, Hannah cries out for her new master. When Mrs. Henry interrogates her, Hannah is quick to mention that she is "one of that miserable class" (117) of slaves, and she also reveals that a "prayer was on [her] lips" during the fall into the ravine that claimed her master's life. In the first moments of consciousness, in her first encounter with Mrs. Henry, Hannah takes the opportunity to define herself as a slave and as an honest and religious woman. Subjugating the fears that must have accompanied a revelation of her legal status to the pleasure she gains in revealing her status as a "true woman," Hannah wins Mrs. Henry's admiration. That this admiration is valuable to Hannah becomes evident when she lauds Mrs. Henry's moral rectitude when the latter claims she is too virtuous to keep Hannah as a slave.

The Henry plantation, with its neat style and harmonious décor, is the most idyllic domestic space (outside of freedom) that Hannah inhabits within the narrative. Not surprisingly, the residents living within the idealized space are uniformly courteous, diligent, and reverential. As Hannah walks the grounds with Mrs. Henry, she describes the slave quarters on the plantation:

> looking over their little truck patches and gardens, all of which gave evidence of being neatly attended in the absence of weeds and the appearances of thrifty growth in the various plants, vegetables, and flowers, designed for use and ornament. Various groups of persons . . . all of whom seemed impressed with a reverential feeling of the sanctity of the day, and of regard for their mistress, were seated on little low benches at their doors, quiet[l]y enjoying the beauty of the evening. They all rose with courteous reverence to salute us as we passed, and invited us to walk over their grounds, and gather such flowers as we liked. I shall not soon forget the pleasing intimation of a devotional character impressed upon each little party (138).

I have quoted this passage at length because it represents the acme of plantation life for the slave, and Hannah's appreciation of the neat homes and simple gardens that pass for slave quarters seems to indicate her own willingness to accept such a life. The slaves on the Henry plantation are not dissatisfied with their treatment, nor are they anxious to run away; if only Hannah could have this life, she too would be satisfied because she would be given the freedom to live out her values.

In order to persuade Mrs. Henry of both her fidelity and her morality (perhaps in an effort to secure herself a place on the Henry plantation), Hannah is willing to behave in ways that seem atypical for a slave intent on resisting domination. Soon after her walk with Mrs. Henry, Hannah reveals that William is the "ghost" who has been haunting the plantation. In sharing this information, Hannah occupies a liminal space between slave and master—she validates the persistent belief among the slaves that a spirit is haunting the plantation while still serving her mistress's needs. This space between the two plantation communities is where Hannah persistently imagines herself. Though she has no illusions about her station in life, she wants to be a slave whose mental acuity is respected and whose morality is beyond reproach. Thus, when Charlotte and William make their escape from the plantation, Hannah cannot bring herself to leave:

> I answered plainly that however just, or right, or expedient it might be in them to escape my accompanying their flight would be directly the reverse, that I could not lightly sacrifise the good opinion of Mrs Henry and her family, who had been so very kind to me, nor seem to participate in a scheme, of which the

consummation must be an injury to them no less than a source of disquiet and anxiety. Duty, gratitude and honor forbid it. (142)

Certainly, the notion of "duty" to a master extending past the eye of the overseer seems an unlikely feeling for a slave, and William, who has not had the fortune to be enslaved on the Henry plantation, asserts that Hannah's reasoning is flawed: "'And so to a strained sense of honor you willingly sacrifise a prospect of freedom . . . Well, you can hug the chain if you please. With me it is liberty or death'" (142).

William's frustrated rebuke likely echoes the confusion of readers who wonder what place gratitude or honor could have in a system that demands labor without pay and forces people to submit to the whims of their masters. Certainly, Hannah's decision to obey the laws that construe her as property instead of abiding by the natural law described in the Declaration of Independence appears to be a remarkable instance of kowtowing to white power. Yet, once readers understand the calculus underlying Hannah's maddening logic, the dual importance of manifesting gratitude toward her mistress and retaining her honor becomes clear. While William and Charlotte need to run away to preserve the sanctity of their marriage—and thus the sanctity of Charlotte's womanhood—Hannah's escape would only demonstrate her failure to live by the same moral code that forces Charlotte to leave the plantation. The fact that Hannah upholds the same morality that Charlotte evinces is the very reason she cannot join Charlotte in their flight to freedom. Far from simply "hugging the chain," Hannah believes that she is clinging to something far more precious and eternal: her own clear conscience and respectability.

Once the action of the story moves from the Henry plantation to the Wheeler residences, Hannah's self-image and her conception of appropriate female behaviors are well established. The white women she encounters during the remainder of her experience in slavery are antithetical to her middle-class notions and serve as a counterpoint to the cultured, modest ladies who have helped shape her personality. While Crafts describes Mrs. Henry's femininity in terms of her delicate compassion and honesty, the author paints Mrs. Wheeler in a far more severe light. While certainly feminine, Mrs. Wheeler has learned to use her position as a woman to practice dishonesty and coercion. In an effort to keep Hannah for herself, she forces Hannah to write a letter that impugns her own character. Hannah's reaction to this letter and her subsequent sale speaks to the power of the female to do evil:

I never felt so poor, so weak, so utterly subjected to the authority of another, as when that woman with her soft voice and suavity of manner, yet withal so stern and inflexible told me that I was hers body and soul, and that she did and would exact obedience in all cases and under all circumstances. (155)

The most terrifying figure in the novel is not a violent overseer, a lecherous master, or even the nefarious Mr. Trappe. Instead, the arch-villain in Hannah's story is a woman who appears to live according to the same self-sacrificing tenets to which Mrs. Henry and Aunt Hetty subscribe, but who is in fact a vain, jealous, conspiratorial mistress who gains power by appearing to have none.

The author continues to demonstrate Mrs. Wheeler's laziness and vanity in a variety of anecdotes, Mrs. Wheeler's episode in blackface most notable among these. This portrait of the spoiled mistress contrasts with the idealized depictions of the female characters that helped Hannah define her personality. Nonetheless, Hannah desires that her new mistress think well of her and that she should remain Mrs. Wheeler's favorite. When Maria attempts to displace Hannah as Mrs. Wheeler's waiting maid, Hannah laments the change in her own fortune: "[Mrs. Wheeler's] conversations were all with Maria; her presents were all to Maria. She scarcely noticed me at all, while I vainly wondered in what I had offended" (203). Clearly, Hannah values her position as the favorite servant; it is a position she has attained in every home she has served in.

However, Maria is able to displace the virtuous Hannah by behaving like their mistress: "[Maria] was an adept in the art of dissembling and her countenance would be the smoothest and her words the fairest when she contemplated the greatest injury" (203). Maria and Mrs. Wheeler are dangerous women; both wholly self-interested, they use their power within the domestic sphere to demean Hannah and damage her reputation. However, when Hannah is finally ordered to leave the Wheeler home, she is "desolate" because she has been "accused of a crime of which [she] was innocent" and fallen in Mrs. Wheeler's estimation (205). Despite her hatred for her mistress, Hannah is distraught because her formerly good name has been sullied. In revealing a concern for her honor and her station among her peers, she chooses to regard herself as a free woman and thereby resist the impulse to regard herself as a slave. Had she resorted to the same dishonesty that Mrs. Wheeler and Maria practice, Hannah would have validated the results of such duplicitous behavior; instead, she refuses to allow ends to justify her means.

Hannah's dismissal from the house is most galling to her because she will be forced to associate with the same slaves whose lot she decried upon arriving at the Wheeler plantation. These poor creatures do not have access to the knowledge that Hannah has and are incapable of joining her in the fulfilling life she imagines for herself. Hannah speculates on the thoughts of the field servants when she first rides past them: "To see people ride in carriages, to hear such names as freedom, heaven, hope and happiness and not to have the least idea how it must seem to ride, any more than what the experience of these blessed names would be" (201). Certainly, Hannah means to condemn the system of slavery through her comments, but she also condemns the ignorance of her fellow slaves. Though Hannah realizes she is a slave, she isn't one of the benighted lot she views from the carriage. As she was on her walk with Mrs. Henry, Hannah is separate from the rest of the servants; this physical distance helps reinforce the intellectual space she imagines between herself and her fellow slaves.

Because Hannah has consistently viewed herself apart from other slaves, and because she is extraordinarily self-conscious, it is no surprise that the prospect of association with and marriage into a lower caste would drive her to escape:

> Had Mrs Wheeler condemned me to the severest corporal punishment, or exposed me to be sold in the public slave market in Wilmington I should probably have resigned myself with apparent composure to her cruel behests. But when she sought to force me into a compulsory union with a man whom I could only hate and despise it seemed that rebellion *would be a virtue*, that duty to myself and my God actually required it, and that whatever accidents or misfortunes might attend my flight nothing could be worse than what threatened my stay. (206, italics added)

Finally, Hannah accepts her own rebellion against the caprices of slavery. She has been unwilling to escape from bondage by lying or deceiving because her personal morality must sanction her flight. Once her middle-class dream—manifested in the combination of the pleasing domestic space and a respectful relationship she enjoys at the end of the novel—is threatened, Hannah realizes that she must run away. Here again, Hannah reveals her desire to live as a "true woman" would, just as Hazel Carby suggests: "the black woman repeatedly failed the test of true womanhood because she survived her institutional rape, whereas the true heroine would rather die than be sexually abused."[23] The same devotion to duty and God that held Hannah in slavery despite opportunities to escape is what ultimately drives her into the wilderness. It is in the wilderness that Hannah's faith and devotion to God—along with the dutiful, virtuous behavior this faith engenders—are tested and, ultimately, validated.

Whether the ending of this tale conforms to what actually happened to the historical Hannah Crafts, or whether the author wrote a conclusion that explicitly rewards virtue in order to give *The Bondwoman's Narrative* a moral is out-side the scope of this essay. What is clear in the ending, however, is that Hannah has obtained her freedom and that her ability to do so is in large part due to her continued devotion to God and personal morality. This devotion, which is remarkable in both its rigidity and in the fortune that attends it, determines Hannah's behavior more than her master or mistress ever can. God and Christian morality are her master and mistress, and in rejecting her earthly owners for these eternal powers, Hannah proclaims her own unwillingness to submit to enslavement. Though she does not evince the physical resistance of her real-life contemporaries, Hannah is unwilling to compromise the moral guidelines she creates for herself, thus averring her individuality within a system that seeks to deny it. More than this, she is willing to test her faith in the wilderness—a dangerous environment from which only God's approval can allow her to emerge. From the satisfied light of this approval, the author of *The Bondwoman's Narrative* proudly asserts that complete freedom for the slave could only be at-tained in concert with—and perhaps even because of—Christian virtue.

Notes

I would like to thank the Center for the Study of the American South at the University of North Carolina at Chapel Hill for a research grant that allowed me the time to complete this essay. I would also like to thank William L. Andrews, Philip F. Gura, and Linda Wagner-Martin for their insightful readings and valuable comments on earlier drafts of this essay.

1. Hannah Crafts, *The Bondwoman's Narrative*, ed. Henry Louis Gates, Jr. (New York: Time Warner, 2002), 3. All subsequent page references refer to this edition.

2. I will use "Hannah" to name the character within the novel and "Crafts" to name the author of *The Bondwoman's Narrative*. This is done to avoid conflating the historical Hannah Crafts with the incidents and people named in what may have been a partially or wholly fictive work.

3. Contrast this with Olaudah Equiano's *The Interesting Narrative of the Life of Olaudah Equiano*, which regards the trials of slavery as evidence of God's benevolence. For Equiano, torment is only prelude to salvation, whereas Crafts believes that God in no way sanctions the suffering within slavery.

4. In Frances Smith Foster, *Written By Herself: Literary Production by African American Women, 1746–1892* (Bloomington: Indiana Univ. Press, 1987), Foster suggests that "In amalgamating the various example of appropriate language and literature into their own creations, [African American women] became . . . actors redefining the uses and possibilities of literature and language that served their own purposes" (22). Crafts's narrative, which evidences both her indebtedness to a wide range of literary figures and her unique understanding of slavery, is an example of such an amalgamation. This essay examines the "purposes" behind Crafts's novel.

5. See Henry Bibb, *Narrative of the Life and Adventures of Henry Bibb, an American Slave, Written by Himself* (New York: 1849); and William Wells Brown, *Narrative of William W. Brown, a Fugitive Slave, Written by Himself* (Boston: American Anti-Slavery Society, 1847).

6. For this and later references to Douglass's work, see Frederick Douglass, *Narrative of the Life of Frederick Douglass, an American Slave. Written by Himself*, ed. William L. Andrews (1845; reprint, New York: Norton, 1995).

7. In Crafts's descriptions of the wilderness and her professions of faith, readers may hear echoes of Puritan captivity narratives such as Mary Rowlandson's *The Sovereignty and Goodness of God . . .* (1682). Such similarities are particularly interesting within an African American narrative because, within the wilderness, escaping slaves usually relied upon their own resources and the assistance of others far more than the protection of a benevolent God. One exception to this rule is Sojourner Truth's *Narrative*.

8. Melvin Dixon, *Ride Out the Wilderness* (Urbana: Univ. of Illinois Press, 1987), 26.

9. Ibid.

10. See Lawrence Levine, *Black Culture and Black Consciousness* (New York: Oxford Univ. Press, 1977). Levine suggests that "stories which detailed the fate of those who forgot their dependence upon God were common among the slaves and the freedmen" (92). However, he also notes that much of the folklore popular on the plantation would have taken a practical form, since "the situation of the slave and freedman made survival a paramount concern" (97). In other words, most slave storytellers would have understood that virtue was necessarily bounded by the exigencies of a life in bondage and would be unlikely to promulgate stories that presented an uncomplicated approbation of virtuous behavior. Though I am not suggesting that Crafts's story is uncomplicated, it is most certainly a unique volume in the pantheon of slave tales.

11. Lori Merish, *Sentimental Materialism* (Durham: Duke Univ. Press, 2000), 139. Merish also notes that "woman's fiction" of the post-Reconstruction era "often highlighted the traditionally 'feminine,' domestic themes of marriage and motherhood as markers of black women's accession to full (civil) subjectivity" (260). Certainly, Crafts's work evidences Hannah's humanity and at least suggests her ability to function as a civil subject within the domestic sphere. For more on this idea, see Gillian Brown, *Domestic Individualism* (Berkeley: Univ. of California Press, 1990), especially 39–60.

12. Nina Baym, *Woman's Fiction* (Urbana: Univ. of Illinois Press, 1993), 27.

13. See William L. Andrews, "Hannah Crafts's Sense of an Ending," in *The Bondwoman's Narrative Educational Companion* (New York: XanEdu, 2002) for more on the ending of the novel. Andrews also notes the parallels between woman's fiction and *The Bondwoman's Narrative*; he suggests that the former may have indeed been instrumental in shaping the latter.

14. See Harriet Jacobs, *Incidents in the Life of a Slave Girl*, ed. Jean Yellin (Cambridge: Harvard Univ. Press, 2000).

15. See Dickson D. Bruce, Jr., *The Origins of African-American Literature, 1680–1865* (Charlottesville: Univ. Press of Virginia, 2001). Bruce describes the common trope of the "virtuous mulatta" who is destroyed by her encounter with the malicious slave owner (294–297). Certainly, Mrs. De Vincent plays this role in *The Bondwoman's Narrative*, but her virtue is not attended by the same fortitude and faith that Hannah demonstrates. Therefore, it seems that Crafts would have readers believe that unfailing virtue can overcome the villainy of characters like Mr. Trappe and Mrs. Wheeler.

16. Hazel Carby, *Reconstructing Womanhood* (New York: Oxford Univ. Press, 1987), 30.

17. Barbara Welter, "The Cult of True Womanhood, 1820–1860," in *Dimity Convictions: The American Woman in the Nineteenth Century* (Columbus: Ohio State Univ. Press, 1976), 21–41. See also, Carby, *Reconstructing Womanhood*, 23.

18. See Booker T. Washington, *Up From Slavery*, ed. William L. Andrews (1901; reprint, New York: Norton, 1996).

19. Contrast Hannah's virtuous behavior with that of a character like Uncle Tom, whose submission makes him a martyr; see Harriet Beecher Stowe, *Uncle Tom's Cabin or, Life Among the Lowly* (Boston: John P. Jewett, 1852). The difference between Hannah Crafts and Uncle Tom is that the former installs her self-image as her master; Hannah only takes orders that allow her to conform to the ideal she wishes to embody and thereby denies the power of the master despite her apparently deferential and submissive behavior.

20. Baym, *Woman's Fiction*, 44.

21. Merish's analysis of authors such as Sedgwick, Stowe, and Kirkland in *Sentimental Materialism* suggests that the codes of middle-class domesticity that Hannah so ably deciphers would have been especially resonant for both the author and, perhaps, her imagined readers as well.

22. Since slaves "inherited" their status as chattel from their mother, the idea that white blood could somehow mitigate the effect of this all-determining inheritance is questionable at best. Hannah realizes that as a slave, she has inherited nothing but the color that defines her for whites, and that to maintain a self-image based on inheritance would only be a validation of the arbitrary laws that rendered her a slave in the first place.

23. Carby, *Reconstructing Womanhood*, 34.

IV

AFRICAN AMERICAN GOTHIC

13

The Art of Ghost-Writing
Memory, Materiality, and Slave Aesthetics

RUSS CASTRONOVO

The materiality of Hannah Crafts's novel, *The Bondwoman's Narrative*, proves its authenticity. Imprints of a thimble, stains of iron-gall ink, threads of cloth in the paper: these traces confirm the physical materials of this manuscript as products of the 1850s. Another "sign of genuine age in a document," according to Joe Nickell's "Authentication Report," is an almost spectral presence of letters and words that transferred the mirror image of Crafts's handwriting between facing pages as the manuscript sat unpublished for the last 150 years (293). This "ghost-writing" (293) conjures up the hand of Crafts, an afterimage of her labor in using a goose quill pen to author a tale of the physical as well as spiritual trials that beset her narrator, Hannah. Ghosts give testimony of a faded knowledge about the past. What is half there provides confirmation of historical presence; shadows substantiate the bondwoman's reality.

Ghost-writing authenticates the material existence of Hannah Crafts's labor that produced her manuscript. Scientific testing and analysis of the pages reveal these facts *about* the novel. Literary and cultural analysis of the hauntings, spirits, and morbid superstitions *within* the novel offer evidence of a different sort of materiality. In this case, authenticity and the real do not lie solely in her manuscript as artifact; an argument about the legitimacy and historical relevance of *The Bondwoman's Narrative* lies in its status as a text, specifically its use of the ghost story as a means of documenting the materiality of slave labor so often swept under the ideological carpet and disavowed by aesthetic discourse. Crafts's ghost-writing is not that gothic after all but is rather a critical aesthetic response to the everyday horrors of slavery.

Hovering about this tale of mystic encounters, local legend, and gothic superstition is a commentary on aesthetics and artistic production.[1] This other, more figurative sort of "ghost-writing" seems ideally suited for such reflections since aesthetics is, in many respects, a ghostly discourse that disconnects artistic production from historical and embodied contexts. In Crafts's hands, however, ghosts do not suffer disembodiment, and neither does art flit above the difficult conditions of a world made all too real by the gothic effects of the South's peculiar institution. Ghosts in *The Bondwoman's Narrative* recall real persons disappeared by slavery and substantiate memories threatened by auctions, family separation, and social death. Crafts's ghost-writing recuperates the faded, unacknowledged, and repressed memories of the slave community. The novel's retelling of slave superstition constitutes an archaeological unearthing of what Crafts at one point identifies as the "sweat and blood and unpaid labor" that lies unseen behind the art prized by the master class (14).

This insistence on the materiality of art and aesthetic production flies in the face of prevailing nineteenth-century theories of beauty, which validated art's freedom from and transcendence of material conditions, especially the conditions of its own production. The otherworldly pretensions of American aesthetics at this time structured civic philosophy as well: the beautiful was also politically beautiful since the capacity to forget material conditions, to live a life apart from repressive institutions or dehumanizing markets, amounted to the highest entitlement. Art was not just for art's sake. The opposition between transcendent forms and an embodied materiality was deeply racialized. The privilege of inhabiting an abstract plane above the material realm of the everyday was reserved for whiteness. Having no traffic with a world of social contingency, whiteness became a ghostly form in which freedom signified liberation from corporeality and history. In short, white political identity was idealized as a supreme state of disconnection, a final and absolute detachment from the vicissitudes and unpredictability of political life itself. Freedom was about an aesthetics of death.[2] A fascination with corpses, suicides, clairvoyants, and spirits cuts across so many public spheres (antislavery rhetoric, women's rights, socialist reform) in the nineteenth-century United States that the afterlife (or at least talk about the afterlife) served as a common discursive arena for both whites and blacks. While famous white abolitionists like Lydia Maria Child and Harriet Beecher Stowe took an interest in clairvoyance and spiritualism, black writers routinely spoke of a better life in the hereafter, conflating political emancipation with the spiritual goal of being "free at last." Frederick Douglass, Harriet Jacobs, and Louisa Picquet all either attended séances or received patronage from white abolitionists with an abiding faith in the millennial promises of white spirits.

By virtue of its ghost-writing, *The Bondwoman's Narrative* locates itself squarely in this terrain as a means of assessing an aesthetic ideology of disconnection and its corresponding politics of disembodiment. Crafts's novel can be usefully situated in terms of this broader cultural engagement with aesthetics and death. In 1841, Ralph Waldo Emerson located the beauty in "the power to detach" (Emerson 433), which heightens perception by freeing an object from context so that it can be studied and appreciated apart, on its own and for itself. Although Emerson's essay, "Art," argues that beauty should be understood with a pragmatic sensibility of democratic usefulness, his aesthetic theory nonetheless echoes with the implications of unfreedom. The compulsory nature of Emerson's aesthetics at first appears counterintuitive given his emphasis on detachment as a step toward liberation that proceeds by removing the beautiful object from contingency. In a world of distraction and interruption, the beautiful is necessarily in a compromised position, competing with an array of sights and sounds for our attention. Once divorced from context, once separated from an "embarrassing variety," beauty is free to work its range of effects on our senses (Emerson 432). But such freedom goes hand in hand with unfreedom: the beautiful is also "the tyrant of the hour" that clamors narcissistically for all attention be reserved for itself alone (Emerson 433). Emerson seems untroubled by the potential arrogance of this position since he sets out with the presupposition that "the beautiful" and works of genius will speak in a universal voice. Art after this fashion is endowed with the capacity to "overpower the accidents of a local and specific culture," which is a good thing since Emerson is embarrassed by the popularity and variety of second-rate literature and theater churned out in the United States (Emerson 435). In the name of ennobling democratic civilization, Emerson throws up an appreciation of beauty and art as a barricade to the leveling of culture. Art serves the dominant class by dominating the cultural scene of mid-century America.

No crude apologist of elite culture is Emerson, however. The complexities—and contradictions—of his position save him from simply retreating to beauty and art as reactionary forces that can stave off the coming anarchy of culture made cheap by vulgarity, commodification, and popularity. Art promises to elevate the common people, providing oppressed humanity the future prospect of a social world based on fairness and symmetry. But for the moment the poem that prefaces Emerson's "Art" counsels "Man" to use aesthetics as a mode of political and social resignation:

'Tis the privilege of Art
Thus to play its cheerful part,

Man in Earth to acclimate,
And bend the exile to his fate (Emerson 429)

Four years later, in 1845, Frederick Douglass would give proof of Emerson's theory in his bitter attack on slaveholders who encouraged slaves to indulge in supposedly "cheerful" activities to "bend" them to their "fate" as perpetual bondpersons. During the Christmas holidays slaves were presented with a few days' liberty of dancing and fiddling, which functioned as "safety-valves, to carry off the rebellious spirit of enslaved humanity" (Douglass, *Narrative* 300). Coercion takes the form of leisure.[3] While Douglass stood in the glow of sympathetic antislavery audiences and talked about the political implications of "juba" beating and other aspects of slave culture's aesthetics, Hannah Crafts explored these issues in obscurity.[4] As an early African American novelist laboring outside the antislavery limelight, she engages these aesthetic questions via ghost-writing, an indirect and shadowy transcript of the slave culture that indistinctly marks the art objects of the slaveholding class as well as the gothic conventions imported to her own narrative.

Whether beauty operates as philosophical precept that detaches and liberates the object from context or functions in a more pragmatic sense to bend exiles and slaves to their fates, in either case it disregards the specific and often painful conditions of embodiment. Ghost-writing in *The Bondwoman's Narrative* challenges these prevailing ideologies of art and aesthetic experience. In light of Crafts's novel, the first component of Emerson's aesthetics—that the "beauty of art lies in detachment" (Emerson 432)—is revealed as an impossibility for those who lack the luxury of forgetting about the contingencies and "accidents of a local and specific culture." The second component—that art reconciles human beings to oppression—seems callous advice if offered to people living within the South's domestic institution. The narrator of *The Bondwoman's Narrative* first encounters the aesthetic when she is commanded to perform household tasks in a series of unused rooms crammed to the hilt with marble statues, oil paintings, rich carpets, and drapery. Almost immediately, the aesthetic overpowers her, its "tyrant" influence, to recall the language of Emerson, dominating her senses. Hannah feels as though she has "entered a new world of thoughts, and feelings and sentiments" while she loiters in hallways lined with portraits of the dead (17). Her aesthetic response seems decidedly nonphysical and spiritual; the "haunting air" inspired by these paintings detaches her from everyday existence and elevates her to a new plane of consciousness bearing little connection to her present (16).

But does Hannah really abide Emersonian precepts about aesthetic objectivity?[5] Her notion of art is doubly spectral, on the one hand promoting detachment, while on the other representing, as Crafts observes of the portraits in the slaveholder's gallery, the departed with "eyes [as] motionless and void of expression as those of an exhumed corpse" (16). In this stylized universe of morbid disembodiment, things are often not as they seem. Instead, things are much more than they seem, which is to say that events, persons, and memories are much more historically real than an aesthetics of disembodiment and disconnection can imagine. And insofar as this perspective fetishizes notions of purity by distancing the individual from the messy contingencies of the everyday, such aesthetics are white aesthetics.[6] Thus while the slaveholder's family portraits evoke shadows and the supernatural, Hannah insists on a materialist critique. Even as the slaves appreciate these *objets d'art* as signs of their master's transcendent wealth, "it never occurred to us to inquire whose sweat and blood and unpaid labor had contributed to produce it" (14). Hers is a negative critique ("it never occurred") that reverses the direction of aesthetic contemplation so that what once was detached becomes attached, that what once was spirit returns to the flesh. A negative materialist critique—and this is what ghost-writing is—has disturbing implications for the aesthetic ideology of whiteness that sustains the planter class. At a general level, the master's expensive furnishings, paintings, and other emblems of civilization never outstrip the blackness that they purportedly transcend. And, at a more specific and intimate level, the resemblance between the master's bride to the portrait of a "slave woman belonging to [her] father, whose countenance was nearly white," later sold off from the family plantation, hints at the "white" wife's secret African heritage (46). For the "white" mistress, art conjures up pictures of the dead that desublimate her privileged existence, threatening to condemn her to a life of drudgery. The slave mother's portrait is an example of ghost-writing par excellence in which the departed, the vanished, and the disappeared return to flout any possibility of amnesia, aesthetic objectivity, or other type of disconnection as they lay claim to their bearing on the present. In the aesthetics of ghost-writing, the Emersonian pretension that art will "overpower the accidents of a local and specific culture" finds itself overpowered by a rather specific set of material considerations, namely, the interconnections of black and white identities within American slave culture.

In part because these artifacts are so powerfully resonant, Hannah is instructed by the housekeeper not to dawdle in the rooms filled with art. Asked to account for her presence in this haunted part of the house, Hannah responds that she is merely "looking at the pictures" (17). But a slave cannot "merely" look at pictures in a world overdetermined by aesthetic representations of the dead. Her explanation seems innocent enough, asserting only rudimentary visual literacy and not the more dangerous verbal literacy she has been learning in secret. The housekeeper accepts her explanation and even questions whether an "ignorant thing" such as Hannah could receive any lasting impression from art (17). Hannah has received much more than a lesson in aesthetic disinterestedness, however. Her contact with portraiture provides a political education as well:

> Though filled with superstitious awe I was in no haste to leave the room. . . . I was not a slave with these pictured memorials of the past. They could not enforce drudgery, or condemn me on account of my color to a life of servitude. As their companion I could think and speculate. In their presence my mind seemed to run riotous and exult in its freedom as a rational being, and one destined for something high and better than this world can afford. (17)

Looking at the dead, she intuits that her quickened emotions and inspired intellect pose a serious challenge to the status quo of racial subordination. Often idealized as an absolute state of disconnection and disembodiment, "riotous . . . freedom" in American political thought, especially within antislavery rhetoric, hinges on a morbid fascination with death.[7] As the climactic chapter title of William Wells Brown's *Clotel; or, the President's Daughter* puts it, "Death is Freedom" (Brown 216). Crafts shares this deathly political logic, but, once again, her negative materialist critique reverses the direction, or in this case, switches the target, of murderous desire. Surrounded by images of the white dead, Hannah indulges in a Romantic release that equates liberation with the human soul's capacity to aspire, often defiantly, to planes higher than earthbound limits.[8] In addition to this rather conventional musing, she also participates in a much less common strategy, which, instead of embracing death for the slave, takes aim at the slave master. Even this aim is expressed as misdirection: she concentrates her vision not on the master but on his ancestor's portrait.

The first time that *The Bondwoman's Narrative* does violence to Sir Clifford's portrait comes when Hannah's master, irritated by the groaning branches of a linden tree, commands that the tree be chopped down. The result of his words is phantasmatic as the portrait crashes to the floor. "Who done it?" asks Hannah from the security of retrospection, revealing the difficulty of forgetting her former life within an institutional regime where blame could be quick and punishment immediate (29). The "invisible hand of Time" is singled out as the culprit, but the novel also hints that occult forces are responsible for this attack on the image of white patriarchy (29). The tree is not simply an object within the natural world; more importantly, the linden functions as a supernatural mnemonic. Slaves are lashed to the linden for brutal punishment. And,

from the linden, the victims have promised to haunt the big house and its occupants. As the material artifact of the master's art is dislodged by curses from
beyond the grave, white aesthetics are tripped up by slave aesthetics. Although
this scene seems to rely solely on gothic conventions, Crafts drops hints about
the Africanist sources of haunting and other gothic effects in claiming that
"people of my race and color" are somehow predisposed to spiritual matters
(27). Interestingly, this sort of essentialism also comes into play earlier when
Hannah traces her aesthetic sensibility, particularly her interest in "fancy pictorial illustrations and flaming colors," to her black ancestry (5). The ghostly
workings of slave aesthetics bring white art back to earth; the legend of a slave
woman's promise to return from the dead returns whiteness to the scene of
the murder. Slave superstition—itself an emanation of a black narrative aesthetic—acts as a material witness to the transcendence and erasure practiced
by a white art of forgetting. Matters of the spirit in nineteenth-century
African American life, according to Katherine Clay Bassard, perform community, "engaging in and (re)producing cultural forms and practices" that
build the identity of a people (Bassard 128). These "forms and practices"—
linguistic usage, modes of expression, kinship relations—are as matter-of-fact
as they are supernatural and as aesthetic as they are spiritual. In staging a confrontation between slave aesthetics and dominant art, *The Bondwoman's Narrative*
provides a historical record of the intangible chords of memory that stand just
beyond white artistic structures much as a linden tree used as a whipping post
stands within earshot of the master's window.

The Bondwoman's Narrative assaults Sir Clifford's image a second time in
putting white family portraits on the auction block. A series of woes besets
the plantation household as the relationship between white master and mistress falls prey to concubinage, adultery, suspicion, and distrust. Black sexuality—especially as it is subject to the predatory control of white men—spells
trouble for the white domestic intimacy necessary for the continuation of
master's legally recognized line. No matter how embarrassing this sexuality
could prove for the master class and its own self image as dignified and genteel, little scruple seemed to accompany the public commodification of slave
women that was calculated to arouse the financial as well as prurient interest
of potential buyers. As William Wells Brown recounts the sale of "the president's daughter," he carefully observes how her price steadily goes up by $100
increments until "a paper certifying that she [Clotel] has good moral character," that is, an affidavit of her virginity, is presented at which point the jump
in price doubles to $700 (Brown 66). In place of exposed slave women,
Crafts's narrative archly abandons the white family portraits to public sale:
"Sir Clifford's portrait and its companions of both sexes, had been publicly

exposed in the market and knocked down to the highest bidder" (194). The family's decline is complete. The white progenitor and his lawful heirs now suffer the trial of family separation suffered by slave families. It could be argued, however, that the white family experiences only a facsimile of the black family's anguish since the white family's images and not its bodies are subjected to sale. Whiteness does not escape so easily, however. Crafts's critique reaches to other levels precisely by returning the aesthetics and image of whiteness to the scene of black materiality, to the scene of the crime. Art is not allowed to hover above the historical world divorced from the conditions and people that create and sustain it.

The crossed-out words in the manuscript provide evidence of a deliberate intention to saddle white aesthetics with the contingencies of black materiality. Originally, it seems, Crafts simply wanted to communicate the sale of the portrait collection objectively and without any vindictiveness. Upon revision, however, she apparently embellished her description of the process, specifying how the white images are "knocked down." Even as this addition to the manuscript details how the paintings are sold at auction, it also invests the bloodless images of whiteness with enough corporeality that they can be dragged through the marketplace The impersonal nature of public financial speculation blends with the violent physicality of being "knocked down." Frederick Douglass had already used this phrase in 1845 to recount his battle with the slave-breaker Covey as he reaches for a stick to club the rebelling slave: "He meant to knock me down" (Douglass, *Narrative* 298). Covey's intentions backfire, and the teenage Douglass teaches him a lesson about corporeality. But neither Hannah the character nor Crafts the author can get their hands on the master in *The Bondwoman's Narrative*. How does one "knock down" a master who is present only as a painted image? How does one strike at a ghost? Indeed, Hannah's master preempts any possibility of retaliation by taking his own life. Hannah is nonetheless able to get back by locating his suicide in "the drawing room—that ancient one where hung the family pictures" (72). He literally cannot live up to his own aesthetic image that validates the master class as urbane, dignified, and qualified to rule over others. Not only does Crafts return the aesthetic image of whiteness to contexts of black materiality; she also returns the image of whiteness to the corruptible white body. If the political privilege associated with whiteness inheres in its abstraction and detachment, Crafts's shows how this aestheticized perspective originates in a specific set of cultural conditions involving (de)racialized bodies.

At the tangible level of a manuscript page with words crossed out, a negative materialist critique comes into play once again, reversing the conventional trajectories of escape and freedom. Privileged with an existence freed of physical want and labor, her master would seem to escape retribution. But the very aesthetic that accomplishes his disembodiment also poses a mortal threat to both his body and genealogy. The art that effects the master's escape becomes the means of engineering his death. In contrast to fugitive slaves like Clotel who achieve a morbid freedom in the body's suicide, Hannah comes closer to freedom when death is visited on the bodies of white men. After her master's suicide, she falls into the possession of Mr. Saddler who next meets his end when his wagon overturns. Although Hannah is also injured in the accident, her rather fine sense of morality remains intact, and she admits to her status as a slave despite the fact that her light complexion would allow her to pass. The white woman who nurses her back to health at first presumes the dead white man to have been Hannah's "near relative," and Hannah herself writes that "I almost doubted my identity" after the wreck (115–116). Aboard a northbound steamship on her way to freedom, Hannah overhears that Mr. Trappe, the man in the business of dredging up ghosts from the past to extort "white" women with forgotten black ancestors, has been murdered. Beyond the reach of her nemesis, Hannah can safely report, "There is a hush on my spirit in these days, a deep repose a blest and holy quietude. I found a life of freedom . . . " (237). She effectively displaces materiality—in its most undeniable form—onto the men who claimed her as a material possession. The materiality and historicity of their whiteness—possessive, corruptible, and mortal—liberates her "spirit"; in fact, the actuality of their deaths allows her to attend to matters of the spirit.

—

So far in this discussion, Crafts's ghost-writing seems limited to imagining whites as both haunted and incorporeal, enjoying the privileges of not inhabiting a body. Blacks, in contrast, remain burdened by the unpredictable and objectifying effects of corporeality. Owners like Mrs. Wheeler continually force Hannah to jump to satisfy their whims just as unscrupulous speculators like Mr. Trappe threaten the stability of families presumed to be white. Slavery is about contingency, whereas mastery is about the absolute. Neither families nor selves have any right to integrity or wholeness under slavery. If "the possibility of wholeness," according to Johnella Butler, sets an important criteria for "the African American aesthetic," then Hannah and her compatriots, like *The Bondwoman's Narrative* itself, remain caught within the divisiveness of white conventions and institutions (Butler 178). Although Butler states that practitioners of an African American aesthetic refuse the "traumatic, binary fragmentations of matter and spirit," in early portions of her novel Crafts tends to make whites much more intimate with ghosts and immaterial spirits while restricting blacks to scenes of painful embodiment.

Yet as the otherworldly turns of the novel intensify, Crafts no longer abides the racial segregation of dark matter and whitened spirits. The gothic stratagem employed by Charlotte and William to allay suspicion about their plans for escape neatly integrates ghostly apparitions and slave bodies. During her convalescence at the Henrys, Hannah observes the bittersweet union of Charlotte and William who belong to different masters. After a severe beating, William runs away and haunts Charlotte's room at the Henry household. A ghost story does the trick of explaining the unexplained noises and sightings created by the fugitive. Never crediting the "strange reports of an unearthly visitant," Hannah somewhat smugly sets her rational skepticism against the superstition of the other slaves (132). While old Jo, whom Crafts is careful to identify as "a negro" perhaps because of his folk beliefs, clamors in comic fashion, "de ghost, de ghost, sabe me from the ghost," Hannah coolly tells her readers, "I found enough in the stern realities of life to disquiet and perplex, without going beyond the boundaries of time to meet new sources of apprehension" (132–133). Indeed, Hannah resists the gothic narrative mode that would lead her deeper into the mystery and perhaps threaten William and Charlotte with exposure by unveiling the romantic facts behind the ghost story. She instead views an unsentimental narrative mode as her ethical responsibility, stating that she "should only be an observer" (136).[9] Questioned by her mistress about the hauntings, Hannah confronts a dilemma. She does not want to appear as ignorant or superstitious as old Jo, but neither does she want to give up the fugitive. With some deft equivocation, she admits that the house is visited by a spirit but "not a spirit separated from the flesh" (139). Fusing matter and spirit, ghost and slave body, *The Bondwoman's Narrative* allows black bodies to experience the privileges of disembodiment. Hannah does not begrudge William the otherworldly disguise that conceals his slave body. Neither does she deny him his body. His master's punishment already has denied William the right to his body in the most brutal way. In order to escape the social death of slavery, William does not have to experience literal death—as do Clotel and the other tragic mulattas of abolitionist fiction. Unlike gothic sentimentalism, the art of ghost-writing does not partition body and spirit.

Even though Hannah dances around the question about the spirit's identity, she soon spills all to her mistress but not without sticking to an early realist mode, communicating only what she "had observed and witnessed" (139). Her unsentimental commentary functions as affidavit to the deep connections that draw slave husband and wife to one another. Black people really do have souls—even though American moral, legal, and scientific cultures had spuriously established that African American destiny was compromised by matters of excessive embodiment. If "the black image in the white mind" negatively associated blacks with uncontrolled libidinal desire and weak moral character, Crafts's ghost-writing about the newlyweds, Charlotte and William, positions their bodies within the spiritual relationship of conjugal union.[10] Indeed, at a practical level, William's disguise as a ghost serves as a ploy for the couple's escape. This link between ghosts and freedom is further established by Hannah's next owner who explains how Southern officials residing in Washington, D.C., have had their slaves lured away by an antislavery senator and his mulatto aide-de-camp. She tells Hannah that the "senator assisted in *spiriting* them away" (151, emphasis added). Her language suggests the spirit as a plane beyond a master's control. The domain of the spirit need not be divorced from corporeality as a privileged site of disembodiment but instead remains intimately connected to the African American bodies that temporarily disappear from white sight.

Although Charlotte and William successfully "spirit" themselves away, Crafts as author seems still trapped within the gothic tradition of the ghost story—and its racialized conventions. By the time Crafts began work on *The Bondwoman's Narrative,* "An Authentic Ghost Story" had already been put into wide circulation as Chapter 42 of Harriet Beecher Stowe's *Uncle Tom's Cabin.* The crazed, child-murdering quadroon, Cassy, becomes the madwoman haunting Legree's attic, manipulating supernatural rumors to discourage the curious from investigating any strange noises or sights coming from hers and Emmeline's hiding place. As a ghost, Cassy "either carried a duplicate key" or enjoyed "a ghost's immemorial privilege of coming through the keyhole . . . with a freedom that was alarming" (Stowe 449). Her freedom and privilege certainly come from the "most hackneyed clichés of Gothic tradition," which, as Karen Halttunen points out, saturate this episode in Stowe's novel (Halttunen 123). But it is also important to view this tradition as implicitly racialized. The freedom and privilege Cassy enjoys are a white woman's: donning a white sheet, she induces Legree to see her once sexualized body as the spectral image of his saintly mother. Legree's earlier vision of "that pale mother rising by his bedside" prepares his immobility and impotence upon seeing a shrouded slave woman standing by his bed in "ghostly garments" (Stowe 399, 450). Given her status as a quadroon concubine, Cassy has no doubt stood by his bed on other occasions. At this supremely gothic moment, however, Cassy's spirituality grants her the disembodied sanctity of white womanhood, protecting her from sexual abuse. Even after the gothic game is over and Cassy and Emmeline flee the plantation, the fugitives retain this whiteness as Stowe describes how "some of the Negroes had seen two white figures gliding down the avenue towards the high road" (Stowe 451). From where does their white-ness come? Are we seeing their bodies still shrouded in white sheets or evi-dence of their light skin? Working at the morbid junction of African Ameri-can superstition and dead white mothers, these women exploit an ambiguity that renders identity fluid, making their bodies hard to pin down. Cassy and Emmeline are next seen on a steamer out of Cincinnati bound still further north to Canada. They have successfully "spirited" themselves away.

The freedom that Stowe's slave women find in this radical seizure of the gothic departs from the oppressive interiors and haunted rooms typically as-sociated with the genre. Indeed, for Stowe herself, the gothic marked "a place of anxiety and psychic confinement" (Halttunen 129). As a genre, then, the gothic potentially poses a double threat for a black writer like Crafts. At one moment, its shadowy plots and half-buried traumas can paralyze individuals, and at the next, its overdetermined racial associations of whiteness and dis-embodiment can imprison the black body. Gothic effects ooze and seep throughout *The Bondwoman's Narrative*: secret rooms are discovered in plantation mansions; arteries spontaneously burst in a rush of blood; human skeletons are unearthed; torture forms part of the daily landscape; beautiful women haunt the place of their murders; corpses seem to rise up to communicate mysterious messages from beyond the grave. Can Crafts's novel plot its story with gothic narrative conventions but still remain free of its ideological over-tones that sentence blacks to the constraints of hyper-embodiment? The an-swer seems to be "no"—but only if unseen noises, visitations, apparitions, and supernatural phenomena are seen solely as the province of a gothic dis-course on whiteness.

If, on the other hand, spirits and deathly emanations have Africanist ori-gins, then Hannah's encounters with gothic conventions may not be that con-ventional at all. "Spell-bound" by a vision of a walking corpse, Hannah while alone in the woods falls into a trance-like paralysis that she compares to an "embodied death" (222). Suffering a phantasmagoria as profound as any of Poe's mesmerized or buried-alive subjects, she experiences the psychological distress of the gothic—plus an unexplainable something more. Her distress has origins of a diasporic nature wholly alien to the gothic Calvinism that be-devils Stowe: unable to move or call out, Hannah experiences a trance evoca-tive of West African religious practices that survived in the New World.[11] Still, Hannah would be the last person to claim an affinity with the practi-tioners of hoodoo or conjure. By contrasting her rationality to the gullible disposition of slaves like old Jo whose language bears marks of the black ver-nacular, Hannah privileges a white narrative genre over an Africanist cultural legacy. From a diasporic perspective, however, the gothic is not a white genre but a hybrid discourse of multiple origins. Trances, revenants, and spiritual portents cannot be identified as either black or white, regardless of Hannah's intention to disavow elements of slave culture or Crafts's conscious use of Stowe-like scenarios. Despite conscious intention, black cultural practices speak from within the unconscious of Crafts's New World gothic. Her slave aesthetic makes art out of memories and traditions that are buried and nearly forgotten.

Although Hannah herself is deaf to these vernacular and Africanist cultural echoes, her various self-transformations in *The Bondwoman's Narrative* resound with occulted memories that challenge the neat divisions between rationality and superstition, between matter and spirit. Her passage from the land of slavery to the freedom of the North thus becomes indistinguishable from passage from one world to the next. During her escape, she falls into a profound delirium as she sits up one night with the corpse of fugitive slave. The corpse that seemingly "press[es] its cold leaden hand against my heart" embodies the social death of slavery that drains the life of its victims (222). Hannah's hallucination that confuses death and social death suggests the otherworldly accuracy of second sight. Once she exits this psychological crucible filled with "horrors" and "anxieties of suspense" of being alone with a corpse, she passes through the valley of the shadow of slavery's social death toward freedom (222). But the dead will not be forgotten in her journey. Dead bodies and ghosts refuse separation—and they appear constantly in the pages of this novel, recalling masters to crimes that they would otherwise soon forget and slaves to relationships and communities that they struggle to keep intact. It would thus be a misreading to view these spectral encounters as a simple incorporation of gothic effects popular in the sentimental literature of the time. Instead, Hannah's frequent contact with the dead and dying amounts to a realistic tallying of slavery's consequences.

Crafts's fictive nineteenth-century transcript of second sight anticipates the late-twentieth-century anthropological work of Karen McCarthy Brown with a vodou priestess of Brooklyn. In a follow-up essay to her 1991 study, *Mama Lola*, Brown reverses the direction of the Middle Passage and travels with the priestess and her daughter to Benin. The three pause before the "Tree of Forgetting," which, as legend has it, "slaves on their way to the ships bound for the Americas were made to walk three times around this tree, a ritual act intended to wipe all memory of the Dahomean homeland from their minds" (Brown 30). At the site of historical trauma, Mama Lola falls to her knees and recovers an ancestor's memory, a past not her own, as she confronts a past buried by the slave trade. "Transatlantic slavery is to history as black holes are to the reaches of space," writes Brown (31). So, too, Crafts's narrative passes around the linden, mentioning again and again the tree that serves as the grisly location of slave beatings. But the linden is not simply a site of abjection. Its straining branches recall Hannah to the curse uttered by a dying slave woman lashed to its trunk: "I will come here after I am dead. . . . I will brood over this tree, and weigh down its branches, and when death, or sickness, or misfortune is to befall the family ye may listen for ye will assuredly hear the creaking of its limbs" (25). In each case, spiritual matters dislocate the traumatic subject, casting the self amid a wider and often undocumented history. Just as Mama Lola's response to the African vestiges of the Middle Passage reveals the "human connectedness operative in Vodou" (Brown 30), Hannah's response to the gothic effects of slavery reaffirm relationships, so often pulled apart by slavery, that exist only as memory.

—

Through ghost-writing Crafts intervenes in mainstream aesthetic discourse. Indebted to but suspicious of the gothic, this narrative logic fuses spiritual and otherworldly effects to the body's materiality within institutions of American racial bondage. Like the gothic, ghost-writing concentrates on death and the macabre, but in contrast to gothic sentimentality it is insistently grounded in the specifics of history. Life without this sort of materiality would be closer to death. Crafts's entry into aesthetic discourse is therefore also a political maneuver that questions the correlation of whiteness, disembodiment, and freedom. Ghost-writing offers material testimony of the family separations, corporeal abjection, and trauma that detached individuals from one another and their bodies under slavery's social death.

Hannah finds an afterlife to slavery not through death's final release but in the North. Still, freedom does not necessarily spell an end to the threat of division. "I must not omit telling who are my neighbors," she writes because to overlook this community would be to recreate at the level of narrative the institutional indifference toward other human beings that characterizes slavery (239). She counts Charlotte and William among her neighbors and recovers her long-lost mother. Just because William no longer has to disguise himself as a ghost to live with his wife does not mean that *The Bondwoman's Narrative* is now free of gothic trappings. Nor do the new relationships that Hannah forms with "the friends of the slave in the free state" mean that her novel is no longer haunted by the racialized conventions required to tell her story in the first place. Her challenge is to use the aesthetic of ghost-writing, an aesthetic potentially freighted with gothic trappings, without dividing body and spirit, sacrificing the materiality of memory, or privileging disembodied whiteness. Writing itself becomes the answer to this challenge. A tactile activity, writing as a material object constitutes an undeniable historical realness that matches the "silent unobtrusive way of observing things and events" practiced by Crafts's heroine. Both an aesthetic activity and a material artifact, her layered sense of writing fuses the imagination to everyday contingencies of the here and now. In contrast to the push within Emersonian aesthetics toward transcendence and disconnection, Crafts insists on recognizing writing as a tangible product. She thus does not merely write but instead writes about her writing:

> I have yet another companion quite as dear—a fond and affectionate husband. He sits by my side even as I write and sometimes, shakes his head, and sometimes laughs saying "there, there my dear. I fear that you grow prosy, you cannot expect the public to take the same interest in me that you do" when I answer "of course not, I should be jealous if it did." (238)

Her conjugal community appears at this intimate scene of her writing. Each confirms the other: her husband's presence situates her writing amid lived relations just as her book-in-progress confirms the connectedness of husband and wife by providing a material occasion for domestic banter and dialogue. Wife, husband, and manuscript work together to ensure that no one becomes a ghost. Whereas Frederick Douglass in 1845 claimed radical autonomy by self-authenticating his individuality with the embodied materiality of his writing ("My feet have been so cracked with the frost, that the pen with which I am writing might be laid in the gashes" [Douglass, *Narrative* 271]), Crafts locates her free self at the confluence of her writing and another being, her husband. This insistence on connection renders her stance no less radically poised against a system, as the story of Charlotte and William attests, which had no respect for slave community or marriage. By implication, Crafts's husband is not the only one looking over her shoulder at her writing. Readers of *The Bondwoman's Narrative*, she suggests, will also validate her story by consuming it as a written document. Ironically, her husband's self-deprecating jest proved too accurate: for over a century and a half as Crafts's novel lay unpublished, "the public" did not take an interest in her story. But because of the materiality of her manuscript, we take an interest in *The Bondwoman's Narrative* today.

In addition to this eerily accurate prediction about "public . . . interest," her husband's reaction to her writing takes shape as an acute aesthetic judgment. The self-deprecating humor that her novel turns "prosy" or uninteresting when it touches on him, her "fond and affectionate husband," also labels her work as commonplace. But such an evaluation need not be seen as critical or derogatory. Instead, her husband credits her with a commonplace aesthetic that privileges everyday intimacy over disconnection and attachment over detachment. What her aesthetic privileges, then, are domestic experiences and relationships that nineteenth-century black people, living in a nation in which family separation and community disintegration was both legal and profitable, do not have the privilege to enjoy. She and her husband are deeply tied to one another, something impossible under slavery or within the studied estrangement of an Emersonian aesthetic perspective. Lest readers understand this conjugal bond as restraining to him, she quickly adds that her husband "is, and has always been a free man" (238). Such "prosy" or unimaginative writing memorializes the lost and taken-for-granted affinities between people: its untranscendent qualities insist on human interconnection. "Prosy" writing is ghost-writing, too. The voices from beyond the grave, unearthly visions, and shrouded specters of ghost-writing are not extraordinary or mysterious; there is nothing gothic about such episodes. Rather, these manifestations are ordinary for slaves like Charlotte and William or for Hannah herself, all of whom understand personhood as mediated by memories and people that exist beyond the self. With this closing gesture that so complexly situates Crafts's writing among lived historical relations, *The Bondwoman's Narrative* ensures that readers think of this novel not simply as text but in terms of the tangible nature of its handwritten pages.[12] After all, it is at the material level of the physical manuscript that ghost-writing most graphically appears.

Notes

1. Nineteenth-century descriptions of slavery's gothic effects attempt to communicate the psychological as well as physical horror of bondage. Such descriptions, however, at once tend to sensationalize bondage and fictionalize its historical significance. For more on this point, see Goddu, Halttunen, DeWaard.

2. I make these arguments in *Necro Citizenship*.

3. Douglass's denunciation of aesthetic activity is more nuanced than complete rejection of leisure and pleasure as "part and parcel of . . . gross fraud" foisted on his companions (*Narrative* 300). Douglass's scorn here concerns the slaveholder's aesthetic, which needs to be distinguished from his earlier description of a slave aesthetic best embodied in the slave songs that "breathed the prayer and complaint of souls boiling over with the bitterest anguish" (*Narrative* 263).

4. On "juba" or "jubilee beating," see Douglass, *My Bondage and My Freedom* (155).

5. The ideology of aesthetic detachment, of course, does not originate with Emerson, who most probably is giving a pragmatic inflection to Kant's *Critique of Judgment*.

6. "White aesthetics" should not be construed as a monolithic claim about white people, a group identity that has been historically striated by class, region, and other factors. Instead,

the idea of white aesthetics helps express the connections and overlap between a discourse of objectivity and cultural meanings of race in an era of slavery.

7. See Castronovo 25–61. Hannah certainly adheres to this eroticized morbidity with her description of her mistress's death: "A gleam of satisfaction shone over her face. There was a gasp, a struggle, a slight shiver of the limbs and she was free" (100).

8. Compare, for instance, Douglass's Romantic apostrophe to the ships on Chesapeake Bay: "Those beautiful vessels, robed in purest way, so delightful to the eye of freemen, were to me so many shrouded ghosts, to terrify and torment me with thoughts of my wretched condition . . . . 'You are loosed from your moorings, and are free; I am fast in my chains, and am a slave! . . . You are freedom's swift-winged angels, that fly around the world; I am confined in bands of iron!'" (*Narrative* 293).

9. From the first paragraph, Crafts establishes her interest in what may best be described as a type of proto-realism: "It may be that I assume too much responsibility in attempting to write these pages . . . but rather a silent unobtrusive way of observing things and events, and wishing to understand them better than I could" (5). Foregrounding her narrative mode in this fashion is important in laying a foundation for the truth claims conveyed in the novel.

10. See George Fredrickson, *The Black Image in the White Mind*.

11. Halttunen discusses the Beechers' combination of "gloomy Calvinism" and gothic sensibility (129–130). For more on the translation of West African religious practices to the New World, especially as they appeared in discourses of white reform, see Castronovo 159–168, and Wardley. Or, consider the dying words of the fugitive slave in *The Bondwoman's Narrative* who murmurs, "There are no slaves there. . . . Neither is there sorrow or sighing there, nor parting of friends" (220). This scene at once recalls the glorious deathbed visions of little Eva and St. Claire in *Uncle Tom's Cabin* and African American currents within New World Christianity. For an authoritative discussion of African American religious perspectives, see Raboteau.

12. The novel's final sentence provides still one more closing gesture: "I will let the reader picture it all to his imagination and say farewell," she writes of her domestic scene (239). While she accepts the commonplace aesthetic that comes with "prosy" writing, Crafts also appeals to the pictorial and imaginative faculties of the reader. She thus encourages the reader to continue the aesthetic commentary plotted in her novel.

Works Cited

Bassard, Katherine Clay. *Spiritual Interrogations: Culture, Gender, and Community in Early African American Women's Writing.* Princeton: Princeton University Press, 1999.

Brown, Karen McCarthy. "Telling a Life through Haitian Vodou: An Essay Concerning Race, Gender, Memory, and Historical Consciousness." In *Religion and Cultural Studies.* Ed. Susan L. Mizruchi. Princeton: Princeton University Press, 2001.

Brown, William Wells. *Clotel; or, the President's Daughter: A Narrative of Slave Life in the United States.* New York: Carol, 1969.

Butler, Johnella E. "*Mumbo Jumbo,* Theory, and the Aesthetics of Wholeness." In *Aesthetics in a Multicultural Age.* Ed. Emory Elliot. New York: Oxford University Press, 2002.

Castronovo, Russ. *Necro Citizenship: Death, Eroticism, and the Public Sphere in the Nineteenth-Century United States.* Durham: Duke University Press, 2001.

Crafts, Hannah. *The Bondwoman's Narrative.* Ed. Henry Louis Gates, Jr. New York: Warner Books, 2002.

DeWaard, Jeanne Elders. "The Crime of Womanhood: Ambivalent Intersections of Sentiment and Law in Nineteenth-Century American Culture." Ph.D. Diss. University of Miami, 2002.

Douglass, Frederick. *My Bondage and My Freedom.* Urbana: University of Illinois Press, 1987.

———. *The Narrative of the Life of Frederick Douglass, an American Slave, Written by Himself.* In *The Classic Slave Narratives,* ed. Henry Louis Gates, Jr. New York: Mentor, 1987.

Emerson, Ralph Waldo. "Art." In *Essays and Lectures.* New York: Library of America, 1983.

Fredrickson, George M. *The Black Image in the White Mind: The Debate on Afro-American Character and Destiny, 1817–1914.* New York: Harper and Row, 1971.

Goddu, Teresa A. *Gothic America: Narrative, History, and Nation.* New York: Columbia University Press, 1997.

Halttunen, Karen. "Gothic Imagination and Social Reform: The Haunted Houses of Lyman Beecher, Henry Ward Beecher, and Harriet Beecher Stowe." In *New Essays on Uncle Tom's Cabin,* ed. Eric J. Sundquist. Cambridge: Cambridge University Press, 1986.

Kant, Immanuel. *The Critique of Judgement.* Trans. James Creed Meredith. London: Oxford University Press, 1952.

Raboteau, Albert J. *Slave Religion: The "Invisible Institution" in the Antebellum South.* New York: Oxford University Press, 1978.

Stowe, Harriet Beecher. *Uncle Tom's Cabin, or Life Among the Lowly.* New York: Signet, 1966.

Wardley, Lynn. "Relic, Fetish, Femmage: The Aesthetics of Sentiment in the Work of Stowe." In *The Culture of Sentiment: Race, Gender, and Sentimentality in Nineteenth-Century America,* ed. Shirley Samuels. New York: Oxford University Press, 1992.

14

Hannah crafts.

PRISCILLA WALD

This essay is about the absence of ghosts in *The Bondwoman's Narrative*. In fact, I will argue that it is not a haunted text. My assertion will surprise many readers, considering the images of shadows "flitting past through the gloom," the supernatural thrills, mysterious beings, and corpses in the woods that permeate this work, and the centrality of the legend of the linden that explains the curse on the house of Crafts's first master. Certainly, Crafts uses the form of the ghost story and other gothic conventions. But I will argue that she does so in order to refuse them—conspicuously. And that conspicuous refusal—especially in the legend of the linden—allows her to foreground the importance of her own authorship as both cultural expression and political act, as she articulates her ideas about the relationship of fiction to politics.

Of course, a work does not need ghosts to be haunted, and as many critics have argued, race relations—particularly in the institution of slavery—gave rise to many scenes of haunting. While Thomas Jefferson is not typically thought of as a gothic author, he offers an especially powerful example of such a scene, when, in Query XIV of his *Notes on the State of Virginia*, he enumerates "the most remarkable" of the 126 new acts proposed as part of the intended revisions to the state's code of laws.[1] Among them he lists a provision for emancipation of "all slaves born after passing the act" to be accompanied both by their colonization abroad and the simultaneous recruitment of white settlers. Anticipating the question, "Why not retain and incorporate the blacks into the state, and thus save the expense of supplying, by importation of white settlers, the vacancies they will leave?" he ominously explains that "deep rooted prejudices entertained by the whites; ten thousand recollections, by the blacks, of the injuries they have sustained; new provocations; the real distinctions which nature has made; and many other circumstances, will divide us into parties, and pro-

213

duce convulsions which will probably never end but in the extermination of the one or the other race."[2] Implicit in his political analysis is his apparent knowledge of what the descendants of Africans will recollect and how they will respond. And implicit in that assumption is his expression of white guilt. Keenly aware of, and deeply troubled by, the injustice of enslavement, Jefferson summons a haunting presence embodying the guilty conscience of white Americans and the foundational inconsistencies of the fledgling nation.

The sense of a haunting here comes not only from the sense of guilt but from the pressure of what Jefferson does not acknowledge. Conspicuously absent from his analysis is the racial intermingling, biological and social, that would make the separation of "black" and "white" (to say nothing of nature's "real distinction") impossible in all senses. The incorporation of "blacks into the state" that he deems impossible has been in place from the outset. Economically, socially, ideologically, "white America" is contingent upon what Toni Morrison, in a well-known formulation, calls "the ghost in the machine."[3] Embedded in the list of historical grievances, the phrase "the real distinctions nature has made" demonstrates the obscurity of the process by which two fictions—Africanism and Americanism—are historically materialized: how, again in Morrison's words, "Africanism is the vehicle by which the American self knows itself as not enslaved, but free; not repulsive, but desirable; not helpless, but licensed and powerful; not history-less, but historical; not damned, but innocent; not a blind accident of evolution, but a progressive fulfillment of destiny."[4]

It is in the nature of contingencies to haunt, if by *haunting* we understand the felt pressure of what has been refused or repressed. "In haunting," writes Avery Gordon, "organized forces and systemic structures that appear removed from us make their impact felt in everyday life in a way that confounds our analytic separations and confounds the social separations themselves."[5] Ghosts and hauntings are dangerous. Their presence attests to discrepancies that they can equally expose to view or obscure, which is why both Gordon and Morrison find the analysis of our hauntings so crucial to the project of social justice.

No wonder, then, that the institution of slavery furnished such rich material for what Teresa Goddu has termed an "American Gothic."[6] The contradictions of racism and the institution of slavery, which so troubled Jefferson and the Constitutional Congress, made those injustices especially rich sites for ghosts and hauntings. In the United States, as critics including Goddu, Morrison, Gordon, and Kari Winter have persuasively argued, the institution of slavery and the race relations it expressed and ultimately shaped have informed the development of the genre from the outset. Whether, as Winter argues, affinities between slave narratives and gothic novels influenced the development of both, or, as Goddu maintains, slavery invariably "haunts the American gothic,"[7] attention to the correlation yields insight into the literary, cultural, and political history of the United States.[8] Such an inquiry, moreover, attests to the relevance not only of literary critical analysis to an understanding of history, but also of literature to politics. That latter insight was well known by the writers of slave narratives, a genre sponsored at least in part (and in a variety of complicated ways) by abolitionists in the promotion of their cause. And it was equally comprehended by Hannah Crafts, as her own tantalizing (non)use—or conspicuous refusal—of gothic conventions in *The Bondwoman's Narrative* makes clear.

But the very familiarity of the gothic as a set of literary conventions also posed problems for the authors of actual narratives of enslavement. As critics such as Goddu and Saidiya Hartman have pointed out, the use of the gothic leads to what Goddu calls "the slave narrative's double bind: the difficulty of representing a gothic history through gothic conventions without collapsing the distinctions between fact and fiction, event and effect,"[9] without, that is, having the politics subsumed into the literary, thereby muting the reader's response and failing to achieve the desired effect.[10] The story they could sell, as many of the narrators discovered, was not necessarily the story they wanted to tell.[11] Moreover, for authors such as Crafts, the immediacy of slavery involved neither guilt nor repression, and the presence of black America was certainly not something she would deny. There is no dearth of ghosts and hauntings, of course, in African American literature, and their meanings are as various as the authors who invoke them. But Crafts did not choose to tell a ghost story; *The Bondwoman's Narrative* begins with a tantalizing tale that flirts with the conventions of the gothic and appears to summon slavery's ghosts only to refuse them explicitly and unconditionally. And she uses an almost-but-not-quite ghost story to underscore the terms of her own authorship in her very obviously *fictional* (although plausibly autobiographical) tale of a bondwoman's escape from enslavement.

As in any recently recovered literary work (especially an unpublished manuscript), the question of authorship is of central concern. But it assumes particular importance in what may be the first known novel by a black woman. In his introduction to the first published version of this manuscript, Henry Louis Gates, Jr., writes, "I have to confess that I was haunted throughout my search for Hannah Crafts by Dorothy Porter (Wesley)'s claim that—judging from internal evidence—Hannah Crafts was a black woman because of her peculiar, or unusually natural, handling of black characters as they are introduced to the novel."[12] I believe that Gates's locution—especially the use of *haunted*—would have delighted Crafts, for it links the idea of haunting to the particular pressures of African American female authorship in the mid-nineteenth-century United States, a relationship that is registered especially in the novel's tauntingly haunting moments. "African American women knew what had happened to Phillis Wheatley and to her work," notes Frances Smith Foster. "They knew Wheatley's literary achievements may have facilitated her eventual freedom but they also knew that it had not protected her finally from the ravages of racial discrimination and poverty. They knew it took more than words to change society and they knew that their words would be subjected to interpretations engendered by non-literary expectations and assumptions."[13] They knew, in other words, the possibilities, perils, and paradoxes of their authorship. They also knew that since their concerns and forms of self-expression were not conventional in the literary world of mainstream white America, they had to engage in a particular struggle with those conventions; they had, as Foster notes, to test "American literature for its ability to accommodate their own testimonies. And they were modifying that tradition, wherever necessary, to accommodate the inclusion of those testimonies."[14] That struggle, and the consequent modification, are evident in *The Bondwoman's Narrative* in Crafts's conspicuous refusal of gothic conventions and readers' expectations: specifically, when she dissociates haunting from ghosts and reclaims it as an aesthetic, a gesture that insists on a social analysis as (and because) it underscores the terms of her authorship.

i

Near the beginning of *The Bondwoman's Narrative*, Crafts's middle-aged master decides to marry, and in the course of preparing for the return of the bridal party, she is sent to close the windows of a distant apartment of the large house. The housekeeper, Mrs. Bry, explicitly tells her not to loiter in the rooms along the way, and Crafts assures her that she won't. Narrating her passage, Crafts prepares us for a haunting. She describes the "inexpressibly dreary and solemn" experience of "passing through the silent rooms of a large house, especially one whence many generations have passed to the grave" (14–15). She finds herself wondering about them and proclaims her susceptibility to a gothic—or uncanny—moment:

> Involuntarily you find yourself thinking of them, and wondering how they looked in life, and how the rooms looked in their possession, and whether or not they would recognise their former habitations if restored once more to earth and them. Then all we have heard or fancied of spiritual existences occur to us. There is the echo of a stealthy tread behind us. There is a shadow flitting

past through the gloom. There is a sound, but it does not seem of mortality. A supernatural thrill pervades your frame, and you feel the presence of mysterious beings. It may be foolish and childish, but it is one of the unaccountable things instinctive to the human nature. (15)

The conventions of storytelling, with which she is clearly familiar, lead us to believe that she is setting the scene for a ghost story and that the story will have something to do with the housekeeper's injunction and Crafts's promise not to loiter.[15] The receptivity to a haunting under such conditions is "instinctive" and "unaccountable" and appears unrelated to her experience of enslavement. Placing her emphasis on the susceptibility to a particular feeling, she identifies it as a feature of humanity. The passage manifests her interest in how literary and social conventions cause particular scenes or experiences to evoke predictable sensations or responses—how we are socialized, that is, into an aesthetic.

Among a few relatively unimportant grammatical infelicities, the pronominal inconsistency—the switch back and forth between "we" and "you"—seems only to signal the casual pronoun use of a storyteller, and of one, no less, who begins the novel by confessing her awareness of her "deficiencies" and describing herself as "neither clever, nor learned, nor talented" (5), a confession that is itself conventional. The narrative, which is, after all, in manuscript form, actually supports only the claim of someone not fully tutored in (or, perhaps, attentive to) the particularities of grammar and spelling and the mechanics of punctuation. It certainly does not lack artistry or an awareness of literary conventions and traditions. And in view of the narrative that follows, the inconsistency of pronouns, however accidental it appears or may even be, is nonetheless meaningful. Musing about feelings, she uses the second person: "Involuntarily *you* find *yourself* thinking of them" and "a supernatural thrill pervades *your* frame and *you* feel the presence of mysterious beings." Between these insertions of the second person, her use of the first person plural marks the memory of the stories that have conditioned both the receptivity ("all *we* have heard or fancied of spiritual existences occur to *us*") and the imagined change in the physical environment ("the echo of a stealthy tread behind *us*"). Thinking of the people who once inhabited the house puts Crafts in mind of their estrangement: she is more familiar with the rooms than even their erstwhile owners would be if they were to return. That sense corresponds to the lapse into second person, at once a familiarizing direct address and a dissociation from her own feelings (a kind of defamiliarizing). Thoughts about past inhabitants in effect inspire her to assume the role of storyteller, as she shapes the experiences and sensations of her reader ("you"). Crafts moves into the group ("we") when she describes how we all have been conditioned—largely by stories ("all we have heard or fancied of spiritual existences")—to experience the world in a particular way. The passage marks a digression from the account, and the pronouns register a productive tension between Crafts's sense of herself as at once subject to and in control of those conventions.

Significantly, following this passage, the story does not go where literary conventions suggest that it should. In place of ghosts, we get two legends, and in place of the consequences we assume she will face as a result of disregarding Mrs. Bry's command, we get, from the latter, a bemused—if somewhat acerbic—remark, which occasions a philosophical meditation on her condition from Crafts. Both legends tempt us to ghost stories that prepare us, like the wandering Crafts, for "the presence of mysterious beings." Yet, neither goes quite where conventions would dictate.

Expecting ghosts, the narrator and her readers enter into the family drawing room in which hang portraits of each successive master of the estate, beginning with its founder, Sir Clifford De Vincent, and their wives. The portraits remind her of a story that has been elevated to the status of a legend, recounted by Mrs. Bry, that Sir Clifford, having ordered portraits of himself and his wife to be hung in the drawing room, cursed any "person who should ever presume to remove them" as well as "any possessor of the mansion who being of his name and blood should neglect to follow his example" (15). Thus had he decreed the visual analogue to the patriarchal dynasty he clearly intended to found. The first heir to deviate was the current occupant, who had hung his portrait prior to marrying and without the festivities that traditionally accompanied the hanging of the portraits.

Crafts reinforces the sense of foreboding generated by that detail (her master's evident disregard of Sir Clifford's curse) when she follows it with the observation that "memories of the dead give at any time a haunting air to a silent room" (16). But again she defies expectations when "the golden light of sunset" casts the playful "shadows of a linden" over the features of the portraits, which the shadows proceed to animate (16). Past tense shades into present as a "stern old sire with sword and armorial bearings *seems* moodily to relax his haughty aspect," a war veteran "*assumes* a gracious expression it never wore in life," a "halo of glory" descends on a bride, a young mother's hair floats over herself and her child, and even "the frozen cheek of an ancient dame *seems* beguiled into smiles and dimples" (16, emphasis added). Far from a spectral haunting, in which the narrator would experience these changes as emanating from without, this scene describes something much more like an enchantment, in which Crafts foregrounds the play of her own imagination. With the tense change, she calls attention to her double roles as perceiver and artist; she conspires with the sunlight on the linden to animate the portraits, an interaction that is clearly transformative. Against the meaning of the portraits that Sir Clifford evidently intended to instantiate, Crafts offers her own artistic revision and, in the process, depicts her more general struggle with the fixity of conventional forms.

Sir Clifford cannot control the effect of the portraits, which are subject not only to Crafts's reinterpretation but also to the changing conditions under which they are viewed. As dusk descends, the playful shadows turn dark and somber, changing her own master's "usual kind and placid expression to one of wrath and gloom . . . , the lips turgid with malevolence" (17). In turn, however, Crafts feels not haunted, but inspired. "I was not a slave with these pictured memorials of the past," she insists. "As their companion I could think and speculate. In their presence my mind seemed to run riotous and exult in its freedom as a rational being, and one destined for something higher and better than this world can afford" (17). Where Sir Clifford intended to reify the authority and entitlement of the masters of Lindendale in the portrait gallery, Crafts emphasizes their mutability. She is liberated by her ability to animate them, to play with their meaning and thereby express her artistry, which breaks down barriers of time and status and enfranchises speculation. As a manifestation of her artistic agency, her authorship becomes a figure of her liberation.

Mrs. Bry comes upon Crafts just as the latter has completed the task for which she had been sent, closing the windows not because she had been sent to do so but because, she explains, "the night air had become sharp and piercing, and the linden creaked and swayed its branches to the fitful gusts" (17). The housekeeper responds to Crafts's simple explanation of what she has been doing ("looking at the pictures") with disdain rather than the anger we had been led to expect: "'Looking at the pictures' she repeated 'as if such an ignorant thing as you would know any thing about them'" (17). It is an odd response, since Crafts has just told us that Mrs. Bry had been the one to tell her about the legend. Interestingly, Mrs. Bry in effect fails to claim (or, it seems, to remember) her own act of authorship. And her words make clear that she certainly cannot imagine Crafts in that role, a skepticism through which Crafts marks her (white) audience's likely response to her narrative.

As many authors of African descent had learned (and as Frederick Douglass, in particular, had publicly decried), white America characteristically found it difficult to imagine black authorship, an extension of their inability to imagine fully equal personhood. Hence Crafts's seemingly incongruous response:

> Ignorance, forsooth. Can imagination quench the immortal mind or prevent its
> feeling at times the indications of its heavenly origin. Can it destroy that deep

abiding appreciation of the beautiful that seems inherent to the human soul? Can it seal up the fountains of truth and all intuitive perception of life, death and eternity? I think not. Those to whom man . . . teaches little, nature like a wise and prudent mother teaches much. (17–18)

The meditation is noteworthy because it is so disjunctive. The setup of the incident makes us expect a ghost story and a punishment. Neither is forthcoming. Instead, we get a paean to aesthetics and the imagination. Crafts refuses to be haunted by the portraits because haunting requires that she surrender her agency. As the more elaborate legend of the linden, with which she follows this incident, suggests, Crafts locates her act of authorship, which she offers as the most profound antidote to the deadening effects of enslavement, precisely in the disjunction between the conventions and the story she tells: in the defiance, that is, of the reader's expectations, as they are established through literary and social conventions. In this way, Crafts jars her potentially resistant readers into a different kind of listening. Drawing on Robert A. Stepto's assertion that "distrust of the American reader and of American acts of reading [is] a primary and pervasive motivation for Afro-American writing,'" Foster contends that "African American writers [who] cannot trust Anglo-American readers to respond to their texts as peers . . . develop literary strategies that initiate 'creative communication' by getting readers 'told' or 'told off' in such a way that the readers do not stop reading but begin to 'hear' what the author is saying."[16] The animation of the portraits and the meditation that follows may help resistant readers begin to hear the story that Crafts wants to tell.

ii

The legend of the linden follows logically from the scene in the drawing room. First, Crafts introduces Sir Clifford, the would-be legend-maker, and his central role in family lore. Second, she establishes the linden as the medium through which she effects first the portraits' and then her own transformation. The linden, of course, does not produce the effects on its own; rather, as she emphasizes, the "golden light of sunset" casts completely different shadows through the tree's branches from the darkness of night. And those effects would be meaningless without the author's perceptions. Finally, she expresses a sense of foreboding in regard to the current master of Lindendale.

Just prior to the master's return with his bride, Crafts describes—again, in gothic terms—the ominousness of the wind—"how particularly anxious it seemed to enter the drawing-room in the southern wing, rattling the shutters, and shrieking like a maniac, and then breathing out a low gurgling laugh like the voice of childhood" (20). Compounding the "awe and dread" (20) experienced by members of the household, "the linden lost its huge branches and swayed and creaked distractedly, and," reports Crafts, "we all knew that was said to forbode calamity to the family" (20). For "it had not been concealed from [the servants] that a wild and weird influence was supposed to belong to" the linden (20). The passive voice suggests a seemingly disavowed creation of a legend, as though, perhaps, its credibility and pervasiveness lay in the absence of an author. But Crafts is interested in precisely that process, and she focuses her account of the legend on its source and its effects. As with ghost stories in many narratives of enslavement, the legend of the linden recounts the horror of a slave owner's breathtaking cruelty.[17]

The linden had been planted by and flourished under the care of Sir Clifford, whom she here describes as a "stern old man" known as "a hard master to his slaves" (20). With the added observation that "few in our days could be so cruel" (20), Crafts demonstrates how Sir Clifford had accomplished at least to some extent what he had clearly intended with the portraits: a legendary status. The linden, we learn, "was chosen as the scene where the tortures and punishments were inflicted. Many a time had its roots been manured with human blood. Slaves had been tied to its trunk to be whipped or sometimes gibbeted on its branches" (20–21). Again, the passive voice suggests a refusal of attribution, but here Crafts uses it to convey the deferral of responsibility that is a hallmark of the institution of slavery. Sir Clifford uses the linden, however, as a kind of theater of cruelty in which to enact scenes of horror that are perhaps intended to deaden both the enslaved and the enslaver, albeit in drastically different ways.

The legend of the linden springs from Sir Clifford's "direst act of cruelty, and the one of a nature to fill the soul with the deepest horror" (21). With this description, Crafts prepares us for literary conventions, this time of the slave narrative (with its gothic features). Here is the conventional scene encouraged by abolitionists wishing to represent the profound horrors of the institution and thereby presenting the representational bind I referred to earlier; just as the tale of the slave owner's cruelty represents how such scenes of brutality are morally deadening for the slave owner and can promote the deadening effects of despair for the enslaved, so the literary conventions of horror and cruelty represented by the gothic genre risk blunting the reader's sensibility to the crimes enabled by the institution of slavery. So Crafts's dilemma, like that of all who narrate such scenes, is how to countermand those potential consequences of literary conventions. By summoning and then transforming them, Crafts evokes and then confounds her reader's expectations. In that way, she calls attention to the choices she makes as an author—in this case, both to use and to refuse certain literary conventions.

The legend concerns a particularly vicious punishment that Sir Clifford exacts on an old servant, Rose, who had been the nurse of Sir Clifford's son and was therefore particularly beloved by the family. Rose's children had evidently been sold, and the only being who remained for her to love was her youngest daughter's dog whom the daughter had especially enjoined her mother to care for. The dog was "white and shaggy, with great speaking eyes, full of intelligence, and bearing a strong resemblance to those of a child" (21). To Rose there seemed to be no distinction. Against the humanity of the dog, Crafts underscores the pettiness (and inhumanity) of Sir Clifford, who "in all his state and haughtiness could demean himself sufficiently to notice the trespass of a little dog" (22). And she underscores his petty tyranny further by juxtaposing the source of his rage (the *little* dog) with the magnitude of his self-importance: "Sir Clifford made it a boast that he never retracted, that his commands and decisions like the laws of the Medes and Persians were unalterable" (22). Sir Clifford orders Rose to kill her dog, and when she refuses to do so, he has them both suspended from the linden, in sight but out of reach of one another.

Crafts is careful to illuminate the strategies of slavery as she underscores Sir Clifford's efforts to dehumanize the enslaved by ordering them to perpetrate the actual crimes; he commands Rose to kill the dog herself and some of "the obsequious slaves" to hang Rose and the dog from the tree. Crafts conveys the efficacy of these tactics again through the use of passive voice:

> An iron hoop being fastened around the body of Rose she was drawn to the tree, and with great labor elevated and secured to one of the largest limbs. And then with a refinement of cruelty the innocent and helpless little animal, with a broad iron belt around its delicate body was suspended within her sight, but beyond her reach. (23)

Passivity, signaled by the passive voice, constitutes a strategy of the peculiar institution. To the enslaved it represents their surrender of agency. It allows the enslavers to deny responsibility for the barbarous acts they perpetrate. For Crafts, it is the figurative antithesis of authorship.

The legend of the linden represents one of the very few such digressions (and the longest one) in the book. Crafts lingers on the scene of torture in which Sir Clifford forces the two principals to witness each other's suffering. In the 1845 *Narrative of the Life of Frederick Douglass, an American Slave, Written by Himself,* the young narrator famously recounts witnessing the beating of one of his aunts from a closet in which he is sequestered. He describes the act of witnessing this scene as his "entrance to the hell of slavery."[18] For Crafts, the depths of cruelty manifested by Sir Clifford inhere in adding to Rose's unbearable physical tortures the need to witness the suffering of her beloved companion, whom she seeks ceaselessly to comfort throughout their shared ordeal.

Sir Clifford is heedless to the entreaties of his wife and son to pardon Rose and her dog, and when he refuses, his wife asks that he at least end their torture with death, since "the sight of their agonies and the noise of their groans would haunt her to her dying day" (24), but he remains unyielding. On the last night of their lives, a storm compounds their torment with consequences for the entire household. Rose's wailing, the dog's howling, and the tree's creaking are evident through the noise of the storm. Crafts writes that "slumber entirely fled the household of Sir Clifford. His Lady heretofore one of the gayest of women was never seen to smile afterwards" (24). The legacy of a haunted mansion is assured for any reader even remotely familiar with gothic fiction, and the curse with which Rose responds when Sir Clifford, on discovering the dead body of the dog in the morning, proposes to take the servant down from the tree is as expected:

> At the sound of his voice she opened her blood-shotten lack-lustre eyes,—and her voice as she spoke had a deep sepulchral tone. "No" she said "it shall not be. I will hang here till I die as a curse to this house, and I will come here after I am dead to prove its bane. In sunshine and shadow, by day and by night I will brood over this tree, and weigh down its branches, and when death, or sickness, or misfortune is to befall the family ye may listen for ye will assuredly hear the creaking of its limbs" and with one deep prolonged wail her spirit departed. (25)

The length of this digression and its placement near the beginning of the novel certainly lead the reader to believe that it will be central to the plot. And, indeed, the foreboding that Crafts experiences while viewing the portrait of the current master of Lindendale, and the ominousness of the curse that Rose levels against the family, both recounted in the context of wedding preparations, do prepare us for his ill-fated marriage. But the fate of the marriage in no way suggests supernatural intervention. On the contrary, the institution of slavery (with no help from a curse) is directly and explicitly to blame. The new Lady of Lindendale runs away from her new home and husband when her father's lawyer, who has followed her to Lindendale, threatens to reveal to her husband her African ancestry. Crafts does not give us the opportunity to know how her kind and placid husband might have responded to this discovery, for after discovering his wife's flight (accompanied by Crafts) and the reason for it, he commits suicide.

It is of course tempting to see Crafts attributing the master's fate to Rose's curse, but she never does so explicitly, and her actual narration refuses the connection. Indeed, the portraits in the drawing room that so fascinated her represent an unbroken lineage of patriarchs following from Sir Clifford who do not appear to have been cursed. And the lawyer, the apt-named Mr. Trappe, is the direct agent of the master's fate, while the earthly institution of slavery enables him to perpetrate his evil actions. Rose's inability to bring divine vengeance on the master of Lindendale, however, does not mean that she fails entirely to haunt the house. She gives meaning to the creaking of the linden, exacting her revenge by creating a legend that speaks to the horror of the institution of slavery and the particular cruelties that it enables. Rose haunts, in other words, *as an author,* and Crafts is her heir. Crafts illustrates the efficacy of Rose's curse/narrative when she describes how her master, on hearing the creaking of the linden at the celebration of their homecoming, "called for music, and prepared to dance . . . striving to obliterate some *haunting* recollection" (29, emphasis added). But in an important distinction between Rose and Crafts as authors, the former does not consider the full effects of her narrative. All hear the creaking of the linden as a signal of calamity for the family (despite evidence to the contrary), but it also memorializes the act of cruelty by which Sir Clifford laid down the law(lessness) of slavery. In other words, as she uses the master's tools, Rose risks playing into Sir Clifford's own symbolic use of the tree. She tries to change the meaning of who is being punished—and she certainly demonstrates that slavery dehumanizes the enslavers more fully than the enslaved—but she also reinforces one of the strategies of enslavement: the use of terror and superstition in the service of subordination.[19] In her preface, Crafts wonders if she has "succeeded in portraying any of the peculiar features of that institution whose *curse* rests over the fairest land the sun shines upon . . . in showing how it blights the happiness of the white as well as the black race" (3, emphasis added). Curses, for her, are the consequences of earthly institutions rather than supernatural intervention, and resistance to them depends upon recognizing them as such.

iii

In *The Bondwoman's Narrative,* Crafts takes control of the term "haunting," which she uses to describe earthly rather than supernatural events, and her use of the term involves changing its typical relation to temporality. The word is more often associated with Mr. Trappe than anyone or anything else. Crafts dislikes him when she first perceives him. She describes her terrified mistress as seeming to be "*haunted* by a shadow or phantom apparent only to herself, and perhaps even the more dreadful for that" (27), and Trappe is "the figure of that old man, with his dark clothes, and darker eyes . . . incessantly *haunting* and pursuing" (35, emphases added). All roads seem to lead back to Mr. Trappe. Even when, fleeing and disguised, Crafts and her erstwhile mistress decide to take shelter for a night with an apparently kind family, they learn that, ironically, they are domiciled in the home of Trappe's relatives, where he discovers them. Crafts realizes that he is "dogging [their] footsteps and would be haunting [them] everywhere" (63). Trappe is of course not a ghost; he is not even particularly uncanny. His motivation is clear: he is greedy and corrupt. With the repetition of *haunting*, Crafts insists on the banality of evil: it is entirely—and unfortunately—of this world, and the institution of slavery is one of its chief manifestations. The mistress is haunted by, and Trappe haunts as a result of, knowledge of a secret that cannot be revealed because of the institution, which haunts, therefore, more by what it evokes for the future than by what it summons from the past.

And Trappe seems omnipresent not because he is somehow supernatural but because he is powerful and determined. He is only as haunting and as inescapable as mortal power (and an unjust society) can make him. Eventually, Crafts and her erstwhile mistress are indeed apprehended because they are recognized as fugitives, and they are returned to Trappe because that is how the system works. Crafts recounts first the death of the former Lady of Lindendale, from a broken heart, and then her own experiences enslaved in two different families prior to her escape from bondage. She reports being content in the first family, where she is brought following an accident, and surprised to be treated so kindly. Yet, even here (and even though she asks the mistress to buy her so that she can remain with the family), slavery casts its pall. One night, following the wedding of a bondwoman who lived with the family to a man enslaved on the neighboring plantation, Crafts watches "the gay groups collected on the smooth green, and chasing each other through the flying dance, or laughing and chatting in a great state of mirthful enjoyment" and wonders "if they were really so happy— . . . if no dark shadows of coming evil never *haunted* their minds" (120, emphasis added). While gothic ghosts conventionally embody the return of a repressed past (and perhaps a corresponding present), the institution of slavery creates a haunted *future*. That, for Crafts, is its greatest crime: "There can be no certainty, no abiding confidence in the possession of any good thing. The indulgent master may die, or fail in business. The happy home may be despoiled of its chiefest treasures, and the consciousness of this embitters all their lot" (94). Of course no future is ever certain, but slavery represents *human* arbitrariness superimposed on the exigencies of chance. The institution is predicated on the concerted effort to deprive the enslaved of any part of their agency.

Crafts makes clear that in narrating a story of enslavement, and an accompanying critique of the institution of slavery, she cannot afford the luxury of a ghost story—the thrill of a horror that can be aestheticized through familiar literary conventions. The true "horror" of slavery—the ghost that haunts the enslaved—is the shadow of a future subject to the arbitrariness of human oppressors. Past horrors are not repressed because there is no veneer to obscure the horror. They are remembered and projected onto a future that allows for no contentment. Rose, for example, haunts not as a ghost but as a memory of the all-too-natural and all-too-human crimes that an owner of slaves may at any time *legally* perpetrate on another human being.

Significantly, the one "ghost" that Crafts encounters turns out to be the bridegroom from the very wedding that gave rise to her ruminations about the haunted future. Because nightly conjugal visits are not in his master's plan, he must sneak in to see his wife (and to plan their escape from bondage). On these visits, he is mistaken for "an unearthly visitant" (132) by many of the household servants, although never by Crafts, who regards that superstition as a sign of oppression. The enlightened mistress of the house, Mrs. Henry, confesses her surprise to Crafts that such a belief would flourish in her household when she had "always striven to instruct [her servants] better than to put any confidence in such wild and unfounded reports" (139). But however enlightened her household, it cannot withstand the corruptions of the institution.

Beneath the titillating terror of a ghost story—and the hijinks of a bridegroom making conjugal visits—is a far more horrendous story of a barbaric institution, which confounds Mrs. Henry's best intentions. Whether instructing her servants or encouraging their marriages, Mrs. Henry cannot countermand its corrosive effects. Several times Crafts remarks on her resolve never to marry while she is enslaved: "Marriage, like many other blessings," she explains, "I considered to be especially designed for the free, and something that all the victims of slavery should avoid as tending to perpetuate that system" (206). Literally, procreation adds to the master's property. But families—beloved companions for whom one feels responsible—can also bind one more firmly to the system. Such is the perversion of the institution of slavery. Charlotte, the bride of the "ghost," causes her husband, William, to question his resolve to flee (although ultimately they both escape successfully). Crafts's second (and successful) flight, on the other hand, is prompted precisely by her cruel mistress's "bestowing" her on a man she does not love.

In *The Bondwoman's Narrative*, as in most abolitionist discussions of slavery, the institution destroys the marriages of slaveholders as well. The fate of Crafts's first master and mistress, as we have seen, is its direct result. But their successors, too, fall victim to its corruption, as Crafts learns when she encounters a former acquaintance from Lindendale while with her last master and mistress in Washington, D.C. In one of the few digressions since the legend of Lindendale, she recounts the narrative through which she became acquainted with their fate. Evidently, the English mistress was unprepared for, and distressed by, her husband's infidelity with the bondwomen on his plantation, and her haughty response to him and cruel treatment of them alienates him further from her. Their mutual animosity escalates until finally she sustains severe injuries as a result of a quarrel. While bedridden, she undergoes a transformation, becoming "a gentle, humble lamb-like follower of Christ" (192) and earning her husband's love, but too late for them to enjoy. She never recovers, and "from the hour of his wife's death" her husband "had never seemed like himself, probably in consequence of grief, more probably in consequence of remorse" (193). Rose would no doubt be gratified to learn of the end of Sir Clifford's lineage and the subsequent dismantling of Lindendale,

> that the Linden with its creaking branches had bowed to the axe, and that great changes had been wrought inside the house as well as out; that some of the ancient rooms, whose walls ceiled with oak were brown with age, had been newly renovated, and now shone in all the glory of fresh paint and plaster. Above all that Sir Clifford's portrait and its companions of both sexes, had been publicly exposed in the market . . . and knocked down to the highest bidder. 'Sic transit gloria mundi.' (194)

With the *linden*, Crafts of course invokes Rose's curse, yet there is nothing supernatural even hinted at in the fate of the owners of Lindendale. Rather, again, their misfortunes can be directly attributed not to Rose's curse (or an act of divine vengeance) but to the earthly institution of slavery itself. The linden unceremoniously bows to the axe, signaling the end of the cursed dynasty, but the newly renovated house is ready for new occupants, with no effect on the *curse* of slavery. And the fate of Sir Clifford's portrait, however ironically it marks the futility of hubris and invokes the fate of his own bondpeople, is hardly in fact comparable to the latter. Summoning the linden, in other words, Crafts makes an authorial choice that honors the memory rather than credits the ghost of Rose. Trappe's victims, too, are avenged when he is murdered by the sons of a family with African roots that he had ferreted out for his own personal gain. Slavery needs no actual ghosts.

But Crafts also makes clear that her insights, like her authorship, are hard won. Toward the end of her account, just prior to her successful establishment in the North, she finally demonstrates (rather than abstractly narratives) her own susceptibility to otherworldly terror. Having attended a fellow fugitive on her deathbed, she is left alone with the dead body in a deserted cabin in the woods when the brother of the dead woman goes out to look for food. When he fails to return, Crafts can barely resist turning the corpse into a ghost. She recalls that "a great and unaccountable terror seized" her (221). The ensuing account verges on a gothic scene:

> My apprehensions were increased tenfold by the mysterious voices of the night. Mutterings, chatterings, and sounds of fearful import echoed through the gloom. Owls shrieked hediously to which was added the dismal howling of wolves. Then the corpse seemed to leer horridly, to gibe and beckon and point its long skinny fingers towards me, and though I knew that this was all fancy, though I had sense enough left to perceive even then the absurdity of my fears I could not overcome them, I could not pray for the protection of Heaven; Heaven seemed to have turned its face against me. (221–222)

With "sense enough to perceive . . . the absurdity of [her] fears," Crafts struggles against her susceptibility to common cultural anxieties: fear of death and the woods at night. It is hard to imagine too many readers who would not share her terror, and that conventionality is her point. Throughout the narrative, she recounts her struggle with conventions and susceptibilities. Here, in the woods at night, a fugitive (neither enslaved, nor free), she fully inhabits a liminal position, and here she most pointedly enacts that struggle.

In her account of the preceding deathbed scene, she had stressed the distinction between this scene and its cultural (and literary) analogues. She is, in fact, quite contemptuous of how "the ceremonial attendant on the dying hour burdens it with unmeaning pomp, and . . . the hush and sanctity of the . . . occasion give way before the elaborate and commonplace manifestations of condolence and sympathy" (218). By contrast, she and the dying woman's brother "could weep in silence and privacy. Public opinion came not to dictate the outward expressions of [their] grief" (220). Her terror, on the other hand, challenges her control, making her obviously susceptible to a more conventional response. "It was the longest night of my existence," she writes, "and I shall never forget its horrors. I, who had learned to sleep as calmly and composedly on a bed of leaves as in a palace chamber, was thus alarmed and terrified by ['the immediate presence of the dead' is crossed out in the manuscript] I know not what" (222). The terror punctuates as it expresses her liminality. In effect, it brings her back into the "we" of the passage with which I began: "all we have heard or fancied of spiritual existences occur to us."

Replacing "the immediate presence of the dead" with "I know not what," Crafts underscores the complexity of her fear. She knows its ostensible cause, but her point is beyond her ability to understand and name precisely because it is so conventional. It is an "unaccountable terror" like the "presence of mysterious beings" that she senses when Mrs. Bry sends her through Linden-dale to shut the windows, which she also describes as "unaccountable." It cannot be explained by the objects themselves, but it attests to a common susceptibility: the *sensation* of terror, that is, not the ghost. However long the night she endures, it never witnesses the corpse's actual animation. But it does show how difficult it is to maintain her perspective. She cannot, after all, stay in the woods, a fugitive—or, perhaps, an author—forever. As she prepares to establish herself in the North, she acknowledges her susceptibility to conventions. And since her entire narrative has counterposed her authorship to the language of haunting, she acknowledges the struggle with conventions that is at once a part of authorship and a mark of the limitations of freedom.

At the conclusion of the introduction to the novel, Gates speculates about "the unusual name of Crafts (plural)" and wonders if she had chosen it "as an homage to Ellen and William Craft, to whose cross-dressing disguise Hannah refers twice in her novel" (lxxii). Such a choice would certainly fit her authorial self-consciousness, and the name would likely have appealed to her all the more as it evokes the *craftiness* of the disguise. With the use of *Crafts*, moreover, the author may also have intended to underscore the activity *(crafting)* that she stresses throughout the narrative as she offers an account and analysis of enslavement. Embedded in her signature, in other words, is a sentence that may tell us what the author of *The Bondwoman's Narrative* most wanted us to know about herself: Hannah crafts.

Notes

1. Thomas Jefferson, *Notes on the State of Virginia* in *Thomas Jefferson: Writings* (New York: Library of America, 1984), pp. 123–325, p. 263.

2. Ibid., p. 264.

3. Toni Morrison, "Unspeakable Things Unspoken: The Afro-American Presence in American Literature," *Tanner Lectures on Human Values,* delivered at the University of Michigan on October 7, 1988.

4. Toni Morrison, *Playing in the Dark: Whiteness and the Literary Imagination* (Cambridge: Harvard University Press, 1992), p. 52.

5. Avery Gordon, *Ghostly Matters: Haunting and the Sociological Imagination* (Minneapolis: University of Minnesota Press, 1997), p. 19.

6. Teresa A. Goddu, *Gothic America: Narrative, History, and Nation* (New York: Columbia University Press, 1997), p. 3. U.S. history, by which I mean the dominant narratives of the past as they are typically taught and written about since the nation's inception, contains abundant examples of the haunting presence of the institution of slavery. It is, however, worth considering the particular ghosts and hauntings yielded by other examples of racist oppression, such as Indian Removal (and genocide), as they find expression in different regions, historical moments, and cultural forms. Lucy Maddox has written compellingly about the centrality—and haunting presence—of Indian Removal to the mid-nineteenth-century literary works that came to be known as "the American Renaissance." See Lucy Maddox, *Removals: Nineteenth-Century American Literature and the Politics of Indian Affairs* (New York: Oxford University Press, 1991). See also Renee Bergland, *The National Uncanny: Indian Ghosts and American Subjects* (Hanover, N.H.: University Press of New England, 2000).

7. Goddu, *Gothic America*, p. 3.

8. See Kari J. Winter, *Subjects of Slavery, Agents of Change: Women and Power in Gothic Novels and Slave Narratives, 1790–1865* (Athens: University of Georgia Press, 1992).

9. Goddu, *Gothic America*, p. 137.

10. See Goddu, *Gothic America*; and Saidiya V. Hartman, *Scenes of Subjection: Terror, Slavery, and Self-Making in Nineteenth-Century America* (New York and Oxford: Oxford University Press, 1997).

11. On politics and the market, see Augusta Rohrbach's essay, "A Silent Unobtrusive Way: Hannah Crafts and the Literary Marketplace" in this collection.

12. Henry Louis Gates, Jr., "Introduction," to *The Bondwoman's Narrative*, by Hannah Crafts, ed. Henry Louis Gates, Jr. (New York: Warner Books, 2002), p. lxv.

13. Frances Smith Foster, *Written By Herself: Literary Production by African American Women, 1746–1892* (Bloomington: Indiana University Press, 1993), p. 18.

14. Ibid., p. 19.

15. On Crafts's erudition, see the Appendices to *The Bondwoman's Narrative*, especially Appendix C and the web site created for the text at bondwomansnarrative.com.

16. Foster, *Written By Herself*, p. 107.

17. A possible model for Crafts could be Harriet Beecher Stowe's 1852 *Uncle Tom's Cabin*, in which the bondwoman Cassy destroys her especially vicious master, Simon Legree, by playing on his superstitions and guilt. See in particular Goddu's reading of Cassy's use of ghosts, which she reads as a "gothic tale within the novel's already gothicized plot" and argues that it "shows the gothic operating on yet another level: it allows the objects of torture and terror to haunt back" (Goddu, *Gothic America*, p. 143). With her own work most likely dating from sometime between 1853 and 1861, Crafts was almost certainly familiar with Stowe's novel when she wrote *The Bondwoman's Narrative*. On the dating of the text, see Gates, "Introduction," pp. ix–lxxiv. It is interesting to think about Cassy as an author figure, but one who, unlike Crafts, uses the master's tools to dismantle the master's house.

18. *Narrative of the Life of Frederick Douglass, an American Slave, Written by Himself*, ed. David W. Blight (New York: St. Martin's Press, 1993), p. 42.

19. Cassy similarly escapes from and destroys Simon Legree through her ingenious perception of his weakness, but in so doing she too plays into the superstitions by which her fellow bondpeople are enslaved.

15

"I found a life of freedom
all my fancy had pictured it to be"

Hannah Crafts's Visual Speculation and the Inner Life of Slavery

CHRISTOPHER CASTIGLIA

In her afterword to the volume *Black Popular Culture*, Michele Wallace laments the lack of critical attention to "vision, visuality, and visibility" as means by which whites, through "an unrelenting and generally contemptuous objectification," have generated "meaning" for African American bodies.[1] Without an analysis of visual representations of race, Wallace warns, African Americans "are in danger of getting wasted by ghosts . . . , by effusions and visual traces that haunt us because we refuse to study them, to look them in the eye."[2] Exemplifying the "revolution in vision" Wallace calls for, Carrie Mae Weems's *From Here I Saw What Happened and I Cried* (1995–1996) features nineteenth- and twentieth-century images of African Americans, rephotographed, enlarged, and tinted an eery red. The images are mounted in frames, the glass of which are etched with texts calling attention to racial stereotypes, such as "SOME SAID YOU WERE THE SPITTING IMAGE OF EVIL" and "YOU BECAME MAMMIE, MAMA, MOTHER & THEN, YES, CONFIDANT–HA." The texts superimposed on the photos further name the disciplinary knowledges that render contempt "objective"—"YOU BECAME A SCIENTIFIC PROFILE," "A NEGROID TYPE," "AN ANTHROPOLOGICAL DEBATE," "& A PHOTOGRAPHIC SUBJECT"—and codify "race" in a hierarchical visual structure (in which, for instance, the anthropologist, as viewer, has authority over the "negroid type," whose image is photographed, named, and given meaning).

At the same time as the superimposed texts saturate the underlying images with "meaning" (of race, of sexuality, of social position), the faces in Weems's portraits are notably opaque; almost any image could be removed from its frame and placed under another text, to similar effect. This is part of Weems's point: there is no correspondence between the image and the meaning assigned to it, which serves the interest of the viewer, rather than objectively naming any quality of the viewed. One label explicitly notes this opacity, stating, "BORN WITH A VEIL YOU BECAME ROOT WORKER JUJU MAMA VOODOO QUEEN HOODOO DOCTOR." The opacity of the face's surface—its veil—serves to rupture the correspondence between image and interpretation, between historical experience and the "meanings" that overtake and manage those experiences. At the same time, Weems, in challenging the power of stereotypes to fix and foreclose visual meaning, authorizes the contemporary viewer to see differently, to imagine other "meanings" for the photographs, and in the very act of proliferating meaning to challenge the stronghold of singular interpretation over the signifying power of visual representation. Asking questions rather than didactically imposing answers, Weems invites viewers, in her words, "to refigure and reintroduce the black subject to ourselves."[3] In short, Weems refuses to allow visuality to remain simply a mechanism of racism's control of bodies, insisting instead on the power of imaginative interpretation to generate new ways of occupying bodies, identities, social relations.

Beyond refusing the imposition of definitive meaning by white interpretive authorities, the phrase "BORN WITH A VEIL" creates a space of black interiority as well. Behind the stillness of Weems's photographed faces lies a space of desire, rage, ambition, and affect, the markers of a humanity denied by objectifying labels. Even Weems's title, *From Here I Saw What Happened and I Cried*, insists on the connection between witnessing (seeing) and affect (crying), between vision and interiority, that points to the second absence Wallace names in her essay. "Parallel to the visual void in black discourse," Wallace writes, "and intersecting with it, is the gap around the psychoanalytic."[4] While Wallace leaves the connection unexplored, psychoanalysis's reliance on visual dynamics is clear, from Freud's Oedipal complex, beginning with the child's viewing of the primal scene and ending with the psychic equivalent of Oedipus's self-blinding, to Lacan's mirror stage, predicated on Narcissus's misrecognition of his image in the water as his true "self." Both the Oedipal complex and the mirror stage are central to psychoanalysis's theorization of identification, the process through which the subject takes shape in relation to a seen "other" (either the sexualized parent for Freud or the differentiated reflection for Lacan). In these conceptions of identification, what you see is what you *are*, vision apparently pre-existing the interpellative moment in which spectacle is given cultural meaning. Wallace's formulation of revolutionary vision—looking the traces of history "in the eye"—invokes an identificational moment as well, "history" here taking the form of a pictured face, of portraiture. In revolutionizing visual theory, however, Wallace allows the viewer control over the process of identification as well, refusing the "ghost" of identities that white-interpreted representations seek to name and control.

Expanding Wallace's connection of identification and vision, *From Here I Saw What Happened and I Cried* adds to psychoanalysis's naive visual theory an awareness that vision itself is framed by ideological narratives that attempt to overdetermine the outcomes of identification by saturating images with supposedly fixed meaning (the meaning of "mother," of "different," of "self"). Weems therefore asks viewers, "Can you identify with the image *as framed by the superimposed texts?*" Inviting viewers to join in generating multiple interpretations, Weems allows them to re-imagine identification as a variable project of creation rather than the foreclosing of imagination by identity's proper names. Drawing the veil between image and interpretation, Weems opens the possibility for identificatory transformation in the viewer as well. The opening of identification through a reconception of visual meaning has particular implications for women viewers, especially in relation to images of African American women (the series begins and ends with the same image of an African woman in profile, arguably establishing her as the "I" of the title and hence the grounds for subjective identification in the series). The visual theory of the Oedipal complex becomes particularly tricky for women, since their identificatory vision is, according to Freud, of the mother's "lack," granting the daughter a vision of nothing, and therefore essentially a nonvision. For a woman to insist on vision in the moment of identification, as Weems does, therefore denies the misogynistic construction of womanhood as absence and insists on the material presence of women's experience as and of visual spectacle.

In what follows, I want to explore the dynamics of vision and identification in another African American artist who reproduced portraiture not in photography but in words (a common nineteenth-century practice art historians call *ekphrasis*). In *The Bondwoman's Narrative*, Hannah Crafts, like Carrie Mae Weems a century and a half later, challenges the practices of visual speculation that posit a direct correspondence between outside and inside, between what is shown on the surface (of bodies, texts, historical actions) and what those physical traces purport to reveal about obscure "insides" (character, psychology, meaning). Foregrounding and resisting the panoptical regimes underlying slavery, Crafts echoes Frederick Douglass, who tells of the overseer who slithered through the fields to spy on the slaves, and Harriet Jacobs, who bored a small hole in the wall of her cramped hiding place in order to watch her children play below as well as to spy on her lecherous master, thereby reversing his scopophilic control of her body. In both narratives, whites justify their ownership of slaves by reading the brutalized actions produced by the deprivations of slavery as evidence of inner, racialized "character," a practice Toni Morrison rends gothic in *Beloved*, in which the overseer Schoolteacher keeps account books of the observed "traits" that supposedly mark racial "types" and therefore justify the brutal and invasive appropriation of enslaved bodies.

Crafts undermines the visual economies of slavery by thematizing the ruptures between representation and meaning, between outer sign and inner truth. These moments of rupture occur in *The Bondwoman's Narrative* in the depictions of portraits, in which Crafts, appropriating the gothic convention of the portrait that reveals a hidden, usually horrible truth (one might think, for instance, of the Pyncheon portrait in Hawthorne's *The House of the Seven Gables*), rendering the direct correspondence between outer signs and inner truth suddenly unfamiliar and unsettling, slavery's nightmarish uncanny. At the same time, Crafts refuses to abandon vision to the brutal economies of slavery. Rather, as a writer and an artist Crafts reclaims vision as a means toward optimistic identifications that generate potentially more enabling, if (because) more fragmentary and patchwork, life narratives. Having troubled the visual economies that assert ownership of bodies in the presumed possession of the inner truth of images, Crafts reinscribes meaning, not as a quality of the seen but as a practice of the seer, not as economic investment but as imaginative and often unpredictable identification.

To say that Crafts complicates the apparent correspondence between visual representation and inner truth is not to say that *The Bondwoman's Narrative* is unconcerned with the inner workings of affect and psychology. On the contrary, Crafts's complex affective responses to slavery—fraught with desire and disavowal, guilt and gall—suggest that writing was for Crafts on some level a very personal effort at psychic resolution, albeit a highly literary one rich in allusion and aesthetic complexity. *The Bondwoman's Narrative* explores a slave woman's desire for her absent mother and the consequent unpredictable identifications, especially with white women, which, as Jennifer Fleischner persuasively argues, characterize the narratives of many slave women.[5] Those narratives (and to a large degree, Fleischner's analysis) assume a natural identificatory bond between slave mothers and daughters, making black "identity" the psychic ground for which cross-racial identification is a misrecognition. Such an analysis ignores not only the ruptures Crafts insists upon between vision and meaning but the inscription of the Oedipal narrative within a bourgeois domesticity forbidden to slaves. The "lack" represented for Freud by the mother's absent penis—which itself shows that what is "seen" is not "there" at all but is a projection of the seer—becomes enlarged in *The Bondwoman's Narrative* into the literal absence *of* a mother, a "lack" that propels Hannah not into psychic blindness, as it does Oedipus, but into a process of inventive identification based precisely in the creative possibilities of sight. At the same time, Crafts's narrative registers rage at the absent biological mother through Hannah's repeated disavowal of other black women and of the heterosexual romance plot that structures "womanhood" and hence the very domestic grounds of Oedipal identification. Throughout the narrative, Hannah endeavors to *un*define herself racially through repeated *dis*identifications with other black—and particularly other escaped slave—women, giving rise to repeated expressions of rage and grief, which are recuperated only through a reunion with her mother that Crafts codes as fantastic and phantasmagoric.

The Bondwoman's Narrative startlingly depicts black betrayal as the result not only of systems of distrust and disloyalty fostered by white owners and overseers (dynamics highlighted, for instance, in Frederick Douglass's narrative) but of the constitution of a slave's psyche within disavowals of blackness itself. In these rageful moments, Crafts registers horror not simply at identification with the wrong people but with the process of identification itself: all identifications, as Crafts suggests in her critique of portraiture's capacity to represent the complexity of human desire and rage, is *mis*identification. At the same time, Crafts's narrative is suffused with desire not for freedom or for a husband and children nor even for restored maternity but for an imaginative intimacy between women, particularly women of undecided racial identity. In this, Crafts seemingly echoes sentimentalism's espousal of "the female world of love and ritual." Yet Crafts's desires are more sexual, more violent, and more aesthetic than sentimentalism has been credited with, possibly marking Crafts's erotic desire for women, but just as likely pointing to the eroticized drive toward imaginative collective invention that animates *The Bondwoman's Narrative* from beginning to end. In narrating these desires and disavowals, Crafts offers what is to my mind the fullest known account of the psychology of race in antebellum America. In Hannah Crafts we see "double consciousness" not simply as an ideological schizophrenia imposed *upon* black folks, as DuBois represented it, but constitutive of a prolonged and painful ambivalence toward the uncertainties of identification—what we might call a *meta-anxiety*—that complicates both the heroic disentanglements from slavery characteristic of slave narratives such as Douglass's and the purity of sentiment ("right feeling") espoused by sentimental works such as Stowe's *Uncle Tom's Cabin*. *The Bondwoman's Narrative* insists, then, on having it both ways: narrating the psychological dynamics of slavery and freedom while simultaneously noting how race and gender block the "truthful" confessions of inner life—of identification, affect, and desire—upon which psychology depends. Even while Crafts invites readers to trust in pictures ("I will let the reader picture it all to his imagination," the novel's final sentence declares [239]), she shows how opaque portraits are, especially whey they attempt to "picture forth" the inner truth of "identity."

Throughout *The Bondwoman's Narrative*, vision is racialized. From the beginning, Hannah names among the characteristics that mark her as a slave, despite her white skin, her "fancy [for] pictorial illustrations and flaming colors" (6).[6] Among the slaves, she reports, "It was our privilege to look and listen. We loved the music, we loved the show and splendor" (29). An early clue is given to the black ancestry of Hannah's new mistress when Hannah notes the apparently white woman's "habit . . . of seeming to watch everybody as if she feared them or considered them enemies" (27). While slaves' vision brings them pleasure, the gaze of masters and overseers, scopophilic and panoptic, makes slaves feel "surrounded by watchful prying eyes" (207). Even while their eyes pry, however, whites, in *The Bondwoman's Narrative* remain visually inept, exemplified by Hannah's master, who is "not given to habits of observation" (35). Clear racial demarcations arise, then, from visual practices, with pleasure and insight belonging to blacks, invasive prying and metaphoric blindness to whites.

Just as the racial identities of plantation populations were notoriously murky, however, so *The Bondwoman's Narrative* troubles the clear distinctions between blindness and insight, most obviously in Crafts's gothic antagonist, Mr. Trappe, who speculates not only by trading in the bodies of slaves—as one character states, Trappe "'buys only for speculation'" (112)—but by seeing beyond appearances to the secrets contained in the heart's interior: "He loved to probe the human heart to its inmost depths," Hannah reports, "and watch the manifestations of its living agony" (108). Insight, for Trappe, is a potent means of possession, causing Hannah to feel "that in both soul and body I was indeed a slave" (108). Possession of interior states—of the "heart" and the "soul," of the excesses of the physical body—allow Trappe to own slaves not simply through the mastery of their bodies but rather by the affective orchestration of a slave's psyche, and hence of his or her consent. Using his "insight" to produce for slaves an interior (always subject to his definitions), a realm of sentiment and desire beyond the physical labors commanded through the body, Trappe is able to take it away again. Making it his business to trace the hidden genealogies of prominent, wealthy women "far back to a sable son of Africa" (98), Trappe marshals the indeterminacies of antebellum race to the detriment not of the slaveholders who insisted upon the purity of racial identity but rather their creolized victims.

Although Trappe turns "in-sight" into a cynical and destructive instrument of possession, his production of interiority and its subsequent mastery is subtly aestheticized, resting upon a logic of visual representation that begins with the supposedly direct correspondence between surface and depth, which is then extended to the correlation of appearance and character, action and consent. Although his traffic in deceptive appearances might have rendered Trappe skeptical about representation's evidentiary status, it is nonetheless a portrait's ability to speak the truth of its subject's racial identity that grants him his extraordinary power over Hannah's mistress. Showing her a small portrait, Trappe inquires,

> "Do you know it."
> "It resembles me," I answered "though I have never sate [sat] for my likeness to be taken."
> "Probably not, but can't you think of some one else whom it resembles."
> "The slave [Charlotte] Susan"
> "And it was hers, and it is yours, for never did two persons more resemble each other." (47)

The power of visual speculation that gives Trappe the confidence to assert a correspondence between representation and truth, genealogy and identity, robs Hannah's mistress of her power to consent. Her "likeness" is "taken" in both senses: through visual speculation she is "seen" to be the equivalent of her representation, a literalness that allows Trappe, in a dynamic of economic speculation, to "take" her for all she has, thereby ending her power of self-determination. At the same time, mirroring the matrilineal logic of slavery (in which children inherit the status of their slave mothers), Trappe asserts a correspondence not only between representation and identity but between generations as well: the overdetermined moment of legal and Oedipal identification, in which the slave daughter necessarily becomes the "likeness" of her mother, here rests on a representational correspondence that the ambivalent language of only proximate equivalence—"likeness," "resembles"—challenges.

If assertions such as Trappe's of the unvarying and fixed nature of the creole woman's identification (with her "likeness" in the form of her portrait and of her mother)—an identification to which I'll return shortly—white identifications, equally specularized in *The Bondwoman's Narrative*, produce equally ambivalent results. In the novel's first chapter, Crafts introduces the control masters claim over dynamics of representation and meaning, a control central to the rituals of display underlying the gallery of portraits that is the emotional center of the home of Hannah's master. Having hung his own portrait in the gallery alongside that of his wife, the original owner of the house, Sir Clifford De Vincent, Crafts reports,

> denounced a severe malediction against the person who should ever presume to remove them, and against any possessor of the mansion who being of his name and blood should neglect to follow his example. And well had his wishes been obeyed. Generation had succeeded generation, and a long line of De Vincents occupied the family residence, yet each [one] inheritor had contributed to the adornments of the drawing-room a faithful transcript of his person and lineaments, side by side with that of his Lady. (16)

De Vincent's "malediction" comprises, in effect, three imperatives: first, to "truthful" transcription (the imperative to picture oneself forth); second, to static correspondence between generations (a denial of the possibilities of history producing difference or change); and third, to heterosexuality (a prediction that every master will have a lady who can guarantee the generational transmission of property).

Hannah, sent to check arrangements before the arrival of the new mistress, undermines the speculative assumptions of De Vincent's malediction, however. Pausing in the gallery before the portraits, Hannah muses,

> There is something inexplicably dreary and solemn in passing through the silent rooms of a large house, especially one whence many generations have passed to the grave. Invariably you find yourself thinking of them, and wondering how they looked in life, and how the rooms looked in their possession, and whether or not they would recognize their former habitation if restored once more to earth and them. Then all we have heard or fancied of spiritual existence comes to us. (14–15)

Hannah's mediation seems to credit De Vincent's assumption: future generations will still possess, visually, their belongings, the generational transmission of property, carried out reproductively, descendants whose racial purity (i.e., their whiteness) is clearly pictured forth. At the same time, no sooner does Hannah introduce De Vincent's phantasmagoric prediction than she introduces the possibility of *mis*recognition, that spectacle will not produce clear possession. Here Crafts establishes an important pattern, at once social and aesthetic, that she repeats throughout the novel: beginning with an assertion of exact correspondence (fancied images=past generations) tied to possession (members of previous generations gaze on their belongings), Crafts subordinates possession to "fancy" (viewership), giving rise to a moment of failed recognition (the possibility that things might not look the same across time) that in turn gives way to a moment of imaginative speculation ("all we have heard or fancied"). The result is that "inner-ness" is still possible (Hannah uses this scene, after all, to express her own ambivalence about the mistress's arrival and her desire and resentment about the wealth exhibited in the mansion's furnishings), but it is separated from direct correspondence to visual "outsides" and is made, instead, the terrain of imagination, now the property of viewers, not of owners. Putting possession in the eye of the beholder, this scene tellingly inverts slavery's usual dynamic, making the owners the viewed, slaves the viewers. This process, more than "race," "generation," or "possession," Crafts makes instinctual ("a supernatural thrill pervades your frame, and you feel the presence of mysterious beings. It may be foolish and childish, but it is one of the unaccountable things instinctive to the human nature" [15]). Slaves' instinctual vision, as Hannah demonstrates, is invested not in finding "meaning" contained in the spectacle, but rather in the generative creation of images to articulate slavery's unspeakable ambivalences, its haunting ghosts.

Slavery is haunted, first and foremost, by its attachment of speculative vision to ownership. Hannah manifests the literalizing gaze of white masters by turning their very eyes into cold, unfeeling monuments, attesting to the lack—of imagination, of affect, of compassion—at the heart of white self-representation: "Memories of the dead give at any time a haunting air to a silent room. How much more this becomes the case when standing face to face with their pictured resemblances and looking into the stony eyes motionless and void of expression as those of an exhumed corpse" (16). Again, however, a moment of slippage between representation and interiority opens the possibility for imaginative transformation on the part of the viewer: "But even as I gazed the golden light of sunset penetrating through the open windows in an oblique direction set each rigid feature in a glow. Movements like those of life came over the line of stolid faces as the shadows of a linden played there" (16). Under Hannah's gaze, the portraits become nicer: relaxed, gracious, dimpling with smiles. Relieved of the burden of exerting transparent overlap between appearance and identity, the portraits become, for Hannah, an instrument for imaginative identification, not as a coerced correspondence between inner essence and outer show but rather as a moment of creative projection, a wish fulfillment on the part of the spectator rather than a victory of possession on that of the spectacle.

> Though filled with suspicious awe I was in no haste to leave the room; for there surrounded by mysterious associations I seemed suddenly to have grown old, to have entered a new world of thoughts, and feelings and sentiments. I was not a slave with those pictured memories of the past. They could not enforce drudgery, or condemn me on account of my color to a life of servitude. As their companion I could think and speak. In their presence my mind seemed to run riotous and exult in its freedom as a rational being, and one destined for something higher and better than this world can afford. (17)

By turning the presumed "reality" of representation into "mystery," thereby undermining the power of men like Trappe to assert and manage her affective consent, Hannah opens up a world of possibility and entitlement centered on an interiority—"a new world of thoughts, and feelings and sentiments"—asserted without being "pictured forth," a potential now rather than a "nature" and hence a doom.

Whites remain oblivious throughout *The Bondwoman's Narrative* to the visual potential Hannah discovers, as when the head housekeeper, Mrs. Bry, upon discovering Hannah gazing at the portraits, scoffs at her, "'Looking at the pictures,' she repeated 'as if such an ignorant thing as you are would know anything about them'" (17). Lacking Hannah's speculative imagination, whites remain haunted by the ambivalence of portraiture, as when her new mistress "passed on to examine beneath a broad chandelier the portrait of Sir Clifford. The image regarded her with its dull leaden eyes. She turns away and covers her eyes" (29). Desiring to "pass" for white by disguising her own racial indeterminacy, the ambiguity of the portraits terrifies the mistress, who can continue her masquerade only by imposing upon herself the blindness associated with other whites in the house. The odd shift from past to present verb tense, giving the description the feel of stage direction, invites the reader into a moment of speculation as well, a meta-spectatorship in which, viewing the mistress viewing the portrait, we are invited to see her inability to see life in(to) the portrait as a prediction of her ultimate loss of control over the meanings permitted to her own "likeness." Unlike her mistress, Hannah does not turn away from the portrait or from the potentials of representation; rather, as the household celebrates the new mistress's arrival, "beyond them and over them, and through the mingled sounds of joyous mirth and rain and wind I saw the haughty countenance of Sir Clifford's [frowning] pictured semblance" (29). Crafts here puts the possibility of portraiture's exact correspondence to its subject under erasure, crossing out "frowning" (which would treat the picture as the face itself) and substituting in its place "pictured semblance," a phrase that again inserts representation's only proximate relation to what it pictures forth.

The inability to engage representation creatively particularly haunts Hannah's master, who, rather than subverting the De Vincent imperatives in order to achieve his own imaginative ends, defies them on their own terms. Striving "to obliterate some haunting recollection, or shun from his mental vision the rising shadows of coming events" (29), the master chooses "to dissent from this custom" and has his portrait, without that of a spouse, hung without "the usual demonstration of mirth and rejoicing" (16). Thinking to kill his ancestor by refusing the imperatives the latter attached to representation, Hannah's master proves as literal as the original De Vincent, with whom he also shares an ignorance of the changes wrought upon representation (and hence upon possession) by generational history. When De Vincent's portrait ominously crashes to the floor as the new mistress is welcomed to the house, Hannah speculates:

> Time had been there and solemnly and stealthily spread corrupting canker over the polished surface of the metal that supported it, and crumbled the wall against which it hang. But the stately knight in his armor, who placed it there had taken no consideration of such an event, and while breathing his anathema against the projector of its removal dreamed not of the great leveler who treats the master and slave with the same unceremonious rudeness, and who touches the lowly hut or the lordly palace with the like decay. (30)

Unable to recognize the structure supporting his house—or the labor supporting the wealth represented by that house—the master undermines his benevolent self-representation. Hannah's vision makes his fate clear: while she transforms the portraits of his ancestors into companionable images of mirth and kindness, her master's portrait "seemed to change from its usually kind and placid expression to one of wrath and gloom, and the calm brow . . . wrinkled with passion, the lips turgid with malevolence" (17). In the end, Hannah's master kills himself in the presence of his ancestors' portraits, manifesting the violence of speculation and the inflexible (fated) identifications it produces, while the portraits themselves, in a neat inversion of the slave trade, are "publicly exposed in the market [to the highest] and knocked down to the highest bidder. Sic transit gloria mundi" (194). Refusing to see life in the portraits for similar reasons that they refuse to see humanity in their slaves, white self-representation becomes implicated in—rather than placed in commanding transcendence over—the deadening objectifications of economic speculation.

Hannah understands her visual acumen as the result not of biology or "nature" but of her placement within the social structures of slavery: "I have said that I always had a quiet way of observing things, and this habit grew upon me, sharpened perhaps by the absence of all elemental knowledge. Instead of books I studied faces and characters, and arrived at conclusions by a sort of sagacity that closely approximated to the unerring certainty of animal instinct" (27) Trained by slavery's hypocrisies to question the truth of surfaces, Hannah is able to discern, to her advantage, the distinction between appearances and character. Like numerous slave narrators before her, Hannah can see through the soft-spoken benevolence of white owners such as Mrs. Wheeler, who "was an adept in the art of dissembling" and whose "countenance would be the smoothest and her words the fairest when she contemplated the greatest injury" (203). Hannah also learns to manipulate appearances to deceive those who would control her, as when a slave trader declares, "'I believe that Hannah can be trusted. I almost know she can. I see it in her countenance, and I've got eyes that [most often] are seldom deceived in the human face [']'" (110). In the end, Hannah's divorce of character from appearance allows her to form unlikely alliances across lines of race and gender, as when she and her escaped mistress are recaptured and placed in a jail for safekeeping. Hannah quickly begins to form a bond with the ugly and apparently menacing jailor: "Notwithstanding the repulsiveness of his appearance," she reports, "there was something genial and clever in the man" (86), whose looks "concealed a really kind and obliging disposition" (86). Hannah's willingness to see through appearances opens up the possibility that white readers, too, will identify with the jailor's kindly "deeper" self, whatever their previous relation to histories of cruelty and constraint. So confident is she in her pedagogy in the skills and advantages of imaginative vision that the last sentence of *The Bondwoman's Narrative* leaves the reader not simply to interpret but to join Hannah in the act of imaginative creation—interpretation *as* portraiture—that allows identification across time and experience: "I will let the reader picture it all to his imagination and say farewell" (239).

Hannah's identification with white owners ("As their companion") in the portrait gallery leads her to be recuperated by a long absent and longed-for maternity: "those to whom man [learns little nature] teaches little, nature like a wise and prudent mother teaches much" (18). Hannah's displacement of maternity onto nature avoids the thorny problem of embodiment, which, in the southern economy, would necessitate the naming of the mother's race. For all Hannah's visual imagination—obscuring as it does the correspondence between "race" as maternal history and "race" as fated character—identification necessarily remains as critical to Hannah's story as it was for any slave attempting to negotiate between a bondage coded as black and a freedom coded as white. Despite Hannah's challenge to the surface significations that would give access to a slave's psychology, her narrative gives evidence of the often violent conflicts of identification and disavowal that, as I will argue in the following section, make *The Bondwoman's Narrative* a deeply and disturbingly psychological text.

By the end of her story, Hannah has learned to use her orphaned status strategically, telling strangers she meets, "I was an orphan who had been left in destitute circumstances, and that I was endeavoring to make my way on foot to join the relatives of my mother who lived at the north. This account, so true and simple, greatly won the sympathy of all especially the women" (212). Yet Hannah acknowledges that her quest for maternal "joining" is "true" as well as simple or strategic. From the beginning of her tale, Hannah laments, "I was not brought up by any body in particular that I know of" (5), adding, "It sometimes seems that we require sympathy more in joy than sorrow; for the heart exultant, and overflowing with good nature longs to import a portion of its happiness. Especially is this the case with children. How it augments the importance of any little success to them that someone probably a mother will receive the intelligence with a show of delight and interest. But I had no mother, no friend" (8). The shift from mother to friend signifies Hannah's efforts to create maternal bonds with a series of amiable women, from Aunt Hetty, who teaches Hannah to read, to her mistress, who treats Hannah and her other female slaves "rather as companions than servants" (35), to Mrs. Henry, who nurses Hannah when she is seriously injured in a carriage accident. That all these women are white (or, in the case of her mistress, a white-identified creole) complicates Hannah's desires, necessarily conflating the sympathy associated with maternal love with the possessive control associated with whiteness. It is this uneasy conflation that, in large measure, makes identification such a troubled and troubling process for Hannah.

Identification involves internalizing qualities of another into oneself, and Hannah, identifying with white mother-figures, quickly learns to synthesize sympathy and control in her own maternal posturings. Describing her relationship to her fellow slaves, Hannah reports,

How much love and confidence and affection I won it is impossible to describe. How the rude and boisterous became gentle and obliging, and how ready all were to serve and obey me, not because I exacted the service or obedience, but because their own loving natures prompted them to reciprocate my love. How I longed to become their teacher, and open the door of knowledge to their minds by instructing them to read but it might not be. (12)

Obtaining obedience and consensual labor through sympathetic kindness, Hannah eerily echoes white slave owners like Mr. Trappe, who explains his mastery over slaves in similar terms, "'I have always found that the simplest request [has more power to obtain what you] goes farther than the loudest command. If a woman is stubborn or obstinate ask her a favor, coax her, flatter her and my word for it she'll be pliable as wax in your hands'" (89). A similar philosophy prevails on the Henry farm, where the "overseer was gentle and kind, and the slaves were industrious and obedient, not through fear of punishment, but because [they felt it to be their duty] loved and respected a master and mistress so amiable and good" (123).

Although Hannah enjoys her position as mother-figure to her fellow slaves and to the white children of her master, a position that allows her, through white identification, an unprecedented amount of power, her desire to *have* a mother predominates, and when her mistress offers her the chance to escape, Hannah quickly declares that, much as she loves her "children," "I loved my mistress more" (50). Hannah's willingness to place herself under the control of white mothers soon teaches her a painful lesson in the controlling manipulations underlying sympathetic nurture. When, after several months enjoying Mrs. Henry's benevolent care, the kindly white woman tells Hannah her new master is coming to claim her, Hannah begs Mrs. Henry to buy her, but she refuses, holding Hannah's request at bay with a hand "so white and soft and beautiful" (125). Hannah offers to work as a field hand for the Henrys, pleading,: "'all I ask is to feel, and know for a certainty that I have a home, that some one cares for me, and that I am beyond the gripe [grip] of these merciless slave-traders and speculators [']" (125). Mrs. Henry shows her so much "sympathy and such an affectionate tenderness" (126) that Hannah goes as far as to consensually surrender complete obedience, "'You have no idea how good I will be, or how exactly I will conform myself to all your wishes'" (126).

One suspects that, at this point, Hannah is realizing that affectionate sympathy and cold-hearted control are not mutually exclusive, yet to drive the point home, Mrs. Henry tells Hannah that on his deathbed her father commanded his daughter's promise to avoid the slave trade in every form (127): "'And now dear Hannah, do you wish me to break that vow?' she asked. I could not say that I did, and yet my heart rose against the man, who in a slave-holding country could exact such a promise" (127). Crafts subtly indites white abolitionists whose benevolence caused increased hardship for slaves and the condition of whose consciences became more important than the material well-being of African Americans. Horrendous as its consequences are, however, the willful control of fathers, being explicit, allows Hannah a space of resistance; the benevolence of Mrs. Henry, on the other hand, brooks no opposition, forcing

Hannah, mortified when she sees the hurt her pleading has caused Mrs. Henry, to apologize for her very desire for even the small comforts labor on the Henry farm would afford her (128). Earlier, when Hannah and her mistress stop during their flight from Trappe to rest in the home of a kindly man and woman who oppose slavery, the fugitives are seduced by their hostess's kindness into a momentary security, until, that is, they realize the woman is Trappe's sister and that she is also boarding their tormentor in her house (62–63). Kindness and brutality, Hannah discovers, are usually kin. Although her experiences with mother-figures occasionally work to her advantage—as with Aunt Hetty, who teaches Hannah to read, hides her in her flight from Trappe and gives her the money to travel to the north—more often identification, as Hannah's experience with portraits has shown her, involves complicated networks of desire, control, and possession; when the identification is motivated by a need for maternal comfort, the process is all the more complex and disturbing. In opposition to the depiction of sympathetic white mothers in novels like *Uncle Tom's Cabin*, in *The Bondwoman's Narrative*, the hand that rocks the cradle literally rules the plantation, if not the world.

The ambivalence such complexities produce manifests itself in the astonishing violence visited—often by Hannah's narration itself—upon potential mother figures. The hypocritical Mrs. Wheeler is transformed by Hannah into "a spoiled child that never cares for what it has, but is always wanting something new" (154). In the end, Mrs. Wheeler is done in by Hannah's "forgetfulness": having purchased for her mistress a face cream that turns Mrs. Wheeler's face black and causes her social ostracism (165–67), Hannah's unconscious (she neglects to inform Mrs. Wheeler of a story she has heard about this transformative cream) effects the "deserved punishment of an act of vanity" (169). Another white mistress who would flatter herself with benevolent self-representations is treated to a similarly violent outcome. Mrs. Cosgrove, whose insistence that her husband's slave mistress and their illegitimate baby be sold to a trader causes the distraught slave to kill the baby and herself, and who later has another of her husband's mistresses driven from the house (177–78), boasts of "'the consolation of having once performed my duty in giving freedom to a poor slave'" (183). In the end, however, Mrs. Cosgrove's suspicions drive her to an accident that leaves her permanently crippled, a violence that transforms her into an impotent "manifestation of love" (192).

Hannah's most ambivalent identification is with her creole mistress (so ambivalent is Hannah toward this maternal figure that she never even grants the mistress a name), to whom Hannah is bound by kindness, and by her identification with a fellow orphan, whose "mother was a slave, then toiling in the cotton fields of Georgia" (44). This bond pulls Hannah into a plot that, due to her mistress's emotional and physical weakness and her attraction for the ubiquitous Trappe, places both women in grave danger. Once again, kindness quickly gives way to a controlling cruelty on the mistress's part and a retributive violence on Hannah's. Living in an abandoned shack for several months, the mistress becomes "querelous and complaining, upbraided me as a cause of all her difficulties, and heaped the strangest accusations of conspiracy on my head" (67). "After a while," Hannah reports, "my mistress became decidedly insane, and her insanity partook the most painful character. She fancied herself pursued by an invisible being, who sought to devour her flesh and crush her bones" (67). Despite Hannah's representation of her mistress as insane, she *is* being pursued by an "invisible being"—Trappe—and although Hannah bases her sense of her mistress's insanity on her "terrified imagination" which "began to conjure strange fancies," such as stories of persons devoured by swarms of rats, Hannah herself wakes to find "a huge rat . . . was nibbling at my cheek" (79). Hannah confesses, "I gazed in fascinated horror at the cavity" (79) into which the rat disappears, horror and desire joining in the ambivalent drive toward maternal identification that keeps Hannah tied to a woman she now perceives as dangerously deranged. Hannah's unconscious understands the maternal source of her violent ambivalence, even if her conscious mind doesn't: "A pleasant slumber sealed my eyelids, and I enjoyed a blessed dream of my mother, whom I had never seen" (80).

The fictional nature of maternal identification—which conjures images of a mother she has never seen—allows Hannah the same imaginative control over the process of identification she asserts in relation to the identifications invited by portraits. This control is challenged, however, when Hannah's biological mother appears at the end of the narrative "aged and venerable, yet so smart and lively and active, and Oh: so fond of me" (237). This largely implausible reconciliation—the two women happen to be living in the same New Jersey community, where the older woman recognizes certain distinctive marks on Hannah's body—is necessary to narrative closure, freedom being coded as successful generational identification, despite what Hannah has realized about the dangerous yoking of that narrative to slavery's possession of black bodies (or, more appropriately, of consensual labor through the management of desire). Perhaps because of this ambivalence, Hannah allows the resolution to occur off-stage, thus blocking the reader's identification with her supposed pleasure:

> We met accidentally, where or how it matters not. I thought it strange, but my heart yearned toward her with a deep intense feeling it had never known before. And when we became better acquainted, and fonder of each other's society, and

> interested in each other's history, I was not half so surprised as pleased and overwhelmed with emotions to which I could find no name, when she suddenly rose one day, came to me, clasped me in her arms, and sobbed out in rapturous joy "child, I am your mother." And then I—but I cannot tell what I did, I was nearly crazy with delight. (238)

The odd phrase "crazy with delight," echoing as it does other moments in the text when maternal identification has resulted in irrational anger and even madness, complicates the happy resolution that this reunion nominally signals.

Hannah's ambivalent identification with her biological mother raises a fascinating problem for theories of race and identification.[7] One might well understand Hannah's violent ambivalence toward other maternal figures, as I have suggested, as a result of her cross-racial identifications. This explanation would naturalize, however, her already racialized "proper" status as "black." That is, the very difficulty Hannah has in identifying with white women might seem to make "natural" her self-understanding as "really" black. Yet "blackness" itself, as it is defined under slavery, is largely a product of the white imagination, and there is no more reason to assume that Hannah would have any less ambivalence toward the colonized subject position "black" as she does toward the mastering position "white." Her ambivalence toward her mother might therefore be understood not simply as the Oedipal struggle endemic to the process of maternal identification but also as a hesitation before the mirror (stage) of racial identification.

Not surprisingly, Hannah's relationship to blacks in *The Bondwoman's Narrative* is just as violently ambivalent as her relationship to white mothers. In addition to what Henry Louis Gates, Jr., notes as the classist distaste of black field servants—she refers to the field hands, for instance, as the "vile, foul, filthy inhabitants of the huts" (20–25)—her more subtle and prolonged antagonism seems reserved for figures with whom she *should* identify: other escaped slaves, especially women.[8] Interestingly, this antagonism is articulated not in relation to race but in relation to sexuality: the escaped slaves against whom Hannah expresses the most anger are women who escape in tandem with their husbands (Charlotte with William) or with men Hannah initially believes to be their husbands (as with Jacob and his sister). Crafts even uses the word "elopement" to describe escapes from slavery, figuring such escapes as movements into a romance plot that, for Hannah, is perilously analogous to slavery: "The slave, if he or she desires to be content," Hannah cautions readers, "should [ever think of] always remain in celibacy" (131). While on some level this might be a gesture toward white female readers, making their domestic imprisonment analogous to slavery and hence inviting sympathetic identification, or a realization, such as that expressed by Harriet Jacobs, that affectionate bonds become a means to hold women in slavery. I want to suggest, however, that one might read this antagonism as another form of Crafts's intervention in generational transmission, as well as a potent exercise in the need to *disidentify* with black womanhood in order to open a space of imaginative freedom that would permit Hannah to be what Crafts's title perpetually fixes her as: a bondwoman.

Hannah's ambivalence toward sexualized black women becomes apparent in her response to Charlotte, the slave of the benign Mrs. Henry, whose plot to escape with her husband, William, provokes Hannah's determination "to acquaint Mr. Henry of my suspicions" (135). "How could I acquit my conscience of cruelty and wrong if through discoveries made and information given by me the happiness of Charlotte and her husband should be destroyed, by his subjection for the second time into servitude" (136), Hannah rationalizes, yet it's worth noting that in these ethical deliberations, Hannah expresses no concern for *Charlotte's* continued subjection under slavery. Hannah, who resolves to betray Charlotte to Mrs. Henry, soon finds that she has *over*-identified with white ownership, expressing more concern for Mrs. Henry's property than the white woman herself. Mrs. Henry tells Hannah, "having eyes we had better not see, and having ears we should not hear. That she hoped and trusted Charlotte's good sense would prevent her taking any rash or precipitous step likely to embarrass either, and that she should make it in her way to give the former a few words of cautious advice" (140). Charlotte, whose resolution to escape is formed by her "'dear husband'" but who also wants "'a female friend to go with us, a good stout-hearted woman who can look danger in the face unblenched, whose counsel could guide us in emergencies, who would be true, and zealous, and faithful; my heart turned to you as the one'" (141), hardly exemplifies the wife bound either to slavery to or exclusively heterosexual intimacy. Nevertheless, when Hannah argues with Charlotte's plan and William reprimands her, "'There, Hannah, now don't dishearten my dear wife,' he said, drawing her affectionately to his bosom. 'Our minds are fixed; they cannot be changed, because we have no alternative. We must either be separated or runaway, and which think you, that an affectionate wife would choose?'" (142) in establishing Charlotte's choice as one between "wife" and "slave," William effectively overdetermines Hannah's choice:

> During this long speech I had time to collect my thoughts, and I answered plainly that however just, or right, or expedient it might be in them to escape my accompanying their flight would be directly the reverse, that I could not lightly sacrifice the good opinion of Mrs. Henry and her family, who had been

so very kind to me, nor seem to participate in a scheme, of which the consummation must be an injury to them no less than a source of disquiet and anxiety. Duty, gratitude and honor forbid it. (142)

Naming the odd nature of her apparent identification—"And so to a strained sense of honor you willingly sacrifice a prospect of freedom" (142)—William fails to recognize how much his own definition of Charlotte as a "wife," hence figuring escape as a romantic "elopement," determines Hannah's distance from the unfortunate other woman.

A similar dynamic occurs when, after she *does* escape, Hannah, wandering in the woods, comes across a man and a woman, the latter sick with a fever. The tenderness between man and woman echoes the relationship between William and Charlotte, producing a similar crisis of identification in Hannah:

Toward morning, however, the paroxysm of her fever subsided, and she sunk into a gentle slumber. Her companion folded her garments closely around her, and then stretching himself by her side seemed to prepare for repose. Presently my thoughts became confused, with that pleasing bewilderment which precedes slumber. I began to lose the consciousness of my identity, and the recollection of where I was. Now it seemed that Lindendale rose before me, then it was the jail and the white towers of Washington, and—but the scene all faded; for I slept. (215)

Finding that they are brother and sister and not lovers, Hannah befriends Jacob and helps him care for his sister, who soon thereafter dies.

"My dear sister," he said bending his mouth to her ear.
"I hear, but I can't see you. Is the sun arisin?"
"It is, it is."
"It [*sic*] see it now; it is comin, a light, a very bright light."
The sun came, the light arose, the light of righteousness.
Dead.

The ambivalence evidenced by the abrupt way Hannah announces the woman's death (and by Crafts turning her subjective "I" into an objective "It") is detectable as well in her defensive digression into the unlikely subject of mourning conventions. Concluding that "We could weep in silence and privacy. Public opinion came not to dictate the outward expression of our grief" (220), Hannah, relieved that no one can see that she mourns *improperly*, opens the possibility that she did not mourn at all.

Hannah's guilt soon gives rise to self-retribution: left alone with the corpse while Jacob hunts for food, Hannah reports, "I retreated to my hut in which the sad wreck of mortality lay stark, stiff, and immovable. Was it the presence of death, or that my nerves were weak and agitated, but a great and unaccountable terror seized me. I shuddered in every limb, great drops of sweat started to my forehead, and I cowed down in the corner like a guilty thing" (221). Hannah's guilt arises specifically from the unmourned corpse, who "seemed to leer horribly, to gibe and beckon and point its long skinny fingers towards me, and though I knew that this was all fancy, though I had sense enough left to perceive even then the absurdity of my fears I could not overcome them, I could not pray for the protection of Heaven; Heaven seemed to have turned its face against me" (222). Hannah seems to undergo a process not of mourning but of what Freud describes as melancholia, the subject's inability to surrender a lost love object, aspects of which the melancholic pulls into herself in order to preserve the presence of the lost love. Whereas Freud's melancholia is an identificational process necessary to the griever who faces disintegration with the loss of her love, Hannah experiences melancholia as a dynamic of forced merger: "The corpse seemed to rise and stand over me, and press with its cold leaden hand against my heart. In vain I struggled to free myself, by that perversity common to dreams I was unable to move. I could not shriek, but remained spell-bound under the hedious benumbing influence of a present embodied death" (222). Unable to free herself from enforced identification with a murderous identity, an "other" misunderstood as the "same," Hannah restores her equilibrium only by removing identification from the interior space of her psyche, making it "present embodied death," and thereby allowing her to narrate, and hence gain some interpretive control over, the figure of black womanhood.

Having disavowed her identification with black women and having recognized the violent control instituted by her identification with white women, Hannah is left with a self-produced and imaginative identity pieced together, like *The Bondwoman's Narrative* itself, from historical events and fictional genres, between outward show and inner desire, options for storytelling and the drive toward self-determination that makes stories necessary. Hannah learns to treat identities the way she treats the portraits that are their representational equivalent: she takes a speculative freedom that refuses the direct correspondence between seeming and being. Yet the acts of imaginative freedom that divorce outer show from inner life risk accommodating the historical forces that insist on direct correspondences and clear identifications—the slave economy and the legal apparatus that upholds it—rather than working, materially, to change them. In this regard, Mrs. Wright—one of the most complex figures in the text—offers an important caution. A white woman arrested when she helps a beloved servant, sent to the slave trader by her husband, escape, Mrs. Wright meets Hannah and her mistress when they are imprisoned by Trappe's agents. The aptly named Mrs. Wright seems in many ways a perfect candidate for Hannah's maternal identification. Like Hannah, she disrupts the chronological order necessary to generational descent, telling Hannah, "'I cannot recall names and events in their proper places'" (81). Like Hannah, she favors "habits of intimacy" (82) outside conventional domesticity, leaving husband and children to help her beloved servant escape. Like slaves in general, she becomes the victim of a kind of social death: after an epidemic kills her family and ruins their property, "she ceased to be spoken of even by those who had experienced the most of her kindness" (84). Above all, Mrs. Wright articulates more clearly than any character in *The Bondwoman's Narrative* the destructive hypocrisy that forces subjects "'to profess approbation when you cannot feel it, to be hard when most inclined to melt; and to say that all is right, and good, and true when you know that nothing could be more wrong and unjust [']" (84), thereby rending outward show from inner truth, causing the psychic damage of slavery.

Oddly, however, Hannah does not identify with Mrs. Wright, however perfect her credentials, for Mrs. Wright offers a sad warning about the dangers of imagination itself. By "constant habit and association," Hannah reports, Mrs. Wright transforms her cell into a luxurious palace, connecting it "with ideas of home, a home that the state with great trouble and expense prepared for her, even as it makes provision for its acknowledged head" (84). In the most perverse maternal identification in the narrative, Mrs. Wright tells Hannah, "'very motherly and good is the state'" (81). As "'her eyes wandered over the rough stone walls, and the high dark ceiling with an admiring and complacent look" (81), Mrs. Wright turns speculation into the most dangerous form of accommodation, the inverse of the white masters who would make it a tool of possession and control. An emblem of captivity fictionalized, making a pleasurable aesthetic from the material hardships of state coercion, Mrs. Wright possibly expresses the ambivalence about turning slavery into a novel that may have prevented Hannah Crafts from seeking a publisher for *The Bondwoman's Narrative*.

Despite her imaginative acumen, Mrs. Wright's palace remains haunted by the specter of slavery. And understanding that surfaces are poor indications of character or meaning, she also strives to achieve psychic freedom by finding a satisfactory manifestation of her restless desires. Caught between outward show and inner desire, Hannah, however imaginative she is in her speculative interpretations, also remains haunted. Hannah purports not to believe in ghosts, boasting that, unlike other slaves, "I seldom [never] gave way to imaginary terror. I found enough in the stern realities of life to disquiet and perplex, without going beyond the boundaries of time to meet new sources of apprehension" (132). Yet ghosts appear whenever Hannah confronts the violence done to women by men, as when the slaves believe a ghost is haunting the plantation but Hannah realizes the mysterious visitor is William come to visit Charlotte (134) or when she is told that the shack she and her mistress have been living in is haunted by "a beautiful girl" murdered inside" (69). Ghosts also rise when Hannah encounters the bodily control of slavery, as when she tells Trappe, "'the thought of you must always be a haunting curse to my memory'" (108). In both cases, Hannah is haunted by the residual traces of an identification with victimhood—with black womanhood and with the controls of slavery—that she is never able to shake. The association of haunting and identification becomes explicit when Hannah describes her mistress, caught like Hannah between whiteness and blackness, struck "with horror of what she is" (96). Identifications haunt Hannah because they bear remnants of the material violence caused by historical slavery, individualized in the inner space of the slave's psyche: "I am superstitious, I confess it; people of my race and color usually are, and I fancied then that she was haunted by a shadow or phantom apparent only to herself, and perhaps even the more dreadful for that" (27). It is the psychic turmoil of slavery—the violent splits of desire and disavowal—that is most troubling to Hannah, who, anticipating Fanon's important work on the psychodynamics of race and colonialism, declares, "those who think the greatest evils of slavery are connected with physical suffering possess no just or rational ideas of human nature. The soul, the immortal soul must ever long and yearn for a thousand things inseparable to liberty. Then, too, the fear, the apprehension, the dread and deep anxiety always attending that condition in a greater or less degree" (94). Faced with these tumultuous and conflicting emotions, the slave woman can protect herself only by insisting, as Hannah does repeatedly in her reading of portraits, that things—and people—are not always what they seem.

Notes

I am grateful to Ernestine Jenkins for bringing the work of Carrie Mae Weems to my attention, and to Augusta Rohrbach and Christopher Reed for their extremely careful and generous comments on earlier drafts. Above all, I am grateful to Henry Louis Gates, Jr., for his meticulous research in bringing *The Bondwoman's Narrative* to print.

1. Michele Wallace, "Afterword: 'Why Are There No Great Black Artists?' The Problem of Visuality in African-American Culture," *Black Popular Culture*, ed. Gina Dent (Seattle: Bay Press, 1992), 335, 333–346.

2. Ibid., 344.

3. Quoted in Thomas Pickle, Jr., "Reading Carrie Mae Weems," *Carrie Mae Weems: Recent Work, 1992–1998* (New York: George Braziller Publisher, in association with the Everson Museum of Art, 1998), II.

4. Wallace, "'Why Are There No Great Black Artists?'" 344.

5. Jennifer Fleischner, *Mastering Slavery: Memory, Family, and Identity in Women's Slave Narratives* (New York: New York Univ. Press, 1996).

6. Hannah Crafts, *The Bondwoman's Narrative*, ed. Henry Louis Gates, Jr. (New York: Warner Books, 2002). Hereafter cited by page number in the text.

7. My thinking on racial identification draws upon Diana Fuss's elaboration of Franz Fanon's project in *Black Skin, White Masks*. "'Fixed' by the violence of the racist interpellation in an imaginary relation of fractured specularity," Fuss writes, "the black man, Fanon concludes, 'is forever in combat with his own image' (*B*, 194)" (143). For Hannah Crafts, vision is not only fractured by the racial power-knowledges produced through slavery but is put under erasure by the visual "lacks" imposed by structures of gender identification. From both vantages, Hannah learns that "by imposing upon the colonial other the burden of identification (the command to become a mimic Anglo-European), the Imperial Subject inadvertently places himself in the perilous position of object—object of the Other's aggressive, hostile, and rivalrous acts of incorporation" (146). The white master's status as object of the black female gaze is literalized in *The Bondwoman's Narrative*, as I argue, by the scenes of Hannah reading her master's portraits. Through these readings, Hannah insists on her own ambivalence, rage, and desire, thereby refusing what Fuss describes as the colonizer's "sovereign right to personhood by purchasing interiority over and against the representation of the colonial other as pure exteriority" (145). Hannah exemplifies what Fuss, through Fanon, names as a principal psychic weapon of the weak, the power "to identify and disidentify simultaneously with the same object, to assimilate but not to incorporate, to approximate but not to displace" (146). Diana Fuss, *Identification Papers* (New York: Routledge, 1995).

8. Henry Louis Gates, Jr., "Introduction" to *The Bondwoman's Narrative*, by Hannah Crafts, ed. Henry Louis Gates, Jr. (New York: Warner Books, 2002), lxv-lxvii.

16

Gothic Liberties and Fugitive Novels

The Bondwoman's Narrative *and the Fiction of Race*

KAREN SÁNCHEZ-EPPLER

The cover of Warner Books' beautiful edition of *The Bondwoman's Narrative* evokes the manuscript status of this work, a stack of pages tied together with rough cord. The image highlights the weave of rag paper centered on an elegant embossed swirl. These trappings of authenticity are not drawn from the manuscript itself. Joe Nickell's detailed authentication report finds "no evidence of the manuscript having been tied in a bundle with string or ribbon," describes embossments bearing the name of a Springfield paper manufacturer, and pages that have been calendered smooth.[1] Warner Books knows that authenticity must be fabricated, that a real nineteenth-century manuscript inevitably falls short of our aesthetic ideals for such an object: it doesn't make a compelling cover. For similar reasons, at the center of all this retexturing lies an embossed rubric that does not appear on Hannah Crafts's title page: "A Novel." These words are as clear a marketing ploy as the swirls that surround them; they announce a book that might be the first novel produced by a black woman anywhere, a book that could be the only novel written by an African-American woman who had been a slave. For modern readers to recognize this manuscript as a novel is to claim priority, uniqueness, and aesthetic worth more significant than would accrue to a slave narrative. Though viewed as that too, this text is surely an extraordinary find, the only such holograph we have. Thus, the insistence of its jacket-cover on the status of this text as "a novel" reflects the relative prestige of fiction in the world of early twenty-first-century literary values. Yet, and this is what for me makes this text so interesting, the anxieties over authenticity and the investment in the comparative prestige and power of the novel that underlie Henry Louis Gates,

Jr.'s and Warner Books' decisions of how best to present this manuscript are inherent to the text itself.

The value of fiction was not so evident and secure in the mid-nineteenth century, when Puritan hatred of the lie and settler disdain for the frivolous still lingered in an increasingly commercial and entertaining literary marketplace. For an account of slavery written by a fugitive slave, fiction could be politically damning as well, since the utility of the slave narrative depended on its capacity to expose the truth about slavery. The extraordinary success of *Uncle Tom's Cabin* offers one of the strongest indicators of the growing prestige of the novel at mid-century, the widespread nature of this new conviction that fiction could redirect the real. Crafts's writing, her complex, uneven relation to fictional forms, provides compelling insights into the attraction of the novel at this crucial moment of literary and political history.

In a manner as canny and self-conscious as the fabricated authenticity of Warner Books' twine and the unequivocal promotion of this text as "A Novel," Hannah Crafts titles her manuscript:

The Bondwoman's Narrative
By Hannah Crafts
A Fugitive Slave
Recently Escaped from North Carolina

The name, or possible pseudonym, Hannah Crafts, stands as a hinge between two titles with very different generic implications. The first has the timbre of the past: picturesque, literary, individualized, and sharply gendered. It is a fine title for a novel. The second looks much more like the title of other slave narratives: it rings with the factual, generalized, political, and recent. Together, *The Bondwoman* mirrors and opposes *A Fugitive Slave.* "Bondwoman" was in the 1850s a quaint way of referring to slavery, a term loaded with the biblical and poetic. Most slave narratives of this period use the term "slave" or "fugitive" in their title as Crafts does in the phrases that follow her name.[2]

The name "Hannah Crafts" poised on this manuscript page between the novelistic and the factual emphasizes how issues of authenticity and genre structure the very notion of authorship. Michel Foucault, interrogating the concept of authorship, remarked that "if a text should be discovered in a state of anonymity . . . the game becomes one of rediscovering the author. Since literary anonymity is not tolerable." There is no doubt that in the face of this text whose authorship remains so elusive, so largely unfettered to facts, the de-

sire to find and verify Hannah as that "fugitive slave" seems particularly pressing.[3] The "author function" is ideological, Foucault contends, "the author is
the principle of thrift in the proliferation of meaning," a mechanism "by
which one impedes the *free* circulation, the *free* manipulation, the *free* composition, decomposition, and recomposition of fiction."[4] Clearly Foucault's critique of authorship, articulated through names like "Aristotle," "Homer,"
"Shakespeare," and "Flaubert," does not quite register the position of the slave
author or the extent to which readers in the nineteenth century and now continue to find ways of "resisting," as Frances Foster puts it, rather than insisting upon African American authorship.[5] The recognition of slave authorship
may confirm and delimit the value and meaning of the slave narratives in ways
congruent with Foucault's account, but it simultaneously serves to confirm the
value and meaning of the writer in a manner not required by his highly canonical exemplars. The resistance to slave authorship, the tendency to doubt that
these texts were really produced by men and women who had been held as
slaves, denotes a skepticism not easily disentangled from racism, a resistance to
the idea that one who had been denied self-ownership could possibly provide
the "genius" and "perpetual surging of invention" attached to the notion of
authorship.[6] If this manuscript does indeed prove to be the work of "a fugitive slave," it will be our most potent evidence against such denials, a manuscript unmediated by the editorial hand of a white press. To insist on the relevance of authorship and authenticity for *The Bondwoman's Narrative* reiterates an
argument about black intellectual ability that appallingly continues to gape
open even 230 years after the publication of Phillis Wheatley's *Poems on Various
Subjects Religious and Moral*, with its authenticating affidavit signed by eighteen
eminent white Bostonians. But if Foucault's critique of authorship does not
consider the peculiar predicament of the slave text, reading his essay in relation to *The Bondwoman's Narrative* highlights the specifically emancipatory
rhetoric of his denunciation of the author function—for what he perceives to
be shackled by the figure of the author is precisely a series of traits and possibilities that he repeatedly identifies as "the free."

Young Hannah, sent upstairs to close a window in the portrait gallery of
Lindendale, exults in just such a rapturous, interpretive freedom:

> Though filled with superstitious awe I was in no haste to leave the room; for
> there surrounded by mysterious associations I seemed suddenly to have grown
> old, to have entered a new world of thoughts and feelings and sentiments. I was
> not a slave with these pictured memorials of the past. They could not enforce
> drudgery, or condemn me on account of my color to a life of servitude. As
> their companion I could think and speculate. In their presence my mind

seemed to run riotous and exult in its freedom as a rational being, and one designed for something higher and better than this world can afford. (17)

The text glosses Hannah's feelings of liberation as proofs of her rational and
immortal soul. But the freedom described in this passage appears suffused
with the superstitious and mysterious, not the rational, and if it confirms
Hannah's connection to "something higher and better than this world can afford," that something seems more akin to "a new world" of art and imagination than to Heaven. What "runs riotous" in this passage is the very capacity
for interpretation and proliferation of meaning that Foucault celebrated as
"the free circulation, the free manipulation, the free composition, decomposition, and recomposition of fiction." Such liberty has a decidedly literary quality. Hannah Crafts's freedom here resides not in her authorship—for it is as
author that she contains this riotousness in the conventional terms of the rational and spiritual—but rather in her position as viewer, interpreter, reader.
"No one could prevent us making good use of our eyes," Crafts remarks of
the liberty to explore her master's mansion that accompanies young Hannah's
labors of cleaning it (14). Hannah's feeling of freedom in the portrait gallery
derives from a double act of "recomposition." If young Hannah sees in these
pictures "companions" rather than owners, she does so through a complex
process of interpretation and denial that rejects the artistic and ancestral intentions behind such portraiture, refusing to view them as signs of lineage,
possession, and power. So, too, in writing this scene Crafts adopts and alters
the conventions of gothic fiction, for generic norms hold the act of viewing
an ancestral portrait as testimony to the inescapable tentacles of the past, the
inevitable entrapment of blood. Crafts re-imagines the gothic genre, just as
Hannah re-interprets the ancestral portraits, and for both it is this readerly rejection of expected or authorized meanings, the openness to counter-factual,
counter-intentional invention, that makes this scene so liberating.

The Bondwoman's Narrative is an extremely hybrid work. The opposition of the
novelistic and factual displayed on its title page is further fractured by the
wide range of fictional forms from which this text draws—testimonial, sentimental, gothic, satiric, pious, sensational, and more. This mixing of genres is
not unique to this book; indeed such hybridity proves to be a quite general
characteristic of African American writing in the 1850s. The questions of authenticity of identity and genre that permeate the present publication of this
manuscript—was she a slave? was she black? is this a novel? is it true?—echo
nineteenth-century concerns. Such questions arise, of course, from a bed of
essentialist assumptions: that slaves are black, that freedom is white, that novels falsify, that race and genre ought to be, if ever they could be, pure. The

power of Crafts's interpretive freedom derives from her persistent disruption of all such axioms. If this produces a text that at times appears excessive, disjunctive, even chaotic, the roughness of Crafts's seams makes visible the act of linkage and actively expresses the difficult and complex relations between racial identity and literary form during the 1850s, a set of tensions that pervades not only the proliferation and standardization of slave narratives during this period but also the production of the first African American novels.[7]

Before returning to Crafts's text, I want to briefly rehearse the extent to which these issues of authorship, authenticity, verisimilitude, and generic instability characterize African American writing during this decade. William Andrews dubbed the formal dilemma of the slave narrative as the tension between the roles of "eye-witness" and "I-witness," foregrounding how the position of author served two essentially contradictory functions simultaneously: the authorial voice of the slave narrative provides both a transparent lens onto slavery and a self capable of personal and cultural expression.[8] A tug-of-war between the political value of fact and the ontological validations of narration thus lies at the heart of the double-bind of slave authorship. Neither witness provided much space for a version of self or story more capacious than the stereotyping needs of abolitionist politics. The novelistic strategies of narration (scenic description, dialogue, etc.) employed by writers like Harriet Jacobs, instance the effort to use the tools of fiction to expand the representational possibilities of the slave narrative. Such efforts resulted in a great deal of generic complexity, and much of the best critical work on *Incidents* explores the play between genres.[9] The possibilities that fiction offered for navigating the limitations posed by what Carla Peterson terms the "essentialized notions of black selfhood" at stake in the slave narrative prompted even such successful narrative writers as William Wells Brown and Frederick Douglass to turn their hands to fiction.[10] The desire of these ex-slave authors to write fiction was not matched by a public interest in publishing or reading such works, in marked distinction to the extraordinary popularity of *Uncle Tom's Cabin* (1852), published just the year before Douglass's *Heroic Slave* and Brown's *Clotel* (both 1853).[11] Not surprisingly these early African American novels do much to thematize issues of genre. *Clotel*, for example, a generically diverse and notoriously patchwork document, actually reproduces large segments of other texts ranging from portions of Brown's own *Narrative* reset as quotations within a third-person telling of his life, to actual or pseudo-advertisements and newspaper clippings, to a lengthy segment of Lydia Maria Child's short story "The Quadroons." In his "Conclusion," Brown acknowledges the wide range of sources and kinds of materials he has drawn upon for this text: he "made free use" of the stories told him by the many fugitive slaves he helped toward Canada, he is "indebted" to Child and has "taken" from American abolitionist journals, and so on, explaining that "all these combined have made up my story."[12] Andrews describes the theoretical implications of the "liminal world of *Clotel*, where fictive and natural discourse dovetail and can easily be made to look the same." He concludes that these textual strategies work to foreground the nature of narration and the valuing of authenticity as they challenge the "reader to ponder the basis on which one distinguishes between the real and the fictive in any text."[13]

As this literary history suggests, if by the 1850s the conventions of the slave narrative often worked to constrict literary expression, they nevertheless continued to provide an array of narrative practices to be drawn upon in the creation of other African American literary forms.[14] In the intensity of its generic instability, Crafts's text emphasizes the circular structure of this trajectory. Is Crafts mining the novel (gothic, sentimental, melodramatic, satirical) in order to write a slave narrative? Or is she mining the slave narrative in order to write a novel? To recognize this generic circuit is to raise questions about the nature of genre in the first place, to ask what is at stake in our practices of talking about genres as if they were pure, unadulterated forms. Thus *The Bondwoman's Narrative* provides provocative, fruitful ground not just for understanding African Americans' turn toward fiction during this decade but also for raising more general questions about the functioning of genre and the relationship between genre and race. After all, part of what feels so unsettling about Hannah's experience of freedom in the portrait gallery and Crafts's recourse to the gothic is the assertion that in the face of these ancestral portraits "color" doesn't matter, even as we, and surely Crafts, know that in the context of plantation slavery ancestry inexorably refers to race.

Genre bears no necessary relation to truth. Brown titled Chapter 23 of *Clotel* "Truth Stranger than Fiction," a conventional phrase that Crafts echoes in her preface. Still, in the dense intertwining of concerns with genre and with authenticity that surround *The Bondwoman's Narrative*, I am struck by the extent to which Crafts's most markedly fictional scenes (scenes characteristic of the non-realist genres, such as the gothic legend of the linden tree, the sentimental domestic utopia of the Henrys' cottage, and the sensational voluptuousness of Cosgrove's "harem") are associated with aspects of the story for which little external corroboration has been found. Crafts's most convincing realism, by contrast, is associated with passages where her form of naming most suggests actual people (the initial masking of "Wh—r" which was later overwritten with "eele" to spell "Wheeler") and where her description suggests an actual place, both of which have now been verified by the historical record. In short, I perceive a marked symmetry between Gates's ability to locate historical evidence and the shifts in Crafts's literary style. Even as I question the stakes and presumptions behind the "game" of "rediscovering the author," I find I can't help playing too. I want to postulate, as my own early guess at authorship, that Hannah Crafts was indeed a slave of Ellen Wheeler's in Washington, D.C., and possibly for a short period on the Wheeler plantation in North Carolina, but that she did not spend much time on a plantation and that, consequently, her scenes of plantation life are largely based not on her life experience but on her readings.[15] Her first description of the slave quarters closely imitates Dickens's description of a tenement from *Bleak House* but is introduced by a phrase of Crafts's own: "is it a stretch of imagination to say that . . . " (199).[16] Thus Crafts calls attention to the metaphoric qualities of this passage, its literariness. But whose imagination is being stretched here? If I am right in guessing that Crafts's knowledge of plantation slavery largely derives from lore and books, then fiction would serve to present Hannah in a manner closer to what readers' images of "real slavery" might be. The slave narratives, *Uncle Tom's Cabin* and other slavery fictions, and the abolitionist press as a whole had all defined slavery as plantation slavery, making other kinds of slave experience seem inauthentic. As Crafts uses generic conventions to mark the plantation South as gothic, sensational, or novelistic, she highlights the social fiction that this and only this is slavery.

The attitude toward literacy in *The Bondwoman's Narrative* strikes me as another instance of Crafts's distance from the norms of plantation slavery. For all her fascination with the literary, Crafts generally treats the capacity to read as a commonplace accomplishment for a house slave. Literacy is less celebrated in this text than taken for granted. For example, in her first encounters with Mrs. Wheeler, that lady's assessments of Hannah's utility as a personal servant include tests of her capacity to read and write: in the morning she has Hannah dress her hair, then after breakfast,

> Mrs. Wheeler requested me to read for her. I had not gone over two pages, when she called for pillows, which were to be disposed about her person to facilitate slumber; then she inquired if I was musical, adding that Jane used to soothe her to sleep with the guitar. I had played a little on the harp, and so I told her. She bade me get it, and play softly, very softly on account of her nerves. Then settling her person among the pillows, but in such a manner as not to derange her hair she prepared to take a nap. My music, however, did not suit her. It was sharp, or flat, or dull, or insipid anything but what she wished. (152–153)

For Mrs. Wheeler, books and music, like pillows, are luxurious comforts, signs of status and pleasure, and such cultural skills become just another sort of labor that a lady might extract from her slaves. There is no sense in this passage that slave literacy could be associated with liberation or viewed as a threat to the plantation system. Indeed, Mrs. Wheeler quickly turns Hannah's capacity to read and write into the means of acquiring her servitude: "That afternoon she dictated a letter for me to write" (153). Unlike Frederick Douglass's attempt to write his own pass, Hannah is constrained to write the fallacious and self-damning text that will procure her own purchase. Mrs. Wheeler's dictation reveals her dishonesty, her willingness to lie about Hannah's traits in the hopes of buying her at a lower price. Mrs. Wheeler knows how to use Hannah's literacy to abuse and defame her. But Crafts gets revenge in these passages, reclaiming reading and writing not as skills to be exploited but as marks of cultural status and refinement. In these terms Mrs. Wheeler's incapacity to hear or appreciate Hannah's reading and music betrays the mistress's finicky and selfish character; her responses define her as a creature of wishes, vanity, and delicate nerves, but utterly lacking in discernment, integrity, and real culture.

The best historical assessments suggest that the levels of literacy that Mrs. Wheeler and Hannah view as ordinary were in fact quite unusual: it appears that slave literacy rates hovered around five percent of the slave population and were disproportionately associated with house slavery and/or urban settings.[17] Presuming that Gates is correct in identifying Mrs. Wheeler's previous servant "Jane" as the Jane Johnson whose escape from the Wheeler family while in Philadelphia prompted the notorious Passmore Williamson case, one of the test cases of the Fugitive Slave Law, it is worth noting that however satisfactorily Jane may have played the guitar, she signed her testimony in the case only with her mark.[18] Though Crafts's high level of literacy could certainly be attained under slavery, even plantation slavery, I find it more difficult to imagine that anyone who had lived long in the plantation South would view these accomplishments as unremarkable. Crafts, however, does not limit her presentation of the ordinariness of slave literacy to these scenes with Mrs. Wheeler. When, for example, Mr. Trappe equips the house where he keeps the slave women he intends to sell as fancy girls, he does so in a manner that presumes that they may wish to pass their time reading:

> True, the wants of our nature were all supplied. We were provided with delicate food, were furnished with books and embroidery, and ~~might~~ so far as outward appearances were concerned ~~have been~~ we might have been happy. But those who think the greatest evils of slavery are connected with physical suffering possess no just or rational idea of human nature. The soul, the immortal soul must ever long for and yearn for a thousand things inseparable to liberty. (94)

The longings of the immortal soul for liberty often appear in slave narratives as linked to literacy. Frederick Douglass explains:

> my learning to read had already come, to torment and sting my soul to unutterable anguish. It had given me a view of my wretched condition, without the remedy. As I writhed under it, I would at times feel that learning to read had been a curse rather than a blessing.[19]

Here learning to read prompts just the kind of knowledge and anguish that Crafts describes; both passages recognize that "the greatest evils of slavery" are not "connected with physical suffering" but rather with mental and spiritual deprivation. Douglass depicts the consciousness and torments that derive from his new capacity to read as a large part of what fuels and enables his escape. Reading may not in itself provide "the remedy" to slavery, but Douglass still recognizes and celebrates literacy as "the pathway from slavery to freedom."[20] Crafts, by contrast, oddly includes "books" in the list of amenities that address her "outward" "wants" without affecting her internal needs. The disjunction between Crafts's embrace of the *literary* as a mode and mark of liberation, and her general dismissal of *literacy* as a commonplace accomplishment, stands in marked contrast to the norms of the slave narrative and may even be seen as a conscious critique of that genre's presumption that mere reading and writing were signs of selfhood or liberation enough.[21]

In the writings of ex-slaves, learning to read generally appears as a heroic accomplishment, difficult, often painful, and requiring a great deal of fortitude and resourcefulness. Crafts certainly presents her desire to read as differentiating young Hannah from other slave children, but she represents her acquisition of literacy as an occasion of wish fulfillment far more than as a testimony to personal effort. Like Douglass copying his letters off shipyard boards, or Brown tricking and bribing school boys to teach him, Hannah initially learns to read surreptitiously.[22] "My dream," as she calls the desire to read, "was destined to be realized" in a scene that, with a characteristic layering of genres, Crafts describes both as an instance of divine intervention and as a fairy tale. Aunt Hetty and Uncle Siah teach Hannah to read, prompted by "our Saviour's words" (7). Their text book is "the book of God" (12), and Crafts stresses that these were not merely literacy lessons: "they cultivated my moral nature. They led me to the foot of the cross" (10). Crafts weaves through this pious account the settings and figures of a fairy tale: sitting on the bank of a brook Hannah is approached by "an aged woman" who makes "salves and ointments," lives "in the little cottage just around the foot of the hill," and "who seemed to know my wish before I expressed it" (7). A true fairy godmother, Aunt Hetty transforms the slave girl into a princess, or at least bestows upon her a similar act of recognition: "I feel a warmer interest in your welfare than I should were you the daughter of a queen," she says (8). When the overseer discovers these secret literacy lessons, Hannah's teachers are punished, again in a rich mix of religion and legend:

> in conformity to the inscrutable ways of Providence the strength of these aged servants of the Cross were tried by a more severe ordeal. Alas: Alas that I should have been the means . . . My fancy painted them as immured in a dungeon for the crime of teaching a slave to read. (12–13)

Hannah herself miraculously "escaped the punishment" (12), and most magically of all her beloved Aunt Hetty reappears near the book's end to provide the "silver" and the "plans" that will bring Hannah to freedom in New Jersey (230). In the conjunction of scripture and fairy tale, Crafts associates the acquisition of literacy with supernatural powers. This power, however, clearly emanates not from the mere capacity to read but from these literary traditions and the sanctions that they both give, in their so different ways, to the miraculous.

The reappearance of Aunt Hetty at the close of this story offers a prime instance of the "clumsy plot structures" and "impossible coincidences" that characterize this text (the phrases are Ann Fabian's [xxvi]). Such traits may be a legacy of sentimental fiction or an attribute of unschooled writing, but they also proclaim the power of fiction to remake the world. Only the will of God or the literary suspension of disbelief can make the impossible, possible. A coincidence in a text is something produced not out of the logic of circumstance but only by the fiat of desire, the fictional capacity to grant wishes. That literacy acquisition could be non-traumatic for a slave, or at least that all of its trauma should fall on other, white, people, seems deeply counter-factual. "The first time they caught you trying to read or write you was whipped with a cow-hide, the next time with a cat-o-nine-tales and the third time they cut the first jint offen your forefinger," one ex-slave explained to a WPA interviewer. Another described how when the master discovered that one of his slave women was literate, "he made her pull off naked, whipped her and den slapped hot irons to her all over. Believe me dat nigger didn't want to read and 'rite no more."[23] Literacy may be dangerous to slaves, but the literary enables Crafts to dispel such dangers, eliding and displacing scenes of punishment so that Hannah may remain unscarred.

In these terms, Crafts's partiality to the gothic seems particularly interesting, since the gothic has been generally understood not as a genre that enables the denial or evasion of social dangers but rather as one that seeks to materialize those dangers in the most hyperbolic and malevolent form. Critics have shown how the gothic has been used to express the traps and menace of patriarchy or the inescapable controls of capitalism. The gothic gives form to whatever haunts, threatening that the wrongs of the past will return, hence its most consistent formal features are foreshadowing and repetition, its overarching conceit the return of the dead in the dual form of ghosts and inheritance. Manifesting confinement and yearning for freedom, the gothic is an Old World genre whose relevance for American slavery certainly occurred to other writers of this period, most notably perhaps to Stowe, who has Cassy enact gothic horrors in a performance that enables her escape from Simon Legree.[24] Crafts's uses of the gothic are multiple and diffuse. Gothic motifs recur throughout the text, often erupting in unexpected ways, as in Lizzy's introduction of her story of Cosgrove's "harem"—a tale better described generically as melodrama or sensation fiction—with the assertion that the new master of Lindendale is "haunted" (171). At other times the gothic comes wrapped in unusual effect, as in the humor with which the drunken Jo describes the "ghost" who tread on his toes (133–134 and 138–139). In this play of contradictions, repetitions, and revisions, *The Bondwoman's Narrative* itself often seems haunted by the gothic.

Just a page after the story of Hannah's reading lessons, Crafts initiates the first of this book's many gothic sequences:

> There is something inexpressibly dreary and solemn in passing through the silent rooms of a large house, especially one whence many generations have passed to the grave. Involuntarily you find yourself thinking of them . . . A supernatural thrill pervades your frame, and you feel the presence of mysterious beings. It may be foolish and childish, but it is one of the unaccountable things instinctive to the human nature. (14–15)

Crafts generalizes Hannah's feelings in this scene, insisting that the "you" of the reader feel them too and that indeed such emotions and experiences are "instinctive to the human nature." The gothic presumes a common psyche and common compulsions. It places everyone in the position of the slave, in the realm of the involuntary. Crafts's insistence that these emotions and their triggers function across racial divides has strong political implications, though it is highly unusual to ground such an account of human sameness upon such an obviously artificial impetus. Yet in so doing, Crafts provides this text with a literary lineage, her house of fiction can claim "many generations" of its own and "the echo of a stealthy tread behind us" (15).[25]

The experience Crafts here describes as universal is not, however, so easy to come by; it requires a large and old house, an ancestral mansion. If indeed this scene does feel recognizable to readers it is because we have read it before. Still, these Old World literary spaces do have a clear correlation in the American South: the planter class stands as America's most evident and self-conscious gentry. Their grand houses and the labors of upkeep such dwellings demanded do indeed serve as sites of imprisonment and torture. Moreover, in a nation that ideologically prides itself on the opportunity for self-making, slavery remains a recalcitrant site of inheritance, for the language of generations that intimates aristocratic pedigree has more ominous implications for the slave. As Crafts points out in another scene, the houses of slaves are ancient too: "Many of these huts were even older than the nation, and had been occupied by successive generations of slaves. The greatest curse of slavery is its' heriditary character" (200).

Crafts's deep sense of the relevance of the gothic to the project of writing slavery comes conjoined, however, to an apologetic discomfort, so that if the gothic seems Crafts's favorite literary mode, it also appears as the least stable of her many genres. Even as she embarks upon the gothic, and celebrates the "supernatural thrill" it provides, Crafts dismisses these feelings as "foolish and childish." She knows, however, that the repudiation of gothic terrors will not quell them. Many years later, left alone in the woods with the corpse of a fellow fugitive, Hannah seems to see the dead body leer and beckon "and though I knew that this was all fancy, though I had sense enough left to perceive even then the absurdity of my fears I could not overcome them" (222). Crafts's deployment of the gothic often wavers in this way; clearly one of the attractions of the genre for her stems from this ambivalence, from the sense of the inevitability of terror even if absurd, the ability both to name fears "foolish" and to feel them. Thus in a manner opposite from the warding off of violence that she accomplishes with her fictive wish fulfillment, Crafts uses the gothic to label her terrors as fiction and to redefine them as thrilling. After all, as an account of slavery, the gothic may be not exaggeration but understatement.

The question of race stands at the center of Crafts's ambivalence over the gothic. "I am superstitious, I confess it; people of my race and color usually are," Crafts explains, pleasure and pride ringing through her confession even as she labels as racial characteristics terrors she had previously depicted as universal (27). Later, when Mrs. Henry chides her, "Why, Hannah, superstitious, too," she replies, "Not a particle of it, Madam" (139), distinguishing herself from the other slaves, as well as betraying Lotte and her husband, who, in an echo of Cassy's plot in *Uncle Tom's Cabin,* have used the pretext of ghostly visitations to meet and plan their escape. Here the gothic becomes a tool of racial solidarity, and Hannah's recoil from it and insistence on giving Lotte's mistress a rational explanation of the ghost is one of the moments of the text in which her character appears least sympathetic. Even the hypocritical Mrs. Henry remarks that in such a situation, as people who care for Lotte, "having eyes we had better not see, and having ears we should not hear" (139). Such scenes suggest that to embrace the gothic entails confronting and acknowledging the legacy of race, a connection that goes far to explain Hannah's ambivalent attitude toward the genre. Hannah's sense of freedom in the portrait gallery, we should recall, depended in large part on the insistence that "I was not a slave with these pictured memorials of the past," on the denial that these portraits had anything to do with "color" or "servitude." Her account of the slave huts and the "heriditary character" of slavery appears grounded in a similar act of denial or displacement. The passage continues,

> The father leaves to his son an inheritance of toil and misery, and his place on the fetid straw in the miserable corner, with no hope or possibility of anything better. And the son in his turn transmits the same to his offspring and thus forever. (200)

To describe the inheritance of slavery this way elides one of the greatest evils of the system, for slave law proclaims that servitude passes not through "the father" but through mothers, *partus sequitur ventrem*, rewarding white masters for the rape and concubinage that fathers their own slaves. This elision is all the more remarkable since one of the central plot sequences of *The Bondwoman's Narrative*, the heart of its first gothic tale, concerns Mrs. Vincent's secret inheritance of servitude from her slave mother. In her first description of this new mistress, Crafts notes that "there was mystery, something indefinable about her . . . I fancied then that she was haunted by a shadow or phantom" (27). The mystery that haunts Mrs. Vincent casts its shadow throughout *The Bondwoman's Narrative*, and the ghosts of this gothic are rape and race. Considering the lightness of her skin, which will permit Hannah to pass as both a white boy and a white woman during her escape, might not part of what Hannah confronts in the portrait gallery be the possibility that all these painted Vincents may prove to be her own ancestors too?[26]

In these accounts of the phantom of race, Crafts plays upon its immateriality, emphasizing the absurdity that something this invisible, this impalpable, could make so enormous a material difference. There is little that appears "black" about the bodies of Mrs. Vincent, or Lizzy, or Hannah herself, and yet nothing of the prerogatives of "whiteness" pass to slave children. "Scenting out the African taint" is Mr. Trappe's evil business (232). Trappe documents and profits on the capacity to discern blackness within even the most aristocratic white families and the most beautiful white women, presuming race to be a fact that can be found and proved. Trappe's villainy makes evident the reductive and destructive implications of the role of race detective and hence raises questions about the stakes of interest and desire within Gates's or my own eagerness to determine the race of Hannah Crafts.[27] Like Trappe, like Gates, like me, Crafts also presents herself as an expert reader of racial signs. "Almost white," Hannah's "obnoxious descent could not be readily traced," she explains and then goes on to trace it in "a rotundity to my person, a wave and curl to my hair" (6). Crafts, similarly, covers her first description of Mrs. Vincent with racial signs: "a small brown woman, with a profusion of wavy curly hair" and "lips which were too large full and red" (27). Moreover, her narration loads Trappe himself with tokens of blackness; Crafts so consistently mentions his "great black eyes" (28) and "seedy black" clothes (37), his "dark clothes and darker eyes" (35), that simply spotting a "coat of seedy black" (158) on the streets of Washington is enough to alert Hannah and her readers that Trappe lurks nearby. The conventional darkness of gothic evil doubles as the markings of race. Thus, like her villain, Crafts appears fascinated with reading race, with racial secrets and the pervasiveness of racial mixing. The multiple repetitions of this plot point, however, in the opposite direction from Trappe's legal maneuvers, suggesting that the idea of racial purity itself may be less fact than fiction. In this way Crafts offers a model for reading race that is not "trapped" by it, a model that I have attempted to follow in this essay.

As P. Gabrielle Foreman explicates in her analysis of the passing strategies of Ellen Craft and Louisa Piquet, these fugitive slaves are not "passing for" but rather "passing through" whiteness, using their light complexions as a tool for achieving a freedom in which they can reassert their black identities and their ties to their darker-skinned husbands and mothers. "While dominant national consciousness conflates freedom with whiteness," she writes, "these women are clear that they resist such associations and are working to cleave hierarchically fixed meanings from racial classifications."[28] Once free, Hannah throws off the "disguise" of whiteness, enlisting herself in the free black community of New Jersey, marrying an African American husband, and in the most exuberant and unbelievable of the book's many coincidences, reuniting with her mother. "Can you guess who lives with me?" she asks her readers, emphasizing the implausibility of this happy denouement, "You never could—my own dear mother" (237). Like these other light fugitives, Crafts's mulatta genealogy thus proves ultimately less concerned with identifying white fathers than in producing black mothers. In a conversation with the

"Quadroon" slave Lizzy, Hannah dismisses her friend's pride in her "good family" and the "privelage" of being a "near relative" to "some honorable gentleman" or "some great lady," insisting that such ties "matter little" (33–34).

What matters much for Crafts in the conjuring of racial ghosts is instead the production of blackness. Crafts's penchant for turning "white" characters "black" refracts through a wide range of textual guises and genres. Most dramatically, the tragic story of Mrs. Vincent, Hannah's first mistress who becomes her fellow slave, transmutes into farce and satire as Hannah's next mistress, Mrs. Wheeler, turns black in a chemical reaction of facial powder and smelling salts. Turning her mistresses black, Crafts takes revenge on the system that enslaves her. Her delight in this plot motif counters the surety that nearly all slaves must have some white ancestry with the suggestion that all southern whites may have hidden blackness too. The huts of slaves, Crafts insists are "older than the nation," identifying these black households as a site of national origin.

The tone of these two tales of blackened mistresses appears, of course, antithetical. Crafts voices sympathy and sorrow with the plight of Mrs. Vincent and gleeful ridicule at the comeuppance of Mrs. Wheeler. The story of Mrs. Vincent figures the permeability of race as a mark of solidarity between women. Mrs. Vincent declares that Hannah must "call me mistress no longer. Henceforth you shall be to me as a very dear sister" (48). The claim of sisterhood adopts feminist-abolitionist rhetoric even as it alludes to the secret genealogies of plantation households that may often make slave and mistress sisters. But Hannah continues to call Mrs. Vincent "mistress" in conversation, as Crafts does in narration, so that while the plot consigns her to slavery, the telling of it resurrects the differences of status between these two women. In one of her most psychologically nuanced sequences, Crafts describes how as "my mistress became decidedly insane," she turned "querelous and complaining, upbraiding me as the cause of all her difficulties, and heaped the strangest accusations of conspiracy on my head" (67); that is, as Mrs. Vincent comes closer to the status of her slave, as Trappe's plot and Crafts's proclaim slave and mistress racially the same, Mrs. Vincent's madness recreates the distance between them, as in her paranoia she takes on the oppressive demeanor of the mistress, querulous and complaining. Mrs. Vincent is not the only woman to be driven insane in this book. Mrs. Wright, imprisoned for attempting to help a slave girl escape also goes mad, hallucinating that her jail is a palace and she a queen. That the two "white" women who become most closely identified with the sufferings of slave women lose their minds, their insanity taking the form of delusions—of paranoia or grandeur—mentally inhabiting the counter-factual, suggests a cruel underside to the freedom of the fictive.

The blackening of Mrs. Wheeler, on the other hand, recounts a marvelously inventive and humorous story of racial masquerade and retribution. Crafts's evident pleasure in taking this fictional revenge illuminates the element of racial vengeance in these other tales of uncovering blackness. Moreover, Crafts uses this tale of cosmetic racial crossover to frame and introduce her fullest account of the illicit sexuality that truly produces racially mixed bodies. Mrs. Wheeler's face and hands turn black because of a chemical reaction between a white powder she applies, in an effort to appear more beautiful when she goes to solicit a political appointment for her husband, and the vapors of her smelling salts. As Crafts narrates Mrs. Wheeler's preparations for this outing, her syntax subtly but repeatedly connects Hannah with Mr. Wheeler. So, for example, when Mrs. Wheeler demands the smelling salts, Crafts details how "I went to the house, procured the smelling bottle, Mr. Wheeler advanced to meet me, took the little delicate supporter of weak nerves, and handing it to his wife, the carriage drove off" (165). The collaboration of Hannah and Mr. Wheeler to produce Mrs. Wheeler's blackness suffuses this telling, while these two characters hardly interact at all in any other portion of the book. When Mrs. Wheeler returns, having been insulted by the politicians she solicited, Mr. Wheeler supports Hannah's assertions of innocence, and Crafts amends his wife's retort so as to make explicit the sexual undertones of passages on these pages that link "Mr. Wheeler and myself" (166). "No: no:" Mrs. Wheeler exclaims, "Slaves generally are far preferable to wives in husbands' eyes" (167). Meanwhile, the jokes and "titter"(168) that meet Mrs. Wheeler's petitions on her husband's behalf all derive from the insinuation that she must be Mr. Wheeler's black mistress. Thus, while the classic "tragic mulatta story" of Mrs. Vincent tends to obscure its sexual origins, the farce of Mrs. Wheeler's blackface plays on them. This chapter ends, moreover, with Hannah's coincidental reunion with Lizzy, who tells her the more recent news of Lindendale, where these hints of slave mistresses expand into full sexual exposé: "no Turk in his haram ever luxuriated in deeper sensual enjoyments than did the master of Lindendale" (172).

In general Crafts does not seem particularly anxious about issues of narrative coherence; this text abounds in odd juxtapositions of content, genre, and tone. Lizzy's lengthy account of the Cosgrove harem could easily stand as a short story on its own and could have been told at virtually any other juncture in the text. Yet Crafts makes a marked effort to place it here, directly after the account of Mrs. Wheeler's blackening, as if to emphasize the sexual meanings of this farce, how the rape of slave women and the degradation of slave mistresses intertwine.[29] Most striking of all, she has Lizzy end her tale by describing the renovations of Lindendale and concludes, "Sir Clifford's portrait and its companions of both sexes, had been publicly exposed in the market and knocked down to the highest bidder. 'Sic transit gloria mundi.'" (194). Here the suspicion that runs beneath Hannah's sense of gothic liberty in the portrait gallery that these may well be her ancestors too, the interpretive fiat by which she denies the capacity of these painted figures to confine her by "color" or "servitude," bursts into gleeful inversion. Crafts places the haughty Vincent ancestors, Sir Clifford de Vincent himself, upon the auction block like any slave—the masters are sold. Thus, *The Bondwoman's Narrative* displays with awkward but insistent immediacy the impurity of both genre and race, the ubiquitousness, perhaps even inevitability, of mixture, miscegenation. Crafts, enamored of the power of fiction, registers the recognition that the most potent site of fictional power in nineteenth-century America—and perhaps still now—must be the fiction of race.

Notes

My first readings of *The Bondwoman's Narrative* benefited from the conversations of the seminars on "African-American Literary Recoveries" that I gave at the Universities of Barcelona and La Laguna; the Forschungs-Colloquium at the Kennedy Institute for American Studies, Frei Universitat, Berlin, read and critiqued an early draft of this essay. My thanks to all of these participants and especially to Angels Carabí, Rodrigo Andrés, Teresa Requena, Justine Tally, and Heinz Ickstadt. Thanks also to my colleagues at the University Malaga who helped me to write far from libraries I know, especially the unerring editorial hand of Ruth Stoner, and to the Fulbright Commissions in Spain and Germany, who made all these contacts possible. And thanks to Gabrielle Foreman for e-mailed insights and a willingness to share her provocative essay while it was still in press.

I. Joe Nickell, "Authentication Report," Appendix A to *The Bondwoman's Narrative*, by Hannah Crafts, ed. Henry Louis Gates, Jr. (New York: Warner Books, 2002), 301; on embossments, see 290; on the paper's smoothness, see 292. All subsequent citations of *The Bondwoman's Narrative* and its appendices will be cited parenthetically within the text. As Jerome Christensen points out, Time Warner itself exemplifies "the corporate merger of fact and fiction"; see his "The Time Warner Conspiracy: *JFK, Batman*, and the Manager Theory of Hollywood Film," *Critical Inquiry* 28 (Spring 2002): 591.

2. I have surveyed the catalogues of the Library of Congress and the American Antiquarian Society and found only one "bondwoman" amongst the anti-slavery titles of the 1840s and 1850s: Elizabeth Lloyd's "Appeal for the Bondwoman, To her own Sex" (Philadelphia, 1846). Lloyd's appeal is in verse, a poem written by a white woman to white women, speaking "for" those in bonds. Her use of the term "bondwoman" is consistent with the generally elevated and literary tone of the piece and its biblical flavor. The *Oxford English Dictionary's* citations for "bondwoman," "bondswoman," and "bondmaid" are almost entirely poetic or scriptural. William L. Andrew's bibliography of slave narratives (available at University of North Carolina's "Documenting the American South" web site http://docsouth.unc.edu/neh/neh.html) reveals that while nearly two-thirds of the narratives published between 1830 and 1860 use the word "slave" or "slavery" in their title, not one employs the term bond-

woman or bondman. (I found only two uses of the term "bondage" in titles during this period: Edmund Kelley's *A Family Redeemed from Bondage* [1851] and Frederick Douglass's *My Bondage and My Freedom* [1855].) The only use of "bondwoman" in titling a narrative is Frances Titus's *Narrative of Sojourner Truth: A Bondswoman of Olden Times* (1884). The initial version of Truth's *Narrative*, written by Olive Gilbert and published in 1850, appeared under a much more conventional mid-century title: *Narrative of Sojourner Truth, a Northern Slave, Emancipated from Bodily Servitude by the State of New York in 1828*. The decision to retitle this narrative as that of a "Bondswoman of Olden Times" provides a biblical cadence, an evocation of the past that presents Truth's experiences in slavery as legendary and picturesque. Frederick Douglass's account of Truth, when he first met her at the Northampton Association in the early 1840s, registered this anachronistic tendency in her self-presentation. Its appeal "seemed to please herself and others best when she put her ideas in the oddest forms," he remarked. "Her quaint speeches easily gave her an audience." Frederick Douglass, "What I Found at the Northampton Association," in *History of Florence Massachusetts. Including a Complete Account of the Northampton Association of Education and Industry*, ed. Charles A. Sheffield (Florence, Mass.: Charles A. Sheffield, 1895), 130–132. For a discussion of Douglass's assessment of Truth, see Nell Irvin Painter, *Sojourner Truth: A Life, A Symbol* (New York: W. W. Norton, 1996), 98.

3. Gates himself is well aware of the tension between his desire to see this text as a novel and his chances of identifying Hannah Crafts. Obviously, it is only to the extent that this text proves not to be fiction that it becomes capable of providing clues to the author's identity (Gates, "Introduction," xxxiv–xxxv).

4. Michel Foucault, "What Is an Author?" *The Foucault Reader*, ed. Paul Rabinowitz (New York: Pantheon Books, 1984), "if a text" 109, "author function" 108, "principle of thrift" 118, "by which one impedes" 119. Emphasis mine.

5. Frances Foster, "Resisting Incidents," in *Harriet Jacobs and Incidents in the Life of a Slave Girl: New Critical Essays*, ed. Deborah M. Garfield and Rafia Zafar (New York: Cambridge University Press, 1996), 57–75. See also Satya Mohanty's critique of the ways in which postmodernism has functioned to undermine the cognitive value of experience and social position, that is, the specifics of authorship, and the particular harm that this does to the narratives of oppressed people. Satya Mohanty, *Literary Theory and the Claims of History: Postmodernism, Objectivity, Multicultural Politics* (Ithaca: Cornell University Press, 1997).

6. Foucault, "What Is an Author?" 119.

7. "Chronological Bibliography of North American Slave Narratives," a segment of "Documenting the American South" (see note 2), lists 10 narratives in the 1830s, with a sharp rise to 25 slave narratives published in the 1840s, and 31 in the 1850s. James Olney discusses the standardization of form and content of slave narratives during the 1840s and 1850s in "'I Was Born': Slave Narratives and Their Status as Autobiography and Literature," in *The Slave Narrative*, ed. Charles T. Davis and Henry Louis Gates, Jr. (New York: Oxford University Press, 1985), 148. At present count, the 1850s produced seven African American novels or significantly fictionalized autobiographies: Frederick Douglass's *The Heroic Slave* (1853), William Wells Brown's *Clotel* (1853), Frank J. Webb's *The Garies and their Friends* (1857), Harriet Jacobs's, *Incidents in the Life of a Slave Girl* (written by 1858, published 1861), Martin R. Delany's *Blake; or the Huts of America* (1859–1862), Harriet Wilson's *Our Nig* (1859), and Hannah Crafts's *The Bondwoman's Narrative* (written between 1855 and 1860). For accounts of this turn toward fiction, see William L. Andrews, "The Novelization of Voice in Early African American Narrative," *PMLA* 105 (1990): 23–34; and Carla Peterson, "Capitalism, Black

(Under)development, and the Production of the African American Novel in the 1850s," *American Literary History* 4 (1992): 559–583.

8. William L. Andrews, *To Tell a Free Story: The First Century of Afro-American Autobiography* (Urbana: University of Illinois Press, 1986).

9. See, for example, Valerie Smith on Jacobs's use of the conventions of the sentimental novel, "Form and Ideology in Three Slave Narratives," *Self-Discovery and Authority in Afro-American Narrative* (Cambridge: Harvard University Press, 1987); and Jennifer Rae Greeson, "The 'Mysteries and Miseries' of North Carolina: New York City, Urban Gothic Fiction, and *Incidents in the Life of a Slave Girl*," *American Literature* 73 (2001): 277–309, on the relations between Jacobs's text and the urban gothic.

10. Peterson, "Production of the African American Novel in the 1850s," 579.

11. In his "Introduction" to *Our Nig*, Henry Louis Gates, Jr., discusses not only the absence of any reviews for this African American novel but also the comparative scarcity of reviews even in the black and abolitionist presses for William Wells Brown's *Clotel* or Martin R. Delany's *Blake*, a silence especially evident when compared to the wealth of reviews of slave narratives during these years. Harriet E. Wilson, *Our Nig; or, Sketches from the Life of a Free Black* (New York: Vintage Books, 1983), xxx. Also worth noting is the fact that of the five African American novels published during the 1850s, only *Our Nig* was published in book form in the United States, and that was at the expense of the author and resulted in extremely limited distribution and sales.

12. William Wells Brown, *Clotel; Or, The President's Daughter: A Narrative of Slave Life in the United States* (London: 1853), 224.

13. Andrews, "Novelization," 32.

14. Both Valerie Smith's *Self-Discovery and Authority in Afro-American Narrative* and Hazel V. Carby's *Reconstructing Womanhood: The Emergence of the Afro-American Woman Novelist* (New York: Oxford University Press, 1987) position slave narratives as originary texts for African American women novelists. The connection between narratives and later novels is even clearer in the case of male authors, where the same men produced both sorts of texts.

15. I have no external evidence for this hypothesis, but I do find many aspects of Crafts's text problematic as the work of a woman who had spent much of her life as a plantation slave. Crafts's general sense of isolation, the absence of marks of complex relation or deep ties to other African American slaves, especially in comparison to the extraordinary psychological nuance with which Crafts depicts relations between slave women and the white, or apparently white, women they serve, strikes me as similar to patterns found in other texts written by black women working as slaves or domestic servants above the Mason-Dixon Line (Harriet Wilson, Sojourner Truth, Elizabeth Keckley) and as markedly different from anything described by other slave women who had lived long in the plantation South. Other anomalies that support this view include Crafts's unusual attitude toward literacy (discussed below), the virulence of her repulsion from life in the slave quarters, and other small oddities like the "lime-tree walks" and "orange trees" that could not grow in North Carolina despite Gates's efforts to explain them away (198–199 and Gates's note 272). The skepticism of Justine Tally helped fuel my own. I want to thank, too, Jean Fagan Yellin for her willingness to hear out these doubts.

16. For a juxtaposition of this passage with Dickens's, a similarity first noted by Hollis Robbins, see 332. Robbins also detected the use of *Bleak House* in Crafts's descriptions of Washington, D.C., but there the similarities of Washington gloom and London fog along

these two cities' different rivers appear to me far more an instance of Crafts's glee at recognizing the fit of this description she had read with a city she knew well, rather than the use of her reading to fill a gap in her personal experience. Crafts's descriptions of life in the capital are dense with accurate local details (331–332).

17. See Janet Cornelius, "'We Slipped and Learned to Read': Slave Accounts of the Literacy Process, 1830–1865," *Phylon* 44 (1983): 171–186. Cornelius's data is derived from 3,428 slave narratives gathered by the WPA as well as 93 other slave narratives, interviews, and autobiographies that mention literacy acquisition. Of the ex-slaves whose testimonies are included in the WPA volume, she finds just over 5 percent learned to read as slaves (172). Her data also finds that although less than 4 percent of the slave population was urban, 16.5 percent of literate slaves lived in cities. A full three-quarters of those who learned to read as slaves did so while working as house servants (174–175). Slave manuscripts are very rare; most such documents are letters, and I know of none that demonstrates the kind of competence that one presumes Mrs. Wheeler would have wanted for her correspondence. For example, the letter Vilet Lester wrote to her former owner, in the hopes that her new master would be able to purchase her daughter, displays psychological nuance and linguistic sophistication not unlike Crafts's own. Lester's letter offers enormous insight into the complex dynamics and language of affection between slave and mistress, as well as instancing her sense of the elegant phrases and decorum required of letters, but it is also full of misspellings: "I wis him to buy her an my Boss being a man of Reason and fealing wishes to grant my trubled breast that mutch gratification and wishes to now whether he will Sell her now so I must come to a close by Enscribing my Self you long loved and well wishing play mate as a Servant until death" (Letter of Vilet Lester to Miss Patsey Patterson, August 29, 1857, Special Collections, Duke University Library).

18. Jane Johnson's testimony signed by her mark is included as "Appendix B," 320. However, Katherine E. Flynn's essay in this volume provides evidence that Johnson was in fact literate, in which case her use of a mark would suggest once again the generally guarded nature of slave literacy.

19. Frederick Douglass, *Narrative of the Life of Frederick Douglass, An American Slave, Written by Himself* (1845) in *The Frederick Douglass Reader*, ed. William L. Andrews (New York: Oxford University Press, 1996), 52.

20. Ibid., 48.

21. The particulars are very different, of course. Still, Crafts's attitude toward basic literacy skills reminds me of David Walker's scornful reply to the old man who claimed that his son "could write as well as any white man," "what else can your son do besides writing a good hand? . . . Can he write a neat piece of composition in prose or in verse? . . . did your son learn, while he was at school, the width and depth of English Grammar? To which he also replied in the negative, telling me that his son did not learn those things. Your son, said I, then, has hardly any learning at all." David Walker, *Appeal, to the Coloured Citizens of the World, But in Particular, and Very Expressly, to Those of the United States of America* (1831) (New York: Hill and Wang, 1994), 31.

22. For Douglass's account of learning to read, see chapters 6 and 7 of his *Narrative*; for Brown's, see the "Narrative of the Life and Escape of William Wells Brown" that prefaces the first edition of *Clotel*, 25–28. Harriet Jacobs presents her initiation into literacy as both easier and ultimately less self-affirming than these picaresque stratagems: her mistress taught her to read and spell as a young child, but "this privilege, which so rarely falls to the lot of a

slave," comes tainted with "injustice" and betrayal since this same mistress failed to set her free. *Incidents in The Life of a Slave Girl*, ed. Jean Fagan Yellin (Cambridge: Harvard University Press, 1987), 8.

23. Both passages quoted by Cornelius, "Slave Accounts of the Literacy Process"; she notes that only a few such atrocities would be sufficient "to establish a mythology about the dangers of reading and writing" (174). Crafts's only acknowledgment of the dangers of reading comes with her decision not to teach the slave children in her care since "I could not have even hoped to escape detection and discovery would have entailed punishment on all" (12). This position allows Hannah an unpunished access to literacy while denying similar knowledge to other slave children.

24. Kari J. Winter, *Subjects of Slavery, Agents of Change: Women and Power in Gothic Novels and Slave Narratives, 1790–1865* (Athens: University of Georgia Press, 1992) is the only book-length study I know to explore the relation between these two genres. See also the collection of critical essays, *Haunted Bodies: Gender and Southern Text*, edited by Anne Goodwyn Jones and Susan V. Donaldson (Charlottesville: University Press of Virginia, 1997); and Teresa Goddu, *Gothic America: Narrative, History, and Nation* (New York: Columbia University Press, 1997). For a classic account of the ideological uses of the gothic as an expression of female vulnerability, male coercion, and economic forces, see Mary Poovey, "Ideology and *The Mysteries of Udolpho*," *Criticism* 21 (1979): 307–330. Ruth Parkin-Gounelas, "Learning What We have Forgotten: Repetition as Remembrance in Early Nineteenth-Century Gothic," *European Romantic Review* 6 (1996): 213–226, describes the historical and psychic functions of gothic repetition. For the haunting of Simon Legree, see Harriet Beecher Stowe, *Uncle Tom's Cabin* (1852) (New York: Penguin, 1986), chapters 35 and 39.

25. Interestingly, this scene and most of the other gothic sequences in this book are associated with Lindendale, and Lindendale itself is a markedly "Old World" place. Not only was it founded by "Sir Clifford de Vincent, a nobleman of power and influence in the old world" (15), but even after the demise of the Vincents, its new owner, Cosgrove, marries "an English woman of aristocratic family and connections, and very high" (172) and with Mrs. Cosgrove's death the plantation once again becomes "haunted" (171). That is, Crafts seems to identify the gothic with Europe, enhancing its claim to high cultural, literary status.

26. See Saidiya V. Hartman on slave law's denial of the possibility of rape for slave women, and how this absence in the law often manifests itself in textual lacuna in the narratives of slave women. Saidiya V. Hartman, *Scenes of Subjugation: Terror, Slavery, and Self-Making in Nineteenth-Century America* (New York: Oxford University Press, 1997).

27. The continuing profit of reading race is exemplified by the sentence *The New Yorker* magazine picked to highlight as a caption for Gates's article on *The Bondwoman's Narrative*. They unerringly selected the moment in this early and condensed version of Gates's "Introduction" that most plays upon the self-authenticating quality of race detection: "The author writes as a keen insider, capturing the way black people talked to each other when white auditors were not around, and not as abolitionists thought they did." If Crafts's blackness allows her to recreate how black people really talked, it is Gates's blackness that enables him to verify this act for *The New Yorker's* still predominantly white readership. *The New Yorker*, February 18 and 25, 2002: 105. See also the slightly more cautious version of this point in Gates's "Introduction" (xxiv). At such moments it is jarring to remember that it was Gates himself who most powerfully argued in the 1980s that race is a construction best evoked in quotation marks. See Henry Louis Gates, Jr., ed., *"Race" Writing and Difference* (Chicago: University of

Chicago Press, 1986), and *Figures in Black: Words, Signs, and the "Racial" Self* (New York: Oxford University Press, 1987).

28. Gabrielle Foreman, "Who's Your Mama? 'White' Mulatta Genealogies, Early Photography, and Anti-Passing Narratives of Slavery and Freedom," *American Literary History* 14 (Fall 2002): 508–509.

29. See Nell Irvin Painter, "Three Southern Women and Freud: A Non-Exceptionalist Approach to Race, Class, and Gender in the Slave South," in *Feminists Revision History*, ed. Ann-Louise Shapiro (New Brunswick: Rutgers University Press, 1994): 195–216, for an extraordinarily balanced account of the sexual dynamics within plantation households: "families and societies cannot designate and thereby set apart one category of women as victims. The victimization spreads, in different ways and to different degrees. But where historians have been prone to construe southern family relations within watertight racial categories, the stories [of individual southern women, white and black] pose complicated new questions whose answers do not stop at the color line."

The psychological nuance and detail of Crafts's many portraits of slave mistresses attest to her sense of this entanglement and the heavy costs that slavery extracts from the lives of white women as well as black. Besides Hannah herself, Crafts's depictions of Mrs. Vincent, Mrs. Wright, Mrs. Henry, Mrs. Cosgrove, and Mrs. Wheeler are decidedly the richest characterizations in this book, and they are strikingly different from each other. Ruth Stoner and the Forschungs-Colloquium in Berlin pressed me to think more seriously about the possibility of Hannah Crafts being a white woman, and the sophistication of these many portraits would offer the strongest evidence for such a position. Yet beneath even the most sympathetic of these depictions runs an edge of critique, even vindictiveness, that I find hard to reconcile with such a view. If Hannah Crafts is a mid-nineteenth-century white woman, then she is an extraordinary one not only, as Gates notes, for her unusual lack of prejudice in her approach to black characters but also for the powerful conviction of inherent culpability that informs her approach to even the kindliest of white characters. I find it more compelling to think about the ways that these portrayals depict the racial porosity of suffering under the peculiar institution, the impossibility of maintaining Painter's "watertight racial categories."

17

Trappe(d)
Race and Genealogical Haunting in
The Bondwoman's Narrative

ROBERT S. LEVINE

Near the beginning of *Moby-Dick*, the greenhorn Ishmael, having arrived in New Bedford at night, goes in search of lodgings. Wandering through the "gloom," he eventually comes to the lighted building of "The Trap," "the door of which stood invitingly open." He walks through the door, finds nothing, and "pushed on and opened a second, interior door." He describes what he discovers therein:

> It seemed the great Black Parliament sitting in Tophet. A hundred black faces turned round in their rows to peer; and beyond, a black Angel of Doom was beating a book in a pulpit. It was a negro church; and the preacher's text was about the blackness of darkness, and the weeping and wailing and teeth-gnashing there. Ha, Ishmael, muttered I, backing out, Wretched entertainment at the sign of "The Trap!"[1]

Ishmael discovers "blackness" by penetrating the interiors of an inviting building, and shocked by what he finds, he retreats. The white man does not want to be trapped by "The Trap." Of course Ishmael's recoil here, his determination to hold onto his whiteness, is part of Melville's comic strategy, for immediately following this scene Ishmael sleeps with a cannibal whose face "was of a dark, purplish, yellow color . . . with large, blackish looking squares," and greenhorn no longer, he famously declares: "Better sleep with a sober cannibal than a drunken Christian."[2] Conflating and relativizing (white) Christian and (blackish) cannibal, Ishmael moves us past the anxious racial binary and dichotomy of the encounter with "The Trap." As is consistent with the treatment of race from *Typee* (1846) through *The Confidence-Man* (1857), Melville in *Moby-Dick* ultimately works to display the fluidity of race, even as he conveys his own white anxieties about an identity-threatening racial instability.[3]

Though the scene at "The Trap" is a relatively minor one in *Moby-Dick*, it can be taken as paradigmatic of a significant motif, or trope, of antebellum writings of the 1850s: the ironically presented disclosure of a hidden blackness that poses a threat to whiteness. Ishmael makes his fearful discovery by entering a public building. But the far more trenchant disclosure is generally figured in terms of a house, such as the house of Glendinning in Melville's *Pierre* (1852), the post-Monticello house of Jefferson in William Wells Brown's *Clotel* (1853), the house of Gordon in Harriet Beecher Stowe's *Dred* (1856), and the house of Garie in Frank J. Webb's *The Garies and Their Friends* (1857), among many others. What unifies all of these "white" houses is that they are both physical structures and genealogical houses that are revealed to have "blackness" within. Melville's *Pierre*, among the most powerful of these fictions, subtly hints at that blackness by raising questions about the fathers. The young man Pierre, who comes from a family with a "pride of purity" in its heroic Revolutionary pedigree, discovers that his father may have had a daughter out of wedlock who may well be black, just as Pierre's grandfather, a Revolutionary hero, may have had sexual relations with his slaves. Thus Pierre comes to fear that the "dark, dark, dark" woman to whom he is attracted may be his sister. To the very end, Pierre remains uncertain of his identity, haunted as he is by the "blackenings" within the house of Glendinning.[4]

In numerous genealogical fictions of the period, the author's account of cross-racial entanglement underscores the ludicrousness of understanding a nation's identity and ideologies in relation to a foundational fiction of pure whiteness. In *Clotel*, for example, Brown provides a comic anecdote about Daniel Webster's difficulty in obtaining accommodations because his "dark features" led a landlord "to suppose him a *coloured man*."[5] In the larger context of the genealogical history of Brown's novel, which exposes the connections between Thomas Jefferson's "fathering" of a nation and his fathering of slaves whose apparent "whiteness" allows them and their children, for a while at least, to lay claim to American whiteness and freedom, the landlord's misidentification of Webster's "race" may not have been a misidentification after all.[6] For one of the questions raised by Brown's *Clotel*, Melville's *Pierre*, Stowe's antislavery novels, Webb's *Garies*, Harriet Jacobs's *Incidents in the Life of a Slave Girl* (1861), and many other genealogical fictions of the period is this: Just how stable is the whiteness claimed by the Revolutionary fathers and their ac-

knowledged (and unacknowledged) descendants in light of the nation's misce-
genated past?[7]

Among the many values of Henry Louis Gates's recent recuperation of
Hannah Crafts's fascinating unpublished novel, *The Bondwoman's Narrative*, is to
remind us anew of the shaping impact and dehumanizing force of racial categories in the pre–Civil War United States and to provide us with a text that
has the potential to offer new insights into racial representations and formations of the period. During the 1850s in particular, juridical and scientific
conceptions of racial difference contributed to the oppressions of the Fugitive Slave Law and the Dred Scott ruling, to an intensifying antiblack racism
in the North and a redoubled commitment to slavery in the South, and to an
escalating sectional violence in the Kansas and Nebraska territories and elsewhere. Genealogical fictions like *Clotel* and *Garies* posed a challenge to such
racial reifications and their attendant politics, as did numerous other such fictions of the period, even works like Hawthorne's *The House of the Seven Gables*
(1851) and Melville's *Pierre*, novels that are not immediately thought of in relation to debates on slavery and race. But as Teresa Goddu has argued, questions about slavery, race, and genealogy have always been at the center of what
she describes as the gothic tradition of the American romance, a tradition that
appropriated a central trope of the Continental version of the gothic—the
twisted genealogical lines materialized in the twisting passages of the castle—
as a way of revealing how "the ghosts of America's racial history" continue to
haunt the present. Haunted by the past, Hawthorne explores in *House* the futility of Colonel Pyncheon's project of planting a family that had "his race
and future generations fixed on a stable basis," and he addresses themes that
one wouldn't expect of a staunch Democrat, such as the immorality of master-slave relationships and, in the figures of Judge Pyncheon and Chanticleer,
the absurdity of making pretensions to racial superiority and purity. Goddu
argues that when African American writers worked with gothic modes during
the 1850s, they took a very different perspective from Hawthorne and other
"haunted" white genealogical romancers, for they could choose to "haunt
back."[8] I will be suggesting in this essay that there is no reason to believe that
African American writers couldn't be haunted by race as well.

Most likely written during the mid-1850s, Crafts's *The Bondwoman's Narrative*
shares many of the gothic tropes and unmasking strategies of Melville's *Pierre*
and Hawthorne's *House* and also the genealogical/racial/gothic tropes and
motifs one finds in much antislavery writing of the period, such as Stowe's
Uncle Tom's Cabin and *Dred*, Brown's *Clotel*, Webb's *Garies*, and Jacobs's *Incidents*.
My claim is not that Crafts read and was responding to all of these novels,
though Gates and others have established that Crafts was a wide reader who

was inspired by at least one British genealogical fiction, Dickens's *Bleak House.*[9] It seems probable that she knew Stowe's writings, and I will be considering the specific influence of Hawthorne. But my larger claim is that Crafts knew the contemporary debates on slavery and race and was attempting to make a critical intervention with her novel. My reading of *The Bondwoman's Narrative* will be addressing Crafts's representation of racial genealogies, focusing on the character of Trappe as the novel's principal figure of genealogical disclosure. Trappe exposes the "blackness" in seemingly "white" characters and their houses by studying genealogies. As a scholar-type who holds a sadistic power over such characters, he is clearly modeled on Chillingworth, and I will comment further on the parallels below. But what I find particularly interesting about Trappe is the threat he poses to whites who don't think of themselves as passing or as having entered a house of blackness. I will be arguing that Crafts presents Trappe as a figure of terror in white supremacist culture: he points to the instability, fluidity, and uncertainty of a culture that bases itself on the racial dichotomy and binary emblematized in *Moby-Dick*'s "The Trap." Near the end of the essay I will be addressing Crafts's own anxious relation to both Trappe and what he represents.

Trappe is introduced into the novel at a crucial genealogical moment, when the current master of the Lindendale plantation, where Hannah is a house slave, brings his new bride home. (Neither the master nor mistress are ever given names; and because the character Hannah is only called Hannah, I will use "Hannah" when I am emphasizing the role of the character and "Crafts" when I am emphasizing the role of the writer who created "Hannah.") A long-standing bachelor, the master hopes now to be able to produce an heir for Lindendale, a plantation that goes back a number of generations. It is arguably for this reason, then, that Hannah finds herself perpetually studying her new mistress, but she finds herself equally engaged by Trappe, the old man who seems always to accompany the lady of the house, "a rusty seedy old-fashioned gentleman with thin grey locks . . . and great black eyes so keen and piercing that you shrank involuntarily from their gaze."[10] Moving her gaze between the mistress and the old man, Hannah discerns a disturbing connection between them: "I arrived at the conclusion that each one watched and suspected the other, that each one was conscious of some great and important secret on the part of the other" (28).

Whatever those secrets might be, it is clear that Trappe's knowledge of his mistress's secret has given him a power over her similar to Chillingworth's power over Dimmesdale. The numerous parallels between Trappe and Chillingworth suggest that Crafts turned to *The Scarlet Letter* as a model for her representation of the sadistic uses of hidden knowledge. Like Chillingworth, who eventually moves in with Dimmesdale, Trappe, we learn, used his knowledge of his mistress (and her deceased father) to become part of the household as she was growing up and plans to continue to be part of the household at Lindendale. Also like Chillingworth, Trappe is an elderly scholar who is most at home among "books and papers" (35), who has been spurned by a younger woman, and who seems driven by sadistic desires for revenge. Hawthorne describes Chillingworth as "delving among [Dimmesdale's] principles, prying into his recollections, and probing every thing with a cautious touch, like a treasure-seeker in a dark cavern."[11] Crafts describes Trappe similarly as having "spent his life in hunting, delving, and digging into family secrets, and when he has found them out he becomes ravenous for gold" (45). But what are those secrets, and how intent is he on "gold" as opposed to "treasure"?

The mistress's secret, almost immediately apparent, is that she is "black," which would mean that should she successfully pass as white and produce an heir, the genealogical house of Lindendale, like the genealogical house of Melville's Glendinnings, would by the culture's definition of such matters be blackened. We discern her secret through Hannah, who observes that the mistress has "a profusion of wavy curly hair, large bright eyes, and delicate features with the exception of her lips which were too large, full, and red" (27). Having described herself as a woman who looks white to the eye but whose "African blood" gave "a wave and curl to my hair" (6), Hannah, without quite realizing it, has in effect discovered through the "wavy curly hair" and other physical characteristics of her white-complected mistress a racial sister. In the meantime, she makes her own efforts to plumb Trappe's secret, and quickly learns from the mistress's slave/maid, the quadroon Lizzy, that he is a wealthy lawyer who had assumed guardianship of the mistress ten years earlier based on his discovery in the father's papers of "some important secret" (34). Hannah thus concludes that the mistress chose to marry the master in an effort to escape Trappe, "the shadow darkening her life" (34).

That shadow, of course, is the shadow of race. After eavesdropping on Trappe as he blackmails the mistress, Hannah offers her sympathy to the distraught woman, who then reveals her secret. According to the mistress, at the time of her birth there were parallel black and white female births at the plantation, and that when the white infant died, the black nurse took the newly born "black" baby girl and put her "by her lady's side, when that Lady was to[o] weak and sick and delirious to notice that the dead was exchanged for the living" (44). Such was the entanglement of white and black families that no one really noticed the switch, not even the father, though somehow Trappe discovered what had happened by studying family papers around the time of the father's death. Trappe eventually revealed the secret of her birth to the mistress when she refused his proposal of marriage, offering as his evidence a portrait of a slave named Susan whom the mistress views as an image of herself, even "though I have never sate [sat] for my likeness to be taken" (47). Just as Phoebe in Hawthorne's *House* sees in a portrait of Colonel Pyncheon the congruent identities of the founder of the Pyncheon house and his descendant Judge Jaffrey Pyncheon, the mistress sees in the portrait of Susan her genealogical connection to a slave and realizes that she is under Trappe's control. Finding community with Hannah through the sharing of secrets, the mistress agrees to take flight with her as fugitive slaves, a flight which, as with the fugitive slaves in *Uncle Tom's Cabin*, is enabled by the light complexions bequeathed by their slave-owner fathers and enslaved mulatto mothers.

The attempted flight of Hannah and the mistress from the scrutinizing eye of Trappe parallels the attempted flight of Hester and Dimmesdale from Chillingworth. The Hester-Dimmesdale parallel also speaks to an erotic connection between the two women, as the mistress exchanges a husband for a black woman she regards as a sister. But as in *The Scarlet Letter*, escape is impossible because Trappe knows his victims and anticipates their every move (as Chillingworth knows to book passage with the Spanish vessel that Dimmesdale and Hester had planned to take to Europe). Hannah and the mistress first make their way to the home of a benevolent man and woman with antislavery predilections, only to find that Trappe is the woman's brother and that he is watching them from the next room, "dogging our footsteps, and . . . haunting us everywhere" (63). The women next hide out at a cabin, the site of a former massacre, but Trappe, with the help of slave catchers, eventually tracks them down and gets them under his legal control. The mistress makes her final escape from Trappe in the same way that Dimmesdale escapes from Chillingworth, through a dramatic, willed death that is portrayed as a form of victory: "A gleam of satisfaction shone over her face. There was a gasp, a struggle, a slight shiver of the limbs and she was free" (100).

Just before the mistress's death, when he believes he still has power over her, Trappe reveals his motives and worldview in clear and chilling language. Rationalizing what may appear to some as his evil desires to make money from others' misery, he argues, in effect, that there is no morality, just "conditions" and situations, and that he was a "victim of circumstances" in having by "accident" discovered the secret "that made me acquainted with your lineage" (97). Insisting on his haphazard acquisition of the mistress's secret, he then contradictorily asserts that the discovery of such "accidents" has become his vocation: "You are not the first fair dame whose descent I have traced back— far back to a sable son of Africa . . . Many and many are the family secrets that I have unraveled as women unravel a web. You may think of it as you please, you may call it dishonorable if you like, but it brings gold—bright gold" (98). And yet he identifies as his main motivation, as least in the case of the mistress, not economics but the vengeful sadistic power vouchsafed by the knowledge of her racial antecedents: "I wished to see you humbled at my feet as I had been at yours. I wished you feel yourself standing on the brink of a precipice, and know that my hand could thrust you down to a certain destruction, or pluck you back to safety" (99). Her willed death thus deprives him of something more valuable to him than gold.

In the haunting Trappe, then, there is a disturbing mix of sadistic will to power, knowledge, and greed. As a "black" man in white culture, he himself seems haunted, and there are suggestions in the repeated mentions of his "keen black eyes" (63) and black clothes that his knowledge of racial entanglement is a form of self-knowledge, that he knows whereof he speaks. (In this regard, it should be underscored that despite his knowledge of the mistress's "blackness," he was prepared to marry her.) In her portrayal of Trappe, Crafts ultimately presents him as a figure of terror, as someone who threatens to reveal to white culture that which it already knows about itself and strives to suppress: that "[m]any and many are the family secrets" that the genealogical seeker can "unravel." Nowhere is the tension between knowledge and suppression more apparent than in the opening chapters describing the founding of the house of Lindendale—the very house that Trappe would seem to have successfully preserved in all its white racial purity.

Prior to the actual arrival of Trappe and the bridal party at Lindendale, Crafts describes the founding of the house both as physical structure and genealogical house. The two foundings actually go hand in hand, for the founding patriarch, Sir Clifford De Vincent, had ordered that his and his wife's portraits be hung in the mansion's main drawing room and "denounced a severe malediction against the person who should ever presume to remove them, and against any possessor of the mansion who being of his name and blood should neglect to follow his example" (15). Insisting upon a conjunction of name and blood, Clifford wants the display of husbands and wives to attest to the untroubled transmission of the founder's avowedly white blood through successive generations. His wishes are fulfilled, for "each inheritor had contributed to the adornments of the drawing-room a faithful transcript of his person and lineaments, side by side with that of his Lady" (16). As in Hawthorne's *House*, in which the Pyncheons make use of portraits to insist upon their genealogical distinction from the "blacker" Maules, Clifford similarly aspires to use portraits to insist upon his family's genealogical distinction from the blacks with whom (it quickly becomes clear) they are inextricably entangled.[12] Hannah's description of a representative mother/bride underscores the cultural work performed by the gallery: "Over the pale pure features of a bride descends a halo of glory; the long shining locks of a young mother waver and float over the child she holds" (16).

And yet as she describes the portrait gallery's visual proclamation of a "pure" whiteness, Hannah takes note of a "shadow flitting past through the gloom" (15) of the portrait gallery. To be sure, most of the vividly depicted patriarchs and their ladies are dead, which necessarily imparts a "haunting air" (16) to the room. But Hannah implies more than the mere fact of death. Describing herself as "standing face to face with their pictured resemblances and looking into the stony eyes motionless and void of expression as those of an exhumed corpse" (16), she seems on the verge of some sort of interpretive penetration before she is interrupted by the white housekeeper, Mrs. Bry, who brusquely asks what she is doing in the gallery. "Looking at the pictures" (17), Hannah declares, to which Mrs. Bry replies: "as if such an ignorant thing as you are would know any thing about them" (17).

But as we learn in the subsequent chapter, she *does* know something more about them, for the portrait gallery of Lindendale is not the only site at or near the house that marks family genealogy. The family tree, the linden planted by Sir Clifford when he founded the house of Lindendale, also invokes that history, but from the very different perspective of the slaves. "What tangled skeins are the genealogies of slavery!" Harriet Jacobs exclaims in *Incidents in the Life of a Slave Girl*.[13] And it is precisely such a tangled history of entanglement that Hannah has full access to, and it is this history, we realize, that had prompted her to attempt to discern in the portraits an alternative history of origins and transmission from that vouchsafed by the paired white portraits in the gallery.

That history is of the violent entanglement of master and slave, a violence that speaks not only to the physical cruelty of the master but also to the tenuous basis of the master's white house. As in Hawthorne's *House,* there are two genealogical lines—in this case the white masters and black slaves—that have become entangled because of the "sins of the fathers" (43). The story is simple: At around the same time that Sir Clifford established his portrait gallery, he tied the elderly slave Rose and her beloved dog to the linden tree because Rose had refused to drown her dog. After six horrible days of suffering, both Rose and her dog die. The story of Sir Clifford's torture-murder of Rose is as much a primal first "portrait" of the genealogical house/tree as the idealized portraits in the mansion's gallery. Significantly, Hannah reveals that though the portrait gallery tells the family history to the public, it is the linden that tells the family history to the slaves: "The servants all knew the history of that tree" (20). And the story is not so simple after all.

As in the harrowing accounts of the master's beating of Aunt Hester in Frederick Douglass's *Narrative* and Cassy's tangled sexual history in *Uncle Tom's Cabin,* Crafts suggests a close connection between the master's physical and sexual violence against slave women, a violence that casts its shadow over the whiteness of the family tree. According to the narrator, the linden, literally the family tree, "had its roots . . . manured with human blood. Slaves had been tied to its trunk" (20). The suggestive talk of black blood mixing with the family tree points to the sexually violative nature of the entanglement between Clifford and Rose. Rose had been the nurse of Clifford's son, hinting at her possible maternal relation, and she herself had had a daughter, hinting at Clifford's possible paternal relation (see the discussion of the Cosgroves below). When the daughter becomes older, she is sold into slavery in Alabama, and the aggrieved Rose attaches herself to the dog that had been her daughter's pet, with the dog becoming "to her what a grandchild is to many aged females" (22). We can read Clifford's order that she drown her "grandchild" as suggesting the possibility that Sir Clifford had raped not only Rose but also her daughter, thereby producing a granddaughter that Clifford or his wife would have killed at birth to preserve the genealogical purity of the house. Crafts's designation of the dog as grandchild metaphorically points to the possibility of the intermingling of blood at the house of Lindendale while not insisting on its literal truth. Refusing to drown her "grandchild," Rose is forcibly attached to the tree: "An iron hoop being fastened around the body of Rose she was drawn to the tree, and with great labor elevated and secured to one of the largest limbs" (23). The dog, too, is attached to the tree, suspended from a branch beyond Rose's reach. In refusing to drown the dog, Rose makes herself and the dog permanently part of the tree, as their blood is drawn into its roots.

In Hawthorne's *House,* Matthew Maule, just before his execution, proclaims about Colonel Pyncheon (and by implication the house of Pyncheon): "God will give him blood to drink!"[14] And indeed the Colonel and subsequent generations "drink" blood, regularly dying from unexplained sudden deaths involving apoplectic seizures. Rose makes a similar curse on Clifford's genealogical house just before her execution: "I will hang here till I die as a curse to this house, and I will come here after I am dead to prove its bane" (25). Blood is important to this curse as well, for arguably Rose "appears" as the blood that remains veiled by the portraits, the blood that Trappe discerns coming from outside the house of Lindendale in the form of the proposed new mistress, the blood that streams from the master's "ghastly wound in his throat" (74) when he learns from Trappe that his wife is black, and the blood that will be revealed as permeating the house of Lindendale in the later account of the Cosgroves.

Before turning to the Cosgroves, however, it would be useful to consider the intervening account of the Wheelers in Washington, D.C., which, precisely because of its setting in the federal city, presents a more fully national vision of racial haunting and instability. As with William Wells Brown's presentation of Thomas Jefferson's "black" children and of "black" Daniel Webster, Crafts uses the scenes between Hannah and her new North Carolina master and mistress to challenge national ideological formations that have whiteness at their center. Describing Washington, Crafts emphasizes the muddiness of the place, and the recurrent image of mud indicates the difficulty of making (racial) distinctions, or perhaps more literally is a sign of something much darker than whiteness. It is significant that Hannah observes Trappe in Washington watching over the nation's capital in his "coat of seedy black" (158), and doubly significant, or ironic, that their encounter should occur shortly after Hannah purchases a whitening powder for Mrs. Wheeler (as if Trappe, in watching over the scene, somehow knows much better about "whiteness"). That powder provides one of the fine comical moments in the novel. Like the white women on display in the Lindendale portrait gallery, the white women of the District, as described by Crafts, are obsessed with displaying the purity of their whiteness. The current rage among fashionable women is for a powder that promises to do away with all facial markings that might even hint at blackness: "Tan, or freckless [freckles], or wrinkles, or other unseemly blotches would simultaneously disappear" (158). Mrs. Wheeler applies the "very fine, soft, and white" (165) powder before visiting with a government administrator to appeal for a civil service position for her husband. She returns a transformed woman. Hannah remarks: "the servant admitted a lady, who came directly to Mrs. Wheeler's apartment. I was greatly surprised; for though the vail, the bonnet, and the dress were those of that lady, or exactly similar, the face was black" (165). Or as Mr. Wheeler more directly puts it to his wife: "Your face is black as Tophet" (166).

This scene is strikingly similar to the scene in Frank Webb's *The Garies and Their Friends* (1857) when the racist George Stevens, after being tarred by street toughs of a fire company, is subjected to racist ridicule by those who fail to recognize him as a white man. The reader wants Stevens to learn from his sufferings about the hardships facing blacks, but instead he washes off the tar and remains resolved to foment a murderous riot in black neighborhoods. Similarly, the reader wants the racist Mrs. Wheeler to gain some sympathetic wisdom from what Crafts in the chapter title calls "A Turn of the Wheel" (157). But instead of gaining new insights into the arbitrariness of race and the hurtfulness of racism, she redoubles her efforts to assert her whiteness, choosing to return with her husband to their slave plantation in North Carolina until the nasty gossip about the Wheelers' racial identity comes to an end. The Wheelers' white contemporaries seem particularly annoyed that Mrs. Wheeler's act of requesting a job in blackface displayed the too easy transformation of "white" into "black," as if she threatened to make all of the District's whites into blacks. Their disapproval is voiced most publicly when an "eminent divine in a fashionable sermon held forth for two whole hours on the sin and wickedness of wantonly disguising the form or features" (169).

Unsurprisingly, Mrs. Wheeler seeks an easy, non-Trappe-like explanation of her racial "transformation," which is supplied by Hannah, who remarks that she had read about a chemist who had taken revenge on a woman who jilted him by creating a powder that would "blacken the whitest skin" (167). Angered that Hannah failed to warn her about the powder, Mrs. Wheeler lashes out at her slave, only to find her husband rushing to Hannah's defense. Furious, Mrs. Wheeler states: "Slaves generally are far preferable to wives in husbands' eyes" (167). If that is the case (and that is the suggestion of the novel's emphasis on the genealogical haunting at Lindendale), then over time "white" and "black" will lose their distinctive biological meanings, and the ideological defense of slavery and the ideological concept of the United States as a white nation simply will not make sense. That is the implication of the story that the Lindendale's house slave Lizzy subsequently tells Hannah when she meets with her in Washington.

According to Lizzy, the current master and owner of Lindendale, Cosgrove, is "haunted" (171), and indeed he is, for he feels responsible for having killed his wife. But the person in the story who is most haunted is Cosgrove's English aristocratic wife, proud of what she would like to believe is the pure white "English and aristocratic blood in her veins" (175). In *Pierre*, Melville shows great comic resourcefulness in undermining notions of the supposedly pure, heroic, and known English genealogies of royalty and aristocracy, reminding his readers of the genealogical branches extending back to "the thief knights of the Norman" and coursing off from Charles II and his mistress Nell Gwynne. In a key genealogical chapter in *Dred*, "The Gordon Family," Stowe describes the line running from the founder, "Thomas Gordon, Knight, a distant offshoot of the noble Gordon family, renowned in Scottish history," to Colonel Gordon, father of two "white" children and the "black" slave who is overseeing the plantation.[15] *The Bondwoman's Narrative* conveys a similar skepticism about the purity of "aristocrat blood"; for what the maddened Mrs. Cosgrove finds everywhere in the house of Lindendale, as she begins to explore "its remotest corners" (179), are shadowy secrets: white-to-the-eye children whose genealogies link them to white-to-the-eye slave mothers and Cosgrove. After discovering one group of "white" slave women and children residing in the house, she finds at the end of another winding hall another closed door, behind which are "two boys, with round fat cheeks, great blue eyes, and plump little hands, quite as beautiful and fresh and healthy as if the most favored lady in the land had been their mother" (182). But of course these children too are the issue of Cosgrove's sexual violation of a lightly com- plected slave woman. Such "white" children are ubiquitous in the house, and the phrase "favored lady" ironically undercuts Mrs. Cosgrove's conception of her own lady-like racial purity.

In an oddly sentimental conclusion to the story, we learn that Mrs. Cos- grove's effort to rid her house of blackness by expelling this particular slave woman and her children results in a violent encounter with her husband that leaves her seriously injured. Shortly afterward, she discovers religion and for- gives her husband, and there is a reconciliation between the two (the apparent whites of the house) before she dies from her injuries. But the reconciliation cannot hide the truth that this genealogical house has failed to achieve the vi- sion of its founder. Accordingly, the linden is cut down, the house is rebuilt from within, and the portrait of Sir Clifford is sold at auction.

As Mrs. Cosgrove explored the hidden hallways and rooms of Lindendale, the question of whether she would be able to find any whites in her house seemed to have driven her mad. Her explorations of her house, which com- plement Trappe's genealogical investigations, implicitly raise the question of whether there are any "whites" to be found in the South. That is precisely the white racial anxiety informing the account of Trappe's death near the end of the novel. Hannah hears the story of his "violent death and assassination" (232) aboard a steamboat that is taking her, a fugitive slave, from the South to New Jersey. It should be emphasized, then, that the male passengers who are talking about Trappe are not abolitionists but rather slave sympathizers and slave traders. Earlier in the novel, the slave trader Saddler had said of Trappe that he "has no more feeling than a bit of iron" (112) and that he "cannot be considered a slave-trader, yet his business is quite essential to trade" (113). Similarly, the traders on the steamer regard Trappe, and not themselves, as having "no principle" (232). Why?

The answer, I think, is contained in the vitriolic remarks of one of the slave traders on the steamboat: "[H]e would not have hesitated a moment to sell his own mother into slavery could the case have been made clear that she had African blood in her veins. No blood-hound was ever keener in scenting out the African taint than that old man" (232). The image of the genealogical in- vestigator as "blood-hound" is wonderful here, given that the novel also por- trays actual bloodhounds in pursuit of fugitive slaves. As a bookish, Chilling- worth-like bloodhound, Trappe pursues fugitives not through swamps, rivers, and forests but through paper trails of blood. He pursues, as Saddler had earlier noted, by "prying into secrets, and watching his chance" (113). Crucially, the fugitives he pursues by uncovering their secrets are always "white." The implied concern of the slave traders on the steamboat is that Trappe could have sold his own mother—or any other white southern mother—into slavery, because someone as skillful as he in genealogical history could well have found the papers that would have raised questions about the mother's (and all white mothers') racial identity. In the world of Trappe, no "white" is safe.

But Trappe's world is also the world of the United States more generally—and this truth is suggested by the account overheard by Hannah of the last genealogical pursuit of this bloodhound. Following the death of a wealthy planter, Trappe, governed by his knowledge that the planter's wife was his former slave, hides the papers that would have emancipated the wife and children who, like the slave master's children in Webb's *Garies* and Frances Harper's *Iola Leroy* (1892), believed that they were white. Trappe then reveals the "true" racial identity of these "whites" and consigns them to the slave market, purchasing the females with his usual speculative aims. The sons and brothers subsequently take revenge: One of the males shoots Trappe in the brain, and the tale-tellers and audience on the steamboat clearly approve. No longer do they need to fear that Trappe will visit their houses! Well that they should have been concerned, for *The Bondwoman's Narrative* has failed to provide us with one convincing instance of a racially pure family. The destabilizing work of Trappe and Crafts would seem to go hand in hand.

In this respect, it is ironic that while Hannah presents various women with whom she experiences a sense of solidarity, the character she most resembles in the novel is Trappe. Like Trappe, she has "a silent unobtrusive way of observing things and events, and wishing to understand them better than I could" (5). Like Trappe, she watches over characters as she attempts to make sense of their (racial) identities, and she experiences a certain gratification in the powers of surveillance. Hannah presents herself as someone who needs to use the tools of a Trappe to resist his traps. But even apart from Trappe, she reveals herself as someone who takes great pleasure in uncovering the secrets of others. During her short stay with the Henry family, for example, she becomes obsessed with watching the behavior of the newly betrothed slaves Charlotte and William, convinced that William, who lives on another plantation, has been visiting the house at night. She wants to know more: "I determined at once to fathom the mystery" (134). She secretly follows Charlotte, admitting to her readers that she never asked herself "by what right I presumed to interfere with the secrets of a house where I was myself admitted only by tolerance" (134), even as she felt unease at "the use, or necessity, or even the expediency of my instituting an espionage on the actions of one every way my equal, perhaps my superior" (136). When she finds that Charlotte is harboring the escaped William, she reveals the information to Mrs. Henry, despite her "conscience of cruelty and wrong" (136) in betraying these slaves. It is the antislavery slave-owner Mrs. Henry who decides not to meddle; and it is Hannah who seems cruel when she rejects Charlotte and William's appeal to join them in their escape.

Attempting to present herself as anything but cruel, Hannah regularly announces the importance of religion to her character, and her ability to experience, as she puts it, "a manner of sympathy and consideration for every one" (11). But the power of sympathy, even at its most benevolent, is also somewhat Trappe-like, based as it is on the sympathizer's assumption that by virtue of a superior kind of imagination he or she can know the other.[16] Moreover, as we have seen in the case of Charlotte and William, there are limits to Hannah's sympathy. Hannah's most disturbing failure of sympathy, I would argue, comes near the end of the novel when Mrs. Wheeler banishes her from the plantation house and forces her to live with the field slaves. Anxieties that one could so readily fall from white privilege to black "degradation" are shared by many of the white characters of the novel, and to a certain extent by Hannah as well. The question I would pose, then, against the grain of Henry Louis Gates's heroic research efforts to establish the former-slave status of Hannah Crafts, is why would such fears be so central to the authorial work of the "black" Crafts? A close look at the account of Hannah's interactions with the field slaves is in order.

When the Wheelers return to their North Carolina plantation from Washington, D.C., Hannah confronts head-on the putatively large gap between house and field slaves. The field slaves, she says, live among "fetid straw," "toil beneath the burning sun, scarcely conscious that any link exists between themselves and other portions of the human race," and possess a "mental condition" that can be "briefly summed up in the phrase that they know nothing" (200). She asserts that house slaves, by contrast, are "of a higher and nobler order than those belonging to the fields" (202). Such a sharp distinction between field and house slaves has no precedent that I know of in antebellum African American writing. Douglass, Brown, Delany, and Jacobs all acknowledge the differences between field and house slaves, but as with Douglass's accounts in the *Narrative* and *My Bondage and My Freedom* of the expressive power of the slave spirituals, or Brown's portrayal of the seemingly white-obsessed Sam singing a joyous song at the death of his white master, they also locate a revolutionary and communitarian spirit in those slaves. Like Douglass and many other antislavery writers, Crafts allows that "[d]egradation, neglect, and ill treatment had wrought on them [the field slaves] its legitimate effects" (200), but her insistence on such absolute differences between the two groups of slaves is relatively extreme. Hannah never expresses her revulsion at black field slaves quite so powerfully as when Mrs. Wheeler vindictively expels her from the house and declares that she will become the wife of the field slave Bill. Hannah describes herself as experiencing "horror unspeakable" at the thought of being "doomed to association with the vile, foul, filthy inhabitants of the huts, and condemned to receive one of them for my husband" (205).

Hannah's expression of revulsion at the field slaves will no doubt become one of the critical cruxes of *The Bondwoman's Narrative*. As Gates remarks somewhat defensively in his introduction to the novel, the revulsion makes good sense in terms of class and gender issues. Hannah expresses special revulsion at the prospect of "marriage" to Bill, asserting that marriage should be "voluntarily assumed" (205). An involuntary marriage prescribed by a slave-owner, Gates rightly notes, would constitute a form of rape, and he concludes about this scene: "Rarely, if ever, in the literature created by ex-slaves has the prospect of rape, and the gap in living conditions between house and field, been put more explicitly and squarely."[17] But I wonder if that gap hasn't also been put unrealistically and melodramatically to the service of Crafts's own racial anxieties. Given that the novel has heretofore focused on a history of white masters raping their slaves, why hadn't Hannah expressed revulsion or fear at the prospect of one of her white owners sexually violating her? Does she regard a black rapist as worse than a white rapist? Or perhaps that is not really the main issue here. For having made her point about the forcible nature of the marriage, Crafts nonetheless has Hannah describe the situation at Bill's cabin in language that deflects attention onto other matters as well. The paragraph is worth quoting in full:

> Bill's cabin was in the midst of the range of huts, tenanted by the workers in the fields. In front was a large pool of black mud and corrupt water, around which myriads of flies and insects were whirling and buzzing. I went in, but such sights and smells as met me I cannot describe them. It was reeking with filth and impurity of every kind, and already occupied by near a dozen women and children, who were sitting on the ground, or coiled on piles of rags and straw in the corner. They regarded me curiously as I entered, grinned with malicious satisfaction that I had been brought down to their level, and made some remarks at my expense; while the children kicked, and yelled, and clawed at each other, scratching each other's faces, and pulling each other's hair I stumbled to a bench I supposed designed for a seat, when one of the woman [sic] arose, seized me by the hair, and without ceremony dragged me to the ground, gave

me a furious kick and made use of highly improper and indecent language. Bill, who had retired to the outside of the hut, hearing the noise of the fray came hastily in. It was his turn then. He commenced beating her with a hearty good-will, and she scratched and bit him, furiously. In the rough and tumble they knocked over two or three of the children, besides treading on the toes of some of the women, who irritated by the pain started up and joined the contest which soon became general. (208–209)

Entering the cabin of the field slaves, Hannah can seem like Ishmael entering "The Trap"—such are the distinctions between white and black, house slave and field slave, and such are her desires, acted upon almost immediately, to want to flee from blackness. However much Crafts might wish to attribute the "reeking" filth to the degradation forced upon enslaved blacks by whites, she seems to discern in the cabin something essential about the character of the cabin's inhabitants. But what is especially noteworthy here is that Hannah's revulsion seems focused less on Bill than on the dozen or so women who immediately want to pummel her. She fears that she will become like these women, and those fears are precisely what Mrs. Wheeler had played upon when she banished Hannah to the fields in the first place: "With all your pretty airs and your white face, you are nothing but a slave after all, no better than the blackest wench" (205).

That white can be revealed as black is, I have been arguing, central to the trope of genealogical haunting that informs *The Bondwoman's Narrative* and many other genealogical fictions of the 1850s, and that is what makes Trappe—the man who traffics in such revelations—such a central and frightening character in the book. I am also suggesting that the possibility of white being revealed as black is one of the novel's informing anxieties and that Crafts taps into these anxieties not simply in order to undermine the ideological premises of white supremacy as Brown, say, does in *Clotel* (and I do think that is one of her goals) but also because these are fears that she herself seems implicated in. I am aware that this is a potentially troubling claim, and a claim that cannot be easily supported, given that we know very little about Crafts herself. But the revulsion at blackness near the end of the book, when compared to Hannah's seeming obliviousness to the threat posed to her body by her white masters, seems out of proportion, as if she has finally discovered the nightmare of slavery in the slaves themselves and thus wants to resist the obvious fact, underscored by Mrs. Wheeler's taunting, that she is one of them.

To be sure, when she undertakes her eventual escape from slavery (and the field slaves) by masquerading as a white man, she does offer sympathy and assistance along the way to two blacks, Jacob and his sister, who are attempting to escape from a South Carolina slave plantation. But before her relationship to these fugitive slaves is put to much of a test, the sister dies and Jacob is shot while trying to steal a boat. At which point Hannah's former religious mentor, the white Aunt Hetty, takes her in and eventually sends her off to find refuge in a black community in New Jersey. In the happy final chapter, Hannah talks of how the "hand of providence" (237) also helped to bring her mother and Charlotte and William, the former slaves she had once betrayed, to freedom in New Jersey. Hannah has married an ordained Methodist preacher and has fulfilled her dreams in every way: "I found a life of freedom all my fancy had pictured it to be. I found the friends of the slave in the free state just as good as kind and hospitable as I had always heard they were. I dwell now in a neat little Cottage, and keep a school for colored children" (237).

A happy ending, yes, but a disconcerting ending, too, completely inconsistent with the more troubled and ambivalent accounts we have of "freedom" at the end of Douglass's *Narrative*, Harriet Jacobs's *Incidents*, Harriet Wilson's *Our Nig*, and perhaps most pertinently, Webb's *The Garies and Their Friends*. *Garies* concludes with a happy marriage and group gathering of free blacks and their white abolitionist friends, on the one hand, and a disturbing suggestion of black vulnerability in racist Philadelphia, on the other, as the half-crazed Mr. Ellis, the victim of white vigilantes, remains on the lookout for "another mob."[18] In *The Bondwoman's Narrative*, the short interlude with Jacob and his sister and the closing chapter in New Jersey seem intended to counterbalance the fear and loathing of blackness expressed by Hannah (and Crafts) in Bill's cabin. But the concluding chapter's untroubled celebration of black uplift, "goodness," "undeviating happiness" (239), and interracial harmony reads more like a white abolitionist fantasy than an affirmation of black community.

That said, a politics of black community does inform the key story of the bloody linden tree central to the novel's representation of genealogical haunting. The story is passed on by the slaves of the Lindendale plantation, and as far as that story is concerned, Hannah certainly does appear to be part of the black community. And yet because we do not know the "real" Hannah Crafts, it is ultimately impossible to make categorical claims about her own racial politics, affiliations, and anxieties, and because the novel was never published, we cannot make claims about its audience, reception, and influence. Perhaps all for the good, then, we can only note the critical tensions of an interracial novel that alternately suggests sympathetic knowledge of (and seeming identification with) black and white perspectives. *The Bondwoman's Narrative* is a novel both with and without a history, and that, I want to suggest, will remain a source of its power for twenty-first-century readers.

The fact of the novel's nonpublication makes its recovery and the reception of the novel inextricably intertwined, as we will inevitably read *The Bondwoman's Narrative* in relation to the needs and genealogical structures (the history of African American literature; the history of American literature; the history of African diasporan literature; the history of the Gothic; and so on) of our own various houses of fiction. What are the differences, then, between reading the novel as the first novel written by a formerly enslaved African American woman (which it likely is) and reading it as a novel by, say, a white abolitionist woman with extensive knowledge of the life histories of formerly enslaved African American woman? The differences would seem to be profound. But are they? For one of the truly brilliant aspects of *The Bondwoman's Narrative*— brilliant insofar as Crafts seems to have anticipated the dilemma of racial identity politics with such prescience—is the way that it can trap its bookish, Trappe-like readers who insist on working with essentialized racial categories in order to establish "authentic" identities. As a telling instance of what Werner Sollors has called the "interracial literature" of the not-so-tragic mulatto, and as a novel that makes a mockery of "black" and "white," *The Bondwoman's Narrative*, in Sollors's terms, undermines "the ideology of racial dualism" and poses a challenge to "the resistance to interracial life" that remains prevalent in U.S. culture.[19] At same time, the novel powerfully shows that those racial categories, however fictive they might be as juridical and "scientific" inventions of white supremacist culture, are socially real and affect the lives of characters and readers alike. Is there any way out of this trap except by imagining a happy ending for all? That is the challenge posed by Crafts's implicating genealogical narrative.

Notes

1. Herman Melville, *Moby-Dick; or, The Whale* (1851), ed. Andrew Delbanco (New York: Penguin Books, 1992), p. 10.

2. Ibid., pp. 10, 11, 23, 26.

3. For a masterful discussion of racial critique and anxiety in Melville, see Samuel Otter, "'Race' in *Typee* and *White-Jacket*," in *The Cambridge Companion to Herman Melville*, ed. Robert S. Levine (New York: Cambridge University Press, 1998), pp. 12–36.

4. Herman Melville, *Pierre; or, The Ambiguities*, ed. Harrison Hayford, Hershel Parker, and G. Thomas Tanselle (Evanston and Chicago: Northwestern University Press and The Newberry Library, 1971), pp. 89, 314, 198. For a fuller elaboration of racial and genealogical themes in the novel, see my "Pierre's Blackened Hand," *Leviathan: A Journal of Melville Studies* 1 (1999): 23–44.

5. William Wells Brown, *Clotel, or The President's Daughter*, ed. Robert S. Levine (Boston: Bedford/St. Martin's, 2000), p. 173.

6. For an excellent discussion of genealogical issues in *Clotel*, see Russ Castronovo, *Fathering the Nation: American Genealogies of Slavery and Freedom* (Berkeley: University of California Press, 1995), pp. 212–227.

7. Russ Castronovo has recently argued that analyses of "race" have become a cliché of cultural studies ("Race and Other Clichés," *American Literary History* 14 [2002]: 551–565). Though Castronovo does not deny the role of race in the actual social workings of nineteenth-century U.S. culture, he worries that regular demonstrations by increasingly canny critics of the fluidity, instability, and fictionality of race (the kind of assertions that I will be shamelessly making in this essay) risk being little more than conventional exercises in formalist interpretation that do nothing to address or "subvert" cultural hierarchies.

8. Theresa A. Goddu, *Gothic America: Narrative, History, and Nation* (New York: Columbia University Press, 1997), p. 132; Nathaniel Hawthorne, *The House of the Seven Gables* (1851), ed. Milton R. Stern (New York: Penguin Books, 1981), p. 17. For useful discussions of genealogical fictions, see also Lee Quinby, ed., *Genealogy and Literature* (Minneapolis: University of Minnesota Press, 1995). On race and the antebellum period, see, for example, Thomas F. Gossett, *Race: The History of an Idea in America* (1963; rpt. New York: Oxford University Press, 1997); and Dana D. Nelson, *National Manhood: Capitalist Citizenship and the Imagined Fraternity of White Men* (Durham: Duke University Press, 1998).

9. On the possible composition date of the novel, see Henry Louis Gates, Jr., "Introduction" to *The Bondwoman's Narrative: A Novel*, by Hannah Crafts, ed. Henry Louis Gates, Jr. (New York: Warner Books, 2002), esp. pp. xlvi–liv. On Crafts's reading of Dickens and other contemporaneous writers, see Gates, "A Note on Crafts's Literary Influences," *The Bondwoman's Narrative*, pp. 331–332.

10. Crafts, *The Bondwoman's Narrative*, ed. Gates, pp. 27–28. All future page references will be supplied parenthetically in the main body of the text.

11. Nathaniel Hawthorne, *The Scarlet Letter* (1850), ed. Sculley Bradley et al. (New York: W. W. Norton, 1978), p. 92.

12. Given the parallels between Hawthorne's *House* and *The Bondwoman's Narrative*, one imagines that Crafts was being playfully ironic in naming the founder of Lindendale after the enfeebled Clifford Pyncheon.

13. Harriet A. Jacobs, *Incidents in the Life of a Slave Girl: Written by Herself* (1861), ed. Jean Fagan Yellin (Cambridge: Harvard University Press, 1987), p. 78.

14. Hawthorne, *House*, p. 8.

15. Melville, *Pierre*, p. 10; Harriet Beecher Stowe, *Dred; A Tale of the Great Dismal Swamp* (1856), ed. Robert S. Levine (New York: Penguin Books, 2000), p. 36.

16. See Adam Smith, *The Theory of Moral Sentiments* (1759), ed. D. D. Raphael and A. L. Macfie (London: Oxford University Press, 1976), esp. p. 9. For a thoughtful discussion of the egotistical and sometimes cruel implications of sympathy, see Marianne Noble, *The Masochistic Pleasures of Sentimental Literature* (Princeton: Princeton University Press, 2000).

17. Gates, "Introduction," *The Bondwoman's Narrative*, pp. lxix–lxx.

18. Frank J. Webb, *The Garies and Their Friends*, ed. Robert Reid-Pharr (1857; rpt. Baltimore: Johns Hopkins University Press, 1997), p. 372.

19. Werner Sollors, *Neither Black Nor White Yet Both: Thematic Explorations of Interracial Literature* (Cambridge: Harvard University Press, 1997), p. 242.

"Don't speak dearest, it will make you worse"
The Bondwoman's Narrative, *the Afro-American Literary Tradition, and the Trope of the Lying Book*

ZOE TRODD

Hannah Crafts's Mr. Trappe represents and is aware of the trap located by Henry Louis Gates, Jr. in the "challenge of the great white Western tradition": "if blacks accepted this challenge", Gates writes, they "also accepted its premises, premises in which perhaps lay concealed a trap".[1] Trappe explains the nature of this trap to Hannah and her mistress in chapter seven ('Mr. Trappe') of *The Bondwoman's Narrative*, claiming, in true structuralist fashion, that "'Freedom and slavery are only names attached surreptitiously and often improperly to certain conditions. They are mere shadows, the very reverse of realities'" (p. 97). The theme of words as "shadows, the very reverse of realities", of language as a slippery signifier of reality, runs throughout the novel but is sounded particularly loud in this chapter, when Hannah's mistress dies.

The separation of signifier and signified is apparent when the dying woman begins a dramatic struggle with language: standing before Trappe "she inclines her head and would say 'yes' but has no voice" (p. 96), then is silent, her lips sometimes moving "as if in replying, but" emitting "no voice" (p. 99), or else speaking "with great effort" (p. 98). Trappe elaborates on the discrepancy between name and thing and the slave's uneasy relationship with language ("Freedom and slavery are only names", p. 97), then deliberately confuses her with a pun on the word 'line', mentioning her "lineage" (p. 97), then his own "line" (p. 98), so that she is forced to acknowledge the doubleness of his language, saying, "'I don't understand your meaning'". He explains that he meant his "line of business", but continues to connect the two meanings: his line is to trace back her line, and seconds later Hannah's mistress loses all connection between words and world. Suddenly she understands Trappe's words only in the abstract, not in relation to reality: "it was clear that she heard what he was saying . . . and understood what they meant of themselves, but it was not so evident that she attached meaning to them in any other connection, or felt their intimate relation to herself" (p. 99). Blood bubbles from her lips instead of speech and she dies. The last words she hears are: "'Don't speak dearest, it will make you worse'" (p. 100).

Signifyin(g) upon Hannah Crafts, and riffing on Henry Louis Gates, because "Signifyin(g) is the figure of Afro-American literary history, and revision proceeds by riffing upon tropes",[2] we can use this theme of words as "the very reverse of realities" to set *The Bondwoman's Narrative* in the Afro-American literary tradition. The theme Signifies the novel upon several other texts in the tradition, in particular James Weldon Johnson's *The Autobiography of an Ex-Colored Man*, Zora Neale Hurston's *Their Eyes Were Watching God*, Nella Larsen's *Passing*, and Octavia E. Butler's *Kindred*, and lets it be Signified upon by them. Like *The Bondwoman's Narrative* itself, we can riff on The Trope of the Talking Book; and we might name the revised result 'The Trope of the Lying Book', thereby emphasizing and extending the complicated relationship of The Trope of the Talking Book with language and the written word.[3]

Of course, there are elements of Trappe's trap that are not unique to the Afro-American literary tradition, and others that are mere conventions of sentimental fiction and the slave narrative. Crafts knows that language configures reality, thus acting as barrier between people and the world, but an interest in the slipperiness of language and represented experience is not unique to Afro-American writing; most famously, Shakespeare hints that Hamlet's story will be retold from a different angle by Horatio, and Euripides asks that we reconsider whether Helen was really abducted to Troy or Iphigenia really sacrificed. And of course Crafts echoes her own biblical chapter-head quotations, several of which confirm the treachery of language. We read, for chapter five: "*When men say peace and safety sudden destruction cometh*"; for chapter two: "*When he speaks fair, believe him not; for there are severe abominations in his heart*"; and to these we might add Matthew 5:37: "Plain 'Yes' or 'No' is all you need to say; anything beyond that come from the devil". Even her particular critique of the effects of slavery on language is reminiscent of Ben Jonson's "wheresoever manners and fashion are corrupted, language is, [for it] imitates the public riot".

It is tempting to seize upon other famous moments of despair about language and assume that Crafts also seized upon them. Hamlet's "I have that within which passes show / These but the *trappings* and the suits of woe" (my emphasis) seems particularly relevant, offering as it does a verbal connection to Mr. Trappe and a version of Hannah's repeated statements that words are inadequate to describe events and emotions. Language is not a good friend to Hannah, often eluding her—"I could find no words, and so sat silent and embarrassed" (p. 8)—or tempting her into danger—"It was not for me to reply. The lady would have took it in high dudgeon had I opened my lips to make the most reasonable excuse, and one unreasonable would have been still greater insult" (p. 195). She writes, "My horror, and grief, and astonishment were indescribable. I felt Oh how much more than I tell" (p. 12), and this is repeated several times; in chapters ten and twelve, for example, she writes: "How should I convey in words an adequate idea of a manner refined by education . . . " (p. 124); "It would be a difficult undertaking to describe all the costly and elegant and beautiful things . . . " (p. 148). But this last series of examples connect Hannah more closely to the genres of the slave narrative and sentimental fiction than to Shakespeare: the I-can't-possibly-describe-it device feels like a verbal tic shared with Harriet Jacobs and others of the nineteenth-century slave narrative and sentimental traditions.

To a certain degree, Crafts is even participating in the nineteenth-century slave narrative tradition when her attitude towards language approaches that of complete relativism, for there is something of Frederick Douglass in Mrs. Wright, from whom Hannah learns the lesson that "'all who live in a land of slavery must learn sooner or later; that is to profess approbation where you cannot feel; . . . to be hard when most inclined to melt; and to say that all is right, and good, and true, when you know that nothing could be more wrong and unjust'" (p. 84)—in short, to break the connection between signifier and signified. It is as though Mrs. Wright has observed and is now extending into a general lesson the experience of Douglass who as a slave isn't allowed to tell the truth. He is instead forced, even if asked "a series of plain questions", to "suppress the truth rather than take the consequences of telling it", so that truth becomes relativistic: he doesn't consider it false to answer that his master treated him well, explaining, "I always measured the kindness of my master by the standard of kindness set up among slaveholders around us".[4]

So, like Douglass, Crafts recognizes the "arbitrary relationship between a sign and its referent, between the signifier and the signified", as Gates phrases the problem when discussing the 1845 *Narrative*.[5] But she goes further than Douglass. Hannah notices early in the novel that the "meek gentle smile" and "loving words" of Uncle Siah, although they win the "regard" of others, fail to reveal his "sterling worth" (p. 10), and then she learns, from Trappe and Mrs. Wright most notably, that the separation of signifier and signified with regard to Uncle Siah is not unusual. She realizes, as part of her journey towards freedom, that when slaves "hear such names as freedom, heaven, hope and happiness", they have no "experience of [what] these blessed names would be" (p. 201), and so have no meaning with which to furnish the empty words. In her doomed mistress's life story, Hannah sees how a woman is made a slave, and how a slave is made a woman, but then also how a woman is re-made into a slave by the written word: her mistress is born a slave and not brought up as one, then discovers her identity in the papers given to her by Trappe. She reads and "perceived the worst and what I was, and must ever be" (p. 47). Though the slave then becomes a woman in order to marry Hannah's master, and the woman a slave again when threatened by Trappe after her marriage, the turning point in her self-perception is at this moment of textual confrontation in the presence of the perpetually bookish Trappe, whose rooms are filled with "books and bundles of papers" (p. 46) and who makes "himself at home among the books and papers" at Lindendale (p. 35).

So books make the woman a slave, in a reversal of the well-known Douglass moment. Hannah's address to the "Doctors of Divinity" concludes with a description of two lying books: "The Constitution that asserts the right of freedom and equality to all mankind is a sealed book to them [the slaves in the cotton fields]", she writes, adding: "so is the Bible, that tells how Christ died for all; the bond as well as the free" (p. 201). Crafts may have been suspicious of the Douglass concept of writing oneself into existence with the tools of the Western literary tradition and apparently never tried to write herself into existence publicly: there is no evidence that she tried to publish *The Bondwoman's Narrative*. In this she is kindred of Phillis Wheatley, whose protest is equally buried and also recently unearthed: "On Being Brought from Africa to America" (if we accept it as such),[6] recognizes in its anagram form not only the two different worlds of slave and master but also the doubleness of language and the presence of another voice hidden beneath the heroic couplets of literate white culture. Crafts explores this doubleness of language, represented by Wheatley through the anagram form and sounds a warning to Afro-Americans about the process of proving one's humanity (as Phillis Wheatley herself famously did!) through the mastery of Western languages and literature.

Her relationships to Douglass and Wheatley begin to root Crafts in the Afro-American literary tradition. In addition, though Trappe's trap, "words as shadows, the very reverse of realities", is obviously a major trap of the Western canon, and particularly of twentieth-century texts, a juxtaposition of Crafts, Johnson, Hurston, Larsen, and Butler reveals it to have particular dangers and meanings within the Afro-American literary tradition. While Crafts is a proto-structuralist writer, she is also an early modern black writer. She anticipates Wittgenstein's "the limits of my language mean the limits of my world", but adds, conversely, that a world with slavery in it is limited and thus limits language. We recognize Trappe's "shadows, the very reverse of realities", in the following statement by the linguist Anthony Burgess: "Meaning resides *shadowly* in the morpheme, less so in the word, less so again in the phrase or sentence or paragraph; but meaning only comes to its fullest flower in the context of an entire way of life".[7] Crafts explores the implication of the Burgess statement for slaves: the "entire way of life" in the slave states of 1850s America was responsible for the failure of meaning to come "to its fullest flower" in language, for if, as Trappe asserts, "freedom and slavery are only names attached surreptitiously and often improperly to certain conditions", then improperly applied terms dictated the reality of a slave's existence. Name created reality, and the correct relationship of signifier and signified was turned on its head. We witness in the death scene of Hannah's mistress the death of meaningful or expressive language and understand why our modern distrust of language was preempted by the nineteenth century in a slave narrative.

The death or absence of meaningful language with which to express African American reality is taken up as an issue by several important writers in the black tradition. With its inherent disconnect between signified and signifier, language is as much a source of the African American's "double self-consciousness", or "dual personality", as the dualities of African and American, black and white, ex-slave and citizen, past and present.[8] One of Crafts's connections to the twentieth-century concern with language as signifier, and particularly to Johnson and Larsen, is through the theme of 'passing', for there is a breakdown of signification when the term 'black' is applied to a person who looks white, and the 'white' describes a person who is really black: we see that black and white "are only names attached surreptiously and often improperly to certain conditions. They are mere shadows, the very reverse of realities". The African American "dual personality" is particularly pronounced in characters who can pass not only because they feel both black and white but because the nonsense and relativity of the racial terms is clear in them and to them.

Throughout *The Autobiography of an Ex-Colored Man*, Johnson links the concept of "dual personality" to his narrator's mixed race but also the doubleness of signifier and signified, of reality and representation of reality. His narrator knows that the "literary concept of the American Negro" is so powerful that "it's almost impossible to get the reading public to recognize him in any other setting" (p. 167) and that representations of Negro life have left real Negro experience "a mystery to the whites" (p. 21). He comes to a recognition of the relativity of language through an observation that the word "nigger" has no inherent meaning; it can be an insult or an endearment depending on who says it (p. 92). Having learnt this lesson of relativity with him, we're suspicious when the Texan on the train uses the word 'fact' repeatedly, and, indeed, what he claims as fact is actually being stated as belief: "Down here in the South we're up against facts . . . We don't *believe* the nigger is or ever will be the equal of the white man" (p. 164, my emphasis). The relativity of language parallels the relativity of the narrator's racial identity but also the behavior of the South, which is, "in the light of other days . . . magnificent", but "today . . . cruel and ludicrous" (p. 190).

The potential pain of textual representation is felt by Toni Morrison's Sethe, in *Beloved*, who runs away not when she has learnt to read and write but when she realizes how *she* will be read and written (in two columns, one for her animal and one for her human characteristics). The limits of the "literary concept of the American Negro" is also explored by Butler, whose character Dana, in *Kindred*, learns through her time-travel not to rely on books for her understanding of the world, a similar lesson to that learnt by Johnson's narrator when he sees that "the French life of popular literature . . . [is] different from real French life" (p. 129). Dana spends her time in between visits to the nineteenth century reading books, so that later, when eating the food of 1819, she remembers "horror stories" about the diseases of the time and wishes that she hadn't read about such things so she would at least be free from the dread of them (p. 48).[9] But like Janie in *Their Eyes Were Watching God*, Dana is made to know things "that nobody had ever told her",[10] that she couldn't have experienced through books, thus escaping from the pseudo-reality of the signifier. She comments: "I had seen people beaten on television and in the movies. I had seen the too-red blood substitute streaked across their backs and heard their well-rehearsed screams. But I hadn't lain nearby and smelled their sweat or heard them pleading and praying, shamed before their families and themselves" (p. 36); she reiterates: "most of the people around Rufus know more about real violence than the screenwriters of today will ever know" (p. 48).

Rufus enjoys listening to Dana read: "'It's almost like being there watching everything happen'", (p. 87) he exclaims, but the 'almost' stops us from fully accepting the connection between reading and experiencing. Dana and Kevin are novelists by trade, here experiencing the reality that they would otherwise have to experience second-hand or fictionalize, but even so Kevin pretends to be traveling through the South researching a book (p. 79), and Dana enjoys *Robinson Crusoe* because "as a kind of castaway myself, I was happy to escape into the fictional world of someone else's trouble" (p. 87). She is so bookish that she tears pages from a scratch pad to mark the way through the woods (p. 126), literally imposing pages upon reality, having just been accused by Rufus of talking "'like a damn book'" (p. 125). It is only when she abandons the attempt to be "almost" there "watching everything happen" through books, and experiences reality unmediated by textual signifiers, that she is free and re-leased back to her own time.

Dana is somewhat reminiscent of Larsen's Irene, in *Passing*, who experiences language as powerful signifier and then begins to see and interpret everything in language's terms of signifier and signified. Initially Clare's written word is substituted for Clare herself, through handwritten letters to Irene that become some kind of "literary concept" of Clare. So begins a chain of substitutions and significations that eventually destroys the characters. The letter and hand-writing prompt extensive memories (the whole first section!), and Irene is sur-prised by the power of language as signifier, eventually looking at the letter "with an astonishment that had in it a mild degree of amusement at the vio-lence of the feelings which it stirred in her".[11] Her suspicions about Brian and Clare, which stand in place of reality, and the white teacup, which represents Clare's shattered body at the end of the novel, develop the theme of substitu-tion and representation. Irene comes to see in Clare "an image of her futile searching" (p. 200) and a signification of her own precarious existence and marriage, so that Clare wonders if she is now only a signifier, saying (of Mar-garet Hammer): "'I assure you that from the way she looked through me, even I was uncertain whether I was actually there in the flesh or not'" (p. 154). All the characters' identities seem disrupted by an over-reliance on signifiers, and the novel accordingly often represents conversations or letters in fragments or as one-sided.[12] Eventually Irene faints while trying to represent her identity in the word "I——".

One of the novel's major replacements of signifier for signified is the pre-sentation of events as memories rather than unfolding realities, so that past re-places present—perhaps because 'passing' denies the body's black heritage and history, leaving it only a memory, or signifier, in the passer's life, rather than a living reality. The meeting of Clare and Irene in Chicago, the tea with Gertrude and Clare's husband, and The Negro Welfare League dance are all related as Irene's memories. Of course, Irene may or may not rewrite the past when remembering it: perhaps, for example, Clare's smile at the waiter wasn't really "too provocative" (p. 149). Memory is in fact dangerous for Clare, for it draws her to the people of her childhood. Her statement, when describing her meeting with Margaret Hammer ("'I remember it clearly, too clearly'") might be applied to her situation more generally. Finally, Irene cannot re-member whether she pushed Clare or not, and as one signifier (memory) fails, so another (language, the novel) ends.

Although Crafts has little to say on the subject of memory itself as sig-nifier, she is, like Johnson, engaged with memory as it relates to history, questions of genre, and the unreliability of language as signifier. Johnson's narrator looks at the "fine specimens of young manhood" at Atlanta University and sees the "patriarchal 'uncles' of the old slave regime" (p. 62): the students seem to have a double-existence, straddling two moments. Later, when we realize that the man who lets the narrator ride in his porter's closet to Jacksonville has probably made this imprisonment necessary by stealing his money and clothes, we reread *"doubled* up in the porter's basket" with new attention. Perhaps it means that the narrator has a double existence at this moment: he is both himself *and* a slave in a slave ship, transported by the man who took away his means of traveling freely, cultural memory displacing his current reality so that, again, the African American straddles two eras. Similarly, in Butler's *Kindred,* Dana's movement into the past can be understood as collective memory interrupting and imposing itself upon the present: her double life, lived half in 1976 and half in 1819, begins as America celebrates its two-hundredth anniversary, as though, through her, America remembers its past.

The substitution of memory for present-day reality is dangerous and painful in *Kindred, Passing,* and *The Autobiography* and may indicate an ambivalent attitude towards written history, one major source of collective memory and the ultimate signifier of past reality. Butler is especially keen to remind us of the impossibility of knowing the past, for the past must be expressed in language, and so any connection with it will be incomplete; hence Dana is left incomplete (armless) by her connection with it. A suspicion of written history and historians may be the inevitable product of a suspicion of language as signifier and may lead to a preference for imaginative representation: fiction represents new realities and creates new worlds, thus embracing words as a different *version,* but not necessarily the "reverse", of reality. Hence, Crafts's Mrs. Wright, who has learnt the "words as reverse of realities" lesson that "all who live in a land of slavery must learn sooner or later" (p. 84), lives in a world of "mental hallucination" and imagination (p. 80), and Johnson's narrator dwells "in a world of imagination, of dreams and air castles" (p. 46). He acquires no information from the existing histories of the Civil War, instead getting the "first perspective of the life [he] was entering" from *Uncle Tom's Cabin* (p. 41). He asks us to employ our counterfactual imaginations and visualize his life had he attended Atlanta, had he married the "young schoolteacher" and remained in Jacksonville, had he remained for much longer gambling at the "Club". He is conscious of the dramatic possibilities of any moment and aware that his life is suited to fictional representation: sitting through the opera in Paris he wants to cry out, "Here, here in your very midst, is a tragedy, a real tragedy" (p. 135). Accordingly, *The Autobiography* is only nominally an "autobiography" and clearly an imaginative fictional representation.

Indeed, Johnson and Crafts both write fiction and pretend to pass it as nonfiction, and in *The Autobiography*, *The Bondwoman's Narrative*, and also in *Kindred*, fiction is a more authentic way of engaging with an oral personal history requiring identification that can't be found in textbooks or other examples of written history. Butler toys with the solution of imaginative history to the problem of the 'lying book', showing us, at the novel's opening, Dana and Kevin sorting their books into shelves of fiction and non-fiction, and then the immediate inadequacy of such a divide, for Dana is whisked back to 1819 and says of her experience: "'if you told me a story like this, I probably wouldn't believe it either, but like you said, this mud must come from somewhere'" (p. 16), and "'As real as the whole episode was, as real as I know it was, it's beginning to recede from me somehow. It's becoming like something I saw on television or read about—like something I saw second hand'" (p. 17).

As Gates reminds us in his introduction to *The Bondwoman's Narrative*, "Veracity was everything in an ex-slave's tale, essential both to its critical and commercial success and to its political efficacy within the movement" (lxiv), and Crafts, circling Trappe's trap, more suspicious than Douglass of the concept of writing oneself into existence, resenting the autobiographical form, which automatically focused on her being "recently escaped from North Carolina", may have felt like one of Pirandello's characters, in *Six Characters in Search of An Author*. Indeed, she would have been equally justified in protesting that it would be "a dreadful injustice of other people to judge [her] only by this one action, as [she] dangle[s] there, hanging in chains, fixed for all eternity, as if the whole of one's personality were summed up in that single, interrupted action" (*Six Characters in Search of an Author*, Act I). Her decision to write fiction is perhaps related to the concerns often raised about black autobiography, the loss of individual personality through the demand for facticity, and the control and even generation of stories by white sponsors and abolitionists.

So the claim that Crafts makes for "veracity" in her preface is just token and formulaic, and her fictionalized autobiography is not to be taken literally. It is, as a whole book, an exercise in Signifyin(g). If the roles of signifier and signified are slippery and represented experience is suspect, as she examines, then the nature of written history is by implication complicated. Her awareness of the capacity of words to become unattached from meaning, as experienced by Hannah's mistress and explained by Trappe, may have made Crafts feel trapped by both language and the expectation that she write her "true" story. Perhaps she recognized that, concealed within the autobiographical challenge, a challenge intimately related to the "challenge of the great white Western tradition", so described by Gates, was another version of Trappe's trap. As William L. Andrews writes, "black autobiography served as a kind of sociological crucible in which some of the era's most interesting . . . experiments were conducted in how to tell the truth about experience", but "by the mid-nineteenth century, black autobiographers had recognized that their great challenge was much more than just telling the truth; they had to *sound* truthful doing it".[13] Logically, if *sounding* truthful was the greatest challenge, then in answering this successfully a writer presumably became able to sound truthful about events that had not occurred, so distancing signifier from signified.

But to write imaginative fiction, instead of strict autobiography or history, is to embrace the imprecision of language and its inability to accurately represent reality. It is to escape from its chains and those of the formulaic slave narrative and to begin to resolve the problem of language in a slave state. Loss of faith in language, that psychological impact of slavery, is, throughout the Afro-American canon, made into a Signifyin(g) game with the relativistic myriad of interpretive linguistic possibilities. Crafts, in her decision to write imaginatively, makes an early attack on the barriers between fiction and history, so that the term 'lying book' becomes tautology, thus brushing the solution of Signification up against the problem of signification. She engages with the issue of whether there is any way at all to tell the "truth" about black experience with white words, white requirements for expression, white limits of comprehension, especially when, as Gates writes, "literacy . . . could be the most pervasive emblem of capitalist commodity functions", could be the tool and weapon of the slave-owning state, and the enemy of the Afro-American.

In the same essay, Gates goes on to question how "the black subject [can] posit a full and sufficient self in a language in which blackness is a sign of absence", and, though it is true that meaning is a product of culture, of shared convention, and so all meaning in a slave state must surely draw the chains tighter, such a conclusion denies language any power to protest and transform society.[14] Imagination is one solution to this and to the slipperiness of language as signifier of reality, explored by Crafts with her emphasis on the Gothic and re-explored by Johnson and Hurston in the twentieth century: it is *Their Eyes Were Watching God* that explores at length both Crafts's premise that words can't adequately represent reality and the potential solution through imagination. Hurston makes the case for the value of words as imaginative rather than literal representation. The members of Janie's community seek power in words. They set their words free to walk "without masters" (p. 2), pass "nations through their mouths" (p. 1), and in the courtroom have "their tongues cocked and loaded, the only real weapon left to weak folks" (pp. 185–186). But their words find their true state when working with the imagination, to gossip or tell stories, offer Daisy steamships and "earoplanes" (p.

69), or stage an argument that is "a contest in hyperbole and carried on for no other reason" (p. 63).

Janie's own imagination is expansive but without outlet: from the beginning of her interaction with Jody all supposin' is cut off. We read: "'Jody . . . but s'posin'"—'Leave de s'posin' and everything else to me'" (p. 29). She knows that her imagination goes far beyond that of her grandmother's; that she is one of those people who can "look at a mud-puddle and see an ocean with ships", but that "Nanny belonged to that other kind that loved to deal in scraps. Here Nanny had taken the biggest thing that God ever made, the horizon . . . and pinched it in to such a little bit of a thing that she could tie it about her granddaughter's neck tight enough to choke her" (p. 89). Part of Janie's rebellion against her grandmother is to "look at a mud-puddle and see an ocean with ships", to look at a flood and see a "monstropolous beast" (p. 161). The act of telling her life story to Pheoby, and through Pheoby to the whole community, is one of untying the choking necktie and creating herself before language, that of her community but also of the whole white Western tradition, gets there first. When Butler's Kevin asks Dana to deal with his correspondence for him (p. 136), a request that is echoed by Rufus (p. 226), or to type his manuscripts instead of focusing on her own fiction (pp. 108–109), we know that he is a literary relative of Janie's grandmother and Jody, and that the restriction of Dana's creativity and imagination may be one of the mysterious forces behind the time-travel.

Janie knows that "'talkin' don't amount tuh uh hill uh beans when yuh can't do nothin' else'" (p. 192): that words are meaningless, and signification breaks down completely, when there is no referent. But she also knows that when one uses imagination, then talking *does* amount to something: the reference to a "hill of beans" recalls Janie and Tea Cake working at picking beans, and brings Tea Cake back through the memory. Imagination plus words recreates a whole lost world, and suddenly the world is no longer limited by language. The beginning of the third-person narrating voice in *Their Eyes* coincides with the moment in the story when Janie decides that "her conscious life has commenced at Nanny's gate" (p. 10): her conscious life begins when she shifts to narrating herself in the third person—to imagining herself. Full "of that oldest human longing—self-revelation" (p. 7), she doesn't *just* reveal, but imagines, so that the story becomes a self-creation. The third-person narrative, apparently still her voice, presents scenes that she didn't witness, so that the effect is one of imaginative creation rather than straight remembering.[15] She can describe scenes she hasn't seen because her imagination—her ability to know "things that nobody had ever told her"—has been set free by Tea Cake, who plays an "imaginary instrument" (p. 100) and lets her "tell big stories herself from listening to the rest" (p. 134).

In telling her life story, Janie becomes a "big picture talker ... using a side of the world for a canvas" (p. 54). She enjoys "thought pictures" when they are "crayon enlargements of life" (p. 51). With these "mind-pictures" (p. 20) and the imaginative "canvas", Hurston fuses the imaginative with the visual. The first telling of her story, in the courtroom, is followed by the second telling, to Pheoby, with its vividly visual imaginative similes,[16] and then the third telling, no longer in words, but through "pictures of love and light on the wall". This fusion is similar to that felt by Hannah when she encounters the portraits and finds she can "think and speculate", let her mind "run riotous". The eyes in the portraits that Hannah encounters should be "void of expression as those of an exhumed corpse" (p. 16), but the past is no corpse when represented by visual art: "the stern old sire ... seems moodily to relax his haughty aspect. The countenance of another ... assumes a gracious expression it never wore in life ... Over the pale pure features of a bride descends a halo of glory; the long shining locks of a young mother waver and float over the child she holds; and the frozen cheek of an ancient dame seems beguiled into smiles and dimples". These paintings, which make their subjects *better* than they were in life, are perfect signifiers, signifying reality as it should have been and providing, with the aid of Hannah's imagination, "smiles and dimples", a "gracious expression", and a "halo of glory". It is as though visual art somehow leaps across one Platonic level, representing the original reality, before it was given shape in imperfect human form. If words are "shadows" of reality, then visual art represents reality as it was, before being made a shadowy human shape, diluted and present in the world.

The link made between "picture" and "imagination" by Crafts in the last sentence of *The Bondwoman's Narrative* is another clue that in valuing the imagination she is valuing the visual. Indeed, a second solution to the problem of words as "mere shadows", as the "reverse of realities", might be the recognition of other artistic mediums, namely visual art and music, as better signifiers than language. Hannah senses that visual art is a good signifier, that it offers a rational and true connection to the past but also space for imagination: standing in front of the portraits she seems "to have entered a new world of thoughts, and feelings and sentiments. I was not a slave with these pictured memorials of the past ... As their companion I could think and speculate. In their presence my mind seemed to run riotous and exult in its freedom as a rational being" (p. 17). Her "silent unobtrusive way of observing things and events" (p. 5), that "quiet way of observing things ... sharpened perhaps by the absence of all elemental knowledge", and her practice of studying "instead of books . . . faces and characters" (p. 27), demonstrate that she is more comfortable with observation, faces, the visual image, than with books and language.

Language does represent reality briefly but accurately at the end of the novel. Hannah collapses the difference between its world and its medium, apparently quoting her husband as he speaks, as though the page becomes a recording device: "He sits by my side even as I write and sometimes shakes his head, and sometimes laughs saying 'there, there my dear. I fear you grow prosy, you cannot expect the public to take the same interest in me that you do'" (p. 238). This is the first and last time that her husband is mentioned, so he must be commenting upon this very sentence. But, predictably, doubts are immediately recast on the adequacy of language, and there is further appeal to the visual imagination as the novel ends: "I could not, if I tried, sufficiently set forth the goodness of those about me . . . I will let the reader picture it all to his imagination" (p. 239). The suggested replacement of language by the visual imagination is familiar from *The Autobiography of an Ex-Colored Man*, for Johnson's narrator is as imaginative as Hannah and Janie, and he too combines his imagination with the pictorial to replace language. He writes of the process of learning to read: "I invariably attempted to reproduce sounds without the slightest recourse to the written characters . . . [And] whenever I came to words that were difficult and unfamiliar, I was prone to bring my imagination to the rescue and read from the picture . . . I would sometimes substitute whole sentences and even paragraphs from what meaning I thought the illustrations conveyed".[17]

Although not explored by Crafts, music seems to be another comparatively reliable signifier, able to express thoughts in sound if not in word, so that, as Douglass writes of the slaves' songs in his *Narrative*, the "mere hearing of these songs would do more to impress some minds with the horrible character of slavery, than the reading of whole volumes of philosophy on the subject could do".[18] Music expresses complicated emotions and ideas particularly well for Johnson's narrator. He is a man of mixed emotions and uses the word "half" repeatedly, almost desperately, in an attempt to communicate internal division.[19] He has, for example, a "savage and diabolical desire [but at the same time] a vague feeling of unsatisfaction, of regret, of almost remorse",[20] and he explains at another point that his feelings are "divided between a desire to weep and a desire to curse".[21] Yet he can't find a way to make language do both at the same time, for words seem to create clumsy paradox, such as his "little tragedies" (p. 3). On the other hand, the "strange harmonies . . . either on the high keys of the treble or the low keys of the bass" (p. 8) are subtly expressive: the piano can be "a sympathetic, singing instrument" but also "the source of hard or blurred sounds" (p. 26). Ragtime, with its syncopated melody line played against a straight or routine accompaniment, is a metaphor for conflicting motifs that are also harmonious. The musical duet that the narrator performs is a success, and his "particular fondness for the black keys" (p. 8) reminds us of the symbolic coloring on the piano: black and white keys together make the whole instrument and provide the full expression of meaning. When the narrator's wife, who is "as white as a lily", "the most dazzling white thing" he has ever seen", speaks in "tones of . . . passionate *color*" (p. 198, my emphasis), we realize that tone might better represent meaning than words.

Crafts does not explore musical tones as an expressive medium, but she does play with silence, an important element of musical expression and possibly also of visual communication: Hannah's "way of observing things and events" is "silent", after all, and there is an explicit rejection of sound in the passage describing the portraits, for one of the images "appears to open and shut his lips continually though they emit no sound" (p. 16). Indeed, the third way to step out of the darkness of "shadowy" words is to stay silent. Silence is initially painful and damaging for Hurston's Janie ("'mah wife don't know nothin' 'bout no speech-making'"), who learns to press "her teeth together and . . . hush" (p. 71), but her silent refusal to speak to the townsfolk is a reclaiming of silence (p. 2). In *The Bondwoman's Narrative*, silence is often more powerful than the spoken word: Rose's eventual silence on the Linden, when her "protruding tongue refused to articulate a sound", is ominous and predictive of disaster, as is the presence of Trappe "leaning speechless against a pillar, or sitting silently in a corner" (p. 32). We recognize echoes of Proverbs 10:32, "The righteous man can suit his words to the occasion; / the wicked know only subversive talk", in the contrast between Mrs. Wheeler, who chatters constantly and manipulates the truth in Hannah's dictated letter, and Mrs. Henry, who knows that language cannot adequately represent reality, saying of her father's death: "'I would not describe the scene if I could, and I could not if I would'" (p. 126), then choosing to be silent.

Mrs. Henry is a good model for this third solution of silence, but she fails to implement the fourth, and final, possible solution to the power of signifier over signified, which is to make words fit reality, so that reality is not limited by words. Hannah notes that even this worthy woman falls into the trap of suiting "the action to the word" (p. 115), when, as Orwell writes in his 1946 essay "Politics and the English Language", "what is above all needed is to let the meaning choose the word, and not the other way about". Janie, in *Their Eyes*, tries to reverse the relationship and find a harmony of voice and imagination, of word and thought: she knows, when running away with Jody, that "her old thoughts were going to come in handy now, but new words would have to be made and said to fit them" (p. 32), and she tells Pheoby that at the beginning of her relationship with Tea Cake "'new thoughts had tuh be thought and new words said. After Ah got used tuh dat, we gits 'long jus' fine. He done taught me de maiden language all over'" (p. 115).

Jean Toomer also investigates this solution. In *Cane*, the natural and human world *is* a book rather than the book being *about* the natural and human world: "things are so immediate in Georgia".[22] Halsey is aware that reality is less dramatic, less artistic, than in books: "These aint th days of hounds an Uncle Tom's Cabin, feller. White folks aint in fer all them theatrics these days",[23] and the narrator notes that his own rendering of Carma's story is perhaps inadequate: "this Carma, strong as a man, whose tale as I have told it is the crudest melodrama . . . ".[24] Kabnis put his book aside to listen to the "hills and valleys", which are "heaving with folk songs",[25] and knows that he must shape words to fit his soul and not adapt his soul so that words make sense: "I've been shapin words after a design that branded here . . . Been shapin words t fit m soul . . . sometimes theyre beautiful an golden an have a taste that makes them fine to roll over with y tongue . . . Th form that's burned int my soul is some awful twisted thing that crept in from a dream, a goddam nightmare, an wont stay still unless I feed it. An it lives on words. Not beautiful words . . . Misshapen, split-gut, tortured, twisted words".[26]

Butler explores the same solution in *Kindred*. Dana learns through her time-travel to call things as they are: she understands the literal meaning of "skin you alive", a phrase she heard as a child,[27] and comments on Fowler "literally cracking the whip".[28] Also, though Kevin appears to be perpetually "distant and angry" when he isn't, Rufus is red-haired, and so aptly named—signifier matching signified. The color red runs through *Passing* too, even appearing in Irene *Red*field's name, and it signifies danger in this earlier novel: the child Clare sews "pieces of bright red cloth together",[29] as her father threatens her; "brilliant red patches flamed in Irene Redfield's warm olive cheeks" as her dangerous interaction with Clare recommences;[30] the "bright red arch" that Irene is painting on her lips when she first believes that Brian is having an affair with Clare and the "scarlet spear of terror" that she feels directly afterwards signify danger,[31] as does the "dusky red" in Felise's cheeks just before they meet Clare's husband;[32] Clare is wearing a red dress when she dies, and her lips are described as "full, red", her whole body a "flame of red and gold", just before she falls from the window.[33] After her death the colors turn "purple" and "mauve" (p. 241), as though diluted now that danger has passed, signifier still matching signified.

Crafts also attempts a version of this last solution. As Gates points out in his introduction to the novel, she renders "physical characteristics" as "outward reflections of . . . inner personality", describing Maria as a "wary, powerful, and unscrupulous enemy", *then* a "dark mulatto, very quick motioned with black snaky eyes". "The sign of blackness or race" does not predetermine, as it does in Stowe, for example, "the limited range of characteristics even possible for a black person to possess".[34] Mrs. Wheeler is even made "as black as Tophet", as though to illustrate her degraded nature. The internal defines the external in a time when the external (color of skin) defined everything: when the signifier dominated the signified. No longer are social categories dependent on language but, temporarily, come before it.

Equally important is that, at the moment of Hannah's escape, Crafts both appropriates the problem of signifier and signifier, quite deliberately echoing the reversal that Trappe and Mrs. Wright explain, but also indicating that this reversal may be at the same moment put right. Already planning to escape, Hannah takes up the Bible, one of those lying books (p. 201), opens it at chance "at the place where Jacob fled from his brother Esau" (p. 207), and is thus confirmed in her decision to escape. She will make her life imitate the passage, so that a "literary concept" shapes reality instead of being shaped by it. And yet she had already decided that "rebellion would be a virtue" (p. 206) and that she "would not bear it [the forced marriage]" (p. 207): the passage in the Bible seems also to be imitating her life, so that text represents reality and *not* the reverse. The ambiguity is perhaps a sign that Hannah has learnt how to use the Trope of the Lying Book to her advantage. Butler's Dana gains her freedom by escaping from bookish reality, but Hannah's freedom comes when she fights the enemy with the enemy's weapons, takes bookish reality on its own terms, and blurs its distinctions between reality and textual representation of reality.

In offering a critique of the idea that language and literacy facilitate and represent freedom for the slave, Crafts proposes instead a path to freedom carved by imagination, silence, visual art, and a healing reversal or appropriation of the problematic signifier/signified relationship. She reaches for, but doesn't fully grasp, the Afro-American tool of Signification, which creates whole imaginative and textual worlds and explodes the universal problem of signification (the perpetual separation of signifier and signified) with an embrace of the relativity of language such that "a particular utterance may be an insult in one context and not in another . . . The hearer is thus constrained to attend to all potential meaning carrying symbolic systems in speech events—the total universe of discourse".[35] Signifyin(g), saying one thing to mean another, takes on the problem of language and doesn't solve it but rather glories in it. Crafts seeks, at this early stage in the Afro-American literary tradition, to fashion and explore The Trope of the Lying Book, and further down the road, Signifyin(g), indirect discourse (most famously in *Their Eyes Were Watching God*), 'speakerly texts', and the black vernacular tradition would grapple again with signification and the doubleness of language. With Johnson, Hurston, Toomer, Larsen, and Butler for company, Crafts ponders how words might be made more than "mere shadows, the very reverse of realities", how one might someday say: 'Do speak dearest, it will make you better'.

Notes

1. Henry Louis Gates, Jr., 'Writing, "Race", and the Difference It Makes', in *Loose Canons* (New York: Oxford University Press, 1992), p. 66.

2. Henry Louis Gates, Jr., *The Signifying Monkey* (New York: Oxford University Press, 1988), p. 124. All uses of 'Signifyin(g)' refer to Gates's definitions in this work.

3. The Trope of the Talking Book is explored at length in Gates's *The Signifying Monkey*.

4. Frederick Douglass, *Narrative of the Life* (New York: Penguin, 1986), p. 62. All page references given in the text refer to this edition.

5. Henry Louis Gates, Jr., *Figures in Black: Words, Signs and the 'Racial' Self* (New York: Oxford University Press, 1987), p. 96.

6. Henry Louis Gates, Jr., introduced the anagram, spotted by a freelance writer, in his Jefferson lecture in Washington this year (2002).

7. Anthony Burgess, 'Words', in *Language Made Plain* (London: English Universities Press, 1964), p. 107, my emphasis.

8. W.E.B. Du Bois, *The Souls of Black Folk* (New York: Norton Critical Edition, 1999), p. 10. James Weldon Johnson, *The Autobiography of an Ex-Colored Man* (New York: Hill and Wang, 1960), p. 21. All page references given in the text refer to these editions.

9. Octavia E. Butler, *Kindred* (Boston: Beacon Press, 1988), p. 75. All page references given in the text refer to this edition.

10. Zora Neale Hurston, *Their Eyes Were Watching God* (New York: HarperCollins, 1998), p. 25. All page references given in the text refer to this edition.

11. Nella Larsen, *Passing* (New Brunswick, NJ: Rutgers, 1986, with *Quicksand*), p. 181. All page references given in the text refer to this edition.

12. See, for example, the telephone conversation with Hugh (p. 197), the conversations at Irene's tea-party (pp. 218–219, 222), and Clare's letter (p. 145).

13. William L. Andrews, *To Tell A Free Story: The First Century of Afro-American Autobiography, 1760–1865* (Urbana: University of Illinois Press, 1986), p. 89.

14. 'Writing, "Race", and the Difference It Makes', pp. 65, 51.

15. See, for example: Hicks and Coker talk about Jody and Janie after the newly married pair have passed by (pp. 35–36); Janie is forbidden to attend the mule's funeral, but the narrator describes the scene at the swamp anyway, even imagining the conversation between the vultures; the narrator reports a private conversation between Sam Watson and Pheoby (pp. 110–111).

16. For example: "Logan with his shovel looked liked a black bear doing some clumsy dance on his hind legs" (p. 31); "The morning air was like a new dress" (p. 32); "Matt was wringing and twisting like a hen on a hot brick" (p. 58); "A deep sob came out of Jody's weak frame. It was like beating a bass drum in a hen-house. Then it rose high like pulling in a trombone" (p. 86).

17. Johnson, *The Autobiography of an Ex-Colored Man*, p. 9.

18. Douglass, *Narrative*, p. 57.

19. See, for example, "half vision" (p. 4), "half fright" (p. 5), "half second story" (p. 6), "half success" (p. 30), "half truth" p. 38), "willing to meet them more than half-way" (p. 81).

20. Johnson, *The Autobiography of an Ex-Colored Man*, p. 3.

21. Ibid., p. 135

22. Jean Toomer, *Cane* (New York: Norton Critical Edition, 1988), p. 86. All page references given in the text refer to this edition.

23. Ibid., p. 94.

24. Ibid., p. 13.

25. Ibid., p. 85.

26. Ibid., p. 111.

27. Butler, *Kindred*, p. 202.

28. Ibid., p. 212.

29. Larsen, *Passing*, p. 143.

30. Ibid., p. 145.

31. Ibid., pp. 216–217.

32. Ibid., p. 226.

33. Ibid., p. 239.

34. Henry Louis Gates, Jr., introduction to *The Bondwoman's Narrative*, p. xxv.

35. Claudia Mitchell-Kernan, 'Signifying', quoted in Gates, *Figures in Black*, p. 240.

V

In Search of an Author

19

The Case for Hannah Vincent

NINA BAYM

W e don't yet know who wrote *The Bondwoman's Narrative*. We may never find out. But our own first inclination is to identify her with the escaped slave who tells the story. We make this identification even though *Bondwoman* is obviously a novel, which means that much or most of it is made up. The full title of the previously unpublished 1850s manuscript (*The Bondwoman's Narrative, by Hannah Crafts, a Fugitive Slave Recently Escaped from North Carolina*) aligns it with the many slave autobiographies produced and circulated by abolitionists before the Civil War. Opponents of abolition typically attacked these eloquent but formulaic narratives on the grounds that they had been fabricated or heavily worked over by white editors. Ghostwritten or "as told to" stories were inevitably the norm when so much of the testimony came from people who were illiterate. What a find it would be to unearth a "true" slave's "true" story, one written by him- or herself without the intervention of an editorial crew! Even more significant than the accuracy of events would be the insight provided into the slave's consciousness. It is attractive to imagine that even though *Bondwoman* is clearly a work of fiction, it is such an "authentic" story—but it would be such only if the writer herself had experienced slavery firsthand.

It looks at first as though the desire to find a fugitive slave author has propelled Henry Louis Gates's quest. His heading to the first section of his introduction—"The Search for a Female Fugitive Slave"—seems to make her fugitive status the most important thing about her. Pre-publication press releases for the book, its dust jacket, and all the initial reviews in the popular press, feature and endorse that possibility. Yet in his introduction, even as he makes clear his responsibility to look for a fugitive slave author, Gates also forthrightly chronicles many of the false leads and dead ends he encountered searching for her. Ultimately, his most likely candidate for the real Hannah turns out to be a free African American woman from New Jersey named Hannah Vincent, and I want to follow that lead and propose that if the author is not this precise Hannah, she nevertheless may well have been a free woman. True, if Hannah (as I will call her henceforth) is a free woman, then one cannot generalize about slave literacy; but in my view this is the only loss. To have found the first true novel by a black woman is a find of unprecedented importance.

Understandably, readers don't want to be conned by a false memoir. But if one thinks of *Bondwoman* as a novel, a pure work of imagination, a different and equal if not greater value emerges. Rather than unmediated revelations of a fugitive, we would have a thoughtfully crafted—as the pen name "Hannah Crafts" invites us to imagine—work of art. There is no need to take the position that the story has value only if the author was herself a former slave, for it is ultimately not because of any particular factual detail, or even an accumulation of factual details, that *Bondwoman* works so well; it is because the account rings imaginatively true.

In its own day, the story's many obvious forays into imaginative fiction would have made it extremely vulnerable to anti-abolitionist arguments had it been published. Even abolitionists themselves might have been uncomfortable with the way experiences of slavery are used to experiment with fictional technique. Yet, this very novelizing of experience can also be seen as its strength, and while Gates argues powerfully that *Bondwoman* reflects authentic experiences under slavery (along with an authentic state of mind), he also calls it a novel and expatiates on its high degree of literacy, literary knowledge, and literary talent. In proposing that Hannah was not an escaped slave, I do not mean to assert, as a white woman, what could or could not have been possible for a fugitive slave. We never know what human beings can do until we see them do it. I do think it's more likely, however, that a novel as complex as this one—a novel showing such familiarity with the range of fictional genres current in the 1850s, a novel so full of specific reworkings of well-known literary tropes—would have been composed by a person with a long immersion in imaginative literature. Such an immersion would be much more possible for a free woman than a fugitive slave.

As a preliminary matter, I must emphasize that I do not interpret the comments of the esteemed collector of African Americana, Dorothy Porter (Wesley), who had originally purchased the manuscript for her collection, as meaning that she definitely believed the unknown author to have been a former slave. Her commentary is couched in terms of probability. The auction catalog copy states, "It is uncertain that this work is written by a 'negro'"; Gates interprets this to mean that "*someone* . . . believed Hannah Crafts to have been black" (Gates, "Introduction," p. xii). But the statement can also be read to imply the opposite—that even though the narrative is told in the first person by a black narrator, it's "uncertain" that the author was in fact black. Gates reports that Porter's correspondence says she thinks the unknown author seems to have had firsthand knowledge of estate life in Virginia. But Porter also says the "most important thing" about the manuscript is its apparent authorship by an African American ("Introduction," p. xix)—not, in other words, its apparent authorship by a former slave. I think of myself as remaining true to Porter's priorities in proposing that although the status of the author as a black woman is just about certain, her status as a fugitive slave is not so clear.

Many aspects of the narrative confirm that the author was female and African American. That she was a woman is deducible from the overwhelming preponderance of female characters and the female-centered domesticity of most events in the novel. Men in the book are few and far between; the chief male character, Mr. Trappe, is obviously an invention. That Hannah was African American is inferable from the social nuancing and frankness with which she criticizes other black people, characteristics that Gates elegantly analyzes in his introduction. It is also strongly suggested by the overwhelming preponderance of black characters, for—taking *Uncle Tom's Cabin* as exemplary—abolitionist texts by white authors (and some by blacks as well) tend to have a majority of white characters. A chief aim of such texts was to model appropriate actions and attitudes for white readers vis-à-vis the slave system and individual slaves they might encounter—notably, of course, fugitives—by portraying right and wrong white behaviors.

The abolitionist movement put into circulation numerous texts attributed to black authors who had been slaves. But this does not mean that all African American writers before the Civil War must have had slave backgrounds. On the eve of the Civil War, there were indeed three million people under slavery, but there were almost half a million free blacks as well. These free people had a wide range of options denied to the enslaved, but they endured a huge range of racist practices, and slavery certainly touched them more nearly than it touched white people. Many free blacks worked for the abolitionist cause in numerous ways. They may well have been more effective in harboring and helping fugitives than white people were. Knowledgeable about escape routes and familiar with fugitives' stories, they had a fund of information that could be put to use by a gifted writer. Might a black person who hadn't herself been a slave imagine herself convincingly into a slave's frame of mind? Why not? True, it would take a certain kind of brashness to present herself as a fugitive when she was not one; but since Hannah apparently never attempted to publish the manuscript, she never in fact tried to present herself as anything. That Hannah, therefore, could have been such a free person is at least supported by the original New Jersey provenance of the manuscript. It is also supported by Gates's discovery of a free New Jersey woman tellingly named "Hannah Vincent" in the census rolls—telling because the narrative begins on a Virginia plantation owned by one "Sir Clifford de Vincent." Because slaves were so often endowed with the surnames of those who "owned" them, Gates speculates that there was a real Vincent in Virginia whose name this Hannah might have borne. But if she were a free black, how inventive it would have been for her to imagine a Virginia plantation and give the "master" her own surname!

Authenticity, too, is a slippery concept. We don't dismiss the authenticity of *Beloved* on the grounds that Toni Morrison herself did not experience slavery firsthand. We believe, on the contrary, that she has got it exactly right. We don't complain about the authenticity of *Native Son* because Richard Wright never murdered anybody. We believe, after all, in the power of the novelistic imagination, and those of us who are teachers try to instill this belief in the literal-minded. Many of my undergraduate students over the years have rejected *Uncle Tom's Cabin* because Harriet Beecher Stowe was a white woman from Connecticut. Yet, in Stowe's own day, the novel worked as an inspiration to many African Americans; its account rang true to them. Students, too, often reject the work of Phillis Wheatley, the educated eighteenth-century slave who resided with a Boston family, on the grounds that she wasn't a "real" slave. They object forcefully to her apparent claim, in "On Being Brought from Africa to America," that "'Twas mercy brought me from my pagan land." They ask, "How could she write that?" And they answer, "Because she was not a field hand laboring in the cotton fields, she did not know what slavery was really about." This is, of course, a wrong way to think, but the position is quite understandable. Among the myriad experience-based accounts that might emerge from a slave system, which was at all times barbarous but nevertheless varied significantly from place to place and individual to individual, the "authentic" account is likely to be one that readers have agreed upon as most representative of whatever it is they believe—which means that the "authentic" is frequently a consensus, a convention, an audience creation.

—

I first learned about *Bondwoman* in April 2001, when Gates phoned and asked me to read the manuscript in typescript. As his introduction explains, he was asking several specialists in various aspects of nineteenth-century American literature to react to his find. At this early point in his investigation, Gates was considering the very remote (and quickly abandoned) possibility that the manuscript pre-dated passage of the Fugitive Slave Law in 1850. Because

Hannah says nothing at all about that law, and because antislavery literature after 1850 is typically saturated with references to it, it seemed initially possible that the manuscript dated from the 1840s. Therefore, Gates asked me specifically to watch for material that would make a pre-1850 date impossible, such as references to literary works that came later. Any such reference would mean that although the manuscript might have been partly composed before passage of the Fugitive Slave Law, it was not completed before 1850. Knowing the date would help focus the search for an author.

From the start I was struck by what seemed to be many ingenious reworkings of situations featured in *Uncle Tom's Cabin*, serialized during 1851–1852 and published as a book in 1852. Among examples are the slave-trader's account of a mother's suicide (pp. 104–105 in *Bondwoman*), along with other slave-trader and slave-owner accounts resembling speeches by the slave-trader Haley and the slave-owner Simon Legree. The hanging of a slave and her dog (pp. 21–23) grotesquely sensationalizes the event that motivates George Harris to run away in Chapter 3 of *Uncle Tom*, the drowning of his dog Carlo. (Compare Stowe's "the creature has been about all the comfort that I've had. He has slept with me nights, and followed me around days, and kind o'looked at me as if he understood how I felt" with Crafts's "It fed from her hand, slept in her bosom, and was her companion wherever she went. In her eyes it was more much more than a little dumb animal" [p. 21].) Hannah's secret stowing of clothing for escape in a garret evokes the plans of Cassy and Emmeline to get away from Legree's plantation. Hannah's briefly recounted reunion with her mother parallels Cassy's with Eliza (compare "Cassy caught her up in her arms, pressed her to her bosom, saying . . . 'Darling, I'm your mother!'" [Ch. 43] with "she suddenly rose one day, came to me, clasped me in her arms, and sobbed out in rapturous joy, 'child, I am your mother'" [p. 238]).

This of course answered that question right away from my angle. These and other textual moments are echoes, not exact copies, which in the aggregate point to thorough familiarity with *Uncle Tom's Cabin* and, possibly, with its non-fictional follow-up, *A Key to "Uncle Tom's Cabin,"* as well. (Later printings of the novel were often bound together with the *Key.*) Even the fact that Stowe's Eliza is impelled to run away for her child's sake, not her own, obliquely resembles the frame of mind leading Hannah to break out of a system to which she had sadly reconciled herself (more on this later).

It also seemed to me that the early description of the portraits in the Vincent mansion were vaguely reminiscent of Hawthorne in *The House of the Seven Gables* (1851), but for purposes of dating, the similarities with *Uncle Tom's Cabin* were enough. Evidence from other readers with other perspectives converged definitively on a post-1850 date for the completion of the manuscript.

Most persuasive is the scientific ink-and-paper analysis conducted by Dr. Joe Nickell, but there are also the extremely close borrowings from Charles Dickens's *Great Expectations,* published in 1853, references to Jane Johnson's escape from slavery in 1855, and references to events concerning Mormons and Indians from possibly as late as 1857.

The evidence goes beyond a post-1850 date to support composition during at most a three-and-a-half-year period between late 1857 and January 1861 (the attack on Fort Sumter). One can't imagine this work as being in progress after January 1861, given that it has no references at all to the Civil War. Still, the absence of references to the Fugitive Slave Law, if this was written by a fugitive slave in the 1850s, remained puzzling to me, and as I read the manuscript I kept asking myself how it might be explained.

The puzzle, to my mind, might be answered in two ways, one internal to the manuscript and the other external. The internal explanation would be that the logic of the story had nothing to do with fugitives. However, this is manifestly not the case, because the longest sequence in the novel—the flight of Hannah and her mistress from Mr. Trappe—is all about being a hunted fugitive. The terror of being hunted, indeed, becomes the narrator's leading trope for the psychological experience of being a slave. The external explanation would be that, not being a fugitive herself, the author felt free to focus entirely on conditions in the South. For her, slavery is a southern condition; the North equals freedom.

This is obviously far from an air-tight argument, but it opens the door to imagining Hannah as a free black woman. Then, the idea that Hannah was free is supported when the year 1857 is established as the earliest possible date for completion of the manuscript, because 1857 is a problematical date if the author was a fugitive. Gates, working with references to Hannah's service in the Wheeler family, narrows her escape possibilities to the interval between March 21 and May 4 of that year, when the Wheelers were in North Carolina where they had a plantation. Granted that Hannah is inventing all the way along, so that no particular event can be taken as absolutely true to the facts—still, if one takes her "several weeks" en route at face value, she could have arrived in the North no earlier than the summer of 1857. If one accepts that the manuscript was completed in 1857, she would have had to settle in New Jersey, meet and marry her husband, unite with her lost mother (presumably this element is entirely fictional, but still . . .), find employment as a teacher, and write much or all of the book in just a few months. If she wrote all of it after attaining freedom, she would have worked at an astonishing pace; but if she wrote only part of it, then when did she start, and how did she manage to bring the manuscript with her when she made her break, and how (of course) could she have known that she would eventually make it to freedom? Especially since she tells us toward the end of the story that only the direst circumstances would have motivated her to flee, we must imagine that for most of her time in slavery Hannah was not planning to escape and therefore could not have planned to write a narrative about her experiences.

This means that if she were a fugitive, she would have had to compose the whole thing after her escape. And this in turn makes the partial overlap between some of her references and some of the books in the Wheeler library into something of a red herring. As Gates has stated, Wheeler's books were typical rather than unique. Again, one has to ask—not how she had access to books, which was certainly possible for house slaves—but how she had access to pens, ink, paper (lots of paper) and the entire technology of writing, which is so very different from (and more expensive than what is required for) the far simpler act of reading. Hannah's narrative tells us how she learned to read (although she cagily never shows herself reading any book except the Bible) but never how she learned to write.

We, today, who learn and teach writing and reading as mutually constituting and reinforcing skills, easily forget that the two activities are intrinsically separable and historically have been separated until quite recently. Literacy studies of the New England colonies, for example, have shown that many more people could read than write; the people who marked contracts with an "x" often could read those very contracts but could not write even their names. The general populace in Bible-centered New England learned to read, but only those whose work demanded it (ministers, statesmen, merchants— along with their wives, like Anne Bradstreet) learned to write. It is thus not difficult to imagine a slave Hannah who could read, but it is very difficult to imagine such a Hannah who could write and just about impossible (for me, at least) to imagine a Hannah with access to the necessary tools for producing a weighty manuscript full of literary allusions like *Bondwoman*.

If one grants that a fugitive Hannah would not have started the manuscript until she reached freedom, then one has to push completion up to the very eve of the Civil War to allow her the time to write it. Of course, a free black woman might also have completed a manuscript late in 1860; but evidence continues to point to late 1857 as the most likely completion date. How much simpler it is to posit an author who was free, a woman with a modicum of formal schooling, herself a schoolteacher with access to books and magazines, with a firm sense of her audience (more on this below), and with time to compose in relatively favorable circumstances.

Does this theory invalidate *Bondwoman*'s authenticity? Obviously in a sense it does; but in another sense it does not. Hannah says of herself early on that she invites confidence and earns trust; the real Hannah could have met and talked to numerous fugitives passing through the free community in which she resided. She could have heard and absorbed stories secondhand; she had obviously read widely in the literature of slavery. She had the material and the imagination to make these her own. If *Bondwoman* synthesizes and adapts testimony from a range of sources that are themselves authentic, and if it produces its impact partly by presenting this testimony in the first person, its documentary value remains very high. True, one cannot use it to generalize about slave literacy; but the value of the testimony for slave experience is not undercut by this. As defenders of the authenticity of *I, Rigoberta Manchu* have pointed out, the *testimonio* oral tradition not only allows but actually requires the first-person speaker to voice the collectivity, including events that did not actually occur to that speaker but that did occur to those whose lives are being voiced. Even as I write this, evidence is emerging to put in question whether Olaudah Equiano was born in Africa, as his narrative claims, or in the Carolinas, as he indicated on various legal documents in England. If, rather than being a sufferer on the middle passage, Equiano heard, absorbed, and preserved for all time the stories of those who did suffer, we are still greatly in his debt. And, again, since Hannah made no attempt to publish her manuscript, it is unfair to accuse her of making false claims.

By the 1850s, first-person novels were omnipresent. Dickens, Thackeray, Bulwer-Lytton, Hawthorne, Melville, and Poe are just a few of the literary lions who were writing first-person novels and tales. And the fact that *Bondwoman* is, ultimately, a novel is to me the most important thing about it. Scholarly investigation has made it clear that the two other antebellum candidates for novels by black women—Harriet Wilson's *Our Nig* and Harriet Jacobs's *Incidents in the Life of a Slave Girl*—are in fact lightly fictionalized autobiographies. In *Bondwoman* we have the opposite: an apparent autobiography that is in fact a novel, the first such work we now have by an African American woman, and a very exciting example of sophisticated literary experimentalism as well. The work melds a range of literary types: not only the first-person *bildungsroman*, then in vogue, but also the domestic novel (this is my preferred term for what other critics often call the "sentimental" novel), the gothic, the slave narrative, the fairy tale (the kindly old couple in the woodland cottage who teach Hannah to read), comic satire (the blackening cosmetic that so embarrasses Mrs. Wheeler), current events reportage (politics in D.C., the Mormons, the Indians), historical fiction (the appearance of "real" characters in the novel, including—I think—John Wheeler and his wife), and the picaresque, whose episodic ligaments bind together all the novel's other segments.

The result is obviously an imaginative creation, but one that is true the way all good fiction is when it testifies to the power of story-telling as much or even more than it validates itself by factual accuracy. Consider just one example: the hanging of Rose and her dog. I am assured by my medical kin that even a clumsily hanged individual will live for fifteen minutes at most, but Hannah's old woman and her dog live for five excruciating days! It is preposterous, in a sense, but imaginatively far more effective, as Hannah draws that death scene out to the last degree.

—

When I read the text for the first time I felt—it was an intuition, but I haven't changed my mind about it—that Hannah was not a fugitive slave but a free woman. But like others of us who read the manuscript, I worried over the question of why Hannah did not try to publish it. I have come to think that this was the wrong question to ask, because it rises from our contemporary assumption that anybody who writes fiction writes to publish. But, thanks to work by many literary scholars specializing in different eras and nations, we are increasingly aware of the existence of so-called "manuscript cultures" in diverse social circles—that is, cultures where writing was produced but where for diverse reasons publication was never an issue.

It wasn't until the eighteenth century in the Western world that authorship for a mass audience became a possibility. The possibility depended on the emergence of certain kinds of technologies of print and distribution that hadn't existed earlier. It also depended on the development of business and proprietary attitudes toward writing that were outgrowths of market capitalism. In some cases (as in the Chesapeake Bay area in the eighteenth century), publishing for the masses was considered socially beneath the class status of the writers; in other cases (as in parts of New England), one wrote imaginatively only to entertain family and friends; and in still others across the social spectrum, writing (as in diaries) was a private activity meant for oneself alone. It is likely, that is, that an enormous amount of written material not only was never published but was never directed toward that end.

If Hannah was the schoolteacher she claims to be at the end of her novel, if she is the free Hannah Vincent found by Gates—a schoolteacher—then here is another situation where writing might be produced without an intention to publish. In fact, here is a situation in which publication could damage the writer's agenda. This is the situation of writing for one's students, something that in fact every professor who has ever written a lecture, or any teacher who has ever written out a lesson plan, knows very well. If the lecture is published, the teacher loses control over it. It is no longer available for oral delivery, because it's possible for people to "read the book."

There was a great deal of such writing in the nineteenth century, as there still is today. Textbooks were expensive and often ill suited for young people; teachers prepared their own. Moreover, they often wrote for intervals of student relaxation. We know of the existence of such materials because, on occasion—especially toward the end of a teacher's career—they did get into print, often as "vanity" publications given to the retiree's former students. If the students were girls, reading of this kind might be reserved for the sewing hour that was a regular feature of the class day. Ellen Tucker Emerson (Ralph Waldo's older daughter) wrote home about such reading hours in the elite boarding school she attended for three terms, run by Catharine Maria Sedgwick's sister-in-law. From four to five P.M., during the sewing hour, Mrs. Sedgwick read biographies and other published popular work to the students. In 1854, the educator Almira Hart Phelps, widely known for a best-selling botany text, published *Ida Norman; or, Trials and Their Uses,* a novel that (according to her preface) she began working on in 1846 and read in weekly installments to students "with a design of imparting moral instruction to the young under a form more interesting to the young than that of didactic essays." Other schoolteacher-authors who published original material of this kind at some point in their careers include Susannah Rowson and Hannah Webster Foster. Their published volumes are only the tip of a huge pedagogical iceberg.

Let's imagine, then, that Hannah's *Bondwoman,* with its "serviceable" (i.e., plainly legible, hence easy to read) rather than "elegant" handwriting, was composed for reading to students, chapter by chapter, over time. This theory allows one to perceive what may be the novel's most crucial stylistic feature: it was intended for a specific and all-black audience, which makes it doubly unique among early recovered works by African Americans. Almost all known antebellum books by black people addressed themselves to white readers, who were the purchasers of most print materials, and whose support for ending slavery was the ultimate aim of most black writing at the time. The next known prominent example of an all-black literary intention is not found until the 1890s, when a sizable black reading audience at last emerged as a determinant of African American writing. Frances E. W. Harper wrote *Iola Leroy* (1892) for an audience of African American Sunday School students. The great surge of African American writing in the 1920s not only depended on white patronage but also addressed itself mainly to white readers. In short, *Bondwoman,* as the earliest known example of any American work implying an audience of all African American readers (or, more accurately, auditors), is an extraordinary find.

Imagine, then, a novel-loving but pious teacher who wants to show fiction's power for good to her students and wants also to instruct these students in the ghastly realities of a system that touches them (free though they are) very closely. Then, rather than reading a Hawthorne tale to them, or a Poe story, or an extract from Charles Dickens, or a fugitive's account, or a chapter from *Uncle Tom's Cabin*, she adapts all these to her audience's situation and unifies them through an attractive protagonist who is also the narrator. If, at the conclusion of a long course of such reading, she intimates that she and the narrator are the same person, she produces a splendid effect that reminds students emphatically of the strange and wonderful status that storytelling occupies in the human world. If she was the kind of popular teacher I imagine her to be, these reading sessions would have been the highlight of the student experience.

So, then: *Bondwoman* may be a first-person fiction about slavery, constructed as a picaresque, funneling real experience through a wide range of literary models. It may be written by a free black woman schoolteacher to read to her students and never imagined as a candidate for publication. My reference to sewing above implies what I also think is likely: that the implied audience is specifically female, as is suggested by the almost exclusive focus on women's experience. And the diverse homilies on—to quote Gates—"breeding, education, morals, manners, hygiene" ("Introduction," pp. lxvi–lxvii) suggest, as he points out, an espousal of an antebellum ideology that is both bourgeois and domestic, an espousal forerunning the emergence of a "true" black bourgeoisie late in the nineteenth century (see also Gates's note to p. 142 [p. 249]). Rather than an unmediated disclosure of one fugitive's class mentality, pitting the house slave's gentility against the field slave's animalism (a mentality possibly representative, possibly not), this is a thoughtful exposition of a bourgeois ideology for the young audience that Hannah is instructing in their responsibilities as free black women. But, if she is not reflecting an "actual" slave mentality, neither is she distancing herself from such a mentality by presenting herself as superior to the slave whose story she ventriloquizes. Rather, she shows both that Hannah's superiority is something internal, available to all who work for it, but nevertheless requiring a degree of freedom for its development; she shows also that the very horrors of slavery require of those who are free the utmost commitment to bettering themselves. They are to better themselves not only for themselves but on behalf of those who don't have their inestimable advantage of being free.

Here, again, the heavy emphasis on marriage—that institutional bulwark of bourgeois life and the mainstay of bourgeois femininity—narrows the story's message decisively to women. It implies a narrative told by one woman to other women, or women-to-be, or women-in-training. The handling of the motif aligns *Bondwoman*'s values not with the sentimental seduction novels of the late eighteenth century but with the American domestic novel of the 1850s. In this extremely popular genre, the woman's happy ending always involves a good marriage. But at the same time, such a marriage rewards the protagonist's particularly national, even "Yankee," exhibition of independence and strength of character under trying circumstances, as well as her demonstration of willingness to live unmarried if she cannot marry an admirable man. In the evolution of fiction by white women in the United States, the eighteenth-century novel of seduction and female victimization had given way during the 1820s to this newer, more up-to-date, and more "American" formula whereby women developed themselves as responsible, moral agents with the strength to control their own destinies without abandoning their basic feminine nature.

Hannah's polemic against slave marriages of course reminds her auditors that slave women have no protection against what is much more accurately thought of as rape than seduction. But the story does not follow the pattern of a sentimental seduction novel, the kind popularized in the United States through the vogue of Susannah Rowson's *Charlotte Temple*, wherein the hapless heroine is seduced, abandoned, and then dies. Because the "rape" that Hannah flees from involves marriage to a black man, her polemic attributes an interesting kind of agency to women under slavery, one that may actually be more relevant to the circumstances of a free audience than to an audience of the enslaved.

The polemic invites two different readings. On the plot level, Hannah resists being "married" off to a vile field hand, which would drop her radically in the social scale that exists within slavery. On the expository level, Hannah generalizes from her refusal, saying that no slave woman should ever marry under any circumstances at all, because, no matter who her husband might be, she will become the unwitting creator of additional slave lives. Thus, Hannah makes it absolutely clear that the precondition for any marriage at all, regardless of what kind of cultural or even legal sanction that marriage appears to enjoy, is freedom. The "legality" of a slave marriage whose offspring are legally slaves, to her, is a cruel imposture.

Harriet Jacobs's *Incidents in the Life of a Slave Girl* also associates freedom with marriage, but from a very different angle. Jacobs's narrative makes black-black marriage an attractive but impossible ideal. Her story focuses on the forced black-white sexual connection to produce sympathy and outrage among white women readers. Jacobs shows that marriage is never a natural condition but always a legal construct, an institution sanctioned, defined, protected, and monitored by laws. As an individual operating in a lawless society, she does not imagine that a slave woman could remain celibate, and she decides to deploy her sexual allure within very narrow limits, electing one white sexual partner in order to forestall being raped by another. (It is worth noting that she miscalculates; what she thinks will happen—she'll be left alone by her tormentor, her children will be emancipated by their white father—doesn't happen, and eventually she has to run away.) Hannah's argument, developed within an all-black context, is much more abstract than Jacobs's. For Jacobs, celibacy among slave women is impossible, and it is precisely the supposed sexual laxness of black women that she attempts to analyze and deny. Hannah claims in effect that even were slaves' marriages legal, they would be immoral because it is always immoral to create a slave. Therefore, she argues for celibacy among slave women at all times. If celibacy becomes impossible, they must run.

The threat of a forced—but apparently legal—marriage is Hannah's motivation. She says: "nothing but this would have impelled me to flight. . . . I knew too much of the dangers and difficulties to be apprehended from running away ever to have attempted such a thing through ordinary motives" (p. 207). She knows, because she has already tried it. But this earlier, failed breakout attempt, the novel's longest single incident, had occurred out of loyalty to her fleeing mistress, a mulatto successfully passing as white who is hunted ruthlessly by a mysterious man, Mr. Trappe, whose life purpose is to "trap" and sell her back into slavery. This gothic plot device is unconvincing, if realism is the desired narrative impression. But whatever aims the device is meant to serve, it allows Hannah to be a loyal, faithful, even loving servant without making her into the complaisant tool of slavery that she'd have been if this same mistress were a white woman.

Still, Hannah at heart is no rebel but distinctly a person inclined to make the best of whatever situation she finds herself in. Not for her the masculine resistance on behalf of Enlightenment principles of rationality, freedom, and equality; not for her, of course, resistance on account of the assault on one's manhood by slave abuse. She tells us that "the life of a slave at best is not a pleasant one, but I had formed a resolution to always look on the bright side of things, to be industrious, cheerful, and true-hearted, to do some good though in an humble way, and to win some love if I could" (p. 11). This cheerful self-abnegation brings a modest earthly reward, at least for a time; she is "trusted and confided in" (ibid.). Here, Hannah clearly adapts a female domestic paradigm to slavery, striving to be exactly the kind of good, useful woman celebrated in one middle-class domestic narrative after another. This is "sentimentalism" in the key sense that its philosophical underpinnings are sympathy, fellow-feeling, compassion, benevolence, but it is far from the stock sentimentalism specializing in victims and tears. To the contrary, Hannah is never a victim.

But a compassionate character like this is not likely to act vigorously on her own behalf, although she will readily act to help others, especially the less fortunate. Her persecuted mistress is obviously such a one. And, when the threatened abuse involves creating another enslaved human being, flight can be justified on behalf of that other, if not for oneself. And thus it happens that Hannah takes flight the second time to avoid doing harm to others. This lesson, whatever its relevance to the situation of a slave woman, has incredible potential power for the free young women who I imagine listening to this story as it is read to them. It brings home more clearly than anything else could both that they owe their opportunities for marriage to their freedom and that freedom is not held for oneself alone.

In historical reality, many slaves attempted to run away and many succeeded. But most stayed put, and Hannah likely gives a good representation of the prevailing state of mind among those who bore with the institution rather than faced the dangers of flight. Still, possession of one's own sexuality—a specifically female marker of bourgeois selfhood—does outrank every other possible escape motive for her. When celibacy, or "chastity," is added to Gates's cluster of "breeding, education, morals, manners and hygiene" the female aspect of these other genteel virtues becomes all the more clear, as does the extent to which these are not private virtues but public goods. In domestic and historical fiction by white women including, for example, such well-known early examples as Lydia Maria Child's *Hobomok* (1824) and Catharine Maria Sedgwick's *Hope Leslie* (1827) the woman brings to nation-building her gentility, her refinement, her breeding, education, morals, manners, and hygiene—thus indicating that these (like her chastity) are woman-specific attributes that are powerfully important for the inevitable historical progress of civilization toward enlightened, democratic refinement. Says Caroline Kirkland in *A New Home—Who'll Follow?* (1839) of women on the frontier: "As women feel sensibly the deficiencies of the 'salvage' state, so they are the first to attempt the refining process, the introduction of those important nothings on which so much depends."

Thus, I imagine that this highly literate, omnivorously reading schoolteacher had absorbed, distilled, and applied the essential ideology motivating white women's domestic fiction to her narrative and created a heroine who resembled such fiction's domestic ideal. She did this not because she wanted to be "white" but because she understood the ideology to be an American inheritance, an American opportunity. She refashioned it to fit the aspirations of a free, nascent, black female bourgeois class within which women's special attributes would be cherished and usefully employed. And she did this a full generation before the emergence of a tradition of black women's domestic literature described by such scholars as Hazel Carby (*Reconstructing Womanhood: The Emergence of the Afro-American Woman Novelist*, 1987) and Claudia Tate (*Domestic Allegories of Political Desire: The Black Heroine's Text at the Turn of the Century*, 1992). Perhaps Hannah was in advance of her time; or perhaps, in the archives of unpublished materials there exist many numerous initiatives like hers, for the "betterment" and "uplift" of the rising generation of African American women.

———

I have been writing as though it were a foregone conclusion that Hannah was a free black woman, but of course the question must remain open until the author is decisively identified. But note now that in addition to having settled, married, found employment, and written the narrative in short order, a fugitive Hannah would have had to have fully absorbed a bourgeois ideology in this same brief space of time. It could have happened; but the free Hannah would have had much more opportunity—a lifetime, in effect. What then, of her apparent firsthand knowledge of Virginia and North Carolina, of slave escape routes, of the Wheeler connection?

Well, Gates tells us that Wheeler "became for a month or so the most famous slaveholder in the whole of America, and all because of an escaped female slave" ("Introduction," xlii). What would it mean to be famous—not to mention the *most* famous—if not that the man, his situation, and his views were circulated by the press throughout the public sphere, affording easy access to the information for literate persons with an interest in slavery? If his had been an obscure case, then (to me at least) the Wheeler connection would carry more weight than it does as a high-profile news story. In the context of a brief notoriety, Wheeler's appearance as a real person in the text aligns the work with the conventions of historical fiction, which require that one or more actual historical personages at least make cameo appearances for the sake of verisimilitude. In every antebellum novel about the American Revolution, for example, George Washington must make an appearance; this moment gives "authenticity" to what is otherwise clearly a fiction.

Then, too, some facts—or absence thereof—would also seem to militate against Hannah's having had a "real" connection with the Wheelers. I've already addressed (perhaps at tedious length!) the short window her escape allows for the massive adjustments necessary to identify her with the author of *Bondwoman*. I add now that if the escape occurred within Gates's time frame, one has also to wonder when she had hidden her escape clothing in the garret or, for that matter, wonder how to reconcile the explanation of her extraordinary motive for escape with the anticipation of a need to escape (p. 210). It seems telling, too, that Wheeler's diaries do not mention acquiring a slave replacement for the absconding Jane but do note employing non-slave serving women as replacements. Nor—most crucial for me—does he record the second occurrence of a slave woman's escape (which is what Hannah's would have been), only two years later. Wouldn't a man, who by his own lights had been so publicly burned by the first escape, have likely made some reference to this repetition? Having lost his court case for restitution over the loss of Jane, he might understandably be too embarrassed to disclose publicly that the event had happened again. Since, too, this was an unaided escape, he'd have nobody to sue this time.

But even if Wheeler kept silent in public, one would expect some venting in the diary. The absence does not constitute proof, and there are certainly some details about the Wheelers in *Bondwoman* that would seem to argue for firsthand experience with the family. Perhaps—to push my own perspective—these were gleaned from the newspaper accounts she read. Perhaps Hannah did indeed know the household in some way, even if she was not a slave within that household. If Hannah's knowledge of the Wheelers is perhaps more than one might expect if she was merely a bystander who read about Jane Johnson's escape (or even if she had somehow met Johnson), her knowledge of estate life in Virginia and other aspects of southern life and slave conditions, I believe could be gleaned from many a novel about the South, or even from a good school geography. A geography would also provide the names of towns, rivers, agricultural produce, and even the names of prominent residents. Samuel Goodrich's *Universal Geography* of 1833, a 900-plus-page tome in my personal library, contains information about Virginia's boundaries and extent, mountains, rivers, bays and harbors, climate, soil, "face of the country," "natural curiosities," geology, mineral springs; it lists all the counties and describes several cities (but not Milton, which was a hamlet not a city), summarizes Virginia history, manufactures, government, religion, and education. This geography also contains over seventeen pages of small type about life, customs, and manners in the South. It's the kind of book a person might consult before setting down a description of a place, for, oddly, a place is always most accurately represented "firsthand" if good research lies behind the representation. "Nature writing" is always an amalgam of personal impression and data from outside sources; so is news writing. And historical writing is always a re-creation based on research, since all of us live only in the present moment

Among research sources, one might count a number of popular novels set in the South—for example, by George Pendleton Kennedy, William Gilmore

Simms, "Mrs." E.D.E.N Southworth, or Eliza Dupuy. These books featured many detailed descriptions of southern plantation life. As for escape routes, fugitives on their way to Canada regularly passed through the free communities of New Jersey. Newspapers and journals were full of pro- and antislavery rhetoric and anecdote. The abolitionist press had a strong presence in the middle states; one of the most important of the antislavery publications, the weekly *National Era* (in which *Uncle Tom's Cabin* appeared in serialized form), was published in Washington, D.C. The *Era* contained much more than straight abolitionist reportage, including accounts of legislative sessions in the capital, poems, stories, and other materials. It might well have been a source for Hannah's comic account of political shenanigans in the national capital. A strongly acquisitive talent like hers could have absorbed all this diverse material from various print sources, synthesized it, and made it her own.

The census records for Hannah Vincent are clearly garbled, but there she is, coming close to filling the bill, as Gates makes clear. As I've already said, it is especially intriguing to imagine that—since no Vincent family has been unearthed in the region of Virginia where the novel begins—this Hannah attached her own name to the imagined owner of the fictional Poe-like Virginia plantation where Hannah spends her childhood. This adroitly turns the tables on the many masters who imposed their surnames on their slaves. It makes Hannah the author of her own antecedents in the best tradition of imaginative self-invention. A free Hannah Vincent, associated with the Methodist church and resident in Burlington, New Jersey, in her twenties or thirties during the crucial decade of the 1850s, would seem to fit well the external criteria for authorship of this narrative. The internal criteria—inventiveness, imagination, skill, passion, love for and appreciation of the power of fiction to tell the truth, commitment to the future of her students as free women citizens of the United States—are not to be located in any census.

Some readers will be disappointed if it turns out that Hannah was never a slave. And perhaps further research will unearth a fugitive slave woman who wrote this narrative. But as the first known pure work of imagination by an African American woman, *The Bondwoman's Narrative* should be considered even more of a discovery than it would be were it a purely factual narrative. From a cultural perspective, it gives us a glimpse of antebellum African American middle-class female pedagogy in the making. From an artistic perspective, it brings to light the work of a true literary genius.

20

The Outsider Within

The Acquisition and Application of Forms of Oppositional Knowledge in Hannah Crafts's The Bondwoman's Narrative

RUDOLPH P. BYRD

Each of us is here now because in one way or another we share a commitment to language and to the power of language, and to the reclaiming of that language which has been made to work against us.

—Audre Lorde, *Sister Outsider: Essays and Speeches*

The African American women's literary tradition, as is their history, is an amalgam, a mixture of diverse elements, some carefully and purposefully created and some a matter of coincidence or convenience. At the same time, this literature is an entity, an interstice, a nexus, and it is not deducible simply by identifying its components. It exists in its own right. . . . As literature the productions of African women may be subjected to the various theoretical perspectives. . . . To attempt to comprehend it without attention to its context is to ignore the elements that its creators and its readers certainly did not ignore.

—Frances Smith Foster, *Written By Herself: Literary Production by African American Women, 1746–1892*

"Belonging yet not belonging presents peculiar challenges."[1] This is the first of several truths asserted by Patricia Hill Collins in her insightful and influential *Fighting Words: Black Women and the Search for Justice* (1998). Along with such scholars, activists and writers such as Angela Davis, bell hooks, Valerie Smith, Beverly Guy-Sheftall, and Alice Walker, Hill Collins is one of the leading theorists in Black feminist thought. Hill Collins's prominence as a theorist in this now well-defined field of social theory is based upon not only the critical success of *Fighting Words* but also upon the influence of her ground-breaking *Black Feminist Thought: Knowledge, Consciousness, and the Politics of Empowerment* (1990). In *Black Feminist Thought*, Hill Collins provides an historical framework for understanding the emergence of a Black feminist standpoint in the work of such Black feminists as Davis, Guy-Sheftall, hooks, Walker, and Audre Lorde while also examining the manner in which African American women have managed the competing obligations of family, work, and activism. Eight years later in *Fighting Words*, Hill Collins examines again many of the themes and questions at the center of *Black Feminist Thought* while also exploring new ground through her analysis of the issues that Black feminist thought confronts as social theory as well as the issues it raises for social theory. Positing the life of Sojourner Truth as a rich site for the analysis of the goals and possibilities of Black feminist thought, Hill Collins argues that the power, credibility, and relevance of this or any other social theory depends in part upon its capacity to "move people towards justice."[2] In both of her books, Hill Collins contests the dominance of white feminists and their promulgation of theoretical positions that render Black women marginal and invisible, and in the second she offers a trenchant critique of the ideologies of Black nationalism and its current iteration, Afrocentrism. Also in both books, Hill Collins develops with increasing depth and acumen the concept of "outsider within," a concept which she argues convincingly captures the complex social location of African American women. Hill Collins's concept of "outsider within" is, I would like to suggest here, a useful theoretical framework for examining the position and choices of Hannah, the protagonist in Hannah Crafts's *The Bondwoman's Narrative* (2002), a novel now available for the first time to a national and international readership through the masterful editing of scholar Henry Louis Gates, Jr. As a mulatto slave in antebellum America, Hannah occupies the peculiar position of belonging and yet not belonging, that is to say, of "outsider within." Moreover, as the protagonist in this novel, she reveals the very peculiar challenges she confronts and overcomes, as well as the peculiar forms of knowledge she acquires from this marginal social location.

According to Hill Collins, the stance of the "outsider within" has its origins in the complex operations of racism, sexism, the limitations of class, and other forms of oppression upon the lives of African American women. More specifically, she maintains that the condition of the "outsider within" derives from the economic position that many African American women occupied as domestic workers. In *Black Feminist Thought*, Hill Collins writes that the vocation of domestic worker "allowed African-American women to see white elites, both actual and aspiring, from perspectives largely obscured from Black men and from these groups themselves." In analyzing accounts of Black domestic workers, Hill Collins discovered "the sense of self-affirmation [that Black women] experienced at seeing white power demystified." She argues that this complex process of demystification produced "a curious outsider-within stance, a peculiar marginality that stimulated a special Black women's perspective." Occupying the position of "outsider within," African American women have acquired, Hill Collins maintains, a "distinct view of the contradictions between the dominant group's actions and ideologies."[3]

In *Fighting Words*, Hill Collins develops further this intriguing concept based upon the migratory habits of African American women domestic workers who were intent upon deriving whatever benefits they could from an economic and social system whose objective was their continued subjugation. Like all migrations, the journey across the color line produced in these African American women a change of consciousness, or what Hill Collins terms a "distinct view" of the contradictions of the social and political order from which they were largely excluded by virtue of race, gender, and class. In her more recent elaboration of the concept of "outsider within," Hill Collins continues to endow it with the capacity to "describe social locations or border spaces occupied by groups of unequal power."[4] She writes further that under "conditions of social injustice, the outsider-within location describes a particular knowledge/power relationship, one of gaining knowledge about or of a dominant group without gaining the full power accorded to members of that group."[5] Extending and complicating the scope and implications of the concept of "outsider within," Hill Collins argues that in their position as domestic workers African American women "possessed access to what James Scott . . . calls the 'hidden transcripts' of *both* Black and White communities. In this case, Black women had access to the private knowledges that groups unequal in power wanted to conceal from one another."[6] "Theorizing from outsider-within locations," writes Hill Collins, "reflects the multiplicity of being on the margins within intersecting systems of race, class, gender, sexual, and national oppression, even as such theory remains grounded in and attentive to real differences in power. . . . In other words, theorizing from outsider-within locations can produce distinctive oppositional knowledges that embrace multiplicity yet remain cognizant of power."[7]

In what particular ways does the protagonist in Hannah Crafts's novel embody Hill Collins's concept of "outsider within"? Put another way, how does the life of the protagonist in this antebellum novel, which is an amalgam of the slave narrative and sentimental fiction, reflect the multiplicity of positions and the attendant acquisition of the special forms of knowledge that flow from a very distinctive species of marginality? In her position as "waiting maid," Hannah learns more about the habits, machinations, and cruelties of her masters and mistresses than doubtless she would care to learn, but never-theless the knowledge she acquires in the subordinate position of "outsider within" provides her with a very special perspective or "angle of vision" on the operations of power in the plantation household. The "hidden transcripts" or "private knowledges" that Hannah acquires as she moves from slavery to free-dom are forms of knowing that in general terms encompass, I would like to suggest here, the relations of power within the context of slavery. More specifically, these "private knowledges" endow Hannah with a deepening in-sight and perspective on the dynamics of power between master and slave, be-tween mistress and slave, and between master and mistress. These "hidden transcripts" or "private knowledges" produce in their totality what Hill Collins terms "distinctive oppositional knowledges" that catalyze Hannah to resist and overcome the hegemony and power of the slaveholding class. These are the questions and positions I wish to engage in the course of this essay. As I do so my argument is based upon the belief that Hannah Crafts shares cer-tain aspects of the life of her protagonist, that is to say, she is a mulatto, a former slave, and a "keen observer of the dynamics of slave life."[8] I am aware of the debate regarding Crafts's racial ancestry, but I am persuaded by the im-pressive "circumstantial evidence" that Gates summons in his well-argued in-troduction that Crafts was both a "black woman and a former slave."[9]

Born into slavery, Hannah is emblematic of the condition of "outsider within" by virtue of her status as a slave in antebellum Virginia. As chattel property, she belongs to or is the possession of someone else. Lacking free-dom, she does not belong to herself, or rather she is not in full possession of the very limited range of possibilities available to African American women, free or enslaved, of her generation. Doomed to what Orlando Patterson has termed a "social death," Hannah occupies a marginal position in the social and political order of antebellum America.[10] In the opening paragraphs of the novel, she describes her orphaned status as a slave on the plantation of Lin-dendale in Virginia as well as the manner in which she comes to understand the dynamics of power between master and slave:

> I was not brought up by any body in particular that I know of. I had no train-ing, no cultivation. The birds of the air, or beasts of the field are not freer from moral culture than I was. No one seemed to care for me till I was able to work, and then it was Hannah do this and Hannah do that, but I never complained as I found a sort of pleasure and something to divert my thoughts in employ-ment. Of my relatives I knew nothing. No one ever spoke of my father or mother, but I soon learned what a curse was attached to my race, soon learned that the African blood in my veins would forever exclude me from the higher

walks of life. That toil unremitted unpaid toil must be my lot and portion, without even the hope or expectation of any thing better. This seemed the harder to be borne, because my complexion was almost white, and the obnoxious descent could not be readily traced, though it gave a rotundity to my person, a wave and curl to my hair, and perhaps led me to fancy pictorial illustrations and flaming colors.[11]

Growing up without a knowledge of her antecedents, Hannah soon acquires a knowledge of her condition and the defining features of the relationship between master and slave through, as she suggests, the retelling of the Old Testament story of the curse of Ham by pro-slavery advocates. Further, she writes that the realties of her condition as a slave are soon impressed upon her through the harsh regimen of plantation life where her childhood was lost completely to the exigencies of plantation labor. As a slave, Hannah embodies in many respects the quintessential expression of the "outsider within," for in this position where she possesses not rights but only obligations she gains a knowledge, according to Hill Collins, of the "dominant group without gaining the full power accorded to members of that group." Of course, Hannah's social location of "outsider within" is complicated by the fact of her mixed ancestry, that is to say, by the fact that she is physically white and racially mixed. Although she states that the "obnoxious descent could not be readily traced," in other words that she could pass for white, she is nevertheless a slave because of the inflexibility of the one-drop rule in circulation and rigidly enforced then and now (one drop of Negro blood doth a Negro make), as well as the rule promulgated by slaveholders that the slave child shall inherit the condition of the mother. In this novel of passing that sounds many of the themes that would be treated by such African American writers as Frances E. W. Harper and Charles Chesnutt, the ambiguity of Hannah's racial status introduces plainly an additional level of complexity to her position of "outsider within." As a mulatto, she is a symbol of the degeneracy of the slave system and also a threat to a social and political order that prizes racial purity. Interestingly, at the point of her second escape Hannah stretches and complicates further the condition of "outsider within" in this early novel of passing by making the crucial decision to conceal the fact of her race and sex by passing successfully as a white man. During the final stage of her journey from slavery to freedom, the narrator undergoes yet another transformation. At the insistence of Aunt Hetty, the white woman possessing anti-slavery views who teaches Hannah to read and write, she leaves Wilmington, North Carolina, by ferry for free territory disguised or passing as a white woman. As a slave and as a mulatto, as well as an individual who successfully demonstrates under perilous conditions that race and gender are social constructions, Hannah embodies many of the contradictions that Hill Collins attributes to the social location of "outsider within."

Occupying this position of multiplying contradictions while also migrating between the Black world and the white world, between the world of the free and the world of the enslaved, Hannah informs us that as a house servant she acquired a knowledge of the social order of slavery through observation. Shortly after the arrival of the mistress with whom she would make her first attempt to escape slavery, she reveals herself as a perceptive observer of the operations of power during one of many ritual dinners honoring the new bride of Lindendale:

> As one of the waiters I saw the company at supper. There were jeweled ladies and gallant gentlemen. There were youthful faces and faces of two score that strove to cheat time, and refuse to be old. There was a glare and glitter of deceitful smiles and hollow hearts.
>
> I have said that I always had a quiet way of observing things, and this habit grew upon me, sharpened perhaps by the absence of all elemental knowledge. Instead of books I studied faces and characters, and arrived at conclusions by a sort of sagacity that closely approximated to the unerring certainty of animal instinct. (27)

Hannah's highly developed powers of observation and her seemingly astute judgment of character are the foundation for the development of what Hill Collins terms "an angle of vision" on the operations of power between master and slave within the plantation household.[12] Existing on the margins of the social order of the plantation household yet, paradoxically, essential to its operations, the narrator soon develops through her careful study of "faces and characters" a special perspective on white supremacy. Plainly, her survival in this complex and dangerous social order depends upon her ability to read and interpret the signs and symbols that signify her position as slave, or as "outsider within."

In an earlier passage in the novel, Hannah's position as "outsider within," that is to say her precise location within the context of the master/slave paradigm, assumes an almost metaphorical cast. Having volunteered to close the windows in one of the upper rooms in the plantation, she finds herself for the first time in the portrait gallery leading to the southern turret. The white maid Mrs. Bry insists that Hannah perform this task without loitering in the beautiful and private rooms of Lindendale, but our young protagonist ignores this admonition. Crafts's short migration from the parlor to the portrait gallery is not only a journey from the public to the private spaces of Lindendale but also a journey through its history as revealed in the idealized representations of the ancestors of the current master of this Virginia plantation. Upon entering the portrait gallery, she is cognizant of the beauty of the room, the history it enshrines and her relationship as a slave to this history:

> Though filled with superstitious awe I was in no haste to leave the room; for there surrounded by mysterious associations I seemed suddenly to have grown old, to have entered a new world of thoughts, and feelings and sentiments. I was not a slave with these pictured memorials of the past. They could not enforce drudgery, or condemn me on account of my color to a life of servitude. As their companion I could think and speculate. In their presence my mind seemed to run riotous and exult in its freedom as a rational being, and one destined for something higher and better than this world can afford. (17)

In the presence of what many would term her racial and social superiors, Hannah masters her sense of "awe" and imagines herself not as a slave but rather as a "companion" to the ancestors of Lindendale. Through the power of her imagination, she transcends for a moment her twin position of slave and of "outsider within" in the very place where that position is also simultaneously reinforced, for one such as she will never be represented in this gallery. This migration from the parlor to the inner sanctum of Lindendale has produced a striking alteration in Hannah's consciousness. This carefully drawn moment in the gallery of Lindendale where history, race, gender, and caste are trumped temporarily by the assertion of both a powerful will and an expansive imagination recalls W.E.B. Du Bois's imagined colloquies with Shakespeare, Balzac, Dumas, and others "above the Veil" of race described in *The Souls of Black Folk* (1903).[13] Like Du Bois in his visionary encounter with his alleged white superiors with whom he imagines a world free of the stain of white supremacy, in the presence of the powerful ancestors of Lindendale Hannah also imagines herself as a "rational being, one destined for something higher and better than this world can afford." Significantly, Hannah does not surrender this nascent sense of possibility and the marked feeling of equality with the aristocracy of Lindendale even after she is upbraided by Mrs. Bry for disobeying her order not to loiter in the private rooms of the plantation: "Looking at the pictures," she repeated, "as if such an ignorant thing as you are would know any thing about them" (17). While she makes no reply to Mrs. Bry's chastisement, one which reveals the manner in which race and caste have determined her perception of this young slave, in her private musings captured in the chapter's final paragraph Hannah plainly has the last word, as it were. She asserts to the reader of her novel that ignorance is not the defining feature of her condition; on the contrary, she believes that those "to whom man teaches little, nature like a wise and prudent mother teaches much" (18).

As Hannah negotiates the personalities and the histories that mark the route between the public and private spaces of Lindendale and the other plantations she inhabits during the course of her tale, she acquires what Hill Collins terms "the hidden transcripts" or the "private knowledges that groups unequal in power wanted to conceal from one another."[14] In the case of Hannah, the "hidden transcripts" and "private knowledges" often, though not always, assume the form of secrets. In an early passage in the novel, she recalls how many sought her out for support and sympathy and in the process made her the custodian of many confidences: "By and by as I grew older, and was enabled to manifest my good intentions, not so much by words, as a manner of sympathy and consideration for every one, I was quite astonished to see how much I was trusted and confided in, how I was the made the repository of secrets, and how the weak, the sick, and the suffering came to me for advice and assistance"(11). As Hannah matures into womanhood, it is not only the weak but also the powerful who entrust their secrets to her. As the "repository of secrets," Hannah rivals Mr. Trappe as the keeper of the secrets of both the vulnerable and the privileged. The difference, however, between Hannah and the aptly named Mr. Trappe is that unlike this slave speculator who masquerades as a solicitor, she does not use the "private knowledges" she acquires to entrap and exploit others. These "private knowledges" form the basis for her decision to resist through flight the hegemonic powers of the slaveholder. Strengthened by these "private knowledges," which in their totality function as "distinct oppositional knowledges," Hannah makes the courageous decision, as I will show, to liberate others as well as herself.

Hannah's knowledge of the dynamics of power that define the relationship between master and slave is revealed to her, as I have suggested, at an early age in a variety of ways. Beyond her many personal experiences which sometimes assume the cast and weight of metaphor, she acquires a widening perspective on the relationship between master and slave through the tales told by slaves on the Lindendale plantation in Virginia. One such melodramatic tale is the "legend of the Linden," the haunted tree planted by Sir Clifford, an ancestor to the current heir of Lindendale, who in his cruelty is responsible for the death of Rose, a slave "who had been nurse to his son and heir, and was treated with unusual consideration by the family in consequence" (21). Rose had developed a special tie to a dog given to her by her daughter who was sold away from the plantation. The little dog "was her treasure, and sole possession, and the only earthly thing that regarded her with fondness, or to whose comfort her existence was essential" (22). According to plantation lore, Sir Clifford took offence at Rose's pet and ordered her to kill it, but because of her deep attachment to the dog, who was the last living link to her daughter, the old slave woman refused. As a result of her defiance, Sir Clifford orders that both Rose and her dog be gibbeted to a large linden. Notwithstanding the entreaties of his wife and son, the enraged Sir Clifford watched Rose and her beloved pet hang suspended from the bough of a linden for little more than five days before both died. Moments before her death, Rose pronounces the following curse upon Sir Clifford and the descendants of Lindendale: "I will hang here till I die as a curse to this house, and I will come here after I am dead to prove its bane. In sunshine and shadow, by day and by night I will brood over this tree, weigh down its branches, and when death, or sickness, or misfortune is to befall the family ye may listen for ye will assuredly hear the creaking of its limbs . . . " (25). Retribution is visited upon the heirs of Sir Clifford; indeed, Hannah leaves little doubt that the tragic end of the marriage of the current master and mistress of Lindendale, a seeming aneurism and suicide within months of their marriage, is a manifestation of the enduring power of Rose's curse. A precursor of Paul Laurence Dunbar's "The Haunted Oak" in *Lyrics of Lowly Life* (1896) or tales of slavery and the supernatural set forth in Charles Chesnutt's *The Conjure Woman* (1899), "the legend of the Linden" documents one of the many atrocities that constitutes only a small part of the "hidden transcript" between master and slave.

From her position of "outsider within," Hannah's enlarging education on the relations of power between master and slave also includes knowledge of the slave's relationship to the mistress. In this instance, the narrator does not summon plantation lore in order to explore aspects of this relationship but rather reconstructs her own divergent experiences with two mistresses, the first being the mistress of Lindendale and the second the mistress of the North Carolina plantation from which she makes her final escape.

Predictably, Hannah's first impressions of the new mistress of Lindendale are based upon her highly developed powers of observation. In a passage laden with the tropes of sentimental fiction, Crafts leaves little doubt that the recently arrived mistress of Lindendale is burdened with a secret:

> My mistress required little assistance and I had full leisure to examine and inspect her appearance. . . . I did not see, but I felt that there was a mystery, something indefinable about her. She was a small brown woman, with a profusion of wavy curly hair, large bright eyes, and delicate features with the exception of her lips which were too large, full and red. She dressed in very good

taste and her manner seemed perfect but for an uncomfortable habit she had of seeming to watch everybody as though she feared them or thought them enemies. I noticed this, and how startled she seemed at the echo of my master's footsteps when he came to lead her down stairs. I am superstitious, I confess it; people of my race and color usually are, and I fancied then that she was haunted by a shadow or phantom apparent only to herself, and perhaps even the more dreadful for that. (26–27)

While the narrator suggests that she is more superstitious, by virtue of "my race," than perceptive, we soon discover that in performing the duties of "waiting maid" that Hannah's reading of the interior life of her mistress is correct.

Hannah's suspicions regarding "the shadow or phantom" haunting the life of her mistress are intensified by conversations she has with Lizzy, the mistress's "first maid." As a "Quadroon, almost white, with delicate hands and feet, and a person that any lady in the land might have been proud of," Lizzy is far more knowledgeable about her mistress's past than she reveals; indeed, she possesses "private knowledges" based upon a certain kind of education acquired in plantation society (33). In a chapter predictably entitled "A Mystery Unraveled," Hannah finds herself once again the "repository of secrets." Increasingly overwrought as a consequence of living with the possibility of the discovery of her secret, her new mistress reveals the story of her past:

And then in broken and incoherent sentences she related the story of her life— how she had been brought up, and educated by a rich gentleman, whom she called father, and by whom she was introduced into society as his daughter— how she had been taught by him to consider her mother as dead, and how she had since ascertained through Mr. Trappe, that whoever might be her paternal relative, her mother was a slave then toiling in the cotton fields of Georgia. Then she clasped her hands, and moaned and sorrowed, refusing to be comforted.

"Can you be certain that his information is correct" I inquired "and that he does not merely seek to torment and trouble you?"

"It is true, all true, I have had sufficient proofs. Only one thing is wanting to complete the chain of evidence, and that is the testimony of an old woman, who it seems was my mother's nurse, and who placed me in her lady's bed, and by her lady's side, when that Lady . . . was to[o] weak and sick and delirious to notice that the dead was exchanged for the living." (44)

The very sympathetic Hannah knows that her mistress speaks truthfully of her past as she earlier had overheard an exchange between her and Mr. Trappe in which elements of this classic story of miscegenation and slavery were revealed.

It is a version of the southern story of race, slavery, and passing that Mark Twain would explore almost fifty years later in his novel *Pudd'nhead Wilson* (1894). Doubtless, Hannah feels a deeper bond to her mistress not only because of her decision not to be blackmailed into a marriage by Mr. Trappe but also because of the similarities in their origins and racial makeup, which, as a consequence of the difference in their social station, goes unremarked between them. Strangely, this is a silence that is never broken notwithstanding the fact that Hannah comes to regard her mistress as a "sister or a very dear friend" (44).

Plainly, the "private knowledges" that Hannah acquires from her mistress are ones that could topple the social order of Lindendale. These forms of knowledge reveal the ways in which the mulatto—I am thinking now of the mistress of Lindendale—is a threat to the social order of slaveholding society, and also the degree to which power relations in this society turn upon this secret knowledge of race and ancestry. It is these "private knowledges" that constitute "the hidden transcripts" that Hannah, by virtue of her position of "outsider within," now possesses. Interestingly, she notes that her master remained blissfully unaware of the drama unfolding within his own house. "Our master was an easy good sort of man," observes Hannah, "fond of his wife, but not given to habits of observation. It never occurred to him that the burden of a great misfortune was on her mind, or that other causes than ill health occasioned her lowness of spirits, her avoidance of society, and long detention in her rooms" (35). Of course, the master eventually learns of the dark realities that threaten to destroy his marriage and position in society, and it is this knowledge that results, as we discover, in his suicide. Fully in possession of these "hidden transcripts," Hannah advises her mistress to forsake her ties to Lindendale, including her marriage. Both mistress and slave become runaways and in the process forge a sisterhood based upon their joint decision to resist the definitions and corrupting power of slavery: "Hand in hand we listened, all was still; we went down stairs softly, the hall was deserted; we opened and shut the door—again listened and looked, but no one was near—then paused, lingered a moment, turned to the house with a farewell glance, and then . . . turned to the wide expanse of field and forest and meadow, crossed by intersecting roads, and hurried away" (51). In this crucial juncture, the "hidden transcripts" or "private knowledges" constitute the basis for the "distinctive oppositional knowledges" that motivate Hannah to liberate herself and as well as another. Unfortunately, flight does not result in the acquisition of freedom, for her mistress dies of an apparent aneurism while still a runaway, and Hannah, through a series of financial transactions in which she herself, ironically, plays the role of amanuensis, finds herself once again a slave and the waiting maid of yet another mistress.

There are many important and striking differences between the first mistress and the second mistress. Unlike her predecessor, the second mistress to whom Hannah functions as a "Lady's maid" is apparently not a mulatto but is instead a woman of undisputed Anglo-American descent. Moreover, as the author of this tale, Crafts makes the crucial decision to provide the name of this second mistress, whom she calls Mrs. Wheeler. As Gates reveals in his introduction, the Mrs. Wheeler who appears in the second half of this novel is none other than the wife of John Hill Wheeler, assistant secretary to President Franklin Pierce.[15] As Gates argues in his carefully researched introduction, this historical information is crucial in determining the period of this holograph's composition, which, as he reveals, took place during the decade of the 1850s. Further, the fact that Gates was able to confirm the existence of Mrs. John Hill Wheeler underscores for us the autobiographical nature of this work of fiction, for Crafts, according to Gates, was a slave of the Wheelers. Plainly, Crafts's knowledge of the operations of plantation life is not based solely upon her reading of slave history and her knowledge of oral history but also upon her twin experience of slave or "outsider within." This fact endows her novel with a certain authority, for Crafts conceives and orders the various parts of this tale out of her own wide experience as chattel. This autobiographical element also endows her novel with a certain ambiguity, for until other scholars extend and complete the impressive work of authentification begun by Gates, we will be compelled always to speculate about the possibility of the historical existence of each character we encounter in this antebellum novel. In the character and person of Mrs. Wheeler, Crafts's narrator provides us with another perspective on the nature of power in the plantation household between mistress and slave.

The perspective that Hannah acquires of elite plantation society in both Washington, D.C., and North Carolina through the person of Mrs. Wheeler is far from flattering. As the twin and opposite of her first mistress, Mrs. Wheeler embodies the vanity, corruption, and the cruelty of persons of her class who are motivated only by comfort and power. While Hannah reveals the dark way in which power manifests itself in a presumably white woman, there are also moments of humor, as revealed in her first encounter with her soon-to-be-mistress. Having been without a "Lady's maid" for some weeks because the slave who once occupied that position has acquired her freedom in what Gates tells us is a much celebrated escape of the 1850s, Hannah's first charge is to "dress" Mrs. Wheeler's hair.[16] As she sets about to perform this duty armed "with combs, brushes, and pomatum [pomade]," what emerges is a portrait of the mistress that is in marked contrast to the idealized representations of southern white womanhood elevated to the level of dogma within the cult of true womanhood emerging during this period:

"I was too feeble to think of attempting it myself, and since Jane ran off, there
has been no one to whom I could think of entrusting my head, till Mrs. Henry
so warmly recommended you."

"I am much obliged to Mrs. Henry I am sure.["]

"Jane was very handy at almost everything" she continued. "You will seldom
find a slave so handy, but she grew discontented and dissatisfied with her condition, thought she could do better in a land of freedom, and such like I
watched her closely you may depend; there, there, how you pull."

The comb had caught in a snarl of hair.

"Forgive me madam, but I could not help it; the hair is actually matted." (149)

As Hannah sets about to order the confusion of her mistress's hair there
are, predictably, other setbacks or snarls. Encountering other "matted" sec-
tions of hair, the tendered-headed Mrs. Wheeler begins to complain of Hannah's not so gentle technique of dressing hair:

"Hannah Hannah, why I can't stand such rough usage."

"I do my best, madam, but your hair is in a dreadful state."

"I know that, but do be careful," and she continued the rehearsal of Jane's conduct. (150)

For a variety of reasons, this is a remarkable scene in African American literature of this period. According to Frances Smith Foster, the "most prominent African American writers of the antebellum period are Jarena Lee, Zilpha
Elaw, Nancy Prince, Harriet E. Wilson, Frances E. W. Harper, and Harriet Jacobs."[17] If Crafts had found a publisher for her novel during this period, that
is to say, if she had overcome the racism "during the era of the most fervent
social reform" that ironically resulted in the development of what Foster
terms "woman's literature . . . along separate paths," she would doubtless be
listed among this group of pioneering figures in African American literature.[18]
What is remarkable about Crafts's hair-dressing scene is that nothing like it
appears in the fiction of Lee or other African American writers of this period.
It stands apart as a scene in which the power of the mistress is undermined
and ridiculed through the performance of a duty that necessarily involves a
degree of intimacy between mistress and slave. For those interested in the politics of hair in American culture, I suspect that this is a scene that will be ref-
erenced often for its irony, humor, and its subtle subversion of the power relations between mistress and slave.

The growing intimacy between Hannah and Mrs. Wheeler yields the first
of many insights that reveals the complexity of the relationship between mis-

tress and slave. Ever the perceptive observer of human behavior from her position of "outsider within," Hannah, in the process of dressing Mrs. Wheeler's
hair, addresses a readership that is presumably unaware of the closeness and
dependency that mark an otherwise hierarchical relationship:

> Those who suppose that southern ladies keep their attendants at a distance,
> scarcely speaking to them, or only to give commands have a very erroneous im-
> pression. Between the mistress and her slave a freedom exists probably not to be
> found elsewhere. A northern woman would have recoiled at the idea of com-
> municating a private history to one of my race, and in my condition, whereas
> such a thought never occurred to Mrs. Wheeler. I was near her. She was not
> fond of silence when there was a listener, and I was pleased with her apparent
> sociality. (150)

While Hannah would soon discover that she enjoys less and less the company of her mistress, this observation reveals the shifting, subtle nature of the
evolving relationship between mistress and slave that would predictably produce in her a less than exalted view of the mistress in particular and the slaveholding class in general. In his introduction, Gates cites William Andrews's very
perceptive reading of this moment in Crafts's novel, which recalls, as he points
out, a similar moment in the slave narrative by Elizabeth Keckley entitled *Behind
the Scenes, or Thirty Years a Slave, and Four Years in the White House* (1868). According
to Andrews, what is important about these two texts is that "a black woman is
trying to get her white readers to realize that the relationship between white
and black women in slavery was not one of mere dictation, white to black, or
mere subjugation of the black woman by the white woman."[19] As Gates points
out "Andrews's observation convincingly reinforces Crafts's authenticity both as
a black woman and a former slave."[20] I also would add that Crafts and Keckley
occupied in a variety of social locations the position of "outsider within," and
in these locations they acquired "the set of hidden transcripts" that demystified
for them the operations of white supremacy.

Another humorous but finally bitter episode that serves to reveal the complexity of Hannah's position of "outsider within," as well as mark a pivotal
moment in her relationship with Mrs. Wheeler, is one that contains elements of
minstrelsy. Hannah observes that her second mistress "had been a belle in youth,
and the thought of her fading charms was unendurable" (157). Having been
made aware of a new beauty aid by an acquaintance similarly preoccupied with
averting the unwelcomed effects of aging, Mrs. Wheeler dispatches Hannah to
the chemist in order to acquire "a box of the Italian Medicated Powder" that re-
putedly possesses the capacity to make old skin young again. Mrs. Wheeler

wastes no time in making use of the powder; indeed, she applies it shortly before she goes out on an errand for her husband. Upon her return, Mrs. Wheeler learns of an unexpected side effect of the "Italian medicated powder," which she discovers in the presence of first Hannah and then her husband:

> In two hours a carriage stopped at the door; the bell was rung with a hasty jerk, and the servant admitted a lady, who came directly to Mrs. Wheeler's apartment. I was greatly surprised; for though the vail [sic], the bonnet, and the dress were those of that lady, or exactly similar, the face was black.
>
> I stood gazing in mute amazement, when a voice not in the least languid called out "What are you gazing at me in that manner for? Am I to be insulted by my own slaves?"
>
> Mr. Wheeler just that moment stepped in. She turned towards him, and the mixture of surprise and curiosity with which he regarded her was most ludicrous.
>
> "Are you all gone mad?" inquired the not now languid voice. "Or what is the matter?"
>
> "You may well ask that question," exclaimed Mr. Wheeler, sobbing with suppressed laughter. "Why, Madam, I didn't know you. Your face is black as Tophet.["]
>
> "Black?" said the lady, the expression of astonishment on his countenance transferred to hers.
>
> "Hannah bring the mirror."
>
> I complied.
>
> She gazed a moment, and then her mingled emotions of grief, rage and shame were truly awful . . . . (165–166)

As we discover by reading further in Crafts's novel, "Mrs. Wheeler's face was the topic of the city" (169). There were many, as "the Lady's maid" tells us, who were at great pains to explain behavior so uncharacteristic of a person of Mrs. Wheeler's standing: "Some viewed it in the light of a little masquerade; and thus taken it became extremely funny. Others considered it to have originated in a wager, and thought the lady rather debased herself. Very few regarded it as it really was, the deserved punishment of an act of vanity" (169). In some of the most humorous and well-paced writing in the novel, Hannah delivers her harshest judgment of Mrs. Wheeler. And this is a judgment that is based upon what Hill Collins terms "private knowledges," for as Hannah notes earlier in the novel, "I was near her" (150). Being "near her," Hannah has no illusions about her mistress and perceives her as cruel, mercurial, and vainglorious. Very plainly, the problematic and undignified behavior of Mrs. Wheeler has demystified further for Hannah the so-called sanctity of white womanhood and the operations of power within slaveholding society. Occupying the position of "outsider within," Hannah's perception and judgment of Mrs. Wheeler destabilize the pedestal that so many white women of her era occupied either willingly or by coercion, while also revealing the rather shallow foundations for the defense of white womanhood within the context of white supremacy.

Feeling that she may have lost face, as it were, as a result of this unrehearsed performance of blackface, Mrs. Wheeler swears Hannah to secrecy. The "Lady's maid" notes that partly because of the effects of this humiliating episode, the Wheelers leave Washington and return to North Carolina. Through the machinations of Maria, "a dark mulatto, very quickly motioned with black snaky eyes," Mrs. Wheeler becomes convinced that Hannah has broken her confidence and broadcast this peculiar instance of minstrelsy among the slaves on her North Carolina plantation. For this alleged betrayal, Mrs. Wheeler expels her from the big house to the slave quarters where she informs Hannah with marked contempt, "You can herd with them" (205). Confronted with banishment as well as an unwanted marriage with the slave Bill, who has designs upon her, Hannah is fully aware of the humiliating and bitter implications of her fall from status: "Accused of a crime of which I was innocent, my reputation with my Mistress blackened, and most horrible of all doomed to association with the vile, foul, filthy inhabitants of the huts, and condemned to receive one of them for my husband my soul actually revolted with horror unspeakable" (205).

The revolt engendered in her soul results in the outward and, for her, ultimate manifestation of revolt: flight. Hannah's determination to defy and resist the unjust punishment meted out to her by Mrs. Wheeler is reflected in the final sentence of the chapter significantly entitled "Escape": "This done [the cutting of her hair and the donning of her disguise], I quenched the light, cautiously descended as I went up, let myself out by a back door, stood a moment to collect my thoughts and then starting *ran for my life* [emphasis added]" (210). Like the heroines of the sentimental productions of the nineteenth century, Hannah vows to protect her virtue. Unlike the heroine of Thomas Dixon's *The Clansman: An Historical Romance of the Ku Klux Klan* (1905), whose pursuit by a crazed mulatto leads to her suicidal jump from a cliff captured in dramatic filmic strokes in D. W. Griffith's *Birth of a Nation* (1915), Hannah chooses not suicide but life and freedom through a carefully planned escape in which she passes ultimately as a member of the social and racial group responsible for this final degradation. Hannah imagines flight rather than suicide as the most effective means of resistance. Arguably the first African American woman novelist, Crafts, in arranging for her heroine to choose life

and freedom over suicide, inaugurates a pattern that would distinguish the fiction of African American women from that of Anglo-American women. This
is a pattern that Alice Walker remarks upon in her reading of Kate Chopin's
The Awakening (1899) and Zora Neale Hurston's *Their Eyes Were Watching God*
(1937), two canonical texts in what we now term women's literature, in which
heroines faced with a set of events that define their "quest for self-definition"[21]
make radically different choices: Edna Pontellier chooses suicide or rather to
drink endlessly from the sea, while Janie Crawford chooses self-assertion and
to pass onto other Black women her tale of survival, power, and transformation.[22] In spite of the jeopardy, multiplying difficulties, and her marginal
social location of "outsider within," Hannah embodies the powerful idea of
resistance and struggle conveyed in "distinctive oppositional knowledges":
forms of knowledge that are self-emancipatory. Originating from the social
location of "outsider within," it is this defiant and liberating stance that
would emerge as the defining pattern and theme in the fiction of many
African American women writers from Crafts to Hurston to Walker. It is a
stance that would produce what Foster has argued is a distinctive literary tradition by African American women "essentially concerned with testifying
against that which would confine or repress their experiences and with testing
the possibilities of language to replace rejected versions of self, art, and society with more accurate and positive representations."[23]

As the possessor of the "hidden transcripts" or "private knowledges," Hannah testifies knowledgeably about the interplay of power that defines not only
the relationship between master and slave, between mistress and slave, but also
between the mistress and the master. While she possesses a knowledge of
some of the features of this last social configuration derived from her observation of the marriages of her first and second mistresses, the chief means by
which she conveys the complexity of the dynamics of power between master
and mistress is through a story narrated to her by Lizzy, the quadroon. As we
might recall, Hannah first meets Lizzy while at Lindendale and is reunited
with her during a sojourn in Washington, D.C. Lizzy's melodramatic tale centers upon the secrets of the marriage between Mr. and Mrs. Cosgrove, the current master and mistress of Lindendale.

An "English woman of aristocratic family and connections," Mrs. Cosgrove
is an alien in alien culture and by virtue of this fact shares to a certain extent
Hannah's condition of "outsider within." Although an outsider, as the wife of
the master of Lindendale she occupies a powerful position; indeed, the only
figure in this social hierarchy whose power supercedes her own is that of Mr.
Cosgrove. As an alien, Mrs. Cosgrove does not possess firsthand knowledge of
the customs of plantation life, including one of the most common, which is

the system of concubinage whose purpose is to satisfy the lust while augmenting the wealth of the master. As Lizzy informs an attentive Hannah, for some time her mistress was unaware of the existence of this custom at Lindendale because of the plantation's physical and social architecture:

> Hitherto the lady had known nothing of her husband's favorites. The mansion, you know, was large and irregular in its dimensions, besides being built in a kind of rambling style, that precluded the occupant of one part from knowing anything of the other. In obedience to his orders they had kept themselves secluded and out of sight, and the servants were forbidden to mention them in her presence under the penalty of the severest punishment. (173)

Inevitably, such deceptions are soon found out, and through what might be termed an instance of domestic slippage, Mrs. Cosgrove learns of "her husband's [several] favorites." Lizzy narrates a display of accusations, sarcasm, and deception, and also something resembling appeasement between the master and mistress over the existence of what she terms "those hussies." In order to restore some element of peace to his now failing marriage, Mr. Cosgrove agrees to sell "his favorites." This decision unleashes a sequence of bloody events that, as we learn, further destabilize this marriage. According to Lizzy, one of the master's "favorites," distraught over her sale, fatally stabs her child and tosses it into "the arms of its father. Before he had time to recover from his astonishment she had run the knife into her own body, and fell at his feet bathing them in her blood" (177). In reconstructing this tale of matricide and suicide, Hannah documents the many varieties of suffering to which the system of concubinage gives birth. While violating the sanctity of the marriage between master and mistress and igniting discord between them, this exploitative social system also reduces slave women and their children to a precarious, vulnerable, and discredited existence.

According to Lizzy, after these events the marriage of the Cosgroves deteriorates further. While Mr. Cosgrove appears to have agreed to the sale of his "favorites," he does not surrender them all to the auction block. Mrs. Cosgrove soon discovers this second deception, which leads her husband to establish a residence for his concubine and their children away from the plantation. The continuing deception on the part of the master intensifies the escalating rage and jealousy of the mistress. Crafts writes that "they bickered and quarreled without any hope or prospect of reconciliation. Their happiness ruined, their domestic peace a wreck" (186). The hostilities reach their apex in a confrontation, according to Lizzy, in which the master blocks the path of the mistress as she negotiates her way on horseback to Rock Glen, the new home of the concubine. According to Lizzy, Mrs. Cosgrove loses her balance as a result of a blow delivered by her husband, so enraged is he by what he regards as this unwarranted interference in his personal affairs as well as this unprecedented challenge to his patriarchal powers. The accident that follows the blow reduces Mrs. Cosgrove to the condition of an invalid. While there is a reconciliation between the Cosgroves it comes, sadly, just before Mrs. Cosgrove's painful death, which is occasioned by injuries that are physical, psychic, and emotional in nature. In reconstructing the dissolution of the marriage of the Cosgroves, Hannah discovers and reveals that the relationship between master and mistress is sometimes marked by betrayal, jealousy, and violence. She also makes apparent the unequal distribution of power in the plantation household. While the mistress may exercise a degree of power within the context of white supremacy, her power is always and inevitably curtailed by the power of male supremacy, that is to say, of patriarchy. In privileging Lizzy's tale, Hannah is careful to reveal the special suffering and loss of Black women in the contests of power between master and mistress. All of this and more is contained in the "hidden transcripts" that Lizzy passes to Hannah in the form of a tale that reveals the hidden aspects within the social order that doubtless impinged upon the marriages of her first mistress as well as that of Mrs. Wheeler.

While *The Bondwoman's Narrative* opens with Hannah's initiation into the knowledge of the operations of power between master and slave, in the penultimate chapter of the novel she acquires an important piece of private knowledge as a runaway. Doubtless this private knowledge is the basis for what she describes as the "hush on my spirit," the "deep repose," and "a blest and holy quietude" that pervades the life she enjoys at the conclusion of the novel as a free woman who has been reunited with her mother and who also is the wife of a free-born ordained Methodist minister (237). Passing as a white woman traveling on a ferry from Wilmington, North Carolina, to free territory, Hannah overhears a conversation between two gentlemen who are strangers to her. Incredibly, their conversation concerns the final days of Mr. Trappe, the slave speculator who has been the source of considerable anxiety and suffering for Hannah since her first encounter with him at Lindendale. Carefully piecing together the fragments of a private conversation, she learns that Mr. Trappe has been assassinated apparently by members of a Black family he had attempted to sell into slavery by destroying all evidence of their free status. In reconstructing this timely exchange between two strangers, Hannah's reaction to this "private knowledge" is registered only in a fragment of an apparent aphorism: "evenhanded justice returns the ingredients of the poisoned chalice to our own lips" (232). Wishing not to exult after learning about the much deserved and violent death of a man who was nothing short of a predator, Hannah displays a marked economy in expressing her own views regarding Mr. Trappe's passing as she passes from a state of bondage to a state of freedom.

Hannah carries this vital piece of private knowledge with her into freedom, and it is a knowledge that doubtless informs her efforts to create a new life in that much desired state. Crafts writes of the sense of peace that settles upon the life of her protagonist after this second successful attempt to escape slavery. While she fashions for us a "happy ever after ending," its sweetness is tempered when we recall the realities of the lives of African American women of the nineteenth century. In shedding the status of slave, Hannah does not completely shed the condition of "outsider within." The change of status does not eradicate completely a condition which, more and more, is both a political condition as well as an existential one, for both are indissolubly linked to the other. As an African American woman who would live out her life in nineteenth-century America, Hannah would remain by virtue of her race and gender on the margins of the operations of power and also keenly aware, to be sure, of what Hill Collins terms "the contradictions between the dominant group's actions and ideologies." Or put another way, even in freedom, Hannah, like her creator Hannah Crafts, would remain, as Gates astutely observes in his introduction, a "keen if opinionated observer from within."[24] It was in this social location of "outsider within," this social location of contradictions, that Hannah first acquired a knowledge as well as a particular perspective or "angle of vision" on the operations of power between master and slave, mistress and slave, and master and mistress. While occupying this social location she acquired not only the "hidden transcripts" but also her freedom, and it would be from this same location that she would defend and enlarge her freedom not only for herself but also for others. Throughout the novel, Hannah embodies the powerful idea of resistance and struggle specific to what Hill Collins terms "distinctive oppositional knowledges." These are forms of private knowledge, as I have been suggesting here, that are self-emancipatory.

To recall and amend an earlier statement by Hill Collins, for Hannah, belonging yet not belonging would always present peculiar challenges as well as certain forms of knowledge. For Hannah Crafts, the mulatto, autodidact, and former slave of John Wheeler who also shares the social and psychological condition of her protagonist, the writing of this first novel by a female fugitive slave doubtless revealed to her the many possibilities that exist within forms of testimony and the process of testing and reclaiming a language "that has been made to work against" her. In testing and reclaiming a written language that was illegal for her to acquire and to use at the time of the novel's composition, Crafts creates a novel that inaugurates many of the themes and patterns of the fiction of many African American women writers. Further, in this antebellum novel that is an amalgam of the slave narrative and sentimental fiction, she fictionalizes perspectives and experiences that are representative of those of African American women of her era and subsequent ones who occupy the social location of "outsider within." Above all, as a former slave and arguably the first African American woman novelist, Crafts is a powerful voice of the South whose text inaugurates a national tradition of novelistic writing by African Americans that includes such writers as Harriet Wilson, Frances E. W. Harper, Charles Chesnutt, Zora Neale Hurston, Richard Wright, Ralph Ellison, James Baldwin, Paule Marshall, Ishmael Reed, Charles Johnson, Alice Walker, Ernest Gaines, Toni Morrison, and many others. These writers would extend and complicate in extraordinary ways many of the situations, themes, and questions first addressed by Crafts in her very hybrid antebellum novel.

Notes

1. Patricia Hill Collins, "Learning from the Outsider Within Revisited," *Fighting Words: Black Women and the Search for Justice* (Minneapolis: the University of Minnesota Press, 1998), 3.

2. Ibid., 251.

3. Patricia Hill Collins, *Black Feminist Thought: Knowledge, Consciousness, and the Politics of Empowerment* (New York: Routledge, 1991), 11.

4. Hill Collins, *Fighting Words*, 5.

5. Ibid., 6.

6. Ibid., 7.

7. Ibid., 8.

8. Henry Louis Gates, Jr., Introduction to *The Bondwoman's Narrative*, by Hannah Crafts, ed. Henry Louis Gates, Jr. (New York: Warner Books, 2002), lxxii.

9. Ibid., lxxi. Throughout his introduction, Gates makes a strong case for Hannah Crafts as Black and a former slave. Gates's solid points regarding Crafts's portrayal of Black characters, her claim of African ancestry, her analysis of the relationships between field slaves and house slaves, and her knowledge of the dynamics of power between master and slave are persuasive evidence of her caste and racial background, that is to say, that she was a mulatto and a slave, a mulatto who, as Gates argues, "chooses her blackness." Moreover, William Andrews's perceptive analysis of moments in Elizabeth Keckley's slave narrative and Crafts's novel considerably weakens the reading of Crafts as a free white female. Since there is evidence that Crafts was a slave and a mulatto, then it follows, using the racial calculus of her era and our own, that she was neither white nor free. I am convinced that Crafts is a mulatto and former slave not only for the reasons provided by Gates and Andrews, which are, in part, elaborations of a position held by Dorothy Porter, but also because of the manner in which Crafts portrays white characters, particularly white women. Crafts's portrayal of white women is largely balanced, which is to say that she is interested more in complex portrayals rather than idealized ones. In her portrayal of white women, especially Mrs. Cosgrove and Mrs. Wheeler, she seems intent upon destabilizing the pedestal or not portraying white women in only the most flattering terms. For example, Crafts's description of Mrs. Cosgrove ascending a ladder and disappearing unceremoniously into a second-story window, her petticoats tumbling in behind her, in search of ad-

ditional evidence of her husband's infidelity, is a scene that is both hilarious and subversive of an exalted view of white women. Additionally, Crafts's scene of Hannah dressing Mrs. Wheeler's matted hair is one which thoroughly undermines the perception of white women as beautiful, fastidious, clean, and without flaws. It is a scene that offers a powerful critique of the politics of beauty in general and hair in particular. The hair of white women, its straightness and length, has been always perceived as one of their most coveted assets and a point of envy for Black women. The unstated message of this scene is that although Hannah is a mulatto and slave, her hair is a better grade and in better condition than the hair of her mistress. While I will offer further commentary on these scenes in later parts of this essay, I would assert now, in this effort to clarify further this important matter of Crafts's racial background and social status, that it is doubtful that even the most progressive white woman of the nineteenth century could write such scenes. The pride she would feel as a consequence of her race and gender would make it difficult to impossible for her to imagine, let alone portray, white women in such realistic and also unflattering terms. Crafts's portrayal of white women arises from the sensibility and point of view of someone occupying a subordinate position in relation to them, that is to say, of the position of "outsider within." It is this point of view or perspective that accounts for Crafts's complex portrayal of white women, and for the humor and insight that flow from such portrayals. As I am convinced of Crafts's racial and caste status, this belief necessarily shapes the manner in which I view her novel in relation to the African American literary tradition. Although the evidence is not conclusive, nevertheless I am persuaded that Crafts, as a mulatto and former slave, is the author of what is arguably the first novel by an African American writer. The argument I advance in this essay is based upon this position.

10. Orlando Patterson, *Slavery and Social Death: A Comparative Study* (Cambridge: Harvard University Press, 1982), 51.

11. Hannah Crafts, *The Bondwoman's Narrative*, ed. Henry Louis Gates, Jr. (New York: Warner Books, 2002), 5–6. All further references to this text will appear in parentheses.

12. Ibid., 6.

13. W.E.B. Du Bois, "Of the Training of Black Men," *The Souls of Black Folk* (1903; New York: Penguin Books, 1989), 90.

14. Ibid., 7.

15. Gates, "Introduction," *The Bondwoman's Narrative*, li.

16. Ibid., xlvi–l.

17. Frances Smith Foster, *Written By Herself: Literary Productions by African American Women, 1746–1892* (Bloomington: Indiana University Press, 1993), 83.

18. Ibid., 82.

19. Gates, "Introduction," *The Bondwoman's Narrative*, lxxi.

20. Ibid., lxxi.

21. Sandra M. Gilbert and Susan Garber, *Madwoman in the Attic* (New Haven: Yale University Press, 1979), 76.

22. Alice Walker, "Saving the Life That Is Your Own: The Importance of Models in the Artist's Life," in *In Search of Our Mothers' Gardens: Womanist Prose* (New York: Harcourt, Brace & Jovanovich, 1983), 6.

23. Foster, *Written By Herself*, 12.

24. Gates, "Introduction," *The Bondwoman's Narrative*, xxv.

21

The Bondwoman and the Bureaucrat

THOMAS C. PARRAMORE

In his youth, John Hill Wheeler was a southern princeling who, some may have supposed, would one day become President of the United States or, perhaps, Chief Justice of the Supreme Court. As the scion of a large and well-to-do family, he had advantages few of his contemporaries enjoyed. He was born in 1806 to Mary Elizabeth Jordan Wheeler, the first of three wives of merchant shipowner John Wheeler, in the northeastern North Carolina village of Murfreesboro, in Hertford County.[1]

From his New Jersey-born father, an astute and widely esteemed business-man and deeply committed Baptist layman, the son absorbed traits of charac-ter and industry that portended a life of solid achievement. The father was an erstwhile member of the town corporation, academy trustees, Bible Society, justices of the peace, the local chapter of the American Colonization Society, and long-time village postmaster. John Hill Wheeler was assured that he would be able to acquire as much education as he could absorb.[2]

The elder Wheeler, owing to his numerous New York, New England, and West Indian mercantile associates, was often the first person in town to hear news from abroad. He groomed his son John, one of his nineteen offspring, by sending him, at age six, for primary schooling with Baptist Rev. James Wright, at Potecasi Creek, in adjacent Northampton County. In 1813, the son entered the celebrated Hertford Academy in Murfreesboro, where he was a beneficiary of the expert teaching of Massachusetts-born Rev. Jonathan O. Freeman, widely regarded as one of the most effective teachers in the state. John Hill's village schoolmates and acquaintances included future U.S. Senator Solon Bor-land and future North Carolina Chief Justice William Nathan Harrell Smith.[3]

In 1820, at age fifteen, he was allowed (or sent) on a voyage to Bermuda and back in one of his father's ships, the *Pacific*. He also had a role in a locally produced drama, Kotzebue's "The Stranger," as adapted by William Dunlap. In 1821, he was off to Columbian College (now George Washington University), in Washington, D.C., where he enrolled at age fifteen in the preparatory department. As a college student, he mingled and matched wits with some of the most promising young men in America before his graduation in 1826 "with distinction." He was chosen in 1824 by his fellow students to give an address before the visiting General Lafayette to persuade him to join a club to which the students belonged.[4]

In 1827, he returned home to study law under attorney Henry W. Long of Murfreesboro and, soon afterward, Chief Justice John Louis Taylor of the state supreme court. He was admitted to the North Carolina bar in 1828 (though he was never to practice law), while he was earning, at the same time, a Master of Arts degree at the University of North Carolina.[5] His qualifications for eventual distinction in public life were already impressive; his willingness to work hard toward his goals a demonstrated fact.

Young Wheeler's initial bid for public office began immediately after receiving his law license. Returning home to Murfreesboro, he declared himself a Democratic candidate for the state House of Commons during his busy year, 1827, at age twenty-one. He sought to win public approval by disclaiming "any other desire than to be useful" to his fellow citizens and vowing not to appear at musters and other public events where "ardent spirits" were in evidence or "any other drink whatsoever." He won the election and became the youngest member of the commons. His career was already taking on what might be called, at this early age, meteoric proportions.[6]

As a legislator, a key aim for Wheeler was to promote a bill to open northeastern North Carolina's Roanoke Inlet, a shallow Outer Banks aperture that was injurious to the maritime commerce of the region. He spoke at Democratic meetings throughout his district, taking a leading part in discussions of the area's tepid commerce and how to revive it. Blocked, however, in Raleigh, by those who felt that the state legislature should guard vigilantly the sacred keys to the treasury, his bill failed to pass. It was his first setback in public life and seemed unimportant. He was re-elected to his seat in 1828 and 1829.[7]

Wheeler's career seemed to profit, in part, from his personal charm. He had "a warm heart," wrote a eulogist, a "classic wit, [and] mirth-creating humor." He became "a favorite in all circles in which intelligence, refinement, and graceful address were desired." But his first electoral setback was a defeat in his "severely contested and gallant canvas" of 1831 for the U.S. House of Representatives by a much more experienced politician.[8] Still only twenty-five years old, his future continued to look highly promising. If not president, he would perhaps become a leader in the Senate.

A token of Wheeler's charm and powers of persuasion was his marriage in 1830 to Mary Elizabeth Brown, nineteen-year-old daughter of a respected Washington, D.C., minister. (They evidently met while he was in college.) Mary was one of the country's foremost polymaths, well versed in mathematics, natural philosophy, astronomy, chemistry, botany, anatomy, physiology, geography, and history. She read Latin and Greek and could "carry on a conversation in the former with classical efficiency and perfect facility." She also was proficient in several modern languages, "especially French and Spanish."

So "minutely exact was her knowledge," wrote an admirer, "that she was frequently appealed to by gentlemen of liberal education to decide questions of literary criticism, or scientific discussions." In addition, she pursued expertise in music and art, attaining "superior excellence" in both. Despite her father's influential Washington ministry, she rejected opportunities to join a church, but her Bible was "filled with notes and reflections marked with her hand," and evangelical in character.[9] Such an accomplished young wife could not be less than an asset to John Hill Wheeler's high aspirations.

In the late summer of 1831, Wheeler and, presumably, his new wife were visiting his family in Murfreesboro, when on the morning of August 22, a Southampton County, Virginia, man ran into town screaming that the slaves were in rebellion sixteen miles north. They had just killed his wife and ten children. Thomas Weston, an elderly resident, came out on his porch to hear the news and dropped dead when he heard it. Fearing an attack on their town, residents placed its black population under strict confinement and recruited a "home guard" to keep them under surveillance as well as to fend off attackers. A town-and-county militia force of infantry and cavalry was then dispatched to the scene of Nat Turner's Revolt, the bloodiest slave uprising in American history.[10]

The militia apparently participated in the capture and murder of numerous suspects, whose heads were mounted on poles as a grisly warning to all. Wheeler himself is said to have raised a group of volunteers, which may have comprised the homeguard. His younger brother, Samuel J., a student at Union College in Schenectady, New York, was a militia officer. Their father, John Wheeler, from his vantage point as postmaster of the town nearest the scenes of violence, relayed reports of events to newspapers in Norfolk, Virginia, Washington, D.C., and elsewhere—and thus to the world at large. Meanwhile, panicked Murfreesboro citizens shot and beheaded an unidentified free black man for the crime of walking through town in the general direction of Southampton County. They also murdered and beheaded another for acting strangely while driving a white woman and her daughter.[11]

Ironically, Murfreesboro in the 1820s was one of only eleven towns in North Carolina with a chapter of the American Colonization Society, which sought to free slaves and send them to Africa. It was a misguided but well-meaning idea to try to resolve the slave question, and it was supported by many benevolent men with philanthropic aims. John Hill Wheeler's father was one of its principal local supporters and is said to have tried to persuade all of his own slaves to accept their freedom and passage to Africa, an offer accepted by an indeterminate number but probably not many. Over the years before 1850, the town's slave-masters freed nearly a hundred bondmen for this purpose.[12]

It is possible that John Hill Wheeler, like others of this period (including, possibly, his wife), had been traumatized by the slave insurrection. At any rate, it marked a watershed in his life, after which his aspirations seemed less likely to be fulfilled. For the next five years, he neither sought nor held state public office save for a three-year stint as clerk to a delegation chosen to settle old spoliation claims with France. But he had only begun to sip the wine of despair.[13]

In September, 1832, he and Mary lost their first-born child, Richard M. J., within a few weeks of the demise of Wheeler's revered father, John Wheeler. To cap the climax of his misfortune, his beloved Mary died in 1836, as did their third child, Julian S., a year later, leaving Wheeler with only his infant daughter, Elizabeth.[14] His life, for the time being at least, had lost its early savor.

Long years afterward, Wheeler wrote in his diary: "This is the anniversary of the death of my Sainted Mary 19 years ago—In the stillness of midnight my mind reverted to this mysterious Providence—and though I cannot know [in life,] I shall know hereafter the reasons for so mournful a dispensation. May the Lord sanctify his acts and make me worthy to be with her in glory."[15]

At last weathering his multiple crises, Wheeler, in 1837, accepted appointment from President Van Buren to the coveted new post of superintendent of the Charlotte (North Carolina) Branch Mint and held the office through the four years of Van Buren's administration. Soon after his appointment, he also acquired a handsome plantation, "Ellangowan," on the Catawba River, near Charlotte, and took up a part-time role as gentleman planter. Within a year, he courted and married another estimable young woman, Ellen Oldmixon Sully of Philadelphia, a daughter of America's most distinguished painter, Thomas Sully. She is said to have been a minor artist herself. Their first child, Charles S., was born in 1839.[16]

Wheeler's native optimism was soon restored by his new family, official duties, and surroundings. Always fascinated with history, he launched a project, about 1841, to write a history of North Carolina, a task never before accomplished by a native son or daughter. He was also nominated by Mecklenburg

County Democrats for the state House of Commons in 1842, a testament to his resurgent ambitions, as was his election as grand master of the state's Freemasons for the 1842–1843 term. (He had to decline the legislative bid from Mecklenburg County because his farm was in neighboring Lincoln County.) Over his objections, he was also named colonel of a locally recruited army regiment bound for the Mexican War, but he resigned before it left for the front. He was often thereafter referred to as "Colonel Wheeler."[17] Back in the public eye, he was anxious once more to renew his pursuit of greatness.

In 1842, he was elected state treasurer. Relocated by this victory to Raleigh, the state capital, he began to search for and study original documents bearing on the early history of his state and in 1844 published his *Indexes to Documents Relative to North Carolina*, from a list of records compiled by another researcher in London in 1827. But he may have overextended himself in the process, for he suffered defeat by the Whigs for re-election as treasurer in 1844. Two years later, he lobbied fellow Democrats to nominate him for governor, but the effort failed.[18]

Wheeler was buoyed, however, by the publication in 1851 of his epochal *Historical Sketches of North Carolina, 1584 to 1851*, which made him a household name across the state and with leading figures beyond, including America's foremost historian, George Bancroft. It was soon found, however, to contain a witch's brew of errors, literary and historical. Nonetheless, its 10,000-copy first printing sold out, a major publishing success. Whigs found it so partial to Democrats that they dubbed it "the Democratic Stud Book," but many Democrats deemed it the greatest book ever published in the state, errors notwithstanding. It remained for decades the standard history of the state. Not the least of its virtues was creating in North Carolina a pride in its past, evidence that it was more than just "a vale of humility between two mountains of conceit." A second edition appeared in 1873.[19]

Recognizing that he was not a professional at the historian's trade, Wheeler was quite aware that he was not the most qualified person to write such a book but did so because no one else would. In May, 1853, he wrote to Governor William A. Graham that he wished "some other and abler hand" had written it. He was pleased, however, to see "others now in the field who may be tempted in hours of their leisure and retirement to give to their Country and posterity the result of their patient investigations."[20]

In June 1853, Colonel Wheeler was rumored to be in line for the humble post of chargé d'affaires to Sardinia. "How the mighty are fallen," cracked a Whig newspaper, but it turned out to be a false report. About this time, however, he was named by President Franklin Pierce as his secretary to sign land warrants, a golden opportunity to observe the presidency at close hand and the daily machinations of the federal government, in short, to become a Washington insider. Within a year, however, he was elected from Lincoln County to another term in the House of Commons and surrendered his post in Washington.[21]

Except for brief intervals, the colonel was to hold one or another federal post until his post–Civil War retirement. He became, in fact, a perpetual presence on Capitol Hill and at the White House, often made possible by the intercession of his growing circle of federal functionaries and friends in high places.[22] Professional officeseekers stood in low esteem with the public, though many able operatives made their livelihood this way, some becoming valuable and dedicated civil servants. But Wheeler's old dream of high national office no longer guided his dreams.

Wheeler remained a valuable Washington insider, one who knew where to turn for advice on any question and where the best opportunities lay. He gleaned a firsthand knowledge of whom to turn to on any question. This knowledge made him a valuable advisor to presidents and led to friendships between himself and Presidents Jackson, Van Buren, Buchanan, and postwar president Andrew Johnson. Key congressmen and others also appreciated him for his charming and risible manner. He acquired a fine house in the capital to answer the needs of his wife and two teen-aged sons, and in 1853, he sold his North Carolina plantation and moved permanently to Washington.[23]

Late in 1853, Wheeler learned that he had been chosen by Pierce as the second American Minister to Nicaragua. Up to this point, the colonel had not been in the national spotlight, but this mission was of critical importance, owing to the fact that the United States was vying with Great Britain for leverage in Central America. There was also the matter of preserving the right of American gold-hunters and others to cross Nicaragua by land rather than having to sail around Cape Horn. Critics decried the fact that the new minister could not speak Spanish and had no diplomatic experience, but Wheeler, a quick learner, began his Spanish lessons almost at once. He felt that he could count on his coveted personal traits to make up for his want of diplomatic background. He left Washington for Nicaragua in January 1854, accompanied by his wife and sons.[24]

Reaching his destination, the new minister found a delicate and complicated situation. A civil war was in progress, partly owing to mistakes of his predecessor, former Senator Solon Borland of Arkansas, who had grown up with Wheeler in Murfreesboro. It was impossible to tell which side in the war he should recognize as the legitimate government. But, a tireless worker, he accomplished all the main objectives assigned to him in a few months. His decided racial and class biases, however, riled Central American leaders.[25] He looked forward to returning to the United States with a record of gratifying successes.

In mid-June, 1855, with Wheeler ill from "a tropical fever," Filibuster William Walker and a contingent of fifty-eight American freebooters, landed on the Pacific coast of Nicaragua with the aim of seizing control of the country. As Wheeler watched from the sidelines (Walker had Nicaraguan citizenship), the invaders, soon much increased, fought their way to control of most of the country. When Walker asked Wheeler to intervene to arrange a truce between his own and Nicaraguan forces, the minister complied, drawing a stern rebuke from Washington that he had gone beyond his instructions.[26]

Wheeler returned briefly to Washington in early 1855 for consultations with Secretary of State William C. Marcy on Nicaragua's turmoil and the role he was expected to play there.[27] Before he could set sail back to Central America, however, an incident occurred that would make his name both famous and infamous across the land.

On July 18, Wheeler and three of his slaves, Jane Johnson and her sons, en route with him to Nicaragua, waited on the deck of the steam ferry to take them to New York and his ship. (Wheeler was taking them to Nicaragua to serve his wife and children.) As the steamer prepared to cast off, a small body of abolitionists rushed aboard, sighted Wheeler and his party, and snatched the slaves away over his resistance. Wheeler promptly filed for a habeas corpus to regain his property, and the federal district court upheld his claim on the ground that the state of Pennsylvania had no authority to "divest the rights of property of a citizen of North Carolina."[28]

The larger issue at stake was the requirement of the new Fugitive Slave Act ordering that any slave trying to flee his or her master was to be apprehended and returned to the owner. Passmore Williamson, leader of the abductors, appeared in court arguing that Jane and her offspring had fled voluntarily, which was evidently true. Williamson denied that he had any control over the fugitives, for which statement he spent two months in jail, but Wheeler was unable to locate either Jane or her offspring.[29] Before he reached Nicaragua and his family, he was the laughingstock of abolitionists, an honorable and mistreated victim in the eyes of slaveholders.

Wheeler, irascible and defiant, was depicted in the press as arguing over the case with an abolitionist in a Philadelphia drugstore. The colonel declared that Williamson had threatened to cut his throat and that his opponent should be "down in prison with that damn'd Williamson." After he stormed out, witnesses agreed that he had acted the part of "a black-guard."[30]

This was clearly not the kind of reputation Wheeler had for so long sought. Yet his friendship with William Walker, meanwhile, flowered into strong mutual admiration. Walker, a short, slim, and rigidly pious Tennessean, was admired by many as a highly charismatic figure. Wheeler may not have noted the difference between himself and Walker; whereas Wheeler sought Nicaragua for the United States, Walker dreamed of building an empire of his own. Wheeler's avowed aims were to "educate" Nicaragua's people, develop their resources, and legitimize slavery there. For these purposes, he favored U.S. annexation of Central America. Moreover, further acquisitions in Central America could be carved into slave states to offset, for the South, new free states in the West. Pierce was already the first president "to pioneer territorial aggrandizement as an arm of the incoming administration."[31]

It is an open question, however, whether Wheeler escorted three slaves across the states of Maryland and Pennsylvania in deliberate defiance of the Fugitive Slave Act. There were, after all, sea routes to Central America that entailed no travel through states where slavery had been abolished. That the experience brought him the greatest celebrity of his life may only have been coincidental.

Forewarned not to do so, Wheeler, unheeding, continued to cooperate with Walker, eventually recognizing a group cobbled together by the filibuster as the legitimate government of Nicaragua. By this time Wheeler was known in Central America as "el ministero filibustero," and he was summoned to Washington to explain himself. In November 1856, he met with Secretary Marcy, on whose recommendation Pierce asked for Wheeler's resignation and, after several months' delay, received it. Owing perhaps to allies in key offices, he was reappointed by President Buchanan in 1857, but, still ill with tropical fever, and perhaps disgusted with a lack of official resolve, he declined the position. (Apparently his work had been re-evaluated and found, under the circumstances, to have been excusable, if not laudatory.) Walker's career later ended in front of a Nicaraguan firing squad.[32]

It appears, then, that Wheeler saw the prospect of his own government's control of much or all of Central America as too important to leave to the quibbling of Washington bureaucrats. He would act boldly to achieve his ends, believing that success in those directions would eventually rebound to his credit and mitigate the political difficulties he was creating for himself and his party.

The acquisition of California and most of Mexico had, for a while in the 1850s, induced in men like Wheeler faith in a forthcoming Pax Americana. Central America would be annexed and colonized by the United States, slavery would be instituted there, and America would rise triumphant over its great new empire. The South might recover its power in Congress. The goal seemed so worthwhile and certain of fulfillment that filibusters might defy official policies of the United States and present it with a fait accompli few politicians could afford not to embrace. Wheeler saw his chance to be midwife to the undertaking and enable his country to make one of greatest forward leaps in its history.[33]

Wheeler, however, like Solon Borland before him, was a poor candidate for the role he played. He had little respect for the Nicaraguans and Negroes he met in Central America and said so loudly and clearly in a book-length manuscript he compiled of the country's history. All alike, he wrote, "have conclusively proved . . . that they were incapable of self-government." He was especially hard on the Roman Catholic Church, which, from his perspective, was the source of "all the civil convulsions and bloodshed" in Central America. The priests, "with few exceptions," were guilty of every crime, "and their daily acts in every civilized country would subject them to the severest penalties of the Criminal Law." Long before Kipling summoned the United States to "take up the white man's burden," Wheeler believed that the United States was destined to rule over Central America.[34]

Wheeler's Achilles' heel was his rampant bigotry in religion, race, and class, which can be traced back to at least 1830 when, as a young legislator in Raleigh, he unsuccessfully opposed a bill to reaffirm the exemption of Quakers from enrollment in the state militia. A source of his attitude was, in all likelihood, his family's energetic endorsement of certain evangelical Protestant prejudices prominent in the Old South. With regard to Mexico, he had written in 1846 that it was "a nation whose whole history is marked by tyranny, and perfidy."[35] In short, he was not the sort of man a divided nation could afford to have in sensitive places. It needed uniters, not more dividers.

Of his mission to Nicaragua, Wheeler wrote in 1857 to his supporters in Murfreesboro that "I bore myself as became the high functions I was entrusted with—and if I did not fulfill the wishes of some who are opposed to the success of American enterprises, and who down all progress in science and art, and the good will of every friend of liberty," so be it. The value of Nicaragua, "the luxuriant soil, so capable of the production of cotton, corn, sugar, coffee, indigo, and every article so essential to our comfort, is only exceeded by its geographical importance to the United States." Nicaragua's own "happiness, the cause of liberty, . . . the development of a region now wild and uncultivated, and then ultimate destiny, all point" to its eventual rule by the United States.[36]

In Murfreesboro, this was raw meat. Dr. Samuel J. Wheeler, the colonel's brother, visiting Cuba for his health in 1853, wrote letters to Raleigh's *Biblical Recorder*, a Baptist paper, in terms nearly identical to the colonel's, about that Catholic island. In 1855, an editorial, entitled "Romanism," in the *Murfreesboro Gazette*, of which he was editor, declared that "Romanism is a curse to any land." Five years later, a chapter of the Knights of the Golden Circle (KGC), calling for American annexation of all lands in or bordering on the Caribbean, was installed in Murfreesboro, the first town in the state to come under the KGC's malignant influence.[37] Relations between the United States and Central America were, owing to the work of Borland and Wheeler, off to a poor start with long-lasting negative consequences.

It appears from the writings of the Wheeler brothers that religion fueled their prejudices at least as much as race and class. Protestantism, greed, and fear were being enlisted throughout the South in the service of Manifest Destiny. The brothers, since the Mexican War, for which John Hill Wheeler helped raise a regiment, and in which, a third brother, Junius B. (along with Solon Borland) fought, had zealously advocated both race and religion as requisite grounds for the conquest of Central America.[38]

Not long after his arrival back in Washington, Wheeler, still handicapped by his tropical fever and a recently amputated finger, set out with Ellen for North Carolina for a six-week visit to his sister Julia and her family at Mulberry Grove plantation, ten miles south of his native Murfreesboro. A large and prosperous enterprise, the plantation belonged to Julia's husband, Dr. Godwin C. Moore. According to Wheeler's diary, they took a steam ferry from Washington to Norfolk or Portsmouth, then a train to Boykins Depot, Virginia, a few miles north of the North Carolina line, and finally went by carriage to the plantation.[39]

His brother Dr. Samuel J. Wheeler, a regular correspondent to the *Petersburg* (Virginia) *Daily Express,* observed that President Buchanan meant to reappoint the colonel to his ministerial post, "should diplomatic relations be renewed with Nicaragua." But the candidate, he wrote, "seems to be disposed to retire from public life and seek a renovation of his health in the enjoyment and quietude of private life."[40] Such was the colonel's resigned attitude in the spring of 1857. For a moment, he had stood atop the mountain, but his vision of the other side had failed him.

There remained, however, a curious postscript to Wheeler's career that has only come to light at the beginning of the twenty-first century. Apart from Jane Johnson, he may have owned another female slave, one who fled from him to freedom and then wrote an autobiographical novel about her experiences in slavery. The case for "Hannah Crafts," evidently the first former slave woman to write a novel, is made by Professor Henry Louis Gates, Jr., head of Harvard University's Department of Black Studies. The question at issue is an elusive and puzzling one and has drawn widespread attention across the United States.

In *The Bondwoman's Narrative,* the narrator, Hannah, an attractive "brown mulatto" maid-servant of Mrs. Wheeler, accompanies the Wheelers south, presumably on their 1857 visit to North Carolina. After a short time, a jealous slave named Maria reports Hannah to Mrs. Wheeler for repeating a very embarrassing tale about Hannah's mistress. In a rage, Ellen arranges for Hannah to marry, against her will, a coarse black field hand who lusted for her. Rather than accept this fate, Hannah, a refined and highly literate young woman, manages to escape north to freedom and write her "autobiographical novel," setting forth an outline of her life in slavery.[41]

Professor Gates, who bought Hannah's unpublished manuscript at an auction, has gone to heroic lengths to try to verify, among other details, the people, geographies, and topographies she depicts, especially as it relates to Virginia and North Carolina. He has found many associations of Hannah's fiction with apparent fact. Moreover, his technical investigators have verified that the manuscript was written in the mid-to-late 1850s, that its paper and ink are compatible with those years, that Hannah's writing seems to have been that of a right-handed female slave—or former slave—and so on.[42]

With these findings to draw on, Gates has been able to validate enough of the substance of the novel to identify it as a fictionalized version of "Hannah's" life story, including the six-week visit to North Carolina in the spring of 1857. Hannah herself obligingly states that she escaped from Wheeler in North Carolina. The time was soon after the colonel had returned from Nicaragua, sick with tropical fever, when he may have felt that the southern climate could benefit him. Moreover, having resigned his ministerial post, there was no work requiring his presence in Washington. As far as existing records show, this was the only verifiable opportunity Hannah seems to have had to visit North Carolina.[43]

The novel, then, appears in many respects to be what it purports to be, that is, a fictionalized autobiography by a self-educated fugitive female slave. Literary analysts have declared that her depictions of "master-slave power relations" in Virginia, North Carolina, and Washington "ring true." Thus Professor Gates concludes, not surprisingly, that there is sufficient warrant to believe that the novel is, at least in some considerable part, Hannah's own true life story.[44]

All is not well, however, with these findings and suppositions. The compatibility of fact with fiction eventually ceases, and the circumstances of Hannah's visit to North Carolina, at least, may be shown to be fictitious. On close examination, it becomes quite evident that Hannah never set foot in North Carolina, a fact that casts a long shadow of doubt over her whole narrative.

To begin with, Hannah tells of her steamboat trip, presumably in 1857, from Washington to Wilmington, North Carolina and Colonel Wheeler's nearby plantation. But Wheeler owned no land in North Carolina after selling his Lincoln County property in 1853. His trip was not to Wilmington but by steamer down Chesapeake Bay and overland from Portsmouth, Virginia, to Mulberry Grove, the home of his sister and brother-in-law, the Godwin C. Moores. But no such place as Hannah describes—"a large rice plantation" near Wilmington with lime and orange trees, its fields of cotton (in summer rather than properly in spring) "sweeping down to the river's edge" (rather than to drainable low ground)—has ever existed in North Carolina or, indeed, anywhere else.[45]

The same is true of Hannah's description of slavery at the fictitious Wilmington site. There, slave huts were "ranged on the backside . . . as far from the habitation of their master as possible. "They were built" with little reference "to neatness and convenience," had "no garden or bright flowers . . . no whitewashed wall." The slaves dwelt in overcrowded hovels, in and among which all the slaves "lived promiscuously." At Mulberry Grove, with its 200 slaves on 3,000 acres, according to one who grew up there, the "negroes dwelt in a village fronting the residence, and each family possessed just such a cabin as it desired. Some were limited to a single room, while others rejoiced in outhouses and kitchen. Each and all had his own hen-house and garden."[46] The fictitious Wilmington site, then, served abolitionists' ends well enough, but not the requirements of autobiography.

As to the circumstances of "Hannah" provoking Mrs. Wheeler's wrath and that lady's subsequent order that she be forced to marry a repellant field hand, the facts do not support her narrative. No such union could have taken place without the permission of the plantation's Dr. Moore, who, famous for his relative mildness and sensitivity toward his slaves, would certainly not have given it. Further, since Mulberry Grove lay within twenty-five miles of the Virginia line, it would not have required, as "Hannah" writes, some two weeks (or two days, for that matter) to escape from North Carolina.[47]

Lastly, no such person as "Hannah" is mentioned in John Hill Wheeler's diary of his 1857 trip to Mulberry Grove or in any other of his known writings. In the diary, Wheeler speaks frequently and at some length about Jane Johnson's highly publicized escape from him in 1855, but he is totally silent on "Hannah." He finds no reason to pursue her either before leaving Mulberry Grove for a short visit to Charlotte or upon his return. It does not appear that he sent advertisements to, say, the Norfolk and Richmond papers seeking her capture. So far, then, no scrap of evidence verifies Hannah's testimony that she was ever Wheeler's slave.

In a novel, of course, a writer is at liberty to invent whatever characters and venues come to mind. Such creations may serve the story well, but they are not autobiographical. Since no credible case can be adduced that any element of the North Carolina material in the novel is autobiographical, "Hannah's" professed experiences in both Virginia and Washington also fall under deep suspicion. It is not enough to establish that some of the surnames she mentions are found in mid–nineteenth-century Virginia censuses or that some of the places she mentions appear on nineteenth-century Virginia maps.

Too many of the manuscript's researchers appear to have strained to prove, rather than test, Hannah's basic accuracy. She is credited by one or more researchers with having been "intimately familiar with the areas of the South where the narrative takes place"; some note that her avowed escape route, which she fails to reveal in any detail, "is one sometimes used by runaways." It is highly dubious that unspecified "internal evidence" makes it "apparent that the work is that of a Negro." It is meaningless that Wheeler's large library contained nearly every title Hannah mentions in her account, for so did many other libraries of the time, large and small. Claims that Hannah "was intimately familiar with Mr. and Mrs. John Hill Wheeler" are also suspect,[48] since the information she passes on about them was a matter public record in virtually every periodical during, and for some time after, the 1855 Passmore Williamson case.

The allegedly factual aspects of the novel, along with its unquestionably imagined ones, are too readily absorbed into its analysis. The editor feels that his introduction makes it clear that the North Carolina part of "Hannah's" tale is altogether fictitious. Yet the reader still finds in the analysis "Hannah's" professed "horror at moving from the Wheeler [sic] home to the 'miserable' huts of the field-slaves . . . ." Her "depictions of life in Virginia, North Carolina, and Washington . . . rang true," and so on. These statements are framed so as to cause the reader to suppose that they should all be viewed as factual. The same occurs in the book's "Textual Annotations," where reference is made to "Wheeler's visit to North Carolina and Hannah's escape from the plantation there . . . ."[49]

It may, perhaps, be argued that such references are meant only to characterize Hannah's own deliberate fictions, not those of Gates and his editorial team. The latter, however, are often not expressed as presumptively fictitious but as demonstratively factual. This sort of ambiguity, on which Gates's analysis leans heavily, weakens the argument for their autobiographical significance.

None of this, of course, in any way subverts the strong supposition that "Hannah's" novel is the earliest known to have been written by a former slave woman. The inherent importance and value of the narrative is undiminished by an admission that it is not, after all, an autobiography. For the latter argument to prevail, it will require a far more disinterested analysis and fortuitous findings.

John Hill Wheeler, having experienced no untoward event in North Carolina in 1857, returned there briefly in 1859 with Tennessee Senator Andrew Johnson, who came on a state visit. He resigned his most recent office, "in the statistical bureau," in 1861, when the Lincoln administration made clear that it was earmarked for a Republican. Wheeler's latest historical interest was in editing the story of a notorious North Carolina Tory of the Revolution, as related by the subject, *The Narrative of Colonel David Fanning* (1865).[50]

By this time an elderly Unionist, the colonel sat out the American Civil War as a non-combatant, applying at first for an appointment to the faculty of the University of North Carolina and, soon afterward, making plans to open a law practice in Murfreesboro. Neither plan materialized, although Washington's Peter Force and other prominent figures sent letters to the university in his behalf. In 1863, at his own expense, he made his way through the Union blockade to London in order to copy more historical documents bearing on colonial North Carolina. Ironically, his son Sully was a Union naval officer during the war, and Woodbury, a second son, was a Confederate soldier, while his brothers Samuel J. and Junius B. served, respectively, as a Confederate major and a Union colonel.[51]

Absorbed more than ever, at the war's end, in his historical pursuits, the colonel helped organize the North Carolina Historical Society, edited the *Legislative Manual and Political Register of the State of North Carolina for the year 1874*, and completed, in 1882, his *Memoirs and Reminiscences of North Carolina and Eminent North Carolinians*. The latter contained much useful information and many of the documents he had discovered on his visit to London. The book was published posthumously in 1884.[52]

If Colonel Wheeler were "Hannah's" master, he may have merited her professed low opinion of him and his wife, the prerogative of any slave toward any master. Despite his outburst while debating the Philadelphia abolitionist, he was, on the whole, a sociable and "clubable" man, faithful to his wife, loyal to both his Union and Rebel kin, and a relatively mild slave-master (neither Jane Johnson nor "Hannah" accuse him of abuse). He was also an able speaker and an avid reader—his library held at least 1,882 titles, most of which, to judge from his diaries, he read.[53]

He resisted dishonoring either his country or his state during the war, always a man deeply rooted in his native North Carolina soil. His long pursuit of office seems to have been motivated as much by a desire to serve his country as by the hope of personal gain. His grievous racial and religious bigotry was shared by many white Americans, North and South.

Yet John Hill Wheeler, the wunderkind of the 1820s, may have died regretting that he never attained the heights he had once believed himself so well suited to inhabit. That he failed to do so may be attributed in some degree to the early influence of religious and racial intolerance, which he never overcame, and, perhaps, to his direct exposure to Nat Turner's Revolt. It was his fateful appointment to the Nicaraguan ministry that exposed these cancerous growths and laid bear his inner demons. Thereafter, he never held nor deserved a significant office of public trust.

Notes

1. Joseph S. Fowler, "Memoir of the Author, Colonel John Hill Wheeler, of Hertford County, North Carolina," preface, John Hill Wheeler, *Memoirs and Reminiscences of North Carolina and Eminent North Carolinians* (Columbus, Ohio: Columbus Printing Works, 1884), iii; Randall O. Hudson, "The Filibuster Minister: The Career of John Hill Wheeler as United States Minister to Nicaragua, 1854–1856," *North Carolina Historical Review* 49 (Winter 1972), 282.

2. Diary of Dr. Thomas O'Dwyer, Southern Historical Collection, University of North Carolina, Chapel Hill, N.C., March 11, 26, June 15–16, July 5, Aug. 24, Nov. 8, 1825; "Lists of Justices of the Peace, 1800–1850," Governor's Office, Division of Archives and History. John Wheeler was named justice of the peace in 1808.

3. Fowler, "Memoir of Col. John Hill Wheeler," iii; Thomas C. Parramore, "Borland, Solon," in *Dictionary of North Carolina Biography*, ed. William S. Powell (Chapel Hill: University of North Carolina, 1996), s.v.; Diary of John Hill Wheeler, 1860, "Diary of Events" at year's end.

4. Fowler, "Memoir of the Col. John Hill Wheeler," iii; Thomas Schoonover, "John Hill Wheeler," in *American National Biography*, 23, ed. John A. Garraty and Mark C. Carnes (New York: Oxford University Press, 1999), 140.

5. J. G. DeR. Hamilton, "Wheeler, John Hill," *Dictionary of American Biography*, 20 (Columbus, Ohio: Columbus Printing Works, 1884), 50.

6. *Halifax* (N.C.) *Roanoke Advocate*, Aug. 30, 1830.

7. *Edenton North Carolina Gazette*, Feb. 27, Dec. 9, 1830.

8. Hamilton, "Wheeler, John Hill," 50.

9. Samuel J. Wheeler (?), *Raleigh Biblical Recorder*, Dec. 7, 1836.

10. Wheeler, *Memoirs and Reminiscences*, 210.

11. *Halifax* (N.C.) *Roanoke Advocate*, Sept. 9, 1831; Robert S. Parker to Mrs. Rebecca Maney, Aug. 29, 1831, John Kimberly Papers, Southern Historical Collection, University of North Carolina, Chapel Hill, N.C.; Wheeler, *Memoirs and Reminiscences*, 210; Schoonover, "John Hill Wheeler," 139.

12. John W. Moore, "Historical Sketches of Hertford County, N.C.," *Murfreesboro Albemarle Enquirer*, May 3, 1877.

13. S. J. Wheeler (?), *Raleigh Biblical Recorder*, Dec. 7, 1836.

14. Albert Gallatin Wheeler, *The Genealogical and Encyclopedic History of the Wheeler Family in America* (Boston: American College of Genealogy, 1914), 258.

15. Henry Louis Gates, Jr., "Introduction," *The Bondwoman's Narrative*, by Hannah Crafts (New York: Warner Books, 2002), liii.

16. Fowler, "Memoir of the Col. John Hill Wheeler," xxii; Hamilton, "John Hill Wheeler," *Dictionary of American Biography*, 20 (New York: Charles Scribner's Sons, 1936), 140. For reference to "Ellangowan," see John H. Wheeler, *Historical Sketches of North Carolina* (Philadelphia: Lippincott, Granbo, and Company, 1851), xxii.

17. H. G. Jones, "Wheeler, John Hill," in *Biographical Dictionary of North Carolina*, ed. William S. Powell (Chapel Hill: University of North Carolina Press, 1996), s.v.; *Wilmington* (N.C.) *Daily Journal*, May 13, 1873.

18. J. H. Wheeler to Edmund Ruffin, Dec. 6, 1851, in *The Papers of John Willis Ellis*, I, ed. Noble J. Tolbert (Raleigh: Edwards and Broughton, 1920), 96, 123; William Hooper to Willie P. Mangum, Feb. I, 1846, in *The Papers of William A. Graham*, I, ed. J. G. deR. Hamilton (Raleigh: State Division of Archives and History, 1961), 391–392.

19. Jones, "Wheeler, John Hill"; Noble J. Tolbert, ed., *The Papers of John Willis Ellis* (Raleigh: State Division of Archives and History, 1964), 96, 113.

20. John H. Wheeler to James Iredell, in *The Papers of William A. Graham*, 3, 126–127.

21. Jones, "Wheeler, John Hill," 167; *Norfolk American Beacon*, Sept. 16, 1853.

22. Fowler, "Memoir of the Col. John Hill Wheeler," viii.

23. Letter of George Stevenson to T. C. Parramore, April 25, 2002.

24. Hudson, "The Filibuster Minister," 280–281; John Hill Wheeler Diary, Sept. 16, 1854; diary for Nov. 26, 1854.

25. Hudson, "The Filibuster Minister," 283–286; Schoonover, "John Hill Wheeler," 140.

26. Robert E. May, *The Southern Dream of a Caribbean Empire, 1854–1861* (Baton Rouge: Louisiana State University Press, 1973), 89–90, 94–103, 109.

27. Hudson, "The Filibuster Minister," 288.

28. Jones, "Wheeler, John Hill," 168; *Frederick Douglass's Paper*, Aug. 10, 1855.

29. Hudson, "The Filibuster Minister," 287, 292.

30. *Frederick Douglass's Paper*, Aug. 10, 1855.

31. Charles H. Brown, *Agents of Manifest Destiny: The Lives and Times of the Filibusters* (Chapel Hill: University of North Carolina Press, 1972), 109.

32. J. H. Wheeler, "A New Work on Nicaragua, The Centre of Central America; Its Past History, Present Position and Future Prospects," mf. copy, John H. Wheeler Papers, Southern Historical Collection; May, *The Southern Dream of a Caribbean Empire*, 251–253.

33. For a thorough discussion of this issue, see May, *The Southern Dream*; James M. Woods, "Borland, Solon"; Schoonover, "John Hill Wheeler," s.v.

34. Hudson, "Filibuster Minister," 296.

35. *Greensboro* (N.C.) *Patriot*, May 5, 1855; *Raleigh Biblical Recorder*, Feb. 4, 1852; Hamilton, *The Papers of William A. Graham*, 127–129.

36. *Petersburg* (Va.) *Daily Express*, June 22, 30, 1857.

37. *Raleigh Biblical Recorder*, Feb. 4, 1853; quoted in *Greensborough* (N.C.) *Patriot*, May 5, 1855; *Murfreesboro Citizen*, Aug. 2, 30, 1860.

38. Hamilton, *The Papers of William A. Graham*, 494–495.

39. John Hill Wheeler's diary for March through May, 1857, mf., Southern Historical Collection.

40. *Petersburg Daily Express*, Mar. 30, 1857.

41. Crafts, *Bondwoman's Narrative*, 196.

42. Gates, "Introduction," xviii–lvi.

43. Ibid., lv; "Textual Annotations," 276,

44. Gates, "Introduction," lxxi–lxxii.

45. Letter from George Stevenson to T. C. Parramore, April 25, 2002; Crafts, *Bondwoman's Narrative*, 198–199; diary of John Hill Wheeler, March 3–April 9, 1857. Stevenson's letter is accompanied by a copy of the deed in which Wheeler sells his farm, in October 1853, to Henry W. Conner.

46. Crafts, *Bondwoman's Narrative*, 198–199.

47. Ibid., 214.

48. Gates, "Introduction," xii; xvi, xvii, xix, lvi; "Textual Annotations," 322–333.

49. Gates, "Introduction," xxv, xxxiv–xxxv.

50. Jones, "Wheeler, John Hill," 168; for Fanning's narrative, see reprint by the Reprint Company, Spartanburg, South Carolina, 1973; J. G. deR. Hamilton, ed., *The Papers of Thomas Ruffin*, 3 (Raleigh: Edwards and Broughton, 1920), 141.

51. Jones, "Wheeler, John Hill"; Gates, "Introduction," xlv; *Petersburg Daily Express*, Oct. 9, 1861; T. C. Parramore, "Wheeler, Junius Brutus," in *Dictionary of North Carolina Biography*, ed. William S. Powell, s.v.; J. H. Wheeler to Thomas Ruffin, in Hamilton, ed., *Papers of Thomas Ruffin*, 3: 141.

52. Jones, "Wheeler, John Hill," s.v.

53. Wheeler's diaries, passim; Crafts, *Bondwoman's Narrative*, 159–160.

22

Jane Johnson, Found! But Is She "Hannah Crafts"?

The Search for the Author of The Bondwoman's Narrative

KATHERINE E. FLYNN

Genealogists, historians, and literary scholars all struggle with a common problem: identity. Genealogists must correctly identify individuals in order to reconstruct families, extend lineages, or track genetic traits. Historians must identify their subjects correctly and put those lives into familial context if they are to accurately interpret the events and the attitudes that have shaped society. Literary scholars are regularly challenged with identifying authors of manuscripts—as are many genealogists who find unsigned works amid their family's trove of relics from the past. Yet even when historic manuscripts are skillfully mined for clues, researchers are frequently stymied in their efforts to find documentary evidence of human lives to match those details.[1] The challenge is especially great in the case of manuscripts that could be pseudonymously authored. One must not only search for an individual of an unknown or suspected name but also establish that the name attached to the manuscript is fictitious. Moreover, pseudonymous works that purport to be based on real events tend to alter facts and identities within their narrative to protect the author's anonymity. Henry Louis Gates's discovery of a manuscript titled "The Bondwoman's Narrative" well illustrates both the difficulties and the possibilities involved in this type of challenge. Gates, who chairs the Afro-American Studies Department at Harvard University, recently published the manuscript under the same title, and he has chronicled the difficulties of his search for its author in both the introduction to the book and in the popular media.[2]

Written in the first person, *The Bondwoman's Narrative* is a rarity—a "fugitive slave novel" in unedited, holographic form—and possibly the earliest known novel by an African American woman. In Gates's opinion, "here we . . . en-counter the unadulterated 'voice' of the fugitive slave herself, exactly as she wrote and edited it."[3] Finding the woman who gave life to that voice has been a challenge for numerous researchers. Gates's own work, coupled with an expert forensic analysis of the manuscript,[4] convincingly establishes three facts:

- The manuscript was written between 1853 and 1861.
- The author was a marginally educated African American woman, whose hesitant penmanship, many strike-throughs, erratic capitalization, "eccentric" punctuation (even to the placement of apostrophes and quotation marks on the base line, in the manner of commas) all suggest someone "who struggled to become educated."[5]
- The slave owner from whom "Hannah Crafts" escaped was one John Hill Wheeler, a North Carolinian in political service in Washington, D.C.

Historic records suggestively link "Hannah Crafts" to one Jane Johnson, a Wheeler slave who escaped in 1855 and became the center of a court case that was an international cause célèbre. Gates draws various parallels between details in the novel (which actually refers to Jane's escape) and details about Jane herself. But he also notes the variances between them that might exclude Jane from further consideration, and he presents other possible theories, as well.

Notable among the negative considerations is this: court documents show Jane placing her mark upon each of her 1855 affidavits, whereas "Hannah Crafts" avers that she learned to read as a child and had become the mistress of a "school for colored children." However, prior efforts to trace Jane as a free woman have failed,[6] making it impossible to know whether she might have acquired some education after her escape.

This chapter presents the writer's search for Jane Johnson, documents Jane's identity, and traces her to her death. Beyond that, it identifies—and eliminates—an actual, contemporary schoolteacher of the name Hannah Crafts, it analyzes the evidence that suggests "Hannah Crafts" is a pseudonym, and it marshals evidence that strongly suggests "Hannah" was the Wheeler slave Jane (Williams) Johnson Woodfork Harris.

Historic Background

In July 1855, John Hill Wheeler, U.S. Minister to Nicaragua, returned briefly to Washington to deliver a packet of treaties—then departed again via train to

Philadelphia, where he planned to sail to New York and on back to his post. Traveling with him was his slave woman Jane Johnson, whom he had purchased in January 1854 but had left behind when dispatched to Nicaragua later that year, as well as Jane's two young sons. Wheeler stopped in Philadelphia at the home of his father-in-law, the celebrated portraitist Thomas Sully, intending to stay only long enough to collect a trunk his wife needed. But the party missed the early afternoon boat out of Philadelphia that Wheeler had planned to take.[7]

Meanwhile, Jane had her own plans—specifically, to escape once they reached New York—but she saw an even better opportunity that July afternoon. While Wheeler took dinner at the hotel, she furtively sought help. One hotel worker sent for William Still, a black leader in the Underground Railroad, who notified Passmore Williamson, a prominent white abolitionist. Still and Williamson rushed to the hotel only to find that the Wheeler party had already left for the steamer. Catching up with Jane on the boat's deck, they informed her that under Pennsylvania law all she had to do to be free was leave the boat. There ensued a minor scuffle with Wheeler, as Jane fled with her sons to a waiting carriage.

Incensed, Wheeler sued Williamson, asserting that his slaves had been taken against their will and demanding their return. When Williamson denied any knowledge of their whereabouts, he was imprisoned without bail. Poor Passmore Williamson didn't stand a chance in front of Judge John Kintzing Kane. Wheeler had influential friends in Philadelphia as well. His father-in-law, Thomas Sully, was a prominent portrait painter who had lived for over two decades in Philadelphia. There was a very tight connection between Sully and Kane stretching back over many years. John K. Kane was one of Sully's major financial backers for a famous trip to England to paint the young Queen Victoria. When Sully returned to Philadelphia there was a famous court case in 1838 over the portrait and its copies. Sully's lawyer in the case was none other than John Kintzing Kane.[8]

At a hearing on 30 August, Jane made a bold appearance, testifying that she had fled of her own volition, then hurriedly left the courtroom under the protection of abolitionists and state authorities. A carriage chase ensued through the streets, as she and her protectors evaded federal marshals attempting to enforce Wheeler's rights.

After Jane Johnson fled that surreal Philadelphia courtroom scene in 1855, narrowly escaping reenslavement by Wheeler, where did she go? What happened to her and her two sons, Daniel and Isaiah? And what of her other unnamed "children in Virginia" Wheeler alluded to during the drama on the boat and in court?

The Clues

A scant profile of Johnson's life up to 1855 emerges from the testimony in the case. She was born sometime between 1814 and 1830, in Washington itself; and she had at least two children: Daniel, born about 1844; and Isaiah, born about 1848. Their birthplaces may have been Virginia; and at least one other child may have been left there.[9] Wheeler had bought Jane in Richmond, Virginia, from a Cornelius Crew around New Year's Day, 1854.[10] Although some contemporary records created by whites call her Jane *Wheeler*, she consistently called herself Jane *Johnson*. Two other clues in known records would lead to discovering her life after she attained freedom:

- The first was a single line in the records of the October 1855 court proceedings. On Williamson's behalf, Jane filed an affidavit attesting that he did not coerce her. To create that affidavit, on 25 September, she appeared "in person" in the U.S. Court for the District of Massachusetts—a court seated in Boston.[11]
- The second was a letter said to have been written to Passmore Williamson in March 1856 by William Cooper Nell, a charter member of the Boston Vigilance Society who reported that he had seen Jane and her children and all were well.[12]

Obviously, the place to look for Jane was Boston, not Philadelphia or New York.

Identifying Jane Johnson

1860 Federal Census

The standard finding aid to the pre-1870 federal censuses (popularly called the AIS indexes) are not *every-name* indexes. Rather, they include only heads of households and individuals living in a dwelling headed by someone of a different surname.[13] Within these limitations, one finds six Jane Johnson entries for Massachusetts—four of them in Boston and surrounding Suffolk County. Consulting the actual census returns for each Jane revealed none that matched the profile. If she were still alive and still resided in Boston but had married before 1860, her husband would be considered the head of household and she would appear under his unknown surname. However, both of her sons would still have been minors. Assuming that they continued to use the Johnson surname, then the rules of the index would call for the inclusion of at least one of them. The subsequent search for "Daniel Johnson" produced six listings, one of which led to a household group that fit the profile of Jane and her family.[14]

Lawrence Woodfork[?]		40, male, black, cook, born Virginia, literate
Jane	"	38, female, black, born D.C., *literate*
Daniel Johnson		16, male, black, born Virginia, attended school during year
Isaiah	"	12, male, black, born Virginia, attended school during year
Ellen A[?]	"	11, female, black, born Virginia, attended school during year

NOTES:

- No tick mark appears in the column for spouses wed within the past twelve months.
- A total of fourteen individuals, in three family groups, occupied this dwelling.

All details appear to fit our target's profile—ages, birthplaces, and names—except for Ellen. Was she a child of Jane, even though Jane had mentioned only a son left in Virginia? If so, how and when did young Ellen get to Boston? Or was she a child of Lawrence? *Of utmost significance is the statement that Jane could read and write—although, just five years before, she had affixed her X to each of her court documents.*

In one other respect, the census entry and the index presented a research problem. On the original manuscript, the surname of Lawrence and Jane is difficult to decipher. The indexers interpreted it as *Wadford*. An examination of several pages of the census, closely comparing the enumerator's letterforms, suggested that *Woodfork* was more probably correct. The Boston 1860 directory confirmed that reading, placing Lawrence *Woodfork* at "3 Revere St Ct." Charles Ringold, one of the other family heads who shares the dwelling in the 1860 census entry, is also listed in the directory at the same address.[15]

Boston Marriage Records

The statewide marriage index offers only one Jane Johnson in Boston during 1855–1960 and no Lawrence Woodfork or any conceivable surname variant.[16] The cited record for this sole Jane identifies her as a white woman born in Scotland. However, the statewide index includes only marriages for which a minister's return was filed, while Boston kept its own city index for both marriage intents and marriage returns. The several Jane Johnson intents include the following:[17]

Lawrence Woodford, "col'd," of Boston, aged 39 years, a laborer, second marriage.
    Born in Essex County, Virginia; son of Thomas.
Jane Johnson, "col'd," of Boston, aged 25 years, second marriage.
    Born in Caroline Co., Va.; daughter of John Williams.
Application: 13 August 1856, by "LW" [Lawrence Woodford].

The details in the record provide both clues and contradictions to be resolved. The surnames shown for Jane and her father, together with the statement that this would be her second marriage, suggest that her husband in slavery was a Johnson. Her stated birthplace conflicts with all others that cite Washington; yet, even this "contradiction," in data supplied by her future husband, may suggest another county in which she had lived.

The most obvious site for the marriage seemed to be the Independent Baptist congregation worshipping at the African Meeting House on Smith Court and Joy Street, Beacon Hill.[18] This building, the oldest standing African American church in America, is now part of Boston's Museum of Afro American History.[19] Museum staffers, who have extensively researched the whereabouts of records relevant to the church's history, point to statistical summaries and minutes at the Trask Library, Andover Theological Seminary in Newton, Massachusetts. However, this facility reports no marriage entries within its holdings for the congregation.[20]

The Neighborhood

A complete survey of Boston's city directories from 1854 forward places Jane and her family in a vibrant community amid some of the most influential African Americans of her time (see Table I). But it was not a stable residence; the family would move almost every year for the next several years. All of their residences lay on the north slope of Beacon Hill, whose black residents in 1860 constituted one of the largest concentrations in the North. (Typically, the southern part of Beacon Hill was home to the most prosperous white families and hotels in Boston, serviced by the blacks who lived nearby.)

The African American leaders of Beacon Hill were a wellspring of activism, lobbying not only for the abolition of slavery but also for black rights in the North—including the protection of fugitive slaves, access to public places, and integrated education. In halls just blocks from her home, Jane would have heard such men as William Cooper Nell, the first black historian, and John Rock, the first black attorney to practice before the U.S. Supreme

Table I   Locations of Jane (Williams) Johnson Woodfork Harris in Boston, 1856–1872

Year	Name	Address	Map Site (FIGURE 1)
1856	Lawrence Woodfork	65 Southac (present Phillips St.)	1
1857	Lawrence Woodfork	1 Southac Ct.	2
1858	Lawrence Woodford	8 Grove	3
1859	Lawrnce Woodfalk	3 Revere St. Ct.	
1860	Lawrence Woodfork	3 Revere St. Ct.	
1861	Lawrence Woodfork	31 Bridge St.*	5
1862	*Not found*		
1863	Mrs. Jane Woodfolk	2 Thompson Ct.	6
1864	Mrs. Jane Woodfolk	22 Vine	7
1865	Jane *Harris* (widow)	22 Vine	7
	Daniel Johnson (sailor)	22 Vine	7
	I. Johnson (55th Mass. Rgt.)	22 Vine	7
1866–70	*Not found*		
1871	Mrs. Harris	5 Fruit Street	8
1872	Jane Harris (widow)	5 Fruit Street	8
	Isaiah Johnson	5 Fruit Street	8

* Now North Anderson Street

Sources: **1856:** *Boston Directory for the Year 1856, Embracing the City Record, A General Directory of the Citizens, and a Business Directory* (Boston: George Adams, 1856), 365. **1857:** *Boston Directory for the Year 1857.* . . (Boston: George Adams, 1857), 380. **1858:** *Boston Directory for the Year 1858.* . . (Boston: George Adams, 1858), 395. **1859:** *Boston Directory for the Year Ending June 30, 1860.* . . (Boston: Adams, Sampson & Co., 1859), 436. **1860:** *Boston Directory . . . for the Year Commencing July 1, 1860* (Boston: Adams, Sampson & Co., 1860), 458. **1861:** *Boston Directory . . . for the Year Commencing July 1, 1861* (Boston: Adams, Sampson & Co., 1861), 475½. **1863:** *Boston Directory . . . for the Year Commencing July 1, 1863* (Boston: Adams, Sampson & Co., 1863), 385. **1864:** *Boston Directory . . . for the Year Commencing July 1, 1864* (Boston: Adams, Sampson & Co., 1864), 391. **1865:** *Boston Directory . . . for the Year Commencing July 1, 1865* (Boston: Adams, Sampson & Co., 1865), 192, 224–25. **1871:** *Boston Directory . . . for the Year Commencing July 1, 1871* (Boston: Sampson, Davenport & Co., 1871), 333. **1872:** *Boston Directory . . . for the Year Commencing July 1, 1872* (Boston: Sampson, Davenport & Co., 1872), 343, 400.

Court, as well as the fiery abolitionist William Lloyd Garrison and Abraham Lincoln himself. Next door to Jane and Lawrence during Jane's first year in Boston (but only that year) were the famed Lewis and Harriet Hayden—Lewis being an escaped slave who achieved business success and prominently led the Boston Vigilance Society. He and Harriet housed and protected literally hundreds of fugitive slaves seeking safety in Boston or safe passage to Canada, suggesting perhaps that the Haydens might have provided Jane and her children their first shelter.[21]

The Treasurers Accounts of the Boston Vigilance Society do record on 10 November 1855 the reimbursement of $39 to William Manix for the board

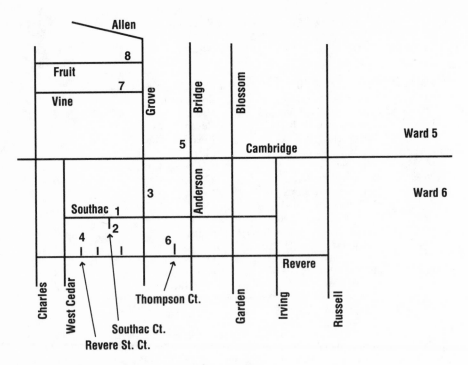

Not drawn to exact scale, but roughly 1" = 0.1 mile
Revere Street Court is present-day Bellingham Place

Sources: Map of Part of Ward 6, Boston (Philadelphia, G.M. Hopkins: 1874). Also, Boston [Mass.] Street Laying-Out Department, *A Record of the Streets, Alleys, Places, etc. in the City of Boston: with an Appendix Containing a Description of the Boundary, Wards and Aldermanic Districts of the City and a Codification by the Corporation Counsel of the Legislative Acts [in] Force January 1, 1902, Authorizing the Laying out and Construction of Public Works, in the City of Boston, and Making of Assessments Therefor* (Boston: Municipal Printing Office, 1902). The author gratefully acknowledges the expertise of Kathryn Grover, an independent scholar and an author of "Historic Resource Study: Boston African American National Historic Site," who pointed out the errors in the original publication and supplied the sources for the corrections.

Fig. I.   Sites of Jane's Residences on Beacon Hill 1856–1872

of Jane Johnson and two children followed by $4.85 for shoes and other expenses for the same. On 22 November 1855 Robert Wallcut was paid $10 for the furniture he provided Jane Johnson. On 13 February 1856 Wallcut was paid $10 for expenses for Jane Johnson.[22] William Manix was an African American fugitive slave who ran a boardinghouse at 83 Southac housing several fugitive slaves.[23] Robert Wallcut was not only a member of the Boston Vigilance Society but also the white publisher of the abolitionist newspaper *The Liberator* and several abolitionist books.

The Civil War Years

Instability would continue to rock Jane's life, as she struggled to make a life as a free woman. Despite their own trials, Jane and Lawrence sheltered fugitive slaves on at least two occasions, 25 December 1857 and 13 April 1859.[24] The city directories attest Lawrence's absence after mid-1861, and the city's death records explain it. An entry for Lawrence Woodfork (indexed as Wood*falk*) reports that he died on 9 December 1861, aged forty-six and a resident of 31 Bridge Street. His parents are given as Thomas and Millea[?], his birthplace as Essex County, Virginia.[25] Not surprisingly, considering the five moves they had made in the five years of their marriage, he left no estate for probate.[26]

As the directories imply, the widowed Jane eventually remarried; the Boston registers offer the following:[27]

> William Harris, "col'd," of Boston, aged 37 years, a mariner, second marriage.
> Born in Oldtown [Allegany County], Maryland; son of Samuel and Polly.
> Jane WOODFORK, "col'd," of Boston, aged 26 years, second marriage.
> Born in Washington, D.C.; daughter of John Williams and Jane.
> Married: 20 July 1864, by Peter Ross, M.G. [Bishop, A.M.E. Church]

Again, the details of the record present contradictions, although the bride's identity is not in doubt. Given that Harris should have been Jane's third husband, not her second, did she consider her slave marriage to be of no legal consequence? Agewise, she should have been in her mid-forties; surely it was not vanity that reduced her age to twenty-six, considering that she already had a grown son. Or did her new husband simply know little about her? Whatever the case, he did not remain long in her life. As the directories show, by 1865 she was again a widow.[28]

That year's directory also provides a window into another corner of Jane's world, one lit by the pride and shadowed by the agony of mothers who send young sons to war. Isaiah was only about fifteen (but claimed to be eighteen) when he enlisted in the Fifty-fifth Massachusetts Volunteer Infantry, a "colored" unit formed from the overflow of recruits for the famous Fifty-fourth Massachusetts. Mustering in as a drummer in Company K, in June 1863, he directed that all letters were to go to "Mrs. Jane Woodfork No 2 Revere St Boston Mass (mother)."[29]

Odds are that Jane—like many widowed mothers—was also to receive his pay. The men of Isaiah's unit had been promised pay equal to that of white soldiers: thirteen dollars a month. When the paymaster doled out wages of only ten, both "colored" units refused to accept any pay until they were treated equally. The governor offered to make up the difference from state funds, but the units refused on principle; it was more a matter of equality than money. Not until June 1864 did Congress right this inequity. In the interim of fifteen months, Isaiah and his fellow soldiers received nothing, causing tremendous hardships at home.[30]

Isaiah's unit was mustered out on 29 August 1865 at Charleston, South Carolina. All of the men are said to have returned to Boston; and the regimental history published in 1868 places Isaiah in Boston,[31] although he does not appear in the city directories of 1866–1871. His fate after 1872 is unknown. Between 1890 and 1901, one Isaac Johnson of Xenia, Ohio, fraudulently collected a pension on his service—creating a file that produced one other personal detail. Amid several depositions taken from members of the Fifty-fifth in 1901, Ransom Chatman of Company K discussed the real Isaiah: "He was a little dark complex'd boy, nothing more than a boy, and enlisted as a drummer. He was the [white] Captain's pet."[32] Four repositories hold extant photographs of members of the Fifty-fifth, but none depict Isaiah Johnson;[33] and federal files of headstone requests for Civil War veterans include nothing for him.[34]

The Postwar Years

Jane and her offspring disappear for five years after the war's close. She and both sons, apparently, were there to answer the door at 22 Vine when the compiler of the city directory canvassed Boston for the 1865–1866 directory (see Table 1). But they seem to have left Massachusetts before the 1865 state census enumerator made his rounds, and they were still elsewhere when the 1870 federal census was compiled.[35] Moreover, they have not been located within the 1870 AIS indexes for New Jersey, North Carolina, Virginia, or Washington, D.C., or in more specialized census databases.[36]

Did Jane, once she no longer had to fear reenslavement, return to the South to search for the son who was sold away from her—or for her parents or siblings? Did her grown sons, who had been to sea and off to war, decide to try their luck elsewhere—prompting Jane to follow them? The postwar uprooting of freedmen in the southern states is well known; but the postwar mobility of those northern blacks who had fled enslavement in Dixie and the extent to which they may have looked southward after 1865 have not been adequately studied. All efforts to document Jane's activity in the immediate postwar years have proven fruitless thus far.

Whatever her choices and actions, Jane reappears in Boston in 1871, set-
tling at 5 Fruit Street. The next year's directory, placing her and her son Isaiah at the same address, had barely gone to press when she died of dysentery
amid a city-wide epidemic attested by numerous other entries recorded in and
around her own.[37]

Dates of death & registration: 2 and 3 August 1872
                         Name: Jane Harris "cold" [colored]
            M[aiden] N[ame]: Williams
                           Age: 59 years
                       Address: 5 Fruit St. Ct.
      F[emale] W[idow of]: William
                  Birthplace: Washington, D.C.
    Parents & birthplaces: John [and] Jane Williams; Washington, D.C.
 Cause of death & duration: Dysentery, 14 days
        Place of Interment: Woodlawn
                   Informant: L. Jones [Lewis L. Jones, undertaker; 50 LaGrange St.][38]

No probate proceedings were launched for Jane, and her death went unno-
ticed by area papers.[39] Her burial at Woodlawn Cemetery (a facility opened at
Everett, five miles north of Boston, to accommodate the overflow from the
city) created little additional information; the age and death date on file there
is the same given in the civil registration of her death, but she is buried alone
in a double plot. The record does not state who bought the plot or when it
was purchased. Jane's grave is identified by only a cheap metal plot marker,
similar to many in her section.[40]

The Direct Link

After all this research was complete, the alleged Nell-Williamson letter was
tracked to the Chester County Historical Society in Pennsylvania. Indeed, two
letters were found there. Together, they were even more valuable than anticipated. The published reference to the letter had merely stated that one William
C. Nell wrote Passmore Williamson from Boston, supposedly in March 1856,
to say that he had seen Jane and her children and that they were well. It gave no
specifics as to where Nell encountered her, where she lived, or what her new circumstances actually were. The historical society's staff reports no letter for the
reputed date but found two others to and from the same individuals that clinch
her identification as Jane (Johnson) Woodfork, wife of Lawrence:[41]

Boston, December 3, 1855

Dear Mr. Williamson,

When I called upon You at Moyamensing prison last October with the committee from the National Convention of Colored Americans I omitted to mention that I met Jane Johnson and her two Boys at the Cars in Boston after her escape from Wheeler, in my capacity as a member of the Vigilance Committee, and was subsequently engaged in securing Home and employment for her: on each occasion she was full of gratitude to You and the other noble friends who rescued her.

I also intended soliciting Your autograph and will feel much obliged if the same be forwarded to the antislavery office Philadelphia or to my address 21 Cornhill Boston.

I remain in the cause of Freedom for all

Fraternally Yours,

William C. Nell

Boston May 26, 1856

Respected Friend,

Accept my thanks for the volume kindly forwarded me.

Jane Johnson called in this morning and expressed much pleasure on hearing from you. She requested my informing you that *she now lives No 1 Southack Court*—and is quite well. Her Boys are progressing finely at School, for all these advantages of freedom she feels heartfelt gratitude for your exertions.

Gratified in the opportunity of communicating as above I remain

Fraternally Yours,

Wm. C. Nell

Nell's second letter, sending Jane's address to Passmore, is critical for at least two reasons. First, the address is exactly the same one listed for Lawrence Woodfork in the 1857 directory—proving beyond doubt that the Wheeler slave for whom Williamson spent three months of his life in jail was Jane (Williams) Johnson Woodfork Harris. Second, it establishes that Jane and her family were already on the road to literacy in 1856: her request that Nell send her address to Williamson suggests that she wished to correspond with him directly, rather than through Nell. Whether she could read by this point or whether she anticipated having Lawrence or her sons read Williamson's letters to her remains uncertain.

Eliminating "Hannah Craft(s)"

Any argument that Jane Johnson might be "Hannah Crafts" requires a reasonable elimination of the possibility that a viable candidate of this name might have existed. Gates's introduction to the published *Bondwoman's Narrative* reports the details of his search that, in the end, turned up no possibilities.[42] Using the 1860–1880 census indexes and the electronically published database to the Freedman's Bank records,[43] he identified—and effectively eliminated—several individuals named Hannah and Maria H. Craft or Kraft. The fact that he found no Hannah *Crafts* is ordinarily inconsequential, given the vagaries of census spellings.

Although Gates's search seems to have included all appropriate states and variant spellings, one census limitation appears not to have been considered: the indexes he consulted are not *every-name indexes*, and wives who used the same surname as their husbands were systematically eliminated. Although the online genealogical libraries of several commercial firms are filling the void with every-name search engines as well as digitized page images, that process is not complete for all states. Thus, identifying a married Hannah or an unmarried one in a household of the same surname would require viewing the actual household for each and every Craft(s) entry, locale by locale.

This procedure does, indeed, identify a schoolteacher by the name of Hannah Crafts—not in New Jersey as "Hannah Crafts" claimed but in Boston, from 1860 to 1903. More precisely, she was Hannah Frederika Crafts, born about 1837–1838 to Mathew (Mathias) Crafts, a Prussian immigrant who progressed from "laborer " to "deputy wharfinger," and his wife Hannah, who had been born in Massachusetts about 1810. The Crafts were white. The censuses and the city directories show that the family remained in the same neighborhood, despite political changes that shifted them from Wards 4 to 2 between 1850 and 1860. The younger Hannah would continue to live in Ward 2, East Boston (in the family home at 87 Webster and later at 131 Webster) until her death, as a spinster, on 12 August 1903.[44]

No record places Hannah near Jane Johnson's community along the line between Wards 5 and 6. The known schools at which Hannah taught during Jane's lifetime—Monmouth Street Primary and Lexington Street Primary—are in her own immediate neighborhood. No evidence discovered to date suggests that she had any contact with members of the abolitionist movement, the Underground Railroad, or Boston's escaped-slave population. Nor has research revealed any trace of other creative writings by her, published or unpublished.

Finding a real Hannah Crafts, schoolteacher—and one in Boston itself—begs the obvious question: Could *The Bondwoman's Narrative* have been written by Hannah Frederika Crafts? Nickell, the forensic expert who evaluated the manuscript scientifically and contextually, presents compelling evidence that seemingly rules out this Hannah. Two of his points are particularly germane:[45]

- The writer of the novel was a woman with a reasonably advanced vocabulary but minimal proficiency with the written language.
- The writer was almost certainly black and intimately familiar with slavery. A single, twenty-something white female, reared in Boston with no first-hand knowledge of slavery, would not likely write with such verisimilitude about master-slave sex and rape, or even the gritty details of daily relationships. The writer of this narrative was clearly a person who knew the life she wrote about—regardless of whether the details she related were totally autobiographical or an amalgam of situations she lived within.

Modern writers who are (or have) good researchers can invent a variety of characters who have no connection to their life experiences. One might even argue that Hannah Frederika Crafts simply fantasized a novel out of whatever abolitionist literature she had read. But one fact cannot be explained away so easily: the penmanship of *The Bondwoman's Narrative* is simply not that of a formally educated Bostonian schoolteacher, reared in an upwardly mobile family. Beyond this theoretical or psychological evaluation, one piece of hard evidence settles the matter. Hannah Frederika Crafts and her mother, Hannah (Lewis) Crafts both left signatures whose penmanship in no way matches that of the author of *The Bondwoman's Narrative*. (See Figure 2.) To argue that this teacher engaged a scribe to pen a novel using her own name pushes the argument beyond reasonable limits.

Is Jane Johnson "Hannah Crafts"?

One theory posed by Gates is that "Hannah Crafts" may be a pseudonym for the Wheeler runaway Jane Johnson. In considering this possibility, he notes both similarities and differences between the meager details known for Jane and the life account given by "Hannah Crafts." However, this hypothesis—one of several he proposed—foundered upon two shoals: the known illiteracy of Jane and the failure to track her life as a free woman. Now that both handicaps have been removed, the case for "Hannah Crafts" being Jane Johnson

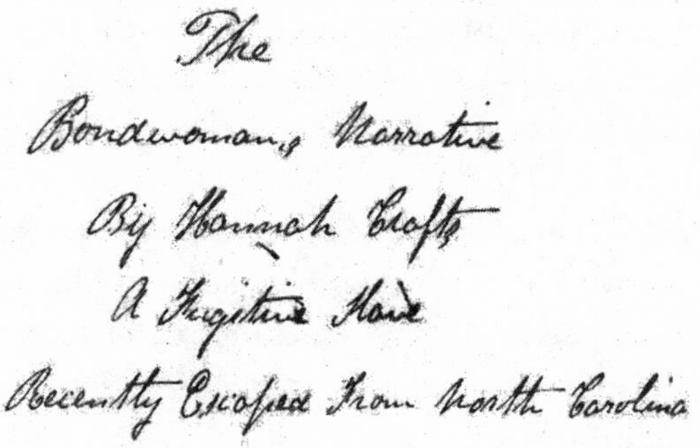

The

Bondwoman,s Narrative

By Hannah Crafts

A Fugitive Slave

Recently Escaped from North Carolina

Sample 1
"Hannah Crafts," Author
from manuscript's title page (ca. 1860–61?)
as reproduced in Gates, *The Bondwoman's Narrative*, p. 1

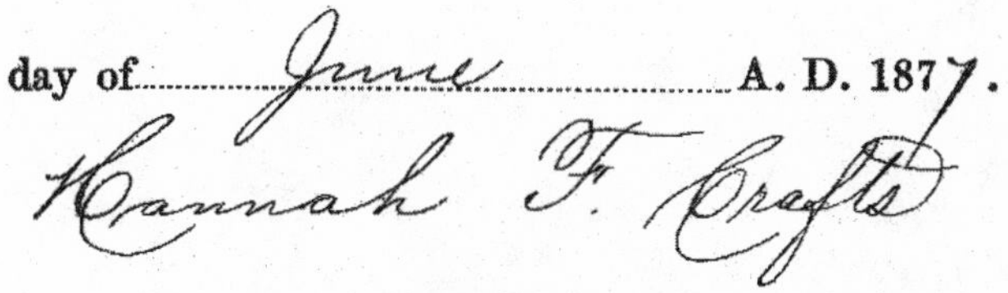

day of *June* A. D. 187**7**.

Hannah F. Crafts

Sample 2
Hannah Crafts, Schoolteacher
(Jane Johnson's contemporary in Boston)
from Matthes Crafts Estate File, no. 59299 (1876), Suffolk Co., Mass.

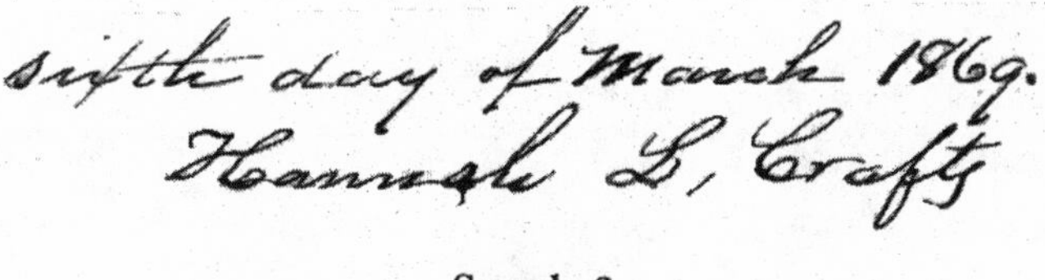

sixth day of March 1869.

Hannah L, Crafts

Sample 3
Hannah Crafts, Sr., widow of Matthes Crafts
(also Jane Johnson's contemporary in Boston)
from Matthes Crafts Trust File, no. 49376 (1869), Suffolk Co., Mass.

Fig. 2. Comparative Signatures

needs reexamining, positing new facts against the arguments made by Gates and against other points, as well.

The core challenge remains the same: *The Bondwoman's Narrative* is a *novel*, although it purports to be based on fact. With any such work, it is hard to discern the line where fiction blends into true events, people, and places. Nonetheless, its genre had already established certain conventions. Pseudonyms were common—the famed Harriet Jacobs, for example, wrote her 1861 *Incidents in the Life of a Slave Girl* under the name "Linda Brent." Even though abolitionists encouraged escaped-slave writers to "be as . . . exact as possible, to name names and to embrace verisimilitude as a dominant mode of narrative development,"[46] those who wrote before the Civil War had serious reasons to change details about their lives, their masters, and their flights. Under the Fugitive Slave Act of 1850, their escape from the punitive arms of their masters was tenuous, and most still had family in bondage who might suffer retaliation. On the other hand, Gates notes, "*fictions* of slavery—whether *Uncle Tom's Cabin* or Mattie Griffith's *Autobiography*—tend *not* to contain characters named after the author's actual contemporaries."[47]

Table 2 summarizes the key points of similarity and disparity introduced by Gates. These are the basics upon which the following analysis builds, as it considers two questions: *Did the Wheelers experience one slave escape or two?* And, *Are the details now known for Jane compatible with evidence the manuscript presents?*

One Escape or Two?

"Hannah" states that she was purchased by the Wheelers as a lady's maid to replace "Jane," who had run away (published version, p. 149). Presuming that "Jane" of the novel was the escapee Jane Johnson, Gates dated the purchase of "Hannah" at 1856 (probably summer 1856) and combed Wheeler's extant diaries for references to a subsequent runaway who might be "Hannah." He found none, but he notes that volumes for the last half of 1856 and the first half of 1858 are missing and then concludes: "Judging from the relevant information contained in Wheeler's diary, Hannah's escape would most likely have occurred between March 21 and May 4, 1857."[48]

Many significant factors contradict this timetable and suggest that *"Hannah" belonged to the Wheelers before 1855.*

Wheeler Family Residence

Between mid-1853 and mid-1854, the primary Wheeler residence was Washington, where John Hill Wheeler served President Franklin Pierce as an assistant secretary. The family departed Washington after his August 1854 appointment as Resident Minister to Nicaragua. Although he briefly returned in the summer of 1855, his family did not. Wheeler was recalled in October 1856, but he had already sent his wife and sons back to the states for their safety in May of that year.[49] Between then and the resumption of the diary entries in January 1857, their residence(s) remains unknown.

Table 2   "Hannah Crafts"—Jane Johnson: Previously Established Points of Similarity and Disparity

Hannah	Jane
Similarities	
• "Hannah" begins her narrative in Milton, Charles City County, Virginia.	• Jane's earliest known origins were in Richmond, Henrico County, the county adjacent to Charles City.
• "Hannah" repeatedly identified her owners as Wheelers.	• Jane was owned by John Hill Wheeler and his wife Ellen.
• "Hannah" came to the Wheelers in Washington, from Virginia, after the Christmas holidays (p. 156).	• Jane was bought by Wheeler, in Virginia, on New Year's Day and brought to Washington.
• "Hannah" states she was bought to replace "Jane" who ran away (pp. 149–52).	• Wheeler's diary extensively discusses Jane's escape, but mentions no loss of any other slave (although parts of the diary are missing).
• "Hannah" describes herself as a mulatto who pretended to be white amid her escape. However, she also writes somewhat enviously of Lizzie, a fellow slave, who was "a Quadroon, almost white, with delicate hands and feet" (p. 33).	• Jane was described by William Still as "chestnut color." The engraving Still published depicts dark skin and African features.
Disparities	
• "Hannah" is single and argues with great emotion for celibacy by slave women (pp. 206–7).	• Jane married and bore at least three children in slavery.
• "Hannah" says she was literate from an early age and even wrote letters on behalf of Mrs. Wheeler (pp. 153–54).	• Jane did not sign her name to affidavits immediately after her escape.
• "Hannah" writes of going from Washington to North Carolina with the Wheelers and describes the trip by boat (pp. 196–99).	• Jane was owned by Wheeler in August 1854, when he left Washington for a trip to his North Carolina plantation—and he customarily traveled by boat. However, he is not known to have taken his family or domestic slaves with him while Jane was part of the household.
• "Hannah" places herself in New Jersey at the time she wrote her novel and does not mention Boston (pp. 237–39).	• Jane's only known locales, after her escape, were Philadelphia and New York.

NOTE: *Page numbers refer to hardcover edition*

In short: if "Hannah" were indeed purchased in Virginia by Mrs. Wheeler and brought to Washington as a replacement for Jane who escaped en route to Nicaragua in 1855, then Hannah could not have been purchased before summer 1856, and her winter introduction to Washington could not possibly have occurred before 1857.

During that winter 1856–1857, however, the Wheelers were not in Washington, Virginia, or North Carolina. Wheeler returned from Nicaragua with a severely infected finger that was amputated in January 1857. The surgery—and apparently the recovery as well—took place in Philadelphia, while the Wheelers stayed at the home of Mrs. Wheeler's father.[50] Not until 14 February did he return to Washington, and on 24 March he left for North Carolina—the event Gates cited as the opportunity for "Hannah" to escape. This timetable means that "Hannah," who professed familiarity with Washington's political and social scene, would have spent only thirty-seven days there—whereas Jane spent at least nine months in the Wheelers' Washington household.

Wheeler's misfortune is doubly significant to the identity of "Hannah." First, if she had been with the family in January 1857, their continued presence in Philadelphia would have made her free; no dramatic escape from the South would have occurred. Second, the failure of "The Bondwoman's Narrative" to mention this amputation—a traumatic event for a man who earned his living by the pen—is only one of many miscues within the narrative that suggest the author fled the Wheelers prior to 1857.

The Weather

"Hannah" describes in great detail the winter scene that greeted her when she arrived at the Wheeler home in Washington: mud, slush, fog, and gloom (pp. 156–157). However, those would not have been the conditions she observed in the winter of 1856–1857. Washington and northern Virginia were hit then with a snowstorm and blizzard of historic proportions—one that meteorological history dubs "The Great Cold Storm." Over two feet of snow fell on 18–19 January 1857, causing enormous drifts. Temperatures plummeted to below zero, creating a multistate catastrophe. Richmond was cut off from the capital for over a week, and the Chesapeake Bay and all the rivers in Virginia froze over.[51] Had "Hannah" been in Washington that winter, she would have described a paralyzing snowstorm, not the city's typical "mud, slush, fog, and gloom."

Jane Johnson, on the other hand, saw Washington with the Wheelers only in January 1854, when the city's weather indeed matched that described by "Hannah."

"Hannah's" Timetable

The events related by "Hannah," *if she were Jane's replacement,* would add nearly a year to the date of her earliest possible arrival in Washington. According to her chronicle, when Mrs. Wheeler came to visit the Henrys in northern Virginia and began to plot for "Hannah's" purchase as a replacement for Jane, "It was now . . . summer" (p. 148). Given the Wheelers' known schedule, that meeting would have been either the summer of 1856 or that of 1857.

Meanwhile, by the narrative's timetable, "Hannah" would have passed the terrible storm of the winter of 1856–1857 as a runaway in a northern Virginia jail (chapters 7 and 8). That portion of the narrative might explain why her description did not include the paralyzing snowstorm in Washington, but it cannot explain why the storm went unmentioned. Amid subzero temperatures that froze all rivers in Virginia and left drifts up to twenty feet high across northern Virginia, the coziness of prisoners would not have been a high priority for the jailers who had to haul in the firewood.

Political Events

Miscues

"Hannah" relates several conversations dealing with political matters that took place in the period after her move into the Wheelers' Washington home. Conspicuously missing is any discussion of the March 1857 grand inaugural of a new president. As a patronage appointee in the capital, Wheeler would have used every opportunity to maneuver at these activities. The narrative, in fact, focuses upon his efforts to curry political favor, but the grand inaugural and change of administration go unmentioned.

Conspicuously present in the narrative, however, is Mrs. Wheeler's complaint about a "senator from Ohio" who was surreptitiously helping Washington-area slaves abscond (p. 151). Ohio's Salmon P. Chase, the staunch abolitionist lawyer nicknamed "attorney general for fugitive slaves," served only from 1849–1855 and then went home to assume Ohio's governorship in early 1856.[52] Clearly, the Washington story "Hannah" tells about the Ohio senator occurred before the end of 1855.

Equally telling is the passage in which "Hannah" writes of the president's wife (p. 157). Buchanan, who took office in 1857, was a bachelor. However, the president in office from January to August 1854, the period during which Jane served the Wheelers in Washington, was indeed a married man. If "The Bondwoman's Narrative" had been written by an active member of the abolitionist community, striving for veracity, that kind of anachronism would not likely appear. But it *is* the kind of unthinking supposition that Jane would have made: no longer part of the gossipy environment of Washington, struggling to support a family at subsistence level, she likely did not follow the newspapers closely enough to know that the new president was, indeed, a bachelor.

Significant Overlaps

Other details uncannily overlap the real experiences of the Wheelers *during the time Jane served them.* John Hill Wheeler, as a North Carolina assemblyman in 1851, campaigned for James Cochran Dobbin to occupy the state's U.S. senate seat. Dobbin lost, but Wheeler won his undying friendship. When Dobbin was appointed Secretary of the *Department of the Navy* in 1853, he prevailed upon the president to find a position for Wheeler; and in August 1854, Wheeler was handed the Nicaraguan appointment.[53]

Meanwhile, "Hannah"—early in her Washington chapter—writes of Wheeler's bid for a position in the *Department of the Navy.* Considering the number of bureaus and departments that the manuscript's author could have chosen to weave fancy around (if that were indeed the case here), it begs disbelief that "Hannah" accidentally portrayed her Mr. Wheeler as a political suitor of the Navy Department.

Moreover, Wheeler's return from Nicaragua in late 1856 was a recall suffered amid disgrace; however, he did not tender his resignation until the president personally insisted in March 1857. The end of Pierce's administration that month also marked the ouster of Wheeler's mentor, Dobbin, who returned to North Carolina and died before the year was out. As one authority reports: "Thus was ended the diplomatic and indeed the political career of John Hill Wheeler."[54]

And again, the events painted by "Hannah" parallel the *January–August 1854* political life of Wheeler—not his life in 1857 or thereafter. If "Hannah" were Jane's replacement, narrating her own experiences with the family, then 1857 political events are inexplicably missing.

Wheeler's Plantation

Other events in narrative also suggest Wheeler's ownership of "Hannah" prior to his Nicaraguan appointment. Soon after her purchase, "Hannah" left Washington with them by boat for their North Carolina plantation. There, she observed "orange trees . . . dropping with fruit" and a cotton field with "snowy fleece bursting richly from the pod" (p. 199). Wheeler's diaries relate two such trips: one in August–September 1854, as he wrapped up affairs in preparation for his new post in Nicaragua, and one in March–May 1857, shortly after his return. The description "Hannah" gives is consistent with September harvest conditions in North Carolina.

Wheeler had, in fact, sold his plantation at Beattie's Ford in June 1853, prior to his purchase of Jane.[55] But, as his diary shows, his North Carolina trips thereafter included visits to his sister, Julia Wheeler Moore, whose husband owned a plantation in Hertford County.

Wheeler's Escaped Slaves

The Wheeler diaries, throughout the 1850s, mention various servants but none named Hannah. They contain numerous entries in which Wheeler discusses his escaped slaves, but the only ones mentioned are Jane and her children. Gates suggests that another runaway could have occurred during one of the two gaps in the diary—late 1856 or early 1858. However, Wheeler's fierce resentment over the loss of his slave property is a recurring theme. He petitioned North Carolina's governor and assembly to legally assist citizens of the state who traveled in the North, claiming, "This course would foil these fanatics with their own weapons"; and as late as January 1860, his diary shows, he was still writing to the Pennsylvania courts, plying his suit to recover Jane. Toward the end of 1863, when he penned a very short summary of important life events, he recorded the date 18 July 1855 and wrote acrimoniously: "My servants (Jane, Isaiah, and Daniel) seized and stolen by a band of Abolitionists."[56]

If "Hannah" had absconded on the heels of Jane, it strains credulity to think he would have ignored the loss of "Hannah" while brooding only over the loss of Jane and her boys.

Is Jane's Evidence Compatible?

Literacy

The evidence attests that Jane acquired some measure of literacy between 1855 and 1860. In the wake of her escape from Wheeler, she had to affix her mark to her affidavits. Over the next ten months, Nell's letters report that Jane had found employment and that her sons were doing well at school; he says nothing about educational efforts by Jane herself. Still, the first census to enumerate Jane as a free woman asserts that she could read and write. *Could she, in four years, have acquired sufficient literacy to pen a novel?* The forensic analysis of the manuscript's craftsmanship suggests a *vocabulary* equivalent to the eleventh grade by modern standards. However, the script is merely serviceable, the text naively "borrows" from Dickens and others, and both the plot and the style would be far more accurately described as "fervent but workmanlike" than "fresh and imaginative."[57]

Lacking an actual specimen of Jane's handwriting, the best one can do is to evaluate her progress in the context of her community. Toward that end, this research project has analyzed the 1860 census data for all adult people of color in Ward 6 who were born in any slave state, the District of Columbia, or Africa. In the main, these individuals' occupations are said to be *laborer, waiter, cook, jobber,* and *service.* Their ranks included only one clergyman and two physicians. Of the total ($n = 286$), 82 percent were born in either Virginia or Maryland (53 percent, Virginia; 29 percent, Maryland), and *fully 85 percent were literate.*

Clearly Jane was immersed in a community in which literacy was expected of people of color. Indeed, economic viability when competing for jobs against white and black laborers born in Canada and the North would have required it. Just as clearly, the support system for fugitive slaves that was set up by Boston's Vigilance Committee included not only housing and employment but adult education as well.

So, what of the discrepancies between Jane's educational background and that claimed by "Hannah"? The narrator of the novel asserts that she learned to read and write at an early age and even boasts of writing letters on behalf of Mrs. Wheeler—but that assertion is highly dubious. The identity of the Wheelers has been resolved beyond reasonable doubt. The period in which "Hannah" lived in their household has been tightly narrowed by the forensic evidence to a year or so in the mid-1850s. Wheeler's wife at that time (his second wife) was the well-educated daughter of the famed portraitist Thomas Sully, for whom Thomas Jefferson had sat.[58] In stark contrast, the penmanship of "The Bondwoman's Narrative" is that of someone self-taught—rough and irregular, hyphenating words at the start of lines instead of the end, and confusing apostrophes and quotation marks with commas to the point of placing all three types of marks on the base line.[59] In no way would she have been able to pen a letter for her mistress that would have met the standards expected of a cultured white lady, a child of privilege, whose husband was then an assistant secretary to the president of the United States.

The literary habits of "Hannah" also point to other elements in the story that seem to be more exaggerated or wishful than simply invented. As Nickell observes, the author's vocabulary was extensive and heavily polysyllabic.[60] Gates further notes that she prefaced each chapter with a quotation from the Bible or a classical work and that the impreciseness of the quotations indicates she was writing from memory. He also demonstrates that the claim by "Hannah" to have stolen into her master's library during childhood, to read all his books, does seem to be rooted in some germ of fact. In 1850, Wheeler cataloged the books in his North Carolina home—over 1,200 volumes—and the extant list includes several classic works that "Hannah" quoted or paraphrased in her narrative.[61] *However, according to her narrative, "Hannah" did not become a Wheeler slave until she was a mature young woman; and she describes a childhood spent elsewhere.*

It would, in fact, be overreaching to conclude from her familiarity with these works that "Hannah" actually *read* them during her two or so years with the Wheelers. Another plausible explanation comes from James Moore, a descendant of Wheeler's sister Julia Wheeler Moore, who reports that the Wheeler family had a tradition of reading aloud to one another in the evening. Wheeler's diaries, in fact, record at least two occasions of his reading to his family from the Bible and from Shakespeare's *Hamlet.*[62] "Hannah," as Mrs. Wheeler's personal maid, would have thereby been exposed to the classic works in the Wheeler library—passages only heard and later recalled from memory. Jane Johnson, as Ellen Wheeler's personal maid in Washington, would have had the same exposure. The effects of such exposure can be seen in a reporter's description of Jane during her testimony in Philadelphia. He reported, "Jane is a fine specimen of the best class of Virginia housemaids, with a certain lady-like air, propriety of language and timidity of manner that prepossesses the audience in her favor. . . . She was very polite in her manners and spoke of 'colored gentlemen,' 'white gentlemen,' and 'colored ladies,' as though ladies and gentlemen had been her associates all her lifetime . . . ."[63]

Marital Status

Presenting herself as chaste in slavery, "Hannah" passionately argued for slave women to remain celibate (pp. 205–207). Jane, ostensibly, felt otherwise. After all, she bore three children before her escape. However, one could counter that Jane, writing as "Hannah," was expressing emotions she had learned the hard way—convictions reached out of the anguish of watching a child sold away from her.

A striking parallel might be drawn between the radical reduction of Jane's own status in August 1854 and Mrs. Wheeler's consignment of "Hannah" to "a crime against nature" among the "promiscuous . . . dirty . . . obscene . . . vile, foul, [and] filthy inhabitants of the huts"—as "Hannah" described them (pp. 199–205). With the appointment of Wheeler to Nicaragua and the Wheelers' decision to leave Jane behind, she plummeted mightily from her own coveted post as a lady's maid in the nation's capital. Apparently left on a rural plantation,[64] she—like "Hannah"—would have been resented by the entrenched staff at the manor house. The tale "Hannah" wove there, of being falsely accused by another housemaid and condemned by her mistress to couple with one of those "brutalized creatures in the cabins," might well have been Jane's own fall from grace.

More concrete is the parallel between the union "Hannah" claimed for herself in freedom. Having "ever regarded marriage as a holy ordinance" (p. 205), "Hannah" became the wife of a Methodist minister (p. 239). Jane, the evidence shows, was also Methodist. When she wed in 1864, her new husband was a sailor with no known roots in Boston. Surely it was not he who insisted that the marriage be sanctified by a bishop of the African Methodist Episcopal Church.

Motivation

Whoever "Hannah" was, she was driven to write this manuscript by powerful emotions. She dwelt extensively on the sexual exploitation of slave women—not just by masters and slavers but by callous mistresses who would force their bondwomen into sexual partnerships that repulsed them. Her discussions of the Wheelers repeatedly held them up to ridicule. At first, in the manner of many novels of that era, she identified her last owners only as W———r. As an escapee subject to the Fugitive Slave Act, which empowered slave owners to seize their "property" across state lines—even outside the South—"Hannah" had much at stake. But by the end of her catharsis, as her tale of mistreatment at the hands of the Wheelers became more passionate, she abandoned both convention and caution and named outright the family that had pushed her beyond endurance.

Who, in fact, had more reason than Jane Johnson to expose the Wheelers' shallowness and cruel disregard for the lives and feelings of other humans? John Hill Wheeler had torn her away from one son and likely from the husband who was her children's father. Within months of that purchase, the Wheelers appear to have deposited her—a genteel, urban housemaid—among their uncultured, unwashed field hands in the country. On that fateful 1855 trip, Wheeler was moving her and her remaining sons out of the country; and strong forces in Pierce's administration already favored the expansion of slavery into Cuba and Central America.[65] For Jane, the planned escape on the coastal portion of that journey was a matter of *act now or forever suffer.* Even after she escaped, Wheeler's influence as a presidential appointee made him a frightening foe. He did, in fact, do everything in his power to reclaim her. If he could succeed in having a white abolitionist imprisoned without bail, he could have had her seized as well—if he had known her whereabouts.

The Pseudonym

The name "Hannah Crafts" is uncommon enough to raise another question: Why would Jane choose it? Did her path cross that of the real Hannah Crafts, schoolteacher, there in Boston? The literary style displayed by "Hannah Crafts" suggests that she was not so much an original thinker as a borrower—someone so uncomfortable with her own worth, so unsure of the value of her own words, that she borrowed passages from other authors that expressed her own feelings particularly well. When narrating personal events, her writing is raw and unsophisticated. But in her background descriptions, the alliterations and other rhetorical devices suggest that she borrowed even more passages than those already detected.

Clearly, she borrowed the name "Hannah Crafts" also—and the one she chose is not so odd a choice. *Craft* (without the final *s*) was a name revered in Boston's abolitionist circles because of the activities of William and Ellen Craft. For Jane to use *Craft* or *Crafts* as a pseudonym would offer an echo of the verisimilitude that slave escapees were urged to use. Perhaps in seeking to preserve her own anonymity while creating that aura, Jane chose the name and occupation of someone there in Boston whom she had met and admired—in the same manner that she attributed to her fictional husband an occupation she obviously respected.

The Manuscript Itself

Questions still swirl around the manuscript itself. When was it written? Why was it not published? How did it survive in manuscript form? The evidence is meager, but suggestive.

By whatever means Jane acquired literacy, it was a hard-earned skill. The exigencies of daily life—employment, child rearing, housework, tending to the needs of a husband, and the continual uprooting of the family household—would have left her with limited time to develop fluency with the written language. It could well have taken several years of hours stolen here and there to become comfortable enough with the process and its accouterments (she principally used sharpened goose quills, quill-pen knives, ink-eraser knifes, and writing sand[66]) before she had the self-assurance to develop a plot, characters, and conversations in ink on costly paper.

Considering these factors, her venture likely overlapped the onset of the Civil War. The expectation of a swift Northern victory likely eased her fear that Wheeler could reclaim her. But it would also have affected the market—not just affordability but public craving—for a novel designed to argue the evils of slavery. Nickell's forensic analysis determined that the manuscript had been written on individual folios and handsewn together, without covers. Not until the 1880s was it bound professionally. Yet even the outside pages that originally had no protection from wear, insects, or other elements are in remarkably good condition. These facts argue against haphazard storage in steamy attics or damp basements by someone who did not appreciate the value of her effort.

Jane died suddenly in 1872. One son lived with her at that time; his life thereafter is unknown. Possibly, he produced offspring who preserved their grandmother's manuscript, well-wrapped, in the family trunk where valuables were stored in that era. An equally plausible explanation for its preservation is suggested by the nature of Jane's community—a tightly knit concentration of some of the nation's most intelligent African Americans. One of her oldest friends in Boston was the first black historian, William Cooper Nell. While her work may not have found a publisher in her lifetime, the community would have known of its existence; and those who risked their lives to help Jane and others escape bondage would not have wanted her story lost. Nell, who died in 1874,[67] his heirs, or others in his circle may well have preserved the manuscript until someone, in 1948, sold it to a collector for $85: the equivalent in today's currency of $632.39.[68] Amid America's economic recovery from World War II, the writings of black women were not commercially hot items.

Did Jane have the means, motive, and opportunity to write "The Bondwoman's Narrative"? Her motivation is beyond question as discussed previously. Most arguments revolve around means and opportunity. Jane arrived in Boston to a community of highly literate African Americans where literacy was critical to survival in the competition for employment. Moreover, this community had blacks of the highest education and intelligence leading the Vigilance Committee to aid fugitive slaves. She had access to the education and the support necessary to achieve the degree of literacy demonstrated in the book. Recall that her background was not that of a field slave but rather a lady's maid who had the bearing and intelligence to personally attend the wife of the assistant secretary to the president with close connections to cabinet members.

Finally, there is the question of opportunity. It is easier to believe that a black woman in Boston, surrounded by other fugitive slaves writing and publishing books to great fanfare, would be inspired to attempt such a feat herself than to accept that a woman in an obscure, rural New Jersey community far from any publishers or connections would sit down and write a three-hundred-page book addressed to the public.

One of Jane's closest contacts in Boston was Nell, who, aside from being the first black historian, was a journalist for the abolitionist newspaper *The Liberator* and an author of a published book. Nell introduced another fugitive slave author, Harriet Jacobs, to Lydia Child. Child eventually edited Jacobs's fugitive slave narrative, *Incidents in the Life of a Slave Girl*, published in 1861 under the pseudonym "Linda Brent." Nell worked at the same address as *The Libera-*

tor's publisher, Roger F. Wallcut, who also published several slave narratives and abolitionist books, and who also assisted Jane when she first arrived in Boston. Thus, Jane was immersed in, and well connected to, a culture of black participation in literacy in all its forms.

Conclusion

Identifying the authors of anonymous or pseudonymous works—even those that purport to be autobiographical—is typically a detective game in which the investigator must build a circumstantial case. Historical researchers are rarely as lucky as Vassar professor Donald Foster, who pegged Joe Klein as the author of *Primary Colors,* because the authors of historical manuscripts are rarely alive to admit authorship after they have been detected. Still, with thorough research and careful analysis, the genealogist can build a convincing case for even the most elusive types of identities.

The present case *is* circumstantial but strongly suggestive that Jane Johnson and "Hannah Crafts" are one and the same person. Beyond this point, an essential question stands: *Was this Jane's own writing, was it the work of an amanuensis, or was it written by someone who felt compelled to exploit her story?* Concrete evidence that she penned the manuscript herself—a matching sample of her handwriting, perhaps—has not surfaced.[69] On the other hand, neither the penmanship nor the style of writing matches that of other known writers, such as William C. Nell and Lucretia Mott, with whom she was acquainted. Research continues, and the publication of these findings may generate knowledge of more documents not yet known.

Black-authored works on the subject of slavery, penned during the years of frenzy that led to the Civil War, are not rare. The authorship of most has been challenged, and most have withstood the challenge—the 1857 "pseudo-slave narrative" of Mattie Griffith being a notable exception that was quickly admitted.[70] In the case at hand, if one proposes that "The Bondwoman's Narrative" was penned by a surrogate before Jane acquired sufficient literacy to author it herself, then one needs a rationale for cloaking Jane in the anonymity of "Hannah." Jane's very status as a cause célèbre would have meant that *Jane's story—presented explicitly as Jane's story*—would have "sold copy." Only Jane herself, once she developed some proficiency with the tools of writing, would have seen any benefit in marketing a manuscript that exposed the Wheelers while protecting her own privacy.

Jane's unique legal records and the contemporary accounts by her associates present her as a woman of innate intelligence, with a clear purpose and the will to gain freedom for herself and her children—in short, a formidable woman in her era. (One study, for example, has shown that only 19 percent of fugitive slaves were women.[71]) That Jane dared to plan and actually achieved freedom, with two young children in tow, is a significant feat. Her saga is impressive in its own right, as one of the few that has been documented among millions of enslaved lives. As simply Jane, she represents an important chapter in America's ongoing experiment to realize the ideals to which it aspires.

Jane (Williams) Johnson Woodfork Harris lies in a nameless grave, with only a numbered marker to identify her remains, but her story has survived.

Genealogical Summary

I. **Jane**[2] **Williams** (John[1]) born about 1814 in Washington, D.C.[72]; died 2 August 1872, in Boston, Suffolk County, Massachusetts.[73] She was the daughter of John Williams and Jane [—?—], both born in Washington.[74] She married (1) probably by slave rites in Virginia about 1843, [—?—] **Johnson**; (2) by marriage intent filed 13 August 1856 in Boston, **Lawrence Woodfork**, who had been born in Essex County, Virginia, during March 1835, to Thomas Woodfork and Millea(?) [—?—], and died 7 December 1861, in Boston;[75] and (3) on 20 July 1864, in Boston, **William Harris**, a sailor who had been born about 1827 in Oldtown, Allegany County, Maryland, as the son of Samuel and Polly [—?—] Harris,[76] and died (perhaps at sea) about 1864–65.[77]

Born into slavery, Jane may have lived in Caroline County, Virginia.[78] Her earliest known owner was Cornelius Crew of Richmond, Henrico County, Virginia, who sold her and two of her children to John Hill Wheeler of Washington about New Year's Day 1854.[79] On 18 July 1855, she and those children escaped from Wheeler in Philadelphia while en route to Nicaragua.[80] In late summer 1855, she settled in Boston, aided by both cities' Vigilance Committees,[81] and then spent the next ten years in various tenements on the north slope of Beacon Hill. She appears to have lived somewhere other than Massachusetts, New Jersey, North Carolina, Virginia, or Washington from 1866 to 1870 but returned to her Boston neighborhood the year before she died of dysentery.[82]

Known and possible children of Jane[2] Williams and [—?—] Johnson are[83]

2   i. DANIEL[3] JOHNSON, born about 1843–44 in Virginia.[84] He went to sea as a young man, made one isolated appearance in Boston's 1865 city directory,[85] and then dropped from known records.

3   ii. UNKNOWN SON, born perhaps 1845–46; sold away from Jane in Virginia.

4 iii. ISAIAH JOHNSON, born about 1847–48 in either Virginia[86] or Washington;[87] served as a drummer in the Fifty-fifth Massachusetts Regiment during the Civil War and rejoined his mother in Boston in 1865.[88] He is last on record there in Boston, 1872.[89]

5 iv. (?) ELLEN "JOHNSON," born about 1848–49 in Virginia.[90] Although a ditto mark attributes the Johnson surname to her on the 1860 census, it appears more likely that she was the daughter of Lawrence Woodfork, given Jane's personal testimony that she had only one child left behind in Virginia, a son. Nothing further is known about Ellen.

© 2002 Katherine E. Flynn, Ph.D., CGRS ℠.

Notes

A scientist by profession and a genealogist by avocation, I first became intrigued by the research problem while reading media accounts of the narrative's discovery. This article was previously published in a slightly modified version in *National Genealogical Society Quarterly* 90 (September 2002): 165–190. There was a subsequent update in *National Genealogical Society Quarterly* 91 (March 2003): 40. I thank Dr. Henry Louis Gates Jr. for his encouragement of this independent study, as well as many others for assistance in the acquisition and interpretation of records: Marie Varrelman Melchiori, CGRS, CGL, who specializes in National Archives research; David C. Dearborn, FASG, of the New England Historic Genealogical Society Library, Boston; Ernest Emerich of the Library of Congress; Kathryn Grover; Mary M. Huth of the University of Rochester; Phillip Lapsansky of The Library Company, Philadelphia; Kelley Nee of the Massachusetts Historical Society; Betsy Lowenstein of the Massachusetts State Archives; Lisa Starzyk-Weldon and Stephen Nonack of The Boston Athenaeum Library; Amber Meisenzahl of Boston's Museum of Afro American History; Paul Maniff of Woodlawn Cemetery, Everett, Mass.; Judith McCarthy, Registrar, City of Boston; Jefferson Moak of the National Archives Philadelphia Branch; Ellen Endslow, Pamela Powell, and Diane Rofini of the Chester County (Pennsylvania) Historical Society; the staff of Swarthmore College Library; and Robert and Kathy (Woitel) Flynn, Anthony and Lisa Trippe, and James Daniel and Kathleen (Kuhle) Flynn.

1. As a rare genealogical case study in the identification of anonymous authors, see Ralph A. Pugh, "Rescuing an Early American Artisan-Diarist from Anonymity," *National Genealogical Society Quarterly* 78 (March 1990): 33–38.

2. Hannah Crafts, *The Bondwoman's Narrative*, ed. Henry Louis Gates, Jr. (New York: Warner Books, 2002); Gates, "The Fugitive," *The New Yorker* (18–25 February 2002): 104–108, 113–115.

3. Gates, "Introduction," *The Bondwoman's Narrative*, xiii.

4. The forensic analysis was made by Joe Nickell, Ph.D., formerly a Certified Genealogical Records Specialist, whose expertise in historic hoaxes has exposed the fraud of the "diary of Jack the Ripper" and established the authenticity of Abraham Lincoln's famed "Bixby letter." Nickell discusses his analytical techniques in several monographs, including *Detecting Forgery: Forensic Investigation of Documents* (Louisville: University of Kentucky Press, 1996). For his full analysis of the "Hannah Crafts" manuscript, see Nickell, "Authentication Report," *The Bondwoman's Narrative*, Appendix A, 283–315.

5. Gates, "Introduction," *The Bondwoman's Narrative*, xxxi.

6. Prior to Gates's efforts, a four-year search for Jane was made by Lorene Cary, author of the novel *The Price of a Child* (New York: Alfred A. Knopf, 1995), which is loosely based on Jane's story.

7. Unless otherwise indicated, this section is a summary of the following works:

- *Case of Passmore Williamson: Report of the Proceedings . . . in the Case of* The United States of America ex rel. John H. Wheeler *vs.* Passmore Williamson . . . (Philadelphia: Uriah Hunt & Son, 1856); digitized online http://memory.loc.gov/cgi-bin/query/r?ammem/llstbib: @field(NUMBER+@band(llst+029)):.

- *Narrative of Facts in the Case of Passmore Williamson* (Philadelphia: Pennsylvania Anti-Slavery Society, 1855); digitized on line www.hti.umich.edu/cgi/t/text/text-idx?c=moa;idno= ABJ1564.

- William Still, *The Underground Rail Road: A Record of Facts, Authentic Narratives, Letters, &c.* (Philadelphia: Porter & Coates, 1872), 88–98; digitized online www.ecpclio.net/ megafile/msa/speccol/sc5300/sc5339/000047/000000/000001/restricted/L1117 /html/031645–0016.html.

- Lucretia Mott to Martha Coffin Wright, letter, 4 September 1855, Mott Collection, Friends Historical Library, Swarthmore College, Swarthmore, Pennsylvania. Mott accompanied Jane to the courtroom and describes the events in this letter. The part of this letter that discusses Jane has never been published.

8. Carrie Rebora Barratt, *Queen Victoria and Thomas Sully* (Princeton: Princeton University Press in association with The Metropolitan Museum of Art, 2000), 58, 77–78.

9. *Narrative of Facts in the Case of Passmore Williamson*, 4, reports Wheeler's reference to Jane's "children" in Virginia. Still, *Underground Rail Road*, 89, quotes Wheeler as claiming Jane had three children left behind in Virginia; but p. 90 quotes Jane saying only one child had been sold far away from her "without hope of seeing *him* again [emphasis added]," and p. 91 quotes her as saying that she had "only left one boy in the South."

10. *Narrative of Facts in the Case of Passmore Williamson*, 14.

11. *Case of Passmore Williamson*, appendix, 164–166.

12. This archived letter is mentioned in a 26 September 1995 *Boston Globe* review of Cary's novel; see www. english.upenn.edu/~lcary/books/price/bosglobe.html. At the research point chronicled above, its exact location and content were unknown. Efforts to locate it began while research continued in parallel veins. Later it was found out that Phillip Lapsansky of The Library Company of Philadelphia had seen the letter and drew Cary's attention to its existence in 1995.

13. An approximately 315-volume series spanning ca. 1790–ca. 1870, by Ronald Vern Jackson et al., published by state under the general format *[State] 1860 Census Index* (various locales: Accelerated Indexing Systems, 1971–1999).

14. 1860 U.S. census, Suffolk Co., population schedule, Boston, Ward 6, sheet 163, p. 801 (penned no.), dwell. 842, fam. 1001 (Lawrence Woodfork); National Archives (NARA) microfilm publication M653, roll 521.

15. *The Boston Directory, Embracing the City Record, a General Directory of the Citizen, and a Business Directory for the Year Commencing July 1, 1860* (Boston: Adams, Sampson & Co., 1860), 363 (Ringold), 458 (Woodfork).

16. *Massachusetts Marriage Index, 1841–1895*, 326 microfiches (Oxford, Mass.: Holbrook Research Institute, 1988), fiches 47–70, covering original vols. 7–9.

17. Boston marriage records, intent no. 1721; full transcript from original record supplied by Judith McCarthy, City Registrar, via e-mail on 19 June 2002, because the original is too fragile to photocopy.

18. William S. Parsons and Margaret A. Drew, *The African Meeting House: A Sourcebook* (Boston: The Museum of Afro American History, 1990).

19. Barbara A. Yocum, *The African Meeting House: Historic Structure Report* (Lowell, Mass.: Building Conservation Branch, North Atlantic Region, National Park Service, 1994), 35–36, 259–263.

20. E-mail message to author from Diana Yount, Associate Director of the Franklin Trask Library, 4 June 2002. The Library is the repository for the archives of The American Baptist Churches of Massachusetts.

21. Parsons and Drew, *The African Meeting House*, 39, 78–81.

22. Francis Jackson, *Treasurers Accounts The Boston Vigilance Committee* (Boston: The Bostonian Society, no date), 48. This source was supplied by Kathryn Grover.

23. Kathryn Grover and Janine V. de Silva, "Historic Resource Study: Boston African American National Historic Site" (unpublished, 31 December 2002), 124. Copy supplied to author by Kathryn Grover.

24. Jackson, *Treasurers Accounts The Boston Vigilance Committee*, 54, 58.

25. Lawrence Woodfork/Woodfalk entry, Death Records Book 1861, no. 3707, and certified death certificate no. 012592, issued to author 11 June 2002 by Registry Division, City of Boston.

26. Probate Index, Suffolk County, Mass., 1636–1893, searched by New England Historic and Genealogical Society Research Service, report dated 5 June 2002 to author.

27. Marriage Book 1864, no. 1499, Registry Division, City of Boston. For Ross, the minister who performed the ceremony, see John Jamison Moore, *History of the A. M. E. Zion Church in America* (York, Pa.: Teachers' Journal Office, 1884), 24, 26, 367.

28. The city directory for 1865 lists several William Harrises in Boston. The directory's identification of Jane as a widow implies that her husband was not alive but does not rule out the possibility that he was living separately. Examining the death records for all William Harris entries in Boston between 1864 and 1872 produced no relevant entries. Given William's livelihood, possibly he died elsewhere.

29. Isaiah Johnson compiled service record (priv., Co. K, Mass. 55th Regt., Col'd.), NARA M1801, roll 47.

30. For Isaiah's unit, see Charles B. Fox, *Record of the Service of the Fifty-fifth Regiment of Massachusetts Volunteer Infantry* (1868; reprint, Freeport, N.Y.: Books for Libraries Press, 1971); Frederick H. Dyer, *A Compendium of the War of the Rebellion*, 3 vols. (1908; reprint, Dayton, Ohio: Morningside House, 1979), 2: 1266; Massachusetts Adjutant's Office, *Massachusetts Soldiers, Sailors, and Marines in the Civil War*, 9 vols. (Norwood, Mass.: Norwood Press, 1931–1937), 4:

715–761; Wilbert H. Luck, *Journey to Honey Hill* (Washington, D.C.: Wiluk Press, 1976); James M. McPherson, *The Negro's Civil War* (New York: Ballantine Books, 1991), 240; and Noah Andre Trudeau, ed., *Voices of the 55th: Letters from the 55th Massachusetts Volunteers, 1861–1865* (Dayton, Ohio: Morningside House, 1996).

31. Fox, *Record of Service of the Fifty-fifth Regiment*, 148.

32. Isaac Johnson (drummer/priv., Co. K., 55th Regt., Mass. Vol. Inf.), Civil War invalid pension application 528183, certificate 650621, Record Group 15, Records of the Veterans Administration, NARA–Washington; see particularly Deposition E, Ransom Chatman (9 July 1901), p. 34.

33. The four repositories are (1) Massachusetts Historical Society, Boston, which holds records of the 55th Officers Association and Charles Fox's Papers; (2) Massachusetts State Archives, Boston, which holds the Hartwell Collection of photographs; (3) U.S. Army Military History Institute, Carlisle, Penn.; and (4) Cornell University Archives, Dr. Burt Wilder Papers, which includes war photographs and postwar letters from soldiers.

34. *Card Records of Headstones Provided for Deceased Union Civil War Veterans, ca. 1878–ca. 1903*, NARA M1845, roll 11.

35. This search was made via the new online database compiled by Ann S. Lainhart; see New England Historic Genealogical Society, *People of Color in the Massachusetts State Census, 1855–1865*, www.newenglandancestors.org/research/database/poc, searched 20 July 2002. My own line-by-line search of the original censuses for Wards 5 and 6 did not yield Jane or her sons. One Daniel Johnson lived in Ward 5, as a domestic servant in a hotel, but cannot be confirmed as the target; see 1870 U.S. census, Suffolk Co., Boston, Ward 5, p. 316 (stamped), dwell. 3, fam. 3 (Robert B. Brigham household); NARA microfilm M593, roll 643.

36. In addition to the previously cited AIS indexes, see *African Americans in the 1870 Census Index* and *Massachusetts 1870 Census Index*, Family Tree Maker's Family Archives CD-ROMs 165 and 284 (N.p.: Genealogy.com, n.d.); search printouts provided by AncestralFindings.Com, 5 and 14 August 2002.

37. Jane Harris entry, Death Records, Book 1872, no. 4511, Registry Division, City of Boston.

38. The firm was still in existence as late as 1890; see *Boston City Directory* (Boston: Sampson, Murdoch & Co., 1890); exact page number not provided in online version www.ancestry.com. Neither the Massachusetts Board of Registration for Embalming and Funeral Directing nor the Massachusetts Funeral Directors Association reports any information on this mortuary; their records do not go back to that date.

39. Suffolk Co., Mass., Probate Index, 1636–1893, checked by the New England Historic and Genealogical Society Research Service, 5 June 2002, yields no record for Jane Harris. The Boston Athenaeum Library's obituary index by Dorothy Wirth, "*Boston Evening Transcript*, 1830–1874," also omits her.

40. Paul Maniff, Woodlawn Cemetery, e-mail to author, 24 May 2002, citing grave 74, row 2, Pilgrim's Rest, North Section; research visit and photograph, 10 June 2002, by Robert and Kathy (Woitel) Flynn.

41. Letters of William C. Nell to Passmore Williamson, 3 December 1855 and 26 May 1856, "Passmore Williamson Visitors Book," MS 76710, Chester County Historical Society, West Chester, Penn. The transcripts provided by the society are reprinted here with its permission. Emphasis is added to the second letter.

Dorothy Porter Wesley and Constance Porter Uzelac, eds., *William Cooper Nell: Nineteenth-Century African American Abolitionist, Historian, Integrationist: Selected Writings 1832–1874* (Baltimore: Black Classic Press, 2002), 419, 432, and 452. This book by Dorothy Porter Wesley (a previous owner of the "Hannah Crafts" manuscript) and completed by her daughter Constance Porter Uzelac was published after the first version of this article went to press. It contains both of these letters in full text along with another letter from Nell to Amy (Kirby) Post dated 12–13 August 1855 where Nell reports Jane's arrival in Boston and describes her as being an impressive woman. The latter letter is in The Isaac and Amy Post Collection, Department of Rare Books and Special Collections, Rush Rees Library, University of Rochester, Rochester, NY.

42. Gates, *Bondwoman's Narrative*, lvii–lxii; specifically at p. lviii Gates states: "No Hannah *Craft*ses are listed in the entire U.S. federal census between 1860 and 1880," [italics added], although he found and considered "several women named Hannah Craft" and "Hannah Kraft."

43. *Freedman's Bank Records*, CD-ROM (Salt Lake City: Family History Dept., The Church of Jesus Christ of Latter-day Saints, 2000).

44. For a sampling of records treating Hannah Frederika Crafts, see 1850 U.S. census, Suffolk Co., pop. sch., Boston, Ward 4, p. 7 (stamped no.), dwell. 75, fam. 101 (for Hannah F. Crafts, age 13); NARA M342, roll 335. 1860 U.S. census, Suffolk Co., pop. sch., Boston, Ward 2, p. 18 (penned number), dwell. 96, fam. 157 (for Frederika Crafts, age 22); NARA M653, roll 520. 1880 U.S. census, Suffolk Co., pop. sch., Boston, Ward 2, enumeration district [ED] 587, sheet 7, dwell. 45, fam. 65 (for Hannah Crafts); NARA T9, roll 552. 1900 U.S. census, Suffolk Co., Boston, Ward 2, ED 1180, sheet 6, dwell. 68, fam. 116 (Hannah F. Crafts); NARA T623, roll 676. *Boston City Directory* (Boston: various publishers, 1868–1900), for Hannah F. Crafts. Death Records, Book 1903, no. 6724, Registry Division, City of Boston. Hannah F. Crafts obituary, *Boston Herald*, 13 August 1903.

45. Nickell, "Authentication Report," 283–315.

46. Gates, *The Bondwoman's Narrative*, xxxii.

47. Ibid., xxxv, emphasis added.

48. Ibid., lv–lvi, 260–261.

49. These events are variously chronicled in Papers of John Hill Wheeler, MS 16736.1 (microfilm, 4 rolls), Library of Congress, Washington; particularly see diary entry of 1 May 1856 for the return of his wife and children. Also see John H. Wheeler to William L. Marcy, 16 May 1856, in *Diplomatic Correspondence of the United States: Inter-American Affairs, 1831–1860*, 12 vols., ed. William R. Manning (Washington, D.C.: Carnegie Endowment for International Peace, 1932–1939), 4:528; and U.S. Dept. of State, *Nicaragua*, www.state.gov/r/pa/ho/po/com/11061.htm for appointments to and removals from service in Nicaragua.

50. Summary of key events in Wheeler's life, at end of 1863 diary, Papers of John Hill Wheeler, roll 2, end of 1863 diary (unpaginated).

51. Barbara McNaught Watson, "Washington Area Winters: Snow, Wind, Ice, and Cold," and "Virginia Winters . . . ," National Oceanic and Atmospheric Administration, *National Weather Service Forecast Office: Baltimore–Washington*, www.erh.noaa.gov/er/lwx, using keyword "Historic Events," then "D.C.-Winters" and "Virginia-Winters"; last reviewed at press time.

52. Harry L. Coles Sr., "Salmon P. Chase," Ohio Historical Society, *Ohio Fundamental Documents*, www.ohiohistory.org/onlinedoc/ohgovernment/governors/chase.html.

53. Wheeler's diary records at least 19 visits with Dobbin from May to August 1854. When Wheeler left for Nicaragua, he gave a painting of Washington by Thomas Sully to Dobbin in thanks; see John H. Wheeler, *Reminiscences and Memoirs of North Carolina and Eminent North Carolinians* (Columbus, Ohio: Columbus Printing Works, 1884), 152.

54. Randall O. Hudson, "The Filibuster Minister: The Career of John Hill Wheeler as United States Minister to Nicaragua, 1854–1856," *North Carolina Historical Review* 49 (July 1972): 280–297, particularly 296.

55. Lincoln Co. Deed Book 42:476, Register of Deeds, Lincolnton.

56. For the first quote, see John Hill Wheeler, *The Wheeler Slave Case* (Raleigh: State of North Carolina, ca. 1857), 182; the only known copy is today at Special Collections, Duke University, Winston-Salem, N.C. For the second quote, see summary of key events in Wheeler's life, op. cit.

57. Nickell, "Authentication Report," 305–306; Gates, "A Note on Crafts's Literary Influences," *The Bondwoman's Narrative*, 331–332.

58. Thomas Schoonover, "John Hill Wheeler," in *American National Biography*, ed. John A. Garraty and Mark C. Carnes, vol. 23 (New York: Oxford Univ. Press, 1999), 139–140; Still, *Underground Rail Road*, 94–95.

59. Sample pages from the manuscript of "The Bondwoman's Narrative" can be viewed online; see Pro Quest Information and Learning Co., *The Bondwoman's Narrative Companion*, www.bondwomansnarrative.com/learn/book/mss/# .

60. Nickell, "Authentication Report," 306.

61. Gates, "Textual Annotations," *The Bondwoman's Narrative*, 242; 321–330 lists books from his catalog.

62. James Moore, Director, R. F. Sink Memorial Library, Fort Campbell, Ky., to author, phone communication, 30 April 2002. For the diary entries, see dates of 25 June 1854 and 26 January 1861.

63. *The Liberator*, Boston, Massachusetts, 7 September 1855, page 143, column 4.

64. Wheeler's records do not state specifically where he left Jane. However, his diary entries show that at least on one occasion, when traveling abroad, he left personal property (including a trunk of important papers that he itemized) with his sister and brother-in-law, the Moores, on their Hertford County plantation.

65. Robert E. May, *The Southern Dream of a Caribbean Empire, 1854–1861* (Baton Rouge: Louisiana State University Press, 1973).

66. Nickell, "Authentication Report," 294–299.

67. "William C. Nell, 1816–1874," in *American Authors, 1600–1900*, ed. Stanley J. Kunitz and Howard Haycraft (New York: H. W. Wilson, 1938), alphabetical by author.

68. Federal Reserve Bank of Minneapolis, "What Is a Dollar Worth?" *Economic Research and Data*, http://minneapolisfed.org/research/data/us/calc.

69. Attempts to find the original of Jane's affidavit, to determine if it was truly signed by an "X", have failed. The court records were indeed traced to *Pennsylvania, Eastern District; Record Group 21, Records of District Courts of the United States*, National Archives-Mid-Atlantic Region, Philadelphia. However, because Judge Kane ruled that Jane Johnson had no standing before the court in Williamson's case, her affidavit was not retained in the court's records. Mr. Jefferson Moak, NARA Archivist, was most generous with his time and expertise in examining these non-filmed records, comparing them to the published accounts and explaining the legal proceedings contained therein.

70. Mattie Griffith, *Autobiography of a Female Slave* (New York: Redfield, 1856). Griffith, white, had been born into a Kentucky slaveholding family and had grown up witnessing the institution about which she wrote.

71. John Hope Franklin and Loren Schweninger, *Runaway Slaves: Rebels on the Plantation* (New York: Oxford University Press, 1999), 210–213, and 328–332.

72. *Philadelphia Public Ledger*, Philadelphia, Pennsylvania, 31 August 1855, page 1. Jane is reported as testifying in court, "I have heard that I was born about the time the British burnt the Capitol at Washington." This historic event took place in August 1814. An approximate birth year of 1814 is compatible with Jane's reported age at her death.

73. Jane Harris entry, Boston Death Records, Book 1872, no. 4511; Still, *Underground Rail Road*, 91.

74. Boston marriage intent no. 1721; and Marriage Book 1864, no. 1499.

75. Boston marriage intent no. 1721; and Lawrence Woodfork/Woodfalk entry, Boston Death Records Book 1861, no. 3707.

76. Boston Marriage Book 1864, no. 1499.

77. *Boston Directory . . . for the Year Commencing July 1, 1865*, 192.

78. This possibility is suggested by the fact that when Jane's second husband filed their intent to marry, he stated Caroline Co., Va., as her birthplace.

79. See affidavits by Jane printed in Still, *Underground Rail Road*, 88–98.

80. The circumstances are narrated at length in ibid., in *Case of Passmore Williamson*, and in *Narrative of Facts in the Case of Passmore Williamson*.

81. William C. Nell to Passmore Williamson, 3 December 1855 and 26 May 1856, transcribed in this paper.

82. For her residences, see the city directory entries abstracted in Table 1. For cause of death, see Jane Harris entry, Boston Death Records, Book 1872, no. 4511.

83. Searches have been completed for all three in the statewide marriage and death indexes through 1879. No relevant entries were found. However, research remains to be done in Boston's Marriage Index, which includes intents omitted from the statewide index.

84. 1860 U.S. census, Suffolk Co., pop. sch., Boston, Ward 6, sheet 163 (penned no.), dwell. 842, fam. 1001 (Lawrence Woodfork household).

85. *Boston Directory . . . for the Year Commencing July 1, 1865*, 192.

86. 1860 Lawrence Woodfork household, cited above.

87. Isaiah Johnson, muster record, previously cited.

88. Ibid.; *Boston Directory . . . for the Year Commencing July 1, 1865*, 192.

89. *Boston Directory . . . for the Year Commencing July 1, 1872*, 343, 400.

90. 1860 Lawrence Woodfork household, cited above.

23

Searching for Hannah Crafts

JOE NICKELL

The Bondwoman's Narrative presents a fascinating mystery.[1] While the hand-written manuscript is ostensibly the only known novel written by an escaped African American slave, we must emphasize *ostensibly*, since the author's identity is unknown beyond her purported name, "Hannah Crafts," on the title page, along with her claim to be "A Fugitive Slave Recently Escaped from North Carolina."

Manuscript Analysis

Nevertheless, Professor Henry Louis Gates, together with Laurence J. Kirsh-baum, Chairman of Time Warner Trade Publishing, gave me a wonderful opportunity to meet the mystery author when they commissioned me to authenticate the manuscript. It was hand-delivered to my lab, and I lived with it for six weeks. During the days I subjected the ink and paper to a battery of tests to see if they were consistent with their purported 1850s authorship, while also scrutinizing the author's handwriting and writing materials for clues to "her" identity. I spent nights at home reading a typescript of the novel to see what additional indications of authorship could be gleaned.

I employed a number of forensic techniques to examine the 301-page manuscript, including stereomicroscopic, chemical, and spectral (e.g., ultraviolet) analyses. As detailed in my subsequent report,[2] everything I discovered was consistent with the author's basic persona and a pre–Civil War date of composition.

All of the writing materials were correct for that period. The 1850s represented something of a watershed for writing accouterments,[3] and those used for the manuscript—including a quill pen (rather than a steel pen), iron-gall ink (instead of some later variety such as nigrosine), and writing sand (to blot the ink, in lieu of blotting paper)—were all common to the 1850s. Also the paper is rag content, lacking the wood pulp that began to be commercially used in 1867. Indeed the manuscript was penned on folios of writing paper, mostly two varieties bearing stationer's embossments of the Southworth paper company, one of them known to have been used in the 1856–1860 period.

In addition to pen, ink, and paper, the writer also had a pen knife and probably an ink-eraser knife, a sander (filled with common sand), a box of vermilion wafers (paste discs used to affix correction slips), and small (possibly sewing) scissors. Seemingly lacking a textured seal (used to impress the paper over wafers to produce a better bond), the author appears to have employed a thimble for that purpose, as well as needle and thread to sew the manuscript together. The combination of writing and sewing materials suggests the writer was a woman.

The manuscript's "serviceable" handwriting (it is neither elegant nor untutored) is of a type that succeeded American round hand and preceded Spencerian script; known as modified round hand, it was taught from about 1840 to 1865. Given the evidence for composition in the 1850s and the writing's absence of archaic forms, this suggests a relative young writer.

The internal evidence of the manuscript was likewise instructive. Because the novel makes specific reference to "the equestrian statue of Jackson" in Washington, D.C. (erected in 1853), but omits any reference to secession or war, a date of circa 1853–1861 is indicated. The novel presents an array of polysyllabic wording, literary phrasings, and classical allusions, yielding (by today's standards) an eleventh-grade readability level. Yet the occasional poor spelling coupled with the eccentric punctuation suggests someone who, I concluded, "had struggled to learn."

My task was mostly limited to what I could glean from the manuscript, not from external historical and genealogical searches. Those were being done by Professor Gates and others. I did express the view that the geographical and other references, along with the author's point of view and insights (as a young, African American, Christian woman), were "credible."[4]

A Plantation Slave?

Now Professor Gates has asked me to review some of the intriguing findings of several skilled researchers. I am especially happy to assess certain proposed "suspects" in the case of "Who is Hannah Crafts?"—to consider them in light of my own analytical "profile" of Hannah and, conversely, to reconsider that profile in light of the new evidence.

One clue in the manuscript led to a particular North Carolina politician and slaveholder. I had noticed that the name "Wheeler" in the narrative had been underlined in several places, and a closer inspection with the stereomicroscope showed that the word had first been written as if to conceal the identity—as in "Mr. Wh——r" and "Mrs Wh——r"—but then was later filled in with the missing letters "eele" in each instance to complete the name.[5] Professor Gates soon found that the reference was to an actual North Carolina man, a slave owner named John Hill Wheeler.[6]

All theories as to the identity of Hannah Crafts must necessarily come to terms with the Wheeler connection. Either she was an escaped slave of Wheeler's, or somehow she acquired sufficient information to create a more or less convincing persona as such for her novel. In his introduction, Professor Gates has set forth the evidence for the former possibility. He demonstrates that Hannah's portraits of black slaves were sharply delineated rather than generalized as a group. He establishes close parallels with the Wheelers, showing that the novel's mention of the Wheelers' runaway slave "Jane" is surely based on the real-life incident of John Hill Wheeler's escaped slave, Jane Johnson.

Gates finds other parallels between the characters and places of *Bondwoman's* and the people and environs of the relative portions of North Carolina and Virginia. He also observes that many of Hannah Crafts's literary borrowings were from books that were to be found in the library of John Hill Wheeler.[7]

There are skeptics to be sure. Thomas C. Parramore, in his "The Bondwoman and the Bureaucrat," questions the evidence Professor Gates has amassed. He seems to accept the findings that indicate a date of 1853–1861 for the manuscript's composition; however, he mischaracterizes the handwriting evidence, stating that Gates's "technical investigators" (in this case me) had claimed "that Hannah's writing seems to have been that of a right-handed female slave—or former slave."[8]

Now the handwriting is that of a right-handed person, but I never claimed it indicated the writer was either female or a slave. I did have other indications for the former, but I never stated that the "writing"—whether Parramore means handwriting or simply text—indicated its author was a slave. We do not have a manuscript test for slaveness; therefore, all scholars can do, until the author's identity is confirmed, is to apply their best judgment to the evidence. But as Alexander Pope wryly observed, "'Tis with our judgements as our watches, none go just alike, yet each believes his own."[9] The matter is complicated because the evidence on which judgments depend comes largely from *The Bondwoman's Narrative*; as Nina Baym points out in her "The Case for Hannah Vincent," it is "obviously a novel, which means that much or most of it is made up."[10]

Parramore believes he can establish "that Hannah never set foot in North Carolina, a fact," he says, "that casts a long shadow of doubt over her whole narrative." Although she writes of traveling with the Wheelers by steamboat from Washington, D.C., to Wilmington, N.C., to visit their plantation, Parramore observes that Wheeler had previously sold that land. However, Gates cites another plantation belonging to Wheeler's relatives that might fill the bill.[11]

Parramore also dismisses Hannah's description of slave life, which he finds does not match that of Wheeler's actual plantation. "The fictitious Wilmington site, then," he insists, "served Abolitionist ends well enough, but not the requirements of autobiography." Yet in using the very word *fictitious* he prompts the obvious counterpoint to his argument: the narrative is not an autobiography but a novel.

Parramore finds still other evidence that Hannah's descriptions are inaccurate, and just as often Gates has already either refuted or rationalized the criticisms, depending on one's point of view. For example, Parramore cites John Hill Wheeler's diary, noting that it "speaks frequently and at some length about Jane Johnson's highly publicized escape from him in 1855, but is totally silent on 'Hannah.'" Yet Gates has noted that the second half of 1856 is missing from the diary and the first half of 1858 is "damaged or illegible."[12]

Parramore's skepticism is shared by writer John Bloom, whose article "Literary Blackface?" was published in "conservative" venues.[13] Bloom suspects "Hannah Crafts" was a "do-gooder white woman pretending to be black," basing his view on some of the same arguments made by Parramore. Of course, it remains to be seen just who Hannah Crafts was, but the evidence of her eccentric punctuation and the relative plainness of her handwriting (lacking the diminutive size and elegant penmanship often affected by educated Victorian ladies) indicate a level of unsophistication on the author's part. And her perspective as an apparent African American woman—described effectively by other writers in this collection of essays—merits more than a hand-waving dismissal.

The Search for "Hannah"

The concern of such naysayers, that Professor Gates has rushed headlong to conclude Hannah Crafts was in fact a fugitive slave, largely ignores the evidence Gates has marshaled to support that hypothesis; his attempts to challenge and potentially disprove it; his efforts to identify the author, whoever she might be; and his continuing openness to others' contrary views: witness this book.

Gates conducted an extensive search for Hannah Crafts. None of the re-sulting "suspects" seemed to be plausible candidates for the author of *Bond-woman's*. Gates discovered several females named Hannah Craft who were white and had not resided in the South. He found a black Hannah Kraft in Mary-land but then learned she was born in 1850 and therefore would have been too young to have written the novel; besides she was illiterate.[14]

Gates also uncovered a Maria H. Crafts in New Orleans, but, in addition to some uncertainty about her race, her handwriting failed to match that of "Hannah Crafts" on the novel's title page. Although some twenty years had elapsed and her handwriting could therefore have changed, and although we really do not have a true *signature* for "Hannah Crafts" (only her *written name* on the title page), I did not think that Maria H. Crafts had written *The Bond-woman's Narrative*.[15]

Subsequently, genealogical researcher Katherine E. Flynn uncovered two more possibilities, and these—a Boston teacher and her mother—even had the final *s* on their surname. They were white, but, as Flynn acknowledged, "One might even argue that Hannah Frederika Crafts simply fantasized a novel out of whatever abolitionist literature she had read."[16]

Nevertheless, Flynn obtained signatures of both Hannah F. and her mother and determined—correctly—that neither matched the handwritten name "Hannah Crafts" on *Bondwoman's* title page. Flynn adds, "To argue that this teacher engaged a scribe to pen a novel using her own name pushes the argu-ment beyond reasonable limits." That is certainly true, all the more so because the manuscript is not a fair copy (a post-corrections copy) but an actual com-posing copy.[17]

Two other candidates for authorship whom Professor Gates mentioned—both representing intriguing possibilities—have been revisited by Katherine Flynn and by Nina Baym. Both would place firm quotation marks around the name "Hannah Crafts."

Was "Hannah" Jane Johnson?

Katherine Flynn has done a wonderful job of tracking down a real-life escaped slave of John Hill Wheeler. Jane Johnson gained her freedom in Philadelphia in 1855 with the help of a black Underground Railroad activist, William Still, and a white abolitionist, Passmore Williamson. After the dramatic events of her escape and subsequent legal contests, she faded into obscurity.[18]

Flynn, however, a skilled genealogist, pursues some productive clues and tracked Jane Johnson (née Williams) to Boston, following her as she married Laurence Woodfork (in 1856), was widowed (1861), remarried (to William

Harris, 1864), and again widowed (the following year). Her whereabouts are unknown from 1866 to 1870, and Flynn wonders if she returned to the South to look for one son who had been sold from her or perhaps accompanied her other two sons (who had been an infantry drummer and a sailor) as they moved elsewhere. She reappeared in Boston in 1871, then died of dysentery the next year.[19]

Although Professor Gates had considered Jane Johnson as a possibility for "Hannah Crafts," he rejected her candidacy because she was apparently illiterate. However, Flynn was prompted to reopen the case. Noting that the hypothesis of Jane Johnson as "Hannah" had "foundered upon two shoals: the known illiteracy of Johnson and the failure to trace her life as a free woman,"[20] Flynn removed both barriers. While tracking Johnson from her escape in 1855 until her death in 1872, she learned that Jane was actually literate.

At least the 1860 census so reported, which means that Johnson (or her husband) apparently answered yes when the enumerator asked whether she could read or write. This census record is *prima facie* evidence for Johnson's literacy, which Flynn notes appears to be corroborated by a letter from one William C. Nell of Boston. He had written to the abolitionist who helped Johnson escape, Passmore Williamson, saying that a grateful Johnson wanted her address passed on to him. This request, Flynn observes, "suggests that she wished to correspond with him directly, rather than through Nell," but she concedes: "Whether she could read by this point or whether she anticipated having Laurence or her sons read Williamson's letters to her remains uncertain."[21]

And there is the problem. Just how literate had Jane Johnson become in the five years since she signed court documents with an X?[22] Not only did "her mark" attest to her illiteracy then, but her co-rescuer (with Williamson), William Still, said of her that she "seems to possess, naturally, uncommon good sense, *though of course she has never been allowed to read*" (emphasis added).[23] This contradicts "Hannah Crafts's" claim to have been taught reading and writing by an elderly white couple and to have been reading since childhood. She says, "while the other children of the house were amusing themselves I would quietly steal away from their company to ponder over the pages of some old book or newspaper that chance had thrown in [my] way."[24] Moreover, while Jane Johnson had commendably learned to read and write over the subsequent five years, it seems unlikely in the extreme that she would have progressed from being totally illiterate to writing a novel of the quality of *The Bondwoman's Narrative* in so short a time.

There are other reasons for doubting Jane was Hannah. What Flynn lists, in her table of similarities and disparities,[25] as a similarity—Hannah's color—is to my mind instead a dissimilarity. In *Bondwoman's*, Hannah is sufficiently light-skinned to disguise herself as a white boy. Indeed, at one point, Mrs. Wheeler shrieks at her, "With all your pretty airs and your *white face*, you are nothing but a slave after all, and no better than the blackest wench"[26] (emphasis added). In contrast, a portrait of Jane Johnson does not show a "white" face but rather is fully consistent with William Still's description of her as being of "chestnut color" or another's as "a tall, dark woman, with two little boys."[27]

Of course, perhaps once again we must allow for fictionalization. But what about the presence in the novel of *both* "Jane" (who is clearly John Hill Wheeler's escaped slave Jane Johnson) *and* "Hannah" (whom Flynn supposes to be a fictionalized Jane)? Many things are possible, but we must seriously question whether Jane, if she were "Hannah," would slander herself by questioning her own morals and implying that she was a religious hypocrite. Specifically, Hannah Crafts has the "good, accomplished, and Christian-like" Mrs. Henry tell Mrs. Wheeler: "Hannah is a good girl; she has good principles, and is I believe a consistent Christian. I don't think your Jane was either."[28]

I doubt that this attack on Jane Johnson's character would be one that the real Jane would advance publicly herself—not for novelistic purposes such as verisimilitude, not as a clever ploy to disguise her true identity, nor indeed for any other rationale I can imagine. I think the characterization also argues against the *Bondwoman's* author having interviewed Jane Johnson. Rather it suggests that the similarities between "Hannah" and Jane—very real similarities as Professor Gates and Dr. Flynn have indicated—may be yet another example of the author's use of published sources.

"Hannah Crafts" or Hannah Vincent?

Another interesting candidate for "Hannah Crafts" is suggested by Nina Baym, a professor at the University of Illinois at Urbana–Champaign.[29] Like Katherine E. Flynn, Professor Baym has returned to a possibility that Professor Gates had shelved, in this case a New Jersey resident named Hannah Vincent.

Gates's discovery of Vincent stemmed from Hannah Crafts's assertion that she had been a slave of the Vincents (originally DeVincents) in Virginia and that slaves frequently adopted the surnames of their owners. Gates's search of the 1850 and 1860 censuses turned up one Hannah Ann Vincent of Burlington, New Jersey. That seemed significant because the manuscript's provenance reportedly traces back to New Jersey and, at the end of the novel, Hannah Crafts claims she lives in New Jersey. The state was also a haven for escaped slaves.[30]

Following Gates, Baym develops the evidence for Hannah Vincent as the real author of *The Bondwoman's Narrative*. In addition to the name and New Jersey connection, there are several other correspondences that make her a seemingly strong possibility. Like "Hannah Crafts," this Hannah is a mulatto, young at the time *Bondwoman's* was composed (she was born circa 1828), a Methodist, and a teacher.

However, Hannah Vincent was not an escaped slave but a free black woman. Thus, Baym argues, she is a more likely candidate for the authorship of such a "complex" novel. As mentioned earlier, Hannah Crafts "borrowed" passages from a number of literary works. Hollis Robbins, a Princeton graduate student, has shown that passages were unmistakably lifted from Dickens's *Bleak House*, and the current list of additional identified sources is extensive.[31]

Gates believes these new findings are still compatible with authorship by an escaped slave. The epigrams at the beginnings of chapters had always indicated a familiarity with many literary works, and in fact, Gates points out that all of the works (with the single exception of *Bleak House*) had been in the library of slave owner John Hill Wheeler. It even included an issue of *Scientific American* that seems clearly the source for an incident in the novel, described by Gates as "one of the most curious scenes in 19th-century African American literature." (The scene, in chapter 13, has Mrs. Wheeler using a new, wrinkle-eliminating cosmetic developed by "a Signor with an unpronounceable name"; hilariously, in accidental combination with her smelling salts, it turns her face black. Similarly, the *Scientific American* of June 11, 1853, describes the work of an Italian chemist named Brugnatelli whose white silver-nitrate powder would turn black when exposed to ammonia. That very issue of the magazine was in the Wheeler library.)[32]

Professor Baym, however, demonstrates logically that the novel would have to have been composed after Hannah's escape. "And this in turn," she says, "makes partial overlap between some of her references and some of the books in the Wheeler library into something of a red herring. As Gates says anyway, Wheeler's books are typical rather than unique." Baym goes on to argue:

> Again, one has to ask—not how she had access to books, which was certainly possible for house slaves—but how she had access to pens, ink, paper (lots of paper) and the entire technology of writing, which is so different from (and more expensive than what is required for) the far simpler act of reading. Hannah's narrative tells us how she learned to read (although she cagily never shows herself reading any book except the Bible) but never how she learned to write.[33]

"How much simpler it is," Baym concludes, "to posit an author who was free; a woman with a modicum of formal schooling, herself a schoolteacher with access to books and magazines." Baym strongly suspects that *Bond-*

woman's is not like some other novels by black women of the period, namely "lightly fictionalized autobiographies," but rather is "an apparent autobiography that is in fact a real novel." If she is correct, *The Bondwoman's Narrative* would still be "the first true novel by a black woman" and "a find of unprecedented importance."[34]

Will the Real Hannah . . . ?

The search for "Hannah Crafts" necessarily continues. We still cannot *decisively* prove or disprove any of several generic possibilities (Hannah was an escaped slave, or a free black, or even a white abolitionist); neither can we positively confirm or eliminate certain specific candidates (an as-yet-unidentified Hannah Crafts on the one hand, or on the other, Jane Johnson, Hannah Vincent, or someone else writing under a pseudonym). One person's conviction is another's unlikely scenario.

It reminds me a bit of the perpetual hunt for the true identity of Jack the Ripper, in which an author proposes a seemingly likely candidate—until the next one comes along. According to one commentator on the Ripper industry, "The common reader like myself found each identification quite convincing as he read it, and kept changing his mind about which was the Ripper."[35]

What is needed in the case of *The Bondwoman's Narrative* is more precise evidence, such as handwriting may be able to provide. Such evidence has already helped eliminate some persons with the name of Craft, Kraft, or Crafts. Should other candidates be discovered and specimens of their handwriting located, we would have a much more objective basis for making a determination. Until then, we are plagued by not knowing how much of the manuscript is truly autobiographical.

It is essential for scholars to remember that the burden of proof is on the advocate of an idea and not on someone else to prove otherwise. And it is necessary to guard against bias; as one scientific investigator urges, we must cultivate "the intellectual discipline of subordinating ideas to facts." As he explains: "A danger constantly to be guarded against is that as soon as one formulates an hypothesis, parental affection tends to influence observations, interpretation and judgment; 'wishful thinking' is likely to start unconsciously." He adds, "The best protection against these tendencies is to cultivate an intellectual habit of subordinating one's opinions and wishes to objective evidence and a reverence for things as they really are, and to keep constantly in mind that the hypothesis is only a supposition."[36]

In that spirit, I offer an updated profile of "Hannah Crafts." We are still looking for a female writer, who was relatively young at the time of composition, which dates from between 1855 (the escape of Wheeler's slave, Jane Johnson) and 1861 (the advent of secession and war). Her identity as an African American slave rings true, but perhaps that is because, as Nina Baym observes, "the account rings *imaginatively* true" (emphasis added).[37]

She was almost certainly not Jane Johnson and could well have been a free black, someone like Hannah Vincent. She had such an unusual ability to see blacks as individuals that it is unlikely (though not absolutely impossible) she was white. Whatever her race, she appears to have struggled to become educated. That, together with some possible indications of frugality (she recycled paper for correction slips and used quills rather than more expensive steel pens), suggests she was not a middle-class Victorian lady. She was certainly a Christian and very likely a Methodist.

The new evidence of the author's extensive literary borrowings and re-workings suggests, as Nina Baym says, that the novel was "composed by a person with a long immersion in imaginative literature."[38] Possibly she had written poems and short prose pieces before trying a novel, and she may have produced other literary works afterward. We should expand our search, especially looking for handwriting to compare with that of "Hannah Crafts." We may yet learn her true identity.

Notes

1. Hannah Crafts, *The Bondwoman's Narrative*, ed. by Henry Louis Gates, Jr. (New York: Warner Books, 2002).

2. Joe Nickell, "Authentication Report: *The Bondwoman's Narrative*," June 12, 2001; Appendix A of ibid., pp. 283–315.

3. Joe Nickell, *Pen, Ink & Evidence: A Study of Writing and Writing Materials for the Penman, Collector, and Document Detective* (New Castle, Del.: Oak Knoll, 2000).

4. Nickell, "Authentication Report."

5. Ibid.

6. Gates, "Introduction," *The Bondwoman's Narrative*, pp. ix–lxxiv.

7. Gates, "A Note on Crafts's Literary Influence," *Bondwoman's*, pp. 331–336; Bryan C. Sinche, "John Hill Wheeler's Library catalog," Appendix C of Gates, *Bondwoman's*, pp. 321–330.

8. Thomas C. Parramore, "The Bondwoman and the Bureaucrat," Chapter 21 of this volume.

9. Alexander Pope, *Essay on Criticism* I.

10. Nina Baym, "The Case for Hannah Vincent," Chapter 19 of this volume.

11. Gates, Textual Annotations," *Bondwoman's*, pp. 271–272 (see note 6).

12. Gates, "Introduction," p. li.

13. John Bloom, "Literary Blackface? The Mystery of Hannah Crafts," United Press International, reprinted by *National Review Online*, July 26, 2002.

14. Gates, "Introduction," lviii–lx.

15. Ibid., lx–lxi.

16. Katherine E. Flynn, "Jane Johnson, Found! But Is She 'Hannah Crafts'? The Search for the Author of *The Bondwoman's Narrative*," *National Genealogical Society Quarterly* 90 (September 2002): 165–190.

17. Nickell, "Authentication Report," p. 297; Kenneth Rendell, letter report to Laurence Kirshbaum, Chairman, Time Warner Trade Publishing, April 26, 2001.

18. Gates, "Introduction," pp. xlvi–lvi; Flynn, pp. 167–168.

19. Flynn, pp. 168–176.

20. Ibid., p. 179.

21. Ibid., pp. 168–169, 175–176.

22. William Still, *The Underground Railroad* (Philadelphia: Porter and Coates, 1872), pp. 94–95; cited in Gates, *Bondwoman's*, pp. 319–320.

23. Still, quoted in Gates, *Bondwoman's*, p. xlix.

24. Crafts, *Bondwoman's*, pp. xxii–xxiii.

25. Flynn, "Jane Johnson," Table 2, p. 180.

26. Crafts, *Bondwoman's*, p. 205.

27. William Still, quoted in Flynn, "Jane Johnson," p. 180; quoted in Gates, "Introduction," p. xlviii.

28. Crafts, *Bondwoman's*, pp. 125, 152.

29. Baym, "The Case for Hannah Vincent."

30. Gates, "Introduction," lxi–lxii.

31. See Hollis Robbins's essay in this volume.

32. Ibid.

33. Baym, "Hannah Vincent."

34. Ibid.

35. Martin Fido, Foreword to Stuart P. Evans and Keith Skinner, *Jack the Ripper: Letters from Hell* (Gloucestershire, England: Stroud, 2001), p. vii.

36. W. I. B. Beveridge, *The Art of Scientific Investigation* (New York: Vintage, n.d.), p. 63.

37. Baym, "Hannah Vincent."

38. Ibid.

VI

Reviews

24

The Bondwoman's Narrative
An 1850s Account of Slave Life

MIA BAY

Who was Hannah Crafts? The author of *The Bondwoman's Narrative*, an autobiographical novel written in the 1850s, describes herself as "a fugitive slave, recently escaped from North Carolina," making her text a remarkable historical find.

Published from a manuscript bought at auction by eminent scholar Henry Louis Gates Jr., it is quite probably the first novel written by an African-American woman, as well as the only novel written by a female fugitive slave. Previously unpublished and unedited, it is also one of the few purely firsthand accounts of the slave experience available. Crafts' story offers us, as Gates notes, a virtually unparalleled opportunity "to gain access to the mind of the slave in an unmediated fashion." (xxxii)

Such claims, of course, hinge on the authenticity of Crafts' manuscript, a subject all but laid to rest in Gates' long introduction to the book. Although Gates never manages to identify the real-life Hannah Crafts—who probably wrote under a pseudonym—he presents a formidable array of evidence authenticating her story. Moreover, Crafts speaks for herself as well, presenting a credible and compelling commentary on life under slavery. Indeed, one of the most surprising features of this altogether surprising work is that The Bondwoman's Narrative need not be read for its historical importance alone. It is an immensely entertaining and illuminating novel.

The distinctive charms of Crafts' novel lie in its unusual combination of genres. A slave narrative rich with insights about slavery, Hannah Crafts' tale is also a page-turner enlivened by conventions drawn from both gothic and sentimental novels. Always interesting, if only intermittently well written, *The Bondwoman's Narrative* uses these fictional genres to mobilize all the dramatic potential inherent to its setting in the slave South, and then goes over the top. As its narrator and heroine, the young "almost white" Hannah Crafts faces not only the evils of slavery, but ghosts, curses and great gusts of the ominous weather so typical to gothic fiction. Indeed, inclement weather heralds adversity so unfailingly in this novel that any mention of wind or clouds makes you brace yourself in anticipation of some gloomy dramatic development. And you never have to wait very long. Arriving on cue, such developments multiply improbably, in the sentimental tradition exemplified by Charles Dickens, whose prose is unabashedly cribbed by Crafts at several junctures in the novel.

Propelled by the supernatural and coincidental as well as by the vicissitudes of slavery, the plot moves quickly. Hannah is not the only near-white woman in this tale. A staple in nineteenth-century fiction, beautiful quadroons and mulattos abound here, and one of them turns out to be Crafts' first slave mistress, a woman whose "wavy, curly hair" and "large, full" lips prefigure the revelation that she is not what she seems. (27) Switched at birth with a dead white child, Hannah's mistress grows up with no knowledge of her true racial identity, until her secret is discovered by the novel's sinister villain, the aptly named Mr. Trappe, who threatens to expose her. She and Hannah then flee Linden, their decaying plantation home, where an ancient slave curse hovers over the planter's family, boding ill for her mistress, even after she recognizes Hannah as her "very dear sister." (48) Much drama ensues, as the two are captured and Hannah's former mistress' fortunes continue to decline. Hannah has better luck, narrowly escaping being sold into the "fancy trade"—a market for slave concubines centered in New Orleans.

Her flight is only the beginning of her adventures, which take her to freedom through a series of owners. Most notable among them are Mr. and Mrs. Wheeler, the characters in the book that can be most readily linked to real people. In both name and personal details, Crafts' Wheelers bear a remarkable resemblance to Mr. and Mrs. John Hill Wheeler, a North Carolina couple whom Henry Louis Gates Jr. uses to help date and document Crafts' narrative. Like the fictional Wheeler described by Crafts, John Hill Wheeler was an "ardent and passionate defender of slavery" who held several offices in Washington, D.C. (xlii) More tellingly, both the real Wheelers and Crafts' characters lose a slave named Jane, who escaped with the aid of Northern abolitionists. John Hill Wheeler's fugitive slave was named Jane Johnson, and the details of her flight are well known since she testified in the "Case of Passmore Williamson" (1855), a famous legal case that Wheeler brought against the abolitionists who helped her escape. Meanwhile, Crafts mentions no litigation, but her novel displays an intimate familiarity with the Wheeler household in the aftermath of Jane's escape—leading Gates to speculate that Crafts might have served the Wheelers as a house servant.

If she did, she was not happy there. In the novel Mrs. Wheeler purchases Hannah Crafts largely as a substitute for the recently departed Jane, who had served as her personal maid and hairdresser. Possibly shedding a new, if banal, light on the discontents of the real-life Jane Johnson, as well those of her successor, Crafts paints Mrs. Wheeler as a disagreeable, exacting and self-absorbed mistress. Jane's departure obsesses Mrs. Wheeler primarily because Jane "ran off" leaving her with "no one to whom I could think of entrusting my head." (149) Mourning the ill-kempt hair that she has had to "endure from losing Jane," Mrs. Wheeler takes comfort in the notion that Jane will "suffer more, probably"—presumably from the ill effects of a freedom she sought only under the influence of men from "'Hio [Ohio]," as Wheeler terms the abolitionists. (149, 150)

As represented in Crafts' novel, Mrs. Wheeler's complaints to her new slave maid about the escape of her predecessor also speak to the careless intimacy of the mistress-slave relationship. Discussing Wheeler's "rehearsal of Jane's conduct," Crafts comments: "Those who suppose that southern ladies keep their attendants at a distance, scarcely speaking to them, or only to give commands have a very erroneous impression. Between the mistress and her slave a freedom exists probably not to be found elsewhere. A northern woman would have recoiled at the idea of communicating a private history to one of my race, and in my condition, whereas such a thought never occurred to Mrs. Wheeler. I was near her. She was not fond of silence when there was a listener." (150)

Both in her commentary on Mrs. Wheeler and elsewhere, Crafts transcends the melodrama of her fictional genres to address the complexities of the slave experience. Yet she also uses fictional conventions to illustrate the slave experience, making particularly good use of the gothic sense of foreboding that she so frequently represents with references to weather. Anxiety about the future, Crafts both emphasizes and dramatizes, is central to the slave experience. The worst of slavery, she writes, is not the "physical suffering," but "the fear, apprehension, the dread and deep anxiety always attending the condition in a greater or lesser degree. There can be no certainty, no abiding confidence in the possession of any good thing. The indulgent master may die, or fail in business. The happy home may be despoiled of its chiefest pleasures, and the consciousness of this embitters all their [the slaves'] lot." (94)

Little wonder then that the weather is so bad in Hannah Crafts' slave South. Tragedy is always around the corner, and the slaves are not the stalwart, heroic figures common to antislavery fiction by white authors—such as Harriet Beecher Stowe's Uncle Tom. Instead, they live in a gothic nightmare dramatically recollected in *The Bondwoman's Narrative*.

25

The Shape of Absence

HILARY MANTEL

The Swann Galleries' auction of African-Americana, which takes place in New York in February each year, is a marketplace for the printed artefacts generated by over two hundred years of black history. There are film posters, books, album covers; further back, bills of sale for slaves. This year's auction included a brochure from a Charleston estate sale of 1859, offering '229 Rice Field Negroes, An Uncommonly Prime and Orderly Gang'. From the 1830s came a silk handkerchief, an Abolitionist keepsake from England, with a picturesque and sentimental vignette of a black mother rocking her baby under a palm-tree; the inscription is 'Negro woman who sitteth pining in captivity'. In a 19th-century oil on canvas, a young half-clad black man gazes pensively out of the frame, towards some distant shore of his imagination. The portrayal is described as 'respectful', is dated 1823 and is perhaps the work of a black artist: an unidentified person from the dusty past, still awaiting the attention of scholars who will offer him a grand entrance into history.

The 2001 auction offered jazz photographs and religious texts, and the memorabilia of black figures from Joe Louis to Malcolm X. There was an autograph letter from Frederick Douglass, the escaped slave who published his autobiography in 1845 and became a leading Abolitionist. There were documents that shed light on the intimate workings of the 'peculiar institution' which so many defended as natural, necessary and ordained by God. In 1854 a family is selling their slave Frances, aged 17, to a dealer in Richmond. Frances is trained as a chambermaid.

She does not know that she is to be sold. I could not tell her; I own all her family, and the leave taking would be so distressing that I could not. Please say to her that that was my reason, and that I was compelled to sell her to pay for the horses that I have bought, and to build my stable . . . I am so nervous that I hardly know what I write.

The letter brought almost five thousand dollars; Henry Louis Gates paid about twice that for the unpublished manuscript of a three-hundred-page novel, undated, by an author whose name at the time meant nothing. It seems little enough for what Gates calls 'history in waiting'; his tone is almost gloating as he describes the auction's annual riches: 'Dozens of potential PhD theses in African American literature are buried in this catalogue.' Gates has helped black studies to progress from what he calls a 'self-esteem machine' to a serious and valued discipline and his latest achievement is to put the obscure manuscript he bought at auction into the US bestseller lists. What Gates discovered in the Swann Galleries' list was almost certainly the first novel written by an escaped female slave, and possibly the first novel ever written by a black woman.

This is what history feels like, under the hand, under the microscope: the manuscript's cloth binding is broken, but all its numbered pages are intact. The paper is machine made, of linen and cotton fibres, not wood pulp, and has blue guidelines to write on; the pen that touched this paper was a goose quill, and the pigment was acidic iron-gall ink, which leaves faint mirror-writing on the facing page, fluorescing traces like a ghost of the text. The handwriting is serviceable rather than elegant. The manuscript has been corrected in various ways: most simply, by wiping off the ink and writing over the error, a technique which works with smooth paper; or, if the mistake was discovered after the ink had dried, by scratching off a word with a small knife. If the correction was longer, a paragraph perhaps, the writer attached a slip of paper to cover the unwanted text. These correction slips were cut, experts suggest, with sewing scissors, and the paste wafers that made them adhere to the page have been pressed down with a thimble. Visitors to Jane Austen's cottage at Chawton notice that Jane's sewing box is bigger than her writing box. It may have been the same with Hannah Crafts.

Where had this manuscript been? Its early adventures are uncertain. Before 1948 it seems to have been in an attic in New Jersey. Then it was bought by the black historian and bibliographer Dorothy Porter Wesley; after her death, it came to auction and to Gates. The catalogue description said that it was 'uncertain' that the MS was the work of a black person, but the fact that Wesley had acquired it suggested to Gates that she had a strong belief that the author was black. Gates submitted it for examination to, among others, the expert who had exposed the 'Jack the Ripper Diaries' as a fraud. The issue of authentication was vital, and went beyond the nature of the artefact itself.

Granted that the paper, ink and other external markers dated it to somewhere between 1855 and 1860, and given that the handwriting, the diction, the vocabulary were faithful to the period, how can we know that the writer was black and, as the title page claimed, 'A Fugitive Slave Recently Escaped from North Carolina'?

You may wonder why anyone would bother to fake such an identity, but who would have imagined that anyone would dare fake the memoirs of a Holocaust survivor? Yet it seems to have happened. More to the point in this instance is the embarrassing memory of Alex Haley's *Roots*. In 1976 the book was marketed as ground-breaking black history. It proved to be not just fiction, but plagiarised fiction. Fakery and accusations of fakery are part of the history of black writing. The 19th century gave rise to a great many publications by African Americans—autobiographies, religious tracts and poems—but sometimes white authors pretended to be black. Mattie Griffith, the author of *Autobiography of a Female Slave* (1856), revealed herself to be white within weeks of publication. Even where the hand that held the pen was black, a certain blurring of the boundaries of authenticity is evident in many texts. The stories of escaped slaves were intended to serve as propaganda for Abolition, and they were often edited by white supporters of emancipation. They had to sound authentic rather than be authentic, which meant that they had to conform to a white readership's idea of how an educated black should sound. When Frederick Douglass toured as a speaker for the Anti-Slavery Society, he was advised not to sound 'too learned', in case his audiences didn't believe he had been a slave.

Henry Louis Gates is an expert on slave narratives. (It was he who rescued from obscurity the first novel published by a black woman. *Our Nig*, by Harriet E. Wilson, came out in 1859; Wilson was born in the North and had never been a slave.) Gates argues that the warm reception of *Uncle Tom's Cabin*, published in 1852, made the white-for-black ruse unnecessary; one could be a commercial success without indulging in the peculiar impertinence of draping oneself in a borrowed skin. In time, Harriet Beecher Stowe's bestseller became a byword for its patronising treatment of its black characters, and Gates suggests that other novels by whites show similar stereotyping, a set of assumptions which would have found them out even if the reviewers had not. He was able to see correspondence relating to Hannah Crafts's manuscript from its previous owner, Dorothy Porter Wesley, who had written: 'There is no doubt she was a Negro because her approach to other Negroes is that they are people first of all. Only as the story unfolds, in most instances, does it become apparent that they are Negroes.'

Gates made stern and so far unsuccessful efforts to track down the author, by the usual methods of historical research. 'Hannah' is the name she has chosen for herself as protagonist, but was perhaps not her real forename; 'Crafts' may be a tribute to Ellen Craft, who with her husband, William, made a daring escape from slavery in 1848 disguised as a white male. Whoever 'Hannah' was, she lives now in the pages of her book, and we need to look within the text to find out who and what she was: and since it has many autobiographical elements, we can locate, if not her presence, then the shape of her absence. To Gates the manuscript has particular value because it is unpublished, unedited, unmediated. Hannah offers us the chance for a 'pristine encounter'. That is an odd way to describe it, because the reader has his or her own expectations, produced by more or less knowledge of slavery and slave narratives; Hannah, for her part, has a sensibility that is anything but pristine. Her narration is highly self-conscious; her manner of relation, her vocabulary are drawn from the 19th-century Gothic novel and from the novel of sentiment. Her story is told through tropes and motifs that are well-worn because they are serviceable, and her expressed emotions are tutored ones. She has read the Bible closely, and begins each chapter with a well-chosen citation. She knows Dickens well enough to lift a chunk of *Bleak House* and change foggy London into foggy Washington. But her borrowing is intelligent, because she sees into Dickens's metaphor. Here are two nations, two cities, suffocating in the fog of irrationality and injustice, where the law and its servants and its victims swim in a miasma of oppression. And Hannah herself, as portrayed in the novel, would make a perfect Dickens heroine. The sternest trials leave her sweet character unsoured. In the worst exigencies, she injures no one, and ends her story in 'blest and holy quietude', in a little white cottage, with a fond husband, a revered and aged mother, and adoring children gathered at her knee. The children are not, curiously, her own. However she tries to smooth the surface of her tale and fit it for the ear of the novel-reading public, the brutalities of its subject-matter cannot be softened for long. *The Bondwoman's Narrative* is like a parcel badly wrapped in silk, and what's inside has spines and teeth.

Though Hannah ends up as a Dickens angel, she begins like Jane Eyre, open-eyed and cautious: 'When a child they used to scold and find fault with me . . . I was shy and reserved . . . I had none of that quickness and animation which are so much admired in children, but rather a silent unobtrusive way of observing things and events, and wishing to understand them better than I could.' Hannah knows no father or mother. The first nurturing figure in her life is a sort of fairy godmother, an elderly white woman who teaches her to read. There is much of the dispossessed princess about Hannah. She has already realised that the 'African blood in my veins' excludes her from any future but that of 'unremitted unpaid toil', and this is hard to understand and hard to bear, because 'my complexion was almost white.' How does her African blood show? It 'gave a rotundity to my person, a wave and curl to my hair, and perhaps led me to fancy pictorial illustration and flaming colours'. No white Abolitionist could have created a more effective stereotype—but then people caricature themselves very efficiently, when they have to show themselves to the outside world. People with the histrionic talent to display their sufferings will turn to stereotype to reach their audience—hence the Irish joke and the Jewish joke and the teeth-baring horror of the nigger minstrel show. But perhaps it is true that Hannah enjoyed pictorial illustration and flaming colours. Her storytelling is coarse and lurid: perfect for Hollywood. And the casting? She'd probably find Halle Berry a shade too dark.

Hannah is a house slave, and her home is Lindendale, a great house whose walls are lined with ancestral portraits, with 'stony eyes motionless and void of expression'. The glow of the evening sun kindles a kind of annihilation in their painted features, and Hannah feels a shudder of superstitious awe; but superstition is for field slaves, and Hannah knows that the people in the portraits are dead and cannot harm her. Nevertheless, Lindendale is the focus of many blood-soaked legends; and the reader feels Hannah take a deep breath as she sits down (quill-pen, sewing scissors, thimble) to recount at length (rag paper, watermarked, smooth) the story of an old slave woman and her small dog, gibbeted alive on the linden tree and left to die, in public view, over the course of several days. If Hannah were alive now, she would be well employed in writing appeals for animal shelters and Help the Aged. When she takes her time, she can wring the human heart with great confidence and efficiency, and no matter how many novels you read this year, it is likely that the old woman and her pooch will be among your top spooks on New Year's Eve. No wonder the linden tree creaks, and the portraits fall from the wall, when a bride comes to Lindendale!

She is a beautiful young woman, a brunette with rather full lips; she seems nervous from the outset, and soon runs mad on a regular basis. The sinister Mr Trappe, who 'claimed to have been the guardian of my mistress previous to her marriage' knows her secret—she has African blood—and is blackmailing her. Hannah and her new mistress run away, and undergo harrowing adventures. They live in the woods, on berries and wild fruits, but are tracked down by agents of the far-reaching Trappe, and are imprisoned in 'Egyptian' darkness, in a dungeon where they fear being eaten alive by rats. A pencilled correction (by whom?) has changed 'Egyptian' to 'Stygian'. But the first thought was right. When God plagued Egypt, it was with 'darkness that may be felt'; God's people are led out of Egypt and into freedom. Hannah may not win prizes for spelling—Gates leaves her mistakes in—but her range of reference is astonishing. On the same page as her 'Egyptian' darkness she tells us that 'persons have been known to sleep on the rack'; this is the 'witches sleep' that gives victims of torture a break from agony, a tiny physiological pause. It is a sad attested fact, though it may also be (someone will check it out and tell us) a staple of Gothic narratives. The Gothic is an apt form in which to express the feelings of the powerless. It is apt where the workings of cause and effect are veiled, as they are from the slaves; it is no use for them to reason about their situation, because they are the victims of caprice, and rationality cannot save them. Gothic convention can survive, and diversify, because of its emotional and situational truth. It is always vastly exaggerated, and at the same time, there is always some culture, some spot on the map, where it is all literally true. There are dungeons, for the body and soul. There are lime pits in which the right-thinking are plunged, till their identity is leached away. There are perjurers and liars, and no one, of any shade, who can be relied on; truth is more than skin-deep. It's all, as Hannah says, 'hedious'. Just stand still, and something will have the flesh off your bones.

From the dungeon (where Hannah's sanity is saved by a vision of her mother) she is delivered back to Trappe. Here is the slave owner's voice, raised in self-justification, counselling submission to the status quo:

> We are all slaves to something or somebody. A man perfectly free would be an anomaly, and a free woman even more so. Freedom and slavery are only names attached surreptitiously and often improperly to certain conditions . . . they are mere shadows the very reverse of realities, and being so, if rightly considered, they have only a trifling effect on individual happiness.

Hannah has thought deeply about the meaning of justice and its workings, and about individual as well as collective injuries. Her literary methods may be crass, but as a politician she is intelligent, analytical and persuasive, and when she begins to strip away the layers of hypocrisy and self-deception in the society into which she was born, she is both unsparing and subtle. She knows despotism, and has seen its miserable face. Her preface tells us that she hopes to show how slavery 'blights the happiness of the white as well as the black race'. Her slaves have souls to save, so do their masters; each is impeding the other in this endeavour. The Christian religion is a subversive force, or so the masters fear; the slaves start to believe that everyone is equal in the sight of God. It persuades them that 'one thing is right and another thing wrong'— whereas properly speaking, they should surrender all moral sense to their owners. For Hannah, slavery is a brutal physical reality, but it is also a demeaning spiritual state. 'My conscience never troubles me,' says Trappe, and when a trader comes calling, his philosophy gives way to crude bargaining: 'Now I'll tell you what . . . You won't find a nicer bit of woman's flesh to be bought for that money in old Virginia. Don't you see what a foot she has, so dainty and delicate, and what an ankle.' But the trader is put off, because he suspects Hannah is 'skittish'. Women turn skittish, he remarks, when they are parted from their children, though that is not Hannah's reason; from being skittish they turn suicidal, and run away, and have to be pursued with dogs; once the hounds have ripped them apart, their market value is decreased.

Hannah's novel is frank about the sexual abuse of black women, which reinforces the South's 'domestic institution' by breeding more slaves, and in addition poisons the marriages of the whites. She describes how white mistresses and black maids grow close to each other—the mirror, the hairbrush—and recognises the similarities in their plight; these similarities do not, of course, guarantee fellow-feeling, because the weak are cruel to those weaker than themselves. The topic is freighted with ambiguity, in history as in Hannah's fiction. The many women involved in the Abolitionist movement were quick to make parallels between slaves and all women, but this was not necessarily a feminist argument; sometimes, grotesquely, it was its opposite. Some Abolitionists argued against slavery on the grounds that it prevented proper family life—a wife could not be properly obedient to her husband if she owed obedience to her white master. And the pro-slavers feared that if slavery were abolished, the institution of marriage would be threatened; to emancipate slaves meant giving freedom to a body of people unfit for it, and women were like blacks in their natural lack of capacity for self-determination. Both slavery and marriage were institutions of private life, with which government should not meddle; but owners were entitled to make marriages among slaves, controlling their intimate lives, making and breaking their families at will.

Hannah's worst moment—the event that precipitates her flight to freedom—comes when she crosses her white mistress who, as punishment, decrees that Hannah should be married to a field slave. 'With all your pretty airs and your white face, you are nothing but a slave after all and no better than the blackest wench.' Hannah has determined never to marry while she is a slave— she refuses to give birth to a child whose innocent body will perpetuate the system. But when she is exiled to the cabin of her prospective husband, her senses as well as her principles revolt. She is to be married to a man

> whose person, speech and manner could not fail to be ever regarded by me with loathing and disgust. Then to be driven in to the fields beneath the eye and lash of the brutal overseer, and those miserable huts, with their promiscuous crowds of dirty, obscene and degraded objects, for my home I could not, would not bear it.

A day picking cotton makes her fingers bleed. This is Hannah, who can not only read, but play the harp! Deeply colour-conscious, shaped by her superior education, she has no access to the minds of the field slaves, and she makes no effort to imagine herself into their skins. The degraded men and women she describes are voiceless and outside history. It is likely they will defy the most probing investigations of Gates's PhD squad. They have lives, but no biography; they are less chronicled than a white man's dog. Only a novelist could give them a voice, but Hannah doesn't try; real life is taking over now.

Hannah's vengeful mistress had a real existence. The novel's first mentions of the family designate them 'Wh——' but later the writer takes courage and fills in the name: 'Wheeler'. From this, Gates has identified John Hill Wheeler, a lawyer, functionary, plantation owner and sometime member of the state legislature of North Carolina, who became briefly famous through a 1855 court case in which he attempted to regain possession of a fugitive slave called Jane Johnson. Jane's story, in fictionalised form, is part of Hannah's narrative, and it seems likely that Hannah was also employed in the Wheeler household, and overheard the private conversation of the family. Gates thinks that she may have been Jane's replacement as lady's maid, serving the Wheeler household in 1856 and escaping the following year. John Hill Wheeler kept a diary, parts of which are intact; a theatre-goer, he records seeing John Wilkes Booth in the part of Shylock, and thinking him a very promising actor. His library, rather than his diary, is likely to have been important to Hannah: he owned the works of Walter Scott, *Gulliver's Travels*, two volumes of Byron, the Brontës' novels, *The Beauties of Shakespeare Regularly Selected from Each Play*, several of Dickens's works, the letters of Burns and Gray, and a volume called *Whom to Marry and How to Get Married! or, The Adventures of a Lady in Search of a Good Husband*.

Hannah runs away disguised as a boy, and after many adventures—not quite as lurid and preposterous as those that have gone before—she reaches a place of safety and a new life. How? Before the Civil War, the North did not provide a sure asylum. Under the Fugitive Slave Act of 1850, it was legal for the owners of runaways to reclaim them if they could, and so it was necessary for escapees to disguise their identity. They could never be sure to live unmolested, and therefore many former slaves kept going until they reached Canada—it was wise to get clear of the Land of the Free, in order to claim rights in your own person. What seems likely is that the real Hannah 'passed for white', both during her escape and in later life, and that this prevented her from trying to get her manuscript published. It is a cruel trade-off: self-suppression as the price of safety.

Hannah as a novelist may be a thing of shreds and patches, but so are we all. The idea of disguising her influences would probably have made no sense to her, because she was as proud of her learning as she was of her near-white complexion. Her descriptions of houses, plantations and landscape show how thoroughly she has internalised the aesthetic values of her masters; she has no eye of her own. When pathos changes to broad comedy, you feel her heart isn't in it; somebody has told her that readers appreciate light relief, and grimly she doles it out. But she knows how to excite horror, and how to move her reader, and how to people her narrative. Her black characters are more complex than her white ones; they are victims of slavery, but not all victims are good. Some slaves are deceitful and malicious, and few measure up to Hannah's own high Christian standards. Her white characters are products of their politics, but while all Abolitionists are saintly, among the pro-slavers she deals in degrees of hypocrisy, guilt and moral deformity. Living at the white person's feet, less noticed than the furniture, she acts as a mirror, a tape recorder, a microphone.

The Abolitionist preference was for facts, facts, facts: not for fantasy, which can be forged. Slave writers were urged to be specific, to skewer names and dates and places, as protection against the owners' frequent allegation that slave narratives were the product of white Northern do-gooders with too little information and too much imagination. In her preface, Hannah declares her book to be a 'record of plain unvarnished facts', but a glance at any page shows it to be something far more artful. So why did Hannah choose to write a novel, not an autobiography? She prefers to tell a story about herself, and perhaps that story had been necessary for her psychological survival. Long before she was free in fact, she had escaped in imagination. She had extracted herself from degrading circumstances and inserted herself into others, more flattering, as a persecuted heroine in a romance. The novel shows us that she has been able to protect her psyche, and keep its core intact; an autobiography would merely assert it. Autobiographies display the triumph of experience, but novels are acts of hope. There are, after all, degrees of freedom. Did liberation consist of the capacity to sell one's labour in a factory, and live in a slum in the cold North? Hannah has elected a better fate for her persona: self-determination, domestic happiness, even a reunion with her lost mother. It is a most touching example of art as solace. The novel has uses in both the outer and the inner world. Do people ever write just one? There's work for the legion of PhD students; scouring the attics and lumber-rooms of America for traces of that unique hand, 'neither an untutored hand nor an example of elegant penmanship', legible and without flourishes, and 'consistent with the writing of a woman'.

26

Literary Blackface?

The Mystery of Hannah Crafts

JOHN BLOOM

W as Hannah Crafts really a black woman? Was she really a slave? How do we know she wasn't a tea-sipping housewife in Morristown who wanted to help abolish slavery?

I'm just not as convinced as everyone else seems to be that this "new" slave novel is authentic.

Just Who Is Hannah Crafts?

In case you missed the ballyhoo, 16 months ago an obscure 301-page hand-written manuscript was offered for auction at the Swann Galleries in New York. The title page read "The Bondwoman's Narrative by Hannah Crafts, a Fugitive Slave, Recently Escaped from North Carolina."

The catalog said that the manuscript appeared to be from the 1850s and that it was "uncertain that this work is written by a 'negro,'" but that there was textual evidence to suggest that it was written by a slave—for example, "her escape route is one sometimes used by run-aways."

Only in these fast-moving sensation-starved times of ours could an ignored 150-year-old manuscript of questionable provenance become, in a single year, a major literary event. *The Bondwoman's Narrative* was touted on the front page of the *New York Times* in November, excerpted in *The New Yorker* in February, and by March it was *already* out there on the shelves of Barnes & Noble, touted as a major discovery by a slew of past Pulitzer Prize winners.

The book was designed to exude authenticity. The cover is made to look like someone's idea of a yellowed, frayed-edge manuscript tied with twine, and the text itself is reprinted with all the spelling and syntax mistakes and numerous cross-outs left intact. (I'm not sure why, because they're distracting, and none of them reveal anything about the author or the story.) More important, it was being promoted without apology by Warner Books as "the first known novel written by an African American woman who had been a slave."

Now. I'm willing to believe that you could buy a previously unknown manuscript and, by diligent investigation, eventually prove that it was written by a certain real person on a certain real date. But in this case we went from "uncertain that this work is written by a 'negro'" to "first known novel written by an African American woman" in less than a year, and that includes the time the book was at the printer.

Surely there had to be some major breakthrough. Did a descendant of the pre–Civil War author come forward and positively identify her? Did a reference to the book turn up in memoirs or letters or diaries from the period? Did the records of the Underground Railroad or the Freedmen's Bureau identify Hannah Crafts or make reference to her novel?

Not only did none of these things happen, but no one ever even found Hannah Crafts in the census records or genealogy libraries. So what exactly is going on here?

Taken for a Ride?

You get a clue from the cover of the book, where the name "HENRY LOUIS GATES, JR." is in a bigger type size than the name of the author! Gates is, of course, the chairman of Harvard's Afro-American Studies Department and probably the most famous scholar of black history and literature in America. And it was Gates, in fact, who purchased *The Bondwoman's Narrative* from Swann Galleries last year. So obviously, as a literary event, this has as much to do with Gates as it does with the quality of the lost novel.

Gates even tells us in his introduction that he felt a thrill when he found the manuscript in the auction catalog. "If the author was black," he says, "then this 'fictionalized slave narrative'—an autobiographical novel apparently based upon a female fugitive slave's life in bondage in North Carolina and her escape to freedom in the North—would be a major discovery, possibly the first novel written by a black woman and definitely the first novel written by a woman who had been a slave."

He buys the manuscript even before he reads it—he was the only bidder—and then sets out to find out who Hannah Crafts was and authenticate her race. When you think about it, this alone is a strange thing to do—as if proving she was black is more important than finding out what her thoughts, dreams and aspirations were, or, more to the point, whether she wrote anything of lasting value.

At any rate, Gates sets out on his quest, and here's what he finds: The ownership of the manuscript can't be traced prior to 1948. That's when it was sold for $85 by Emily Driscoll, a manuscript and autograph dealer on Fifth Avenue. The buyer was Dorothy Porter Wesley, a librarian and historian at Howard University, who asked Driscoll where she got it and was told it came from "a scout in the trade"—a freelance peddler of literary material. All the scout could remember is that he picked it up somewhere in New Jersey. Porter Wesley died in 1995, so presumably it was sold at auction by the heirs to her estate.

This means that, from the 1850s until 1948, the unpublished manuscript was in someone's attic, or perhaps a succession of attics, but whoever preserved it didn't care enough about it to even attach a note to it, and the last non-academic owner thought it was worth less than $85. So obviously either the original author had no living descendants or else at some point the old musty manuscript had ceased to be a family keepsake, indicating that the people who ended up with it thought it had flea-market value at best. Then, when it finally got into the hands of a respected bibliophile, she simply held it for 47 years without attempting to publish it.

Nevertheless, it *was* a very old manuscript. Authenticating the date turned out to be fairly easy. Dr. Joe Nickell, an historical document examiner in Amherst, New York, was hired by Warner Books, and he confirmed that the paper, the ink, the method of binding, and the style of handwriting all put it in the 1850s. Then there was internal evidence. The author refers to the equestrian statue of Andrew Jackson in Washington, D.C., that was erected in 1853, so it had to be written after that date. And even though it's a novel about slavery, there's no reference to the Civil War, so obviously it was prior to 1861.

Nickell even went so far as to say it was written by a woman. He found evidence that a thimble had been used to make some corrections, and by analyzing the eccentric punctuation, spelling and vocabulary, he was able to estimate that the writer had the equivalent of a modern 11th-grade education.

That's all well and good, but it was up to Gates to continue the research and prove that Hannah Crafts was really a fugitive slave. The reason the question has to be asked is that at least ten novels were published before the war by white authors pretending to be black slaves.

But Gates dismisses this idea out of hand. He cites the example of *Uncle Tom's Cabin* by Harriet Beecher Stowe, relates how much money it made in multiple editions, and wonders why a white author would pretend to be black when you could make a killing without doing that. "There was no commercial advantage to be gained by a white author writing as a black one . . ." he writes. ". . . My fundamental operating principle when engaged in this sort of historical research is that if someone *claimed* to have been black, then they most probably were, since there was very little incentive (financial or otherwise) for doing so."

At this point, if I were enrolled in Professor Gates's graduate seminar, I would be vigorously waving my hand so that I could say, "Doctor Gates, I myself am a writer who has used fictitious authorship, written in styles that aren't my own, and imagined myself to be living in other times and places, all without considering how much money it would make me. And if I might add, professor, most authors don't have the slightest idea what will or will not make money."

In other words, the "Why would someone do this?" theory just doesn't seem academically sound to me, especially since we know at least ten people *did* do it. And the reasons for pretending to be black aren't hard to find at all. What better argument for abolishing slavery could there be than having a young attractive articulate spunky black heroine who soldiers on against cruel fate and the inhumanity of man with the help of God and her own gritty fortitude?

How do we know that *The Bondwoman's Narrative* is any different from, say, *Autobiography of a Female Slave*, the 1856 novel that was written by Mattie Griffith, later exposed as a white abolitionist?

The answer is that we don't. As much as you *want* Professor Gates to succeed in his historical quest—you're rooting for him to find the faded yellow document that proves the existence of Hannah Crafts—he never really comes up with any convincing proof.

The novel itself is highly enjoyable, by the way, although I think part of its charm is its quaintness. We're not used to reading 19th-century sentimental novels anymore, and so there's an exoticism about it that wouldn't exist for readers who were already steeped in, say, the Brontës or George Eliot. (George Eliot is, come to think of it, an excellent example of somebody who quite successfully used literary ventriloquism in 19th-century fiction—a woman pretending to be a man.)

The Bondwoman's Narrative includes an excellent ghost story, a scarily villainous lawyer named Mr. Trappe, a comic-relief sequence in which the mistress of the slave girl uses an experimental skin ointment that turns her black, an interlude in a rat-infested dungeon, many stories-within-the-story, and quite a few Gothic adventures and chilling death scenes as the heroine is batted from place to place before eventually dressing as a man, passing for white, and escaping to New Jersey. It's also full of amazing coincidences, as novels of the time tended to be.

Unfortunately, there's nothing in the book that couldn't have been researched, imagined or observed by a white author. Normally I would say it doesn't matter—in some ways it's actually a *better* Americana story if it's an abolitionist woman writing it—but since the whole sales campaign is based on this "first black woman" premise, we should at least be honest enough to say it's unproven.

Trust, But Verify

Gates searched through the census indices in an effort to find all people named Hannah Crafts—there weren't any—as well as the names of all the other characters in the book. He only found two real people who appear to be beyond dispute modeled after people in the story. They are John Hill Wheeler, owner of a slave plantation in Lincolnton, North Carolina, and the U.S. minister to Nicaragua at the time of the book's action, and Wheeler's wife Ellen.

A large section of the book takes place at an estate very much like that of Wheeler, and at a Washington residence that also matches what we know of Wheeler. When the author first wrote the book, she called her heroine's master "Mr. W———." At some later time she went back and wrote in the name Wheeler, as though there was no longer any reason to protect the man's identity. (Wheeler died in 1882, so perhaps the emendation was made then.)

Wheeler was a diehard defender of the institution of slavery, an author, and, fortunately for us, a man who wrote in a diary every day of his life. That diary ended up in the Library of Congress, so Gates is able to track where Wheeler was and what he was doing for most of his life.

Wheeler was notorious for a couple of things. He was minister to Nicaragua when it was conquered by the American William Walker. Walker reestablished slavery in that nation, and Wheeler was so supportive of the man that he went ahead and recognized the Walker government without getting permission from the State Department first. As a result he was recalled to Washington in 1857 and relieved of duty.

More to the point, Wheeler was the plaintiff in a famous fugitive-slave trial called the "Case of Passmore Williamson."

The facts of the case were these. Wheeler was traveling from Washington, D.C., to New York, where he was to take a ship to Nicaragua, when he stopped in Philadelphia on July 18, 1855. Traveling with him were a slave named Jane Johnson and her two young sons. In Philadelphia he had to wait a few hours for the boat to New York, so he went to Bloodgood's Hotel for dinner. Separated from her master, Jane Johnson spoke to whatever black people she could find and told them that she was a slave and wished to be free.

Very quickly the black workers in the hotel got word to William Still, chairman of the Acting Vigilant Committee of the Philadelphia Branch of the Underground Railroad, and he ran to the office of a man named Passmore Williamson, who was secretary of "The Pennsylvania Society for Promoting the Abolition of Slavery, and for the Relief of Free Negroes unlawfully held in Bondage, and for improving the condition of the African Race."

Both men, Still and Williamson, hurried to the hotel, but Wheeler had already departed for the boat. They got a description, ran to the boat, found Wheeler and his slaves, and implored Jane Johnson to come with them. Wheeler tried to interfere, of course. There was some shoving and threatening that got pretty serious, but the result was that Jane Johnson and her sons were taken away and Wheeler never saw them again.

What the men had done was a violation of the Fugitive Slave Act of 1850, so the following day Wheeler swore out a warrant against Williamson and the other men. Eventually Williamson served three and a half months in jail, two black men served a week for assault and battery, and Still was acquitted. Jane Johnson actually testified at the trial, but her appearance was somehow arranged so that she couldn't be seized or arrested—and by that time Wheeler was in Nicaragua anyway.

The importance of this story is that, in chapter 12, the fictional character Mrs. Wheeler makes reference to a runaway slave named Jane, indicating that "Hannah Crafts" was purchased as a replacement for Jane. Gates uses this textual evidence to further narrow down the date of the novel; it had to have been written after 1855.

But I think that the "Case of Passmore Williamson" is also what proves that the action of the novel is *not* based on real events. Here's why: We know from Wheeler's diary that he never gave up trying to get Jane Johnson back. He keeps the legal case alive even while he's serving in Nicaragua, and as late as January 10, 1860—four and a half years later—he's petitioning the Pennsylvania legislature for either restitution or the return of "my Negroes."

And yet, throughout this whole period, he never refers in his diary to a runaway slave corresponding to "Hannah Crafts," much less the loss of a runaway slave who is the personal servant to his wife. Gates notes that part of Wheeler's diary is missing—the latter half of 1856—and that much of the year 1858 is damaged or illegible. But even so, are we to believe that the man would doggedly pursue three runaways for five years—referring to them not once but several times—while ignoring the loss of another slave entirely? If "Hannah Crafts" ran away from John Hill Wheeler, why is she never mentioned by any name in this meticulous and detailed diary? Even if she ran away during the latter half of 1856, it's hard to believe he would not continue his efforts to get her back, just as he did with Jane Johnson.

All we know, then, is that the writer of *A Bondwoman's Narrative* was familiar with the Wheelers—and, by her description of them, thought they were silly, selfish and cruel buffoons (especially the wife). Gates bolsters the opinion of "Hannah Crafts" by going out of his way to quote all the racist comments he can find in Wheeler's diary—and yet none of them prove the existence of Crafts as a household slave. Based on what he knows of the movements of Wheeler, Gates dates Hannah's "escape" from the Wheelers as occurring between March 21 and May 4, 1857.

Ultimately Gates's belief that the author was a slave comes down to a close interpretation of the text itself. He says her writing shows an intimate knowledge of estate life in Virginia and North Carolina. (A white person could have the same knowledge.) He says that "her approach to other Negroes is that they are people first of all"—showing, by example, that she sometimes introduces black characters without saying that they're black, and only confirming their blackness later. This argument borders on the obscurantist. Anyone who had imaginatively entered into the life of a black woman would write in the same manner.

Then there's the issue of her education. Gates would have us believe that a woman in her twenties, escaping in 1857 from a slave state that forbids the education of blacks, would complete a 301-page novel before 1861, and that this novel would show an intimate familiarity with, among other things, the conventions of sentimental novels, Gothic novels, "the law of the Medes and Persians," the "lip of Heraclitus," and words like "magnanimity," "obsequious," "vicissitudes," "hieroglyphical" and "diffidence."

Gates's explanation? She was a house slave who had access to Wheeler's library. Gates even includes an appendix listing some of the 1,200 titles in that library, since Wheeler was as meticulous about cataloguing his collection as he was about keeping his diary.

Are we really to believe that a man like Wheeler—one of the most diehard pro-slavery proponents in the country—allowed his slaves to have free run of his library, or that "Hannah Crafts" was so resourceful that she could sneak in there so often that she got the equivalent of a modern 11th-grade education by teaching herself? Even allowing for three years of freedom before she wrote the novel, she would have to be one of the quickest studies in the history of literacy. At the very least this strains credulity.

In the novel, Hannah is taught to read and write by an elderly couple in a nearby cottage who teach her in secret—a not too likely scenario that, among other things, would allow precious little time for study while she was at the beck and call of an entire household.

But the most telling thing, to me, about Hannah Crafts's story is the nature of her heroine. She has an unshakeable Christian faith. She believes strongly that literacy will set her free. She has such strength of character that she never gets truly angry about the bigotry all around her. Her decision to flee is caused, in fact, not by the horrid treatment by her white owners, but by her being forced to marry a field slave. She considers it legalized rape and won't sacrifice her virtue.

What do all these qualities convey? Exactly what the right-thinking white middle class of the North valued most dearly—faith, character, virtue. Everything about her is designed to be attractive to a concerned matron in Scranton or a progressive lawmaker in Boston.

And why did this "Hannah Crafts" never publish the novel? Perhaps because she did finish it around 1860 or 1861, and by that time there was no more need for moralizing about slavery. If she were black, it would still be a good story in 1866. If she were a do-gooder white woman pretending to be black, there wouldn't be much of a point anymore, would there? It would be the kind of thing you tie with twine and place in the attic.

John Bloom writes a number of columns for United Press International. This piece first appeared on UPI and is reprinted with permission.

27

Desperate Measures

The Bondwoman's Narrative, *by Hannah Crafts*

IRA BERLIN

One of the more remarkable truisms about our relationship to the past is that the sources of historical inquiry expand with interest. The recent surge of interest in slavery has produced a profusion of new sources, from the logs of the slave ship Henrietta Marie to the artifacts exhumed at the African burial grounds in New York City. Few new sources have aroused as much excitement as Hannah Crafts's *The Bondwoman's Narrative*, apparently the first novel written by a black woman in the United States. Announced on the front page of the New York Times and extravagantly praised by a bevy of Pulitzer Prize winners, *The Bondwoman's Narrative* offers new insights into the nature of slave society and the multiple ways slavery shaped the lives of Americans, white and black.

At the outset, it should be acknowledged that *The Bondwoman's Narrative* is not great literature. Rather it is a dull, sometimes tedious read filled with the stock figures of 19th-century African-American fiction—abused slaves, villainous masters, spiteful mistresses, mercenary slave traders, tragic mulattoes and compassionate strangers. Its plot—and often its very language—is borrowed from Dickens and other contemporary literary icons, so much so that its editor, Henry Louis Gates Jr., has subsequently had to concede that the author of *The Bondwoman's Narrative* rifled "through her master's books to quilt together formal elements from the Gothic and sentimental novels as well as slave narratives." Its narrative is sustained by unconvincing coincidences—babies switched (black and white), good fortune betrayed and evil trumped by pure hearts—that have been worn thin in the hands of numerous others. Its arguments that the virtues of evangelical Christianity, force of literacy and

strength of character will triumph are transparent appeals to middle-class abolitionists. In fact, the most engaging writing in *The Bondwoman's Narrative* can be
found in Gates's long introduction.

The contrast between Gates's exhilarating tale of the discovery of Crafts's
manuscript in an obscure catalogue of African-American ephemera and
Crafts's leaden prose could not be more striking. Anyone who doubts that
scholarship is high adventure need only consult Gates's rousing account. But,
for all its dogged thoroughness, his search for the real Hannah Crafts never
yields the woman who claims to be "A Fugitive Slave Recently Escaped from
North Carolina." As a result, Crafts's origins, race and sex remain a matter of
conjecture, and that doubt calls into question any appraisal of *The Bondwoman's
Narrative*. After all, the significance of the book does not rest on its primacy
but on its validity as a first-hand view of African-American slavery.

While Gates has failed to find proof positive of Hannah Crafts's identity,
he has connected the author of *The Bondwoman's Narrative* to the manuscript's
protagonist with a mountain of circumstantial evidence. His examination of
the physical aspects of the manuscript (the age of the paper, the quality of the
ink), analysis of its language (syntax, vocabulary, spelling), and exploration of
the context of the story validate Crafts's claim as author and Gates's claim for
significance. The clincher for Gates—and I think for most readers—is his
identification of John Hill Wheeler, a minor Democratic politico from North
Carolina, as Crafts's owner and of the close correspondence between
Wheeler's life and Crafts's narrative.

Like Frederick Douglass, William Wells Brown and Harriet Jacobs, Crafts
views slavery from the inside, in her case, the Big House in antebellum Virginia and North Carolina. It is an extraordinary story that more than makes
up for its turgid prose by revealing the nature of slavery in pre–Civil War
America. Crafts points her readers to the sexual vulnerability of slave women,
especially house servants, and the abuse that followed. But there is more to
The Bondwoman's Narrative than the slaveowners' dreary presumption that sexual
access was just another of the master's prerogatives. Indeed, once the conventions of 19th-century literature and the clichés of antislavery moralism are
peeled away, Crafts's narrative is about as good a guide to antebellum slave
life as one could find. Perhaps the most prominent theme of *The Bondwoman's
Narrative* is how the threat of sale traumatized black people. During the 19th
century, some 1 million slaves were forcibly deported from the Atlantic
seaboard and shipped to the Southern interior. This enormous forced reloca-
tion sundered marriages, destroyed families and ravaged communities. Slaveowners understood that slaves feared sale far more than the lash and employed the threat of sale both as a means of discipline and as way of

destabilizing black society. Crafts, like other slaves, shaped her life to avoid the separation that sale entailed.

Crafts's narrative also gives a sense of the complexity of slave society, and of how relations among slaves were as critical to understanding slavery as relations between master and slave. Hannah Crafts's decision to run away—upon which her life, as well as the novel, turns—originates not in the gross abuse of her owner, but in the fear that she will be forced to marry a field hand, whose ignorance and gross demeanor—he is depicted here as unrelentingly vile, foul and filthy—disgusts her far more than her owner's unwanted advances. Much of the tragedy of slavery was found not simply in the master's monopoly of force and willingness to use it, but in the ways in which the perversity of the institution twisted the lives of everyone it touched.

The importance of *The Bondwoman's Narrative* lies neither in its many "firsts" nor in the author's attempt to elevate her story into high adventure, but in her unconscious and sometimes unthinking revelations about the commonplaces of black life in bondage. Little wonder that the obscure reference to a manuscript by a former slave set Gates off in search of Hannah Crafts, or that others will join the search.

ABOUT THE AUTHORS

William Andrews is the E. Maynard Adams Professor of English at the University of North Carolina at Chapel Hill. He is the author of *The Literary Career of Charles W. Chesnutt* (1980) and *To Tell a Free Story: The First Century of Afro-American Autobiography, 1760–1865* (1986). He has edited or co-edited thirty volumes, including *The Norton Anthology of African American Literature* (1997); *The Oxford Companion to African American Literature* (1997); *The Literature of the American South: A Norton Anthology* (1997); and *Slave Narrative* (2000), a volume in the Library of America.

Nina Baym is Swanlund Endowed Chair and Center for Advanced Study Professor of English, as well as Jubilee Professor of Liberal Arts and Sciences, at the University of Illinois at Urbana-Champaign. She is General Editor of *The Norton Anthology of American Literature* and has published many books and articles on American literary topics, including three books about nineteenth-century American women writers. In 2000 she received the Hubbell Medal for lifetime achievement in American literary studies from the American Literature Section of the Modern Language Association.

Ira Berlin is professor of history at the University of Maryland and the author of "Many Thousands Gone: The First Two Centuries of Slavery in North America."

Dickson D. Bruce, Jr., is professor of history at the University of California. His books include *Violence and Culture in the Antebellum South* (1979); *Black American Writing from the Nadir: The Evolution of a Literary Tradition, 1877–1915* (1989); and *The Origins of African American Literature, 1680–1865* (2001).

Lawrence Buell is Professor and John P. Marquand Professor of English, and Chair, Department of English at Harvard University. Professor Buell teaches courses in the history of American literature and culture and has a particular interest in environmental(ist) discourses, issues of cultural nationalism, and comparatist approaches to American literary study including transatlantic and postcolonial models of inquiry. He is the author of *Literary Transcendentalism* (1973), *New England Literary Culture* (1986), *The Environmental Imagination: Thoreau, Nature Writing, and the Formation of American Culture* (1995), and *Writing for an Endangered World Literature, Culture, and Environment in the United States and Beyond* (2001).

Rudolph P. Byrd is Associate Professor of American Studies and Director of the Program of African American Studies at Emory University. He is author of *Jean*

Toomer's Years with Gurdjieff and editor of *I Call Myself an Artist: Writings by and about Charles Johnson.*

Christopher Castiglia is Associate Professor of English at Loyola University in Chicago. He is the author of *Bound and Determined: Captivity, Culture-Crossing, and White Womanhood from Mary Rowlandson to Patty Hearst* (University of Chicago Press, 1996) and *Interior States: the Romance of Reform and the Inner Life of a Nation* (forthcoming, Duke University Press), as well as numerous articles on queer culture and on antebellum race and democracy.

Russ Castronovo is Jean Wall Bennett Professor of English and American Studies at the University of Wisconsin–Madison. He is the author of *Fathering the Nation: American Genealogies of Slavery and Freedom* (1995) and *Necro Citizenship: Death, Eroticism, and the Public Sphere in the Nineteenth-Century United States* (2001), and co-editor with Dana Nelson of *Materializing Democracy: Toward a Revitalized Cultural Politics* (2002).

Ann Fabian teaches American Studies and History at Rutgers University in New Brunswick, New Jersey. She has written on gambling and personal narratives in the United States in the nineteenth century and is currently working on a book on the collection and display of human skulls.

Shelley Fisher Fishkin is (as of September 1, 2003) Professor of English and Chair of the Department of American Studies at Stanford University. She is the author of books including *Lighting Out for the Territory: Reflections on Mark Twain and American Culture; Was Huck Black: Mark Twain and African American Voices;* and *From Fact to Fiction: Journalism and Imaginative Writing in America.* She is editor of *The Oxford Mark Twain* and the *Oxford Historical Guide to Mark Twain* and is co-editor of *Listening to Silences: New Essays in Feminist Criticism; The Encyclopedia of Civil Rights in America; People of the Book: Thirty Scholars Reflect on Their Jewish Identity;* and Oxford's "Race and American Culture" book series.

Katherine E. Flynn has been since 1997 a Certified Genealogical Records Specialist SM. She holds a B.A. in chemistry and philosophy from the College of St. Catherine, an M.A. in organic chemistry from Yale University, a Ph.D. from Northwestern University in synthetic organic chemistry and was a Visiting Scholar at the University of Cambridge.

William Gleason is associate professor of English at Princeton University and the author of *The Leisure Ethic: Work and Play in American Literature, 1840–1940* (Stanford, 1999). He is currently working on a study of architecture, race, and American literature.

Catherine Keyser is pursuing her Ph.D. at Harvard University in the Department of English and American Literature and Language. She is a Jacob K. Javitz Fellow and a 2001–2002 Honorary Mellon Fellow.

Robert S. Levine is Professor of English and Director of Graduate Studies at the University of Maryland, College Park. He has published six books, including *Conspiracy and Romance* (Cambridge University Press, 1989); *Martin Delany, Frederick Douglass, and the Politics of Representative Identity* (University of North Carolina Press, 1997); and *Martin R. Delany: A Documentary Reader* (University of North Carolina Press, 2003).

Hilary Mantel's novels include *A Place of Greater Safety, An Experiment in Love* and *The Giant O'Brien*.

Joe Nickell is author of the "Investigative Files" column for *Skeptical Inquirer* magazine. He received a Ph.D. from the University of Kentucky in 1987 and is the author of numerous books, including *Inquest of the Shroud of Turin* and *Secrets of the Supernatural*. He is Associate Dean of the Center for Inquiry Institute.

Thomas C. Parramore is a professor emeritus at Meredith College, Raleigh, North Carolina. He is the author of *Southampton County, Virginia, 1650–1978* (University of Press of Virginia, 1978); *The First Four Centuries* (University Press of Virginia, 1994); and numerous other books and articles on Southern, especially North Carolina, history. He has also written a critique of Nat Turner's Rebellion for a critical volume on the subject to be published in 2003 by Oxford University Press.

Augusta Rohrbach has held a joint appointment with the Radcliffe Institute for Advanced Study and the W.E.B. DuBois Institute at Harvard University after being a Bunting Fellow the previous year. Her published essays have appeared in *International Studies in Philosophy, Callaloo, New England Quarterly*, and *American Literature*. Her book, *"Truth Stranger Than Fiction": Race, Realism, and the U.S. Literary Marketplace*, was published by Palgrave (2002). She received her doctorate from Columbia University in 1994 and taught at Oberlin College for four years. She is currently working on "Ar'n't I a Writer? Trading on Race and Gender and the Literary Marketplace," a full-length study of women writers.

Hollis Robbins is the Director of the Black Periodic Literature Project at the W.E.B. Du Bois Institute at Harvard University. She received her Ph.D. in English and American Literature from Princeton in June 2003. She received a master's degree in Public Policy from Harvard University in 1990. She is the author of numerous articles, including "The Emperor's New Critique" (*New Literary History*, forthcoming).

Karen Sánchez-Eppler is Professor of American Studies and English at Amherst College. She is the author of *Touching Liberty: Abolition, Feminism, and the Politics of the Body* (1993), and of the forthcoming *Rearing a Nation: Childhood and Social Order in Nineteenth-Century America*.

Bryan Sinche is a doctoral candidate in early American literature and American studies at the University of North Carolina at Chapel Hill; he also holds a B.A in English from the University of Michigan. Sinche compiled the catalog of John Hill Wheeler's library that was included in the first edition of *The Bondwoman's Narrative*. He is the managing editor of *a/b: Auto/Biography Studies*.

John Stauffer is Associate Professor of American Civilization and English at Harvard University. His book, *The Black Hearts of Men* (Harvard University Press, February 2002), won the 1999 Ralph Henry Gabriel Prize for the best dissertation in American Studies from the American Studies Association and was co-winner of the 2002 Frederick Douglass Book Prize.

Zoe Trodd has published on black studies and American literature and has won numerous awards for her writing and teaching. She recently co-edited *John Brown and the Coming of the Civil War* (2003) with John Stauffer. She graduated with first-class honors from Newnham College, Cambridge University, England, where she founded and edited a nationally recognized newspaper. She was a Kennedy Scholar at Harvard University (2001–2002) and is now a graduate fellow in Harvard's History of American Civilization department. She lives in England and Cambridge, Massachusetts.

Priscilla Wald is Associate Professor of English and Women's Studies at Duke University and Associate Editor of American Literature. She is the author of *Constituting Americans: Cultural Anxiety and Narrative Form*.

Jean Fagan Yellin is the author of *Harriet Jacobs: A Life* (forthcoming, Basic); *Women and Sisters: The Anti-Slavery Feminists in American Culture* (1990); and *The Intricate Knot: Black Figures in American Literature, 1776–1863* (1972). Jean Fagan Yellin is the editor of an edition of *Uncle Tom's Cabin* (1998). She is perhaps best known for her editions of Harriet Jacobs's 1861 slave narrative *Incidents in the Life of a Slave Girl: Written by Herself* (1987, 2000).

INDEX

Abolitionism, 4, 5, 13, 25, 33, 41, 44, 46–47, 48, 51, 53–54, 58, 61, 62, 64, 106, 114, 129, 132, 134, 136, 140, 141, 158, 196, 204, 215, 221, 244, 258, 259, 260, 268, 315, 316, 389, 421, 424, 428, 430, 440
    abolitionist press, 74, 331, 378
    abolitionist texts, 317
    and Bible, 138–139
    and *Bleak House*, 73–74
    and Constitution, 135
    and Jane Johnson incident, 360. *See also* Williamson, Passmore
    and purchasing slaves' freedom, 133, 141–142
    view of freedom, 54–55, 66
Abzug, Robert, 58
Aesthetics, 196, 197, 198–199, 201, 202, 203, 207, 208, 210, 216, 220, 235
African American writers (antebellum period), 344
Africanism, 214
African Meeting House (Boston), 376
Afrocentrism, 333
AIS indexes, 374–375. *See also* Censuses
American Anti-Slavery Society, 44, 46–47, 118, 424
American Colonization Society, 356–357
American Fugitive in Europe, The: Sketches of Places and People Abroad (Brown), 117
American Renaissance, 27–28
American Revolution, 329
Ammonia, 72, 73, 413
Andrews, William, 19, 27, 258, 259, 303–304, 345

Anti-Slavery Bugle, 118
Appeal in Favor of that Class of Americans Called Africans (Child), 106
Appeal. . . to the Coloured Citizens of the World (Walker), 106
Architecture, 100, 146, 149, 151, 160, 162, 349
    racial theory of, 155
    See also Houses/cottages; Pattern books
Architecture of Country Houses (Downing), 151, 155, 161
"Art" (Emerson), 197–198. *See also* Aesthetics
Auld, Thomas, 141
Aunt Phillis's Cabin; or, Southern Life As It Is (Eastman), 163–164
Austen, Jane, 423
Authenticity issues, 318, 321–322, 329, 343, 345, 419, 423–424, 431–432, 433
Authentic Narrative of James Williams, An American Slave, The, 9–10, 44–47
Autobiography of a Female Slave (Griffith), 386, 424, 434
Autobiography of an Ex-Colored Man, The (J. Johnson), 31–32, 296, 299–300, 302–303, 307
Awakening, The (Chopin), 348

Baldwin, James, 352
Bancroft, George, 358
Banker's Wife, The; or, Court and City, A Novel, 5
Bassard, Katherine Clay, 201
Baym, Nina, 24, 31, 38, 54, 112
Beaumont, Gustave de, 106
Beecher, Henry Ward, 5